UNIVERSITY CASEBOOK SERIES®

JUDICIAL PROCESS

CASES AND MATERIALS

WAYNE MCCORMACK
E.W. Thode Professor of Law
S.J. Quinney College of Law
University of Utah

LOUISA M. A. HEINY
Associate Professor
S.J. Quinney College of Law
University of Utah

FOUNDATION PRESS

444 Cedar Street, Suite 700
St. Paul, MN 55101
1-877-888-1330

Printed in the United States of America

ISBN: 978-1-63460-812-1

To the millions of people depending on the Rule of Law, and their dedicated public servants.

– W. M.

To Bob and Linnea Heiny, two of the best teachers I know; and to the Honorable Lewis T. Babcock, who taught me to pull the trigger—and never drop a footnote.

– L. H.

ACKNOWLEDGMENTS

The authors wish to thank the following people for their help, advice, hard work, and encouragement: Professors Linda Smith, Jojo Liu, Dave Schwendiman, Tony Anghie, and Suzanne Darais; Quinney Fellow Erika Larsen; Emily Aplin; Gary Wilkinson; Ingrid Case; Erik, Sabrina, and Linnea Heiny; Tatiana Bakshaeva; Liz Meyer; the staff and faculty of the James E. Faust Law Library; and the students at the University of Utah S.J. Quinney College of Law.

Karl N. Llewellyn, *Remarks on the Theory of Appellate Decision and the Rules of Canons About How Statutes are to be Construed*, 3 VAND. L. REV. 395 (1950), reprinted with permission of Vanderbilt Law Review.

Maurice Rosenberg, *Judicial Discretion of the Trial Court, Viewed from Above*, 22 SYRACUSE L. REV. 635 (1971), reprinted with permission of Syracuse Law Review.

SUMMARY OF CONTENTS

ACKNOWLEDGMENTS V

TABLE OF CASES XVII

Chapter 1. American Courts & Cases 1
§ 1.1 Structure of the American Judicial System 1
§ 1.2 Federal Courts 2
§ 1.3 State Courts 11
§ 1.4 Anatomy of a Case 13

Chapter 2. The Role of the Law Clerk 17
§ 2.1 General Ethical Considerations 19
§ 2.2 The Requirement of Confidentiality 21
§ 2.3 Conflicts Between Judge and Clerk 24
§ 2.4 Clerk Recusal 27
§ 2.5 The Role of the Clerk—Going Beyond the Record 36

Chapter 3. The Role of Trial & Appellate Judges 45
§ 3.1 Standards of Review 45
§ 3.2 Judicial Review of Administrative Action 67

Chapter 4. Case Assignment & Recusal 87
§ 4.1 Assignment of Cases 87
§ 4.2 Judicial Recusal 97

Chapter 5. Judicial Selection, Retention, & Oversight 123
§ 5.1 Judicial Selection 123
§ 5.2 Judicial Oversight 130
§ 5.3 Judicial Immunity 144

Chapter 6. Specialty Courts 151
§ 6.1 Theories of Punishment 151
§ 6.2 Juvenile Courts 153
§ 6.3 Problem-Solving Courts 162
§ 6.4 The Balance Between Informality and Constitutional Rights 181

Chapter 7. Alternatives to Traditional Litigation 183
§ 7.1 Decline of the Jury Trial 184
§ 7.2 Alternative Dispute Resolution (ADR) 185
§ 7.3 Mandatory Mediation 187
§ 7.4 Mandatory Arbitration Agreements 196
§ 7.5 Pro Se Litigants 200

Chapter 8. Judicial Power & Independence 227
§ 8.1 The History of Judicial Independence 227
§ 8.2 Power and Independence of the Courts 233
§ 8.3 Challenges to Judicial Power 243
§ 8.4 State Electoral Challenges 256
§ 8.5 Administrative Law Judges 258

§ 8.6 International Judicial Independence 262

Chapter 9. Common Law Reasoning & Statutory Interpretation 269

§ 9.1 Decision-Making at Common Law 269
§ 9.2 The Intersection Between Common Law and Statutes 277
§ 9.3 Statutory Interpretation at Work 285
§ 9.4 Statutory Construction in the United States Supreme Court 300
§ 9.5 Grammar and Punctuation 310
§ 9.6 Partially Unconstitutional Statutes 315

Chapter 10. Constitutional Interpretation 317

§ 10.1 Theories of Constitutional Interpretation 317
§ 10.2 The Role of Federalism in Constitutional Interpretation 321
§ 10.3 The Role of History and Tradition in Constitutional Interpretation 331
§ 10.4 Constitutional Interpretation and Unenumerated Rights 340
§ 10.5 The Role of Foreign and International Law in Constitutional Interpretation 368
§ 10.6 Tiered Interpretation and Judicial Philosophy 372

Chapter 11. Civil Law and Other Systems 375

§ 11.1 Comparing the Civil and Common Law Systems 376
§ 11.2 Moving Toward More Unified Models 379
§ 11.3 International Tribunals—Unique and Hybrid Systems 389
§ 11.4 Informal and Religious Courts 394
§ 11.5 IGO and NGO Proceedings 399

Chapter 12. Bias in the Judicial Process 403

§ 12.1 Racial Equality on the Bench 403
§ 12.2 Racial Equality in the Civil System 405
§ 12.3 Racial Equality in the Criminal Justice System 422
§ 12.4 Gender Equality on the Bench 429
§ 12.5 Gender Equality in the Civil System 432

Chapter 13. Writing for Clerks 443

§ 13.1 Types of Writing Projects 443
§ 13.2 Planning the Workload 448
§ 13.3 The Importance of Good Basic Skills 451
§ 13.4 The Seven Deadly Sins of Legal Writing 460

INDEX 465

TABLE OF CONTENTS

ACKNOWLEDGMENTS V

TABLE OF CASES XVII

Chapter 1. American Courts & Cases **1**
§ 1.1 Structure of the American Judicial System 1
§ 1.2 Federal Courts 2
A. History 2
B. Federal Court Structure 4
1. United States Supreme Court 4
2. United States Courts of Appeal 7
3. United States District Courts 8
4. Article I Courts 9
5. Article IV Courts 10
6. Administrative Courts 10
C. Federal Jurisdiction 10
§ 1.3 State Courts 11
A. State Court Structure 11
1. Supreme Courts 11
2. Intermediate Appellate Courts 11
3. Trial Courts 11
B. State Court Jurisdiction 12
C. Concurrent Federal and State Jurisdiction 12
§ 1.4 Anatomy of a Case 13
A. Civil Cases 13
B. Criminal Cases 14
C. Appeals 16

Chapter 2. The Role of the Law Clerk **17**
Bishop v. Albertson's, Inc. 18
§ 2.1 General Ethical Considerations 19
Notes and Questions 20
§ 2.2 The Requirement of Confidentiality 21
Bishop v. Albertson's, Inc. 22
Notes and Questions 23
§ 2.3 Conflicts Between Judge and Clerk 24
Notes and Questions 25
§ 2.4 Clerk Recusal 27
Doe v. Cabrera 28
Notes and Questions 33
Parker v. Connors Steel Co. 34
§ 2.5 The Role of the Clerk—Going Beyond the Record 36
Price Brothers Co. v. Philadelphia Gear Corp. 37
Notes and Questions 40
Mitchell v. JCG Industries 40
Notes and Questions 42

Chapter 3. The Role of Trial & Appellate Judges **45**
§ 3.1 Standards of Review 45
A. The Theory Behind the Standards 45
Maurice Rosenberg Judicial Discretion of the Trial Court, Viewed from Above 45
Notes and Questions 49
B. Standards of Review (The Usual Suspects) 52
1. Issues of Law: De Novo Review 52
2. Factual Determinations by the Trial Court: Clearly Erroneous 52
Anderson v. Bessemer City 53
Notes and Questions 58
3. Factual Determinations by a Jury: Substantial Deference 59
4. Mixed Issues of Law and Fact: It Depends 60
5. Procedural Decisions by a Trial Court: Abuse of Discretion 61
6. Multiple Standards in a Single Case 62
United States v. Charles Thomas Allen, II 62
§ 3.2 Judicial Review of Administrative Action 67
A. The Administrative Procedure Act (APA) 68
B. Federal Agencies 70
1. Social Security 70
2. Immigration Courts 70
Predtechensky v. Immigration and Naturalization Services (INS) 71
C. State Administrative Proceedings 73
The People of the State of Colorado v. Pautler 73
Notes and Questions 79
Heinecke v. Department of Commerce, Division of Occupational and Professional Licensing 80
Notes and Questions 84

Chapter 4. Case Assignment & Recusal **87**
§ 4.1 Assignment of Cases 87
Armstrong v. Board of Education of Birmingham 88
Notes and Questions 95
§ 4.2 Judicial Recusal 97
A. U.S. Supreme Court Recusal Issues 98
Notes and Questions 99
B. Recusal in Lower Courts 101
Caperton v. A.T. Massey Coal Co. 101
Notes and Questions 112
Ligon v. City of New York 112
Notes and Questions 120

Chapter 5. Judicial Selection, Retention, & Oversight **123**
§ 5.1 Judicial Selection 123
A. State Courts 123

B. Federal Courts 126
§ 5.2 Judicial Oversight 130
A. Codes of Judicial Conduct 130
B. Judicial Discipline 130
1. Federal 131
Chandler v. Judicial Council of the Tenth Circuit 132
Notes and Questions 134
2. State 136
Kennick v. Commission on Judicial Performance 137
Notes and Questions 143
§ 5.3 Judicial Immunity 144
Martinez v. Winner 144
Notes and Questions 148

Chapter 6. Specialty Courts 151
§ 6.1 Theories of Punishment 151
§ 6.2 Juvenile Courts 153
A. History 153
B. Juveniles and Due Process 154
In re Gault 155
Notes and Questions 159
C. Current Trends in the Juvenile Courts 160
Notes and Questions 161
§ 6.3 Problem-Solving Courts 162
A. Drug Courts 163
1. History 163
2. Structure and Design 163
B. Due Process 165
People v. Kimmel 165
Hagar v. State 169
State v. Rogers 173
Notes and Questions: 178
C. Mental Health Courts 178
D. Other Specialty Courts 180
§ 6.4 The Balance Between Informality and Constitutional Rights 181
Notes and Questions 181

Chapter 7. Alternatives to Traditional Litigation 183
§ 7.1 Decline of the Jury Trial 184
A. Cause 184
B. Effect 185
§ 7.2 Alternative Dispute Resolution (ADR) 185
§ 7.3 Mandatory Mediation 187
In re Atlantic Pipe Corp. 188
Notes and Questions 195
§ 7.4 Mandatory Arbitration Agreements 196
Notes and Questions 199

§ 7.5 Pro Se Litigants 200
A. Pro Se Parties: Who, How Many, and Why 201
Notes and Questions 202
B. The Problem for Attorneys 204
C. The Problem for Courts 205
Dioguardi v. Durning 207
Notes and Questions 209
Erickson v. Pardus 210
Rowe v. Gibson 213
Notes and Questions 222
1. Sovereign Citizens 223
United States v. Hakeem El Bey 223

Chapter 8. Judicial Power & Independence 227
§ 8.1 The History of Judicial Independence 227
A. The British Experience 227
B. The American Experience 231
§ 8.2 Power and Independence of the Courts 233
A. The Power of Judicial Review 234
Marbury v. Madison 235
Notes and Questions 239
B. Power over State Courts 239
Martin v. Hunter's Lessee 240
Notes and Questions 242
§ 8.3 Challenges to Judicial Power 243
A. Jurisdiction Stripping 243
Ex parte McCardle 245
Notes and Questions 246
B. Impeachment 247
C. Court-Packing 248
Notes and Question 249
D. Directing the Outcome of Cases 249
United States v. Klein 249
Notes and Questions 251
Robertson v. Seattle Audubon Society 252
Notes and Questions 255
§ 8.4 State Electoral Challenges 256
§ 8.5 Administrative Law Judges 258
Association of Administrative Law Judges v. Colvin 259
§ 8.6 International Judicial Independence 262
A. International Standards 262
B. The Continental Experience 263
C. Judiciaries in Times of Conflict 264
1. The Middle East 264
2. Russia 265
3. Eastern Europe 266
4. The Southern Hemisphere 267
5. Conclusion 267

Chapter 9. Common Law Reasoning & Statutory Interpretation 269
§ 9.1 Decision-Making at Common Law 269
A. History of the Common Law 269
B. Common Law Reasoning 270
Karl N. Llewellyn Remarks on the Theory of Appellate Decision and the Rules of Canons About How Statutes are to be Construed 270
C. Common Law Reasoning at Work 272
Chicago, B. & Q. R. Co. v. Krayenbuhl 272
Notes and Questions 275
§ 9.2 The Intersection Between Common Law and Statutes 277
A. Codified Laws on Statutory Construction 278
B. Canons of Statutory Construction 279
William Blackstone Commentaries on the Laws of England Section the Second: Of the Nature of Laws in General 280
Karl N. Llewellyn Remarks on the Theory of Appellate Decision and the Rules of Canons About How Statutes are to be Construed 282
Notes and Questions 283
§ 9.3 Statutory Interpretation at Work 285
A. Inherent Risk Statutes 285
Clover v. Snowbird Ski Resort 285
Notes and Questions 291
B. Comparative Fault Statutes 292
Clark v. Connor 293
Slager v. HWA Corp. 296
Notes and Questions 298
§ 9.4 Statutory Construction in the United States Supreme Court 300
National Federation of Independent Business v. Sebelius 300
Notes and Questions 304
§ 9.5 Grammar and Punctuation 310
Barnhart v. Thomas 310
Notes and Questions 315
§ 9.6 Partially Unconstitutional Statutes 315

Chapter 10. Constitutional Interpretation 317
§ 10.1 Theories of Constitutional Interpretation 317
A. Originalism 318
B. Textualism 319
C. The Living Constitution 320
D. Traditionalism 320
E. Formalism and Functionalism 321
§ 10.2 The Role of Federalism in Constitutional Interpretation 321
District of Columbia v. Heller 321
Notes and Questions 323
United States v. Comstock 324
Notes and Questions 326

Baker v. Carr 327
Notes and Questions 330
§ 10.3 The Role of History and Tradition in Constitutional Interpretation 331
Michael H. & Victoria D. v. Gerald D. 331
Notes and Questions 337
Graham v. Florida 337
Notes and Questions 339
§ 10.4 Constitutional Interpretation and Unenumerated Rights 340
Griswold v. Connecticut 340
Notes and Questions 348
Lawrence v. Texas 352
Obergefell v. Hodges 359
Notes and Questions 368
§ 10.5 The Role of Foreign and International Law in Constitutional Interpretation 368
§ 10.6 Tiered Interpretation and Judicial Philosophy 372

Chapter 11. Civil Law and Other Systems 375
§ 11.1 Comparing the Civil and Common Law Systems 376
§ 11.2 Moving Toward More Unified Models 379
A. ECtHR and Fair Trial 380
Case of Reinhardt and Slimane-Kaïd v. France 380
B. ECtHR and "Administrative" Courts 387
Notes and Questions 389
§ 11.3 International Tribunals—Unique and Hybrid Systems 389
Notes and Questions 392
§ 11.4 Informal and Religious Courts 394
A. Informal Tribunals 394
B. Religious Law and Courts 395
1. Israel 395
2. Shari'a 397
C. Claims and Myths About Shari'a 398
§ 11.5 IGO and NGO Proceedings 399
A. Inter-Governmental Organizations (IGO) 400
B. IGO—Treaties and Arbitration Provisions 400
C. NGO Adjudicators—The Example of International Sports Federations 401

Chapter 12. Bias in the Judicial Process 403
§ 12.1 Racial Equality on the Bench 403
§ 12.2 Racial Equality in the Civil System 405
A. Historically 405
Dred Scott v. Sandford 405
Notes and Questions 409
Plessy v. Ferguson 410
Brown v. Board of Education of Topeka 411
B. Current Issues 414
Fisher v. University of Texas at Austin 415

Schuette v. Coalition to Defend Affirmative Action, Integration and Immigrant Rights and Fight for Equality by any Means Necessary (BAMN) 417
Notes and Questions 421
§ 12.3 Racial Equality in the Criminal Justice System 422
McCleskey v. Kemp 422
Notes and Questions 424
Batson v. Kentucky 425
Notes and Questions 427
§ 12.4 Gender Equality on the Bench 429
Bradwell v. Illinois 429
Notes and Questions 431
§ 12.5 Gender Equality in the Civil System 432
Reed v. Reed 433
Notes and Questions 434
United States v. Virginia 436
Notes and Questions 441

Chapter 13. Writing for Clerks 443
§ 13.1 Types of Writing Projects 443
A. Writing Assignments in Appellate Courts 444
1. Certiorari Memorandum ("Cert. Memo") 444
2. Bench Memorandum 444
3. Single-Issue Memorandum 445
4. Full Case Memorandum 445
5. Precedential Judicial Opinion 445
6. Memorandum Opinion 446
7. Per Curiam Opinion 446
B. Writing Assignments in Trial Courts 446
1. Statement of Facts 447
2. Findings of Fact and Conclusions of Law 447
3. Jury Instructions 447
4. Motions 447
5. Miscellaneous Court Orders 448
§ 13.2 Planning the Workload 448
A. Getting Started 448
B. Drafting 449
C. Editing 449
1. Gross Organization 450
2. IRAC, CREAC, or TRAC 450
3. Topic Sentences 450
4. Sentence Structure and Grammar 450
5. Word Choice 450
6. Spelling 450
7. Citations 450
8. Final Proof 451
§ 13.3 The Importance of Good Basic Skills 451
A. Basic Sentence Structure 451

B. Grammar and Punctuation 451
1. Misplaced Modifiers 451
2. Commas 451
3. Comma Splices 454
4. Split Infinitives 454
5. Ending a Sentence with a Preposition 454
6. Passive Voice 455
7. The Problem of the Singular Gender-Neutral Pronoun 456
8. Who Versus Whom 457
9. That Versus Which 457
10. Commonly Confused Words 458
C. The Bluebook: A Uniform System of Citation 459
§ 13.4 The Seven Deadly Sins of Legal Writing 460
A. Footnotes 460
B. Exclamation Marks 461
C. Over-Emphasis 461
D. Snark 462
E. Verbosity 462
F. Sloth 462
G. Misstatement 463

INDEX 465

TABLE OF CASES

The principal cases are in bold type.

Abaqueta v. United States, 85
Aetna Life Ins. Co. v. Lavoie, 105
American Express Co. v. Italian Colors Rest., 197, 198
American Gen. Fin. Servs., Inc. v. Carter, 285
American Ins. Co. v. Canter, 9
Anderson v. Bessemer City, 53
Argersinger v. Hamlin, 160
Armstrong v. Board of Educ. of Birmingham, 88
Association of Administrative Law Judges v. Colvin, 259
AT&T Mobility v. Concepcion, 197
Atkins v. Virginia, 368
Atlantic Pipe Corp., In re, 188
Auer v. Robbins, 69
Baker v. Carr, 327
Bank Markazi v. Peterson, 255
Barnhart v. Thomas, 310
Batson v. Kentucky, 425, 441
Baumgartner, United States v., 182
Bell Atlantic v. Twombly, 210
Benvin v. U.S. Dist. Court, 136
Betts v. Brady, 49
Bishop v. Albertson's, Inc., 18, 22
Black Rock City v. Pershing County Bd. of Comm'rs, 135
Blodgett v. Holden, 302
Boston's Children First, In re, 119
Bowen v. Yuckert, 314
Bowers v. Hardwick, 349, 351, 354
Bowles v. Seminole Rock & Sand Co., 69
Boy Scouts of America v. Dale, 357
Bradley v. Fisher, 147
Bradwell v. Illinois, 429
Brewer v. Williams, 160
Brown v. Allen, 269
Brown v. Board of Education of Topeka, 411
Brown v. Maryland, 50
Bryant, United States v., 50
Bush v. Gore, 331
Bush v. Vera, 421
Caperton v. A.T. Massey Coal Co., 101, 125, 258
Carolene Products Co., United States v., 373, 461
Carroll Towing Co., United States v., 275
Case of Reinhardt and Slimane-Kaïd v. France, 380
Catchpole v. Brannon, 442
Chandler v. Judicial Council of the Tenth Circuit, 132
Charles Thomas Allen, II, United States v., 62
Cheney v. United States District Court, 99
Chepkevich v. Hidden Valley Resort, L.P., 292
Chevron U.S.A., Inc. v. Natural Resources Defense Council, Inc., 69, 313
Chicago, B. & Q. R. Co. v. Krayenbuhl, 272
Christopher v. SmithKline Beecham Corp., 69
Citizens United v. F.E.C., 125
Clark v. Connor, 293
Clover v. Snowbird Ski Resort, 285
Cohens v. Virginia, 243
Coker v. Georgia, 368
Colegrove v. Green, 330
Colorado, The People of the State of v. Pautler, 73
CompuCredit Corp. v. Greenwood, 197, 306
Comstock, United States v., 324
Conley v. Gibson, 210
Cortez v. University Mall, 299
Craig v. Boren, 434
Curry, In re, 21
Decker v. Nw. Envtl. Def. Ctr., 69
Dioguardi v. Durning, 207, 209
District of Columbia v. Heller, 321
Doe v. Cabrera, 28, 33
Dred Scott v. Sandford, 405
Edmonson v. Leesville Concrete Co., 427
Edwards v. Aguilard, 309
EEOC v. Sears, Roebuck & Co., 435
Eisenstadt v. Baird, 350
Enmund v. Florida, 368
EPA v. EME Homer City Generation, 50, 51
Erickson v. Pardus, 210
Erie R.R. Co. v. Tompkins, 243
Ewing v. California, 338
Fairfax's Devisee v. Hunter's Lessee, 240
Faretta v. California, 201, 202
Field v. Boyer Co., 299
Fisher v. University of Texas at Austin, 98, 415, 421
Flores-Villar, United States v., 99
Forrester v. White, 144
Foster v. Chatman, 427, 428
Franco-Flores, United States v., 182

Frontiero v. Richardson, 434, 437
Garrovillas v. INS, 72
Gault, In re, 45, 154, **155**
Georgia v. Brailsford, 7
Georgia v. McCollum, 427
Gideon v. Wainwright, 49, 159, 202
Gooding, United States v., 50
Graham v. Florida, 161, **337**, 340
Graven v. Vail Assocs., Inc., 292
Grieb v. Alpine Valley Ski Area, Inc., 292
Grievance Administrator v. Fried, 122
Griswold v. Connecticut, **340**, 349, 351, 359
Grutter v. Bollinger, 96
Guice v. State Farm Fire and Casualty Co., 33
Hagar v. State, 169
Hage, Estate of, United States v., 136
Hakeem El Bey, United States v., 223
Hall v. Small Business Admin., 31, 34
Harmelin v. Michigan, 338
Heinecke v. Department of Commerce, Division of Occupational and Professional Licensing, 80
Heydon's Case, 279
Infant Anonymous, In re Adoption of, 59
INS v. Chadha, 326
Interfaith Cmty Org. v. Honeywell Int'l., Inc., 60
J.E.B. v. Alabama ex rel. T.B, 427, 441
Jedrziewski v. Smith, 299
Kahn v. E. Side Union High Sch. Dist., 291
Kennick v. Commission on Judicial Performance, 137
Kent v. United States, 154
Kimel v. Florida Bd. of Regents, 372
Kimmel, People v., 165
King v. Burwell, 305
Klein, United States v., 249
Kopeikin v. Moonlight Basin Mgmt., LLC, 292
Kress v. France, 387
Laird v. Tatum, 100
Lamprecht v. F.C.C., 22
Latta v. Otter, 97
Lawrence v. Texas, **352**, 368
Ligon v. City of New York, 112
Liljeberg v. Health Services Acquisition Corp., 35
Loaisiga-Cruz v. Hosp. San Juan Bautista, 210
Lockyer v. Andrade, 338
Lombardo, United States v., 401
Lorette v. Peter-Sam Inv. Props., 291
Lozada, Matter of, 71
Lynch, Ex parte, 230
Marbury v. Madison, **235**, 239, 305, 318
Martin v. Hunter's Lessee, 2, **240**
Martinez v. Winner, 144
Martinez, United States v., 146
Martinez-Melgar, United States v., 182
Mayberry v. Pennsylvania, 106
McCardle, Ex parte, 245
McCleskey v. Kemp, **422**, 424
McCleskey v. Zant, 425
McCully, In re, 143
McGrath v. Kristensen, 50
McKeiver v. Pennsylvania, 160
McLain v. Training & Development Corp., 298
Merryman, Ex parte, 244
Mettee, In re Estate of, 285
Meyer v. Nebraska, 341
Michael H. & Victoria D. v. Gerald D., 331
Microsoft Corp., United States v., 119
Milavetz, Gallop & Milavetz, P.A. v. United States, 307, 461
Miller v. Alabama, 161
Miller v. Campanella, 213
Miller, United States v., 323
Milligan, Ex parte, 244, 245
Mississippi University for Women v. Hogan, 435
Mitchell v. JCG Industries, 40
Montgomery v. Louisiana, 162
Murchison, In re, 106
National Council of La Raza v. Cegavske, 136
National Federation of Independent Business v. Sebelius, 98, **300**
Nixon v. United States, 135
Northern Pipeline Construction Co. v. Marathon Pipe Line Co., 9
Obergefell v. Hodges, **359**, 461
Olmstead v. United States, 345
Ornelas v. United States, 61
Owens v. Duncan, 218
Parker v. Connors Steel Co., 34
Parsons v. Bedford, 302
Parts and Electric Motors, Inc. v. Sterling Electric, Inc., 53
Pierce v. Society of Sisters, 341
Plaut v. Spendthrift Farms, 251
Plessy v. Ferguson, **410**, 412, 413
Poe v. Ullman, 348
Portland Audubon Society et al. v. Manuel Lujan, Jr., 253
Predtechensky v. Immigration and Naturalization Services (INS), 71
Price Brothers Co. v. Philadelphia Gear Corp., 37

Pullman-Standard v. Swint, 53, 60
Reed v. Columbia St. Mary's Hospital, 222
Reed v. Illinois, 222
Reed v. Moore, 222
Reed v. Reed, 433, 434
Regan v. Taxation With Representation of Washington, 372
Reichman, People v., 75
Reynolds v. Sims, 331
Ring v. Arizona, 80
Ritter, United States v., 121
Robertson v. Seattle Audubon Society, 252
Rodriguez-Lariz v. INS, 71
Rogers, State v., 173
Roper v. Simmons, 161, 340, 368
Rowe v. Gibson, 43, **213**
Rummel v. Estelle, 338
S.M. v. Krigbaum, 182
San Antonio Ind. Sch. Dist. v. Rodriguez, 372
Sandifer v. United States Steel Corp., 42
Sapone v. Grand Targhee, 291
Schaefer v. Putnam, 195
Schmitz v. Cannonsburg Skiing Corp., 292
Schooner Peggy, United States v., 251
Schuette v. Coalition to Defend Affirmative Action, Integration and Immigrant Rights and Fight for Equality by any Means Necessary (BAMN), 417
Scott v. Illinois, 160
Seattle Audubon Society et al. v. F. Dale Robertson, 253
Shelby County v. Holder, 421
Sheppard v. Beerman, 26
Shin v. Sunriver Preparatory School, Inc., 298
Skene v. Fileccia, 291
Slager v. HWA Corp., 296
Solomon v. State of Kansas, 258
Stanford v. Kentucky, 153
Stanley v. Georgia, 349
Stell v. Savannah-Chatham County Board of Education, 89, 93
Stump v. Sparkman, 146, 148
Szetela v. Discover Bank, 199
Talk Am., Inc. v. Michigan Bell Tel. Co., 69
Thompson v. Oklahoma, 161, 340, 368
Torres v. Berbary, 167, 178
Townley v. Miller, 136
Trop v. Dulles, 369
Tumey v. Ohio, 104, 105
U.S. Dist. Court, United States v., 136
U.S. Gypsum Co., United States v., 53
Utah v. Strieff, 428
Valencia, People v., 168
Vaska v. State, 31
Vermont, Estate of, v. Forte, 432
Virginia, United States v., 436
Washington Contract Loggers Assoc. et al. v. F. Dale Robertson, 253
Wellness Int'l Network, Ltd. v. Sharif, 9
White v. Deseelhorst, 292
Whitman v. Am. Trucking Ass'n, 51
Whole Woman's Health v. Hellerstedt, 50, 373
Williams v. Pennsylvania, 403
Yemini v. Great Rabbinical Court, 396
Yerger, Ex parte, 246
Youngstown Sheet & Tube v. Sawyer, 326

UNIVERSITY CASEBOOK SERIES®

JUDICIAL PROCESS

CASES AND MATERIALS

CHAPTER 1

AMERICAN COURTS & CASES

> Leave to the people an independent judiciary, and they will prove that man is capable of governing himself; they will be saved from what has been the fate of all other republics, and they will disprove that governments of a republican form cannot endure. [1]
>
> – Chief Justice John Rutledge, *Speech on a Judiciary Establishment*

The American judicial system has hundreds of appellate courts, trial courts, and administrative courts on both the federal and state sides, not to mention thousands of municipal courts at the local level. Each court has its own jurisdiction, structure, and function. It would be impossible—and painfully boring—to cover every type of court in the American system. Instead, Chapter 1 explores only the basic federal court and state court structures.

§ 1.1 STRUCTURE OF THE AMERICAN JUDICIAL SYSTEM

Article III of the Constitution provides that

> The judicial Power of the United States, shall be vested in one supreme Court, and in such inferior Courts as the Congress may from time to time ordain and establish. The Judges, both of the supreme and inferior Courts, shall hold their Offices during good Behaviour, and shall, at stated Times, receive for their Services, a Compensation, which shall not be diminished during their Continuance in Office.

The Article III system contains 94 territorially defined district courts, two specialized trial courts, 13 courts of appeal (12 regional and one for specialized cases), and one United States Supreme Court. Congress has also created four Article I courts, also known as legislative courts. These tribunals lack full Article III judicial power. Instead, they have exclusive, but limited, jurisdiction over certain types of cases and appeals.

There are also a variety of administrative review tribunals. While these are also often called "courts," administrative tribunals are, in reality, parts of the executive branch or independent administrative

---

[1] Judith S. Kaye, *Safeguarding a Crown Jewel: Judicial Independence and Lawyer Criticism of Courts*, 25 HOFSTRA L. REV. 703, 709 (1997) (quoting 11 ANNALS OF CONG. 739–40 (1802)).

agency structures. Immigration Courts and the Social Security review panels are two of the most active administrative tribunals.

Each state has its own court system, usually consisting of multiple layers. There may be local municipal courts, state trial courts of general jurisdiction, a state-wide intermediate court of appeals, and the state's highest court. The highest court is usually, but not always, known as the Supreme Court of the State of _____. Most states also have a variety of administrative review tribunals.

The relationship between the federal and state courts is a delicate one. While the federal court system is far-reaching, its power is limited. Like the federal government as a whole, the federal courts are limited to the powers granted by the Constitution. At the same time, the Supremacy Clause, contained in Article VI of the Constitution, provides that the Constitution, laws of the United States, and treaties "shall be the supreme Law of the Land; and the Judges in every State shall be bound thereby, any Thing in the Constitution or Laws of any State to the Contrary notwithstanding." Thus, state courts maintain power in certain cases, while being subservient to the federal system in others.

In *Martin v. Hunter's Lessee*,[2] the Supreme Court made clear that the state courts are subordinate to the appellate jurisdiction of the Supreme Court in matters of federal law and diversity jurisdiction. Justice Story, writing for the Supreme Court, made two essential points: (1) the Constitution eliminated many aspects of state sovereignty, and (2) uniformity on matters of federal law is essential to the functioning of the nation.

The relationship between federal and state courts over the past two centuries has occasionally been contentious, but the basic parameters and principles were established early and have never changed.

§ 1.2 FEDERAL COURTS

A. HISTORY

Article III of the Constitution provided a skeletal outline for the federal courts. It created a Supreme Court, as well as "such inferior courts as the Congress may from time to time ordain and establish." It gave the new federal courts three kinds of jurisdiction. First, the courts received what we now call federal question jurisdiction: the power over "all Cases, in Law and Equity, arising under this Constitution, the Laws of the United States, and Treaties." Second, the Supreme Court received "original jurisdiction" over "[c]ases affecting Ambassadors, other public Ministers and Consuls, and those in which a state shall be a party." Finally, the Supreme Court received appellate jurisdiction "[i]n all the other Cases before mentioned"—except where Congress chose to check

2 14 U.S. (1 Wheat.) 304 (1816).

that power. In addition, federal judges were given enviable job security: lifetime tenure and a stable salary.

While all this seems substantial, many of the most fundamental details were left out. How many judges would sit on the court? How many inferior courts would be created, and what jurisdiction would they have? What about an intermediate court of appeals? How would cases be chosen for appellate review, and what schedule would the court use for hearing those appeals? Were the enumerated cases a jurisdictional floor, to which Congress could add, or a jurisdictional ceiling, to which it could not add? What about diversity jurisdiction? How should that be allocated?

Congress fleshed out the details in a series of Judiciary Acts. The first, the Judiciary Act of 1789, filled both mechanical and jurisdictional holes created by the Constitution. It set the number of Supreme Court justices at six: one chief justice and five associate justices. The Act also created the inferior courts mentioned in Article III. Congress created thirteen judicial districts. Each district had one trial court and one circuit court of appeal. These circuit courts of appeal did not have their own slate of judges. Instead, each was comprised of a district judge and two Supreme Court justices "riding circuit."

A smattering of other provisions further defined the mechanics of the court. Congress authorized all people to either represent themselves or to be represented by another person. The Act did not prohibit paying a representative to appear in court, thus leaving room for lawyers. Speaking of lawyers, the Act created the Office of Attorney General, whose primary responsibility was to represent the United States before the Supreme Court. The Act also created a United States Attorney and a United States Marshal for each district. Congress authorized persons who were sued by citizens of another state in the courts of the plaintiff's home state to remove the lawsuit to the federal court. This power of removal helped establish the concept that federal judicial power would be superior to that of the states.

The federal courts' jurisdiction was also further defined. The Supreme Court was given exclusive original jurisdiction over all civil actions between states, or between a state and the United States, as well as jurisdiction over all suits and proceedings brought against ambassadors and other diplomatic personnel. It was given original, but not exclusive, jurisdiction over all other cases in which a state was a party and any cases brought by an ambassador.

Further, both the circuit courts of appeal and the Supreme Court were given appellate jurisdiction, although the overall court structure was different from today's federal courts. The district courts heard only limited cases, such as maritime, admiralty, and minor criminal matters. The three circuit courts had appellate jurisdiction over the district courts. The circuit courts also served as trial courts for the vast majority of federal cases. Each circuit court bench consisted of one district court judge and two Supreme Court justices who rode circuit, visiting the circuit courts twice every year.

The Supreme Court was given appellate jurisdiction over decisions of the circuit courts, as well as decisions by state courts addressing the validity of any statute or treaty of the United States; holding valid any state law or practice that was challenged as being inconsistent with the federal constitution, treaties, or laws; or rejecting any claim made by a party under a provision of the federal constitution, treaties, or laws. A clause granting the Supreme Court the power to issue writs of mandamus was the font of the first case introduced in Constitutional Law: *Marbury v. Madison*. It declared a statute unconstitutional after Chief Justice Marshall read the statute to confer the power of writs outside the Court's appellate jurisdiction.

Notably, the federal trial courts had not yet received original federal question jurisdiction. Although the Constitution allowed it, the first Judiciary Act did not provide for it. Congress briefly created federal question jurisdiction in the Judiciary Act of 1801, but it was repealed the following year and not restored until 1875. The statute is now found at 28 U.S.C. § 1331: "The district courts shall have original jurisdiction of all civil actions arising under the Constitution, laws, or treaties of the United States."

The duties of the Supreme Court justices have remained largely stable over the years. While the justices have always managed an appellate docket, their circuit-riding duties only lasted for the first hundred years. The circuit-riding system prevented the justices from being cloistered and ensured that justices were familiar with practices and procedures all over the country. However, it also resulted in a backlog of Supreme Court cases. Congress created separate circuit court judgeships in 1869 and ended the circuit riding system in 1911. Those duties are now optional, although the justices each have a circuit assignment and field requests for stays, injunctions, extensions of time, and other relief originating in that circuit.

B. FEDERAL COURT STRUCTURE

1. UNITED STATES SUPREME COURT

In some ways, the United States Supreme Court of today is very much like the Court that first sat in February of 1790. Although attorneys who appear before the Court are no longer required to wear a morning suit (a morning coat with tails, matching waistcoat, and striped trousers), other traditions have remained unchanged. The order in which the justices sit on the bench, the color of the justices' robes, and the white quill pens on counsel tables are all a matter of tradition.

While some Court rules are set by statute, most are set internally. The Rules of the Supreme Court of the United States determine much of the day-to-day running of the Court. They govern, among other issues, attorney admission, jurisdiction, oral argument, and the dates and times of argument. Many of the rules are extremely detailed, including the type of paper parties must use ("opaque, unglazed, and not less than 60 pounds in weight"); the color of the cover for each filing (white, orange, tan, light blue, light red, yellow, cream, light green, or dark green, depending on the party and type of document); and the formatting of filed documents ("6 1/8-by-9 1/4-inch booklet format using a standard typesetting process (e.g., hot metal, photocomposition, or computer typesetting) to produce text printed in typographic (as opposed to typewriter) characters").

The majority of the Court's docket is appellate. When a party requests that the Court issue a writ of certiorari, an old English term for "certify the record for review," it files a petition for certiorari explaining the importance of the case and the reasons the Court should choose this case from the thousands that vie for the Court's attention. The opposing party has the opportunity to file a response brief, but many respondents choose not to as a matter of both economy and strategy. State prosecutors' offices and prison officials, particularly, are the targets of hundreds of cases annually. Opposing counsel may signal the relative unimportance of the case by declining to respond. Before the Court grants a petition for certiorari it will always request a response from the respondent. Thus, a request from the Court for a response signals at least a preliminary interest in the case. When a respondent files a response brief, whether by choice or by request, the petitioner is given an opportunity to file a reply. The Court may also request that the Office of the U.S. Attorney General file a brief representing the federal government's position on a particular case.

Since the Judiciary Act of 1925, the Court has had the power to decide which cases it wishes to hear regardless of whether it has appellate or original jurisdiction over the case. The Court receives approximately 10,000 petitions for certiorari each year from which it chooses 75 to 80 cases to hear. It would be impossible for the justices to personally review those thousands of petitions. Instead, the justices' law clerks review the petitions and write memos to advise the justices on the issues, procedural posture, and merits of the various cases. Most of the justices participate in a "cert. pool," spreading the cases amongst the many clerks rather than requiring the clerks in each chamber to review each petition. The Court then lists some cases for weekly conference. The conference is an opportunity for the justices to discuss petitions for certiorari and vote on which cases to accept. In 1925, it was the habit of the Court to discuss every petition for certiorari. Now, however, only those cases specifically chosen by a justice for conference are discussed. Although the conference list is public, the actual conference is private. In recent years, the Court has developed the habit of relisting cases, discussing them at numerous conferences before granting certiorari. It takes four of the nine justices to grant a writ. Thus, the so-called Rule of Four.

Once the Court has granted certiorari, the Chief Justice and Clerk of the Court (not to be confused with a law clerk) set briefing and argument schedules according to the importance of the case and the number of amicus briefs likely to be filed. These "friend of the court" briefs are filed with the permission of the Court by non-parties who have some sort of interest in the case. Frequently, they are filed by professional associations such as the National Association of Criminal Defense Lawyers or the National District Attorneys Association. Academics and attorneys general of different jurisdictions also frequently file amicus briefs.

Next, the parties both file merit briefs, once again following the brief, response, and reply pattern. Again, the appellant goes first. Oral argument is then held. Both audio and written transcripts of the arguments are publically available, but video and still photography is forbidden. After argument, the justices hold a conference. At the start of each conference, each justice shakes hands with every other justice, a tradition begun by Chief Justice Fuller. They sit in a preordained order around a large table with the most junior justice sitting closest to the door and being responsible for getting food, taking notes, and answering knocks at the door. According to current Junior Justice Elena Kagan,

> if there's a knock on the door and I don't hear it, there will not be a single other person who will move. They'll all just stare at me . . . You might ask, "Who comes to the door?" Well, it's *knock, knock*, "Justice X forgot his glasses." And *knock, knock*, "Justice Y forgot her coffee." There I am hopping up and down.[3]

During these conferences, the justices discuss each case, with no justice talking twice before each justice has talked once, and then take a tentative vote. The senior justice in the majority assigns the opinion for drafting. Opinions are drafted and circulated among chambers, usually with editorial or substantive suggestions from other members of the Court. Each justice's chamber functions similar to an independent miniature law firm, researching and drafting independently. When some members of the Court dissent, the most senior justice in dissent assigns a justice to write for the group. As drafts of the majority, concurring, and dissenting opinions circulate, the justices sometimes change their votes. Regardless, the existence of a well-written dissent can force the majority justices to make the majority opinion better. Although the Court issues opinions year-round, it often reserves its most important decisions for the last week of the Term before adjourning for three months.

---

[3] Sandra Sobieraj Westfall, *Elena Kagan: How the Supreme Court 'Hazes' New Justices*, PEOPLE (Nov. 21, 2014, 06:40 PM), http://www.people.com/article/elena-kagan-reveals-supreme-court-hazing.

In addition to appellate jurisdiction, the Court has original and exclusive jurisdiction over "all controversies between two or more States," as well as original but not exclusive jurisdiction over other cases such as those involving ambassadors or other public ministers.[4] Original jurisdiction cases are filed directly in the Supreme Court rather than making their way from the lower courts. Somewhat surprisingly, the Court may still decline to hear cases over which it has exclusive original jurisdiction. It is most likely to hear original cases between states involving boundary and water disputes, but generally rejects cases, such as contract disputes, not deemed worthy of the Court's limited resources.[5]

When the Court agrees to hear an original suit, it will not hold a trial—although one trial was held in the Supreme Court in 1794.[6] Instead, the Court will appoint a special master to gather evidence on factual issues. The Court will then hear oral argument on the special master's report and on legal issues before deciding the case.

2. UNITED STATES COURTS OF APPEAL

The Judiciary Act of 1789 created three circuit courts. The three had both trial and appellate duties.[7] Today, the 94 district courts are grouped into 12 regional circuits (numbered one through eleven, plus the D.C. Circuit). The circuits hear appeals from the federal district courts, as well as appeals from federal administrative agencies. In addition, the United States Court of Appeals for the Federal Circuit has nationwide jurisdiction to hear appeals in specialized cases, such as those involving patent laws, and cases decided by the U.S. Court of International Trade and the U.S. Court of Federal Claims. Thus, we often say that there are 13 courts of appeal, each properly titled "The United States Court of Appeals for the [Numbered or named] Circuit."

Unlike the United States Supreme Court, the courts of appeal do not grant writs of certiorari. Instead, they are required to hear appeals over which they have jurisdiction. This is sometimes called an appeal "of right" because litigants have the right to one appeal from the trial court's judgment. The number of judges assigned to each circuit court varies, but each appeal is heard by a panel of three judges. The panels are chosen randomly—at least in theory. In Chapter 3, we will look at cases where the judges have been caught with a hand in the assignment cookie jar. If a litigant loses its appeal in front of the initial panel, it may ask for a rehearing in front of the same panel, or alternatively (or additionally) a rehearing en banc. A rehearing en banc is generally thought of as an appeal to the entire group of active judges in a particular circuit.

---

[4] 28 U.S.C. § 1251 (2012).

[5] Original Jurisdiction of the Supreme Court, Federal Judicial Center, http://www.fjc.gov/history/home.nsf/page/jurisdiction_original_supreme.html [https://perma.cc/TF9V-D9DS] (last visited July 25, 2016).

[6] Georgia v. Brailsford, 3 U.S. 1 (1794).

[7] History of Federal Judiciary, FED. JUDICIAL CTR., http://www.fjc.gov/history/home.nsf/page/landmark_02.html [https://perma.cc/62AR-LMYG] (last visited July 29, 2016).

However, in large circuits (such as the Ninth) the judges are too numerous to make a full en banc hearing feasible. In these circuits, an en banc panel may be made up of a smaller number of randomly selected active judges. These rehearings are disfavored, and under Federal Rule of Appellate Procedure 35 a court should conduct an en banc proceeding only when it is "necessary to secure or maintain uniformity of the court's decisions" or "the proceeding involves a question of exceptional importance."

Like the Supreme Court justices, the circuit judge panel has a conference after oral arguments, at which an initial vote is taken. Also like the Supreme Court, the most senior judge in the majority assigns the writing of the majority opinion. Drafts of both the majority and dissent are circulated in chambers, with edits and suggestions made by the judges on the panel. Law clerks in both trial courts and courts of appeal typically write bench briefs to help prepare judges for oral argument. These bench briefs may be shared among the chambers and frequently become the basis for the final opinion.

3. UNITED STATES DISTRICT COURTS

The 13 United States district courts originally created by Congress in 1789 have now grown to 94. These courts are often called Article III courts, referring to the Article in the Constitution that created them. They act as both federal trial courts and federal courts of appeal for some administrative courts, such as the Social Security Administration.

Each judicial district usually covers the same geographical area as a single state (and the District of Columbia), although states with large populations are broken into multiple federal judicial districts. Thus, the state of Utah has one judicial district (the United States District Court for the District of Utah), while the state of California has four (the United States District Courts for the Northern, Southern, Central, and Eastern Districts of California). Although the district boundaries mirror the state boundaries, the United States district courts are totally separate from state courts. There are also two special federal trial courts. The Court of International Trade addresses cases involving international trade and customs laws. The U.S. Court of Federal Claims deals with most claims for money damages against the U.S. government.[8]

Each district has multiple sitting judges, as well as multiple sitting magistrates. Unlike federal district court judges, who enjoy lifetime tenure and have broad jurisdiction, federal magistrates are appointed for eight-year terms and have limited jurisdiction. For example, in many districts, magistrate judges are responsible for setting bond in criminal

---

[8] The website of the Administrative Office of the U.S. Courts contains a wealth of information on federal courts, judges, their procedures, statistics, and policies. ADMIN. OFFICE OF THE U.S. COURTS, *Court Role and Structure*, UNITED STATES COURTS, http://www.uscourts.gov/about-federal-courts/court-role-and-structure [http://perma.cc/3CNF-VEZN] (last visited July 25, 2016).

cases, hearing misdemeanor criminal cases, hearing civil rights claims brought by prisoners, and writing proposed orders for the Article III judges. Cases are assigned to the judges on a random and rotating basis.

Each district also includes a U.S. Bankruptcy Court as a unit of the district court. Federal courts have exclusive jurisdiction over bankruptcy cases involving personal, business, or farm bankruptcy. Bankruptcy courts are not Article III courts but are instead created by Congress under its Article I powers. Bankruptcy judges, like magistrate judges, are "judicial officers" of the Article III courts, but do not have the lifetime tenure of Article III judges. Generally, the decision of a bankruptcy judge may be appealed to the district court, but several Circuits have established bankruptcy appellate panels (BAPs). The BAPs are made up of three bankruptcy judges and hear appeals directly from the bankruptcy courts. The BAP is not, however, a mandatory forum. Appellants in these circuits may elect to have their appeals be heard by district court judges instead of the BAP. In either situation, the party that loses in the initial bankruptcy appeal may then appeal to the court of appeals for that circuit.

4. ARTICLE I COURTS

Article I of the Constitution gives Congress the power to "constitute tribunals inferior to the Supreme Court." Article I courts, also called "Legislative Courts," are created by Congress to address specific kinds of cases. They lack full Article III judicial power[9] and, therefore, do not have authority to rule on questions of federal statutory and constitutional law. Additionally, Article I judges do not have lifetime tenure or constitutional salary protections. Article I courts include the U.S. Court of Appeals for Veterans Claims, the U.S. Court of Federal Claims, the U.S. Court of Appeals for the Armed Forces (USCAAF), and the U.S. Tax Court.

The existence and power of Article I courts is controversial, and has been the source of several Supreme Court cases and much legislation. This tension is caused by the fact that Article I courts often look and act much the same as Article III courts, but are subject to oversight by Article III courts. For example, in *Northern Pipeline Construction Co. v. Marathon Pipe Line Co.*,[10] the Court held that a statutory grant of final authority over common law claims to bankruptcy courts (which are not Article III courts) was unconstitutional. Congress responded by giving bankruptcy courts the same essential power, but making it subject to the consent of the parties and the appellate review of the district courts.[11] Similarly, the USCAAF has jurisdiction over courts-martial. In the course of exercising that jurisdiction, it routinely decides important constitutional issues. Its decisions are appealable only to the U.S.

---

[9] American Ins. Co. v. Canter, 26 U.S. 511 (1828).

[10] 458 U.S. 50 (1982).

[11] Wellness Int'l Network, Ltd. v. Sharif, 135 S. Ct. 1932, 1939–40 (2015) (discussing the history of the bankruptcy statutes).

Supreme Court. However, there are some functions, such as issuing orders to military officials outside the limited scope of its jurisdiction, that it cannot perform.

5. ARTICLE IV COURTS

Courts located in the District of Guam, the U.S. Virgin Islands, and the Northern Mariana Islands are Article IV Courts, sometimes called "Territorial Courts." They were created by Congress pursuant to its power under Article IV of the Constitution to govern United States territories. These courts exercise the same jurisdiction as United States district courts, but also exercise local jurisdiction similar to state courts.

6. ADMINISTRATIVE COURTS

Many federal administrative agencies have administrative courts. These courts often determine whether a party is eligible for some governmental protection or benefit under agency regulations. Administrative courts are staffed by Administrative Law Judges (ALJs). These judges are part of the executive branch and have neither the same jurisdiction nor the same job security that Article III judges enjoy. Although they are not part of the judicial branch, ALJs conduct hearings, issue or recommend decisions, and enforce agency regulations. More than 1,100 of the 1,300 federal administrative law judges work for the Social Security Administration. Their decisions are ultimately appealable to the United States district courts.

C. FEDERAL JURISDICTION

The federal courts hear a wide variety of cases. The federal courts exercise diversity jurisdiction over state law claims where the litigants are diverse. Additionally, federal courts exercise federal question jurisdiction over a broad swath of topics:

- Crimes which occur on federal property or involve interstate commerce
- Social security
- Bankruptcy
- Civil rights
- Airline and railroad regulation
- Securities and commodities regulation
- Admiralty
- International trade
- Patent, copyright, and other intellectual property
- Rights under treaties
- Constitutional rights

- Foreign states and foreign nationals
- Habeas corpus claims

§ 1.3 STATE COURTS

A. STATE COURT STRUCTURE

Most state court systems follow a similar pyramidal structure as that of the federal system. In practice, however, there may be many more types of courts or fewer opportunities for appellate review. Each state has at least one trial-level court and one supreme court (sometimes known by another name), but the layers above and below vary widely. Each state has its own method of assigning panels, determining jurisdiction, and determining when discretionary or mandatory review is appropriate.

1. SUPREME COURTS

All states have at least one level of appellate review. Some, like New Hampshire, have only one level of appellate review. Other courts have an intermediate court of appeal, with their supreme courts providing discretionary appeal only. Although the highest court in many states is titled "Supreme Court," some ultimate appellate courts have other names. For example, the New York court system calls its supreme court the "Court of Appeals" and its trial courts "Supreme Courts."

The highest courts in many states promulgate rules of procedure and evidence. They also generally govern the state bar, including the admission, conduct, and discipline of lawyers.

2. INTERMEDIATE APPELLATE COURTS

Many states provide an intermediate appellate court. These serve to provide litigants with an appeal as of right. Not all states, however, give their intermediate appellate court full jurisdiction over all appeals. For example, Texas divides cases between a Court of Criminal Appeals and a Court of Civil Appeals. In an even more complicated division, the Utah Court of Appeals hears all criminal cases except first-degree crimes and capital cases. It also hears a portion of civil appeals, although some civil appeals are diverted directly to the Utah Supreme Court. The Utah Supreme Court may, in turn, send a case back to the Court of Appeals for consideration. The idea behind these and similar systems is to enable one court to become the expert in a particular area of law.

3. TRIAL COURTS

While all states provide various trial courts, the number and type vary widely. In some states, all trial work falls to one court, usually called a district court. Others are significantly striated. Colorado, for example, has district courts, which hear civil cases and felonies; county courts, which hear misdemeanor criminal cases; and municipal courts, which hear traffic violations and petty crimes such as public urination and prostitution. Some states also have separate and specialized juvenile, probate, water, or small claims courts. These are often divisions of a district court.

B. STATE COURT JURISDICTION

Although much of the law school curriculum is devoted to federal cases, most litigants find themselves in state, county, and municipal courts. These courts hear a wide variety of cases:

- Crimes which occur within state, county, or city boundaries with no federal connection
- State constitutional claims
- Basic tort, contract, and property disputes
- Family law
- Civil claims based on state law or regulations
- Regulation of trades and professions (such as lawyers)
- Partnerships and corporations
- Worker's compensation
- Probate
- Traffic violations
- Most juvenile law cases

C. CONCURRENT FEDERAL AND STATE JURISDICTION

State courts also have concurrent jurisdiction with federal courts over many types of cases. The court in which a case is heard is largely a result of litigant strategy. Often plaintiffs have the choice of filing a case in either federal or state court. Location, cost, judicial specialization, and concerns about judge or jury bias all play a part in the strategy. Defendants sometimes remove cases originating in state court to federal court for the same reasons.

State and federal courts have concurrent jurisdiction over a variety of cases:

- Crimes punishable under both federal and state law, although a single incident may involve separate federal and state crimes
- Juvenile criminal law where the crime is punishable under both federal and state law
- Federal constitutional issues
- Some civil rights claims
- Some class actions
- Some environmental regulations

- Federal claims over which the federal courts do not have exclusive jurisdiction

§ 1.4 ANATOMY OF A CASE

A. CIVIL CASES

Every civil case begins with an alleged wrong, whether a contract that was breached, a doctor who misdiagnosed a patient, or a tree planted on the wrong side of a property line. While wise parties will try to resolve the case through mediation or negotiation, playing nice, or just saying "sorry," those who choose the judicial process begin with a complaint filed by the plaintiff. The complaint is a description of the particular claims of wrongdoing and a demand for relief. The defendant has the option of filing an answer to the complaint or filing a motion to dismiss all or some of the claims under Federal Rule of Civil Procedure 12. These are the usual suspects covered in Civil Procedure: motions to dismiss for lack of subject matter or personal jurisdiction, improper venue, insufficient process or service of process, or the most popular—failure to state a claim for which relief can be granted under Rule 12(b)(6).

A "failure to state a claim" occurs under two circumstances. First, it occurs when the plaintiff has written a perfectly nice complaint but has pled a cause of action that doesn't exist. Second, it occurs when the plaintiff fails to plead a necessary element of a claim. If the defense attaches any evidence to the motion (generally in the form of affidavits or other paper documentation), the Rule 12 motion is converted into a Rule 56 motion for summary judgment. Where the judge finds an error in the complaint that would warrant dismissal, she will sometimes grant the plaintiff "leave to amend the complaint"—essentially permission to file a second, presumably improved, complaint.

Once the case gets past these initial hurdles, the parties participate in one or more pretrial conferences designed to allow the judge to help guide the case. Alternative dispute resolution, such as mediation or arbitration, is required in some jurisdictions. The parties then exchange discovery, including required disclosures, depositions, interrogatories, affidavits, documents, tangible items, and physical or mental examinations. The massive amount of discovery created by digitization has caused many jurisdictions to put strict limits on the amount of discovery that must be provided.

When discovery is complete, parties often file Rule 56 motions for summary judgment. Rule 56 recognizes that it is the job of a jury to make findings of fact, while it is the job of a judge to draw conclusions of law. Where there is no factual dispute, there is no need for a jury. The judge can simply make legal conclusions and apply them to the case. Sometimes this occurs because the parties agree on the facts, so there is no need for a trial. The judge simply decides on the proper law and applies it to the agreed-upon facts. More frequently, one party is arguing that the other can't prove the necessary facts, so there is no need for a trial.

When a motion for summary judgment does not dispose of all of the claims, the parties file trial management motions such as proposed jury instructions. Generally, a jury trial follows, although not all civil litigants are entitled to a jury trial and not all civil litigants choose a jury trial. When the parties choose a bench trial the case goes much faster; but either side may demand a jury in many instances.

Regardless of whether the parties choose a jury trial or a bench trial, the pattern is the same. The plaintiff's attorney makes an opening statement. The defense attorney may make an opening statement immediately after the plaintiff's opening but may alternatively choose to wait until the plaintiff rests her case. The plaintiff presents evidence first. After the plaintiff rests her case, the defendant will move for a judgment as a matter of law, often called a "half-time" motion. The motion mirrors a summary judgment motion. It argues that the plaintiff has not presented sufficient evidence for a reasonable jury to rule in her favor. These motions are generally denied. Having spent the time and energy on a trial, the court is more likely to allow the case to proceed to jury than to grant a half-time motion and find herself reversed on appeal. Because of the appellate standards of review, an appellate court can easily reverse a judgment as a matter of law. A jury verdict, however, is almost bulletproof on appeal. No judge likes to be told she got it wrong, and although most judges enjoy the trial process, most don't want to see the same case come back around.

Now it's the defendant's turn. The defendant's attorney makes an opening statement if she hasn't already done so, and then presents her evidence. Once the defense rests, counsel may once again move to dismiss the case. Once again, the odds are excellent that the motion will be denied. The case then goes to the jury, and the jury will render its verdict. That verdict is translated into a "judgment" by the judge. The judgment is just a piece of paper that finalizes the case and triggers a right to appeal. The parties are then free to file post-judgment motions, for example a request for attorneys' fees or a request to raise or lower a jury's monetary verdict. For a losing party who can afford the cost and time involved in an appeal, the case will move on to the next track: the intermediate appellate court.

B. CRIMINAL CASES

Like a civil case, a criminal case begins with an alleged wrong. Here, however, the defendant allegedly not only has caused an injury (physical or monetary) to a particular person or entity, but he or she also has offended the sovereign.

The criminal case begins with the reported crime, usually followed by a pre-arrest investigation. The investigation may be small or significant. A police officer who responds to a domestic assault may interview only a single person before making an arrest. A detective assigned to a murder case may need lab tests, autopsies, search warrants, and interviews. The investigation must conform to the dictates of the Fourth and Fifth Amendments, whether by obtaining warrants before searching a home or by respecting a suspect's right to remain silent.

An arrest can occur with or without a warrant. Ideally, the officer has a chance to ask an on-call judge to issue a warrant. However, an officer isn't required to ask a fleeing suspect to pause while she calls a judge. If a judge issues an arrest warrant, bond is often set in the warrant. If the police execute a warrantless arrest a defendant will have a first appearance in which the judge will set bond (or determine that no bond is appropriate). A neutral magistrate then will review the arrest for probable cause within 72 hours.

If a police officer or prosecutor initiates the case, the charging document is called an "information" or "criminal complaint." In that instance, the defendant has the right to a preliminary hearing, which is a kind of mini-trial in which a judge or magistrate determines whether there is probable cause to believe that this defendant committed this crime and thus should be "bound over" for trial.

In some jurisdictions, a prosecutor may (or must) go another route: the grand jury. In the federal system and some state systems, such as New York, the prosecutor is required to present a felony case to the grand jury. In others, such as Colorado, the prosecutor has the option of using a grand jury in felony cases. A grand jury considers all the evidence and determines that there is probable cause to believe that this defendant committed this crime. It issues a "true bill," after which the prosecutor files an "indictment." A defendant who has been charged via information has no right to a grand jury review, and a defendant who has been charged via grand jury review has no right to a preliminary hearing. A defendant gets only one bite at the probable cause apple.

After the initial charging documents are filed, the defendant will be advised of the charges against him in an arraignment, hire or obtain appointed defense counsel, and be asked to enter a plea to the charges. Virtually every defendant initially pleads "not guilty," although nationally approximately 97% of criminal cases are resolved prior to trial, usually through a negotiated plea agreement.

For those who do go to trial, the pre-trial and trial proceeds identically to civil trials. Although there is no mandatory mediation, most prosecutors and defense counsel engage in plea negotiations. Both sides also file motions. The most common include motions to suppress evidence, add or dismiss charges, provide discovery, and request early rulings on evidentiary issues.

Additionally, at least some discovery is exchanged. Discovery is often more limited than that required in the civil system. The prosecutor has a duty to comport with constitutional rulings, rules of professional responsibility, rules of criminal procedure, and any statutes governing discovery. In practice, the amount and content of the discovery varies widely by jurisdiction. Some jurisdictions, such as Colorado, have very broad discovery rules. Defendants are entitled to most of the material contained in the prosecutor and police files. In these jurisdictions, defendants are required to turn over very little in return. Other jurisdictions, such as the federal system, have grudging rules of discovery. Where the defendant chooses to request the limited discovery available, he may trigger reciprocal discovery rules. In many jurisdictions, the defendant may also be required to provide discovery for affirmative defenses or claims of insanity.

If the defendant is found guilty of some or all of the charges, he will be sentenced in a later hearing. The parties may file post-conviction motions, including motions to lower the sentence. Some defendants go on to serve their time with no further court involvement. Many, however, appeal the conviction or the sentence. Direct appeals are made in the jurisdiction where the defendant was tried and convicted. State defendants, after exhausting all direct appeals, may ask the federal court to review the case through the vehicle of habeas corpus.

C. APPEALS

The losing party at the trial level begins the appellate process by filing a notice of appeal or a petition for certiorari. In most jurisdictions, the appellee is required to file a response or cross-appeal. There is no oral argument prior to a decision on certiorari. If the appellate court must take the appeal or chooses to take the appeal, the parties may next file motions for stays, injunctions, or release pending appeal. The appellant then files the record with the court. The record includes all original papers and exhibits filed with the district court, as well as the transcript of the trial court proceedings. The record may be one file or a room full of banker's boxes.

As with the United States Supreme Court, the appeal is docketed, and the parties file merit briefs. All courts of appeal have the same sort of procedural rules as the Supreme Court. Somewhat surprisingly, many appellate courts now require that the parties engage in alternative dispute resolution. If ADR fails, the appeal continues just as it does in the Supreme Court, complete with oral argument, judicial conferences, circulation of opinions, petitions for rehearing, and, where allowed and financially feasible, further appeals.

CHAPTER 2

THE ROLE OF THE LAW CLERK

> The judicial clerkship is in a sense a fourth year of law school . . . Judges often take on a professorial role with respect to their clerks which, when done well, provides an abundance of mentoring opportunities on the law, on life as a lawyer, and beyond.[1]
>
> – The Honorable Carl E. Stewart, Chief Judge of the United States Court of Appeals for the Fifth Circuit

When Justice Horace Gray hired the first term law clerk in 1875, he created a cottage industry: the courtroom and chambers as a teaching laboratory.

Clerkships are a rare and elusive thing, and competition for them is intense. There are many more extremely qualified graduates than there are open positions. Judges, particularly on the federal level, get hundreds—or even thousands—of applications for each open position. While students compete for the "best" clerkships, judges also compete for the "best" students. Judges, particularly federal judges, often offer clerkships eighteen months or more before students graduate from law school. As one judge noted, "I think some of my colleagues are frequenting maternity wards to make sure they get the 'best' clerks."

Clerkships are competitive for many reasons, including the training and experience they provide. They are also prestigious, both for the clerk and potential employers. For some areas of the profession, such as teaching, a clerkship is *de rigueur*. In other areas of the profession, a clerkship may open doors at particular firms, or even result in substantial signing bonuses.

Often staying only a year or two, clerks provide invaluable work without which an overburdened system would collapse. In 2014, 390,525 cases were filed in the United States district courts, 55,623 cases were filed in the United States courts of appeal, and 1,038,280 petitions were filed in the United States bankruptcy courts. These numbers don't count hundreds of thousands of other cases heard or supervised by the federal courts, including appeals to the Federal Circuit, cases that hung on from previous years, adversarial proceedings in the bankruptcy courts, and

1 Chief Judge Carl E. Stewart & Associate Professor Montré Underwood Carodine, *The Judge-Law Clerk Relationship: More Than Just a Job*, THE BENCHER, Sept.–Oct. 2014, https://inns.innsofcourt.org/for-members/current-members/the-bencher/recent-bencher-articles/septemberoctober-2014/the-judge-law-clerk-relationship-more-than-just-a-job.aspx [https://perma.cc/LGS2-7PFK]

post-conviction supervision. Law clerks help make it possible for judges to handle the deluge of work that comes with heavy caseloads. No judge could single-handedly complete all the research, writing, reviewing, editing, and cite-checking required in every case assigned to him or her. Law clerks are also fresh from learning a vast amount of the most up-to-date substance and procedure in dozens of areas of the law. Their encyclopedic knowledge of the newest law can make drafting and decision-making faster and more accurate.

In return, law clerks receive equally invaluable training. They sit at the right hand of experienced judges. They see hundreds of cases, motions, arguments, and attorneys in a short period of time. They quickly hone their research and writing skills; learn real-life procedure, substantive law, and strategy; and take away the most valuable lesson—"what works" in court.

Law clerks are often the "back of the house," quietly researching and writing behind the scenes. Judges vary in how much contact they allow their clerks to have with attorneys and the public, from none to frequent. Judges also vary widely in how much freedom they give their clerks. Some ask their clerks for research only, performing all the opinion writing personally. Others ask their clerks to both research and draft opinions, supervising and editing the final product. Others are somewhere in the middle, asking clerks to research and draft bench memoranda and recommended orders or opinions.

Bishop v. Albertson's, Inc.

806 F. Supp. 897 (E.D. Wash. 1992)

■ ROBERT J. MCNICHOLS, DISTRICT JUDGE.

The duties of a law clerk are undefined by statute or otherwise. Unlike other players in the judicial arena who are deemed adjuncts of the Court, such as magistrates and bankruptcy judges, and who exercise authority in their own right, a law clerk is essentially an extension of his judge.

Each judge has his or her own concept of what a law clerk is and does. Some squander talent by relegating clerks to mundane clerical tasks. Some lean too far the other direction by delegating non-delegable judicial duties.

The term "law clerk" is a holdover from days of yore when there was far less law on the books and travel more difficult. The clerk served as the judge's secretary, bailiff, scrivener, administrative assistant, and depending upon the personal wishes of the judge, his bodyguard, chauffeur, and man-Friday. While those same duties still exist to one extent or another, the explosion of legal authority and sheer volume of paperwork attendant to modern practice now focus a law clerk's function on his ability to act as a sieve for the flow of information by distilling reams of briefing and documentation into those facts which are relevant and by extracting those legal authorities which are germane to the issues presented.

When the adversarial process breaks down (as unhappily it sometimes does), it is the law clerk who assists the Court in defining issues and locating authorities which have eluded counsel. If the law clerk is fortunate and the judge wise, the clerk will also be utilized as a sounding board and devil's advocate in the decision-making process.

Career law clerks were a rarity until relatively recently. The term "career law clerk" was in fact unknown in the Article III context until coined by the Judicial Conference in 1985. Now, the practice is growing and salaries have dramatically increased in order to attract qualified individuals willing to commit to the long haul. This progression of promotions was accomplished out of recognition that the existing complement of Article III judges cannot conceivably meet the ever-expanding workload without adequate support staffing.

This shift was not undertaken lightly, nor was it undertaken without recognition that the system daily walks a tightrope. It is important that law clerks not be carried away with delusions of authority they do not have. It is important that litigants appreciate that decisions are made by a constitutional judicial officer. It is important that judges not feel their discretion has in any sense been delegated or their judgment impaired by soliciting and considering input from their clerks. Efficiency and speed of disposition in the adjudicative process are worthwhile goals, to be sure, but the system can never lose sight of the fact that Article III imposes limits not meant to be broken or winked at.

The undersigned selects his clerks with care. Scholastic ability has its place, but the focus is on maturity and judgment. The Court prefers people who have been around the barn once or twice, and who know what is out there behind the barn. Of the ten clerks the Court has employed over the past twelve years, each has displayed discrete strengths and weaknesses, but there has not been a bad one in the bunch. All have been conscientious in their work habits, unflagging in their devotion to expedition of the Court's calendar, and thoroughly honorable in their approach to ethical considerations.

§ 2.1 GENERAL ETHICAL CONSIDERATIONS

Diamond purchasers are always mindful of the four C's: clarity, cut, color, and carat. Similarly, law clerks must always be mindful of four C's: confidentiality, conflicts, competence, and civility.

The duty of confidentiality severely limits what clerks can say outside of chambers. Generally, anything that is not public record is off limits. Clerks should never talk to the media (even "on background"), discuss the case with attorneys, or reveal the judge's decision-making process.

The clerk must watch for conflicts of interest and recuse where necessary. Clerks should check to make sure they, their spouse, and their children have no financial, equitable, personal, or professional interest in the case. Additionally, clerks should inform the judge immediately if they, their spouse, or their children have an actual conflict in the case. These conflicts arise when a clerk has direct knowledge about the case, such as when she was an attorney or witness in the case.

Clerks have a duty to competently and thoroughly research all legal issues. Finally, they must be unfailingly civil—impartial and polite—when dealing with lawyers, litigants, and the public.

These ethical rules are derived from multiple sources. First, as a member of the Bar, clerks are required to follow the Rules of Professional Responsibility promulgated by the state bar. Second, each jurisdiction has its own rules or code of judicial conduct. Generally, if a judge can't do something the clerk can't do it either. Third, various jurisdictions have rules of conduct for law clerks. Fourth, some jurisdictions have statutes requiring recusal in certain circumstances. Fifth, the court in which you work may have Local Rules. Finally, your judge may have rules by which she expects you to abide, regardless of whether those rules exist elsewhere.

The Federal Judicial Center publishes a Law Clerk Handbook[2] that sets out rules of Conduct and Ethics for federal clerks. In addition, it publishes an excellent overview entitled *Maintaining the Public Trust: Ethics for Federal Judicial Law Clerks*.[3] Both provide excellent guidance on the issues clerks are most likely to encounter.

NOTES AND QUESTIONS

1. **I've Been Working Real Hard and I'm Trying to Find a Job.** Many clerks begin, or continue, a job hunt while still clerking. Clerks should be careful during both the application and interview process. Ask your judge before submitting written material from chambers as a writing sample. Clear all potential conflicts with the judge before interviewing.

While interviewing, clerks may accept routine hospitality, including meals. Many employers, particularly large private firms, may offer a variety of additional perks after an applicant accepts a job, including a clerkship bonus, compensation for Bar expenses or Bar preparation fees, or an invitation to a retreat or conference. Clerks should accept only Bar expenses and relocation expenses.

More routine problems occur after a former clerk begins a new job. Former clerks may not appear in any case that was pending with the judge during the clerkship, even if the clerk did not work on it. Some judges will

---

[2] FED. JUDICIAL CTR., LAW CLERK HANDBOOK: A HANDBOOK FOR LAW CLERKS TO FEDERAL JUDGES (2007), https://public.resource.org/scribd/8763855.pdf [https://perma.cc/JVD5-6X7Q].

[3] FED. JUDICIAL CTR., MAINTAINING THE PUBLIC TRUST: ETHICS FOR FEDERAL JUDICIAL LAW CLERKS (2011), http://www.lawschool.cornell.edu/publicservice/upload/Federal-Judicial-Center-Ethics-Brochure.pdf [https://perma.cc/J82J-ZYML].

not allow former clerks to appear in their court at all until a certain period of time has passed. Employers, in a well-meaning attempt to avoid conflicts, may ask former clerks to provide a list of cases on which they worked. This is forbidden. Instead, the former clerk should do a conflicts check as each individual case is assigned.

2. **Tell Me More.** Occasionally an attorney will ask the clerk questions about a particular case during a job interview. Those questions will almost certainly implicate the duty of confidentiality. In a more extreme example, an attorney pretended to be a headhunter, contacted a law clerk about a phony job, and then conducted a series of sham job interviews with the clerk. During those interviews he elicited damaging information about the judge and her deliberative process. The attorney's goal was to have the judge disqualified from hearing his client's case and then have her prior decisions in the litigation overturned. Not only was his strategy unsuccessful, but the attorney was disbarred to boot. The opinion in the disciplinary action makes no mention of the fate of the law clerk.[4]

3. **Feel the Bern.** Clerks are not allowed to engage in political activities whether partisan or nonpartisan. While clerks may vote in general elections, they must put away the campaign bumper-stickers, t-shirts, and lawn signs.

4. **Friends Can Be Enemies.** While posting on Facebook, writing a blog, and tweeting a thought are all commonplace activities, they may conflict with a clerk's ethical obligations to uphold the dignity, impartiality, and independence of the court. Even sending a personal email from a court computer can be problematic. Ask the judge for her policies on internet use.

5. **A Member of the Board.** Clerks should make a list of any groups or organizations to which they belong, whether or not the clerk is in a leadership position. This includes professional, law-related, civic, charitable, or social groups. If the group fundraises, lobbies, or litigates, the judge may require the clerk to suspend his or her membership and involvement for the pendency of the clerkship.

6. **Those Who Can, Teach.** Many judges will restrict their clerks' involvement in writing, speaking, publishing, or teaching during the clerkship. The restrictions may vary depending on the topic.

§ 2.2 THE REQUIREMENT OF CONFIDENTIALITY

The judicial clerk holds a privileged and peculiar position in chambers. The law clerk is a researcher, writer, editor, cite-checker, secretary, supervisor, devil's advocate, sounding board, bailiff, teacher, confidant, and consigliore.

Judges often have great influence over their former clerks' careers, providing advice and all-important recommendations and referrals. Judges often become attached to their clerks. As one judge noted, losing a law clerk is as painful as a divorce.

---

4 In re Curry, 880 N.E.2d 388 (Mass. 2008).

Central to the relationship between judge and clerk is an implied warranty of confidentiality. This is often summarized as "what happens in chambers stays in chambers." Judges must know that their theories, musings, doubts, and confidences will be kept. Without absolute confidentiality, the relationship between judge and clerk collapses.

Because confidentiality is the bedrock of the judge/clerk relationship, it is axiomatic that clerks say nothing about a pending case to anyone. Clerks must also keep the judge's deliberations and thought processes secret, even after the opinion has been released.

Bishop v. Albertson's, Inc.

806 F. Supp. 897 (E.D. Wash. 1992)

■ ROBERT J. MCNICHOLS, DISTRICT JUDGE.

Whatever one might think of the merits of the controversy swirling around Justice Thomas and his confirmation hearing, few fair-minded observers would disagree with the proposition that the circus atmosphere cheapened the process by which individuals are selected to serve as the final arbiters of the law. Beyond the process itself, some of the participants therein, and the Supreme Court as an institution, there was yet another casualty.

Among the potholes in the road to confirmation was then-Judge Thomas' involvement in a controversial and emotionally charged appeal challenging FCC policy in favoring female applicants for broadcast licenses. The policy would ultimately be struck down on equal protection grounds. The merits of the decision are of no moment to this discussion, but the procedure which attended it is. The case [*Lamprecht v. F.C.C.*, 958 F.2d 382 (D.C.Cir.1992)] was argued in January of 1991 and remained under submission during the confirmation hearing. Chief Judge Mikva and Judges Thomas and Buckley already knew what the outcome would be and preliminary drafts of the disposition had been circulated among the members of the panel. In keeping with standard practice, no one else outside of the three judges' immediate staff should have known.

Suddenly, everyone knew when the press reported, with stunning accuracy, what the ruling would be and that Judge Thomas would author it. Judge Buckley makes no bones about who leaked the preliminary drafts. It was one of the twelve law clerks working for the panel members. Not only were the drafts released but an unnamed source employed by the Court opined that the decision was being "delayed by Judge Thomas so as not to imperil his nomination." The nomination was already in trouble for reasons too widely publicized to bear reiteration. That Judge Thomas would put his suspected anti-affirmative action views into practice in *Lamprecht* would not help him in some circles. The accusation that he might delay releasing the opinion to serve political ends was even more damaging.

The scope of possible culprits expanded geometrically when it developed that one of Judge Thomas' law clerks distributed the preliminary drafts to the chambers of other circuit judges not on the panel. From there, of course, the drafts could have been further disseminated by any number of individuals affiliated with the D.C. Circuit.

Judge Buckley describes such leakage as a "willful breach of trust" which "cast[s] a shadow" over every law clerk privy to the drafts. So it is, and so it does. The leak could not have been motivated by a well-meaning but empty-headed desire to enlighten the public as to what the law was or would be. The motive, rather, could only have been to defeat Judge Thomas' nomination. Judge Buckley goes nowhere near far enough in his characterization or condemnation. A law clerk who employs his or her unique privity with the judicial process in an effort to subvert the political process violates the most sacrosanct of canons and is guilty of nothing less than official corruption.

The relationship between judge and law clerk is essentially a confidential one. A law clerk should abstain from public comment about a pending or impending proceeding in the court in which the law clerk serves. A law clerk should never disclose to any person any confidential information received in the course of the law clerk's duties, nor should the law clerk employ such information for personal gain.

NOTES AND QUESTIONS

1. **Whose Opinion Is It, Anyway?** Each case generally gets a designated law clerk. That clerk may put dozens of hours into the case, and the temptation is strong for a law clerk to say, "that's my case." However, the duty of confidentiality requires that the clerk never take credit for the work. The opinion is the opinion of the judge—regardless of how much work a clerk did on the case—and to suggest otherwise is a fireable offense.

2. **Just Stopping By.** In many instances, the requirement of confidentiality is clear. A clerk should always be mindful, however, of circumstances in which a breach might occur. An attorney may call or come into a judge's chambers in hopes of gleaning information about a case. A clerk may also need to field calls from the press. The clerk should never speak to any journalist—on or off the record.

3. **You Should Write a Book.** What is a clerk allowed to disclose after a case has been decided? After her clerkship has ended? After the judge has retired? Most judges expect that the duty of confidentiality continues even after a clerk stops clerking for a judge.

Some controversy was created when the book *The Brethren* was released in 1979. Written by journalists Bob Woodward and Scott Armstrong, the book chronicled the United States Supreme Court under Chief Justice Burger. It included a look into the Court's deliberations on a number of cases. Former law clerks anonymously handed over conference notes, diaries, unpublished opinion drafts, and internal memoranda to aid in drafting the book.

What is the balance between the public's right to know about the inner workings of one branch of government and a judge's expectation of confidentiality? Does a book like *The Brethren* potentially disrupt the confidential nature of the relationship between clerk and judge?

§ 2.3 CONFLICTS BETWEEN JUDGE AND CLERK

Because law clerks spend so much time with their judges, and because those judges are able to exert so much influence over the clerk and her future career, finding a good match is essential. There are no yentas for clerkships. Rather, it is up to the judge and the clerk to interview each other, each trying to find a good fit. If all goes well, the clerk and judge form a bond, often keeping in touch over decades.

When all goes wrong, though, it can go spectacularly wrong. A classic example is the pro se complaint filed by a former law clerk against his judge. In 2015, former New Jersey state law clerk Joseph Dearie filed a complaint against his former judge, Edward Gannon. He also sued the State of New Jersey, the New Jersey Judiciary, and a number of other private parties for due process and First Amendment violations, defamation, civil conspiracy, and intentional infliction of emotional distress.[5] The initial complaint and the amended complaint have been sealed by the court, but the former clerk posted the initial complaint on social media and it is widely available on the internet.[6]

The complaint initially looks full of crackpot allegations. On closer inspection, it contains a few potentially credible assertions, including:

1. collusion among the judge and lawyers to aid insurance fraud and racketeering in the New Jersey waste collection industry;
2. failing to read motions and making decisions based on the lawyer by whom the motion was filed rather than the law or facts in the case;
3. reaching erroneous conclusions in various cases;
4. allowing the clerk to write opinions and signing off on those opinions without reading them;
5. ex parte contact with lawyers in pending cases;
6. choosing clerks based on familial contacts and friendships;
7. appearing on the bench in a state of apparent intoxication;

---

[5] Complaint, Dearie [J.L.D.] v. Gannon, Civil Action No. 2:15–cv–00386 (U.S. Dist. N.J. Feb. 11, 2015).

[6] Staci Zaretsky, *Law Clerk Files Totally Unhinged Lawsuit Against His Own Judge*, ABOVE THE LAW (Feb. 13, 2105, 2:15 PM), http://abovethelaw.com/2015/02/law-clerk-files-totally-unhinged-lawsuit-against-his-own-judge/ [https://perma.cc/A26V-RLR7].

8. retaliating against the clerk when he complained to human resources;
9. requiring the clerk to perform personal errands, such as picking up the judge's dry cleaning; and
10. hearsay allegations of sexual harassment against court employees.

NOTES AND QUESTIONS

1. **Oh, Dearie.** The clerk in *Dearie v. Gannon* alleges a variety of bad acts by Judge Gannon. How many of Judge Gannon's alleged actions were outside the bounds of proper judicial behavior?

Dearie's complaint criticizes Judge Gannon for his performance of judicial tasks. Did Judge Gannon cross an ethical line by failing to review motions and other paperwork personally? What about signing off on a clerk's work without reviewing it? May a clerk publicly criticize the judge based on the clerk's opinion that the judge's ruling got the law or reasoning wrong?

Perhaps most importantly, what should a clerk in Dearie's position do? All states have some version of a Judicial Conduct Commission. In most states, the preliminary investigation of misconduct allegations is undertaken by staff without notice to the judge. Thus, the complainant would be anonymous unless the investigation moves to a formal stage. Chapter 5 discusses judicial discipline in more detail.

2. **A Sad End.** In February 2016 Judge Gannon died "after suffering a head injury from a fall outside a deli."[7] His estate has been substituted as a defendant in the case.

3. **It's Who You Know.** Dearie complains that Judge Gannon hired clerks based on relationships with, and recommendations from, friends and relatives. Is that a problem? Don't employers often hire through the networks of people they know and trust, especially in small towns? Many Supreme Court justices hire clerks funneled to them by a small number of "feeder" judges: circuit court judges who recommend particular clerks to particular justices. The clerks have proved their mettle through earlier circuit court clerkships, and the justices have come to respect the opinion of these lower court judges.

4. **Hired and Fired.** Dearie was dismissed after a row with the judge and was ultimately assigned to another judge. Should clerks be protected by the same employment laws as other public employees? Should a clerk be reassigned if his or her relationship with the judge goes south?

There are a wide variety of employment practices in judicial settings. In some jurisdictions, clerks are protected by the same employment rules that apply to all public employees. In others, some court employees are protected as civil servants, but the judge's personal staff is not.

---

[7] Peggy Wright, *Judge Edward V. Gannon Dies After Fall*, DAILY RECORD (Feb. 17, 2016, 9:42 AM), http://www.dailyrecord.com/story/news/2016/02/16/judge-edward-v-gannon-critical-condition-fall/80443766 [https://perma.cc/H3NK-R3QD].

The Supreme Court has received a fair amount of bad press for historically hiring white male graduates from a few highly-ranked institutions. Justice Brennan, for example, was on the Supreme Court bench for 18 years before he hired a female clerk; it was another seven years before he hired the second.[8] While the justices have hired an increasing number of women in recent years, Supreme Court law clerks are still overwhelmingly white. In addition, most of the feeder judges are white men.

5. **Would You Mind?** When the judge and clerk have a good relationship they might have lunch together, go to dinner for a celebratory occasion, or even go for hikes together. The difficulty arises when the judge asks the clerk to perform personal tasks, such as picking up dry-cleaning. For example, Dearie alleges that Judge Gannon delegated personal tasks, from running errands to researching parking options for a baseball game.

Both clerks and judges need to exercise common sense and good judgment when making these requests or performing these tasks. A clerk should cheerfully perform small tasks that he or she might perform for any other colleague such as picking up a sandwich or coffee when the judge is stuck on the bench. These small kindnesses make the office more collegial and engender good will. Additionally, some state court policies specifically allow clerks to run errands for a judge, including trips to the post office or bank.[9]

However, some state ethics advisory committees have concluded that such requests are unethical.[10] Courts may also have policies forbidding the use of public funds, equipment, or personnel for private business. If policies of this type exist, your predecessor clerks or the court administrative office should advise you. If you are interning for school credit and are uncertain about the best practices, consult the professor or director of the program. If you are an employed clerk and you feel that the judge is taking advantage, consult with an experienced professional such as the court administrator, a former law school mentor, or even another trusted judge in the courthouse. This is where your sound judgment must come into play.

6. **I Have My Rights.** In *Sheppard v. Beerman*,[11] a former law clerk filed a 42 U.S.C. § 1983 case alleging that he was fired in retaliation for protesting judicial misconduct. The clerk alleged that the judge engaged in ex parte communications with the prosecution in a murder case and then ordered the clerk to draft a decision that would benefit the prosecution. The clerk refused, told the judge that he had taken extensive notes of other instances

---

[8] David J. Garrow, *Justice William Brennan, A Liberal Lion Who Wouldn't Hire Women*, WASH. POST (Oct. 17, 2010), http://www.washingtonpost.com/wp-dyn/content/article/2010/10/15/AR2010101502672.html [https://perma.cc/NCQ3-QHRY].

[9] Calvert G. Chipchase Federal District Court Law Clerk Handbook 85 (2007).

[10] Ariz. Supreme Court Judicial Ethics Comm., Advisory Op. No., 97–08 (June 17, 1997), https://www.azcourts.gov/portals/137/ethics_opinions/1997/97-08.pdf [https://perma.cc/T3YC-88XN]; *see also* CAL. COMM'N ON JUDICIAL PERFORMANCE, JUDICIAL MISCONDUCT INVOLVING COURT EMPLOYEES (2016), http://cjp.ca.gov/res/docs/Compendiums/JUDICIAL_MISCONDUCT_INVOLVING_COURT_EMPLOYEES.pdf [https://perma.cc/CFV7-4DP8].

[11] 18 F.3d 147 (2d Cir. 1994).

of judicial misconduct, and threatened to take the notes public. Contretemps followed, and eventually the clerk was fired and his office searched.

The clerk brought First and Fourth Amendment claims, all of which were dismissed by the district court. The Second Circuit reversed in part, allowing one First Amendment claim to go forward. However, the appellate court agreed that the clerk had no expectation of privacy in chambers:

> The working relationship between a judge and her law clerk, as noted by the district court, is unique. Unlike a typical employment relationship where an employer may limit the information she wants to share with her employees, in order for a judicial chamber to function efficiently, an absolute free flow of information between the clerk and the judge is usually necessary. Accordingly, the clerk has access to all the documents pertaining to a case. More importantly, clerks regularly have access to the judge's confidential thoughts on a case. The judge may discuss her feelings with her clerk, or may allow the clerk access to her personal notes. In turn, the judge necessarily has access to the files and papers kept by the clerk, which will often include the clerk's notes from discussions with the judge. Because of this distinctive open access to documents characteristic of judicial chambers, we agree with the district court's determination that Sheppard had "no reasonable expectation of privacy in chambers' appurtenances, embracing desks, file cabinets or other work areas." Accordingly, the district court was correct in finding that there was no violation of Sheppard's Fourth Amendment rights.

7. **I've Got the Goods.** In *Sheppard*, the clerk said he had collected evidence of the judge's misconduct over time. Is there a problem with the clerk's amassing evidence to be used at another time? What should the clerk do if he or she reasonably believes that the judge is engaged in improper activity?

§ 2.4 CLERK RECUSAL

Canon 3(C)(1) of the Code of Judicial Conduct, adopted by the Judicial Conference of the United States, provides that "[a] judge shall disqualify himself in a proceeding in which his impartiality might reasonably be questioned."[12] The ethical standard is now statutorily required: 28 U.S.C. § 455 requires that every justice, judge and magistrate "disqualify himself in any proceeding in which his impartiality might reasonably be questioned."[13] This disqualification may be waived, but the judge is forbidden to accept a waiver unless "it is preceded by a full disclosure on the record of the basis for disqualification."[14]

---

[12] Code of Judicial Conduct, Canon 3(C)(1).

[13] 28 U.S.C. § 455 (2012).

[14] *Id.* § 455(e).

Just as judges are required to recuse themselves when their participation in the case raises even the appearance of impropriety, law clerks are subject to the same rules of recusal. Where a clerk has an actual interest in a case, or a connection to the parties or counsel, she must recuse herself. Further, the mere appearance of an interest or connection is reason to recuse.

Doe v. Cabrera

134 F. Supp. 3d 439 (2015)

MEMORANDUM OPINION

■ REGGIE B. WALTON, UNITED STATES DISTRICT JUDGE.

This civil matter is currently before the Court on the plaintiff's Motion to Disqualify & Memorandum in Support Thereof, which seeks to have this Court recuse itself from further presiding over this matter and vacate several of its recent discovery rulings. The motion is primarily based on comments made by one of the Court's law clerks ("Law Clerk I"), who insinuated in jest to members of defense counsel's law firm, including an attorney who has made an appearance in this matter on behalf of the defendant, that she influenced the Court's decision-making process with respect to certain discovery rulings in this case. To be sure, the Court does not condone these comments even though they were made in jest. There was no factual basis for them, and they should not have been made. For the reasons that follow however, the ill-advised conduct by the law clerk provides no basis for the Court to recuse itself.

I. BACKGROUND

A. The Court's Law Clerks

Law Clerk I began serving as a law clerk for the Court in November 2013. From the onset of [her] clerkship, the Court instructed her that she was conflicted from participating in any cases being litigated by the law firm of Zuckerman Spaeder because her father was a partner at the firm. In accordance with that instruction, the Court told Law Clerk I to have no substantive involvement with this case when it was randomly assigned to this Court, as Zuckerman Spaeder had been retained by the defendant for his defense. The Court tasked Law Clerk II to assist on the case, and Law Clerk I has never provided the Court with any substantive input regarding this case.

During Law Clerk I's tenure in the Court's chambers, she acquired the services of Zuckerman Spaeder to represent her in a personal legal matter. The firm's representation of her lasted from January 2015 through February 2015 with some follow-up discussion in May 2015. Associate Ben Voce-Gardner was part of Law Clerk I's legal team in her personal matter. Through the associate's representation of Law Clerk I on her personal matter, the two became friends and periodically sent text messages to each other, even after the legal relationship concluded. That associate has also appeared on behalf of the defendant in this case. The Court, however, was never aware that this associate provided legal services for Law Clerk I, until the events that gave rise to this motion occurred.

B. The Court's Discovery-Related Rulings And Law Clerk I's Communications With Members Of Defense Counsel's Firm

1. Telephonic Hearing

On June 29, 2015, the parties contacted the Court, seeking to resolve a dispute that had arisen during a deposition of a third party. Law Clerk I answered the phone and stated that Law Clerk II was not available. The parties outlined the discovery dispute to Law Clerk I, and she relayed that information to the Court, while reminding the Court that she was screened from involvement in the case and could not assist the Court any further. When Law Clerk II became available, which was almost immediately after the dispute was presented to the Court, the Court only sought his substantive assistance in handling the dispute. Later during the day after the discovery dispute had been resolved, Law Clerk I sent a text message to the associate, indicating that she had "[dealt] with an over[-]the[-]phone objection in one of [his] cases," and asked whether he was in Washington, D.C. for the deposition. The associate was apparently unaware that a deposition was being conducted in this case on that day.

2. In-Court Motions Hearing

On August 5, 2015, the Court heard oral arguments concerning various discovery-related motions. Law Clerk I and Law Clerk II were both present in the courtroom during the hearing. Later that day, as well the day after the hearing, Law Clerk I reminded Law Clerk II that he needed to help the Court memorialize the Court's oral rulings in paper orders, as the Court had limited availability during the remainder of that week and the following week.

After the Court issued its August 6, 2015 Order, that same day and unbeknownst to the Court and Law Clerk II, Law Clerk I sent text messages to the associate stating that he was going to "owe" her an alcoholic beverage. More specifically, Law Clerk I insinuated that she had contributed to the Court's issuance of its August 6, 2015 Order in the defendant's favor. *See* Aug. 18, 2015 Order, Ex. A (Aug. 11, 2015 Ltr.) at 1 & n.2 (Law Clerk I sending text message to associate that "as of 3:34 [p.m.] today," when the Court issued its order, the associate "owe[d] [her] a beer [(or wine)!]"). Law Clerk I also sent a similarly-worded text message to her father. Law Clerk I has represented that these text messages were made in jest, as she was pregnant and was therefore not drinking alcohol. Nevertheless, realizing the impropriety of the text messages, she informed the Court about them that same night. The following day, August 7, 2015, the Court contacted the parties to schedule an emergency conference to disclose what Law Clerk I had told the Court.

During the emergency conference, which occurred in the courtroom, telephonically, and on the record, the plaintiff orally moved for the Court to, inter alia, recuse itself from this case and to vacate its discovery rulings from the August 5, 2015 motions hearing. The Court denied the motion without prejudice, but allowed the parties to brief the issue of recusal. The plaintiff has renewed her motion in written filings.

II. LEGAL STANDARD

Because judges are presumed to be impartial, the Court must begin its analysis of the allegations supporting a request for recusal with a presumption against disqualification. The party moving for disqualification of the judge must make a showing of an appearance of bias or prejudice sufficient to permit the average citizen reasonably to question a judge's impartiality is all that must be demonstrated to compel recusal.

In applying this objective standard, the Court need not accept every fact alleged by the moving party as true.

The pall that the conduct of a law clerk may cast over the integrity of his or her judge, is covered by the appearance of impropriety notion inherent in Section 455(a). Nonetheless, whatever appropriate ethical foothold law clerks must obtain in the employ of the judiciary; the judge cannot be made an easy victim of the clerk's follies or perceived faults. Both bench and bar recognize that judges, not law clerks, make the decisions. If a clerk has a possible conflict of interest, it is the clerk, not the judge, who must be disqualified.

Finally, a motion to recuse under 28 U.S.C. § 455(a) is committed to the discretion of the Court and denial will be reversed only upon a showing of abuse of discretion.

III. ANALYSIS

A. Imputation Of Actual Bias

The plaintiff contends that Law Clerk I had an "actual bias in favor of Zuckerman Spaeder" and the bias must be "imputed to the [Court]." Her contention is supported by neither the facts nor case authority.

The plaintiff suggests that Law Clerk I "demonstrated [her] actual bias" when she: (1) "slant[ed] or skew[ed] her representation of the [June 29, 2015 telephonic discovery] dispute to the [Court]"; (2) attended the August 5, 2015 motions hearing, so that she could observe the hearing, discuss her observations behind closed doors amongst those in the Court's chambers, and relay any "concerns" expressed in chambers to members of Zuckerman Spaeder; and (3) sent text messages in August 2015 to members of Zuckerman Spaeder "indicat[ing] that she was actively attempting to assist in . . . [the firm's] success."

But these suggestions of bias are precisely the innuendos that the Court will not rely on in resolving the plaintiff's motion. They are speculative and unsupported by any facts, at best, and wildly inflammatory, at worst, i.e., they go so far as to attack Law Clerk I of being untruthful in her declaration. First, with respect to the June 29, 2015 telephonic discovery conference, Law Clerk I presented the parties' discovery dispute consistent with the Court's and Law Clerk II's recollection of the dispute. Second, Law Clerk I's attendance at the motions hearing was not part of a larger ruse to assist Zuckerman Spaeder in this case, as she communicated none of her observations or insights, if any, to either Law Clerk II or the Court after the hearing concluded. Third, although her August 2015 text messages may have implied that she had a personal bias for Zuckerman Spaeder and the defendant, that possible bias never had an opportunity to impact the case, as the Court screened her from working on it.

The plaintiff directs the Court's attention to two cases where courts have imputed a law clerk's bias to a court: *Vaska v. State*, 955 P.2d 943 (Alaska 1998), and *Hall v. Small Business Administration*, 695 F.2d 175 (5th Cir.1983). Each of these cases, however, are easily distinguishable. In *Vaska*, the law clerk substantively assisted the trial court on a case involving the local district attorney's office, and had sexual relations with another attorney in the district attorney's office. Based on these facts, the Court found that "because of [the clerk's] personal relationship with one of the . . . attorneys [in the district attorney's office], [the clerk] may have had an actual bias in favor" of that office. Moreover, the Court also found that there the clerk created a "reasonable suspicion . . . that she was an active partisan who was willing to break the rules to benefit the [district attorney's office]," because the law clerk: (1) sent "a copy of a confidential bench memorandum" to the district attorney on the case; and (2) "attached a sticky note to the memorandum" indicating that she was "battl[ing]" on behalf of the district attorney's office. No significant parallels can be drawn between the law clerk's incredible conduct in *Vaska* and Law Clerk I's actions here.

In *Hall*, the plaintiff filed a class action against the defendant employer, alleging that she and other female employees were discriminated against in violation of Title VII. The case was tried by a magistrate judge, whose sole law clerk previously worked for the defendant employer and had resigned because of allegations of discrimination. The law clerk was also a member of the plaintiff's certified class, and had accepted employment with plaintiff's counsel. Despite the law clerk's ties to the case, she participated in pretrial proceedings, attended the trial and took notes, and worked on the final opinion in the case right before she left her clerkship. Under these circumstances, the magistrate judge's failure to disqualify himself was error, because regardless of "[w]hether or not the law clerk actually affected the magistrate's decision, her continuing participation with the magistrate in a case in which her future employers were counsel gave rise to an appearance of partiality[.]"

Hall is not analogous to this case. Although the plaintiff is correct that *Hall* does not "expressly [hold] that an actual bias is imputed to [the Court only] where the law clerk [substantively] participates in [a conflicted] matter," there is no language in *Hall*, let alone any other case cited by the plaintiff, that compels imputation of a perceived law clerk bias to the Court in this case, where Law Clerk I has not substantively participated in the case. *Hall* "does not create a mandatory rule requiring the recusal of the judge whenever a law clerk employed by that judge has a real or possible conflict of interest." Rather, consistent with *Hall*, this Court had Law Clerk II take control of this case, which did not give rise to a conflict.

B. Appearance of Partiality

No well-informed and reasonable observer could call into question the Court's impartiality under the totality of the circumstances. The Court screened Law Clerk I from this case after determining that there was a conflict, and thus, she has never provided any substantive input about this case to either the Court or Law Clerk II. Incredibly, the plaintiff sees ambiguity where none exists, as she contends that she is unclear as to what the term "substantive input" means in Law Clerk I's declaration. Let the plaintiff no longer wallow in uncertainty: in this case, Law Clerk I has neither conducted legal research on any of the parties' motions nor did she provide any advice to the Court or Law Clerk II as to the merits of any motion or any other matter concerning this case. In other words, when ruling on all motions in this case, the Court has never itself, or through Law Clerk II, relied on any contribution from Law Clerk I. She did no work on the case, and she did not contribute any substantive input about any aspect of the case.

The plaintiff argues that the Court's screening of Law Clerk I was insufficient because she in fact did participate in the case. She represents that she is troubled by Law Clerk I's handling of the June 29, 2015 telephonic discovery dispute, attendance at the August 5, 2015 motions hearing motion hearing, where she allegedly took notes, and reminders to Law Clerk II to docket orders reflecting the Court's oral rulings. Such participation, however, does not cast doubt on the impartiality of the Court. At most, Law Clerk I undertook ministerial tasks that had no bearing on how the Court ruled on any motions in this case.

Further, despite the fact that Law Clerk I insinuated that she somehow influenced the Court's decisionmaking process in favor of Zuckerman Spaeder and the defendant in this case through her text messages to members of the firm, a well-informed and reasonable observer would understand that it is the Court, and not any of its law clerks, that presides over a case and resolves disputes between the parties in the case, and unfounded proclamations to the contrary from a law clerk could not reasonably change that understanding.

Make no mistake about it—Law Clerk I's decision to send text messages to members of Zuckerman Spaeder implying that she had a hand in the Court's orders in this case was regrettable and senseless, especially where such an implication was completely inaccurate. "But . . . the [Court] cannot be made an easy victim of the [law] clerk's follies or perceived faults." At bottom, none of the text messages exchanged between Law Clerk I and members of Zuckerman Spaeder affected any of the Court's rulings.

In sum, the Court finds that the unfortunate text messages exchanged between Law Clerk I and members of Zuckerman Spaeder, coupled with her minimal ministerial and observational role in this case—a case in which she has had no substantive involvement—cannot lead a well-informed and reasonable observer to believe that the Court is partial towards Zuckerman Spaeder and the defendant.

NOTES AND QUESTIONS

1. **That's What You Think.** The court concludes that "the unfortunate text messages exchanged between Law Clerk I and members of Zuckerman Spaeder . . . cannot lead a well-informed and reasonable observer to believe that the Court is partial towards Zuckerman Spaeder and the defendant." Is the court correct?

Following Judge Walton's opinion, the defense requested discovery on the issue of recusal. Judge Walton submitted the motion for reassignment. The second district judge decided that "[g]iven the incomplete state of the record and the need to assure itself that the relevant facts are known, the Court will order [the clerk] and [counsel] to submit to the Court for in camera review all documents reflecting or referring to communications between [the clerk] and any member of Zuckerman Spaeder relating to *Doe v. Cabrera*."[15] No further proceedings have been reported.

2. **The Mere Appearance of Impropriety.** In *Guice v. State Farm Fire and Casualty Co.*,[16] the plaintiff sued State Farm for damage caused by Hurricane Katrina. The court's law clerk had filed a similar suit against Allstate Insurance Company for property damage he sustained in Hurricane Katrina. State Farm asked the court to disqualify a law clerk from participation in *Guise* as well as any other Katrina case in which State Farm was a defendant. The clerk's case against Allstate was settled one month before State Farm filed its motion. The judge insulated the clerk from all cases involving Allstate and Lloyd's of London (the underwriter on the Allstate policy). However, he allowed the clerk to work on cases against other insurers. Was this conclusion correct?

In the oft-cited *Hall* case, the 5th Circuit stated:

> Judicial ethics reinforced by statute exact more than virtuous behavior; they command impeccable appearance. Purity of heart is not enough. Judges' robes must be as spotless as their actual conduct. These expectations extend to those who make up the contemporary judicial family, the judge's law clerks and

---

15 2015 WL 6163687 *6 (D.D.C. Oct. 20, 2015).

16 2007 WL 601208 (S.D. Miss. Feb. 23, 2007).

> secretaries. Because a magistrate's sole law clerk was initially a member of the plaintiff class in this suit, had before her employment with the magistrate expressed herself as convinced of the correctness of its contentions, and accepted employment with its counsel before judgment was rendered, we hold that the magistrate erred in refusing to disqualify himself.[17]

A judge who declines to recuse herself, despite the appearance of impropriety, may find herself reversed on appeal and the case remanded and reassigned. However, appellate courts may balance numerous factors in determining the appropriate remedy for a failure to recuse. An excellent example of that balancing occurred in *Parker v. Connors Steel Co.*

Parker v. Connors Steel Co.

855 F.2d 1510 (11th Cir. 1988)

Opinion

■ FLOYD R. GIBSON, SENIOR CIRCUIT JUDGE:

Appellants, former employees of Connors Steel Company (Connors) and putative class representatives of approximately 600 former Connors employees, appeal an order of the district court granting summary judgment to Connors, H.K. Porter Company, Inc. and United Steelworkers of America, AFL-CIO, CLC in this complicated dispute which followed the closing of Connors's steel plant in Birmingham, Alabama. The employees sued Connors, its parent corporation H.K. Porter (Connors and H.K. Porter are collectively referred to as the "Company"), and the Union alleging fraud, a hybrid § 301/fair representation claim, breach of the duty of fair representation, and breach of a collective bargaining agreement (CBA or agreement) and two concession agreements.

* * *

D. Recusal

After the district court issued its decision, the employees filed a motion requesting the district judge to recuse himself from the case. The memorandum opinion issued by the district court contained a footnote that reads in relevant part:

> For the formulation of this opinion, the Court is indebted to its Law Clerk, William G. Somerville, III, for his careful analysis of the massive discovery materials and his countless discussions with the Court as to how the law should be applied to the material facts as to which there is no genuine issue.

The employees argue that the district judge was required to recuse himself because his law clerk, William G. Somerville, III, was the son of William G. Somerville, Jr., a partner in the law firm of Lange, Simpson,

---

[17] Hall v. Small Business Admin., 695 F.2d 175, 176–77 (5th Cir. 1983).

Robinson & Somerville, the firm representing Connors and H.K. Porter. The employees also allege that Somerville's participation in the decisional process was critical to the court's decision because it was Somerville who reviewed the voluminous discovery documents and determined that there were no material issues of fact that would prevent summary judgment disposition of the case. Additionally, the employees allege that Somerville actually held a hearing with counsel in the absence of the district judge and later reported the results of the hearing to the judge. The employees argue that these circumstances violate 28 U.S.C. § 455 and thus require this court to reverse and reassign this case to another judge.

The Supreme Court very recently discussed § 455(a) and its goal of promoting public confidence in the integrity of the judicial process. In *Liljeberg v. Health Services Acquisition Corp.*, 486 U.S. 847 (1988), the Supreme Court held that scienter is not required in order to find a violation of § 455(a). The Supreme Court stated:

> The judge's lack of knowledge of a disqualifying circumstance may bear on the question of remedy, but it does not eliminate the risk that 'his impartiality might reasonably be questioned' by other persons. . . . Moreover, advancement of the purpose of the provision—to promote public confidence in the integrity of the judicial process—does not depend upon whether or not the judge actually knew of facts creating an appearance of impropriety, so long as the public might reasonably believe that he or she knew.

Inherent in § 455(a)'s requirement that a judge disqualify himself if his impartiality might reasonably be questioned is the principle that our system of "justice must satisfy the appearance of justice." The very purpose of § 455(a) is to promote confidence in the judiciary by avoiding even the appearance of impropriety whenever possible.

Thus, section 455(a) embodies an objective standard. The test is whether an objective, disinterested, lay observer fully informed of the facts underlying the grounds on which recusal was sought would entertain a significant doubt about the judge's impartiality.

We now turn to the objective facts that might reasonably cause an objective observer to question Judge Lynne's impartiality. First, the close familial relationship between Judge Lynne's law clerk and a senior partner in the firm representing Connors and H.K. Porter might lead an objective observer, especially a lay observer, to believe that Connors and H.K. Porter will receive favorable treatment from the district judge. This is compounded by the observation that William G. Somerville, Jr., is a former law clerk to Judge Lynne.

Judge Lynne's practice of giving credit to his law clerk in a footnote may erroneously lead some to believe that the law clerk decided the case. While it has not been suggested that the decision in this case was made by Judge Lynne's law clerk and we have no reason to believe that it was, it is not unreasonable to believe that the public may come to this conclusion. It goes without saying that it would be improper for a judge to delegate the adjudicative function of his office to one that was neither appointed by the President nor confirmed by the Senate.

Finally, we believe that when Somerville held a hearing in Judge Lynne's absence and later reported the results of the hearing to the judge this contributed to the appearance of impropriety.

We believe that these facts might cast doubt in the public's mind on Judge Lynne's ability to remain impartial and at a minimum these facts raise the appearance of impropriety. It has been stated on numerous occasions that when a judge harbors any doubts concerning whether his disqualification is required he should resolve the doubt in favor of disqualification.

We express no opinion on whether any of the above facts standing alone would rise to the level of a § 455(a) violation. We merely conclude that all of these facts taken together raise the appearance of impropriety and may cause one to reasonably question Judge Lynne's impartiality.

A law clerk, as well as a judge, should stay informed of circumstances that may raise the appearance of impartiality or impropriety. And when such circumstances are present appropriate actions should be taken. In the instant case either Judge Lynne or his law clerk must have known of the grounds for disqualification and either of them should have raised the issue. If the issue had been raised and fully disclosed the employees may have waived the grounds for disqualification.

Having determined that a violation of § 455(a) is presented, we now must determine the proper remedy. As in other areas of the law, there is surely room for harmless error committed by busy judges who inadvertently overlook a disqualifying circumstance. There need not be a draconian remedy for every violation of § 455(a).

We believe that in this case Judge Lynne's refusal to disqualify himself was indeed harmless error. In determining the proper remedy for a § 455(a) violation the Supreme Court has suggested the following test. Consider: 1) the risk of injustice to the parties in the particular case; 2) the risk that the denial of relief will produce injustice in other cases; and 3) the risk of undermining the public's confidence in the judicial process. We believe that these factors weigh heavily in favor of our conclusion that Judge Lynne's decision not to recuse himself was harmless error.

§ 2.5 THE ROLE OF THE CLERK—GOING BEYOND THE RECORD

Every judge (and clerk) comes upon poorly or incompletely researched and drafted motions—usually more often than she would like. Every judge and clerk also comes upon poorly litigated cases in which technical matters are not fully explained, a record is not properly preserved, or a lawyer fails to provide the court with sufficient facts upon which to rule.

As a general rule, the court and clerks are not bound by the law presented in the parties' briefs. Most law clerks research legal issues anew, making sure that the court has all the necessary and pertinent law when making a decision. On the other hand, courts and clerks may not make legal arguments for parties, nor may they develop a factual record.

An issue sometimes arises, however, when the parties fail to provide the court with sufficient factual information. Sometimes a court will ask the parties for further briefing, but occasionally cases arise in which judges ask their clerks to perform not only legal research but factual research as well. Therein lies a problem.

Price Brothers Co. v. Philadelphia Gear Corp.

649 F.2d 416 (6th Cir. 1981)

■ JOHN W. PECK, SENIOR CIRCUIT JUDGE.

This is an appeal from a judgment entered in a diversity action for breach of contract and breach of warranties. Plaintiff, Price Brothers Company, a manufacturer of reinforced concrete pipe, brought an action against Philadelphia Gear Corporation, claiming that machine components produced by the defendant and used in Price Brothers' pipe wrapping machine had failed to perform as represented. At the conclusion of a trial to the bench, the district court entered judgment for the plaintiff and awarded $125,864.15 in damages. The defendant appealed both the conclusion as to liability and the award of damages, and the plaintiff cross-appealed, asserting that the damage award was inadequate.

Among the issues raised by Philadelphia Gear's appeal is an assertion that the trial court relied on information outside the record in reaching its decision. As one basis of this contention, Philadelphia Gear alleged that prior to the trial the trial judge's law clerk had traveled from Dayton, Ohio, to Beacon, New York, and had observed the operation of the pipe wrapping machine that is at the center of this controversy. Philadelphia Gear argued that the law clerk's observations were presumably reported to the trial judge, and speculated that this report may have been relied on by the judge in making his findings. Philadelphia Gear asserted that it had no knowledge of the clerk's trip prior to its occurrence, that it therefore had no opportunity to be present when the clerk observed the machine, and that it had no opportunity to review or rebut any report made by the clerk to the judge. Philadelphia Gear argues that the fact finding potentially based on the nonevidentiary observation by the law clerk is clearly erroneous as a matter of law.

It is imperative that a finder of fact avoid off-the-record contacts that might bias its judgment or otherwise impair its ability to fairly and objectively weigh the evidence properly submitted at trial. A judge presiding at a bench trial may not directly or indirectly, through his law clerk or by any other means, conduct an investigation outside the record and use the results of that investigation in determining the facts of a case. It need hardly be mentioned that what a judge cannot do in person he may not do by proxy. The fact that the clerk rather than the judge made the trip and observed the machine in no way alters the problem. The fair and impartial administration of justice demands that facts be determined only upon the evidence properly presented on the record. Furthermore, it is incumbent on the finder of fact to protect the appearance, as well as the fact, or its impartiality. It is fundamental that no judgment can be maintained under circumstances that suggest that the fact finder may have relied on covert, personal knowledge rather than on the evidence produced in open court and subject to review by the parties, the public, and the appellate court.

A view by the fact finder of places or objects related to a lawsuit does not per se destroy the fact finder's impartiality. Where the purpose of a view is to assist the fact finder to better understand evidence properly introduced, and the view itself is not considered as evidence, then the potential for prejudice to a party not present at the view is minimized. In contrast, where the fact finder's observations upon a view are used as evidence to determine the facts, then the procedural safeguards of a trial, including the rules of evidence and the participation of the parties must apply.

Unfortunately, from the record originally presented to this Court it could not be determined if the trial judge's law clerk had observed the pipe wrapping machine, and if such an observation did occur, how it was used by the trial judge. Accordingly, we remanded for an evidentiary hearing on the questions of whether the law clerk had viewed the machine, what the law clerk reported to the trial judge, when the defendant learned of the view by the clerk, whether the defendant consented to the view, and, most importantly, what use the trial judge made in deciding the case of whatever the law clerk had observed.

On remand, a district judge not previously involved in this case conducted a hearing directed at the questions recited above.

The undisputed testimony from the hearing answers several of the questions presented. The law clerk did, at the direction of the trial judge, travel to New York and observed the operation of the pipe wrapping machine at the premises of the plaintiff. Counsel for neither party were present. The clerk's conversations with plaintiff's employees were limited to identifying the machine that the clerk had come to see and identifying a part of the machine in response to a question from the clerk.

It is unfortunate that our remand "for an evidentiary hearing and report" was interpreted by the district judge conducting the hearing to mean that no findings of fact were required of him. We are unable, on the basis of the cold record of the hearing, to resolve conflicting testimony as to when the defendant first learned of the law clerk's view of the machine and whether defendant consented to it. Fortunately, however, the questions answered by the undisputed testimony produced at the hearing and by the trial judge's statement do permit us to resolve the issue of whether the trial judge's fact finding was critically impaired by his law clerk's off-the-record observations and report. Thus, whether the defendant consented to the view by the clerk and is thus estopped from asserting prejudice based on that view become irrelevant.

The view involved in this case was more than a simple observation of the place where a specified event was alleged to have occurred. The subject viewed here, the machine, was under the control of the plaintiff. The plaintiff had the opportunity to manipulate what the law clerk saw in order to present an image most favorable to the plaintiff. The defendant was not present to learn what the law clerk observed, what conversations the law clerk had with plaintiff's employees, or what impressions the law clerk conveyed to the trial judge. Obviously, the defendant could not rebut any of the off-the-record information that the trial judge received from this source. These factors created a presumption of prejudice to the defendant in the trial judge's determination of facts that must be rebutted before his decision can stand.

Based on the undisputed testimony produced at the hearing on remand, we conclude that the presumption of prejudice arising from the law clerk's report of off-the-record observations has been overcome. The law clerk's testimony and the statement of the trial judge establish that the sole purpose of the clerk's trip was to observe the operation of the pipe wrapping machine and describe it to the judge so that he might be better able to understand the evidence to be produced at trial. There is no indication that the trial judge considered the law clerk's report as evidence or that the judge was improperly influenced in his fact finding by the clerk's report. Since the trial judge's fact finding was not based on the off-the-record contact of the clerk's view, any error that may have occurred in not obtaining the parties' consent to that view did not result in prejudice and was harmless. We therefore conclude that the specter of prejudice created by the judge's off-the-record contact with material evidence has been removed, and that the trial judge's findings were not biased by his law clerk's view of the wrapping machine.

[Reaching the merits, however, the court of appeals reversed, holding that the trial court had erred in its conclusions of law.]

■ MERRITT, CIRCUIT JUDGE, concurring.

Such a unilateral, irregular method of judicial investigation and decision conducted at the direction of a court without satisfactory notice by a witness who then privately advised the court of his observations, all without cross-examination turns the rules of evidence upside down and is clearly at odds with our adversary system of justice. A more forceful and conclusive showing is necessary to convince me that this kind of error had no prejudicial effect upon the trial and should, therefore, be disregarded.

NOTES AND QUESTIONS

1. **I Don't Get It.** *Price* highlights a problem inherent in some kinds of complicated cases. While the parties have been immersed in the technical details of a particular topic or device, the judge and clerk may be new to that area of the law or technology. It is the responsibility of counsel to submit the necessary diagrams, explanations, videos, or other tangible items that will help the judge and clerk understand. Without the ability to do independent research, and without understandable guidance from the parties, the court may reach the wrong conclusion.

This issue frequently arises in patent litigation. While judges and clerks are well-educated, many do not have scientific or technical backgrounds. Additionally, patent law is a complicated area that not all clerks studied in law school and that is not tested on the Bar. This knowledge gap, and the almost 30% reversal rate, is one of the reasons that some patent attorneys have called for a special trial-level patent court.

2. **Seeing is Believing . . . and Understanding.** Would it be acceptable for a clerk to look at an object at issue in a case if that object was not provided by either party and the clerk didn't speak to either party about it? For example, what if a smart phone, widely available at stores, was at issue in the case and the judge had the clerk buy the phone and examine it? Judge Posner did something similar in *Mitchell v. JCG Industries*.

Mitchell v. JCG Industries

745 F.3d 837 (7th Cir. 2014)

■ POSNER, CIRCUIT JUDGE.

[Workers at a chicken processing plant brought suit against their employers, arguing that the time they spent "donning and doffing" their sanitary gear should be counted as compensable work time rather than meal time.]

The district judge did not opine on how long the donning and doffing take, a question difficult to answer in the usual way of judicial fact determination. The plaintiffs would testify that it takes 10 to 15 minutes, the employer that it takes only 2 to 3 minutes, and how would a judge or jury know who was telling the truth? The plaintiffs could be filmed changing, but their incentive would be to dawdle; the company could doubtless find a few speed demons among the workers. The limitations of the trial process as a method of finding certain types of fact must be recognized.

One of us decided to experiment with a novel approach. It involved first identifying the clothing/equipment that the defendant's plants use and buying it (it is inexpensive) from the supplier. Upon arrival of the clothing/equipment three members of the court's staff donned/doffed it as they would do if they were workers at the plant. Their endeavors were videotaped. The videotape automatically recorded the time consumed in donning and doffing and also enabled verification that the "workers" were neither rushing nor dawdling. The videotape reveals that the average time it takes to remove the clothing/equipment is 15 seconds and the average time to put it on is 95 seconds. The total, 110 seconds, is less than two minutes, even though the "actors" had never worked in a poultry processing plant and were therefore inexperienced donners/doffers of the items in question.

This was not "evidence"—the intention was to satisfy curiosity rather than to engage in appellate factfinding—but it is information that confirms the common sense intuition that donning and doffing a few simple pieces of clothing and equipment do not eat up half the lunch break. The intuition is compelling; no reasonable jury could find that workers spend half their lunch break taking off and putting on a lab coat, an apron, a hairnet, plastic sleeves, earplugs, and gloves. What a reasonable jury could not find does not create a triable issue of fact.

Regarding the propriety of visual imagery in a judicial opinion, we note the Supreme Court's reference in a footnote in its *Sandifer* opinion to a photograph in our opinion. The Court (which affirmed our decision unanimously) said: "the opinion of the Court of Appeals provides a photograph of a male model wearing the jacket, pants, hardhat, snood, gloves, boots, and glasses." There is no note of disapproval, even though the photograph was not in evidence.

Common sense has a place in adjudication. What could be more absurd than to require as a matter of interpretation of the Fair Labor Standards Act that donning and doffing times during lunch breaks be measured daily for each poultry worker for purposes of calculating overtime pay (a modest fraction of an hour's wage) due each worker twice every day? For the employer to try to quantify that time, across numerous employees and numerous days of work, other than by statistical sampling methods suggested by neither side in this case, would be an undertaking at once onerous and futile. Nor is having to change inconsistent with the plaintiffs' having been "completely relieved from duty" during their lunch break, considering how remote from this simple changing are the "duties" listed in the regulation: "an office employee who is required to eat at his desk or a factory worker who is required to be at his machine."

■ WOOD, CHIEF JUDGE, dissenting.

[The majority's opinion] brushes past serious disputes of fact about how the donning, doffing, and washing actually take place in this workplace. I am startled, to say the least, to think that an appellate court would resolve such a dispute based on a post-argument experiment conducted in chambers by a judge. As the majority concedes, this cannot be considered as evidence in the case. To the extent (even slight) that the court is relying on this experiment to resolve a disputed issue of fact, I believe that it has strayed beyond the boundaries established by Federal Rule of Civil Procedure 56. This is quite different, it seems to me, from including an illustrative photograph whose accuracy presumably could not be contested.

The record here leaves no doubt that the parties do not agree on the central question of the amount of time it takes at these workplaces to don and doff the required clothing and equipment and to wash up. The plaintiffs allege that it typically takes workers from 10 to 15 minutes to don their equipment at the beginning of the workday. They further contend that the sanitary equipment must be put on and removed in an area isolated from the production floor, in order to protect the raw poultry from contamination. The need to go to the approved area adds to the time required to complete the donning and doffing activities. The employer paints a much different picture—one that the majority has decided to credit, despite the fact that this case reaches us on an appeal from a grant of summary judgment. The employer estimates that everything can be accomplished in one or two minutes.

This is as material a dispute of fact as I can imagine, and thus one that should have prevented disposition on summary judgment. The amount of time at issue is a question that must be developed at trial; no amount of common sense, internet research, or personal experience can substitute for that.

NOTES AND QUESTIONS

1. No Experiment Was Conducted in the Writing of This Opinion. Judge Posner's opinion in *Mitchell* references *Sandifer v. U.S. Steel Corporation*. He asserts that *Sandifer* approved the use of visual imagery in opinions.

The issue in *Sandifer* was whether the time steelworkers spent donning and doffing required protective gear was time spent "changing clothes" under the Fair Labor Standards Act. The Supreme Court noted without comment that that Seventh Circuit opinion "provide[d] a [description and] photograph of a male model wearing the jacket, pants, hardhat, snood, gloves, boots, and glasses."[18]

[18] Sandifer v. United States Steel Corp., 134 S. Ct. 870, 874 n.2 (2014) (citing Sandifer v. United States Steel Corp., 678 F.3d 590, 593 (7th Cir. 2012)).

Judge Posner is correct that the Supreme Court cited the photograph without comment. He is also correct that the "photograph was not in evidence." However, Judge Posner ignores one key difference between *Sandifer* and *Mitchell*. The issue in *Sandifer* was not whether the plaintiffs were required to don and doff the items in the picture, nor whether the picture accurately depicted the items that they were required to don and doff. Indeed, unlike *Mitchell*, there was no factual dispute at all. Rather, the issue was one of law: whether the items pictured were "clothing" for purposes of the statute. The clothing itself "was already in the Record" and thus fair game for appellate consideration.

2. But Wikipedia Says . . . . In *Rowe v. Gibson*,[19] the Seventh Circuit considered a grant of summary judgment in a prisoner's 41 U.S.C. § 1983 claim. Indiana prisoner Jeffrey Rowe alleged that the prison showed deliberate indifference to his medical needs by delaying or forgetting to give him heartburn medication. Judge Posner, writing for the majority, did significant internet research on acid reflux, going well beyond the record and citing to internet sources such as mayoclinic.org and WebMD. Judge Posner noted that, although the "web sites give credence to Rowe's assertion that he was in pain . . . the information gleaned from the internet did not create a dispute of fact that was not already on the record." However, the court reversed and remanded based on the prisoner's declaration, as well as "the timeline of his inability to obtain Zantac, the manifold contradictions in Dr. Wolfe's affidavits, and, last, the cautious, limited internet research that we have conducted in default of the parties' having done so."

Judge Hamilton took issue with the inclusion of judicial internet research in the opinion, arguing that that "the majority's decision is an unprecedented departure from the proper role of the appellate court." Judge Hamilton went on to note that:

> The ease of research on the internet has given new life to an old debate about the propriety of and limits to independent factual

[19] 798 F.3d 622 (7th Cir. 2015).

> research by appellate courts. To be clear, I do not oppose using careful research to provide context and background information to make court decisions more understandable. By any measure, however, using independent factual research to find a genuine issue of material, adjudicative fact, and thus to decide an appeal, falls outside permissible boundaries. Appellate courts simply do not have a warrant to decide cases based on their own research on adjudicative facts. This case will become Exhibit A in the debate. It provides, despite the majority's disclaimers, a nearly pristine example of an appellate court basing a decision on its own factual research.

Where is the line between legitimate research and going beyond the record?

3. **Using the Internet.** May a clerk use internet resources to research a topic? It likely depends on both the topic and the source. Much legal research, including Congressional history, is best done on the internet. Additionally, courts regularly cite to the dictionary definition of words used in statutes in order to determine the plain meaning of those statutes. It is becoming more common to see Courts cite to internet dictionaries for those definitions.

Where a court uses internet sources, it should be careful to use sources that are not likely to disappear. This phenomenon, known as "link rot," results in about one in every 200 internet sources disappearing annually. In some United States Supreme Court opinions, such as *Fisher v. University of Texas at Austin (Fisher I)*, the Court has reproduced charts or other internet sources in footnotes in order to preserve them. While neither the White House site ("whitehouse.gov") nor the Oxford English Dictionary (oed.com) is going anywhere, courts cannot assume that other sources are here to stay. Additionally, sometimes long-running sites change domain names, making it difficult to find original sources.

Law libraries have now formed a consortium known as Perma.cc designed to combat link rot. It "helps scholars, courts and others create web citation links that will never break."[20] The Perma website allows any author to input any current internet citation. Perma downloads the material and then generates a new permanent URL.

4. **That's Why I Hired You.** Sometimes a clerk may encounter an area of law in which she isn't well-versed. Clerks often need to use secondary sources in order to learn about a particular area of the law. This type of research is considered "legal" rather than "factual" and is both appropriate and necessary. As a general rule, the clerk is allowed to use any source found in a standard law library, whether primary or secondary.

---

[20] *About Perma.cc*, PERMA.CC, https://perma.cc/about [https://perma.cc/YU3T-XWJ8] (last visited July 28, 2016).

CHAPTER 3

THE ROLE OF TRIAL & APPELLATE JUDGES

> The history of American freedom is, in no small measure, the history of procedure. . . . Procedure is to law what scientific method is to science.
>
> – Justice Abe Fortas, *In re Gault*[1]

No judge gets it right every time. Moreover, "right" is often in the eye of the beholder. Every American court, with the single exception of the United States Supreme Court, is subject to review by some other court. Even state supreme court decisions may, in some circumstances, be reviewed by the federal courts.

The power to review the work of a lower court does not give the reviewing court free rein to change everything it dislikes about a lower court's ruling, nor does it give appellants a second opportunity to try the case. The scope of appellate review is almost always narrower than appellants would prefer. Because the appellate court doesn't examine every issue anew, in almost every case, the appellant is at a disadvantage in the appeals process.

§ 3.1 STANDARDS OF REVIEW

A. THE THEORY BEHIND THE STANDARDS

Standards of review are fundamentally based on the distinction between fact and law. At the trial level, the judge decides the law and the jury (if there is one) determines the facts. The same division exists on appeal, where the appellate court generally decides issues of law anew but accepts findings of fact from the lower court. These simple statements, however, mask a world of complexity.

Maurice Rosenberg
Judicial Discretion of the Trial Court, Viewed from Above[2]

If the word discretion conveys to legal minds any solid core of meaning, one central idea above all others, it is the idea of *choice*. To say

1 387 U.S. 1, 21 (1967) (quotations and citations omitted).

2 22 SYRACUSE L. REV. 635 (1971).

that a court has discretion in a given area of law is to say that it is not bound to decide the question one way rather than another. In this sense, the term suggests that there is no wrong answer to the questions posed—at least, there is no *officially* wrong answer.

Lawyers are instinctively drawn to this meaning of discretion, which is correct as far as it goes. But it is incomplete and, besides, it conceals a confusing duality by lumping together two distinct types of judicial discretion. They can usefully be referred to as *primary* and *secondary*.

When an adjudicator has the primary type, he has decision-making discretion, a wide range of choice as to what he decides, free from the constraints which characteristically attach whenever legal rules enter the decision process.

The other type of discretion, the secondary form, has to do with hierarchical relations among judges. It enters the picture when the system tries to prescribe the degree of finality and authority a lower court's decision enjoys in the higher courts. Specifically, it comes into full play when the rules of review accord the lower court's decision an unusual amount of insulation from appellate revision. In this sense, discretion is a review-restraining concept. It gives the trial judge a right to be wrong without incurring reversal.

As everyone recalls, youngsters often play competitive games without official scorers. The players themselves keep score and when one of them calls out the score in accordance with the contest rules, his tally is commonly accepted.

When the players get older, the stakes higher, and the contest more formal, the common practice is to give up relying on the participants themselves to keep the game within the rules. An official scorer is added to the contest; and along with him go an added set of rules, prescribing the status and binding effect of his calls. In Hart's terms, these are "secondary rules," and their addition, and giving them final word in making rulings, "brings into the system a new kind of internal statement." But even with such rules in the picture, "it is important to see that the scoring rule remains what it was before."

The famous Cornell-Dartmouth "fifth down" football game of 1940 is an example. Field officials have no primary discretion about how many downs add up to four or about how far the offensive team must advance the ball within four downs. Yet, when confused officiating permitted Cornell an extra down and with it the winning, game-ending score, in clear violation of the rules of arithmetic and football, there was no way to rectify the error, correct the call, or revise the game's outcome. The field officials were wrong, but unreversible.

Beginning law students tend to view the process of judicial decision from the third umpire's standpoint. They have washed their minds in cynical acid, as Holmes counselled, and say they believe the law is just what the judge wants it to be: "It ain't nothin' 'til he calls it!" More elegantly, they express too often the notion that, "The law is what the courts say it is." That is true to a degree, but by and large judicial decisions are shaped by rules, not judges' whims. The law does not authorize judges to make up the rules to suit themselves any more than sports allow officials to extemporize the score according to whim. Still, neither law nor athletics tries to review every decision made by an official.

Where secondary discretion exists, neither party may successfully urge before an appellate tribunal that he is entitled to an opposite or different decision, or to a "correct" decision. Even if the appellate tribunal concedes that by its lights the wrong decision has been made, . . . it will not reverse. A trial court determination that is discretionary in this sense has a status or authority that makes it either unchallengeable, or challengeable to only a restricted degree. This form of review-limiting discretion therefore gives the trial judge a right to be wrong without incurring reversal—a limited and variable right, we shall see.

The Supreme Court of Delaware many years ago put into words the effect of this remarkable doctrine when it said that "[a]n exercise of discretion by a trial court may be erroneous but still be legal."

Laymen can be excused if they register bafflement at that concept. How can the attributes of being "erroneous" and "legal" co-exist in a judicial decision, considering that one word means wrong and the other supposedly means *right*? That sort of anomaly is all right for football commissioners—where absurdities are always in season—but how can judges indulge in such nonsense?

A good place to start is with the worm's-eye view of the trial judge. From his perspective all appellate Gaul is divided into three parts for review purposes: questions of fact, of law and of discretion. Well-accepted principles surround the first two matters:

(1) In reviewing findings of fact, [FRCP 52(a) now states that a judge's "Findings of fact, whether based on oral or other evidence, must not be set aside unless clearly erroneous, and the reviewing court must give due regard to the trial court's opportunity to judge the witnesses' credibility."]

(2) In reviewing questions of law, appellate courts usually follow an approach that is brutally simple or simply brutal (depending on whether the process is being evaluated by the trial judge or an observer less intimately concerned). The appellate courts merely ask themselves whether they agree with the trial judge's resolution of the legal issue. If not, they reverse him quick as a flash—unless they determine that the error made was harmless, or waived.

(3) Finally, there are questions of discretion. This is the area in which appellate courts have adopted the remarkably tolerant, generous and permissive attitude already described. By doing this, they limit their prerogatives of review by their own act, without prompting or command

by the legislature and even when they are not constrained by the inhibitions on review of facts which were described above. This magnanimity and toleration of lower court decisions they disagree with is not limited to certain courts or modern times.

An area of trial court discretion is a pasture in which the trial judge can roam and graze freely rendering rulings his appellate betters might not have made, unless and until the higher court fences off a corner of the pasture by announcing that a rule of law covers the situation and has been violated. Until that occurs, the trial judge, wielding discretionary power, need not be right by appellate court lights in order to be upheld. Even if the appellate judges disagree with his call, they will defer to him.

To recognize that many of the trial judge's rulings enjoy the shield of review-limiting discretion is to appreciate only part of the story. There are gradations of discretion, ranging from the toughest, most impenetrable variety to types that are too flimsy to ward off any appellate scrutiny that looks askance at the trial court's ruling.

WHY CONFER DISCRETIONARY POWER ON TRIAL JUDGES?

Five reasons can be identified from the decisions, three of which are not particularly impressive or substantial, and two of which make good sense. First, the lesser reasons.

One is the plain urge to economize on judicial energies. Appeal courts would be swamped to the point of capsizing if every ruling by a trial judge could be presented for appellate review.

A second reason is maintaining morale. A trial judge might become dispirited if he had the sense that every rapid-fire ruling he makes at trial is to be fully reviewable by a clutch of appellate judges who can study, reflect, hear and read carefully assembled arguments, consult their law clerks, debate among themselves and, after close analysis, overturn his ruling.

The third reason for hands-off review is finality. The more reverse-proof the trial judge's rulings, the less likely the losing attorney is to test them on appeal and the sooner the first adjudication becomes accepted and the dispute tranquilized.

The common vice of the first three reasons—economy, morale uplift, and finality—is their failure to provide clear clues as to which trial court rulings are cloaked with discretionary immunity of some strength, and which are not. Remaining for consideration are two reasons that escape this criticism.

One of the "good" reasons for conferring discretion on the trial judge is the sheer impracticability of formulating a rule of decision for the matter in issue. Many questions that arise in litigation are not amenable to regulation by rule because they involve multifarious, fleeting, special, narrow facts that utterly resist generalization—at least, for the time being. When the ruling under attack is one that does not seem to admit of control by a rule that can be formulated or criteria that can be indicated, prudence and necessity agree it should be left in the control of the judge at the trial level.

The final reason—and probably the most pointed and helpful one—for bestowing discretion on the trial judge as to many matters is, paradoxically, the superiority of his nether position. It is not that he knows more than his loftier brothers; rather, he sees more and senses more. In the dialogue between the appellate judges and the trial judge, the former often seem to be saying: "You were there. We do not think we would have done what you did, but we were not present and we may be unaware of significant matters, for the record does not adequately convey to us all that went on at the trial. Therefore, we defer to you."

Review-restraining discretion need not be a synonym for lawlessness and tyranny, as Lord Camden feared. It need not be evil and dangerous if those who confer it, those who wield it, and those who review its exercise are sensitive to the risks and responsibilities it involves; if they understand its proper uses; and if they play fair with the system of justice for which they are custodians.

For in the last analysis, the difference between a government of law and a government of men is not that rules decide the cases in the former and fools or tyrants in the latter. Men always decide cases. The difference lies in whether the men—the judges—are aware of their power, aware of their duties, and true to the common law tradition of administering justice under law.

NOTES AND QUESTIONS

1. A Change is Gonna Come. Review of an opinion may come from higher courts, but occasionally the Supreme Court reviews, edits, and even reverses itself. These changes can come in myriad ways.

First, the Court will sometimes substantively reverse course, even in the face of clear precedent. Often this is because the Court sees that early case law was unworkable or because an earlier dissent becomes more convincing as time goes on. For example, in *Betts v. Brady*,[3] the Court held that indigent state felony defendants had no right to appointed counsel absent "special circumstances." Twenty years later, the Court reversed itself, holding in *Gideon v. Wainwright*[4] that these same defendants had a right to appointed counsel. Justice Black, who wrote the dissent in *Betts*, wrote the majority opinion in *Gideon*.

Second, justices may sometimes essentially reverse themselves, expressing the opposite of a formerly held position. In one case involving a Danish citizen who sat out World War II in the U.S. and then sought naturalization, Justice Jackson noted:

---

[3] 316 U.S. 455 (1942).

[4] 372 U.S 335 (1963).

> I concur in the judgment and opinion of the Court. But since it is contrary to an opinion which, as Attorney General, I rendered in 1940, I owe some word of explanation. I am entitled to say of that opinion what any discriminating reader must think of it—that it was as foggy as the statute the Attorney General was asked to interpret. . . . Precedent, however, is not lacking for ways by which a judge may recede from a prior opinion that has proven untenable and perhaps misled others. *See* Chief Justice Taney, *License Cases*, 5 How. 504, recanting views he had pressed upon the Court as Attorney General of Maryland in *Brown v. Maryland*, 12 Wheat. 419. Baron Bramwell extricated himself from a somewhat similar embarrassment by saying, "The matter does not appear to me now as it appears to have appeared to me then." *Andrews* v. *Styrap*, 26 L. T. R. (N. S.) 704, 706. And Mr. Justice Story, accounting for his contradiction of his own former opinion, quite properly put the matter: "My own error, however, can furnish no ground for its being adopted by this Court . . . ." *United States v. Gooding*, 12 Wheat. 460, 478. Perhaps Dr. Johnson really went to the heart of the matter when he explained a blunder in his dictionary—"Ignorance, sir, ignorance." But an escape less self-depreciating was taken by Lord Westbury, who, it is said, rebuffed a barrister's reliance upon an earlier opinion of his Lordship: "I can only say that I am amazed that a man of my intelligence should have been guilty of giving such an opinion." If there are other ways of gracefully and good-naturedly surrendering former views to a better considered position, I invoke them all.[5]

Finally, the Court has begun publicly noting revisions to its opinions,[6] which in past years had come silently days, months, or even years after the original.[7]

Some of these changes are merely stylistic, such as Justice Breyer's change from the word "offer" to the word "confer" in *Whole Woman's Health v. Hellerstedt*.[8] Others are more substantive. In *United States v. Bryant*,[9] Justice Ginsburg mistakenly wrote that the Major Crimes Act applies "when both perpetrator and victim are Indians." The revised opinion was corrected to note that the Act applies when the perpetrator is an Indian and the victim is "another Indian or other person."[10] In a well-publicized faux pas, Justice Scalia wrote a snarky dissent in *EPA v. EME Homer City Generation*.[11] In

---

[5] McGrath v. Kristensen, 340 U.S. 162, 176–78 (1950)(Jackson, J., concurring).

[6] *2015 Term Opinions of the Court: Slip Opinions, Per Curiams (PC), and Original Case Decrees (D)*, Supreme Court of the United States, https://www.supremecourt.gov/opinions/slipopinions.aspx [https://perma.cc/9CUG-QEB9] (last updated July 15, 2016).

[7] Adam Liptak, *Justices Show How Disclosing Revisions Offers (Confers?) Benefits*, N.Y. TIMES (July 25, 2016), http://www.nytimes.com/2016/07/26/us/politics/supreme-court-opinion-edits.html?hp&action=click&pgtype=Homepage&clickSource=story-heading&module=second-column-region®ion=top-news&WT.nav=top-news&_r=0 [https://perma.cc/EN8E-YJQU].

[8] *Id.*; *see also* Whole Woman's Health v. Hellerstedt, 136 S. Ct. 2292 (2016).

[9] 136 S. Ct. 1954 (2016).

[10] Id. at 1961.

[11] 134 S. Ct. 1584, 1616 (2014).

his *EME* dissent, he complained that the EPA was flip-flopping on an identical issue: taking one position in *Whitman v. American Trucking Association*[12] but a different position in *EME*. Unfortunately, Justice Scalia misstated the position of the EPA in *Whitman*—a case where he authored the majority opinion.[13] He quickly remedied the mistake, changing the section heading from "Plus Ça Change: E.P.A.'s Continuing Quest for Cost-Benefit Authority," to "Our Precedent."[14]

In many of these cases, law professors, commentators, journalists, and the parties act as appellants, quickly noting and publicizing the Court's missteps.

2. **The Cold War Basketball Game.** As noted by Professor Rosenberg, sports are full of discretionary calls and requests for review. In one notorious example, one Olympic men's basketball game spawned three "do-overs" and forty years of appeals.

The finals of the 1972 men's basketball tournament at the Munich Olympics was played by a U.S. team of amateur college players against a Soviet Union team of seasoned veterans. The U.S. had never lost an Olympic basketball game, but trailed in this one until the final moments. With three seconds to play, the U.S. sank two free throws to take a one-point lead. As the Soviet team inbounded the ball to take a desperation shot, the referee on the court halted play with one second left. He later explained that he thought the scorer's table had signaled for a timeout. This allowed the Soviet team to advance the ball to mid-court and attempt an in-bound pass, which was deflected, and the game appeared to be over.

Then Renato William Jones, the head of FIBA (the International Basketball Association) came out of the stands and insisted that three seconds be put back on the clock. While the scorer's table was adjusting the clock, the Soviets made an illegal substitution to put a better passer into the game, and the on-court referee allowed play to resume. Just as the first pass was made, the buzzer sounded to end the game. Jones remained at the scorer's table and insisted that play be started once again with three seconds on the clock. On what was now the third attempt to put the ball into play, the Soviet team was able to make a pass toward their goal resulting in a "game-winning" basket.

The Americans protested, the on-court referee reportedly refused to sign the official score sheet, and the officials at the scorer's table apparently were totally confused about the game clock and timeouts. The United States Olympic Committee appealed the Soviet victory, but a FIBA jury of five, three from Soviet countries, held that the Soviet team had won. Despite the FIBA ruling, the American team refused to accept the second-place silver

---

[12] 531 U.S. 457 (2001).

[13] Whitman v. Am. Trucking Ass'n, 531 U.S. 457 (2001).

[14] EPA v. EME Homer City Generation, 134 S. Ct. 1584, 1616 (2014); Jonathan H. Adler, *Justice Scalia Is Not the Only One Making Errors*, WASH. POST (May 1, 2014), https://www.washingtonpost.com/news/volokh-conspiracy/wp/2014/05/01/justice-scalia-is-not-the-only-one-making-errors/?utm_term=.7d47044b2bdc [https://perma.cc/B78N-K9K6].

medal. The controversy over the game became part of the legend of the Cold War Era.

Members of the U.S. team have petitioned the FIBA and the International Olympic Committee for over 40 years to award the Americans and Soviets duplicate gold metals. A precedent for dual metals was set after a 2002 pairs figure skating judging scandal. Although all participants, including Jones, admit that the head of FIBA had no authority to interfere with the decisions made on the court or at the scorer's table, the IOC lacks the power to overturn the decision of FIBA. As the governing body for the sport, the decision of the FIBA is unreviewable.

What parallels do you see between the basketball game and the judicial system? How did precedent, discretionary actions by finders of fact, and appellate entities work in this case?

B. STANDARDS OF REVIEW (THE USUAL SUSPECTS)

A reviewing court's role is framed by the proper standard of review. In order to determine the proper standard of review, the court begins by asking what kind of decision it is being asked to review. Legal rulings, factual findings, discretionary decisions, and administrative actions all receive a different level of scrutiny. The four most common standards of review are de novo, clearly erroneous, substantial deference, and abuse of discretion.

1. ISSUES OF LAW: DE NOVO REVIEW

Issues of law always receive de novo review. In de novo review, the reviewing court reviews the legal question completely independently. It gives no deference to the conclusions of the trial court. De novo review is the only standard that favors the appellant and is the only appeal in which the appellant truly gets a second bite at the apple.

2. FACTUAL DETERMINATIONS BY THE TRIAL COURT: CLEARLY ERRONEOUS

On the other end of the spectrum, issues of fact decided by a trial court get significant deference. The trial judge is in the best position to view evidence, and thus in the best position to determine the facts. The appellate court cannot watch the trial or a hearing after the fact and make decisions about the veracity of witnesses. The trial judge was able to see which witnesses were nervous or wouldn't make eye contact, and which seemed to be telling the truth.[15]

[15] Studies have shown consistently that people are surprisingly bad at determining who is telling the truth and who is not. *See, e.g.*, Richard Wiseman, *The MegaLab Truth Test*, 373 NATURE 391 (1995); Bella M. DePaulo & Wendy L. Morris, *Discerning Lies from Truths: Behavioural Cues to Deception and the Indirect Pathway of Intuition*, THE DETECTION OF DECEPTION IN FORENSIC CONTEXTS 15 (Pär Anders Granhag & Leif A. Stromwell eds., 2004).

The standard for appellate review of judicial findings of fact is "clearly erroneous."[16] "A finding is clearly erroneous when, although there is evidence to support it, the reviewing court on the entire evidence is left with the definite and firm conviction that a mistake has been committed."[17] When the evidence will support either of two permissible conclusions, a trial judge's choice between the two cannot be considered clearly erroneous. Put far more colorfully by the Seventh Circuit in *Parts and Electric Motors, Inc. v. Sterling Electric, Inc.*,[18]

> To be clearly erroneous, a decision must strike us as more than just maybe or probably wrong; it must . . . strike us as wrong with the force of a five-week old, unrefrigerated dead fish.

With the decreasing number of jury trials, judges more frequently become both the finders of fact and the arbiters of law.

Anderson v. Bessemer City

470 U.S. 564 (1985)

■ JUSTICE WHITE delivered the opinion of the Court.

In *Pullman-Standard* v. *Swint*, 456 U.S. 273 (1982), we held that a District Court's finding of discriminatory intent in an action brought under Title VII of the Civil Rights Act of 1964, is a factual finding that may be overturned on appeal only if it is clearly erroneous. In this case, the Court of Appeals for the Fourth Circuit concluded that there was clear error in a District Court's finding of discrimination and reversed. Because our reading of the record convinces us that the Court of Appeals misapprehended and misapplied the clearly-erroneous standard, we reverse.

I

Early in 1975, officials of respondent Bessemer City, North Carolina, set about to hire a new Recreation Director for the city. Although the duties that went with the position were not precisely delineated, the new Recreation Director was to be responsible for managing all of the city's recreational facilities and for developing recreational programs—athletic and otherwise—to serve the needs of the city's residents. A five-member committee selected by the Mayor was responsible for choosing the Recreation Director. Of the five members, four were men; the one woman on the committee, Mrs. Auddie Boone, served as the chairperson.

Eight persons applied for the position of Recreation Director. Petitioner, at the time a 39-year-old schoolteacher with college degrees in social studies and education, was the only woman among the eight.

---

[16] FED. R. CIV. P. 52(a)(6) ("Findings of fact, whether based on oral or other evidence, must not be set aside unless clearly erroneous, and the reviewing court must give due regard to the trial court's opportunity to judge the witnesses' credibility).

[17] *See* United States v. United States Gypsum Co., 333 U.S. 364, 395 (1948).

[18] 866 F.2d 228, 233 (7th Cir. 1988).

The selection committee reviewed the resumes submitted by the applicants and briefly interviewed each of the jobseekers. Following the interviews, the committee offered the position to Mr. Donald Kincaid, a 24-year-old who had recently graduated from college with a degree in physical education. All four men on the committee voted to offer the job to Mr. Kincaid; Mrs. Boone voted for petitioner.

Petitioner then filed this Title VII action in the United States District Court for the Western District of North Carolina. After a 2-day trial during which the court heard testimony from petitioner, Mr. Kincaid, and the five members of the selection committee, the court issued a brief memorandum of decision setting forth its finding that petitioner was entitled to judgment because she had been denied the position of Recreation Director on account of her sex. In addition to laying out the rationale for this finding, the memorandum requested that petitioner's counsel submit proposed findings of fact and conclusions of law expanding upon those set forth in the memorandum. Petitioner's counsel complied with this request by submitting a lengthy set of proposed findings; the court then requested and received a response setting forth in detail respondent's objections to the proposed findings—objections that were, in turn, answered by petitioner's counsel in a somewhat less lengthy reply. After receiving these submissions, the court issued its own findings of fact and conclusions of law.

As set forth in the formal findings of fact and conclusions of law, the court's finding that petitioner had been denied employment by respondent because of her sex rested on a number of subsidiary findings. First, the court found that at the time the selection committee made its choice, petitioner had been better qualified than Mr. Kincaid to perform the range of duties demanded by the position. The court based this finding on petitioner's experience as a classroom teacher responsible for supervising schoolchildren in recreational and athletic activities, her employment as a hospital recreation director in the late 1950's, her extensive involvement in a variety of civic organizations, her knowledge of sports acquired both as a high school athlete and as a mother of children involved in organized athletics, her skills as a public speaker, her experience in handling money (gained in the course of her community activities and in her work as a bookkeeper for a group of physicians), and her knowledge of music, dance, and crafts. The court found that Mr. Kincaid's principal qualifications were his experience as a student teacher and as a coach in a local youth basketball league, his extensive knowledge of team and individual sports, acquired as a result of his lifelong involvement in athletics, and his formal training as a physical education major in college. Noting that the position of Recreation Director involved more than the management of athletic programs, the court concluded that petitioner's greater breadth of experience made her better qualified for the position.

Second, the court found that the male committee members had in fact been biased against petitioner because she was a woman. The court based this finding in part on the testimony of one of the committee members that he believed it would have been "real hard" for a woman to handle the job and that he would not want his wife to have to perform the duties of the Recreation Director. The finding of bias found additional support in evidence that another male committee member had told Mr. Kincaid, the successful applicant, of the vacancy and had also solicited applications from three other men, but had not attempted to recruit any women for the job.

Also critical to the court's inference of bias was its finding that petitioner, alone among the applicants for the job, had been asked whether she realized the job would involve night work and travel and whether her husband approved of her applying for the job. The court's finding that the committee had pursued this line of inquiry only with petitioner was based on the testimony of petitioner that these questions had been asked of her and the testimony of Mrs. Boone that similar questions had not been asked of the other applicants. Although Mrs. Boone also testified that during Mr. Kincaid's interview, she had made a "comment" to him regarding the reaction of his new bride to his taking the position of Recreation Director, the court concluded that this comment was not a serious inquiry, but merely a "facetious" remark prompted by Mrs. Boone's annoyance that only petitioner had been questioned about her spouse's reaction. The court also declined to credit the testimony of one of the male committee members that Mr. Kincaid had been asked about his wife's feelings "in a way" and the testimony of another committeeman that all applicants had been questioned regarding their willingness to work at night and their families' reaction to night work. The court concluded that the finding that only petitioner had been seriously questioned about her family's reaction suggested that the male committee members believed women had special family responsibilities that made certain forms of employment inappropriate.

Finally, the court found that the reasons offered by the male committee members for their choice of Mr. Kincaid were pretextual. The court rejected the proposition that Mr. Kincaid's degree in physical education justified his choice, as the evidence suggested that where male candidates were concerned, the committee valued experience more highly than formal training in physical education. The court also rejected the claim of one of the committeemen that Mr. Kincaid had been hired because of the superiority of the recreational programs he planned to implement if selected for the job. The court credited the testimony of one of the other committeemen who had voted for Mr. Kincaid that the programs outlined by petitioner and Mr. Kincaid were substantially identical.

On the basis of its findings that petitioner was the most qualified candidate, that the committee had been biased against hiring a woman, and that the committee's explanations for its choice of Mr. Kincaid were pretextual, the court concluded that petitioner had met her burden of establishing that she had been denied the position of Recreation Director because of her sex. Petitioner having conceded that ordering the city to hire her would be an inappropriate remedy under the circumstances, the court awarded petitioner backpay in the amount of $30,397 and attorney's fees of $16,971.59.

The Fourth Circuit reversed the District Court's finding of discrimination. In the view of the Court of Appeals, three of the District Court's crucial findings were clearly erroneous: the finding that petitioner was the most qualified candidate, the finding that petitioner had been asked questions that other applicants were spared, and the finding that the male committee members were biased against hiring a woman. Having rejected these findings, the Court of Appeals concluded that the District Court had erred in finding that petitioner had been discriminated against on account of her sex.

II

We must deal at the outset with the Fourth Circuit's suggestion that "close scrutiny of the record in this case [was] justified by the manner in which the opinion was prepared,"—that is, by the District Court's adoption of petitioner's proposed findings of fact and conclusions of law.

We, too, have criticized courts for their verbatim adoption of findings of fact prepared by prevailing parties, particularly when those findings have taken the form of conclusory statements unsupported by citation to the record. We are also aware of the potential for overreaching and exaggeration on the part of attorneys preparing findings of fact when they have already been informed that the judge has decided in their favor. Nonetheless, our previous discussions of the subject suggest that even when the trial judge adopts proposed findings verbatim, the findings are those of the court and may be reversed only if clearly erroneous.

In any event, the District Court in this case does not appear to have uncritically accepted findings prepared without judicial guidance by the prevailing party. The court itself provided the framework for the proposed findings when it issued its preliminary memorandum, which set forth its essential findings and directed petitioner's counsel to submit a more detailed set of findings consistent with them. Further, respondent was provided and availed itself of the opportunity to respond at length to the proposed findings. Nor did the District Court simply adopt petitioner's proposed findings: the findings it ultimately issued—and particularly the crucial findings regarding petitioner's qualifications, the questioning to which petitioner was subjected, and bias on the part of the committeemen—vary considerably in organization and content from those submitted by petitioner's counsel. Under these circumstances, we see no reason to doubt that the findings issued by the District Court represent the judge's own considered conclusions. There is no reason to subject those findings to a more stringent appellate review than is called for by the applicable rules.

III

Because a finding of intentional discrimination is a finding of fact, the standard governing appellate review of a district court's finding of discrimination is that set forth in Federal Rule of Civil Procedure 52(a): "Findings of fact shall not be set aside unless clearly erroneous, and due regard shall be given to the opportunity of the trial court to judge of the credibility of the witnesses." The question before us, then, is whether the Court of Appeals erred in holding the District Court's finding of discrimination to be clearly erroneous.

Although the meaning of the phrase "clearly erroneous" is not immediately apparent, certain general principles governing the exercise of the appellate court's power to overturn findings of a district court may be derived from our cases. The foremost of these principles, as the Fourth Circuit itself recognized, is that "[a] finding is 'clearly erroneous' when although there is evidence to support it, the reviewing court on the entire evidence is left with the definite and firm conviction that a mistake has been committed." This standard plainly does not entitle a reviewing court to reverse the finding of the trier of fact simply because it is convinced that it would have decided the case differently. The reviewing court oversteps the bounds of its duty under Rule 52(a) if it undertakes to duplicate the role of the lower court. If the district court's account of the evidence is plausible in light of the record viewed in its entirety, the court of appeals may not reverse it even though convinced that had it been sitting as the trier of fact, it would have weighed the evidence differently.

The rationale for deference to the original finder of fact is not limited to the superiority of the trial judge's position to make determinations of credibility. The trial judge's major role is the determination of fact, and with experience in fulfilling that role comes expertise. Duplication of the trial judge's efforts in the court of appeals would very likely contribute only negligibly to the accuracy of fact determination at a huge cost in diversion of judicial resources. In addition, the parties to a case on appeal have already been forced to concentrate their energies and resources on persuading the trial judge that their account of the facts is the correct one; requiring them to persuade three more judges at the appellate level is requiring too much. As the Court has stated in a different context, the trial on the merits should be "the 'main event' . . . rather than a 'tryout on the road.' "

IV

Application of the foregoing principles to the facts of the case lays bare the errors committed by the Fourth Circuit in its employment of the clearly-erroneous standard.

Based on our own reading of the record, we cannot say that either interpretation of the facts is illogical or implausible. Each has support in inferences that may be drawn from the facts in the record; and if either interpretation had been drawn by a district court on the record before us, we would not be inclined to find it clearly erroneous. The question we must answer, however, is not whether the Fourth Circuit's interpretation of the facts was clearly erroneous, but whether the District Court's finding was clearly erroneous.

Our determination that the findings of the District Court regarding petitioner's qualifications, the conduct of her interview, and the bias of the male committee members were not clearly erroneous leads us to conclude that the court's finding that petitioner was discriminated against on account of her sex was also not clearly erroneous. The District Court's findings regarding petitioner's superior qualifications and the bias of the selection committee are sufficient to support the inference that petitioner was denied the position of Recreation Director on account of her sex. Accordingly, we hold that the Fourth Circuit erred in denying petitioner relief under Title VII.

In so holding, we do not assert that our knowledge of what happened 10 years ago in Bessemer City is superior to that of the Court of Appeals; nor do we claim to have greater insight than the Court of Appeals into the state of mind of the men on the selection committee who rejected petitioner for the position of Recreation Director. Even the trial judge, who has heard the witnesses directly and who is more closely in touch than the appeals court with the milieu out of which the controversy before him arises, cannot always be confident that he "knows" what happened. Often, he can only determine whether the plaintiff has succeeded in presenting an account of the facts that is more likely to be true than not. Our task—and the task of appellate tribunals generally—is more limited still: we must determine whether the trial judge's conclusions are clearly erroneous. On the record before us, we cannot say that they are. Accordingly, the judgment of the Court of Appeals is *Reversed.*

NOTES AND QUESTIONS

1. **Paper Records.** Prior to 1985, some courts applied a different standard of review to Rule 52 determinations. Rule 52 currently provides that "[f]indings of fact, whether based on oral or other evidence, must not be set aside unless clearly erroneous, and the reviewing court must give due regard to the trial court's opportunity to judge the witnesses' credibility." Prior to 1985, the Rule did not contain the language "whether based on oral or other evidence."

As a result, reviewing courts often varied the standard of review based on the type of evidence provided to the trial court. Some appellate courts reviewed findings based on documentary evidence de novo, some applied a "less rigorous" standard of review, and some held that "clearly erroneous" still meant the same regardless of the nature of the evidence before the trial judge. Courts that applied a more rigorous standard of review reasoned that, when a final judgment was entered on the basis of briefs and exhibits with no live witness testimony, the appellate court was in as good a position as the district court to make a decision based on a purely paper record. The Advisory Committee recognized this argument but concluded instead that:

> [t]hese considerations are outweighed by the public interest in the stability and judicial economy that would be promoted by recognizing that the trial court, not the appellate tribunal, should be the finder of the facts. To permit courts of appeals to share more actively in the fact-finding function would tend to undermine the legitimacy of the district courts in the eyes of litigants, multiply appeals by encouraging appellate retrial of some factual issues, and needlessly reallocate judicial authority.

2. **Try to Keep Up.** Some courts are slow to catch on to new ideas. The Utah version of Rule 52 was amended to track the federal language in 1987. More than a year later, the Utah Court of Appeals decided *In re Adoption of Infant Anonymous*.[19] The natural mother relinquished her parental rights in a proceeding before Judge Murphy. Later, she asked a different judge in a different proceeding to set aside the adoption. The second judge granted her motion on a purely documentary record, and the adoptive parents appealed.

> Appellants challenge Judge Moffat's written finding that the natural mother's oral and written consent to adoption before Judge Murphy was not knowingly given because she was not clearly apprised of the finality of signing the written consent. Normally we would review this determination by the factfinder under the standard set forth in Utah R. Civ. P. 52(a), giving great deference to the trial judge's ability to assess the credibility of witnesses and setting aside the finding only if clearly erroneous. However, because no evidentiary hearing was held, Judge Moffat had before him only the affidavits of the natural mother, the counselor, and the obstetrician, described above, the transcript of the June 24 appearance before Judge Murphy, and the natural mother's written consent to adoption executed that day. Because the trial court's finding was based solely on these written materials and involved no assessment of witness credibility or competency, this court is in as good a position as the trial court to examine the evidence de novo and determine the facts.

The appellate court apparently either did not know about the rule change or failed to recognize its purpose. How seriously should we be concerned about an intermediate court's failure to track rules changes as they occur?

3. FACTUAL DETERMINATIONS BY A JURY: SUBSTANTIAL DEFERENCE

Appellate courts give even more deference to decisions by juries. Like a trial judge, the jury is in the best position to make findings of fact, and it does so in a trial that can't be replicated or viewed at the appellate level. Furthermore, the jury represents the judgment and values of the

---

[19] 760 P.2d 916 (Utah Ct. App. 1988).

community. The standard of review for jury findings is usually "substantial deference." The appellate court will review the record to determine whether there was evidence from which reasonable minds could have reached the conclusion reached by that jury. The appellate court will not disturb a jury verdict unless the appellant can show that there is no substantial evidence to support it, considering the evidence in the light most favorable to the verdict and with all reasonable inferences deducible from the evidence drawn in support of the verdict.

A trial judge is generally said to be lord of the law while juries are rulers of the facts. In truth, many judges put a thumb on the scale of fact-finding through their evidentiary rulings and jury instructions.

4. MIXED ISSUES OF LAW AND FACT: IT DEPENDS

A mixed question of law and fact occurs when "the historical facts are established, the rule of law is undisputed, and the issue is whether the facts satisfy the legal rule."[20] This determination might take place in different contexts. Sometimes, the trial judge will make legal determinations while the jury both finds facts and determines whether those facts satisfy the legal rule. In other contexts, the trial judge makes legal determinations, finds facts, and determines whether those facts meet the legal rule.

> For example, imagine that a man is appealing his conviction under a law that states "it is a crime to be tall." What kind of question is: "Was the trial court correct to find the man 'tall'?" Can we answer it solely by determining the facts of the case? No, because even if we know the fact that the man is five feet ten inches, we do not know if he is "tall" in the sense that Congress intended the word "tall" to mean. Can we answer it solely by determining what the relevant law means without knowing the man's height? No, because even if we know that the statute defines "tall" as "six feet or taller," we do not know how tall the man is. Thus, we have a mixed question of fact and law. Once we know the facts of the case (that the man is five feet ten inches tall), and what the relevant law means (it is a crime to be six feet tall or taller), we can answer "no" to the question "Was the trial court correct to find the man 'tall'?"[21]

As in other appeals, the trial judge's rulings on the law are reviewed de novo. However, the proper standard of review for the application of the facts to the law is somewhat unclear. The jury's factual determination is reviewed with much deference, but its decision regarding whether the

---

[20] *Mixed Question of Law and Fact*, U.S. COURTS FOR THE NINTH CIRCUIT, http://cdn.ca9.uscourts.gov/datastore/uploads/guides/stand_of_review/I_Definitions.html#_Toc199130794 [https://perma.cc/9F3J-UDYS] (last visited Aug. 2, 2016) (citing e.g., *Pullman-Standard v. Swint*, 456 U.S. 273, 289 n.19 (1982).

[21] Interfaith Cmty Org. v. Honeywell Int'l., Inc., 399 F.3d 248, 269–70 (3d Cir. 2005) (Ambro, J., concurring).

facts fit the legal standard less so. The more fact-dominated the question, the more likely that the court will use a clearly erroneous standard.[22]

This bifurcation of the question is exemplified by the question of negligence. The judge determines as an initial matter whether the defendant owed a legal duty and the scope of that duty. Then the finder of fact determines whether the duty was breached. That means that both judge and jury are looking at whether the defendant committed a "legal wrong." The reviewing courts generally will review the statement of law de novo but review the fact of negligence with more deference. The cases are not clear on how much deference to give for the very reasons that Professor Rosenberg describes in his analogy about the breadth of the pasture for discretionary judgments.

Similar issues arise in reasonable suspicion and probable cause determinations. In *Ornelas v. United States*,[23] the Supreme Court held that a determination of reasonable suspicion or probable cause consists of two components. First, the district court finds historical facts. The appellate court reviews this portion of the decision for clear error. Second, the district court asks whether the "historical facts viewed from the standpoint of an objectively reasonable police officer, amount to reasonable suspicion or to probable cause." The appellate court reviews this portion of the decision de novo.

5. PROCEDURAL DECISIONS BY A TRIAL COURT: ABUSE OF DISCRETION

Finally, judges have discretion, particularly under the Federal Rules of Evidence, to make many management decisions. These might include whether to impose sanctions, whether to grant a continuance, or whether to compel the production of documents. Discretionary decisions also include criminal sentencing and many rulings on the admissibility of evidence. The standard of review for these discretionary decisions is, not surprisingly, "abuse of discretion."

When the context provides for trial court discretion, the appellate court will give the trial judge considerable latitude to decide the question either way without being reversed. This does not, of course, mean that the trial court is never reversed on a discretionary issue—it is just exceedingly difficult to convince an appellate court to do so. Appellate courts will reverse, despite the difficult standard, when the trial court rules irrationally, erroneously interprets a law, or relies on a record that contains no evidence to support the decision.

---

[22] *Id.* at 270–71 (Ambro, J., concurring) (discussing this "sliding scale" approach among the circuits in the context of a civil injunction).

[23] 517 U.S. 690 (1996).

6. MULTIPLE STANDARDS IN A SINGLE CASE

Occasionally, a single case will use several of these standards. The appellant and appellee in one particular case may be challenging a trial court's legal determinations, factual findings, and application of a statute or common law principle to the facts. *United States v. Charles Thomas Allen* is an excellent example of a case with multiple standards of review at play. It involves bumbling burglars who rob a college library in a plan reminiscent of the Keystone Kops.

United States v. Charles Thomas Allen, II

516 F.3d 364 (6th Cir. 2008)

■ ALICE M. BATCHELDER, CIRCUIT JUDGE:

Defendant-Appellants Charles Allen, Eric Borsuk, Warren Lipka, and Spencer Reinhard appeal from the district court's imposition of 87-month prison sentences. All four defendants claim an identical error in the sentence calculation and the government cross-appeals, claiming an identical error in all four sentences.

I.

[The defendants were four college students who hatched a plan to steal rare books from the special collections library at Transylvania University and sell them at Christie's auction house in New York City. They made an appointment as visiting scholars to review seven "objects of cultural heritage." These included a variety of books, manuscripts, illustrations, and woodcuts dating from 1425. They varied in value from $10,000 to $4,800,000.

[The defendants arrived at the library in disguise, wrestled the special collections librarian to the ground, and zapped her in the arm with a stun pen before threatening her by name and binding her hands and feet with zip ties.

[Lipka and Borsuk then began to collect the valuable items and prepared to carry them on a pink bed sheet from the library by way of an elevator to a first-floor emergency exit. They encountered another librarian and dropped several items before fleeing with five objects. One librarian chased after the defendants, managing to scratch their car with a key for identification purposes. Other librarians returned the dropped items to their proper places before the police arrived.

[Three defendants hid the stolen items in the basement of their residence, where they were also growing marijuana, while the fourth stayed on campus to take an exam. All four told their parents that they were going on a ski trip over Christmas break. They instead went to New York to meet with a Christie's representative. They set up the appointment through the campus email system.

[After an investigation, police executed warrants on February 11, 2005, apprehended the four men, and recovered all five objects undamaged. Police also recovered three stun guns (though not the "stun pen" allegedly used in the robbery), notes pertaining to the planning of the robbery, and clothes worn by the men to the robbery and the meeting at Christie's. A federal grand jury indicted each of the men on six counts: (1) conspiracy to commit robbery (2) aiding and abetting robbery; (3) conspiracy to commit offenses against the United States; (4) aiding and abetting the theft of objects of cultural heritage; (5) aiding and abetting transportation of stolen goods; and (6) aiding and abetting possession and concealment of stolen goods. They each pleaded guilty to all counts.]

In March 2005, Allen and his attorney had contacted the government to offer information that they hoped would lead to a reduction in Allen's prison sentence, pursuant to [United States Sentencing Guidelines] § 5K1.1, on the premise that the information would provide "substantial assistance" in the investigation and prosecution of other, unrelated offenses. Prior to the exchange of any information, the parties signed a "cooperation agreement," which characterized the meetings as "off the record" and specified that Allen would receive direct-use immunity for any information provided, but acknowledged that the government could pursue any leads obtained and could cross examine Allen with the information if he testified in a manner contrary to the information. Allen offered information about certain illegal activities—burglaries, gambling, blackmail, and drug dealing—in which he and others, including certain co-defendants, had been involved or about which he had knowledge. Detectives verified some of the information, but ultimately, neither the state prosecutors nor the AUSA was interested. Finding that the information was not of any particular use to the government, the AUSA declined to file a § 5K1.1 motion.

In October 2005, at a hearing concerning pre-sentencing motions, the district court judge revealed that the AUSA had disclosed to the probation office much of the information given by Allen during the "off the record" meetings in March. And a probation officer had, in turn, relayed this "off the record" information to the district court judge. The district court stated that she thought the AUSA had "dealt unfairly" with Allen by leading him to believe that his information was of value (and would thus likely lead to a § 5K1.1 motion), but the AUSA had not breached the agreement, and consequently, the court denied the motion.

With regard to sentencing, Allen argued that there was no actual loss, based on the theory that all of the objects were recovered undamaged, and argued against the government's use of the estimated values of the objects. Allen also argued for reduction of his sentence on the theory that he was only a "minor participant."

All four defendants argued against an enhancement for use of a dangerous weapon on the theory that the "stun pen" was not actually dangerous. The government opposed these arguments, and a debate ensued about *which* objects should be used for the valuation: just the five actually removed from the library proper . . . or the objects removed from the Special Collections Department ([and] dropped in the stairwell, although it was unknown exactly which volumes these were, because librarians had returned them to their proper places before the police could document the crime scene); or all seven objects targeted by Lipka and Borsuk. Each of these options resulted in a different valuation, and because it was unknown which volumes were actually removed from the Special Collections Department and individual volumes have different values, a debate ensued over the appropriate estimated value of this middle option.

The court determined that it would value the loss based on only the five objects actually removed from the library. [All four defendants appealed on various grounds.] The government cross appealed, arguing that the court erred by excluding the objects dropped in the stairwell from its valuation of loss, and correspondingly, from its computation of the sentencing range. We find no merit to any of defendants' arguments, but because we find that the government's argument does have merit, we will remand for resentencing in conformity with this opinion.

II.

In an appeal from a sentencing order, we must determine whether the district court's determination was reasonable—both procedurally and substantively. Procedural reasonableness requires that we "ensure that the district court committed no significant procedural error, such as failing to calculate (or improperly calculating) the [United States Sentencing] Guidelines range." Only if the district court's sentencing decision is procedurally reasonable, do we then consider the substantive reasonableness. In the present case, we find the sentencing decision procedurally unreasonable, and therefore, we do not reach the question of substantive reasonableness, with its associated presumption of reasonableness for sentences falling within the guidelines range. We review the district court's application of the Sentencing Guidelines *de novo* and the district court's findings of fact for clear error.

A.

Allen argues that the district court erred by refusing to reduce his sentence as a sanction for the government's alleged breach of his cooperation agreement. We disagree.

Allen contends that the AUSA breached the cooperation agreement when he relayed Allen's self-incriminating information to the probation department for inclusion in the PSR. The district court ruled that the agreement had not been breached, in that the information was not actually included in the PSR or used against Allen in any way. The district court also held that the AUSA did not act in "bad faith" when he disclosed the information, so there was no basis for sanctions.

[However,] even if the AUSA breached the agreement, we reach the same conclusion as the district court did with regard to harm—Allen cannot show any harm, inasmuch as the information was neither included in the PSR nor relied upon by the district court in calculating and imposing Allen's sentence.

Allen [next] seeks to sanction the AUSA—to Allen's benefit—for conduct that may have been improper, but which resulted in no harm. This is not a legal basis for resentencing.

Ordinarily, we review the denial of a motion for sanctions for an abuse of discretion. We see no reason to treat this review differently. An abuse of discretion occurs when the district court relies on clearly erroneous findings of fact, improperly applies the governing law, or uses an erroneous legal standard. Allen points to no contentious facts, improper application of the law, or erroneous legal standard; Allen merely believes—and urges this court to agree—that the AUSA's disclosure is deserving of sanctions.

This argument is without merit.

B.

Allen argues that the district court erred by refusing to characterize him as a "minor participant" and reduce his sentence accordingly. We disagree.

The sentencing guidelines instruct the district court to decrease a defendant's offense level based on the defendant's role in the offense. A "minor participant" is a defendant who is less culpable than most other participants, but whose role could not be described as minimal. Allen argues that he was the least culpable of the four, and he should therefore receive a three-level reduction (for something more than "minor participant" but less than "minimal participant").[4] Allen deems himself less culpable because: (1) his ideas and suggestions were routinely rejected during the planning stages, (2) he had no contact with the "public" during either the robbery or the meeting with Christie's, and (3) he was relegated to conducting surveillance, driving the get away car, and accompanying the others on their trip to New York. Thus, according to Allen, his role was not "indispensable," and he should be punished less severely than the other three participants.

The government responds by reminding us that the degree of participation and culpability is a factual determination entitled to review for only clear error. With this in mind, the government points out that Allen was responsible for: (1) visiting the library prior to the robbery to gather intelligence, such as staffing and security; (2) conducting a "stake-

---

[4] The absurdity of this argument should be apparent on its face. If, for example, the robbery had taken a murderous turn involving a shoot out, and the other three, being far better marksmen, had each shot four victims, while Allen's poor aim had allowed him to shoot only one, then—under Allen's least-culpable-participant theory—he would be entitled to downward departure, inasmuch as he would clearly be the least culpable of the four. We think not.

out" of the library to gather even more intelligence; (3) developing the escape route; (4) obtaining and driving the escape vehicle; (5) arranging hotel accommodations in New York; and (6) helping to finance the operation. On Thursday, December 16, Allen—like the other three—went to the library dressed in an "old man" costume. On Friday, December 17, Allen drove the get-away vehicle and ensured the escape from the pursuing librarians, before helping to hide the stolen objects in his residence and dispose of the evidence from his residence. And, Allen helped transport the stolen objects to Christie's in New York and back to Kentucky.

There is no basis for the claim that the district court clearly erred by finding that Allen was just as culpable as the other three participants. This argument is without merit.

C.

All four defendants argue that the district court erred by finding that the use of the "stun pen," under these circumstances, justified the dangerous weapon enhancement. We disagree.

The sentencing guidelines, with regard to "cultural heritage resources," specify a two-level enhancement if a dangerous weapon was brandished or its use was threatened. A "dangerous weapon" includes even "an object that is not an instrument capable of inflicting death or serious bodily injury but closely resembles such an instrument; or the defendant used the object in a manner that created the impression that the object was such an instrument."

In the district court, the defendants produced an expert to testify that the stun pen used in this robbery—advertised as the "Black Cobra 150,000 Volt Stun Gun Pen"—is actually capable of producing no more than 8,000 volts (it is powered by two AAA batteries), and is therefore incapable of causing serious injury, unless it is, perhaps, poked directly into someone's eye. The government did not dispute this assessment and the *actual* dangerousness of this stun pen is not at issue. The issue is whether this stun pen could reasonably be *perceived* as being capable of inflicting serious bodily injury, and the defendants contend that it could not.

Allen's contention that the stun pen "did not resemble a weapon, but instead resembled a pen" is clearly a factual question for the district court and we have no basis or ability to reconsider that question on appeal. Allen's second contention, that "[a]t no time did any of the defendants represent this object as a weapon, or verbally claim they had a weapon," is simply not true. None of the defendants has ever—until now—disputed that Lipka said "B.J., if you just keep on struggling, *it* will only hurt more. Do you want *it* to hurt more?" The clear representation of this statement was that he had a weapon, was using the weapon, and was prepared to use it more, to inflict more pain, unless she submitted. Finally, while it may be true that Mrs. Gooch never actually saw the pen, she certainly felt it, at least according to her testimony, which was unrefuted.

This argument is without merit.

D.

The government argues that the district court erred by considering only the objects actually removed from the library building in tabulating the loss for its sentencing calculation. We agree.

We review a district court's interpretation and application of the sentencing guidelines *de novo,* though we review the district court's findings of fact for clear error. In the instant case, the district court was clearly interpreting and applying the sentencing guidelines. Because we review this interpretation and application *de novo,* we need not dwell on the court's reasoning or reading of precedent, but may start anew.

The government urges two theories on appeal: (1) that the objects to be included in the tabulation are those that the robbers *intended* to take, that intent being evident from the specific identification of those objects in the communications with Christie's and Mrs. Gooch prior to the robbery as well as the handling of those same objects during the robbery; and (2) "taking" includes even those objects abandoned during the course of the escape. We consider each in turn.

Based on our reading of the cases and the guidelines, we hold that a robber "takes" an object when the robber exercises dominion and control over that object, such that the robber has completed the acts necessary to seize that object. In the present case, Lipka and Borsuk took "dominion and control" over [seven rare books in that] the robbers collected all seven of the objects and prepared to carry them away. During this time they clearly had dominion and control over these objects—they moved them at will; they could have damaged them, destroyed them, hidden them, played with them, or—as they did—prepared them to be carried away.

Thus, we conclude that the objects to be used for the valuation of loss include the five objects actually removed from the library proper, as well as [two additional volumes]. Based on this measure of loss, the value—even under the defendants' valuation estimates—is more than $1,000,000, the sentence enhancement is 16 rather than 14, and the advisory guideline range is 108 to 135 months rather than 87 to 108 months. Consequently, we must remand to the district court to reconsider its sentence in light of this opinion.

§ 3.2 JUDICIAL REVIEW OF ADMINISTRATIVE ACTION

Appeals from administrative agency decisions are often more circuitous than are appeals from district court decisions. Often, litigants must first appeal the decision of an ALJ to another administrative body. Appellants may also be required to exhaust all administrative appeals before requesting a review in the district or circuit court. Much of the appellate process in the administrative arena is governed by the federal Administrative Procedure Act and its state corollaries, as well as statutes addressed to specific agencies.

A. THE ADMINISTRATIVE PROCEDURE ACT (APA)

Federal agencies play myriad roles. They are quasi-legislative, responsible for rule-making in a wide variety of areas. They are quasi-executive, determining citizens' rights and responsibilities in many day-to-day activities. Finally, they are quasi-judicial, interpreting their own regulations.

The Administrative Procedure Act (APA) is the federal statute that governs how federal administrative agencies propose, establish, and enforce regulations. It has been called "a bill of rights for the hundreds of thousands of Americans whose affairs are controlled or regulated" by federal government agencies.[24] The APA dictates standards for agency action. It includes requirements for publishing notices of proposed and final rulemaking in the *Federal Register*, provides opportunities for the public to comment on notices of proposed rulemaking, and sets out how affected individuals may appeal the decisions of an agency.

Judicial review of agency action is governed by 5 U.S.C. § 706:

> To the extent necessary to decision and when presented, the reviewing court shall decide all relevant questions of law, interpret constitutional and statutory provisions, and determine the meaning or applicability of the terms of an agency action. The reviewing court shall—
>
> (1) compel agency action unlawfully withheld or unreasonably delayed; and
>
> (2) hold unlawful and set aside agency action, findings, and conclusions found to be—
>
> (A) arbitrary, capricious, an abuse of discretion, or otherwise not in accordance with law;
>
> (B) contrary to constitutional right, power, privilege, or immunity;
>
> (C) in excess of statutory jurisdiction, authority, or limitations, or short of statutory right;
>
> (D) without observance of procedure required by law;
>
> (E) unsupported by substantial evidence in a case subject to [an adjudication required by statute] or otherwise reviewed on the record of an agency hearing provided by statute; or

---

[24] Statement of Senator Pat McCarran (D Nev.), chairman of the Senate Judiciary Committee, Sen. Doc. No. 298, 79th Cong. 2d Sess. (1946).

(F) unwarranted by the facts to the extent that the facts are subject to trial de novo by the reviewing court.

In making the foregoing determinations, the court shall review the whole record or those parts of it cited by a party, and due account shall be taken of the rule of prejudicial error.

Thus, informal agency decisions, such as those conducted by inspections, conferences, and negotiations, stand unless a reviewing court concludes that the regulation is "arbitrary and capricious, an abuse of discretion, or otherwise not in accordance with the law." Formal rule-making or adjudications, including those with trial-like procedures, must be supported by "substantial evidence" after the court reads the "whole record," which can be thousands of pages long. Some agencies refer to their hearing bodies as courts and the hearing officers as Administrative Law Judges. These may seem odd designations for entities and officials located in the executive branch of the government, but the practice provides additional weight and credibility to administrative decisions.

Agency actions that adversely affect an individual, such as licensure revocations, decisions on disability applications, and immigration decisions, receive standard judicial adjudication. By contrast, when an agency is challenged for issuing a regulation that is inconsistent with its statutory mandate or otherwise beyond its rulemaking authority, there usually will be no adjudicatory record for the court to review. In those instances, review is in the nature of a petition for injunctive relief.

In addition to its other duties, an agency is often called upon to interpret its own regulations. That interpretation is entitled to deference unless it is plainly erroneous or inconsistent with the regulation. This highly deferential standard was first articulated by the Supreme Court in *Bowles v. Seminole Rock & Sand Co.*,[25] and revisited and reaffirmed in *Auer v. Robbins*.[26] While *Auer* deference has been challenged in recent years, it remains good law.[27]

In 1984, the Supreme Court tackled the issue of what deference, if any, federal courts must give to agency interpretation of federal statutes that mandate agency action. *Chevron U.S.A., Inc. v. Natural Resources Defense Council, Inc.*[28] held that lower courts should defer to agency interpretations of those statutes unless they are unreasonable. Even if a court finds that another interpretation is reasonable, or even preferable, it must defer. This concept has come to be known as *Chevron* deference.

---

[25] 325 U.S. 410 (1945).

[26] 519 U.S. 452 (1997).

[27] Decker v. Nw. Envtl. Def. Ctr., 133 S. Ct. 1326 (2013); Christopher v. SmithKline Beecham Corp., 132 S. Ct. 2156 (2012); Talk Am., Inc. v. Michigan Bell Tel. Co., 564 U.S. 50 (2011) (Scalia, J., concurring).

[28] 467 U.S. 837 (1984).

B. FEDERAL AGENCIES

1. SOCIAL SECURITY

Most social security claims for benefits begin with an initial determination by a government employee, often one employed by the state in which the applicant lives. Applicants may ask for a reconsideration of the initial determination. Applicants who disagree with the determination may ask for a hearing before an ALJ. Decisions by a social security ALJ are appealable to the Appeals Council. The Council may either decide the case or remand it to the ALJ for further proceedings. Under 42 U.S.C § 405(g), applicants who disagree with the decision of the Appeals Council may file a civil suit in a United States district court.

Although the case before the district court is, in a sense, a new case, the district court judge is still being asked to review the decision of the ALJ. The court may not decide the facts anew, reweigh the evidence, or substitute its own judgment for that of the Commissioner of Social Security. Instead, judicial review is limited to determining whether the ALJ applied the correct legal standards in reaching a decision and whether there is substantial evidence in the record to support the findings.

In addition to the administrative hearing bodies covered by § 706, there are a number of federal decision-makers that are subject to review by special tribunals. Foremost among these are the military courts-martial, which are reviewed by the U.S. Court of Military Appeals. (These should not be confused with the military commissions operating at Guantanamo Bay, which are covered by the Military Commissions Act of 2006.)

2. IMMIGRATION COURTS

Decisions by immigration judges are initially reviewed by yet another administrative body: The Board of Immigration Appeals (BIA). The BIA is located in Falls Church, Virginia. The Board reviews findings of fact by an immigration judge under the clearly erroneous standard of review. However, it reviews questions of law, discretion, and all other issues de novo. Decisions of the BIA may be further appealed, but they skip the district courts. Instead, BIA decisions go straight to the federal courts of appeal.

Predtechensky v. Immigration and Naturalization Services (INS)

62 Fed. Appx. 768 (9th Cir. 2003)

■ Before: BROWNING, PREGERSON, and REINHARDT, CIRCUIT JUDGES.

MEMORANDUM

Alexander Predtechensky petitions for review of a decision of the Board of Immigration Appeals ("BIA"), adopting and affirming a decision of an Immigration Judge ("IJ") denying Predtechensky's motion to reconsider his motion to reopen his application for asylum and withholding of deportation, which had been withdrawn. We review the decision of the IJ.

I.

Predtechensky claims that the withdrawal of his application for asylum and withholding of deportation was "without informed consent" and arose from the ineffective assistance of his former counsel, Garish Sarin. Predtechensky argues that due process requires that he be permitted to pursue the application.

"Ineffective assistance of counsel in a deportation proceeding is a denial of due process under the Fifth Amendment if the proceeding was so fundamentally unfair that the alien was prevented from reasonably presenting his case. Due process challenges to deportation proceedings require a showing of prejudice to succeed." *Rodriguez-Lariz v. INS,* 282 F.3d 1218, 1226 (9th Cir. 2002). In addition, *Matter of Lozada,* 19 I. & N. Dec. 637, 1988 WL 235454 (BIA 1988), imposes certain procedural prerequisites upon motions to reopen based on claims of ineffective assistance of counsel.

The IJ held that Predtechensky had complied with *Lozada,* but found that Predtechensky's account of the events surrounding the withdrawal of his application for asylum and withholding of deportation was not credible, and that Sarin's account of those same events was credible. Having discredited Predtechensky and credited Sarin, the IJ determined that the withdrawal was "knowing and voluntary."

II. *Discrediting Predtechensky.*

The IJ discredited Predtechensky's account because the IJ determined that Predtechensky's motion to reopen, which claimed that Predtechensky had "no idea what was happening" when he withdrew his application, was "inconsistent with [his] conduct on March 27, 2000," when the application was withdrawn. Predtechensky describes the March 27 hearing as follows:

> Mr. Sarin . . . stated to the Immigration Judge that he was requesting a continuance to pursue adjustment of status rather than advise the Judge, as we had discussed, that I wanted to pursue my asylum claim as my wife had filed for divorce. I was

> shocked at his statement and did not know how to react or what I should do. My wife has not yet obtained a divorce and I didn't know if it was still alright to pursue the petition she had filed. I was extremely confused and nervous. The Immigration Judge then stated that I would probably be withdrawing my asylum application on some future date. Although Mr. Sarin was not asked to withdraw my application on March 27, 2000, he did so anyway. I have no idea why. The Immigration Judge then asked me if that is what I wanted to do and I had no idea what to say. I thought Mr. Sarin knew what he was doing so I said yes. However, I realize now that he should have advised the Immigration Judge that my wife had filed for divorce and that he never should have withdrawn my asylum application.

This account explains how and why Predtechensky mistakenly acquiesced in the withdrawal of his application. Contrary to the IJ's assessment, this account is entirely consistent with Predtechensky's conduct, as described in the IJ's decision. Furthermore, the IJ did not even identify whatever it was that she found inconsistent. Because an IJ "must have a legitimate articulable basis to question the petitioner's credibility, and must offer a specific, cogent reason for any stated disbelief," *Garrovillas v. INS,* 156 F.3d 1010, 1013 (9th Cir. 1998), substantial evidence does not support the IJ's decision to discredit Predtechensky's testimony that his withdrawal was not knowing and voluntary.

III. *Crediting Sarin.*

The IJ credited Sarin's account of what happened in the spring of 2000, finding that Sarin had "appeared before this Court many times" and was "a straightforward conscientious individual and zealous advocate for his clients."

The question is whether the record contains substantial evidence in support of the IJ's conclusion that Sarin's account of his own behavior should be credited. Predtechensky's current attorney, Paula Harris, called the IJ's attention to several aspects [of] Sarin's behavior, alleging that they evidenced professional misconduct and served as grounds for discrediting Sarin. The IJ did not address those allegations. And so while we express no opinion on the propriety of Sarin's behavior, we nonetheless conclude that the IJ's familiarity with Sarin's character generally is irrelevant to whether Sarin behaved appropriately in this case specifically. Indeed, the IJ's personal views of Sarin were based on experiences not reflected in the record, and on which she was not permitted to rely. Thus, there was not substantial evidence to support the IJ's decision to credit Sarin.

IV.

Because there was not substantial evidence to support the IJ's decisions to discredit Predtechensky and to credit Sarin, there was not substantial evidence to support the conclusion that the withdrawal of the asylum application was "knowing and voluntary." Predtechensky contends, and the INS does not dispute, that if he did not voluntarily withdraw his asylum application, then it would violate due process to deem his application withdrawn. Predtechensky also has shown prejudice, because if the asylum application were deemed withdrawn, then Predtechensky would be deprived of a right he otherwise would have had, that is, the right to have his asylum claim adjudicated on the merits. Thus the IJ abused her discretion in denying Predtechensky's motion to reconsider his motion to reopen.

Predtechensky should be allowed to pursue his application for asylum and withholding of deportation. We grant the petition for review, vacate the decision of the BIA affirming the IJ's decision, and remand to the BIA with instructions to reopen Predtechensky's application for asylum and withholding of deportation and to order a hearing on the merits of those claims before the IJ.

PETITION FOR REVIEW GRANTED. VACATED and REMANDED.

C. STATE ADMINISTRATIVE PROCEEDINGS

There are many other kinds of administrative courts, hearings, and procedures, many of which exist at the state level. These include attorney and other professional disciplinary and licensing proceedings, as well as Judicial Conduct Commissions. Administrative bodies are required to provide respondents due process whenever an agency action threatens a liberty or property interest. This includes informing the individual about standards of behavior, providing notice of an alleged breach of those standards, and holding a hearing.

The People of the State of Colorado v. Pautler

35 P.3d 571 (2001)

Office of the Presiding Disciplinary Judge of the Supreme Court of Colorado.

OPINION AND ORDER IMPOSING SANCTIONS

[In July 1998, William "Cody" Neal savagely killed three women with repeated blows from a wood-splitting maul. He kidnapped another woman, raped her at gunpoint, and forced her to watch one of the murders. He then kidnapped two additional people, dictated the details of the crimes into a recording machine over the course of 30 hours, and left the apartment. The surviving victims called police and gave them Neal's pager number. At approximately the same time the police, responding to a request for a welfare check, found the bodies of the three murdered women.

[After extended telephone negotiations with Neal, he agreed to surrender, but only after speaking to a lawyer named Plattner. The police determined that Plattner was no longer in practice. They decided not to call the public defender. Instead, Deputy District Attorney Mark Pautler posed as defense attorney "Mark Palmer." At the time, police did not know Neal's location, thought he was armed, and did not know if there were other victims. Neal surrendered after talking to Pautler. The ruse was discovered when Neal told a public defender who came to see him in jail that he was already represented by a public defender. Neal represented himself on the three first-degree murder charges, pled guilty, and was sentenced to death.

[A disciplinary action was filed against Pautler. The Complaint charged Pautler with violating Colorado Rules of Professional Conduct 8.4(c) and 4.3. The trial was held before the Presiding Disciplinary Judge (PDJ) and two Hearing Board members, all members of the bar. The People were represented by Deputy Attorney Regulation Counsel. The PDJ and Hearing Board assessed the credibility of the witnesses, reviewed the exhibits admitted into evidence, considered argument of the parties, and made findings of fact which were established by clear and convincing evidence.]

II. CONCLUSIONS OF LAW

Colo. RPC 8.4(c) provides: "[i]t is professional misconduct for a lawyer to: (c) engage in conduct involving dishonesty, fraud, deceit or misrepresentation." Pautler admits and the facts conclusively establish that he knowingly and intentionally engaged in conduct designed to deceive Neal into believing that he was represented by a public defender during negotiations structured to encourage Neal to surrender. Pautler admits and there can be no doubt that his conduct violates the plain wording of Colo. RPC 8.4(c).

Pautler contends, however, that the circumstances existing at the time of his conduct, namely, the fear that Neal might harm or kill others, the fact that law enforcement agents did not know Neal's location, and the particularly brutal nature of Neal's crimes, justified his actions and constituted a defense to the charges against him. Pautler also contends that § 18–1–901(3)(l) (II)(A), 6 C.R.S. (1999) invests district attorneys with the status of peace officers and allows them to use deception in the exercise of that authority.

Although there is a substantial body of law that allows law enforcement personnel to use artifice and deceit in the exercise of their professional duties, the facts of this case reveal that Pautler was not acting as a peace officer when he attempted to deceive Neal; rather, he was acting within his role as a lawyer. Pautler's own testimony limits his participation in the events to observation, giving legal advice and acting as a consultant. He was not part of the investigative team but rather was their legal advisor. Simply put, Pautler did not engage in the questioned conduct as a member of the investigative team exercising police authority but as an attorney. His conduct, therefore, must be tested against those rules of conduct applicable to all lawyers.

Pautler also argues that "justification" should be a defense to the professional misconduct charges advanced in the Complaint. Colorado Revised Statutes § 18–1–702, 6 (1999) (the "choice of evils" or "justification" defense), although derived from the common law doctrine of necessity, by its own terms does not apply outside the criminal law setting.

Moreover, the Colorado Supreme Court has previously addressed the issue of justification as a defense to professional misconduct charges as raised in this case. In *People v. Reichman*, 819 P.2d 1035 (Colo.1991), Reichman, the District Attorney for La Plata County, filed a fictitious criminal complaint and other documents against an undercover police officer for the purpose of deceiving the court and others in an effort to rehabilitate the officer's undercover identity and operation. The Supreme Court of Colorado specifically rejected the argument that justification provided a defense to professional misconduct charges.

Although the surrender of Neal was a goal with which all reasonable persons would agree under the circumstances in which Pautler found himself on the evening of July 8, 1998, the means by which that goal might be achieved are subject to scrutiny. The [Colorado] Supreme Court, when faced with the necessity to exercise similar scrutiny, stated:

> This court has spoken out strongly against misconduct by public officials who are lawyers . . . . [T]he respondent's responsibility to enforce the laws in his judicial district grants him no license to ignore those laws or the Code of Professional Responsibility. While the respondent's motives and the erroneous belief of other public prosecutors that the respondent's conduct was ethical do not excuse these violations of the Code of Professional Responsibility, they are mitigating factors to be taken into account in assessing the appropriate discipline.

Prosecutors, who are enforcers of the law, have higher ethical duties than other lawyers because they are ministers of justice, not just advocates. They must be forever vigilant that their conduct as attorneys not only meets the minimum standards of conduct set forth in The Rules of Professional Conduct but they must strive to exceed those requirements. They must also carefully carry out their duty to protect the public in the exercise of their prosecutorial responsibilities while maintaining the duties and responsibilities of professional conduct imposed upon them by The Rules of Professional Conduct. They may not choose to satisfy the former at the expense of the latter.

The Complaint in this action also charges that Pautler's conduct violated Colo. RPC 4.3. Colo. RPC 4.3 provides: "In dealing on behalf of a client with a person who is not represented by counsel, a lawyer shall state that the lawyer is representing a client and shall not state or imply that the lawyer is disinterested. When the lawyer knows or reasonably should know that the unrepresented person misunderstands the lawyer's role in the matter, the lawyer shall make reasonable efforts to correct the misunderstanding. The lawyer shall not give advice to the unrepresented person other than to secure counsel."

The elements of Colo. RPC 4.3 differ from those required by Colo. RPC 8.4(c). The application of Colo. RPC 8.4(c) is broad and prohibits deceptive conduct by attorneys in both professional and nonprofessional situations. Colo. RPC 4.3 on the other hand is more limited. It only applies to those professional situations in which an attorney comes into contact with others while representing a client. Its specific application is intended to prohibit a lawyer from misleading an unrepresented person about the lawyer's role in a matter. The rule does not proscribe contact with unrepresented persons, it merely prohibits a lawyer from misrepresenting his role.

Pautler's misconduct in this case falls squarely within the type of conduct Colo. RPC 4.3 was intended to prevent. Pautler's involvement in these events arose solely because he was a deputy district attorney. His role was to observe events as they transpired, to monitor the integrity of the criminal investigation and to render legal advice regarding that integrity. He did so on behalf of his client, the People of the State of Colorado. He was not a neutral, disinterested participant.

Consequently, when he chose to speak with Neal it was incumbent upon Pautler to inform Neal that he represented the People. Moreover, Colo. RPC 4.3 required Pautler to take reasonable steps to correct the misunderstanding which he knew had been created at his instigation regarding his role. Pautler failed to comply with either requirement. To do so would have revealed the deception in which he was an active participant. That is precisely the type of professional misconduct Colo. RPC 4.3 is designed to prevent. Pautler's conduct violated Colo. RPC 4.3.

III. SANCTION/IMPOSITION OF DISCIPLINE

In arriving at the appropriate discipline to be imposed, consideration should be given to the duty violated, the lawyer's mental state, the injury, whether actual or potential, caused by the lawyer's misconduct and the existence of aggravating or mitigating factors which could enhance or diminish the presumptive sanction.

Pautler's misconduct violated duties owed to the legal system, the profession and the public. At the time of his misconduct Pautler knew that his planned course of deception was inconsistent with The Rules of Professional Conduct, knew that his action would likely be questioned by those charged with enforcing compliance with the rules, and made a conscious choice to engage in the deceptive conduct. Moreover, Pautler knew that his chosen course of deception carried with it the very real risk of potentially serious injury to the public. Pautler knew that if his deception were discovered by Neal, it was reasonably foreseeable that all of the negotiating gains made by Deputy Sheriff Zimmerman might be lost, Neal could terminate communication and resume or escalate his murderous crime spree. Pautler's state of mind was not only knowing, it was intentional.

The injury which arose as a direct result of Pautler's misconduct is both actual and potential. Pautler's misconduct caused actual harm to the administration of justice. The evidence established that Pautler's misconduct, at least in part, contributed to a perceived lack of trust between Neal and his lawyers, adversely impacted subsequent judicial proceedings and resulted in additional hearings to explore factual and legal issues created by the deceptive conduct. Although the evidence in this proceeding is not sufficient to accurately quantify the degree or extent of the actual harm caused by Pautler's deceit upon the criminal proceeding, the evidence is sufficient to conclude that there was some measure of harm caused to the administration of justice.

Arriving at an appropriate sanction for Pautler's misconduct, in light of his mental state and the injury arising from it, is difficult. The sanction imposed must recognize the severity of the misconduct, the injury or potential injury resulting from the misconduct, and whether prosecutors should have been on notice that the conduct was improper. Sanctions imposed against prosecutors who engage in deceitful conduct range from no sanction where the misconduct is minor and there is no prior precedent to disbarment where the conduct is serious and precedent had informed the prosecutor that the conduct is improper.

The ABA Standards provide guiding authority for selecting the appropriate sanction to impose for lawyer misconduct. ABA Standard § 5.22, which applies to misconduct by lawyers who serve as public officials, provides that "Suspension is generally appropriate when a lawyer in an official or governmental position knowingly fails to follow proper procedures or rules, and causes injury or potential injury to a party or to the integrity of the legal process." Pautler's misconduct meets or exceeds every requirement set forth in § 5.22.

ABA Standard § 7.2 which applies to all lawyers who violate duties to the profession, provides: "Suspension is generally appropriate when a lawyer knowingly engages in conduct that is a violation of a duty owed as a professional, and causes injury or potential injury to a client, the public, or the legal system." As with § 5.22, Pautler's misconduct meets or exceeds the requirements of § 7.2.

The most important mitigating factor tending to reduce the sanction to be imposed against Pautler was his motive for engaging in the misconduct. Prior to the time this case was formally filed, the People admitted that Pautler's motive to engage in the conduct was to secure the surrender of Neal. Pautler reasserted that motive in testimony in this case. There can be no doubt that apprehending Neal and thereby removing any risk he might pose to others, whether real or suspected, is neither selfish nor dishonest. Indeed it is a motive shared by all. Both the

ABA Standards and [the Colorado Supreme Court], acknowledge that the absence of a dishonest or selfish motive is a factor to be considered in deciding the appropriate sanction.

Just as the absence of a dishonest or selfish motive may be a mitigating factor, the existence of a selfish or dishonest motive may be an aggravating factor. In this case, Pautler had more than a single motive driving his misconduct. Pautler's deception was focused not only on getting Neal to surrender and protecting innocent citizens but also to accomplish the surrender of Neal in such a fashion as to keep Neal talking about his crimes without the benefit of requested legal representation and thereby gain an advantage in subsequent legal proceedings. This secondary motive is supported by Pautler's testimony at trial that he feared that any defense attorney who might be enlisted in response to Neal's request would tell Neal to stop talking, and by the fact that Pautler did not immediately disclose his actions to Neal's public defender once appointed. He allowed the public defender's confusion about the existence and whereabouts of "Mark Palmer" to continue and interfere with the commencement of meaningful representation of Neal. Pautler waited until the public defender discovered his misconduct while reviewing discovery materials some two weeks after the event. This second motive driving Pautler's misconduct, under the circumstances, was selfish and is an aggravating factor which must be considered.

There exists one additional aggravating factor of significant consequence. Pautler testified that given the same or similar circumstances again, he would make the same decisions and engage in the same deceitful misconduct. He gave that testimony with a substantial measure of conviction. By doing so, Pautler evidenced a failure to recognize or even acknowledge the improper conduct in which he engaged. That failure is particularly significant in this case.

Pautler interprets The Rules of Professional Conduct to be ethical guidelines applicable to his professional conduct unless, in his judgment, circumstances dictate conduct at variance with those Rules to achieve what he perceives to be a desirable end. Such an interpretation reduces The Rules of Professional Conduct to meaningless expressions of aspirational goals forever subject to the situational whims of lawyers seeking to do the right thing as they then see it. Once the door of "justifiable deception" is opened, it takes little imagination to speculate about conduct which could result: by other prosecutors in the pursuit of justice, defense counsel in the zealous advocacy of their client's cause, domestic relations counsel in the protection of their client's abused children, and even commercial counsel in the protection of assets of their corporate client. Pautler's interpretation reflects a fundamental misunderstanding of his role within the legal system, the purpose of the Rules and his obligation to conform his conduct to their mandate. That misunderstanding poses a continuing threat to the legal system, the profession and the public.

The PDJ and Hearing Board, after having weighed the relative strengths of the mitigating factors and aggravating factors, conclude that the mitigating factors outweigh the aggravating factors. However, in light of Pautler's misunderstanding of The Rules of Professional Conduct and his role as an integral part of the legal system, the weight of the mitigating factors is not sufficient to deviate from the presumptive sanction of suspension.

It is therefore ORDERED:

1. Mark C. Pautler, registration number 06438, is SUSPENDED from the practice of law for a period of three months.

2. The period of suspension from the practice of law is stayed and Mark C. Pautler is placed on probation for a period of twelve months. During the period of probation, Mark C. Pautler's practice of law is subject to the following terms and conditions:

> A. Pautler will take and pass the Multistate Professional Responsibility Examination.
>
> B. Pautler will take 20 hours of accredited Continuing Legal Education in ethics in addition to that required by C.R.C.P. 260.2.
>
> C. In all professional encounters subject to the prohibitions of Colo. RPC 4.3, Pautler shall be accompanied by and directly supervised by another attorney who has been licensed to practice law in Colorado for at least five years.
>
> D. Pautler shall not engage in any conduct which results in the imposition of any form of discipline as provided in C.R.C.P. 251.6 or C.R.C.P. 251.7; an order of immediate suspension as provided in C.R.C.P. 251.8 or 251.8.5 or the filing of a Complaint provided in C.R.C.P. 251.14.
>
> E. Failure to comply with any term or condition of the probation shall constitute grounds for revocation of the probation and imposition of the period of suspension.

3. Mark C. Pautler is ORDERED to pay the costs of these proceedings within sixty (60) days of the date of this Order.

4. The People shall submit a Statement of Costs within ten (10) days of the date of this Order. Respondent shall have five (5) days thereafter to submit a response thereto.

NOTES AND QUESTIONS

1. Public Pretender. Would the result of Pautler's disciplinary proceeding have been different if Pautler had immediately notified the public defender and court of his deception? If so, how? Would he still be guilty of violating the Rules of Professional Conduct? If so, would the sanction have been different?

2. No Harm Done? Mark Pautler remained with the Jefferson County District Attorney's Office until 2013, rising to the rank of Senior Chief Deputy District Attorney. He is currently a municipal judge in Colorado.

3. Life Without Parole. Neal was sentenced to death by a three-judge panel. The panel system was declared unconstitutional by the United States Supreme Court in *Ring v. Arizona*.[29] Neal was resentenced to three consecutive life prison terms.

Heinecke v. Department of Commerce, Division of Occupational and Professional Licensing

810 P.2d 459 (Utah App. 1991)

■ ORME, JUDGE:

On March 2, 1988, while working at Pioneer Valley Hospital, Heinecke was assigned to care for a psychiatric patient, referred to in these proceedings as Jane Doe. Jane was diagnosed with multiple personality disorder, resulting from, or exacerbated by, a long history of sexual abuse, possibly including ritualistic abuse. At the time of her admission, Jane was also suffering from depression and was considered potentially suicidal. In addition to Jane's other diagnosed problems, her psychiatrist and therapists were apparently concerned there might be some substance to Jane's claim that she had been involved with a satanic cult, whose members were allegedly desirous that she return to the fold. Consequently, Jane's therapists thought that in addition to the opportunity for full-time observation and treatment, hospitalization might also provide her some measure of security and protection against the alleged cult.

Nurse Heinecke took great interest in Jane's care from the outset. Despite the fact that she had gotten married just two weeks earlier, Jane was very receptive to Heinecke's interest, and it was not long before she was calling him at home, when he was off-duty, just to talk or to ask him to visit her.

Heinecke often responded and spent a significant amount of his free time with Jane at the hospital. He soon learned how to "access" and communicate with some of Jane's personalities.[2] Jane became quite attached to Heinecke and often became agitated when he was not with her. Sometimes Jane became so difficult in Heinecke's absence that he was contacted at home and asked to come in while he was off-duty to help calm Jane down.

As a result of the extraordinary amount of attention Heinecke paid to Jane, in mid-March hospital nursing administrators cautioned Heinecke that he was spending too much time with Jane, at the expense

[29] 536 U.S. 584 (2002).

[2] Refraining from editorial comment, we note she was diagnosed as having forty-six different personalities.

of his other patients, and she was becoming too dependent on him. Jane's therapists also warned that Heinecke's excessive involvement was interfering with Jane's progress. Heinecke failed to heed these warnings, however, and sometimes neglected his other duties in order to spend more time with Jane. Consequently, on April 14, hospital nursing administrators ordered Heinecke to stop seeing and working with Jane.

Heinecke responded by requesting an immediate leave of absence from the hospital. When Jane learned that Heinecke would no longer be working with her, she became extremely upset and immediately demanded to be discharged from the hospital.

Because of Jane's situation and the fact that she, her husband, and Heinecke all were in the market for a new housing arrangement, they decided to find an apartment together. Jane and her husband could not afford to pay Heinecke to care for Jane. But because they all agreed that she could not be left alone, Heinecke agreed to stay with Jane and care for her during the day while her husband was at work. Heinecke, in turn, worked at a hospital emergency room at night while Jane's husband was able to be at home with her.

Because of Jane's psychological disorders, her therapist had told both Jane and her husband that they should exercise birth control and take careful precautions to prevent Jane from becoming pregnant. The therapist explained that a pregnancy and subsequent birth of a baby would seriously impede Jane's progress and aggravate her precarious psychological condition. Moreover, because Jane was suffering from an ulcerated urethra and was taking medication for that condition, her physician told her not to engage in sexual intercourse at all. Consequently, despite their newly-wedded status, because of Jane's condition—both mentally and physically—her husband was practicing sexual abstinence.

Heinecke and Jane, however, were not practicing sexual abstinence. One or more of Jane's personalities, we are told, prompted her to become Heinecke's lover. While Jane's husband was away during the day, Heinecke was accessing the amenable personalities and having sex with Jane.

According to Jane's testimony, her "core personality" did not become aware of Heinecke's sexual relationship with one or more of her other personalities until July 14, when her core personality realized that one of her other personalities was having sexual intercourse with Heinecke. Shortly thereafter Jane contacted, and revealed this discovery to, her therapist. Jane's therapist then accessed the other personality, who supposedly told the therapist it had been having an affair with Heinecke.

After this revelation, Jane's therapist triggered what we are told was a rare communication between Jane's core personality and a personality that was sexually involved with Heinecke. This communication revealed that Heinecke had been having sex with one or more of Jane's other personalities three to six times a week for several months. After realizing what was happening, and upon her therapist's advice, Jane and her husband immediately moved out of the apartment they shared with Heinecke. Although it is not certain exactly when Jane started having sex with Heinecke, she became pregnant with his child on or about April 15, 1988.

After learning of Heinecke's actions, Jane's therapist initiated a complaint against him with the Division of Occupational and Professional Licensing. In a disciplinary hearing before the Utah State Board of Nursing, Heinecke admitted his sexual relationship with Jane. He claimed, however, that he loved her and wanted to marry her. Although Heinecke denied, and the Nursing Board did not expressly find, that he engaged in sexual intercourse with Jane while she was hospitalized at Pioneer Valley Hospital, the evidence regarding when she became pregnant may indicate otherwise. In any event, unmoved by Heinecke's claim of purely romantic motives, and comparatively unconcerned with when his sexual relationship with Jane began, the Division revoked Heinecke's nursing license for unprofessional conduct upon the Nursing Board's recommendation.

Heinecke's appeal of the Division's action raises three issues: (1) Were the Division's findings supported by substantial evidence? (2) Did Heinecke have adequate advance notice that his actions might constitute unprofessional conduct, so as to satisfy due process requirements? (3) Were Heinecke's actions within the scope of the Division's disciplinary authority?

SUBSTANTIAL EVIDENTIARY SUPPORT FOR BOARD'S FINDINGS

Heinecke argues adamantly, and at great length, that the Division's findings generally are not supported by substantial evidence. He fails, however, to point out exactly which findings are unsupported by substantial evidence, and how the evidence is insufficient.

[T]he facts we view as critical are not only supported by substantial evidence, they are essentially undisputed: (1) As a licensed nurse, Heinecke cared for Jane Doe at Pioneer Valley Hospital; (2) Jane suffered from serious psychological disorders; (3) through the course and scope of his employment as a nurse, Heinecke learned how to access and manipulate Jane's various personalities; (4) following her release from the hospital, if not sooner, Heinecke engaged in sexual relations with Jane upon successfully accessing one or more of her multiple personalities.

DUE PROCESS

While we are not without some opinion on the matter, it is not the function of this court to judge the professional qualifications or practices of the petitioner. Our function is limited to assuring the legality of and compliance with the process the law has established to regulate the professions in the public interest. In this case, we must decide whether due process requirements were satisfied. We must determine whether or not the statutes and rules governing the nursing profession provided Heinecke with adequate notice that his conduct with Jane might be considered "unprofessional."

Heinecke claims that because he had no advance notice that his sexual relationship with Jane might constitute "unprofessional conduct" for which his nursing license could be revoked, he was deprived of his license, and livelihood, without due process of law. He argues that nothing in the Nurse Practice Act, nor the administrative rules governing the conduct of nurses, specifically prohibits nurses from having consensual sexual relations with past, or even present, patients. Heinecke suggests that, in this day and age, consensual sexual relationships occur between professionals and their patients or clients on a fairly routine basis.[9] Therefore, such behavior, although not necessarily commendable, is unexceptional. Because the boundaries of "unprofessional conduct" are so vaguely defined, Heinecke argues that he had no reason to believe that what he considered to be unexceptional private conduct might subject him to professional discipline under the rubric of unprofessional behavior.

Contrary to Heinecke's arguments, there is no due process violation in this case. As they apply in this case, the statutes and rules governing the nursing profession provided Heinecke with adequate notice of the standards of the nursing profession. The Division of Occupational and Professional Licensing is authorized to revoke any professional's license for unprofessional conduct. The Nursing Board is specifically authorized to recommend that a nurse's license be revoked or suspended if the nurse "is guilty of immoral, unethical, or unprofessional conduct as it relates to the practice of nursing."

"Unprofessional conduct as it relates to the practice of nursing" is admittedly a broadly phrased standard, one which may not have a ready and precise meaning to those outside the profession. Such a general statutory standard is acceptable, however, for three reasons: (1) The subject of professional performance is too comprehensive to be codified in detail. (2) Members of a profession can properly be held to understand its standards of performance. (3) Standards of performance will be interpreted by members of the same profession in the process of administrative adjudication. Moreover, the vagueness objections applicable to penal laws do not apply to the revocation of professional

---

[9] Frankly, we think someone may have been watching too much "L.A. Law" and "General Hospital." We believe, and certainly hope, that the incidence of professionals engaging in sexual relations with their patients or clients is not as widespread as Heinecke would have us believe. While the concern may be reduced in the case of professionals like architects and engineers, who deal more with "things" than people, professionals entrusted with the psyche of their client or patient, whether the domestic relations attorney or the mental health nurse, simply have no occasion, as professionals, to mess around with those whose care has been entrusted to them, especially during periods of actual or potential vulnerability.

licenses. In contrast to the unfairness in imposing criminal liability on a run-of-the-mill citizen under a statute which does not clearly proscribe the conduct complained of, as a result of their training, testing, and licensure, members of a profession are properly charged with knowledge of what conduct is inconsistent with their responsibilities as professionals notwithstanding some lack of precision or comprehensiveness in the statutes and rules governing their licensure.

Although the Utah Administrative Code contains a nonexclusive list of twenty-six specific items that constitute unprofessional nursing conduct as a general proposition, "[any behavior related to the practice of nursing] which . . . could jeopardize the health and welfare of the people [constitutes] unprofessional conduct. . . ." This language provided Heinecke with adequate notice that he should not do anything that could jeopardize the health or welfare of Jane Doe. He cannot argue with a straight face that his conduct did not jeopardize her health and welfare.

Because of Jane's physical condition, an ulcerated urethra, she had been admonished to abstain from sexual intercourse. Because of her psychological disorders, Jane had been strongly admonished to practice birth control. Heinecke knew that having any kind of sexual relationship with Jane, let alone repeated, unprotected intercourse, could aggravate her condition and impede her therapeutic progress. Heinecke ignored better professional judgment, however, and exploited Jane's condition.

The articulated standards of the nursing profession, necessarily general though they are, provided Heinecke with adequate notice that his conduct would be considered "unprofessional." As a nurse, he should have known that his actions would jeopardize Jane Doe's health or welfare. Those actions were therefore unprofessional under any conceivable standard of nursing professionalism. Consequently, we find no due process violation.

The Division's order is entirely appropriate and is affirmed.

NOTES AND QUESTIONS

1. **Everybody Else is Doing It.** Is "unprofessional conduct" a sufficiently specific standard for disciplinary hearings? Respondents have a constitutional right to adequate notice, but courts tend to give deference to the boards that oversee professionals. Could "conduct unbecoming a professional" be adequate for revocation of an attorney's license? Would it be adequate for removal of a judge from office? Both attorneys and judges are subject to codes of conduct that are both detailed and extensive, but which also come with clarifying commentary and numerous published opinions from ethics panels.

What if Heinecke were correct that consensual sexual relationships between professionals and their patients were fairly routine? Can commonplace conduct still be "unprofessional" for disciplinary purposes? Would it be unprofessional if the relationship had not endangered the patient's physical health?

2. Inclusion of Some Is Exclusion of Others. To what extent is it appropriate to leave important determinations, such as the meaning of "unprofessional conduct," for judicial resolution rather than statutory definition? For example, the United Nations Convention Against Torture does not specify what constitutes "torture," although 169 countries are signatories to its prohibition. The European Convention on Human Rights similarly chose not to define it, simply stating that "[n]o one shall be subjected to torture or to inhuman or degrading treatment or punishment." The European Court of Human Rights explained that it would be inappropriate to itemize types of "torture" because any list necessarily would leave open avenues for inventive miscreants to devise other means of cruelty. Not satisfied with this explanation, the Philippines legislature adopted two detailed lists of prohibited forms of torture: 13 physical and 12 psychological.

In the judicial process, any number of statutory and regulatory provisions are left to judicial interpretation. What guides the courts in that effort? Options include history preceding the adopted provision, notes of debates around its adoption, the purpose of the provision, the views of prior courts, the interpretation of similar provisions, and even a court's own determinations of good public policy. Which of these should take precedence? This question is front and center in chapters 9 and 10.

3. Ethics and Evidence. In *Abaqueta v. United States*,[30] an anesthesiologist admittedly palpated the breast of an unconscious patient prior to breast surgery. Experts were divided on whether it was appropriate for the anesthesiologist to "examine" the area of surgery. The Disciplinary Appeals Board of the United States Department of Veterans Affairs credited an expert who testified on national ethical standards over the defendant's mentor and fellow anesthesiologist. On appeal, the federal district court held that the Board's decision was supported by substantial evidence even given the conflicting testimony. The district court also noted that "[i]t is self-evident to the Court that the patient would not have freely given her consent, because the record is bereft of her testimony that she would have agreed to Abaqueta's palpation procedure in the interest of advancing the laudable pursuit of medical knowledge."

Is it proper for a court to find a fact based on the absence of evidence? Is the court improperly shifting the burden of proof? Courts occasionally have taken "judicial notice" of the existence of facts from the absence of evidence in the record under Federal Rule of Evidence 201. The Advisory Committee Notes, however, specifically forbid the use of the judicial notice rule for this purpose.

---

[30] 255 F. Supp. 2d 1020 (D. Ariz. 2003).

CHAPTER 4

CASE ASSIGNMENT & RECUSAL

> [J]udges must transcend their personal sympathies and prejudices and aspire to achieve a greater degree of fairness and integrity based on the reason of law.[1]
>
> – United States Supreme Court Justice Sotomayor

Most judges are able to decide cases in a fair and impartial manner—most of the time. Judges are human, with all the same fallibilities, biases, and prejudices as the rest of us. Consequently, there are numerous systems built into the judicial process to ensure judicial fairness and impartiality. Two of the most significant safeguards are random case assignment and the requirement of recusal. These safeguards work—again, most of the time.

§ 4.1 ASSIGNMENT OF CASES

Nothing in the federal statutes specifically mandates random case assignment. 28 U.S.C. § 137 simply requires that the "business of a court having more than one judge shall be divided among the judges as provided by the rules and orders of the court." The task of developing the rules is left to the chief judge of each district court. In the federal courts of appeal, 28 U.S.C. § 46 is slightly more specific. It provides that the

> United States Court of Appeals for the Federal Circuit shall determine by rule a procedure for the rotation of judges from panel to panel to ensure that all of the judges sit on a representative cross section . . . and . . . may determine by rule the number of judges, not less than three, who constitute a panel.

Even this statute, however, does not mandate any particular system by which judges are chosen to sit on the panel.

Most people rightly assume that cases are randomly assigned to judges. But what does "random" mean? Statisticians will tell you that true randomness is hard to achieve. If cases were alphabetically assigned to judges, you could wait at the clerk's desk until you see the judge you want and jump in line to file your case. If the judges' names are

[1] United States Supreme Court Justice Sonia Sotomayor, A Latina Judge's Voice, Address at University of California, Berkeley, School of Law Judge Mario G. Olmos Memorial Lecture (2001), *in* N.Y. TIMES (May 14, 2009), http://www.nytimes.com/2009/05/15/us/politics/15judge.text.html?_r=0 [https://perma.cc/57X2-NVTN] (paraphrasing United States District Court Judge Miriam Cederbaum).

repeatedly drawn from a hat, one judge might be assigned ten cases while another might be assigned one. Even the act of tossing a coin in order to determine which judge gets a case isn't perfect.

Over the years, clerks' offices devised systems to meet the requirements of the statute or local rule. In the early days, a clerk might crank an old-fashioned "Bingo!" cage before reaching in and pulling out a piece of paper or plastic ball. Other clerks used a Las Vegas card shoe shuffle, making ten cards for each judge, shuffling them, using them all, then reshuffling and putting the cards back in the box. Today there are computerized algorithms for assigning cases. Like anything digital, these can be corrupted or hacked in various ways.

Sometimes, however, case assignment isn't so random. Readers of legal thrillers might picture a lawyer skulking around a back alley in order to pay off a corrupt clerk who then ensures that a particularly friendly judge is assigned to the case. More likely, though still rare, is the judge who manipulates the system to ensure that a particular case is assigned to him.

In the late 1950s and early 1960s a group of Fifth Circuit judges known as "The Fifth Circuit Four" or simply "The Four" used the technique of purposeful assignment in order to ensure that civil rights cases were assigned to panels comprised of judges friendly to civil rights plaintiffs. The Four consisted of three Republicans and one Democrat: Chief Judge Elbert Tuttle, Judge John Brown, and Judge John Minor Wisdom were all Republican, while Judge Richard Rives was a Democrat. Some observers thought them the Fab Four, using the power of the bench to give shape and meaning to *Brown v. Board of Education*. Others thought them the Four Horseman of the Apocalypse, using subterfuge to undermine the rule of law and irreparably damage states' rights.

Armstrong v. Board of Education of Birmingham

323 F.2d 333 (5th Cir. 1963)
Rehearing Denied En Banc July 22, 1963
Dissenting Opinion July 30, 1963
On Petition for Intervention and Stay Sept. 6, 1963

■ Before TUTTLE, CHIEF JUDGE, and RIVES and GEWIN, CIRCUIT JUDGES.

■ RIVES, CIRCUIT JUDGE:

[The district court had refused to enter injunctive relief for school desegregation despite the following finding:]

To summarize, it graphically appears that the Birmingham Board of Education have operated a segregated school system based upon race in the past, are doing so now, and have formulated no plans to discontinue such an operation.

This litigation has now been pending for more than three years. There must, at the very minimum, be a good faith start toward according the plaintiffs and the members of the class represented by them their constitutional rights so long delayed. However, whether the delay which has already occurred is justified or not, it cannot be compensated by hasty or precipitate action under the order of this Court. Our action must be dictated by the concept of "deliberate speed" to the extent of not causing undue or unnecessary confusion in the administration of the Birmingham public schools to the injury of all of the pupils, white and black. It is probably too late, without undue confusion, to require the elimination as to any grade of such dual districts in time for the [1963] fall term.

We decline, therefore, to issue an injunction pending appeal which would go so far as to provide that the maintenance of separate schools for the Negro and white children of Birmingham shall be completely ended with respect to any grade, or when and how the complete desegregation of the public schools may be accomplished. Such matters can be more appropriately determined upon a hearing of this appeal on its merits when a full record will be available. It affirmatively appears at this time, however, on the face of the opinion and judgment of the district court, that the plaintiffs and the members of the class represented by them are entitled to more than mere expressions of opinion and have a right to a judgment legally enforcing the desegregation measures on which the Board has virtually agreed.

In line with the procedure which we followed as to the Savannah, Georgia, schools in *Stell v. Savannah-Chatham County Board of Education*, 5 Cir., 318 F.2d 425, it is therefore ORDERED that the District Court for the Northern District of Alabama enter the following judgment and order:

> It is further ordered, adjudged and decreed that said persons be and they are hereby required to submit to this Court not later than August 19, 1963, a plan under which the said defendants propose to make an immediate start in the desegregation of the schools of Birmingham, Jefferson County, Alabama, which plan shall effectively provide for the carrying into effect not later than the beginning of the school year commencing September 1963 and thereafter of the Alabama Pupil Placement Law as to all school grades without racial discrimination, including the admission of new pupils entering the first grade, or coming into the County for the first time, on a nonracial basis.

Nothing contained in this opinion or in the order directed to be issued by the district court is intended to mean that voluntary segregation is unlawful; or that the same is not legally permissible.

This order shall remain in effect until the final determination of the appeal of the above-styled case in the Court of Appeals for the Fifth Circuit on the merits, and until the further order of this Court. During the pendency of this order the district court is further directed to enter such other and further orders as may be appropriate or necessary in carrying out the expressed terms of this order.

In view of the already long delay, it is ordered that the mandate issue forthwith.

Motion granted.

■ TUTTLE, CHIEF JUDGE (concurring specially).

I, of course, join Judge Rives in the action taken on the appellants' motion for injunction pending appeal, and I join him in the order that is embodied in his opinion. I agree wholeheartedly with all that is said in his opinion, except as it bears on the relief that is to be granted in September, 1963.

It is now, as it has been from the start, the duty of the Board of Education to assume the primary responsibility [of] putting an end to racially segregated schools. In a situation where such a board of education has completely failed to make such a start, and, fortuitously or otherwise, the first appealable order entered by a district court comes so late in the school year that the Board then attempts to say it is too late to do anything by the following school year, I think it is the duty of an appellate court to require a maximum effort by the Board to do what the law clearly requires of it, rather than to accept as a substitute for performance a plea that the Board has not made necessary preparation to permit orderly transition by the opening of the fall term of school.

I believe it would not be consistent with what this Court has previously required in other situations if I did not express the view, strongly held by me, that as a minimum the Board of Education of the City of Birmingham should be required by an injunction of the trial court to arrange that at least one grade of the public schools of that city be completely desegregated by the abolition of dual school zones pending the appeal of this case on the merits in this Court. Since, however, a majority of the court does not require this relief, I join in the order as written by my esteemed colleague, Judge Rives.

■ GEWIN, CIRCUIT JUDGE (dissenting).

My brothers of the majority have spoken in such inaccurate and disapproving terms with reference to the opinion and order of the distinguished trial judge of the Northern District of Alabama who tried this case for several days, that I find it not only impossible to agree with them, but also necessary to write this dissent in order to inform those who may be interested of my opinion of the actual holding of the District Court. The cases cited by the majority condemn the opinion written by them. The opinion and order of the District Court considered together as they should be, destroy every reason asserted in the majority opinion for the unusual action taken in the circumstances of this case by *the issuance of an injunction pending appeal* in the merits.

It should be noted quickly that the majority opinion leaves little to be decided when the case reaches this court on the merits. Under the guise of 'injunction pending appeal' that opinion substantially decides the case and renders moot many questions which could arise when the case reaches the court for final decision after a review of the record. It is recognized that injunctions pending appeal may be used in *exceptional* and *extreme* cases where there is a *clear abuse of discretion* or *usurpation of judicial power*. Such extreme, harsh and unusual action should never be taken as a substitute for a proper decision on the merits. The action in this case is taken without any pretense that the court has taken so much as a hurried glance at the record. There has not been sufficient time for the record to reach the court. In effect my brothers of the majority have concluded that this is an *extreme and exceptional* case, involving either an abuse of discretion or usurpation of judicial power. Accordingly, they have ordered the District Court to issue a 'judgment and order' enjoining the Superintendent and Board of Education of Birmingham, and have directed '* * * that the mandate issue forthwith.' This drastic action has been taken within a few days following the submission of the case on the motion for injunction—not on the merits.

ON PETITION FOR REHEARING BY FULL COURT

■ PER CURIAM.

One of the members of this Court, having in the dissenting opinion requested a rehearing of the case en banc, the Chief Judge polled the Circuit Judges of this Circuit who are in active service to determine whether an en banc rehearing should be ordered by a majority of such Judges. A majority of the Judges of the Circuit in active service, having voted against convening the Court en banc for the purpose of such rehearing, the petition of the appellees for rehearing by the Court en banc is DENIED.

The Petition for Rehearing is Denied.

■ CAMERON, CIRCUIT JUDGE (dissenting).

On July 12, 1963, a panel of this Court composed of Chief Judge Tuttle and Judges Rives and Gewin filed an opinion and order in this case, ordering the District Court for the Northern District of Alabama to enter the judgment therein set forth, the opinion being written by Judge Rives, a special concurrence by Judge Tuttle, and a dissent by Judge Gewin. Judge Gewin requested that the Court in banc reconsider and decide the case and I joined in that request. The Chief Judge advised that the request had been denied by a five to four vote of the members of the Court. I request had [sic] dissent from the action of the members of the Court in refusing this in banc hearing and from the failure of the panel to grant the in banc hearing requested by the appellees in a telegram to each of the Judges of the Court prior to the beginning of the hearing of the case by the panel.

Since the filing of the opinion and order on July 12th by the panel of three Judges the appellees have filed with the clerk of this Court a petition for rehearing and reconsideration of the decision and order of the panel. I am advised that a sufficient number of the petitions for rehearing was filed for the distribution, as requested by appellees, of a copy of the petition to each of the Judges of the Court. I am further advised that no copies of the petition for rehearing were submitted to any of the Judges of the Court except the members of the panel which had heard the case. That panel has, with Judge Gewin dissenting, entered an order declining the prayer for an in banc hearing and denying the rehearing; and orders have been entered accordingly. I respectfully dissent from these actions of the panel and the orders entered in connection therewith.

The decision of this panel involves questions of procedure which have for some weeks plagued and are still plaguing the Court. The Judges of the Court are sharply divided on these questions and not only the lawyers of the Circuit, but the public generally, are displaying open concern with respect to inconsistent positions which they conceive are being taken by the Court.[1] I feel constrained to present in this dissent the result of some studies I have made and some views I entertain with respect to those questions, some of which have been so ably and exhaustively discussed by Judge Gewin in his dissenting opinion, in which I fully concur.

The procedure followed by the majority here is one which, in any opinion, is not sanctioned by the law. The hearing before these three Judges *was not an appeal*. Rather, it was what the Third Circuit has termed something "in the nature of an original proceeding." It was the substitution of a hearing on "injunction pending appeal" for a hearing on appeal. Theoretically the appeal is still pending, but it is apparent that there is little or nothing more to hear since the decision and order of the

---

1 A feature article dated at New Orleans and appearing in the public press of July 20, 1963, presents a widely held conception of the situation. Excerpts from that article follow:

> The U.S. Circuit Court for the Fifth Circuit has blazed new legal trails for nearly a decade in the deep south in the civil rights struggle for which Negroes are now demonstrating.
>
> The Court's 'hard core' majority has moved at every opportunity, within its appellate power, to implement this school decision. Its orders, some without precedent, forced the riot-triggering admission of James Meredith to the University of Mississippi last year.
>
> It often has moved ahead of the Supreme Court to use the 1954 decision as a guideline to order desegregation of other facilities, buses, terminals, libraries, city auditoriums, parks and playgrounds.
>
> It has repeatedly overruled, and often sharply rebuked, Southern district court judges who have refused to accept or carry out the Supreme Court's rulings. * * *
>
> The split was exemplified by the Court's recent 4–4 deadlock over the issue of a jury trial for Mississippi Governor Ross Barnett on criminal contempt charges growing out of his defiance of its orders to integrate Ole Miss. * * *
>
> The four judges who opposed a jury trial for Barnett have stood together consistently in decisions on civil rights cases. They are Chief Judge Tuttle and Judges Richard T. Rives of Montgomery, Alabama, John Minor Wisdom of New Orleans, and John R. Brown of Houston. * * *
>
> These four Judges will hereafter sometimes be referred to as The Four.

majority of the panel are on the merits of the case, deciding in full, without the benefit of any record of the evidence in the lower court, the questions of law and fact which were before that court in its extended hearing.

The majority in the instant case, as has been true in similar decisions rendered in the past few weeks, placed its reliance chiefly upon *Stell v. Savannah Chatham County Board of Education*, 5 Cir., 318 F.2d 425. The injunctive order issued by the majority in the present case is modeled upon the order granted in the *Stell* case. I think that the *Stell* case should not be followed because it was illegally advanced and set for special hearing by the Chief Judge before a panel selected and assigned by him alone. I am unable to find any authority which is vested in the Chief Judge so to appoint a panel to hear a case or to assign a case for hearing such as was attempted by the Chief Judge in that case.

This Court is, of course, a creature of statute. The statute providing for the assignment of Judges is 28 U.S.C. § 46:[2]

> § 46. Assignment of judges; divisions; hearings; quorum
>
> (a) Circuit judges shall sit on the court and its divisions in such order and at such times as the court directs.
>
> (b) In each circuit the court may authorize the hearing and determination of cases and controversies by separate divisions, each consisting of three judges. Such divisions shall sit at the times and places and hear the cases and controversies assigned as the court directs.
>
> (c) Cases and controversies shall be heard and determined by a court or division of not more than three judges, unless a hearing or rehearing before the court in banc is ordered by a majority of the circuit judges of the circuit who are in active service. A court in banc shall consist of all active circuit judges of the circuit.
>
> (d) A majority of the number of judges authorized to constitute a court or division thereof, as provided in paragraph (c), shall constitute a quorum."

The Rules of this Court do not, as far as I can find, provide for the assignment of cases for hearing or for the assignment of judges by the Chief Judge or any one Judge.

I think, too, that a solution of the problems facing this Court will be helped by a study of the handling of racial cases during the immediate past, in which period so much haste has been made and so many procedural innovations have been utilized that the general impression has grown up and has been expressed that this Court has one set of procedures covering racial cases and another set covering all other cases. I have accordingly made a study of the cases as they appear in the

[2] [Ed: subsequently amended in ways not material to this case.]

Federal Reporter, Second Series, involving controversies heard before panels of this Court bearing date within the two years preceding the hearing of the present case on June 26, 1963. I believe this survey to be correct. It covers twenty-five cases. Of the twenty-five cases listed, the majority of the panel in twenty-two of them was composed of some combination of The Four, who constitute a minority of the active Judges. In only two cases did two of the remaining five members of the Court sit together.

Of the Circuit Judges of this Circuit, The Four sat fifty-five times; the other five sat twelve times. The Four wrote twenty-three of the twenty-five opinions, including per curiams: Chief Judge Tuttle wrote six, including four per curiams; Judge Rives wrote six, including two per curiams; Judge Brown wrote four, and Judge Wisdom wrote six, including one per curiam. The per curiam order adjudging Lieutenant Governor Johnson to be in civil contempt was entered by a panel consisting of Judges Rives, Brown and Wisdom, and one of them wrote the opinion. One per curiam was written by one of the five remaining Judges of this Court and one full opinion was written by a district judge.

The handling by Chief Judge Tuttle of three judge district courts in the State of Mississippi is a part of the picture of the crusading spirit which I think has been largely responsible for the errors here discussed and is relevant to the discussion of a solution of the problems before us. The statute providing for such courts is in these words:

> § 2284. Three-judge district court; composition; procedure
>
> In any action or proceeding required by Act of Congress to be heard and determined by a district court of three judges the composition and procedure of the court, except as otherwise provided by law, shall be as follows: (1) The district judge to whom the application for injunction or other relief is presented shall constitute one member of such court. On the filing of the application, he shall immediately notify the chief judge of the circuit, who shall designate two other judges, at least one of whom shall be a circuit judge. Such judges shall serve as members of the court to hear and determine the action or proceeding.

In the performance of the ministerial duty so imposed upon him, the universal practice, except in this Circuit in the last four years, has been for the Chief Judge to appoint the circuit judge resident in the State for which the district court is constituted and one of the district judges resident in such state as the other two members. I have been able to find no instance where this procedure has not been followed except those here mentioned.

The State of Mississippi has residing within its borders one Circuit Judge, three active District Judges, and one senior District Judge designated for active service, all of whom have been at all times mentioned citizens of Mississippi, qualified for the positions they hold, and ready, willing and able to perform the duties incident to service upon such a district court.

Since November 9, 1961 and prior to the submission of the instant case, three district courts of three judges have been constituted to hear racial cases in Mississippi. For the first of these District Courts of the United States for the Southern District of Mississippi, Judges Tuttle, Rives, and Mize were designated; for the second, Judges Rives, Brown, and Mize were designated; and for the third, Judges Brown, Wisdom, and Cox were designated. A member of The Four was substituted for the resident Circuit Judge in each instance, and another member of The Four was substituted for the additional District Judge. The idea that the Chief Judge may thus gerrymander the United States Judges of a State in order to accomplish a desired result is, I think, entirely foreign to any just concept of the proper functioning of the judicial process.

If this Court is to regain the stature it owned on March 16, 1959 when Judge Hutcheson laid down the duties of Chief Judge it must, in my opinion, forsake the special procedures which have been discussed and adhere to those which are "time-tested" and legal. It is important, I think, that "the court as a body" on whom the responsibility rests take hold of the problem and solve it.

NOTES AND QUESTIONS

1. **Propriety, Impartiality, and Morals.** Was it "wrong" for The Fifth Circuit Four to rig case assignment to reach a result that other panels almost certainly would not have reached? The Canons of Ethics emphasize the "appearance of propriety and impartiality." Does a strong moral justification for a certain result override the policy behind judicial impartiality? Is there a time when the need for a particular political result changes the judiciary from impartial referee to policy-driven overseer?

2. **Fab Four or Four Horsemen?** Legal historians generally view the Fifth Circuit Four kindly. There are several histories of the effort to integrate schools and public facilities in the South. Judge Cameron states that from 1961 to 1963, "The Four" sat as the majority in 22 of 25 cases involving racial discrimination. The complete history of the era was chronicled in FRANK T. READ & LUCY S. MCGOUGH, LET THEM BE JUDGED: THE JUDICIAL INTEGRATION OF THE DEEP SOUTH (1978). Ironically, this book was published by an unknown press and is now recognized as the definitive work on an important part of American history. That book, along with the entry on Judge Brown in GREAT AMERICAN JUDGES: AN ENCYCLOPEDIA 136 (2003) state that after Judge Cameron's opinion, the judges of the Fifth Circuit compromised on both procedure and substance to resolve the crisis. Eventually, Judge Brown implemented methods of assigning cases that were fair, yet expedited civil rights matters.

3. Airing the Dirty Laundry. In *Grutter v. Bollinger,*[3] a case that eventually went to the Supreme Court, the Sixth Circuit upheld the University of Michigan law school's consideration of race as one factor in achieving what the majority viewed as a desired and permissible diversity in the student population. Some judges objected to the procedures by which the court of appeals handled the case, arguing that the chief judge had delayed the circulation of a petition for rehearing after the original panel decision until two judges took senior status and were thus ineligible to vote on the petition. In response, Judge Moore took Judge Boggs to task not just for misinterpreting what had occurred, but for publishing his critique at all:

> Because we judges are unelected and serve during good behavior, our only source of democratic legitimacy is the perception that we engage in principled decision-making. This perception is based both in the reality of our practice—I believe that my colleagues, all of them, strive to decide cases in a principled manner—and in the presentation of our decisions to the public in written opinions.
>
> The decisions of this court are not self-executing but instead must be carried into practice by other actors. They will do so only as long as they regard us as legitimate, as we possess neither the purse nor the sword, but only judgment. For this reason, we are often described as the weakest branch, but a court without purse, sword, or legitimacy would be weaker still. This is not to argue that protecting the relative strength of the judicial branch should be our primary concern. Indeed, we have all sworn to uphold the Constitution, and the Nation needs a strong judiciary to check the occasional excesses of the other branches and, more importantly, to preserve the rule of law.
>
> Our ability to perform these crucial tasks is imperiled when members of this court take it upon themselves to "expose to public view" disagreements over procedure. The damage done by such exposés is, at least in part, the responsibility of those who report them, despite the efforts of Judge Boggs and those joining his opinion to disclaim responsibility for their own conduct. It is understandable, however, that they do so, as their conduct in the present case is nothing short of shameful.[4]

In defense of Judge Boggs, Judge Batchelder had this to say:

> In her separate concurrence, Judge Moore expresses her belief that by revealing that history, Judge Boggs—and I, by concurring—undermine the legitimacy of the court and do harm to ourselves, this court and the nation. I believe that exactly the opposite is true. Public confidence in this court or any other is premised on the certainty that the court follows the rules in every case, regardless of the question that a particular case presents. Unless we expose to

---

[3] 288 F.3d 732 (6th Cir. 2002) (en banc), *aff'd*, 539 U.S. 306 (2003).

[4] *Id.* at 753 (Moore, J., concurring).

> public view our failures to follow the court's established procedures, our claim to legitimacy is illegitimate.[5]

4. **The Statistics (Probably) Don't Lie.** Procedures set up by appellate courts to game the system are still with us, or so say a number of statisticians.

In 2014, a three-judge panel in the Ninth Circuit, including both Judge Stephen Reinhardt and Judge Marsha Berzon, invalidated a state ban on same sex marriage. In the four years preceding the case, the Ninth Circuit heard eleven gay-rights cases. Judge Reinhardt was on the panel in four of them. Judge Berzon was on the panel in five. Eighteen of the court's active judges served on zero same-sex marriage cases. The Coalition for the Protection of Marriage argued that the odds of those panel configurations are 441-to-1.[6]

A 2012 study published in the University of New Hampshire Law Review looked at how chief judges appoint district judges to sit on appellate panels. The researchers concluded that there was "clear and consistent evidence that chief judges, in making designation decisions, tend to choose individuals with similar ideologies."[7]

> The Ninth Circuit already had a troubled reputation in the legal academy for its allegedly liberal bent and penchant for being overruled by the Supreme Court. A 2014 study added another criticism: likely non-random case assignment. The study authors concluded that they have a "roughly 98% confidence that the evidence of non-randomness that we detected for the ideological balance of panels cannot be explained by chance alone," zeroing in on the Ninth Circuit as the most likely culprit.[8]

§ 4.2 JUDICIAL RECUSAL

Just as the public assumes that judges are always randomly selected, most also assume that a judge will not hear a case in which he or she has some sort of bias or interest. The Judicial Code of Ethics states that "[a] judge shall disqualify himself or herself in any proceeding in which the judge's impartiality might reasonably be questioned . . . ."[9] The

---

5 *Id.* at 815 (Batchelder, J., dissenting).

6 Petition of Appellee Coalition for the Protection of Marriage for Rehearing En Banc at 4, Latta v. Otter, 771 F.3d 456 (9th Cir. Oct. 13, 2014) (No. 12–17668), http://cdn.ca9.uscourts.gov/datastore/general/2014/10/13/12-17668_PFRëb%2010-13-14.pdf [https://perma.cc/2HXC-LYL9]; Adam Liptak, *Coalition Challenges Selection of Judges in Same-Sex Marriage Case*, N.Y. TIMES (Nov. 10, 2014), http://www.nytimes.com/2014/11/11/us/politics/after-court-loss-opponents-of-same-sex-marriage-challenge-selection-of-judges.html [https://perma.cc/HL6E-B2HK].

7 Todd C. Peppers, Katherine Vigilante & Christopher Zorn, *Random Chance or Loaded Dice: The Politics of Judicial Designation*, 10 U.N.H.L. REV. 69, 90 (2012), http://scholars.unh.edu/cgi/viewcontent.cgi?article=1161&context=unh_lr [https://perma.cc/2CZU-RU7S]

8 Adam S. Chilton & Marin K. Levy, *Challenging the Randomness of Panel Assignment in the Federal Courts of Appeals*, 101 CORNELL L. REV. 1, 6–7 (2015), http://scholarship.law.duke.edu/cgi/viewcontent.cgi?article=6074&context=faculty_scholarship [https://perma.cc/2S2P-5UD4].

9 FEDERAL CODE OF JUDICIAL CONDUCT Canon 3(C)(1); *see also* 28 U.S.C § 455.

Code details a number of instances in which recusal would be either wise or required, including such matters as pecuniary interests of the judge or close relatives, prior statements regarding the merits of a case, and incidental ex parte communications with parties or lawyers.[10] Although a financial interest in one of the parties would normally require recusal, the Commentary to the Canon makes clear that "disqualification is not required if the judge (or the judge's spouse or minor child) divests the interest that provides the grounds for disqualification."[11]

A. U.S. SUPREME COURT RECUSAL ISSUES

The vast majority of recusals take place professionally and quietly, with judges granting (or, more often, denying) motions to recuse and, if necessary, sending the case on for reassignment. In the Supreme Court, however, the story is often different. Unlike their colleagues in the lower federal courts and most state courts, the Supreme Court Justices are not subject to the Code of Judicial Conduct. Although some of the Court's recusal decisions are routine, others are the subject of great debate.

On the more mundane side, new Supreme Court Justices routinely recuse themselves from cases in which they played a part while in practice. Justice Elena Kagan was Solicitor General before being appointed to the Supreme Court. As Solicitor General, she was third-highest ranking official in the Justice Department and responsible for determining the legal position taken by the federal government in cases before the Supreme Court. The Solicitor General is involved in myriad cases every year, including requests and responses for certiorari, representation before the Court when the United States is a party, and amicus briefs. After her appointment, she recused herself from any case in which the Solicitor General's office played a role during her tenure there, even if she did not personally handle the case. In her first year on the Supreme Court, she recused herself from 28 cases—slightly over one-third of the Court's docket that term. Most of these recusals never made the news, with the exceptions of high-profile cases such as *National Federation of Independent Business v. Sebelius*[12] (the Affordable Care Act case in which Kagan declined to recuse) and *Fisher v. University of Texas at Austin*[13] (the affirmative action case in which she did recuse). Justice Thurgood Marshall, also a former Solicitor General, recused himself from an even greater number of cases in his first year on the Court.

However, other motions for United States Supreme Court Justices to recuse are public and noisy affairs. In a widely criticized decision laid out in a 21-page memorandum, Justice Scalia refused to recuse himself in a case involving his friend Vice President Dick Cheney. Cheney was the chair of an advisory committee whose legality was before the Court

---

[10] *Id.*

[11] FEDERAL CODE OF JUDICIAL CONDUCT Canon 3(C)(4); *see also* 28 U.S.C. § 455(f).

[12] 132 S. Ct. 2566 (2012).

[13] 133 S. Ct. 2411 (2013).

in *Cheney v. United States District Court*.[14] Scalia had invited Cheney on a duck-hunting trip in Louisiana while the case was pending in the lower courts. According to Scalia, there was no discussion of the case, nor even much time spent together on the trip. In Scalia's view, friendship was the only basis for recusal. Showing his usual flair, Scalia asked,

> whether someone who thought I could decide this case impartially despite my friendship with the vice president would reasonably believe that I *cannot* decide it impartially because I went hunting with that friend and accepted an invitation to fly there with him on a government plane. If it is reasonable to think that a Supreme Court justice can be bought so cheap, the nation is in deeper trouble than I had imagined.[15]

NOTES AND QUESTIONS

1. **Something's Lost While Something's Gained.** When a judge recuses, is something lost while something is gained? Recusal may lift the specter of partiality but may also leave the Court without a valuable perspective. For example, Justice Kagan's absence may have been felt in cases such as *Fisher*. As the former Dean of Harvard Law School, Kagan was the only member of the Court with direct admissions experience. Further, the absence of a justice may be felt in subtle ways such as the dynamics of negotiating outcomes and writing opinions.

2. **Tie Goes to the Runner—Except When You're Playing in the Supreme Court.** A rarer problem occurs when the Court splits 4-to-4. Without a tie-breaking vote, the lower court's decision is automatically affirmed. This happened when Justice Kagan recused herself in *United States v. Flores-Villar*.[16] That case addressed gender inequality in the way United States citizenship is awarded to children born abroad. Without Justice Kagan's vote the Court split 4-to-4, affirming a Ninth Circuit decision that denied Mr. Flores-Villar citizenship and resulted in his incarceration and deportation. Although the ruling may not have affected Mr. Flores-Villar—he reentered the United States and was removed at least six times before the case even reached the Court—the ruling had a direct effect on thousands of other children who were born to American parents abroad. It may be many years before the Court grants certiorari on a similar case.

3. **That's Not the Issue.** Justice Scalia's argument in *Cheney v. District Court* certainly has rhetorical appeal. However, the price of that appeal may have been a misstatement of the standard for recusal. In several places he correctly states the standard: a judge should recuse himself if his "impartiality might reasonably be questioned."[17] Later, however, he sums up his reasoning by saying, "Since I do not believe my impartiality should be questioned, I do not think it would be proper for me to recuse."[18] Is this a

[14] 542 U.S. 367 (2004).

[15] *Cheney v. U.S. Dist. Court*, 541 U.S. 913, 928–29 (2003).

[16] 564 U.S. 210 (2011).

[17] *Cheney*, 541 U.S. at 916 (2004) (quoting 28 U.S.C. § 455(a))

[18] *Id.* at 927.

distinction without a difference? Would he lose points on a law school ethics exam?

4. **If It Walks Like a Duck . . .** Justice Scalia's decision against recusal in *Cheney* spawned numerous editorial cartoons and pun-filled headlines using the word "duck" as a verb.[19] It even appeared in Jay Leno's *Late Night* monologue. Speaking at Amherst College, Scalia defended his participation in the case, commenting, "That's all I'm going to say for now. Quack. Quack."[20]

Even if Justice Scalia's analysis of the recusal issue were correct, did his memorandum and accompanying commentary bring disrepute to the Court? Does public pressure have any legitimate roll in judicial decision-making?

5. **No Comment.** Justices generally do not comment on their recusal decisions. In *Laird v. Tatum*,[21] Justice Rehnquist denied a motion for his recusal based on testimony that he had given to Congress on behalf of the Justice Department prior to taking the bench. He commented:

> While neither the Court nor any Justice individually appears ever to have done so, I have determined that it would be appropriate for me to state the reasons which have led to my decision with respect to respondents' motion. In so doing, I do not wish to suggest that I believe such a course would be desirable or even appropriate in any but the peculiar circumstances present here.[22]

Conversely, most Justices stay silent in the face of requests to recuse. Activist groups petitioned Justice Clarence Thomas to recuse himself from the Affordable Care Act cases because his wife had worked for a group lobbying against the legislation. He did not respond. Calls for Justice Kagan to recuse herself on the basis of her prior work in the Justice Department were likewise unsuccessful.

In response to the criticism of recusal non-decisions, Chief Justice Roberts stated in his 2011 Annual Report on the Judiciary:

> I have complete confidence in the capability of my colleagues to determine when recusal is warranted. They are jurists of exceptional integrity and experience whose character and fitness have been examined through a rigorous appointment and confirmation process.[23]

---

[19] *See, e.g.*, E.J. Dionne, *Op-Ed, Why Scalia Should Duck Out*, WASH. POST, Mar. 23, 2004, at A19; Ernst-Ulrich Franzen, *Op-Ed, Scalia Should Duck this One*, MILWAUKEE JOURNAL-SENTINEL, Mar. 20, 2004, at 14A; *If It Walks Like a Duck*, LA TIMES (Feb. 13 2004), http://articles.latimes.com/2004/feb/13/opinion/ed-quack13 [https://perma.cc/UWN5-LT23].

[20] Dan Collins, *Justice Scalia Defends Cheney Trip*, CBS NEWS (March 18, 2004 10:35 AM), http://www.cbsnews.com/news/justice-scalia-defends-cheney-trip/ [https://perma.cc/7JJY-9FDR].

[21] 409 U.S. 824 (1972).

[22] *Id.* at 824.

[23] CHIEF JUSTICE JOHN ROBERTS, 2011 YEAR-END REPORT ON THE FEDERAL JUDICIARY 10 (2011), https://www.supremecourt.gov/publicinfo/year-end/2011year-endreport.pdf [https://perma.cc/E92P-E6UH].

Justice Roberts may have confidence in the justices' ability to determine when recusal is warranted, but does the public? Should the justices be required to give their reasons for denying a motion to recuse? Does it give legitimacy to the Court, or waste valuable Court time?

6. **How Remote is Too Remote?** President Richard Nixon nominated Judge Clement Haynsworth of the Fourth Circuit to take the seat on the Supreme Court vacated by Abe Fortas in 1969. The nomination was defeated in the Senate by a vote of 55–45 amid claims that Haynsworth had participated in cases in which he had financial interests. In the most damaging instance, Haynsworth ruled in favor of a party that did business with a company in which Judge Haynsworth had a one-seventh interest—arguably a remote ethical issue.

7. **You Asked What I Thought.** Sometimes judges, as well as clerks, forget the rule against discussing matters outside of chambers. In a January 2003 speech before the Knights of Columbus, Justice Scalia indicated that he thought an appeals court's ruling concluding that the words "under God" in the Pledge of Allegiance violated the Constitution's separation of church and state mandate was flawed. The man who brought the case called on Justice Scalia to recuse himself when the Supreme Court decided to review it. Justice Scalia did so.

B. RECUSAL IN LOWER COURTS

Recusal methods in the lower courts are diverse, in large part because there is little Supreme Court guidance on the issue. The decision is generally left to the judge's personal discretion, although an appeal of that decision may occasionally result in reversal.

Caperton v. A.T. Massey Coal Co.

556 U.S. 868 (2009)

■ JUSTICE KENNEDY delivered the opinion of the Court:

In this case the Supreme Court of Appeals of West Virginia reversed a trial court judgment, which had entered a jury verdict of $50 million. Five justices heard the case, and the vote to reverse was 3 to 2. The question presented is whether the Due Process Clause of the Fourteenth Amendment was violated when one of the justices in the majority denied a recusal motion. The basis for the motion was that the justice had received campaign contributions in an extraordinary amount from, and through the efforts of, the board chairman and principal officer of the corporation found liable for the damages.

Under our precedents there are objective standards that require recusal when the probability of actual bias on the part of the judge or decisionmaker is too high to be constitutionally tolerable. Applying those precedents, we find that, in all the circumstances of this case, due process requires recusal.

I

In August 2002 a West Virginia jury returned a verdict that found respondents A.T. Massey Coal Co. and its affiliates liable for fraudulent misrepresentation, concealment, and tortious interference with existing contractual relations. The jury awarded Hugh Caperton, Harman Development Corp., Harman Mining Corp., and Sovereign Coal Sales the sum of $50 million in compensatory and punitive damages.

In June 2004 the state trial court denied Massey's post-trial motions challenging the verdict and the damages award, finding that Massey "intentionally acted in utter disregard of [Caperton's] rights and ultimately destroyed [Caperton's] businesses because, after conducting cost-benefit analyses, [Massey] concluded it was in its financial interest to do so." In March 2005 the trial court denied Massey's motion for judgment as a matter of law.

Don Blankenship is Massey's chairman, chief executive officer, and president. After the verdict but before the appeal, West Virginia held its 2004 judicial elections. Knowing the Supreme Court of Appeals of West Virginia would consider the appeal in the case, Blankenship decided to support an attorney who sought to replace Justice McGraw. Justice McGraw was a candidate for reelection to that court. The attorney who sought to replace him was Brent Benjamin.

In addition to contributing the $1,000 statutory maximum to Benjamin's campaign committee, Blankenship donated almost $2.5 million to "And For The Sake Of The Kids," a political organization formed under 26 U.S.C. § 527. The § 527 organization opposed McGraw and supported Benjamin. Blankenship's donations accounted for more than two-thirds of the total funds it raised. This was not all. Blankenship spent, in addition, just over $500,000 on independent expenditures—for direct mailings and letters soliciting donations as well as television and newspaper advertisements—" 'to support . . . Brent Benjamin.' "

To provide some perspective, Blankenship's $3 million in contributions were more than the total amount spent by all other Benjamin supporters and three times the amount spent by Benjamin's own committee. Caperton contends that Blankenship spent $1 million more than the total amount spent by the campaign committees of both candidates combined.

Benjamin won. He received 382,036 votes (53.3%), and McGraw received 334,301 votes (46.7%).

In October 2005, before Massey filed its petition for appeal in West Virginia's highest court, Caperton moved to disqualify now-Justice Benjamin under the Due Process Clause and the West Virginia Code of Judicial Conduct, based on the conflict caused by Blankenship's campaign involvement. Justice Benjamin denied the motion in April 2006. He indicated that he "carefully considered the bases and accompanying exhibits proffered by the movants." But he found "no objective information . . . to show that this Justice has a bias for or against any litigant, that this Justice has prejudged the matters which comprise this litigation, or that this Justice will be anything but fair and impartial." In December 2006 Massey filed its petition for appeal to challenge the adverse jury verdict. The West Virginia Supreme Court of Appeals granted review.

In November 2007 that court reversed the $50 million verdict against Massey. The majority opinion, authored by then-Chief Justice Davis and joined by Justices Benjamin and Maynard, found that "Massey's conduct warranted the type of judgment rendered in this case." It reversed, nevertheless, based on two independent grounds—first, that a forum-selection clause contained in a contract to which Massey was not a party barred the suit in West Virginia, and, second, that res judicata barred the suit due to an out-of-state judgment to which Massey was not a party. Justice Starcher dissented, stating that the "majority's opinion is morally and legally wrong." Justice Albright also dissented, accusing the majority of "misapplying the law and introducing sweeping 'new law' into our jurisprudence that may well come back to haunt us."

Caperton sought rehearing, and the parties moved for disqualification of three of the five justices who decided the appeal. Photos had surfaced of Justice Maynard vacationing with Blankenship in the French Riviera while the case was pending. Justice Maynard granted Caperton's recusal motion. On the other side Justice Starcher granted Massey's recusal motion, apparently based on his public criticism of Blankenship's role in the 2004 elections. In his recusal memorandum Justice Starcher urged Justice Benjamin to recuse himself as well. He noted that "Blankenship's bestowal of his personal wealth, political tactics, and 'friendship' have created a cancer in the affairs of this Court." Justice Benjamin declined Justice Starcher's suggestion and denied Caperton's recusal motion.

The court granted rehearing. Justice Benjamin, now in the capacity of acting chief justice, selected Judges Cookman and Fox to replace the recused justices. Caperton moved a third time for disqualification, arguing that Justice Benjamin had failed to apply the correct standard under West Virginia law—*i.e.,* whether "a reasonable and prudent person, knowing these objective facts, would harbor doubts about Justice Benjamin's ability to be fair and impartial." Caperton also included the results of a public opinion poll, which indicated that over 67% of West Virginians doubted Justice Benjamin would be fair and impartial. Justice Benjamin again refused to withdraw, noting that the "push poll" was "neither credible nor sufficiently reliable to serve as the basis for an elected judge's disqualification."

In April 2008 a divided court again reversed the jury verdict, and again it was a 3-to-2 decision. Justice Davis filed a modified version of his prior opinion, repeating the two earlier holdings. She was joined by Justice Benjamin and Judge Fox. Justice Albright, joined by Judge

Cookman, dissented: "Not only is the majority opinion unsupported by the facts and existing case law, but it is also fundamentally unfair. Sadly, justice was neither honored nor served by the majority." The dissent also noted "genuine due process implications arising under federal law" with respect to Justice Benjamin's failure to recuse himself.

Four months later—a month after the petition for writ of certiorari was filed in this Court—Justice Benjamin filed a concurring opinion. He defended the merits of the majority opinion as well as his decision not to recuse. He rejected Caperton's challenge to his participation in the case under both the Due Process Clause and West Virginia law. Justice Benjamin reiterated that he had no "direct, personal, substantial, pecuniary interest' in this case." Adopting "a standard merely of 'appearances,'" he concluded, "seems little more than an invitation to subject West Virginia's justice system to the vagaries of the day—a framework in which predictability and stability yield to supposition, innuendo, half-truths, and partisan manipulations."

We granted certiorari.

II

It is axiomatic that a fair trial in a fair tribunal is a basic requirement of due process. As the Court has recognized, however, most matters relating to judicial disqualification do not rise to a constitutional level. The early and leading case on the subject is *Tumey v. Ohio,* 273 U.S. 510 (1927). There, the Court stated that "matters of kinship, personal bias, state policy, remoteness of interest, would seem generally to be matters merely of legislative discretion."

The *Tumey* Court concluded that the Due Process Clause incorporated the common-law rule that a judge must recuse himself when he has "a direct, personal, substantial, pecuniary interest" in a case. This rule reflects the maxim that "[n]o man is allowed to be a judge in his own cause; because his interest would certainly bias his judgment, and, not improbably, corrupt his integrity." The Federalist No. 10, p. 59. Under this rule, disqualification for bias or prejudice was not permitted; those matters were left to statutes and judicial codes. Personal bias or prejudice alone would not be sufficient basis for imposing a constitutional requirement under the Due Process Clause.

As new problems have emerged that were not discussed at common law, however, the Court has identified additional instances which, as an objective matter, require recusal. These are circumstances in which experience teaches that the probability of actual bias on the part of the judge or decisionmaker is too high to be constitutionally tolerable. To place the present case in proper context, two instances where the Court has required recusal merit further discussion.

A

The first involved the emergence of local tribunals where a judge had a financial interest in the outcome of a case, although the interest was less than what would have been considered personal or direct at common law.

This was the problem addressed in *Tumey v. Ohio,* 273 U.S. 510 (1927). There, the mayor of a village had the authority to sit as a judge (with no jury) to try those accused of violating a state law prohibiting the possession of alcoholic beverages. Inherent in this structure were two potential conflicts. First, the mayor received a salary supplement for performing judicial duties, and the funds for that compensation derived from the fines assessed in a case. No fines were assessed upon acquittal. The mayor-judge thus received a salary supplement only if he convicted the defendant. Second, sums from the criminal fines were deposited to the village's general treasury fund for village improvements and repairs.

The Court held that the Due Process Clause required disqualification both because of the mayor-judge's direct pecuniary interest in the outcome, and because of his official motive to convict and to graduate the fine to help the financial needs of the village.

The Court in citing *Aetna Life Ins. Co. v. Lavoie,* 475 U.S. 813 (1986) further clarified the reach of the Due Process Clause regarding a judge's financial interest in a case. There, a justice had cast the deciding vote on the Alabama Supreme Court to uphold a punitive damages award against an insurance company for bad-faith refusal to pay a claim. At the time of his vote, the justice was the lead plaintiff in a nearly identical lawsuit pending in Alabama's lower courts. His deciding vote, this Court surmised, undoubtedly "raised the stakes" for the insurance defendant in the justice's suit.

The Court stressed that it was not required to decide whether in fact the justice was influenced. The proper constitutional inquiry is whether sitting on the case then before the Supreme Court of Alabama "would offer a possible temptation to the average . . . judge to . . . lead him not to hold the balance nice, clear and true." The Court underscored that what degree or kind of interest is sufficient to disqualify a judge from sitting cannot be defined with precision. In the Court's view, however, it was important that the test have an objective component.

The *Lavoie* Court proceeded to distinguish the state court justice's particular interest in the case, which required recusal, from interests that were not a constitutional concern. For instance, while the other justices might conceivably have had a slight pecuniary interest due to their potential membership in a class-action suit against their own insurance companies, that interest is too remote and insubstantial to violate the constitutional constraints.

B

The second instance requiring recusal that was not discussed at common law emerged in the criminal contempt context, where a judge had no pecuniary interest in the case but was challenged because of a conflict arising from his participation in an earlier proceeding. This Court characterized that first proceeding (perhaps pejoratively) as a "one-man grand jury." *In Re Murchison,* 349 U.S. 133, 133 (1955).

In that first proceeding, a judge examined witnesses to determine whether criminal charges should be brought. The judge called the two petitioners before him. One petitioner answered questions, but the judge found him untruthful and charged him with perjury. The second declined to answer on the ground that he did not have counsel with him, as state law seemed to permit. The judge charged him with contempt. The judge proceeded to try and convict both petitioners.

This Court set aside the convictions on grounds that the judge had a conflict of interest at the trial stage because of his earlier participation followed by his decision to charge them. The Due Process Clause required disqualification. The Court recited the general rule that "no man can be a judge in his own case," adding that "no man is permitted to try cases where he has an interest in the outcome."

The *Murchison* Court was careful to distinguish the circumstances and the relationship from those where the Constitution would not require recusal. It noted that the single-judge grand jury is "more a part of the accusatory process than an ordinary lay grand juror," and that "adjudication by a trial judge of a contempt committed in [a judge's] presence in open court cannot be likened to the proceedings here." The judge's prior relationship with the defendant, as well as the information acquired from the prior proceeding, was of critical import.

Following *Murchison* the Court held in *Mayberry v. Pennsylvania,* 400 U.S. 455, 466 (1971), "that by reason of the Due Process Clause of the Fourteenth Amendment a defendant in criminal contempt proceedings should be given a public trial before a judge other than the one reviled by the contemnor." The Court reiterated that this rule rests on the relationship between the judge and the defendant: "[A] judge, vilified as was this Pennsylvania judge, necessarily becomes embroiled in a running, bitter controversy. No one so cruelly slandered is likely to maintain that calm detachment necessary for fair adjudication."

III

Based on the principles described in these cases we turn to the issue before us. This problem arises in the context of judicial elections, a framework not presented in the precedents we have reviewed and discussed.

Caperton contends that Blankenship's pivotal role in getting Justice Benjamin elected created a constitutionally intolerable probability of actual bias. Though not a bribe or criminal influence, Justice Benjamin would nevertheless feel a debt of gratitude to Blankenship for his extraordinary efforts to get him elected. That temptation, Caperton claims, is as strong and inherent in human nature as was the conflict the Court confronted in *Tumey* and *Monroeville* when a mayor-judge (or the city) benefited financially from a defendant's conviction, as well as the conflict identified in *Murchison* and *Mayberry* when a judge was the object of a defendant's contempt.

Following accepted principles of our legal tradition respecting the proper performance of judicial functions, judges often inquire into their subjective motives and purposes in the ordinary course of deciding a case. This does not mean the inquiry is a simple one. The work of deciding cases goes on every day in hundreds of courts throughout the land. Any judge, one might suppose, would find it easy to describe the process which he had followed a thousand times and more. Nothing could be farther from the truth.

The judge inquires into reasons that seem to be leading to a particular result. Precedent and *stare decisis* and the text and purpose of the law and the Constitution; logic and scholarship and experience and common sense; and fairness and disinterest and neutrality are among the factors at work. To bring coherence to the process, and to seek respect for the resulting judgment, judges often explain the reasons for their conclusions and rulings. There are instances when the introspection that often attends this process may reveal that what the judge had assumed to be a proper, controlling factor is not the real one at work. If the judge discovers that some personal bias or improper consideration seems to be the actuating cause of the decision or to be an influence so difficult to dispel that there is a real possibility of undermining neutrality, the judge may think it necessary to consider withdrawing from the case.

The difficulties of inquiring into actual bias, and the fact that the inquiry is often a private one, simply underscore the need for objective rules. Otherwise there may be no adequate protection against a judge who simply misreads or misapprehends the real motives at work in deciding the case. The judge's own inquiry into actual bias, then, is not one that the law can easily superintend or review, though actual bias, if disclosed, no doubt would be grounds for appropriate relief. In lieu of exclusive reliance on that personal inquiry, or on appellate review of the judge's determination respecting actual bias, the Due Process Clause has been implemented by objective standards that do not require proof of actual bias. In defining these standards the Court has asked whether, under a realistic appraisal of psychological tendencies and human weakness, the interest poses such a risk of actual bias or prejudgment that the practice must be forbidden if the guarantee of due process is to be adequately implemented.

We turn to the influence at issue in this case. Not every campaign contribution by a litigant or attorney creates a probability of bias that requires a judge's recusal, but this is an exceptional case. We conclude that there is a serious risk of actual bias—based on objective and reasonable perceptions—when a person with a personal stake in a particular case had a significant and disproportionate influence in placing the judge on the case by raising funds or directing the judge's election campaign when the case was pending or imminent. The inquiry centers on the contribution's relative size in comparison to the total amount of money contributed to the campaign, the total amount spent in the election, and the apparent effect such contribution had on the outcome of the election.

Applying this principle, we conclude that Blankenship's campaign efforts had a significant and disproportionate influence in placing Justice Benjamin on the case. Blankenship contributed some $3 million to unseat the incumbent and replace him with Benjamin. His contributions eclipsed the total amount spent by all other Benjamin supporters and exceeded by 300% the amount spent by Benjamin's campaign committee. Caperton claims Blankenship spent $1 million more than the total amount spent by the campaign committees of both candidates combined.

Whether Blankenship's campaign contributions were a necessary and sufficient cause of Benjamin's victory is not the proper inquiry. Much like determining whether a judge is actually biased, proving what ultimately drives the electorate to choose a particular candidate is a difficult endeavor, not likely to lend itself to a certain conclusion. This is particularly true where, as here, there is no procedure for judicial factfinding and the sole trier of fact is the one accused of bias. Due process requires an objective inquiry into whether the contributor's influence on the election under all the circumstances "would offer a possible temptation to the average . . . judge to . . . lead him not to hold the balance nice, clear and true." In an election decided by fewer than 50,000 votes (382,036 to 334,301) Blankenship's campaign contributions—in comparison to the total amount contributed to the campaign, as well as the total amount spent in the election—had a significant and disproportionate influence on the electoral outcome. And the risk that Blankenship's influence engendered actual bias is sufficiently substantial that it must be forbidden if the guarantee of due process is to be adequately implemented.

The temporal relationship between the campaign contributions, the justice's election, and the pendency of the case is also critical. It was reasonably foreseeable, when the campaign contributions were made, that the pending case would be before the newly elected justice. The $50 million adverse jury verdict had been entered before the election, and the Supreme Court of Appeals was the next step once the state trial court dealt with post-trial motions. So it became at once apparent that, absent recusal, Justice Benjamin would review a judgment that cost his biggest donor's company $50 million. Although there is no allegation of a *quid pro quo* agreement, the fact remains that Blankenship's extraordinary contributions were made at a time when he had a vested stake in the outcome. Just as no man is allowed to be a judge in his own cause, similar fears of bias can arise when—without the consent of the other parties—a man chooses the judge in his own cause. And applying this principle to the judicial election process, there was here a serious, objective risk of actual bias that required Justice Benjamin's recusal.

Justice Benjamin did undertake an extensive search for actual bias. But, as we have indicated, that is just one step in the judicial process; objective standards may also require recusal whether or not actual bias exists or can be proved. Due process may sometimes bar trial by judges who have no actual bias and who would do their very best to weigh the scales of justice equally between contending parties. The failure to consider objective standards requiring recusal is not consistent with the imperatives of due process. We find that Blankenship's significant and disproportionate influence—coupled with the temporal relationship between the election and the pending case—"offer a possible temptation to the average . . . judge to . . . lead him not to hold the balance nice, clear and true." On these extreme facts the probability of actual bias rises to an unconstitutional level.

IV

Our decision today addresses an extraordinary situation where the Constitution requires recusal. Massey and its *amici* predict that various adverse consequences will follow from recognizing a constitutional violation here—ranging from a flood of recusal motions to unnecessary interference with judicial elections. We disagree. The facts now before us are extreme by any measure. The parties point to no other instance involving judicial campaign contributions that presents a potential for bias comparable to the circumstances in this case.

It is true that extreme cases often test the bounds of established legal principles, and sometimes no administrable standard may be available to address the perceived wrong. But it is also true that extreme cases are more likely to cross constitutional limits, requiring this Court's intervention and formulation of objective standards. This is particularly true when due process is violated.

The West Virginia Code of Judicial Conduct also requires a judge to "disqualify himself or herself in a proceeding in which the judge's impartiality might reasonably be questioned." Canon 3E(1); see also 28 U.S.C. § 455(a) ("Any justice, judge, or magistrate judge of the United States shall disqualify himself in any proceeding in which his impartiality might reasonably be questioned"). Under Canon 3E(1), " '[t]he question of disqualification focuses on whether an objective assessment of the judge's conduct produces a reasonable question about impartiality, not on the judge's subjective perception of the ability to act fairly.' " Indeed, some States require recusal based on campaign contributions similar to those in this case.

These codes of conduct serve to maintain the integrity of the judiciary and the rule of law. The Conference of the Chief Justices has underscored that the codes are "[t]he principal safeguard against judicial campaign abuses" that threaten to imperil "public confidence in the fairness and integrity of the nation's elected judges." This is a vital state interest.

It is for this reason that States may choose to adopt recusal standards more rigorous than due process requires. The Due Process Clause demarks only the outer boundaries of judicial disqualifications. Congress and the states, of course, remain free to impose more rigorous standards for judicial disqualification than those we find mandated here today. Because the codes of judicial conduct provide more protection than due process requires, most disputes over disqualification will be resolved without resort to the Constitution. Application of the constitutional standard implicated in this case will thus be confined to rare instances.

* * *

The judgment of the Supreme Court of Appeals of West Virginia is reversed, and the case is remanded for further proceedings not inconsistent with this opinion.

It is so ordered.

■ CHIEF JUSTICE ROBERTS, with whom JUSTICE SCALIA, JUSTICE THOMAS, and JUSTICE ALITO join, dissenting:

I, of course, share the majority's sincere concerns about the need to maintain a fair, independent, and impartial judiciary—and one that appears to be such. But I fear that the Court's decision will undermine rather than promote these values.

Until today, we have recognized exactly two situations in which the Federal Due Process Clause requires disqualification of a judge: when the judge has a financial interest in the outcome of the case, and when the judge is trying a defendant for certain criminal contempts. Vaguer notions of bias or the appearance of bias were never a basis for disqualification, either at common law or under our constitutional precedents. Those issues were instead addressed by legislation or court rules.

Today, however, the Court enlists the Due Process Clause to overturn a judge's failure to recuse because of a "probability of bias." Unlike the established grounds for disqualification, a "probability of bias" cannot be defined in any limited way. The Court's new "rule" provides no guidance to judges and litigants about when recusal will be constitutionally required. This will inevitably lead to an increase in allegations that judges are biased, however groundless those charges may be. The end result will do far more to erode public confidence in judicial impartiality than an isolated failure to recuse in a particular case.

And why is the Court so convinced that this is an extreme case? It is true that Don Blankenship spent a large amount of money in connection with this election. But this point cannot be emphasized strongly enough: Other than a $1,000 direct contribution from Blankenship, *Justice Benjamin and his campaign had no control over how this money was spent.* Campaigns go to great lengths to develop precise messages and strategies. An insensitive or ham-handed ad campaign by an independent third party might distort the campaign's message or cause a backlash against the candidate, even though the candidate was not responsible for the ads. The majority repeatedly characterizes Blankenship's spending as "contributions" or "campaign contributions," but it is more accurate to refer to them as "independent expenditures." Blankenship only "contributed" $1,000 to the Benjamin campaign.

It is an old cliché, but sometimes the cure is worse than the disease. I am sure there are cases where a "probability of bias" should lead the prudent judge to step aside, but the judge fails to do so. Maybe this is one of them. But I believe that opening the door to recusal claims under the Due Process Clause, for an amorphous "probability of bias," will itself bring our judicial system into undeserved disrepute, and diminish the confidence of the American people in the fairness and integrity of their courts. I hope I am wrong.

I respectfully dissent.

■ JUSTICE SCALIA, dissenting:

The principal purpose of this Court's exercise of its certiorari jurisdiction is to clarify the law. As the Chief Justice's dissent makes painfully clear, the principal consequence of today's decision is to create vast uncertainty with respect to a point of law that can be raised in all litigated cases in (at least) those 39 States that elect their judges. This course was urged upon us on grounds that it would preserve the public's confidence in the judicial system.

The decision will have the opposite effect. What above all else is eroding public confidence in the Nation's judicial system is the perception that litigation is just a game, that the party with the most resourceful lawyer can play it to win, that our seemingly interminable legal proceedings are wonderfully self-perpetuating but incapable of delivering real-world justice. The Court's opinion will reinforce that perception, adding to the vast arsenal of lawyerly gambits what will come to be known as the *Caperton* claim. The facts relevant to adjudicating it will have to be litigated—and likewise the law governing it, which will be indeterminate for years to come, if not forever. Many billable hours will be spent in poring through volumes of campaign finance reports, and many more in contesting nonrecusal decisions through every available means.

A Talmudic maxim instructs with respect to the Scripture: "Turn it over, and turn it over, for all is therein." Divinely inspired text may contain the answers to all earthly questions, but the Due Process Clause most assuredly does not. The Court today continues its quixotic quest to right all wrongs and repair all imperfections through the Constitution. Alas, the quest cannot succeed—which is why some wrongs and imperfections have been called nonjusticiable. In the best of all possible worlds, should judges sometimes recuse even where the clear commands of our prior due process law do not require it? Undoubtedly. The relevant question, however, is whether we do more good than harm by seeking to correct this imperfection through expansion of our constitutional mandate in a manner ungoverned by any discernable rule. The answer is obvious.

NOTES AND QUESTIONS

1. **Let's Play Forty Questions.** In his dissent, Chief Justice Roberts lists more than 40 questions that courts faced with *Caperton*-like claims might have to answer, including how much money is too much money; whether independent, non-coordinated expenditures should be treated the same as direct contributions; and how long the probability of bias lasts. These are all good questions. Does it matter that the majority didn't—and perhaps couldn't—answer them? We generally think of the common law as developing slowly. A court articulates a basic principle, and then considers factual variations as they occur. If the Supreme Court had answered C.J. Roberts' questions would that portion of the opinion be dicta?

2. **Whose Job is it Anyway?** The majority opinion in *Caperton* focuses on righting a wrong. Conversely, Chief Justice Roberts' dissent emphasizes the need to provide the lower courts with a long-term, workable rule. Which reflects the proper role of the Supreme Court? Can the two goals co-exist?

3. **Not My Job.** Justice Scalia asserts that that the Constitution cannot right all wrongs. Chapter 10, dealing with constitutional interpretation, will examine this and modes of constitutional interpretation.

4. **Are We There Yet?** Eighteen years after the original case was filed, the saga of *Caperton* lives on. In 2015, a West Virginia judge ordered a new trial on damages after a third jury awarded Caperton only $5 million in damages. The judge concluded that Massey's trial strategy—to maintain throughout the trial that it owed Caperton nothing but to suddenly suggest in closing statements that the jury should award $5 million—was deliberate and so prejudicial that no curative instruction would have been sufficient to purge the taint.

5. **You Can Put Away Your Waders.** Contrary to Justice Scalia's fear, courts have not been flooded with *Caperton* claims. Moreover, Chief Justice Roberts' concern that the Court would need to revisit *Caperton* has not (thus far) come to pass. Both scholars and bloggers, however, have spent significant time attempting to answer Chief Justice Roberts' 40 questions and considering the impact of the due process clause on judicial recusal standards and statutes.

Ligon v. City of New York

(In re Reassignment of Cases)
736 F.3d 118 (2d Cir. 2013)

■ PER CURIAM:

These cases, motions of which were argued in tandem, deal with an issue of great significance: the constitutional boundaries of practices by the New York City Police Department ("NYPD") that subject citizens to being stopped and frisked. On August 12, 2013, Judge Shira A. Scheindlin, a long-serving and distinguished jurist of the United States District Court for the Southern District of New York, held that the City of New York ("the City") had violated the plaintiffs' Fourth and Fourteenth Amendment rights, and ordered the City to engage in a variety of remedial measures and activities.

On August 27, 2013, the City moved in the district court to stay those remedies, pending an appeal on the merits of the district court's decision. Judge Scheindlin denied the motions. On September 23, 2013, the City moved in this Court to stay the imposition of the district court's remedies. By order dated October 31, 2013, we both granted that stay and, because the appearance of impartiality had been compromised by certain statements made by Judge Scheindlin during proceedings in the district court and in media interviews, we reassigned the cases to a different district judge, to be chosen randomly. We now explain the basis for that order, which is superseded by this opinion.

Background

We emphasize that the merits of this litigation are not before us and are not at issue here. Accordingly, we neither express nor intimate any views on the merits of the underlying actions. This opinion deals only with our procedural decision to direct the reassignment of the cases and turns on how the cases came before Judge Scheindlin and the media interviews she gave during the pendency of these lawsuits.

For the sake of clarity, we recite the procedural history that has led us to this point. In January 2008, the plaintiffs in *Floyd* [*v. City of New York*] filed a class action alleging that the NYPD violated the Fourth and Fourteenth Amendments through a pattern and practice of stopping and frisking without reasonable suspicion. In March 2012, the plaintiffs in *Ligon* filed a class action alleging that the NYPD violated the Fourth Amendment by engaging in a practice of unlawfully stopping, frisking, and arresting persons for trespass because of their presence in or near buildings enrolled by their landlords in an NYPD crime prevention program known as the Trespass Affidavit Program ("TAP").

When filing, the plaintiffs in *Floyd* marked the case on the appropriate form as related to *Daniels v. City of New York*, an earlier case over which Judge Scheindlin presided. Likewise, the plaintiffs in *Ligon* marked that case as related to *Davis v. City of New York*, over which Judge Scheindlin was also presiding. Because *Daniels*, although terminated a month earlier, and *Davis* had been assigned to Judge Scheindlin, *Floyd* and *Ligon* were forwarded to her, pursuant to Rule 13 of the Local Rules for the Division of Business Among District Judges,[4] and she accepted them both as related cases.

---

[4] In relevant part, Rule 13 provides:

(c) Assignment of cases and proceedings that are designated as related.

In a decision dated January 8, 2013, and amended on February 14, 2013, Judge Scheindlin granted the *Ligon* plaintiffs' motion for a preliminary injunction, holding that they had "shown a clear likelihood of proving that defendants have displayed deliberate indifference toward a widespread practice of unconstitutional trespass stops by the NYPD outside TAP buildings in the Bronx." In a separate opinion, Judge Scheindlin granted the defendants' motion to stay any remedies until after the "issuance of a final decision regarding the appropriate scope of preliminary injunctive relief, and the appropriate scope of permanent injunctive relief (if any) in *Floyd*."

On August 12, 2013, following a nine-week trial in *Floyd*, Judge Scheindlin held that the City of New York violated the plaintiffs' rights under the Fourth Amendment and the Equal Protection Clause of the Fourteenth Amendment. The same day, Judge Scheindlin issued an opinion setting forth remedial measures in both *Floyd* and *Ligon* intended to bring the NYPD's use of stop-and-frisk into compliance with the Fourth and Fourteenth Amendments.

On August 16, 2013, the defendants in both cases filed notices of appeal in this court. On August 27, 2013, the City of New York moved in the district court to stay the remedies in *Floyd* and *Ligon*, pending the outcome of the appeals process. On September 17, 2013, Judge Scheindlin denied the City's stay motions. On September 23, 2013, the City moved in this court to stay the district court's August 12, 2013 remedies order.

Following oral argument, this panel, on October 31, 2013, stayed, "the District Court's January 8, 2013 'Opinion and Order,' as well as the August 12, 2013 'Liability Opinion' and 'Remedies Opinion,' each of which may or will have the effect of causing actions to be taken by defendants or designees of the District Court, or causing restraints against actions that otherwise would be taken by defendants." This panel also concluded "that, in the interest, and appearance, of fair and impartial administration of justice, UPON REMAND, these cases shall be assigned to a different District Judge, chosen randomly under the established practices of the District Court for the Southern District of New York. This newly-designated District Judge shall implement this Court's mandate staying all proceedings and otherwise await further

---

(i) Disclosure of contention of relatedness.

When a civil case is filed or removed or a bankruptcy appeal or motion to withdraw the reference of an adversary proceeding from the bankruptcy court is filed, the person filing or removing shall disclose on form JSC44C any contention of relatedness. A copy of that form shall be served with the complaint, notice of removal, appeal or motion.

(ii) Civil cases that are designated as related.

A case designated as related shall be forwarded to the judge before whom the earlier-filed case is then pending who has the sole discretion to accept or reject the case. Cases rejected by the judge as not related shall be assigned by random selection.

action by the Court of Appeals on the merits of the ongoing appeals." We now explain in greater detail the basis for our decision to reassign the cases.

Discussion

Title 28, United States Code, section 455(a) provides that "[a]ny justice, judge, or magistrate judge of the United States shall disqualify himself in any proceeding in which his impartiality might reasonably be questioned." This statute embodies the principle that "to perform its high function in the best way justice must satisfy the appearance of justice."

The goal of section 455(a) is to avoid not only partiality but also the appearance of partiality. The section does so by establishing an "objective standard 'designed to promote public confidence in the impartiality of the judicial process.' " The rule functions as a critical internal check to ensure the just operation of the judiciary. Our Court, sitting *en banc*, has stated that there exists unusual circumstances where both for the judge's sake and the appearance of justice, an assignment to a different judge is salutary and in the public interest, especially as it minimizes even a suspicion of partiality. And as other circuits have correctly noted, if the question of whether § 455(a) requires disqualification is a close one, the balance tips in favor of recusal.

We emphasize at the outset that we make no findings of misconduct, actual bias, or actual partiality on the part of Judge Scheindlin. Following our review of the record, however, we conclude that her conduct while on the bench, which appears to have resulted in these lawsuits being filed and directed to her, in conjunction with her statements to the media and the resulting stories published while a decision on the merits was pending and while public interest in the outcome of the litigation was high, might cause a reasonable observer to question her impartiality. For this reason, her disqualification is required by section 455(a).

A.

The appearance of partiality stems in the first instance from comments made by Judge Scheindlin that a reasonable observer could interpret as intimating her views on the merits of a case that had yet to be filed, and as seeking to have that case filed and to preside over it after it was filed. These comments were made in the earlier case of *Daniels v. City of New York*, in which the City entered into a settlement agreement requiring it, *inter alia*, to establish policies that prohibited racial profiling. Ten days before Judge Scheindlin's supervisory authority under the settlement agreement was set to expire, she heard argument on a motion brought by the *Daniels* plaintiffs to extend the settlement period. The transcript of the hearing indicates that the City had substantially complied with the relief required by the settlement and that the plaintiffs were seeking information from the City beyond that required to be furnished by the settlement agreement.

Observing that the settlement agreement did not entitle the plaintiffs to the relief they sought, Judge Scheindlin counseled:

> THE COURT: [. . .] *why don't you file a lawsuit*
>
> MR. COSTELLO: We did, we are here.
>
> THE COURT: No, you are struggling with the December 31, 2007 deadline in a 1999 case. *And if you got proof of inappropriate racial profiling in a good constitutional case, why don't you bring a lawsuit? You can certainly mark it as related.* How could it not be related to this whole long seven or eight years we have lived together in this case? Because you are trying to put a square peg in a round hole. And trying to force yourselves to argue what the settlement means, that it doesn't mean if you have a timely lawsuit—*you seem to have compiled interesting arguments*[.] Ms. Grossman [attorney for the City] has not rebutted—maybe she did, that's why we didn't do something, because we didn't want them to write this letter, she—let's just say she hasn't substantially responded to your letter. *If one had only your letter, it would look like you have a lawsuit. So instead of struggling to telling [sic] me about a stipulation of settlement, why don't you craft a lawsuit?*

She returned to the idea of bringing a suit alleging that the City had violated their racial profiling policies and suggested a basis for the suit:

> THE COURT: *what I am trying to say—I am sure I am going to get in trouble for saying it, for $65 you can bring that lawsuit*. You can simply—
>
> MR. MOORE: $350
>
> THE COURT: I knew I had it wrong. *The [C]ity violates its own written policy, the City has a policy that violates—they have violated their policy, here is the proof of it, please give us the remedy. Injunction or damages, or whatever lawyers ask for in compliance. So for $350 you can bring that lawsuit and it is timely.*

And again:

> THE COURT: I don't understand why we have to potentially have, you know, months of briefing when it does fit under this stipulation or it doesn't, that Raffo applies or it doesn't that the court has the power to extend the supervision, that we want our immediate appeal to the circuit. *Why do you need that if you have a lawsuit? Bring it. They have a written policy, right?*
>
> MR. GROSSMAN: *Yes, your Honor.*
>
> THE COURT: If you think they are violating their written policy, sue them.

Judge Scheindlin then advised the plaintiffs that if they filed such a suit, they would successfully obtain relevant documents produced by the government:

> THE COURT: . . . There is enough in the public record to craft the suit. And then *in that suit simply say, we want produced all that was produced in the 1999 lawsuit. I don't know how you could lose getting it.* It may be a question of whether it is still going to be under protective order or not. *But I can hardly imagine not getting it. You know what I am saying? It is so obvious to me that any Judge would require them to reproduce it to you* in the same format that you have it, that you will have it again. Whether or not it remains confidential.

After the plaintiffs indicated their willingness to bring the new suit, she repeated her earlier suggestion that the cases were related and indicated her willingness to keep the newly filed case:

> MR. MOORE: To the extent that some of the materials have already been made public.
>
> THE COURT: what's public is public,—If you cite to the Rand study, publicly, nobody can criticize you for that. If they do, they weren't acting in good faith. If I can get the Rand study on the internet, it is public—
>
> MR. MOORE: you can go to the NYPD website, your Honor.
>
> THE COURT: *There you go, that's public. You can use that. And as I said before, I would accept it as a related case, which the plaintiff has the power to designate.*

I think this current motion is withdrawn. Thank you.

We believe that a reasonable observer viewing this colloquy would conclude that the appearance of impartiality had been compromised. We do not mean to suggest that a district judge can never engage in a colloquy with a party during which the judge advises the party of its legal or procedural options. However, we think, particularly in combination with the public statements described below, that a reasonable observer could question the impartiality of the judge where the judge described a certain claim that differed from the one at issue in the case before her, urged a party to file a new lawsuit to assert the claim, suggested that such a claim could be viable and would likely entitle the plaintiffs to documents they sought, and advised the party to designate it as a related case so that the case would be assigned to her.[17]

---

[17] The designation by parties, and acceptance by district judges, of cases as related to other pending matters pursuant to Rule 13 of the Local Rules for the Division of Business Among District Judges, is a routine practice that promotes judicial efficiency and economy. Our decision in this opinion should not be construed as casting doubt on the proper designation and acceptance of cases as "related" in the normal course—that is, when a district judge does not invite the filing of a suit and encourage its direction to their Court. We also note that, for civil matters, the Rule explicitly anticipates cases being marked as related to "earlier-filed case[s] . . . then pending," which is designed to reduce litigants' costs by informally consolidating

B.

This appearance of partiality by Judge Scheindlin at the *Daniels* hearing was exacerbated as a result of interviews she gave to the news media during the course of the *Floyd* litigation. Cases involving public comment by a presiding judge, other than statements in open court, are infrequent. As the First Circuit has remarked, "[j]udges are generally loath to discuss pending proceedings with the media." Of course, not every media comment made by a judge is necessarily grounds for recusal. We note that Judge Scheindlin did not specifically mention the *Floyd* or *Ligon* cases in her media interviews. However, a judge's statements to the media may nevertheless undermine the judge's appearance of impartiality with respect to a pending proceeding, even if the judge refrains from specifically identifying that proceeding in his remarks to the media. Because context is always critical, the relevant question at all times remains whether, under the circumstances taken as a whole, a judge's impartiality may reasonably be called into question. Because there is no *scienter* requirement in section 455, the test is not how a judge intended his remarks to be understood, but whether, as a result of the interviews or other extra-judicial statements, the appearance of impartiality might reasonably be questioned.

In late May 2013, at the conclusion of the evidence in *Floyd*, when public interest from reporting on that trial was high, and months before she had produced a decision, Judge Scheindlin made herself available for interviews by the Associated Press, The New Yorker, and the New York Law Journal.[22] The "lede" of the AP article dated May 18, 2013, read "[t]he federal judge presiding over civil rights challenges to the stop-and-frisk practices of the New York Police Department has no doubt where she stands with the government. 'I know I'm not their favorite judge,' U.S. District Judge Shira A. Scheindlin said during an Associated Press

proceedings in related cases, Here, at the time *Floyd* was filed in January 2008, *Daniels*, to which it was accepted as "related," was closed.

Judge Scheindlin's motion, the subject of the separate opinion we file today, contends that the "District Court's recognition that judicial economy would be served by the invocation of the related case doctrine codified in Local Rule 13 is analogous to the decision of the Motion Panel to issue an order retaining jurisdiction over the appeal herein in the name of judicial economy." To be sure, both Local Rule 13 dealing with related cases in the district court, and the practice in this court by which a motion panel may choose to hear the appeal on the merits, are designed to conserve judicial resources. However, in the court of appeals, because *the case is the same case and not just a related case*, and no litigant is involved with the decision, there can be no forum-shopping.

In any event, the gravamen of why reassignment of these case is necessary is not simply the use of Local Rule 13. It is the appearance of partiality that was created by Judge Scheindlin's conduct throughout the December 21, 2007 hearing in suggesting that the plaintiffs bring a lawsuit, outlining the basis for the suit, intimating her view of its merit, stating how she would rule on the plaintiffs' document request in that suit, *and* telling the plaintiffs that she would take it as a related case, as well as the media interviews she gave during the *Floyd* proceedings.

[22] Jeffrey Toobin, *Rights and Wrongs: A Judge Takes on Stop-and-Frisk*, The New Yorker, May 27, 2013 (attached hereto as Appendix C); Larry Neumeister, *NY "Frisk" Judge Calls Criticism "Below-the-Belt"*, The Associated Press, May 19, 2013 (attached hereto as Appendix D); Mark Hamblett, *Stop-and-Frisk Judge Relishes her Independence*, N.Y. Law Journal, May 20, 2013 (attached hereto as Appendix E).

interview Friday." The lengthy profile of Judge Scheindlin in The New Yorker, for which she agreed to be interviewed, was titled, "Rights and Wrongs: A Judge Takes on Stop-and-Frisk." The writer, implying that Judge Scheindlin was aligned with the plaintiffs, wrote,

> [t]he primary outlet for Scheindlin's judicial creativity has been an enduring battle she has fought with the N.Y.P.D. A federal judge since 1994, she has been hearing lawsuits against the police for more than a decade. In decision after decision, she has found that cops have lied, discriminated against people of color, and violated the rights of citizens. Now, in the midst of a mayoral race, with the Democratic candidates united in their opposition to the stop-and-frisk policies of the Bloomberg administration, the Floyd case represents Scheindlin's greatest chance yet to rewrite the rules of engagement between the city's police and its people.

While nothing prohibits a judge from giving an interview to the media, and while one who gives an interview cannot predict with certainty what the writer will say, judges who affiliate themselves with news stories by participating in interviews run the risk that the resulting stories may contribute to the appearance of partiality. It is perhaps illustrative of how such situations can get out of the control of the judge that, later in The New Yorker piece, the article quotes a former law clerk of Judge Scheindlin: "As one of her former law clerks put it, 'What you have to remember about the judge is that she thinks cops lie.' "

Further, in those two articles, as well as the New York Law Journal article, Judge Scheindlin describes herself as a jurist who is skeptical of law enforcement, in contrast to certain of her colleagues, whom she characterizes as inclined to favor the government. Given the heightened and sensitive public scrutiny of these cases, interviews in which the presiding judge draws such distinctions between herself and her colleagues might lead a reasonable observer to question the judge's impartiality. As the First Circuit put it, "the very rarity of such public statements, and the ease with which they may be avoided, make it more likely that a reasonable person will interpret such statements as evidence of bias."[23]

C.

In our previous order, we referenced the Code of Conduct for United States Judges. We now clarify that we did not intend to imply in our previous order that Judge Scheindlin engaged in misconduct cognizable either under the Code of Conduct or under the Judicial Conduct and Disability Act, 28 U.S.C. §§ 372, et seq. No such finding is required under

[23] In re Boston's Children First, 244 F.3d at 170; *see also* United States v. Microsoft Corp., 253 F.3d 34, 115, 346 U.S. App. D.C. 330 (D.C. Cir. 2001) ("Judges who covet publicity, or convey the appearance that they do, lead any objective observer to wonder whether their judgments are being influenced by the prospect of favorable coverage in the media.").

section 455, and we do not find that there was any judicial misconduct or violation of any ethical duty.

"To reassign a case on remand, we need only find that the facts might reasonably cause an objective observer to question the judge's impartiality, or absent proof of personal bias requiring recusation [sic], that reassignment is advisable to preserve the appearance of justice." Even where there is reason to believe that a district judge would fairly conduct further proceedings on remand, in determining whether to reassign a case we consider not only whether a judge could be expected to have difficulty putting aside his previously expressed views, but also whether reassignment is advisable to preserve the appearance of justice. Such a decision does not imply any personal criticism of the trial judge, and none is intended here. Indeed, for example, in *United States v. Quattrone*, we ordered reassignment because "portions of the transcript raise[d] the concern that certain comments could be viewed as rising beyond mere impatience or annoyance" even though there was no "evidence that the trial judge made any inappropriate statements leading us to seriously doubt his impartiality."

Reassigning a case to a different district judge, while not an everyday occurrence, is not unusual in this Circuit. Nor is reassigning a case to a different district judge an unusual occurrence in our sister Circuits. Indeed, as noted in our accompanying opinion, reassignment is simply a mechanism that allows the courts to ensure that cases are decided by judges without even an *appearance* of partiality.

Conclusion

This opinion explains the basis for our order of October 31, 2013, directing the reassignment of these cases to a randomly selected district judge and supersedes that order. To reiterate, we have made no findings that Judge Scheindlin has engaged in judicial misconduct. We conclude only that, based on her conduct at the December 21, 2007 hearing and in giving the interviews to the news media in May 2013, Judge Scheindlin's appearance of impartiality may reasonably be questioned within the meaning of 28 U.S.C. § 455 and that "reassignment is advisable to preserve the appearance of justice."

NOTES AND QUESTIONS

1. **You've Got a Friend.** On May 1, 2015, a county commissioner in Utah was convicted of leading an illegal all-terrain vehicle ride through a Bureau of Land Management area that was closed to motorized vehicles. The defendant filed a motion to recuse the judge because of the judge's friendship with the attorney for an environmental group that had no role in the case but was a strong advocate for roadless areas. After considering the motion, Judge Robert Shelby rejected the argument that a friendship could cause bias, but nevertheless disqualified himself to "promote confidence in these proceedings and avoid even the appearance of impropriety in connection with

the court's sentencing duties."[24] The government had argued against recusal on the ground that it would be absurd for a judge to eschew all friendships to remain on the bench.

2. Peremptory Disqualification. In 1979, the American Bar Association supported a proposal to implement a peremptory challenge system for judicial disqualification. It would have required judges to recuse themselves on the mere filing of an affidavit by counsel. It never went anywhere.

3. The Long Strange Career of Judge Willis Ritter. Judge Willis Ritter of Utah began his career as a noted "liberal" who gradually became quirkier over the years. In one incident, he heard a request from the Salt Lake Tribune to interview Gary Gilmore, a convicted murderer who had chosen death by firing squad. The Department of Corrections banned interviews on the ground that they would draw attention to the criminal rather than his victims. The case was assigned to the unpredictable Judge Ritter.

> [Ritter] had been known to throw news people in jail for attempting to take his picture. . . . He jailed maintenance workers for making too much noise while court was in session. He once allowed University of Utah Ute fans to watch their basketball team play in the NCAA Tournament in Provo by slapping a stay on the NCAA's local TV blackout of the game. And he created day-long havoc in downtown Salt Lake City with a restraining order against parking tickets.
>
> Ritter order[ed] an injunction against the prison's ban on interviews with Gilmore. What is more, the judge granted exclusive access to The [Salt Lake] Tribune since it was the only plaintiff in the case.[25]

Judge Ritter eventually became the target of several motions for disqualification. In *United States v. Ritter*,[26] a criminal antitrust case, the U.S. applied to the Tenth Circuit for a writ of mandamus ordering his disqualification. After reversing and remanding twice, the Tenth Circuit concluded that

> [b]ased upon all of the facts and considering the broad language of Section 455(a) requiring disqualification in any proceeding 'in which his impartiality might reasonably be questioned,' it is with reluctance that we conclude that the interests of justice require that the cause be tried by another judge, a judge from outside the district . . . . This action is not to be construed as questioning either the integrity or sincerity of the judge. It is a

[24] Michael McFall, *Federal Judge Recuses Himself From Recapture Canyon Case*, SALT LAKE TRIB. (Aug. 28, 2015 7:18PM), http://www.sltrib.com/news/2888396-155/federal-judge-recuses-himself-from-recapture [https://perma.cc/U6VW-HESN].

[25] Paul Rolly, *Calling Willis Ritter*, SALT LAKE TRIB. (June 12, 2010), http://archive.sltrib.com/story.php?ref=/ci_15280221 [http://perma.cc/E7N3-Z92U]. *See also* Parker Nielsen & Patricia Crowley, THUNDER OVER ZION: THE LIFE OF CHIEF JUDGE WILLIS RITTER (2007).

[26] 540 F.2d 459 (10th Cir. 1976).

> practical action which seeks to avoid stress, trouble and complications in the upcoming trial.[27]

4. **We're All Friends—or Relatives—Here.** Sometimes lawyers try to game the system to force a recusal for tactical reasons. For example, plaintiffs may purposely add defendants with whom the judge has a disqualifiable relationship. Attorneys may also purposely add co-counsel who have a close relationship with a particular judge. This technique can be especially effective in small communities, which often have a limited number of judges. For example, in *Grievance Administrator v. Fried*,[28] a small-town Michigan attorney repeatedly added co-counsel to get cases transferred to one of three judges in the county.

Lawyers who engage in such shenanigans are subject to attorney discipline, and judges are justified in refusing to allow additional counsel to join the case in those circumstances. The Fifth Circuit has also condemned the practice, holding that a court faced with such tactics "need not confine itself to grievance proceedings against errant counsel," but may also disqualify the offending lawyer from practice before the court.

---

[27] *Id.* at 464.

[28] 570 N.W.2d 262 (Mich. 1997).

CHAPTER 5

JUDICIAL SELECTION, RETENTION, & OVERSIGHT

> I love judges, and I love courts. They are my ideals, that typify on earth what we shall meet hereafter in heaven under a just God.[1]
>
> – President and United States Supreme Court Chief Justice William Howard Taft

§ 5.1 JUDICIAL SELECTION

Judicial selection and judicial independence are inextricably intertwined. A judge who must solicit donations and run for election is arguably beholden to donors and liable to prejudge cases in order to fulfill campaign promises. Paradoxically, she may be more likely to rule in ways consistent with the "will of the majority," knowing she will have to answer to the voters in order to keep her job. A judge who is appointed on a merit basis with lifetime tenure is largely unaccountable. She may be unwilling to consider the wishes of the citizenry in her decision-making, and may appear out-of-touch. Beholden to no one, she may be more willing to make unpopular yet morally correct decisions, and thus she may better protect the rights of the minority against the tyranny of the majority. The states and federal judiciaries have found different ways to balance the need for judicial accountability with the need for judicial independence.

A. STATE COURTS

At the time of the founding, judges in most states were appointed for lifetime terms. Over time, the period of tenure was shortened. The populist movements in the Jacksonian era prompted states to institute judicial elections in a bid to make judges more accountable. By the start of the civil war, 21 of 30 states used judicial elections. While we now view judicial elections as compromising judicial independence, in the 19th century elections were seen as a way to insulate judges from the powerful party system and the habit of using judgeships as a means of political patronage.

---

[1] Melvin I. Urofsky, *The Taft Court (1921–1930): Groping for Modernity*, *in* THE UNITED STATES SUPREME COURT: THE PURSUIT OF JUSTICE 199, 199 (Christopher L. Tomlins ed., 2005).

A second wave of reforms came in the early 1930s:

> In 1931, Albert Kales, co-founder of the American Judicature Society, proposed a new method of judicial selection whereby a state would create a bipartisan nominating commission composed of both lawyers and laypersons. This commission would identify highly qualified candidates, without regard for their political ties or party affiliation, for appointment by the governor. The governor would then appoint one of the recommended candidates to the bench. The plan also recognized the need for public accountability, and proposed that all sitting judges would regularly face a retention vote, where citizens would have the opportunity to determine whether judges remained in office after their initial terms.[2]

The American Bar Association approved the idea, and in 1940 Missouri became the first state to institute "merit" selection—now widely known as "the Missouri plan" or "commission-based appointment." Judges are nominated by the Governor, usually from a group recommended by a nominating commission, confirmed by the legislature, and then subjected to a retention vote after a certain number of years in office. Thirty states use some version of merit selection for at least some judicial positions. Twenty states allow contested elections—a few with party affiliations, but most without.

The ABA divides state judicial selection methods into five broad categories: commission-based appointment, legislative or gubernatorial appointment, nonpartisan election, partisan election, and combined methods. There is also a wide variety of methods within these categories. For example, only two states provide appointment by the legislature, and one of these uses a "merit selection committee" process from which to draw candidates. In some "combined" states, appellate judges are chosen through a merit system while trial judges are chosen through partisan elections. In Ohio, candidates are nominated in partisan primary elections. In Michigan, candidates for judicial seats may be nominated at party conventions.

Despite these fairly minor differences, every system has one thing in common: elections. Judges either stand for retention elections or compete in contested elections. Retention votes are generally quiet affairs with no campaigning and little voter turnout. Many voters know little about the judges or their performance, and simply vote the straight retention ticket. Judges are rarely removed through retention votes. Between 1936 and 2009 only ten appellate judges and fewer than 100 trial judges around the nation lost retention votes.

---

[2] AM. BAR ASS'N COALITION FOR JUSTICE, JUDICIAL SELECTION: THE PROCESS OF CHOOSING JUDGES 4 (2008), http://shop.americanbar.org/ebus/store/productdetails.aspx?productId=217453 [https://perma.cc/R7BD-DQWQ].

In recent years, however, retention elections have given activists on both sides of the political spectrum a method to remove judges who have ruled in ways they see as antithetical to their ideology.[3] For example, in 2006 a Utah trial judge was ousted after she berated the brother of a man accused of poaching a deer.[4] She also refused to allow a divorced father to baptize his eight-year-old child into the Church of Jesus Christ of Latter Day Saints, as is the custom, because of her resentment over her own baptism at the same age.[5] In 2011, Iowa voters turned out in record numbers to remove three sitting Iowa Supreme Court justices, including the chief justice, who had unanimously ruled in favor of same-sex marriages.[6] Retention votes have also allowed voters to fire incompetent or unethical judges. For example, in Colorado two district court judges, both former district attorneys, were ousted after an investigation revealed that as prosecutors they had failed to disclose exculpatory evidence in a murder case.[7] The defendant in that case was later exonerated by DNA evidence.[8]

Conversely, contested elections are often noisy affairs with lots of money, campaigning, and even dirty or unseemly tactics. Contested judicial elections have been heavily criticized in the past ten years. Generally thought to make judges more accountable, a number of cases and news stories have shed light on the sometimes seedy underbelly of the process. *Caperton v. Massey Coal*,[9] discussed in Chapter 3, gave the public the distinct impression that judges could be "bought" through elections. *Citizens United v. F.E.C.*,[10] which held that the government could not limit corporate funding of independent political broadcasts in candidate elections, opened the floodgates to political money in judicial elections. Exposés like that written by former Alabama Supreme Court

---

[3] *See generally* ALICIA BANNON ET AL., BRENNAN CTR. FOR JUSTICE, THE NEW POLITICS OF JUDICIAL ELECTIONS OF 2011–12: HOW NEW WAVES OF SPECIAL INTEREST SPENDING RAISED THE STAKES FOR FAIR COURTS 1 (2013), http://www.brennancenter.org/publication/new-politics-judicial-elections-2011-12 [https://perma.cc/7U4J-JYT5] ("During the 2011–12 election cycle, many of these judicial races seemed alarmingly indistinguishable from ordinary political campaigns—featuring everything from Super PACs and mudslinging attack ads to millions of dollars of candidate fundraising and independent spending.").

[4] Findings of Fact and Conclusions of Law, In re Honorable Leslie A. Lewis, No. 06-3D-069 (Utah Jan. 12, 2007), http://jcc.utah.gov/dispositions/documents/LewisLeslie-2007 Reprimand.pdf [https://perma.cc/4JW6-7ATA].

[5] *Utah Judge Accused of Religious Bias Against LDS Church*, RELIGION NEWS BLOG (Nov. 3, 2006), http://www.religionnewsblog.com/16445/utah-judge-accused-of-religious-bias-against-lds-church [https://perma.cc/65BL-FYYD].

[6] Mark Curriden, *Judging the Judges: Landmark Iowa Elections Send Tremor Through the Judicial Retention System*, A.B.A.J. (Jan. 1, 2011 6:59 AM), http://www.abajournal.com/magazine/article/landmark_iowa_elections_send_tremor_through_judicial_retention_system/ [https://perma.cc/W6FF-E89M].

[7] *Terry Gilmore And Jolene Blair Ousted Over Handling Of Tim Masters Case*, HUFFINGTON POST (Nov. 3, 2010 5:39 PM), http://www.huffingtonpost.com/2010/11/03/tim-masters-1999-prosecut_n_778574.html [https://perma.cc/7NP8-ER3Z].

[8] *See* Miles Moffeit, *Two Judges Censured over Masters Trial*, DENV. POST (Sept. 9, 2008 3:47 PM), http://www.denverpost.com/2008/09/09/two-judges-censured-over-masters-trial/ [https://perma.cc/WH7D-259Y].

[9] 556 U.S. 868 (2009).

[10] 558 U.S. 310 (2010).

Chief Justice Sue Bell Cobb made the case. In an article titled, *I was Alabama's Chief Judge. I'm Ashamed By What I Had to Do to Get There*, Cobb noted that

> to run for judge means pitching yourself to the public just as if you were running for dogcatcher. Many ads for judicial candidates I've seen are downright terrifying, with would-be judges bashing opponents as if they were evil incarnate. These candidates were portrayed as judges who, if given the chance, would release child molesters and murderers and order them to move in next door. Nothing could be further from the truth. But dignity and fairness are too often the first casualties in these kinds of endeavors.[11]

Lawyers, who are often asked to contribute to judicial campaigns, are also impacted. A phone call from a judge requesting a donation can feel like extortion. "It's human nature: Who would want to risk offending the judge presiding over your case by refusing to donate to her campaign? They almost never say no—even when they can't afford it."[12]

A movement to end judicial elections has been championed by Justice Sandra Day O'Connor under the banner of the Institute for the Advancement of the American Legal System (IAALS).[13] Justice O'Connor has been critical of efforts to politicize the bench and has argued for selection methods that emphasize qualifications and impartiality while still allowing for accountability. The O'Connor Plan, like the Missouri Plan, calls for the use of judicial nominating commissions, gubernatorial appointment, regular performance evaluations, and periodic retention elections. Alaska, Arizona, Colorado, Missouri, New Mexico, Tennessee, and Utah use the O'Connor plan, while 33 other states and the District of Columbia use at least some components of the plan. Interestingly, this prominent Republican Justice has run into both scholarly[14] and right-wing opposition[15] for her efforts.

B. FEDERAL COURTS

The nomination and confirmation process for Article III judges is highly politicized. Article III judges are nominated by the President,

---

[11] Sue Bell Cobb, *I Was Alabama's Top Judge. I'm Ashamed By What I had to Do to Get There: How Money is Ruining America's Courts*, POLITICO MAG. (March/April 2015), http://www.politico.com/magazine/story/2015/03/judicial-elections-fundraising-115503#ixzz41Z1qUQyZ [https://perma.cc/S7ZR-HB7C].

[12] *Id.*

[13] INST. FOR THE ADVANCEMENT OF THE AM. LEGAL SYS., *Quality Judges*, U. DENV., http://iaals.du.edu/quality-judges [https://perma.cc/A4PQ-RT8C] (last visited August 21, 2016).

[14] G. Alan Tarr & Brian T. Fitzpatrick, *Judicial Selection Should Return to Its Roots*, USA TODAY (March 29, 2013), http://www.usatoday.com/story/opinion/2013/03/29/judges-states-missouri/2028705/ [https://perma.cc/VF5T-4BLF] (not actually criticizing Justice O'Connor but advocating for dropping the "merit commission" portion of the Missouri Plan).

[15] Carrie Severino, *Justice O'Connor's Hypocritical Crusade Against Judicial Elections*, NAT'L REV. (June 11, 2013), http://www.nationalreview.com/bench-memos/350694/justice-oconnors-hypocritical-crusade-against-judicial-elections-carrie-severino.

confirmed by the United States Senate, and then appointed by the President.[16] Before nominating a candidate, the President traditionally consults with the senators of the state where the vacancy occurs. If the senator is from the President's own party or is particularly influential the President will generally nominate the Senator's preferred candidate. Once nominated, the candidate's name goes to the Senate Judiciary Committee. Although the candidate was thoroughly vetted by the White House, she will once again be vetted by the Committee. The candidate's background will be checked, including his or her finances, legal opinions, and public statements. If all is well, the Senate Judiciary Committee will generally hold confirmation hearings. Following the confirmation hearing, the nomination proceeds to the full senate. The chair of the Judiciary Committee presides over a debate on the Senate floor, after which a vote of the full senate is taken. A simple 51-vote majority is required to confirm the nomination.

Although the confirmation process appears straightforward, the process can go awry at many different stages. First, some candidates have skeletons in their closets that only come to light after their name is announced. Second, the Senate Judiciary is not required to hold a vote on any nominee. In recent years, many nominees have seen their road to the bench blocked by inaction at the Committee level. Third, a majority of the Committee can vote to oppose the nomination. While the nomination will still traditionally head to the Senate floor, it does so with a recommendation that it be rejected. Next, the nomination can go off-track if a Senator filibusters by refusing to yield the Senate floor. Although a vote for cloture may occur, it takes sixty votes to stop a filibuster. Finally, a majority of the Senate may vote against the nominee. The nominee may also withdraw at any point along the way.

Confirmation hearings are rarely contentious. In fact, Committee hearings for most Article III judges are sparsely attended. However, there are important exceptions, some of which disclose the political nature of judicial appointments. In 1968, sitting Supreme Court Justice Abe Fortas was nominated by President Lyndon Johnson to replace Earl Warren as Chief Justice. A conservative filibuster, fueled by a dispute over a $15,000 fee Fortas accepted for a university seminar, blocked his elevation to Chief. A year later, he resigned from the bench entirely.

Republican Presidents had a run of appointments from 1968 to 1992 and unsurprisingly ran into some difficulties. In 1969, Richard Nixon first tried to elevate Clement Haynsworth from the Fourth Circuit to the Supreme Court. His views on labor and school desegregation were followed by disclosure of a financial stake in a case that he had decided.

[16] In *Marbury v. Madison,* Chief Justice Marshall decided that appointment occurred by signed presidential commission following Senate confirmation, thus Marbury was officially appointed upon signing of the commission by the President. The dispute was over his entitlement to a copy of the commission, apparently because nobody believed he was a magistrate or entitled to draw a salary without documentation—a bit of formalism attributable to the political temper of the times.

After that nomination was narrowly defeated in the Senate, Nixon nominated another Southern conservative, G. Harrold Carswell. The Senate debate on his nomination gave rise to the famous quote from one of his supporters: "Even if he were mediocre . . . , there are a lot of mediocre judges and people and lawyers. They are entitled to a little representation, aren't they, and a little chance?"[17] His nomination was ultimately defeated.

At the other end of the intelligentsia spectrum was President Reagan's nomination of Robert Bork in 1987. His conservative views on a number of issues such as abortion, sexual privacy, race, and the death penalty were the subject of very articulate and blunt statements in the Judiciary Committee hearings. The debate went beyond Washington as well. Senator Ted Kennedy excoriated Bork in a nationally-televised speech delivered less than an hour after President Reagan announced the nomination. In that speech, Senator Kennedy announced that

> Robert Bork's America is a land in which women would be forced into back-alley abortions, blacks would sit at segregated lunch counters, rogue police could break down citizens' doors in midnight raids, schoolchildren could not be taught about evolution, writers and artists could be censored at the whim of government, and the doors of the federal courts would be shut on the fingers of millions of citizens for whom the judiciary is—and is often the only—protector of the individual rights that are the heart of our democracy.[18]

The ideological debate went mainstream in the following weeks, when a variety of advocacy groups mounted a public campaign against Bork's candidacy. Tactics included television ads, full-page advertisements, mass mailings, demonstrations, and intensive lobbying. Opponents even leaked the contents of his video rental history. When his nomination was defeated by the Senate, 58-to-42, it gave rise to the verb "Borked" to refer to being defeated—not because of incompetence—but because of straightforward political disfavor. The Supreme Court seat denied to Bork eventually went to Ninth Circuit Judge Anthony Kennedy.

In 1991, the nomination of Clarence Thomas by the first President Bush created a media firestorm. A somewhat controversial candidate—the National Organization for Women promised to "Bork" him—Thomas seemed a sure bet for confirmation. Although the Senate Judiciary

---

[17] William H. Honan, *Roman L. Hruska Dies at 94; Leading Senate Conservative*, N.Y. TIMES (Apr. 27, 1999), http://www.nytimes.com/1999/04/27/us/roman-l-hruska-dies-at-94-leading-senate-conservative.html [https://perma.cc/MN4H-MLBN].

[18] James Reston, *Washington; Kennedy And Bork*, N.Y. TIMES (July 5, 1987), http://www.nytimes.com/1987/07/05/opinion/washington-kennedy-and-bork.html [https://perma.cc/Q9F2-JPV3]; Nina Totenberg, *Robert Bork's Supreme Court Nomination 'Changed Everything, Maybe Forever'*, NPR (Dec. 19, 2012), http://www.npr.org/sections/itsallpolitics/2012/12/19/167645600/robert-borks-supreme-court-nomination-changed-everything-maybe-forever [https://perma.cc/EZG3-848P].

Committee voted against confirmation, his name went forward to the full Senate and a vote was scheduled. Three days before that vote, NPR broke the story: a law professor and former assistant to Thomas named Anita Hill alleged that Thomas had sexually harassed her. The Senate Judiciary Committee reopened hearings. What followed was days of sordid televised testimony. After a highly contentious hearing in which Thomas accused the Senate of conducting "a high-tech lynching for uppity blacks" he was confirmed by the Senate, 52 to 48. Eleven democrats joined 41 Republicans to confirm him.

Appointments to the lower federal courts rarely engender significant controversy, although there has been a great deal of controversy about the delays involved in confirmations. During the Bush-Obama period of 2003 to 2013, many executive and judicial nominees were held hostage by filibuster threats in the Senate. Obama obtained confirmation of 30 of 42 nominees to the federal courts of appeal. His predecessor, the second President Bush, managed 35 of 52. But in November 2013, there were 59 executive nominations and 17 judicial nominations waiting for Senate vote. At that point, the Senate changed the rules to prohibit filibusters on nominations other than to the Supreme Court. On the merits, President Obama has lost six nominees to federal courts of appeal, primarily because of gay rights and same-sex marriage issues.

These cases pointedly raise the issue of the degree to which "political" concerns are appropriate criteria for Senate consideration. Senators and observers on both sides of the aisle believe that they are. Modern appointees have learned an important lesson from Judge Bork: give as little substantive information as possible in any confirmation hearing. Justice Thomas asserted to the Senate that he had no opinion on cases as controversial as *Roe v. Wade*, while Justice Sotomayor repeatedly emphasized in her confirmation hearings that it is the role of the court "not to make the law," but to "apply the law." Nominees often smoothly demur on questions of constitutional law, attempting to say as little as possible while simultaneously appearing to answer the question. Justice Kagan once acerbically noted that confirmation hearings have become a "vapid and hollow charade." In a 1995 book review, she called the confirmation hearings of Justices Ginsburg and Breyer "official lovefests" in which "both nominees felt free to decline to disclose their views on controversial issues and cases" and the senators greeted their non-answers with "equanimity and resigned good humor."[19]

Article I judges are chosen by Congress for a period of years. They lack both lifetime tenure and salary protections, but they can be reappointed after their initial term. Federal magistrate judges are authorized by 28 U.S.C. § 631. They are appointed for eight-year terms

---

[19] Elena Kagan, *Confirmation Messes, Old and New*, 62 U. CHI. L. REV. 919, 920 (1995) (reviewing Stephen L. Carter, THE CONFIRMATION MESS (1994)).

by a majority vote of the federal district judges of a particular district. They, too, may be reappointed.

§ 5.2 JUDICIAL OVERSIGHT

A. CODES OF JUDICIAL CONDUCT

The ABA Model Code of Judicial Conduct[20] is extraordinarily brief, consisting of just four Canons. Each Canon contains a general statement, followed by specific rules applicable to that Canon. The Code also contains comments from the drafters. But even the specific rules are fairly brief and general in their terminology. The generality of the canons and their accompanying rules leave much to the discretion of individual judges and their own conscience.

CANON 1

A judge shall uphold and promote the independence, integrity, and impartiality of the judiciary, and shall avoid impropriety and the appearance of impropriety.

CANON 2

A judge shall perform the duties of judicial office impartially, competently, and diligently.

CANON 3

A judge shall conduct the judge's personal and extrajudicial activities to minimize the risk of conflict with the obligations of judicial office.

CANON 4

A judge or candidate for judicial office shall not engage in political or campaign activity that is inconsistent with the independence, integrity, or impartiality of the judiciary.

B. JUDICIAL DISCIPLINE

When a judge violates one or more of the Canons, the methods of judicial oversight consist primarily of three options: recusal by the judge for potential conflicts of interest, discussed at length in Chapters 3 and 4; review by a Judicial Conduct Commission; or impeachment.

The range of ways in which judges can get into trouble mirrors those of the rest of society but with some special concerns. The most obvious misconduct would be accepting bribes or favors for rulings on cases, along with sitting on cases in which the judge or judge's family has a financial interest. As the cases below illustrate, other minor transgressions may or may not reflect on the ability to perform as a judge. Conversely, there

[20] MODEL CODE OF JUDICIAL CONDUCT (AM. BAR ASS'N 2007), http://www.americanbar.org/content/dam/aba/migrated/judicialethics/ABA_MCJC_approved.authcheckdam.pdf [https://perma.cc/JP5R-FRVM].

are some things a judge cannot do which may surprise the most careful observer.

1. FEDERAL

Any person may initiate a complaint against a federal judge. The complaint is filed with the clerk of the relevant court of appeals and must allege "that a judge has engaged in conduct prejudicial to the effective and expeditious administration of the business of the courts, or alleging that such judge is unable to discharge all the duties of office by reason of mental or physical disability . . . ."[21] The chief judge of the circuit, as well as the judge about whom the complaint has been filed, reviews the complaint. The chief judge may institute an expedited and limited investigation. The targeted judge may file a written response, although the complainant cannot see the response. The chief judge has wide latitude to dismiss the complaint or issue appropriate corrective action.[22] Either the targeted judge or the chief judge may request review by the five-member judicial council. The council is comprised of two circuit court judges, two district court judges, and the chief judge of the circuit.

The judicial council ultimately may order that the judge be assigned no further cases, issue a private or public censure or reprimand, certify disability of the judge (triggering a statutory provision that allows the judge to retire with either full or half salary),[23] or request that the judge voluntarily retire.[24] While the judicial council has no power to fire an Article III judge, both magistrate judges and bankruptcy judges may be removed from office.

> If the judicial council determines that the targeted Article III judge may have engaged in conduct—(A) which might constitute one or more grounds for impeachment under article II of the Constitution, or (B) which, in the interest of justice, is not amenable to resolution by the judicial council, the judicial council shall promptly certify such determination, together with any complaint and a record of any associated proceedings, to the Judicial Conference of the United States.[25]

The Judicial Conference of the United States is the national policy-making body for the federal courts. If the Judicial Conference believes that impeachment is appropriate, or determines that the judge has been convicted of a felony, it forwards the case to the House of Representatives for further action.[26] The statute refers to Article II as the source for power of Congress to try impeachment cases.

---

[21] 28 U.S.C. § 351(a) (2012).

[22] *See id.* § 352.

[23] *See id.* §§ 354(A)(2)(B), 371.

[24] *See id.* § 354.

[25] *Id.* § 354(b)(2)(A)–(B).

[26] *Id.* § 355(b)(1).

Chandler v. Judicial Council of the Tenth Circuit

382 U.S. 1003 (1966)

Petitioner applied to MR. JUSTICE WHITE, CIRCUIT JUSTICE for the Tenth Circuit, for "Stay of Order of Judicial Council of the Tenth Circuit of the United States" in the above matter, and the application was by him referred to the Court for its consideration and action.

It appearing to the Court from the response of the Solicitor General to the application that the order from which relief is sought is entirely interlocutory in character pending prompt further proceedings inquiring into the administration of Judge Chandler of judicial business in the Western District of Oklahoma, and that at such proceedings Judge Chandler will be permitted to appear before the Council, with counsel, and that after such proceedings the Council will, as soon as possible, undertake to decide what use, if any, should be made of such powers as it may have in the premises, it is hereby ordered that the application for stay be denied pending this contemplated prompt action of the Judicial Council. The Court expresses no opinion concerning the propriety of the interlocutory action taken.

■ MR. JUSTICE BLACK, with whom MR. JUSTICE DOUGLAS joins, dissenting.

United States District Judge Stephen S. Chandler here asks for a stay of an "Order" of the Judicial Council of the Tenth Circuit directing that until further order of the Council, Judge Chandler "take no action whatsoever in any case or proceeding now or hereafter pending" in his court, that cases now assigned to him be assigned to other judges, and that no new actions filed be assigned to him. If this order is not stayed and if the Judicial Council has some way to enforce it, the order means that Judge Chandler is completely barred from performing any of his official duties and in effect is removed or ousted from office pending further orders of the Council. The reason given by the Council for this drastic action is that it "finds that Judge Chandler is presently unable, or unwilling, to discharge efficiently the duties of his office . . . " By refusing to stay the Council's order, the Court necessarily acts on the premise that the Council has a legal right to remove Judge Chandler from office at least temporarily. Though the Court tries to softpedal its refusal to stay the order by referring to it as "interlocutory in character," the stark fact which cannot be disguised is that a United States District Judge, duly appointed by the President and approved by the Senate, is with this Court's imprimatur locked out of his office pending "further proceedings" by the Judicial Council. I think the Council is completely without legal authority to issue any such order, either temporary or permanent, with or without a hearing, that no statute purports to authorize it, and that the Constitution forbids it. Nor can the effect of the order be softened by asserting that Judge Chandler will be permitted to have a lawyer represent him before his fellow judges. Assuming that we have jurisdiction to stay an order from a governmental agency that has no power at all to do what this Council has done, I would stay this "Order" *instanter*.

The Council states that its order was made "pursuant to the power and authority vested in the Judicial Council by 28 U.S.C. § 332." That section so far as relevant reads:

> Each judicial council shall make all necessary orders for the effective and expeditious administration of the business of the courts within its circuit. The district judges shall promptly carry into effect all orders of the judicial council.

There is no language whatever in this or any other Act which can by any reasonable interpretation be read as giving the Council a power to pass upon the work of district judges, declare them inefficient and strip them of their power to act as judges. The language of Congress indicates a purpose to vest the Judicial Council with limited administrative powers; nothing in this language, or the history behind it, indicates that a Council of Circuit Court Judges was to be vested with power to discipline district judges, and in effect remove them from office. This is clearly and simply a proceeding by circuit judges to inquire into the fitness of a district judge to hold his office and to remove him if they so desire. I do not believe Congress could, even if it wished, vest any such power in the circuit judges.

One of the great advances made in the structure of government by our Constitution was its provision for an independent judiciary—for judges who could do their duty as they saw it without having to account to superior court judges or to anyone else except the Senate sitting as a court of impeachment. Article II, § 4, of the Constitution provides that "Officers of the United States," which includes judges, "shall be removed from Office on Impeachment for, and Conviction of, Treason, Bribery, or other high Crimes and Misdemeanors," and Art. I, §§ 2 and 3, state that impeachment can be instituted only on recommendation of the House of Representatives and that trial can be held only by the Senate. To hold that judges can do what this Judicial Council has tried to do to Judge Chandler here would in my judgment violate the plan of our Constitution to preserve, as far as possible, the liberty of the people by guaranteeing that they have judges wholly independent of the Government or any of its agents with the exception of the United States Congress acting under its limited power of impeachment. We should stop in its infancy, before it has any growth at all, this idea that the United States district judges can be made accountable for their efficiency or lack of it to the judges just over them in the federal judicial system. The only way to do that is to grant this stay and I am in favor of granting it.

NOTES AND QUESTIONS

1. **A History of Strange Behavior.** The Tenth Circuit order was rescinded after one month, and Judge Chandler remained on the bench. He took senior status ten years later but still heard occasional cases until his death in 1989. Judge Chandler apparently was irascible and difficult. According to the obituary at his death,

> In 1962 Judge Chandler testified before a United States Senate subcommittee that he was afraid of being poisoned, that his telephone was tapped and that his fellow judges sometimes cursed him. Twice he was removed from hearing lawsuits because of allegations of personal interest or bias and prejudice. He once barred the United States Attorney in Oklahoma City and five other Oklahoma City lawyers from practicing in Federal Court. The Federal appeals court overturned the ruling.[27]

2. **Misbehavior Isn't a Crime.** Justice Black outlines the criteria and procedures for impeachment of "Officers of the United States, which includes judges." Is he right? Justice Black doesn't quote the full language of Article II, which refers to "all *civil* Officers." Assuming that a judge has committed no crime (at least, none that can be proved) but has become incompetent, as was alleged with Judge Chandler, what remedy should exist? Is "good behavior" in Article III different from the "high Crimes and Misdemeanors" of Article II?

In 1804, federal district court judge John Pickering was impeached for "drunkenness and unlawful rulings." His impeachment created Congressional controversy because he had not committed any "high Crimes and Misdemeanors." Despite the controversy, Pickering was tried, convicted, and removed from office.

3. **It's Time to Retire . . . or Resign.** Judges have the option to retire rather than face the gauntlet of a circuit court council and the Judicial Conference. That's what happened in the case of Judge Edward Nottingham. Nottingham was accused of, inter alia, being a regular customer of a Denver prostitution ring, being a regular (and well-tipping) customer of a local strip club called the Diamond Cabaret, using his court computer to access pornography, and threatening to call the U.S. Marshals on a citizen who challenged his use of a handicapped parking space in downtown Denver. Although the case was assigned to the Judicial Council of the Tenth Circuit Court of Appeals, Judge Nottingham resigned before they could take any action. He is now in private practice in Denver.

4. **The Politics of Impeachment.** There have been 14 federal judges impeached in U.S. history. Of those, four were acquitted by the Senate, seven were removed from office, and three resigned. The wisdom of refusing to impeach for political reasons was established early. After the successful impeachment and conviction of Judge Pickering, the Federalists decided to go after Justice Samuel Chase for political bias and partisanship. He was

---

[27] *U.S. Judge Stephen Chandler, 89; Often Feuded With His Colleagues*, N.Y. TIMES (April 29, 1989), http://www.nytimes.com/1989/04/29/obituaries/us-judge-stephen-chandler-89-often-feuded-with-his-colleagues.html [https://perma.cc/PME8-UQ8X].

acquitted by the Senate. No judge has been impeached since without some element of genuine misbehavior, but misbehavior has included drunkenness, general corruption, and "abuse of power." For example, in 2008, United States District Court Judge Porteous of Louisiana was impeached and removed from office by the Senate for basic corruption, including both cash and items such as meals and trips.[28]

5. **We're Not All Equal Here.** Judicial discipline is not always equal. In 2009, Texas federal judge Samuel B. Kent was impeached and forced to resign after being sentenced to 33 months in prison for lying to investigators about sexually abusing two female employees. Conversely, Texas federal judge Walter E. Smith was merely reprimanded in 2015 by the Fifth Circuit for "inappropriate, unwanted physical and non-physical sexual advances" toward a court employee. He was barred from new case assignments for one year.[29]

6. **A Different Nixon.** Walter Nixon, a former Chief Judge of the United States District Court for the Southern District of Mississippi, was convicted by a jury of two counts of making false statements before a federal grand jury and sentenced to prison. The grand jury investigation stemmed from reports that Nixon had accepted a gratuity from a Mississippi businessman in exchange for asking a local district attorney to halt the prosecution of the businessman's son. Because Nixon refused to resign from his office as a United States District Judge, he continued to collect his judicial salary while serving out his prison sentence until removed from office by the Senate. His challenge to the Senate action went to the Supreme Court on the propriety of the Senate's decision to act without receipt of testimony in the full chamber, instead relying on a report of the Judiciary Committee. The Court ruled that the definition of "trial" was a political question left to the discretion of the Senate.[30]

7. **Can't Somebody Do Something?** Refer back to some of the behavior of Judge Willis Ritter of Utah in Chapter 4. If a judge has become untrustworthy, volatile, or abusive to lawyers and court personnel shouldn't the courts have some power to remove him from hearing cases? Is impeachment the only remedy?

Some appellate courts have reassigned cases in these circumstances. In *Black Rock City v. Pershing County Board of Commissioners*, the Ninth Circuit vacated a district court's grant of summary judgment issued after the parties settled the case. In addition to determining that the district court lacked jurisdiction, the Ninth Circuit noted that Judge Robert C. Jones "excoriated and mocked counsel,"[31] "noted his own laughter on the record,

---

[28] Jennifer Steinhauer, *Senate, for Just the 8th Time, Votes to Oust a Federal Judge*, N.Y. TIMES (Dec. 8, 2010), http://www.nytimes.com/2010/12/09/us/politics/09judge.html [https://perma.cc/B8WZ-C66V].

[29] *Professor Arthur Hellman Quoted on Reprimand of Federal Judge for Sexual Harassment*, U. PITTS. SCH. LAW. (Dec. 23, 2015), http://law.pitt.edu/news/news-item/professor-arthur-hellman-quoted-reprimand-federal-judge-sexual-harassment [https://perma.cc/F6H7-AZCV].

[30] Nixon v. United States, 506 U.S. 224, 238 (1993).

[31] Black Rock City v. Pershing County Bd. of Comm'rs, 637 Fed. App'x. 488, 489 (9th Cir. 2016).

repeatedly lobbed accusations of malpractice, described counsel's comments as 'mealy-mouthed,' and suggested that counsel return to law school."[32]

Prior to *Black Rock City*, the Ninth Circuit removed or considered removing Judge Jones from particular cases on at least five other occasions.[33] In some, the judge applied the wrong legal standard, invited claims against the government, or expressed his disdain for the federal government. In most, Judge Jones exhibited clear anti-government bias. In one case, he denied admission to an out-of-state attorney for the United States, reversed himself when the government sought mandamus from the Ninth Circuit, and then applied the rule again in a new case.[34]

Does a district judge's repeated flouting of appellate court orders bring disrepute to the district as a whole? Is there a point at which the judge's behavior becomes grounds for impeachment?

2. STATE

Every state has some sort of judicial conduct commission. The vast majority of complaints against state judges are dismissed. However, every state has a method of disciplining or removing judges who violate the codes of judicial conduct. Although the process varies by state, generally the judicial conduct commission investigates (and may also prosecute) allegations of misconduct. Its findings of fact and recommendation are generally forwarded to the state supreme court, which must then decide whether the appropriate standard of proof has been met and what sanctions are appropriate. In most states, the supreme court either adopts, modifies, or rejects the commission's findings and conclusions. However, in other states the commission's decision is treated as final unless the judge asks for review.

Most state supreme courts have a range of sanctions at their disposal. Some of these are private, including counseling, letters of caution, private admonishments, or appearances before the commission. Others are public, including public warning, reprimand, admonition, monetary fines, censure, suspension with or without pay, or removal. Judges also sometimes retire in lieu of other disciplinary measures.

---

[32] *Id.* at 489 n.3.

[33] *See* United States v. Estate of Hage, 810 F.3d 712, 721–24 (9th Cir. 2016); United States v. U. S. Dist. Court (*In re* United States), 791 F.3d 945, 957–60 (9th Cir. 2015); Nat'l Council of La Raza v. Cegavske, 800 F.3d 1032, 1045–46 (9th Cir. 2015); Benvin v. U.S. Dist. Court (*In re* Benvin), 791 F.3d 1096, 1104 (9th Cir. 2015) (per curiam); Townley v. Miller, 693 F.3d 1041, 1043–45 (9th Cir. 2012) (order) (Reinhardt, J., concurring).

[34] *See La Raza*, 800 F.3d at 1046; *see also In re* United States, 791 F.3d at 949–50.

Kennick v. Commission on Judicial Performance

787 P.2d 591 (1990)

OPINION

■ THE COURT:

The Commission on Judicial Performance (commission) has filed in this court its recommendation that David M. Kennick, a judge of the Municipal Court for the Los Angeles Judicial District, be removed from office. Accompanying the petition were the commission's findings of fact and conclusions that the judge had committed "wilful [sic] misconduct in office" (willful misconduct) and "conduct prejudicial to the administration of justice that brings the judicial office into disrepute" (prejudicial conduct), and was culpable of "persistent failure or inability to perform the judge's duties" (persistent failure).

The commission's findings, which are in eight counts, deal with five factual situations, beginning with the arrest and conviction of petitioner for drunk driving in August 1985. It is found that he was rude and abusive toward the arresting officers and refused to take field sobriety or blood-alcohol tests (count two), that he sought preferential treatment because of his judicial status and asked an officer if "the paperwork could get lost" before it reached the court (count one), and that he was convicted of driving under the influence of alcohol on a plea of nolo contendere (count three). A second group of findings specifies numerous instances of demeaning, rude, impatient, or abusive behavior, and denial of litigants' and attorneys' rights to be heard, both on the bench and in chambers (counts four and six). Next are findings that petitioner favored certain attorneys in appointing counsel for indigent defendants (count five). In another count it is found that in a long conversation with a waitress at a restaurant, petitioner implied she should not worry about a drunk driving arrest (count seven). Finally, it is found that petitioner's excessive absences from the courthouse, and his cessation of work altogether at the beginning of 1987, constituted persistent failure or inability to perform judicial duties (count eight).

Applicable Standards

We turn to the merits of the commission's report and recommendation of removal. Removal may be justified by any of the three forms of dereliction found here: willful misconduct, prejudicial conduct, or persistent failure to perform duties.

Willful misconduct, or "wilful [sic] misconduct in office" (art. VI, § 18, subd. (c)), has two elements: it must be *willful,* i.e., done with malice or in bad faith, and it must be committed in *office,* i.e., while acting in a judicial capacity. The element of bad faith, or malice, must meet a two-pronged test: the judge must have "(1) committed acts he knew or should have known to be beyond his power, (2) for a purpose other than faithful discharge of judicial duties."

Prejudicial conduct, or "conduct prejudicial to the administration of justice that brings the judicial office into disrepute" (art. VI, § 18, subd. (c)), is generally less serious than willful misconduct and may be committed either (1) while acting in other than a judicial capacity or (2) while acting in a judicial capacity but in good faith and without malice. Prejudicial conduct while acting in a judicial capacity means "conduct which a judge undertakes in good faith but which nevertheless would appear to an objective observer to be not only unjudicial conduct but conduct prejudicial to public esteem for the judicial office." The provision that prejudicial conduct must be that which "brings the judicial office into disrepute" does "not require notoriety, but only that the conduct be damaging to the esteem for the judiciary held by members of the public who observed such conduct."

In considering the commission's report and recommendation, we must independently review the record and sustain the charges against petitioner only to the extent we find there is clear and convincing evidence sufficient to prove them to a reasonable certainty. We must then determine, as a matter of law, what if any constitutional grounds for judicial discipline are established by each of the findings thus sustained and whether those grounds support the commission's recommendation of removal. In formulating these legal conclusions, we give great weight to the conclusions of the commission. In resolving disputed issues of fact, however, we give special deference to the determinations of the masters, who were best able to evaluate the truthfulness of the witnesses appearing before them. Each of the three masters who heard petitioner's case was a judge or retired judge of the Los Angeles County Superior Court and thus experienced in assessing credibility.

Misconduct in Response to Arrest and Prosecution for Drunk Driving (Counts one, two and three)

[The court upheld the findings of the commission with regard to prejudicial conduct in the arrest process. It held that the DUI conviction based on a plea of nolo contendere was not a sanctionable offense because the plea had less effect on public perception of the judiciary than would have been likely with a trial. With regard to the remaining aspect of this incident, the judge did not refer to his role as a judge in attempting to have the charges dropped by the station sergeant.]

Accordingly, it has not been proved by clear and convincing evidence that petitioner was acting in a judicial capacity when he sought favorable treatment from Bladow. The conduct of a judge not acting in judicial capacity cannot amount to willful misconduct, for purposes of judicial discipline, regardless of the malice or bad faith involved. We therefore hold that by engaging in the acts charged and proved under count one, petitioner committed prejudicial conduct but not willful misconduct.

Judicial Rudeness and Denial of Due Process (Counts four and six)

Count four charges petitioner with demeaning, rude, impatient, and abusive behavior toward individuals appearing before him, and count six charges him with denying parties or their attorneys the right to be heard.

[(a) & (b) *Demeaning treatment of counsel*

With regard to one incident of aggressive behavior toward an assistant prosecutor, the court held that the evidence did not show any unusually demeaning behavior. With regard to another incident, however, the court found it more aggressive.]

Clear and convincing evidence supports the commission's findings that petitioner's behavior [in the second incident] was demeaning, rude, impatient and abusive, and was treated by him as a laughing matter. We also agree that he was acting in a judicial capacity and in bad faith, and that his actions therefore constituted willful misconduct in office as well as prejudicial conduct.

(c) *Addressing female personnel as "sweetheart"* (par. c)

Paragraph c of count four alleges that petitioner addressed female attorneys and others appearing before him as "sweetie," "sweetheart," "honey," or "dear." The masters and the commission found this charge was true and that the expressions used were unprofessional, demeaning and unjustified by personal friendship or acquaintance.

The commission found that petitioner had used these expressions in open court, but the masters found he had not done so. There was testimony that petitioner had used the terms "sweetie" or "sweetheart" to "females in the courtroom," but the witness did not specify whether court was then in session. Thus, the commission's finding on this point lacks the requisite evidentiary support. It can fairly be inferred, however, that petitioner used the expressions in and about the courthouse during business hours to people he knew principally or solely in connection with his judicial duties. We agree with the commission that petitioner's use of these terms in addressing women under those circumstances was unprofessional, demeaning and sexist, and violated canon 3A(3) of the California Code of Judicial Conduct ("Judges should be patient, dignified, and courteous to litigants, jurors, witnesses, lawyers, and others with whom judges deal in their official capacity"). We therefore adopt the conclusions of the masters and the commission that these acts constituted prejudicial conduct.

(d) *Rudeness to criminal litigants* (par. d)

Paragraph d of count four alleges that petitioner was discourteous, impatient, and demeaning to litigants appearing before him in criminal and civil cases. The masters and the commission found this charge true only with respect to criminal cases.

The commission's findings are amply supported by the testimony of two deputy district attorneys and two deputy city attorneys, all of whom had appeared frequently in petitioner's courtroom. Petitioner called 28 witnesses, including attorneys, bailiffs, clerks and court reporters, who testified to being frequently present in petitioner's courtroom without observing any of this type of misbehavior. The fact that petitioner proceeded properly and courteously on many, or even most, occasions, however, does not excuse the instances of misconduct proved by testimony which the masters found credible. We adopt the commission's findings on paragraph d of count four, as well as its conclusion that the subject behavior constituted prejudicial conduct. We also agree with the commission that petitioner's refusal to listen to defendants who were attempting to address the court, as found under paragraph d of count four, amounted to prejudicial conduct consisting of the denial of parties' full right to be heard, as charged in count six.

(f) *Intimidation of witnesses* (par. h)

Paragraph h of count four alleges that petitioner was rude and intimidating to witnesses, unnecessarily interrupted their testimony, at times harshly admonished them to "just answer the question," and caused them to become upset. The masters and the commission found this charge true.

We find the charges of paragraph h of count four to be true and agree with the masters and the commission that the acts charged constituted prejudicial conduct consisting of both rude, intimidating treatment of witnesses (count four) and denials of the right to be heard (count six).

Favoritism Toward Appointed Counsel (Count five)

Count five charges that petitioner has "shown favoritism to private attorney Theordore Veganes, with whom [petitioner has] jointly owned property in Hawaii since 1976, and to private attorney David Pantoja."

Both the masters and the commission concluded that petitioner had committed prejudicial conduct by favoring Veganes and Pantoja in his appointments of counsel. The commission also concluded, however, that petitioner's favoritism in appointing counsel constituted willful misconduct. In the present case, there is no contention or evidence that any of petitioner's appointments of the allegedly favored attorneys was not fully justified under Penal Code section 987.2 and related sections, or that the attorneys were overpaid for their services.

Nor do we find any other clear and convincing evidence that petitioner acted in bad faith, i.e., that he knew or should have known the appointments were beyond his powers and that he made them for a purpose other than the faithful discharge of his judicial duties. There is evidence that petitioner was not given clear guidelines for allocating the appointments, and that he acted to provide competent counsel whenever needed without conscious favoritism. Though there was other evidence from which inferences of bad faith might be drawn, such evidence appears to have been rejected by the masters, who were best able to judge credibility. We therefore conclude that the conduct charged in paragraph a of count five constituted prejudicial conduct but not willful misconduct.

Ex parte conversations with attorneys who were appearing on appointed cases

As a further instance of alleged favoritism toward Attorneys Veganes and Pantoja, paragraph b of count five charges petitioner with having "[ex] parte conversations in your chambers with these two attorneys on a number of occasions when they were appearing on appointed cases." Petitioner testified that these attorneys sometimes came into his chambers for social visits on days when they were appearing before him in court, but he denied that they ever discussed cases in which he was acting as judge.

We conclude, however, that petitioner's practice of meeting alone in chambers with an attorney representing one side of a case pending before him in the absence of circumstances that would make ex parte communication proper gave rise to an appearance of impropriety. It therefore constituted prejudicial conduct "that brings the judicial office into disrepute."

Improper Suggestion to Waitress Not to Worry About Drunk Driving Arrest (Count seven)

Count seven alleges that on the evening of February 22, 1985, petitioner "sat at a bar in Cigo's Restaurant in San Pedro for a period of several hours and during that period engaged in a conversation with Mary Davis, a waitress at the restaurant, in which [he] *repeatedly* implied that she should not worry about her recent arrest for drunk driving *because [he] could in some manner exert influence to affect the disposition of the case.*" (Italics added.)

We agree that for a judge to give a layperson assurances about the outcome of a prosecution against the latter may imply inside information and thus be inappropriate. We concur in the commission's conclusion that petitioner's conduct charged and found true by the commission under count seven constituted prejudicial conduct.

Persistent Failure to Perform Duties (Count eight)

Count eight alleges that petitioner "persistently failed to perform [his] judicial duties by being frequently absent from the courthouse, maintaining abbreviated working hours and delegating [his] judicial responsibilities to others," and that "this conduct rendered [him] unavailable for judicial services, placed a burden on [his] judicial colleagues, injured the administration of justice, and failed to promote public confidence in the integrity of the judiciary."

Even if a substantial portion of the absences in 1985 and 1986 were excusable by illness or as vacation, there appears no excuse for petitioner's failure to work from the beginning of 1987 to May 14, 1987, the date of his testimony before the masters. Nor does he claim to have made even an attempt to return to his duties from that time until his retirement in July 1988.

Accordingly, we conclude that petitioner's excessive absences from work in 1985 and 1986 and his cessation of work altogether at the beginning of 1987, as set forth in our finding on paragraph b of count eight, constituted persistent failure or inability to perform his judicial duties.

Removal from Office

The commission recommends that petitioner be removed from office. For the reasons heretofore explained, we must decide whether to adopt this recommendation even though petitioner voluntarily retired after it was made. The commission based its recommendation on three of the constitutional grounds for removal: willful misconduct, prejudicial conduct, and persistent inability or failure to perform judicial duties.

[The court reviewed instances of misbehavior by judges. In essence, only those who abused their position to affect the outcome of proceedings were removed from office.]

The testimony of the numerous attorneys and court personnel who testified on petitioner's behalf, particularly in connection with count four, indicates that he was capable of being a competent, conscientious, and fair judge. Viewed as a whole, petitioner's misconduct does not appear so continuing or pervasive as to preclude his reform. Thus, it seems likely that our public censure of each of petitioner's misdeeds would have led him to correct and improve his judicial behavior. Accordingly, we decline to order him removed from office for willful misconduct or prejudicial conduct.

The commission's recommendation of removal from office is grounded not only on petitioner's willful misconduct and prejudicial conduct, but also on his persistent failure or inability to perform judicial duties, based on the commission's finding, which we have adopted, under paragraph b of count eight. Petitioner's failure to work since the beginning of 1987 without any explanation other than vague references to current medical treatment, and without any evidence that he might or could resume his duties thereafter, is alone sufficient to establish this ground for his removal.

Conclusion

For the reasons stated, we order that as of the date this decision becomes final, David M. Kennick shall be removed from his office as Judge of the Municipal Court for the Los Angeles Judicial District on the sole ground of persistent failure or inability to perform his judicial duties. We also censure him for his willful misconduct in office and his conduct prejudicial to the administration of justice as determined in this opinion. He shall be permitted to practice law upon passing the Professional Responsibility Examination required of applicants seeking readmission or reinstatement to the bar.

NOTES AND QUESTIONS

1. **How Bad Is the Problem?** There is no extant database for tracking judicial misconduct proceedings. A report funded by the American Judicature Society surveyed state judicial sanctions from 1990 to 2001. In that study, the author found 110 cases in which judges were removed from office. Sixty-nine were removed for conduct in office, 28 for conduct wholly outside the office, and 13 for both in-office and out-of-office misconduct. The in-office misconduct included insulting behavior, abuse of power, ex parte communications, and sexual harassment. Most of the cases involving conduct outside the office consisted of criminal acts, inappropriate financial arrangements, or the continued practice of law.[35]

The American Judicature Society, a nonpartisan entity dedicated to "improve and preserve the fairness, impartiality and effectiveness of our justice system" dissolved in 2014 for lack of funds.

2. **Where Did I Go Wrong?** Appellate courts have a wide range of sanctions available when a judge "bring(s) disrepute to the judicial office." However, disrepute may be in the eye of the beholder.

In *In re McCully*,[36] the Utah Legislature ordered a general audit of the foster care system. The Legislative Auditor asked Guardian ad Litem David E. Littlefield to provide records on individual children whom Littlefield represented. He objected, arguing the records were privileged. The Auditor issued a legislative subpoena, which Littlefield moved to quash. Littlefield called juvenile court Judge McCully, informed Judge McCully that he expected to subpoena her to testify, and asked her to prepare an affidavit to explain the role and function of the guardian ad litem in juvenile court. Judge McCully prepared the affidavit in lieu of giving testimony. The Utah Supreme Court publicly reprimanded Judge McCully for violating Canon 3(B)(9). That provision provides, "A judge shall not, while a proceeding is pending or impending in any court, make any public comment that might reasonably be expected to affect its outcome or impair its fairness . . . ."

Rule 3.2 of the ABA Code of Conduct allows judges to consult with executive or legislative bodies "in connection with matters about which the judge acquired knowledge or expertise in the course of the judge's judicial duties."[37] As noted by the dissent, Judge McCully provided information on a matter within her special expertise and jurisdiction to a fellow judge who was hearing, not an ordinary adversarial proceeding, but a case involving the structure and roles of her part of the judiciary itself. Who is right? Did Judge McCully violate the rules of conduct? If so, what should she have done instead?

---

[35] CYNTHIA GRAY, A STUDY OF STATE JUDICIAL SANCTIONS (2002), http://www.ncsc.org/~/media/Files/PDF/Topics/Center%20for%20JudicialËthics/Publications/Study-of-State-Judicial-Discipline-Sanctions.ashx [https://perma.cc/BH5G-2N9T].

[36] 942 P.2d 327 (Utah 1997).

[37] MODEL CODE OF JUDICIAL CONDUCT, *supra* note 13, at R. 3.2(B), 3.2 cmt. n.1.

§ 5.3 JUDICIAL IMMUNITY

Some unhappy litigants have gone beyond the formal complaint process and attempted to sue the judge. These suits are often brought under 42 U.S.C. § 1983, a civil rights statute that makes government actors liable if they deprive a person of any Constitutional "rights, privileges, or immunities" while acting under "color of law." These suits usually come to naught. Judges have absolute immunity from liability for acts committed within their judicial jurisdiction. While litigants may seek redress from the appellate or disciplinary process, they may not sue judges directly. The concept has a lengthy pedigree. "Judicial immunity apparently originated, in medieval times, as a device for discouraging collateral attacks and thereby helping to establish appellate procedures as the standard system for correcting judicial error," remained the "settled doctrine of the English courts for many centuries, and has never been denied, that we are aware of, in the courts of this country."[38]

While absolute judicial immunity is frustrating for wronged litigants, it has a valid purpose: to encourage judges to make difficult decisions impartially, and without fear of reprisal. As the United States Supreme Court noted,

> If judges were personally liable for erroneous decisions, the resulting avalanche of suits, most of them frivolous but vexatious, would provide powerful incentives for judges to avoid rendering decisions likely to provoke such suits. The resulting timidity would be hard to detect or control, and it would manifestly detract from independent and impartial adjudication. Nor are suits against judges the only available means through which litigants can protect themselves from the consequences of judicial error. Most judicial mistakes or wrongs are open to correction through ordinary mechanisms of review, which are largely free of the harmful side-effects inevitably associated with exposing judges to personal liability.[39]

Despite criticism from both academic and legal circles, judicial immunity remains the law of the land.

Martinez v. Winner

771 F.2d 424 (10th Cir. 1985)

■ ARNOLD, CIRCUIT JUDGE.

Francisco Eugenio Martinez, known as "Kiko," appeals from the District Court's dismissal of his civil-rights complaint. Martinez claims the defendants deprived him of his civil and constitutional rights, conspired to "get Kiko," and tried to "railroad" him into prison on

---

[38] Forrester v. White, 484 U.S. 219, 225 (1988).

[39] *Id.* at 223.

unsubstantiated criminal charges. He asserts claims based on 42 U.S.C. §§ 1981, 1983, 1985, 1986, and 1988, the First, Fourth, Fifth, Sixth, Eighth, Ninth, Thirteenth, and Fourteenth Amendments to the United States Constitution, unspecified sections of the Constitution of the State of Colorado, common-law tort actions including false arrest, false imprisonment, malicious abuse of process, harassment, gross misconduct, outrageous conduct, and negligence, and violations of the Code of Judicial Conduct and the Code of Professional Responsibility for lawyers. He seeks damages, an injunction, and declaratory relief. The principal defendant is Fred M. Winner, at all relevant times Chief Judge of the United States District Court for the District of Colorado, who presided over plaintiff's trial in 1981 for mailing a letter bomb.

The District Court held that Judge Winner and the federal prosecutors were entitled to immunity from liability for damages for their acts, and that declaratory and injunctive relief were not available in this case. The judge and the federal prosecutors were dismissed from the case, as no relief could be granted against them. The causes of action under 42 U.S.C. §§ 1981, 1985, 1986, and 1988 were dismissed as either inapplicable or because no claim was stated under them. The claims against the remaining defendants were dismissed under Fed. R. Civ. P. 8(a) and 12(b)(6). Martinez was given 20 days to correct the deficiencies in the complaint, but he chose to stand on the complaint as filed. The dismissal of his complaint was therefore with prejudice.

We hold that Judge Winner is absolutely immune from any claim for damages, and that injunctive and declaratory relief against him would serve no purpose. He has left office. As to the other defendants, we affirm in part and reverse in part.

I.

Martinez's complaint arises out of criminal actions against him in both state and federal courts for the possession and mailing of three letter bombs. In 1973 the United States Attorney's office for the District of Colorado decided to prosecute Martinez for possession of unregistered explosives and the sending of explosives through the United States mails. Martinez fled the jurisdiction and did not return until 1980, when he was arrested by federal authorities. The charges in the indictment were split; each of three mail-bomb incidents was tried separately. In 1980 the Denver District Attorney's office also charged Martinez with crimes involving bombing attempts. These state charges were later dismissed upon motion of the prosecution.

During the first trial highly improper conduct occurred. [In 1973, Martinez went to trial on charges of conspiracy, possession of unregistered explosives, and mailing the explosives. Judge Winner presided. "On the evening of the third day of trial, January 29, the trial judge held a secret meeting with the prosecutors, court personnel, and several government witnesses in his hotel room. Neither defendant nor his counsel were notified about this meeting. Judge Winner stated that he believed there was an atmosphere of intimidation in the courtroom caused by some of the spectators who were sympathetic to the defendant and that he wanted hidden cameras to be installed to record the intimidation. Judge Winner informed the prosecutors that he would grant a motion for a mistrial, but advised them not to make such a motion until after the cameras were installed and after the defense presented its case. The judge further indicated that he could provoke defense counsel to request a mistrial. One witness, Officer Tyus, stated that he could cause a mistrial by giving testimony which had previously been ruled inadmissible.[40]]

Martinez alleges that there was a "get Kiko" conspiracy on the part of state and federal law-enforcement agencies, Judge Winner, and others. Plaintiff, a lawyer, says that he was actively using his legal skills to promote the assertion of rights by Mexicanos and other "oppressed" national minorities, including Native Americans. As a result of these activities, and because he himself was a Mexicano, he alleges that law-enforcement agencies conspired to harass and oppress his political and social activism. He claims they carried out unlawful surveillance and investigations, kept a dossier on him, received and passed on information, and issued malicious and inflammatory press releases. He says that false charges were brought against him, charges known to the prosecution to be false, and that the defendants tried to "railroad" him to jail. The "railroading" charge has particular reference to the hotel-room meeting, the details of which we have already described. As a result of these activities, Martinez alleges that numerous constitutional violations occurred and that many common-law torts were committed against him.

II.

Martinez's complaint seeks to allege many claims against many defendants.

In *Stump v. Sparkman*, 435 U.S. 349, 359 (1978), the Supreme Court stated that a judge is entitled to judicial immunity if he has not acted in clear absence of all jurisdiction and if the act was a judicial one. An act is judicial if it is a function normally performed by a judge and the parties dealt with the judge in his judicial capacity. A judge is entitled to immunity even if he acted with partiality, maliciously, or corruptly.

Many of Martinez's arguments against the judge are based on the theory that the acts were ministerial or administrative and therefore nonjudicial. However, an act may be administrative or ministerial for some purposes and still be a "judicial" act for purposes of immunity from liability for damages. Each act must be examined to determine if it was a function normally performed by a judge and if the parties were dealing with the judge in his judicial capacity. No question is raised in this case regarding Judge Winner's jurisdiction.

---

[40] United States v. Martinez, 667 F.2d 886, 887–88 (10th Cir. 1981).

The complaint states that Judge Winner assigned himself, in contravention of local practice and rules, to preside at the Martinez criminal trial, for the purpose of insuring a conviction. Cases filed in federal district courts are to be divided among the judges as provided by the rules and orders of the court. The chief judge is responsible for the observance of such rules and orders and assigns the cases when the rules and orders make no provision. Martinez does not dispute that Judge Winner, as chief judge, had the responsibility to insure that the rules are followed, but he argues that this is an administrative duty, usually handled by deputy clerks. Although it is an "administrative" act, in the sense that it does not concern the decision who shall win a case, the assignment of cases is still a judicial function in the sense that it directly concerns the case-deciding process, and by statute it is the responsibility of the chief judge, Judge Winner in this case. It was within the expectation of the parties that the chief judge would be responsible for the assignment of cases. That Judge Winner may have acted improperly in assigning a case to himself is irrelevant to the issue of judicial immunity. The assignment of a case to himself was a judicial act for which Judge Winner is entitled to judicial immunity.

Judge Winner suggested at the hotel-room meeting that a hidden camera be installed to observe threats which he believed were being made against the jury. Martinez argues that Judge Winner's suggestion was part of a conspiracy to prosecute him, his lawyers, supporters, and spectators for obstruction of justice, and that Judge Winner gathered evidence, directed police and FBI activities, and tried to involve the prosecuting attorneys in his camera "scheme." Suggesting the installation of hidden cameras to observe possible threats to, or intimidation of, the jury falls within a judge's responsibility to maintain order and security in the courtroom.

A judge who allegedly predetermines a case is still protected by judicial immunity. To hold that a judge who is charged with having made a predetermination of guilt is not entitled to absolute immunity would make ineffective the whole doctrine of judicial immunity. Every dissatisfied loser could sue the judge on this basis. "If civil actions could be maintained in such cases against the judge, because the losing party should see fit to allege in his complaint that the acts of the judge were done with partiality, or maliciously, or corruptly, the protection essential to judicial independence would be entirely swept away." *Bradley v. Fisher*, 13 Wall. at 348. Even if Judge Winner made a predetermination that Martinez was guilty, he is still entitled to judicial immunity.

The complaint also states that Judge Winner wrote to the Department of Justice accusing Martinez of being a catalyst for bringing together four terrorist groups, and charging that he was obstructing justice and was involved in bombings and riots. Copies of the letter were then allegedly sent to other members of the federal bench, to defendant Shaughnessy, Chief of the Police Department of the City of Denver, to unspecified others, and to the Denver Post, which published portions of the letter. Martinez also alleges Judge Winner granted an interview to defendant Webb, a television reporter, to induce him to publish the same accusations.

There is no question that Judge Winner is entitled to immunity for writing the letter to the Justice Department and sending copies to the other law-enforcement officials. The letter referred to the trial and Judge Winner's belief that the jury had been intimidated. As stated above, Judge Winner had a duty to notify the proper authorities if he felt a crime was being committed in his courtroom. As to sending the letter to the Denver Post, the complaint alleges only that the letter was sent, not that the judge sent it. Finally, although it is usually inappropriate for judges to give statements to the press about pending cases, here the statement simply repeated the contents of a letter sent to law-enforcement authorities. If, as we have held, the sending of the letter is itself within the judicial immunity, we do not think that repeating the letter's contents to newspeople is so far nonjudicial as to forfeit that immunity.

We conclude that Judge Winner is entitled to absolute judicial immunity from the claims for damages alleged against him in the complaint. As is always the case when a defense of immunity is upheld, some wrongs may go unredressed as a result of this holding. Indeed, we have already held that the hotel-room meeting and subsequent courtroom proceedings were a gross impropriety. The premise of the doctrine of absolute judicial immunity, however, is that it is more tolerable for a few wrongs to go unredressed than for the judiciary to be continuously harassed by suits brought by disappointed litigants. That most of these cases would probably be dismissed on the merits, either on motion for summary judgment or after trial on the merits, is not a complete answer to the dangers posed by this kind of harassment, for being forced to litigate such matters is a significant personal burden, inevitably distracting the defendant judges from their main duty of deciding cases. The public must look to other remedies, including impeachment and disciplinary proceedings before the judicial council of the circuit involved, for such transgressions.

NOTES AND QUESTIONS

1. ***Stump v. Sparkman.*** The leading Supreme Court case on judicial immunity involved a sterilization order issued ex parte by a trial judge at the request of a mother who claimed that her 15-year-old "somewhat retarded" daughter "had been associating with 'older youth or young men' and had stayed out overnight with them on several occasions."[41] The trial judge signed an order for a tubal ligation without notice to the daughter or appointment of a guardian ad litem. Later, when the daughter married and learned what had been done to her, she filed suit. The Court decided that Judge Stump was entitled to absolute immunity. Justice Stewart was

[41] Stump v. Sparkman, 435 U.S. 349, 352 (1978).

virtually apoplectic as he read his entire dissent from the bench. Nevertheless, the principle of absolute immunity stands.

2. **Hiring and Firing.** Although judges have immunity for judicial acts, they do not have absolute immunity for administrative acts. Thus, their hiring and firing decisions may be actionable depending on the jurisdiction.

3. **You Have Other Options.** What other alternatives could be made available to wronged litigants? Could there be some sort of administrative clearinghouse for lawsuits against miscreant judges, allowing the courts to weed out frivolous claims? Many states have adopted this system for medical malpractice claims. Could the courts increase disciplinary actions against judges, or provide more transparency in disciplinary investigations? In many terrorism cases, the courts have said that persons subjected to torture have remedies other than damage actions, such as disciplinary actions against the offender. Is that realistic? What good does that do the wronged person? Many litigants simply want to feel that they have been heard. Is there a way to give litigants wronged by judges that satisfaction?

CHAPTER 6

SPECIALTY COURTS

> Lawyers, of course, are completely comfortable with the notion that the substantive law must change and adapt to meet changing social conditions. But they are distinctly less comfortable with the idea that the structures of the justice system may also need to evolve to meet current demands.[1]
>
> – New York State Chief Judge Judith S. Kaye

Alternatives to litigation go back hundreds of years. The first human communities—many still operating in the world today—relied on "restorative justice" carried out by the tribal or village elders. Disputes in feudal England were often resolved in manorial courts, where the lord of the manor had jurisdiction over his tenants. These early courts boasted both informality and communal decision-making, but they could also be unfair, harsh, and unreviewable. The possibility of disparity and injustice eventually led to formal and appealable judicial proceedings.

Over the past 100 years, however, a variety of less-formal tribunals were once again created to ameliorate some of the strictures of the traditional Anglo-American adversarial judicial system. Juvenile courts arose out of the abuses of late 19th century criminal law, while reforms in the mid-1980s produced homeless courts, drug courts, veterans' courts, and mental health courts. These courts share the common goal of therapeutic treatment and rehabilitative sentencing for certain criminal defendants.

§ 6.1 THEORIES OF PUNISHMENT

What is the purpose of criminal law? To punish the guilty? To make the victim whole? To avenge the offense against the sovereign? To solve the underlying personal or societal problems that lead to criminal behavior? The answer to those questions depends on whom you ask. Criminal courts in the United States are set up to adjudicate guilt and impose the appropriate punishment. Most courts either impose fines or jail time on guilty defendants, although some sentence offenders to rehabilitative programs as well.

There are a variety of theories of punishment in criminal law. These often drive sentencing at both the legislative and judicial level. The

[1] Chief Judge Judith S. Kaye, Lawyering for a New Age, Sonnett Lecture at Fordham University Law School (April 8, 1998).

theories may be broadly categorized as utilitarian, retributive, and rehabilitative.

Utilitarian punishment has several goals, including general deterrence (deterring other would-be criminals from committing a particular crime), individual deterrence (deterring this particular defendant from reoffending), and incapacitation (warehousing criminals so that they cannot reoffend). Critics argue that traditional punishments such as fines and jail time fail to deter crimes and that warehousing citizens has a disproportionate impact on poor and minority communities.

Retributive punishment is designed to give the defendant his "just deserts." It reflects the condemnation of the community; although it is tempered by, and proportionally graded to, the defendant's moral culpability. Retributive justice is designed to affirm a victim's value to the system, although many victims say that the system fails to reach that goal. Critics also charge that it does little to address the root causes or future likelihood of criminal behavior.

Finally, rehabilitation de-emphasizes punishment. Like utilitarian punishment, the goal of rehabilitation is to prevent this particular defendant from reoffending. However, rehabilitative models recognize that, for some people, jail and other punitive measures are a particularly poor vehicle for achieving this goal. Rehabilitative models are often criticized for being soft on crime or coddling prisoners by providing therapy and other services unavailable to the public at large.

Criminal justice in the United States often goes through pendulum swings—sometimes mercurial and sometimes glacial. Society's preference for one type of punishment over another tends to change over time. One well-publicized and particularly violent crime may markedly shift the criminal justice system from a rehabilitative model to a utilitarian or retributive model. Conversely, the recognition that warehousing prisoners is costly, both in terms of public resources and human lives, may shift the system from a utilitarian model to a rehabilitative model.

In the past ten years, many voters and politicians have concluded that the United States has become over-criminalized. While the United States has just over four percent of the world's population, it has about 22 percent of the world's known prisoners. Since 2008, however, the incarceration rates in the United States have steadily declined. In 2008, the country jailed 716 out of every 100,000 residents. By 2014 that rate had dropped to 612 out of every 100,000 residents.[2] While these data may have multiple explanations, the United States is moving from utilitarian sentencing to rehabilitative sentencing. This movement is exemplified by specialty courts that exist around the country.

---

[2] U.S. DEP'T OF JUSTICE, BUREAU OF JUSTICE STATISTICS, PRISONERS IN 2014 (2015), http://www.bjs.gov/content/pub/pdf/p14.pdf [https://perma.cc/8WYC-YPZC].

§ 6.2 JUVENILE COURTS

Juvenile courts hear two separate kinds of cases. The first are juvenile delinquency proceedings, in which minors are charged with criminal offenses. The second are "dependency and neglect" proceedings, in which a social services agency brings a civil case against a parent or guardian alleging that a child has been abused or neglected. In some jurisdictions the two cases are handled by the same judge; in others the cases are heard in separate divisions.

The two courts share a common history. Both arose from efforts in the late 19th century to create a child protection system.[3]

A. HISTORY

Prior to the 20th century, children in the criminal justice system were treated as little adults, subject to the same rules and penalties as all other criminals. At the time of the Founding the common law "theoretically permitted capital punishment to be imposed on anyone over the age of 7."[4]

Beginning in the late 1800s, activists challenged the notion that juveniles should be subject to adult procedures and penalties and face long prison sentences mixed in jails with hardened adult offenders. Moreover, these reformers believed that society had a duty to address the best interests of the child, as well as the interest of the state, in preventing recidivism. Their efforts paid off when, in 1899, Illinois created the first juvenile court. This new court had the mandate to regulate the "treatment and control of dependent neglected and delinquent children."[5] While the new juvenile court lacked many of the Constitutional protections provided to adult defendants, it also lacked the punishments imposed on adult defendants. The emphasis was on treatment and rehabilitation rather than punishment and retribution.

The shift from punishment to treatment was justified by *parens patriae*—the idea that the state stands in for the parent. The court's goal was to shape and mold the child as a parent would. Lawmakers and judges believed that kids are different than adults in a number of ways. First, they are entirely dependent on the adults in their lives. Second, they are still developing cognitively and emotionally. Finally, juveniles have different levels of understanding. The goal was to have a court where juveniles could both understand the proceedings and be understood by the adults around them.

---

[3] John E. B. Myers, *A Short History of Child Protection in America*, 42 Fam. L. Q. 449 (2008), https://www.americanbar.org/content/dam/aba/publishing/insights_law_society/ChildProtectionHistory.authcheckdam.pdf [https://perma.cc/SL3P-56Z6].

[4] Stanford v. Kentucky, 492 U. S. 361, 368 (1989) (citing 4 WILLIAM BLACKSTONE, *Of Public Wrongs*, *in* COMMENTARIES ON THE LAWS OF ENGLAND 23–24 (1969); 1 MATTHEW HALE, THE HISTORY OF THE PLEAS OF THE CROWN 24–29 (1800)).

[5] Illinois Juvenile Court Act of 1899, 1899 Ill. Laws 131.

After its creation, the juvenile system spread to every state in the union, as well as the District of Columbia and Puerto Rico. Today most juvenile courts have jurisdiction over three types of cases. First, they hear status offenses. These are acts that are only crimes when committed by a juvenile. Examples include skipping school, missing curfew, and running away. Second, the courts have jurisdiction over delinquency cases. These are acts that would be a crime if committed by an adult. Finally, they hear child abuse and neglect cases. Juvenile courts supervise the placement of abused or neglected children inside or outside the home, attempt to get parents the treatment necessary to be successful parents and, where appropriate, adjudicate the termination of parental rights. In most states the goal of the court is reunification of the family, although reunification is not always possible.

Jurisdiction of the juvenile court is set by statute. Once the juvenile court has taken a child's criminal case it has options not always available in adult court. For example, children who commit status offenses may be enrolled in diversion programs. These programs allow juveniles to complete certain requirements, such as public service, in return for a dismissal of the case. Some juvenile courts have work programs that allow the child to earn money to pay restitution, after which the criminal case is dismissed. The juvenile court may also have access to a wide variety of rehabilitative programs and services, including mental health and substance abuse treatment. Although the court lacks jurisdiction over the parents in a juvenile's criminal case, it can make treatment available to an entire family. Juvenile courts may sentence children to jail, but the period of incarceration is generally much shorter, and the jail time is often served at a juvenile detention facility rather than an adult jail. The juvenile court loses jurisdiction over the child when the child turns 21. Thus, sentences imposed by the juvenile court cannot extend beyond the child's 21st birthday.

B. JUVENILES AND DUE PROCESS

A series of societal shifts in the middle of the 20th century caused courts to veer away from the *parens patriae* model of juvenile justice. Early juvenile courts emphasized the individual nature of the process, and thus placed judicial discretion above a juvenile's due process rights. However, in the mid-1960s the Supreme Court held that juveniles must be afforded many of the same due process rights adults enjoy.

In *Kent v. United States*[6] and *In re Gault*,[7] juveniles in delinquency proceedings won the right to counsel, the right to notice of the charges against them, the right to cross-examine the witnesses against them, and the privilege against self-incrimination. The Court in *Gault* considered

[6] 383 US 541 (1966).

[7] 387 U.S. 1 (1967).

the historical underpinnings of the juvenile court, but concluded that the benefits of the court did not outweigh its excesses.

In re Gault

387 U.S. 1 (1967)

■ MR. JUSTICE FORTAS delivered the opinion of the Court.

On Monday, June 8, 1964, at about 10 a.m., Gerald Francis Gault and a friend, Ronald Lewis, were taken into custody by the Sheriff of Gila County [Arizona]. Gerald was then still subject to a six months' probation order which had been entered on February 25, 1964, as a result of his having been in the company of another boy who had stolen a wallet from a lady's purse. The police action on June 8 was taken as the result of a verbal complaint by a neighbor of the boys, Mrs. Cook, about a telephone call made to her in which the caller or callers made lewd or indecent remarks. It will suffice for purposes of this opinion to say that the remarks or questions put to her were of the irritatingly offensive, adolescent, sex variety.

[After a series of preliminary steps, a hearing was held in juvenile court a week later. There was no transcript or recording, Mrs. Cook was not present, no witnesses were sworn, and there was a probation report given to the judge but not disclosed to the parties.]

At the conclusion of the hearing, the judge committed Gerald as a juvenile delinquent to the State Industrial School 'for the period of his minority (that is, until 21), unless sooner discharged by due process of law.' An order to that effect was entered. It recites that 'after a full hearing and due deliberation the Court finds that said minor is a delinquent child, and that said minor is of the age of 15 years.'

No appeal is permitted by Arizona law in juvenile cases. On August 3, 1964, a petition for a writ of habeas corpus was filed with the Supreme Court of Arizona and referred by it to the Superior Court for hearing.

At the habeas corpus hearing on August 17, Judge McGhee was vigorously cross-examined as to the basis for his actions. He testified that he had taken into account the fact that Gerald was on probation [but was extremely vague about the exact basis for his finding that Gerald was a "delinquent." The Arizona courts affirmed the judge and the family sought review in the U.S. Supreme Court.]

[The petitioners] urge that we hold the Juvenile Code of Arizona invalid on its face or as applied in this case because, contrary to the Due Process Clause of the Fourteenth Amendment, the juvenile is taken from the custody of his parents and committed to a state institution pursuant to proceedings in which the Juvenile Court has virtually unlimited discretion, and in which the following basic rights are denied:

1. Notice of the charges;
2. Right to counsel;

3. Right to confrontation and cross-examination;
4. Privilege against self-incrimination;
5. Right to a transcript of the proceedings; and
6. Right to appellate review.

II.

From the inception of the juvenile court system, wide differences have been tolerated—indeed insisted upon—between the procedural rights accorded to adults and those of juveniles. In practically all jurisdictions, there are rights granted to adults which are withheld from juveniles. In addition to the specific problems involved in the present case, for example, it has been held that the juvenile is not entitled to bail, to indictment by grand jury, to a public trial or to trial by jury. It is frequent practice that rules governing the arrest and interrogation of adults by the police are not observed in the case of juveniles.

The early reformers were appalled by adult procedures and penalties, and by the fact that children could be given long prison sentences and mixed in jails with hardened criminals. They believed that society's role was not to ascertain whether the child was 'guilty' or 'innocent,' but 'What is he, how has he become what he is, and what had best be done in his interest and in the interest of the state to save him from a downward career.' The child—essentially good, as they saw it—was to be made 'to feel that he is the object of (the state's) care and solicitude,' not that he was under arrest or on trial. The rules of criminal procedure were therefore altogether inapplicable. The apparent rigidities, technicalities, and harshness which they observed in both substantive and procedural criminal law were therefore to be discarded. The idea of crime and punishment was to be abandoned. The child was to be 'treated' and 'rehabilitated' and the procedures, from apprehension through institutionalization, were to be 'clinical' rather than punitive.

These results were to be achieved, without coming to conceptual and constitutional grief, by insisting that the proceedings were not adversary, but that the state was proceeding as *parens patriae*. The Latin phrase proved to be a great help to those who sought to rationalize the exclusion of juveniles from the constitutional scheme; but its meaning is murky and its historic credentials are of dubious relevance. The phrase was taken from chancery practice, where, however, it was used to describe the power of the state to act *in loco parentis* for the purpose of protecting the property interests and the person of the child. But there is no trace of the doctrine in the history of criminal jurisprudence.

Accordingly, the highest motives and most enlightened impulses led to a peculiar system for juveniles, unknown to our law in any comparable context. The constitutional and theoretical basis for this peculiar system is—to say the least—debatable. And in practice the results have not been entirely satisfactory. Juvenile Court history has again demonstrated that unbridled discretion, however benevolently motivated, is frequently a poor substitute for principle and procedure. In 1937, Dean Pound wrote: "The powers of the Star Chamber were a trifle in comparison with those of our juvenile courts . . . ." The absence of substantive standards has not necessarily meant that children receive careful, compassionate, individualized treatment. The absence of procedural rules based upon constitutional principle has not always produced fair, efficient, and effective procedures. Departures from established principles of due process have frequently resulted not in enlightened procedure, but in arbitrariness.

Failure to observe the fundamental requirements of due process has resulted in instances, which might have been avoided, of unfairness to individuals and inadequate or inaccurate findings of fact and unfortunate prescriptions of remedy. Due process of law is the primary and indispensable foundation of individual freedom. It is the basic and essential term in the social compact which defines the rights of the individual and delimits the powers which the state may exercise. As Mr. Justice Frankfurter has said: 'The history of American freedom is, in no small measure, the history of procedure.'

Neither sentiment nor folklore should cause us to shut our eyes, for example, to such startling findings as that reported in an exceptionally reliable study of repeaters or recidivism conducted by the Stanford Research Institute for the President's Commission on Crime in the District of Columbia. This Commission's Report states:

> In fiscal 1966 approximately 66 percent of the 16- and 17-year-old juveniles referred to the court by the Youth Aid Division had been before the court previously. In 1965, 56 percent of those in the Receiving Home were repeaters. The SRI study revealed that 61 percent of the sample Juvenile Court referrals in 1965 had been previously referred at least once and that 42 percent had been referred at least twice before.

Certainly, these figures and the high crime rates among juveniles to which we have referred could not lead us to conclude that the absence of constitutional protections reduces crime, or that the juvenile system, functioning free of constitutional inhibitions as it has largely done, is effective to reduce crime or rehabilitate offenders. We do not mean by this to denigrate the juvenile court process or to suggest that there are not aspects of the juvenile system relating to offenders which are valuable. But the features of the juvenile system which its proponents have asserted are of unique benefit will not be impaired by constitutional domestication. For example, the commendable principles relating to the processing and treatment of juveniles separately from adults are in no way involved or affected by the procedural issues under discussion. Further, we are told that one of the important benefits of the special juvenile court procedures is that they avoid classifying the juvenile as a 'criminal.' The juvenile offender is now classed as a 'delinquent.' There is, of course, no reason why this should not continue. It is disconcerting, however, that this term has come to involve only slightly less stigma than the term 'criminal' applied to adults. It is also emphasized that in practically all jurisdictions, statutes provide that an adjudication of the child as a delinquent shall not operate as a civil disability or disqualify him for civil service appointment. There is no reason why the application of due process requirements should interfere with such provisions.

Beyond this, it is frequently said that juveniles are protected by the process from disclosure of their deviational behavior. Disclosure of court records is discretionary with the judge in most jurisdictions. Statutory restrictions almost invariably apply only to the court records, and even as to those the evidence is that many courts routinely furnish information to the FBI and the military, and on request to government agencies and even to private employers. Of more importance are police records. In most States the police keep a complete file of juvenile 'police contacts' and have complete discretion as to disclosure of juvenile records.

In any event, there is no reason why, consistently with due process, a State cannot continue if it deems it appropriate, to provide and to improve provision for the confidentiality of records of police contacts and court action relating to juveniles.

Ultimately, however, we confront the reality of that portion of the Juvenile Court process with which we deal in this case. A boy is charged with misconduct. The boy is committed to an institution where he may be restrained of liberty for years.

Under our Constitution, the condition of being a boy does not justify a kangaroo court. The traditional ideas of Juvenile Court procedure, indeed, contemplated that time would be available and care would be used to establish precisely what the juvenile did and why he did it—was it a prank of adolescence or a brutal act threatening serious consequences to himself or society unless corrected? Under traditional notions, one would assume that in a case like that of Gerald Gault, where the juvenile appears to have a home, a working mother and father, and an older brother, the Juvenile Judge would have made a careful inquiry and judgment as to the possibility that the boy could be disciplined and dealt with at home, despite his previous transgressions.

If Gerald had been over 18, he would not have been subject to Juvenile Court proceedings. For the particular offense immediately involved, the maximum punishment would have been a fine of $5 to $50, or imprisonment in jail for not more than two months. Instead, he was committed to custody for a maximum of six years. If he had been over 18 and had committed an offense to which such a sentence might apply, he would have been entitled to substantial rights under the Constitution of the United States as well as under Arizona's laws and constitution. The United States Constitution would guarantee him rights and protections with respect to arrest, search, and seizure, and pretrial interrogation. It would assure him of specific notice of the charges and adequate time to decide his course of action and to prepare his defense. He would be entitled to clear advice that he could be represented by counsel, and, at least if a felony were involved, the State would be required to provide counsel if his parents were unable to afford it. If the court acted on the basis of his confession, careful procedures would be required to assure its voluntariness. If the case went to trial, confrontation and opportunity for cross-examination would be guaranteed. So wide a gulf between the State's treatment of the adult and of the child requires a bridge sturdier than mere verbiage, and reasons more persuasive than cliche can provide. As Wheeler and Cottrell have put it, 'The rhetoric of the juvenile court movement has developed without any necessarily close correspondence to the realities of court and institutional routines."

We do not mean to indicate that the hearing to be held must conform with all of the requirements of a criminal trial or even of the usual administrative hearing; but we do hold that the hearing must measure up to the essentials of due process and fair treatment.

■ MR. JUSTICE STEWART, dissenting.

The Court today uses an obscure Arizona case as a vehicle to impose upon thousands of juvenile courts throughout the Nation restrictions that the Constitution made applicable to adversary criminal trials. I believe the Court's decision is wholly unsound as a matter of constitutional law, and sadly unwise as a matter of judicial policy.

Juvenile proceedings are not criminal trials. They are not civil trials. They are simply not adversary proceedings. Whether treating with a delinquent child, a neglected child, a defective child, or a dependent child, a juvenile proceeding's whole purpose and mission is the very opposite of the mission and purpose of a prosecution in a criminal court. The object of the one is correction of a condition. The object of the other is conviction and punishment for a criminal act.

NOTES AND QUESTIONS

1. **One Bad Apple.** The facts in *Gault* undoubtedly represent some of the more egregious abuses in the juvenile system. It is unclear whether *Gault* was emblematic of the juvenile system as a whole. Is this a case of the cure being worse than the disease? Was there another way that the Court could have curtailed a juvenile judge's abuse of discretion without drastically changing the tenor of the juvenile courts nationwide?

2. **The Assistance of Counsel.** In 1963, *Gideon v. Wainwright*[8] held that indigent adults charged with felonies were entitled to counsel. Similarly, in *Gault*, the Court held that that

> the Due Process Clause of the Fourteenth Amendment requires that in respect of proceedings to determine delinquency which may result in commitment to an institution in which the juvenile's freedom is curtailed, the child and his parents must be notified of the child's right to be represented by counsel retained by them, or

[8] 372 U.S. 335 (1963).

if they are unable to afford counsel, that counsel will be appointed to represent the child.[9]

In a series of cases in the 1970s, the Court further defined the limits of the right to counsel. In *Argersinger v. Hamlin*[10] and *Scott v. Illinois*,[11] the Court made clear that the right to counsel applies only when the defendant is subject to jail time. Further, the Court held in *Brewer v. Williams*[12] that the right to counsel attaches at the start of adversarial judicial proceedings. *Argersinger*, *Scott*, and *Brewer* all involved adult defendants.

While *Gault* was about a delinquency hearing, it left open the issue of the right to counsel for status offenses. That issue has largely been solved by statute. The federal Juvenile Justice and Delinquency Prevention Act mandates a right to counsel for status crimes charged in the federal juvenile system. Many states have passed similar statutes, providing for a right to counsel at some stages of the status proceeding, or providing counsel when the child is subject to detention or removal from the home.

3. **Still Trying.** Over the past fifty years, juvenile courts have tried, with varying success, to meet the Supreme Court's mandate that juveniles receive counsel. Juvenile courts struggle with the same issues of funding and quality that have plagued the public defender system around the nation.

4. **A Jury of Their Peers.** Although juveniles have gained many of the same due process rights that adult criminal defendants enjoy, they do not have a constitutional right to a jury trial.[13] Some jurisdictions, however, have extended a right to jury trial to juveniles under some circumstances.[14]

C. CURRENT TRENDS IN THE JUVENILE COURTS

The promise of a kinder, gentler juvenile system was challenged in the 1980s and 1990s, when states began moving more children into the adult system. Responding to a perceived spike in juvenile crime rates, states began passing statutes that allowed more children to be charged—and punished—as adults. The majority of states have amended their criminal statutes to include public safety and punishment of offenders as primary purposes of the juvenile justice courts. Forty-one states have limited the juvenile court's jurisdiction over an increasing number of serious or violent crimes, as well as over repeat offenders. While the statutes vary, many states require that some kinds of juvenile cases initially be charged in adult court, allow prosecutors to directly file some kinds of juvenile cases in the adult court, or require the juvenile judge to

---

9 387 U.S. at 41.

10 407 U.S. 25 (1972).

11 440 U.S. 367 (1979).

12 430 U.S. 387 (1977).

13 *See* McKeiver v. Pennsylvania, 403 U.S. 528 (1971).

14 JUVENILE RIGHT TO JURY TRIAL CHART, NAT'L JUVENILE DEF. CTR. (July 17, 2014), http://njdc.info/wp-content/uploads/2014/01/Right-to-Jury-Trial-Chart-7-18-14-Final.pdf [https://perma.cc/LBL7-MJLP].

hold a hearing to consider whether to transfer a juvenile's case to adult court.

With this change in philosophy has come the ability to charge, and sentence, some juveniles in adult courts to adult prison sentences. The phrase "adult crime, adult time" became a popular rallying cry in legislatures across the nation. In many states, conviction in an adult court may result in incarceration after the age of 21, as well as placement in a state prison rather than a juvenile detention facility. Many juveniles in state prison find themselves subject to the same abuses and lack of rehabilitative resources that reformers in the late 1800s were attempting to cure. Thus, in some states, the nature and purpose of juvenile justice has come full circle.

NOTES AND QUESTIONS

1. **Children and Death.** As states began moving more children into the adult system, children became once again subject to the death penalty. In 1988, the Supreme Court ruled that the execution of children who were under the age of sixteen at the time of the crime violated the Eighth Amendment.[15] However, only one year later, the Court held that execution of offenders who were between sixteen and eighteen at the time of the crime was constitutional.[16] Fifteen years later the Supreme Court reversed course and held that the execution of a child who committed a capital crime while under the age of eighteen was unconstitutional.[17]

2. **Children and Life.** Many states also subjected children to life in prison without the possibility of parole. In 2010, the Supreme Court ruled that it was unconstitutional to sentence a juvenile to life in prison without the possibility of parole in non-homicide cases.[18] Two years later, in *Miller v. Alabama*,[19] the Court concluded that it was likewise unconstitutional to sentence a juvenile to mandatory life in prison without the possibility of parole in homicide cases.[20] While the Court did not foreclose the possibility of life in prison without parole, it concluded that "youth matters in determining the appropriateness of a lifetime of incarceration without the possibility of parole."[21] Instead, children must be given a parole hearing, and states must recognize that life in prison is disproportionate for all but the rarest of children:

> *Roper* and *Graham* establish that children are constitutionally different from adults for purposes of sentencing. First, children have a lack of maturity and an underdeveloped sense of responsibility, leading to recklessness, impulsivity, and heedless

[15] *See* Thompson v. Oklahoma, 487 U.S. 815, 839 (1988).

[16] *See* Stanford, *supra* note 4, 492 U.S. at 380.

[17] Roper v. Simmons, 543 U.S. 551, 574–75 (2005) (abrogating *Stanford*, 492 U.S. 361 (1989)).

[18] *See* Graham v. Florida, 560 U.S. 48, 74 (2010).

[19] 132 S. Ct. 2455 (2012).

[20] *See id.* at 2460.

[21] *Id.* at 2465.

> risk-taking. Second, children are more vulnerable to negative influences and outside pressures, including from their family and peers; they have limited control over their own environment and lack the ability to extricate themselves from horrific, crime-producing settings. Third, a child's character is not as well formed as an adult's; his traits are less fixed and his actions less likely to be evidence of irretrievable depravity.
>
> Our decisions rested not only on common sense—on what "any parent knows"—but on science and social science as well. . . . [D]evelopments in psychology and brain science continue to show fundamental differences between juvenile and adult minds—for example, in parts of the brain involved in behavior control. . . . [T]hose findings—of transient rashness, proclivity for risk, and inability to assess consequences—both lessen a child's "moral culpability" and enhance the prospect that, as the years go by and neurological development occurs, his deficiencies will be reformed.[22]

In 2016, the Court made *Miller* retroactive.[23] Henry Montgomery, a 69-year-old black man, had spent most of his life in prison. In 1963, Montgomery, then age seventeen, was convicted of killing a deputy sheriff. He was sentenced to life in prison without the possibility of parole. Once incarcerated, he became a model prisoner and by all accounts was fully rehabilitated. The ruling in *Montgomery* means that approximately 2,000 prisoners will be entitled to a reconsideration of their sentences. That may become a nightmarish proposition for prosecutors, who will have difficulty tracking down evidence, witnesses, and victim's families in cases that may be decades old.

3. **Collateral Consequences.** The juvenile courts use vocabulary designed to emphasize the difference between criminal cases against children and those against adults. For example, rather than being convicted, children are "adjudicated delinquent." However, in many cases these children are subject to the same collateral consequences as an adult, including sex offender registration, DNA collection, and later sentencing enhancements.

§ 6.3 PROBLEM-SOLVING COURTS

Almost 100 years after the creation of the first juvenile court, the same rehabilitative rationale was applied to adult defendants. As the name indicates, problem-solving courts are not designed to deter or incarcerate defendants. Instead, they recognize that when defendants have drug or alcohol addictions, are mentally ill, or have other major life issues, punitive measures are ineffective. Instead, problem-solving courts attempt to treat and eliminate the underlying cause of the criminal behavior.

---

22 *Id.* at 2464–65.

23 *See* Montgomery v. Louisiana, 136 S. Ct. 718, 732 (2016).

A. DRUG COURTS

1. HISTORY

In the late 1980s, Miami, Florida was in the middle of America's War on Drugs. An overwhelming number of non-violent drug offenses were appearing on the Eleventh Judicial District Court's docket. The court recognized that putting "more and more offenders on probation just perpetuates the problem. The same people are picked up again and again until they end up in the state penitentiary and take up space that should be used for violent offenders."[24] The court opted to focus on rehabilitation instead of punishment. This new "drug court" offered offenders drug treatment in lieu of jail. In return for successful completion of a rehabilitation program, the defendant's case could be dropped, his sentence vacated, or his punishment reduced.

The concept spread rapidly. In 1992, three years after the first drug court was created, there were ten drug courts operating in the United States. Just four years later, that number skyrocketed to almost 140. In 2009, the National Institute of Justice reported that there were about 2,500 drug courts operating in the U.S., and recidivism rates for drug court participants were as low as one-half the recidivism rate of other first-time offenders.[25]

Following the success of drug courts, other alternative court programs emerged. These include mental health, homeless, veterans', and domestic violence courts. All are premised on diversion from the criminal justice system in favor of treatment. But as one might expect with any innovative approach, problems have arisen.

2. STRUCTURE AND DESIGN

Problem solving courts are generally staffed by a non-adversarial and multidisciplinary team. In addition to a judge, prosecutor, and defense attorney, each court is assigned a case manager, treatment provider, and probation officer. Participants are generally required to waive a variety of constitutional rights in exchange for participation in the program. Many enter a guilty plea to a particular crime. The plea and sentence are then held in abeyance. If a defendant successfully completes a treatment program, the sentence, the plea, or both are withdrawn. Therefore, while an arrest might remain on the defendant's record, the conviction will not.

---

[24] Glade F. Roper, *Introduction to Drug Courts*, *in* DRUG COURTS: A NEW APPROACH TO TREATMENT AND REHABILITATION 1, 4 (James E. Lessenger & Glade F. Roper eds. 2007).

[25] The National Drug Court Institute is a federally funded offspring of several federal agencies, including the White House and Department of Justice. *See* WEST HUDDLESTON & DOUGLAS B. MARLOWE, PAINTING THE CURRENT PICTURE: A NATIONAL REPORT ON DRUG COURTS AND OTHER PROBLEM-SOLVING COURT PROGRAMS IN THE UNITED STATES (2011), http://www.nadcp.org/sites/default/files/nadcp/PCP%20Report%20FINAL_2.PDF [https://perma.cc/92AW-RPMU].

Participants in problem-solving courts are generally required to participate in a variety of treatment programs including group therapy, individual therapy, and medication. Many defendants are required to submit to regular drug and alcohol testing. It is not uncommon for offenders to relapse. Judges have a variety of carrots and sticks available to encourage or force compliance. Although the specifics depend on the terms of the program's participation agreement, judges may delay the defendant's release from the program, impose additional drug-testing, modify the terms and conditions of probation, or even sentence a defendant to a short jail term (generally a day or two) without the benefit of a hearing. However, judges also have the power to determine how often a defendant must check in with the court, and often give out small prizes and generous accolades when participants are successfully working toward their goals. Problem-solving court sessions often look more like therapy, with the judge taking on the role of a parent or therapist: often praising, sometimes punishing, and always providing structure and guidance.

Many problem-solving courts attempt to calibrate the level of services they provide to different populations. They calculate both the severity of a defendant's substance abuse or mental health problems and the likelihood that the defendant will fail a less-restrictive program. Prognostic risk and criminogenic need indicate what level of treatment and supervision are necessary. They also help determine what array of punitive measures might be useful to help defendants continue with the program. The higher the risk level, the more intensive the supervision services should be. Courts have found that mixing "high risk/high need" offenders with "low risk/low need" offenders is often damaging to the latter group. For example, mixing defendants with a long history of drug abuse and multiple arrests with a student who has experimented with drugs tends to increase—rather than decrease—the likelihood that the latter will engage in additional criminal activity. Some courts separate the two categories of offenders. Others restrict their drug or mental health courts to high-risk/high-need offenders. Participation in mental health court is often limited to defendants with a demonstrated diagnosis of specific disorders, including schizophrenia and bipolar disorder.

For many years the structure of problem-solving courts was left up to individual judges. In recent years, however, the Department of Justice, the National Association of State Courts, and a variety of professional and advocacy groups have developed curricula, best practices, and assessment tools. State legislatures have begun funding problem-solving courts as an ever-increasing body of data indicates that they help lower recidivism rates, thus saving the state money.

In addition to courts designed to address discrete issues, a few problem-solving courts have taken a holistic community-based approach. The Red Hook Community Justice Center, in the Red Hook neighborhood of Brooklyn, houses a court, case managers, social workers, drug counselors, child care center, and educational programs in one building. Most of the court's employees live in the geographically isolated community, and all prosecutors and defense attorneys stay at the court on long-term assignment. The Red Hook project was chronicled in the ABA Journal and in a PBS Independent Lens documentary.[26] Similar community courts have sprung up in the intervening 15 years, although they are less common than the single-issue model.

B. DUE PROCESS

Not all offenders are successful in the problem-solving court system. Addicts often relapse during treatment. Some commit new crimes, some can't or won't follow the conditions of probation, and others simply disappear.

Many defendants enter guilty pleas as a precondition to drug or mental health court, thus allowing the trial court to impose a criminal sentence upon termination. Courts are faced with deciding what procedure, if any, is required before a defendant may be terminated from a program and sentenced.

People v. Kimmel

882 N.Y.S.2d 895 (N.Y. City Ct. 2009)

■ JOHN L. LAMANCUSO, J.

Whether a defendant who absconds from a treatment court is entitled to a hearing before being terminated from that court and returned to the trial court for sentencing is the dispositive issue presented herein.

History and Procedural Background

On July 20, 2006, defendant pleaded guilty to one count of burglary in the third degree and one count of attempted burglary in the third degree before Honorable John L. LaMancuso, Acting County Court Judge and Presiding Judge of the City of Jamestown Drug Treatment Court (Jamestown DTC). Sentencing was adjourned for defendant's participation in the City of Jamestown Drug Treatment Court.

Pursuant to the terms and conditions of defendant's Drug Court Contract and plea agreement, defendant agreed to the following alternative sentences: (1) upon successful completion of the treatment court program, his case would be returned to Chautauqua County Court for sentencing, and the agreed-upon sentence would be a five-year term of probation; (2) if unsuccessful, the sentence would be a 1-to-3-year indeterminate state prison sentence. In addition, the contract provided

---

[26] Terry Carter, *Red Hook Experiment*, A.B.A.J. (June 1, 2004 10:30 PM), http://www.abajournal.com/magazine/article/red_hook_experiment [https://perma.cc/N286-R678]; *Red Hook Justice*, PBS, http://www.pbs.org/independentlens/redhookjustice/ [https://perma.cc/H5UY-EKKD] (last visited Aug. 29, 2016).

that "any new arrest . . . while I am in the Drug Court Program . . . can be grounds for immediate termination from the program" (Drug Court Contract P 11) and "I understand and agree that after review and recommendation of the Drug Court Team, the Drug Court Judge alone will determine whether or not I have complied with or failed any of the terms of this agreement[.]"

On December 5, 2007, defendant was arrested and charged with aggravated harassment in the second degree. He was arraigned the next day and remanded to the Chautauqua County Jail. While incarcerated, he was seen by the Chautauqua County Mental Health Forensic Services Unit and found to be in need of treatment.

After an assessment by the Jamestown Mental Health Court coordinator found defendant eligible to participate in Mental Health Court, the Chautauqua County District Attorney approved his entry into the program, upon condition that he plead guilty to the charge and agree to the following revised plea agreement: (1) if successful, no more jail, a continuation of the original Drug Court plea agreement (i.e., five-year term of probation on the felony conviction), and a reduction of the aggravated harassment charge to disorderly conduct; (2) if unsuccessful, a one-year definite sentence on the misdemeanor conviction to be merged into the 1-to-3-year indeterminate sentence on the felony conviction.

On January 14, 2008, defendant accepted the People's offer and pleaded guilty to the charge of aggravated harassment in the second degree. Sentencing was adjourned for defendant to participate in the Jamestown Mental Health Court.

The Mental Health Court Contract provides that defendant will

> "keep all appointments for: Court . . . Treatment . . . follow . . . any medical, psychiatric, or substance abuse treatment program assigned by the Court . . . successful graduation will require a minimum of one (1) year of participation in the Mental Health Court program . . . [i]f I fail to complete the Mental Health Court Program, I will return to the Criminal Calendar to be sentenced."

Unlike the Drug Court Contract, the Mental Health Court Contract does not empower the judge to "alone" determine compliance or failure, after review and recommendation of the Mental Health Court team.

Presaging the tumultuous series of events which were to follow, at his first Mental Health Court appearance in January 2008, defendant's failure to attend a "care coordination" appointment was noted in the court file.

In February 2008, defendant was fired from his job. On March 17, 2008, defendant was committed to the county jail for failing to attend appointments, failing to perform community service and failing to fill a prescription. On March 24, 2008, defendant admitted, in open court, that he had not taken any of his prescribed mental health medications since entering the program. On that date, defendant was released on his own recognizance and permitted to remain in the program.

On April 21, 2008, a tantalizing, yet ephemeral ray of hope pierced the gloomy veil, when defendant indicated he had found a new job and had a wedding date scheduled for the next month. The sanguine outlook was, however, all too short-lived.

He failed to appear on April 28, 2008, and was not seen or heard from again for 8 1/2 months. On January 14, 2009, he was apprehended on the court's bench warrant, in addition to being charged with resisting arrest and obstructing governmental administration in the second degree for his alleged conduct at the time of the arrest. He was arraigned on the new charges and, on the felony matter, was committed to the Chautauqua County Jail without bail.

On February 17, 2009, upon defense counsel's motion, the court issued an order for a psychiatric examination pursuant to article 730 of the Criminal Procedure Law. On March 30, 2009, after receiving two psychiatric reports indicating a lack of capacity, the court issued an order of commitment on the felony matter and final orders of observation and dismissal of accusatory instruments on the misdemeanor matters. The Mental Health Court team's recommendation of termination was held in abeyance pending a restoration of competency. Notification of fitness to proceed was received on April 27, 2009, and an order to produce was issued. Defendant appeared from the county jail on May 26, 2009, and defense counsel requested a hearing on the issue of termination.

The team's recommendation is based upon defendant's 8½-month failure to appear and noncompliance with his Mental Health Court Contract and treatment plan. Citing *Torres v Berbary* (340 F3d 63 [2nd Cir 2003]), defendant asserts "[f]actual issues exist as to whether the defendant knowingly or voluntarily acted in ways that should cause a termination from the program." The People contend that no formal hearing is necessary to terminate a person from a problem-solving/treatment court.

Discussion/Analysis

In *Torres*, where the petitioner was discharged from a drug treatment program and where the court denied the petitioner's request for an evidentiary hearing and proceeded to sentence the petitioner to the prison sentence that had been stipulated in the plea agreement in the event the petitioner failed to successfully complete the treatment program, where the court denied the petitioner's request and accepted as true all statements contained in a letter from the program director to the court and simply allowed the petitioner to make an unsworn statement prior to sentencing, the Second Circuit found that due process had been denied in Torres' sentencing. Noting that "[d]ue process has clearly been held to require 'some kind of hearing' before a person is deprived of a liberty interest," the court stated that "due process in sentencing requires at least a showing by a preponderance of evidence to resolve disputed factual issues" and found that the "preponderance of the evidence" standard was not satisfied by a "single report replete with multiple levels of hearsay and speculation."

The Second Circuit's decision in *Torres* was heavily influenced by the "following elements":

> total reliance by the trial court on a hearsay report that itself contains only uncorroborated statements of unnamed informants; omission of any finding by the trial court as to the reliability of the informants or as to reasons for the non-disclosure of their identities; failure of the trial court to conduct some kind of hearing, including provision for the examination of Torres under oath; lack of preponderating evidence of Torres' wrongdoing; and the gross disparity between a sentence that would release Torres to society on a plea to a misdemeanor charge after completion of the Phoenix House program and the four-and-a-half-to-nine-year felony sentence to state prison that he received for violating the original sentence condition.

While due process does not require a full blown evidentiary hearing each time a defendant is discharged from a residential treatment program, a defendant is entitled to a hearing. The hearing does not necessarily require the calling of witnesses or an opportunity for the defendant to cross-examine. Thus, in [*People v.*] *Joseph*, where the court considered the defendant's sworn statement, an oral report of the People based on their interview of the treatment provider staff members and four written reports, where the court applied the *Torres* factors in a methodical fashion, including the "preponderance of the evidence" standard, the court found that defendant "[had] been afforded a hearing consistent with due process" and proceeded with sentencing.

Where the reason for a treatment team's recommendation of termination is not a re-arrest or discharge from treatment based on allegations of fact which are contested, a hearing is not necessarily required (*see People v Valencia*, 3 NY3d 714, 819 NE2d 990, 786 NYS2d 374 [2004] [defendant had entered four different treatment programs, left all four for different reasons, left the last facility without authorization and was returned to court on a bench warrant]). In *Valencia*, the defendant, relying on *Torres*, argued that when an issue is raised as to an alleged violation of a plea agreement, due process requires an evidentiary hearing and finding by a preponderance of the evidence that the defendant violated the plea agreement before sentencing the defendant to prison. Reasoning that "[h]ere, defendant does not dispute that he committed acts that constituted violations of the plea agreement," the Court of Appeals held that the sentencing court made a sufficient inquiry to satisfy due process.

In the matter sub judice, defendant's failure to appear in court and failure to participate in treatment for 8 1/2 months is undisputed and constitutes a violation of the Mental Health Court Contract and grounds for termination. Undaunted, defendant demands an evidentiary hearing seeking to show that his absence may have been caused by factors beyond his control—by the fact that he may have been depressed, or the fact that he may have been manic or the fact that he may have suffered a psychotic episode. To be eligible for mental health court, a participant must have an Axis I disorder. To afford defendant a hearing on whether he "knowingly or voluntarily acted in ways that should cause a termination from the program" is a Pandora's box no treatment court dare open.

Treatment courts operate on the principle that there is both a carrot and a stick. The upside of successfully completing the treatment court program is usually a reduced sentence, typically a sentence of probation, along with, in some cases, a dismissal or reduction of the charge; the downside is the enhanced sentence, i.e., incarceration. "Tying a reduced sentence to successful completion of a drug treatment court is favored by the courts . . . [and] is what a drug treatment court is all about."

The conditions of the Jamestown Mental Health Court Contract were "explicit, objective, accepted by the defendant [and] clearly breached." Defendant failed to keep all appointments for court and treatment. Also, it is inherently unreasonable for a mental health court participant to bootstrap his defense to a breach of the treatment court contract by using the very reason he is in treatment court to begin with, i.e., his mental health diagnosis. Certainty is what makes problem-solving courts so successful. Affording defendant a full-blown hearing on whether he "knowingly or voluntarily acted in ways that should cause a termination" would undermine that certainty in ways that would make problem-solving courts less able to achieve their salutary goals.

Based upon the foregoing, defendant's request for an evidentiary hearing is denied. In lieu of an evidentiary hearing, and in order to satisfy minimum due process requirements, the court will allow defendant to make an unsworn statement and will consider any written and oral arguments of counsel.

Hagar v. State

990 P.2d 894 (Okl. Crim. App. 1999)

■ LUMPKIN, VICE-PRESIDING JUDGE:

Petitioner Steven Lee Hagar was charged with Unlawful Possession of a Controlled Drug and Carrying a Concealed Weapon in the District Court of Seminole County. On November 14, 1997, Petitioner entered a guilty plea to Count I before the Honorable Joseph Wrigley, Special Judge. Count II was dismissed. Pursuant to a plea agreement, Petitioner was ordered to attend the Drug Court Program. Sentencing was delayed until the completion of, or termination from, the Drug Court Program.

On August 28, 1998, a Drug Court termination hearing was held before the Honorable Jerry Colclazier, District Judge, serving as judge of the 22nd Judicial District Drug Court Program. At the conclusion of this hearing, Petitioner's participation in the Drug Court Program was terminated for non-compliance and he was sentenced to ten (10) years imprisonment. On September 4, 1998, Petitioner filed an Application to Withdraw Guilty Plea. A hearing on the motion was held on October 5, 1998, before Judge Colclazier. At the conclusion of the hearing, Petitioner's motion to withdraw was denied. It is that denial which is the subject of this appeal. Petitioner raises the following propositions of error in support of his appeal.

> I. Petitioner's guilty plea was invalid because the trial court failed to establish an adequate factual basis for the plea.
>
> II. Reversible error occurred when the trial court accepted Petitioner's plea without informing him of the elements of each offense charged.
>
> III. Petitioner was denied his right to due process when he was not given an opportunity to appeal from the revocation from Drug Court.
>
> IV. At the hearing revoking Petitioner from participation in the Drug Court program, Petitioner was denied his right to confront the witnesses against him.
>
> V. The sentence imposed against Petitioner is excessive and should be modified.

After a thorough consideration of these propositions and the entire record before us on appeal, including the original record, transcripts, and briefs of the parties, we find the writ of certiorari must be granted and the matter remanded for further proceedings not inconsistent with this opinion.

When evaluating the validity of a guilty plea, we are concerned only with whether or not the plea was entered voluntarily and intelligently. This includes the requirement that the trial court must obtain a factual basis for the plea.

In the present case, the factual basis given was sufficient. The court asked Petitioner if he understood he was charged with possession of a controlled dangerous substance, to which Petitioner responded in the affirmative. The court did not review the elements of the offense. The court summarily concluded "based on paragraph twenty-four, the Court finds a factual basis does exist and the defendant's plea of guilty is accepted." In paragraph twenty-four of the Summary of Facts/Guilty Plea Form, it is written, "I was in possession of CDS (meth)." Petitioner's signature follows.

Petitioner indicated he understood the charges against him and the possible range of punishment and the plea of guilty/summary of facts form was prepared by Petitioner and counsel. We find the trial court correctly found there was a factual basis for the plea of guilty. Accordingly, we find Petitioner's requested relief in Propositions I and II is denied.

In Propositions III and IV this Court addresses for the first time the Oklahoma Drug Court Act (hereinafter "Act"). This Act authorizes creation of a drug court program in each district court of the State. A drug court program is a type of diversionary sentence, "an immediate and highly structured judicial intervention process for substance abuse treatment of eligible offenders which expedites the criminal case, and requires successful completion of the plea agreement in lieu of incarceration." In addition to authorizing drug court programs, the Act sets forth the eligibility requirements for an offender's participation, procedures to be used in admitting an offender to the program, duration of participation in the program, monitoring of treatment progress, and the consequences of both successful and unsuccessful completion of a drug court program.

Under Section 471.7, the drug court judge shall "set a date for a hearing to review the offender, the treatment plan, and the provisions of the performance contract. Notice shall be given to the offender and the other parties participating in the drug court case three (3) days before the hearing may be held." 22 O.S.Supp. 1998, § 471.7(B). The judge is to "recognize relapses and restarts in the program which are considered to be part of the rehabilitation and recovery process, . . . " Additionally, the judge:

> shall accomplish monitoring and offender accountability by ordering progressively increasing sanctions or providing incentives, rather than removing the offender from the program when relapse occurs, except when the offender's conduct requires revocation from the program. Any revocation from the drug court program shall require notice to the offender and other participating parties in the case and a revocation hearing. At the revocation hearing, if the offender is found to have violated the conditions of the plea agreement or performance contract and disciplinary sanctions have been insufficient to gain compliance, the offender shall be revoked from the program and sentenced for the offense as provided in the plea agreement.

Further, "nothing in this provision shall be construed to limit the authority of the judge to remove an offender from the program and impose the required punishment stated in the plea agreement after application, notice, and hearing."

The right to appeal the decision to terminate or revoke an offender from a drug court program is not specifically set forth in the statute. It is this omission which forms the basis of Petitioner's third proposition of error. In the present case, Petitioner entered his plea, the plea was accepted and his sentencing was deferred pending his completion of or termination from the Drug Court Program. When Petitioner failed to complete the Drug Court Program, he was terminated or revoked from the program, and ordered to serve his previously negotiated sentence. This case is comparable to the situation wherein a defendant's sentence is deferred pending the successful completion of certain terms of probation. If the terms are successfully completed, the conviction is erased from the record. If the terms are not successfully completed, a judgment of guilt is entered and the defendant is sentenced.

In revoking or terminating a defendant from a drug court program, the court makes a factual determination involving the existence of a violation of the terms of the plea agreement or performance contract and whether disciplinary sanctions have been insufficient to gain compliance. The consequence of the judicial revocation or termination from Drug Court is to impose the sentence previously negotiated in the plea agreement. Violations of the terms of the plea agreement or performance contract need only be shown by a "preponderance" of the evidence. The decision to revoke or terminate from Drug Court lies within the discretion of the Drug Court judge.

Having compared the interests and procedures involved in the acceleration of a deferred sentence and the termination from a drug court program, the procedures involved in both processes are similar. Further, as the acceleration of a deferred sentence subjects a criminal defendant to a loss of liberty, so too does the revocation or termination from a drug court program. Therefore, as a defendant has the right to appeal to this Court from a decision to accelerate his deferred sentence, we find a defendant has the right to appeal to this Court from a decision to revoke or terminate participation in a Drug Court program.

In the present case, errors in Petitioner's termination from the Drug Court Program require remand to the District Court. Upon remand, if the State elects to again seek termination of Petitioner from the Drug Court Program, the prosecutor has twenty (20) days in which to file an application so stating, with a copy to this Court. Pursuant to statute, notice shall be given to the offender and the other parties participating in the Drug Court case at least three (3) days before the hearing may be held.

In order to meet the requirements of due process, the written notice must set forth the reasons for termination with such clarity that the defense is able to determine what reason is being submitted as grounds for revocation/termination, enabling preparation of a defense to the allegation. The record currently before this Court contains no written notice of an application to terminate/revoke Petitioner from the Drug Court Program. The omission of such a notice violates the statute and the requirements of due process and would cause a reversal of this case on appeal.

Further, the statute requires the judge at the revocation/termination hearing to "recognize relapses and restarts in the program which are considered to be part of the rehabilitation and recovery process", and "shall . . . order progressively increasing sanctions or providing incentives, rather than removing the offender from the program when relapse occurs, except when the offender's conduct requires revocation from the program." In order to meet the requirements of due process, the judge shall state on the record the reasons for the revocation/termination. This is to include the conditions violated and reasons why disciplinary sanctions have been insufficient or are not appropriate.

In the record before this Court, the judge set forth his reasons for terminating Petitioner from the Drug Court Program, however, there is no indication, either in the record or the judge's statement that progressively increasing sanctions were considered or deemed not applicable due to the offender's conduct prior to the decision to terminate.

Petitioner's final proposition of error, an argument that his sentence is excessive, is rendered moot at this time.

Accordingly, the petition for certiorari is granted, the order of the District Court denying Petitioner's application to withdraw plea of guilty is **AFFIRMED**, and the case is **REMANDED** to the District Court for proceedings not inconsistent with this opinion.

State v. Rogers

2006 Ida. App. LEXIS 87, 2006 WL 2422648 (Id. Ct. App. 2006)

■ GUITIERREZ, JUDGE.

Paul Lawrence Rogers appeals from his judgment of conviction for possession of a controlled substance, which was entered after he was terminated from the Ada County Drug Court program. Rogers contends the court violated his constitutional right to due process when it discharged him from the drug court program. He also argues that the court's factual findings, that he had violated conditions of the drug court program, are clearly erroneous. We affirm.

I.

BACKGROUND

Rogers was initially charged with possession of methamphetamine and driving without privileges. Thereafter, the prosecutor filed a motion to transfer the case to the Ada County Drug Court. The Ada County Drug Court Rules ("rules") provide that a defendant must plead guilty to the charge in order to enter the program and if the defendant is terminated from the program the matter proceeds directly to sentencing. The rules further provide that the presiding drug court judge has the final say over who may enter the program and whether a defendant will be terminated from the program for violations of rules. In accord, and in light of a pending plea agreement, the instant case was transferred to drug court, along with a separate case involving unrelated burglary and attempted grand theft charges against Rogers. Rogers pled guilty to the possession of methamphetamine charge and the remaining charges were dismissed. As part of the plea procedure, Rogers filled out and signed a Drug Court Guilty Plea Form, wherein he acknowledged receipt of the Ada County Drug Court Participant Handbook, and a Phase I—Contract. Pursuant to the rules, Rogers was released on his own recognizance.

Rogers participated in the drug court program for over ten weeks. The program included, among other things, mandatory drug testing, attendance in treatment programs, and frequent sessions with the drug court judge. Pursuant to the rules, Rogers' counselor submitted progress reports to the drug court judge on a regular basis. Rogers would then meet with the drug court judge on a relatively informal basis and discuss his progress in the program. At the outset, Rogers performed poorly, including among other violations, numerous positive drug tests and missed treatment sessions. While the drug court judge repeatedly sanctioned Rogers for violating the program's conditions, the judge chose not to terminate him from the program at those times. Eventually, however, Rogers appeared to turn himself around and his performance earned praise from the presiding judge. Then, during a regularly scheduled status hearing at about week ten, the court confronted Rogers with information contained in a progress report, reflecting the details of allegations of Rogers' involvement in a business venture, "Desire, Inc." In response to the judge's questioning, Rogers stated that it "was an adult entertainment company with strippers for bachelor parties and an escort business also." Rogers admitted that he had been recruiting females, including participants in the drug court program, into the business by handing out business cards. Rogers contended that the business was a legal adult entertainment business that he had contemplated before entering drug court. This contemplated business, he said, never got off the ground. The judge did not believe Rogers, stating, "I think what is happening here is that you're enticing female members of the drug court program into prostitution." The judge ultimately told Rogers that he would probably be terminated from drug court but that the court would give him an opportunity at a future hearing to show cause why he should be retained. No written report of violation was filed.

Before the show cause hearing, Rogers wrote a letter to the court stating his desire to stay in the drug court program and further reiterating that Desire, Inc., was not a prostitution ring, that he conceived the idea before entering the drug court program, and that he ended his involvement in the unformed business after entering the program. At the show cause hearing, no witnesses were called, but the judge invited Rogers and his counsel to make statements. Rogers once again said the court's assessment of Desire, Inc., was mistaken and expressed his desire to stay in the program. The judge then terminated Rogers from the drug court program, stating:

> I just want to tell you why I am kicking you out of drug court. I appreciate the fact that you don't think you did anything wrong.

> And that's sort of my point. I'm not going to have you in drug court with 137 people, half of whom are females, where you don't think there is anything in the world wrong with setting up an adult entertainment business called Desires Inc., and charging $50 apiece for a finder's fee and having the girls work outside. I think it certainly was an adult entertainment business and you just can't do anything like that in drug court, particularly where you don't think you are doing anything wrong.

The court then set the matter for sentencing. The case did not, however, transfer to another district court judge for sentencing. Instead, the drug court judge, now apparently acting in his district court capacity, continued to preside over the case.

II.

ANALYSIS

A. Idaho's Drug Courts

As a preliminary matter, a short discussion of Idaho's drug court program is warranted. The introduction of the problem-solving approach in the courts has given rise to innovative diversion efforts such as drug court programs. In 2001, the Idaho legislature enacted the Idaho Drug Court Act, by 2005 amendment now known as the Idaho Drug Court and Mental Health Court Act (the "Act"). The Act provides, *inter alia*, that the district court in each Idaho county may establish a drug court. With the exception of eligibility standards, the Act itself provides no guidance on the inner workings or procedures to be followed by a drug court. Instead, the Act authorized the Idaho Supreme Court to establish a Drug Court and Mental Health Court Coordinating Committee and vested it with responsibility for establishing standards and guidelines and providing ongoing oversight of the operation of drug courts. Effective September 26, 2003, the Committee has adopted guidelines for adult drug courts. These guidelines do not specify exactly how a drug court program must be run and, as specifically stated therein, the guidelines "are not rules of procedure and have no effect of law." In addition, effective August 15, 2005, the Idaho Supreme Court adopted an administrative rule to provide additional direction for the development, establishment, operations, and termination of drug courts and mental health courts. As relevant to the instant appeal, the rule addresses primarily how a drug court is created and it does not mandate that a drug court program must be operated in any particular way.

As of January 2006, Idaho had forty-four drug courts in operation spread out over approximately twenty-three counties and at differing levels of the judicial system within some counties. From the above discussion, it must be assumed that each drug court in Idaho operates uniquely and, therefore, the analysis in this case might not be applicable to any other particular drug court program in the state. Against this backdrop, we proceed to the issue at hand.

B. Termination of Drug Court Participation in Ada County

Rogers contends the drug court violated his constitutional right to due process when it discharged him from the Ada County Drug Court program. Specifically, he contends that he is entitled to the same process afforded to a probationer or parolee, including notice in writing of alleged violations of the conditions of the drug program and the evidence against him, and the opportunity to present witnesses and evidence on his behalf, and an opportunity to be heard.

[I]n this case, taking into account Rogers' concerns, we hold that the rights of drug court participants can be preserved and advanced by employing a contract analysis which, importantly, will not compromise the effectiveness of drug court programs.

Here, the usual criminal process has been superseded by agreement. At the plea hearing, the court explained to Rogers the consequences of being terminated from drug court, stating:

> Let me tell you what I mean by that in a drug court context. If you fail the drug court program, you would be sentenced on the felony offense that you're pleading guilty to this afternoon . . . . And I've got to tell you, Mr. Rogers, a good share of the people who enter drug court don't make it. At least a third, over a third of them, fail it. And they either go to prison or they do a rider.

The district court then discussed the Drug Court Guilty Plea Form that Rogers had filled out and signed. On this form, Rogers indicated that he was pleading guilty, that he sought admission into the drug court program, that he had received and reviewed a copy of the Drug Court Participant Handbook, that he accepted all of the program's conditions and rules, and that he understood he could be terminated from the program by the drug court judge for any single violation. The court ultimately decided to accept Rogers' guilty plea and enter him into the drug court program. Rogers and the drug court judge then both signed a document entitled "Phase I—Contract" which outlined Rogers' drug court responsibilities during its initial phase and stated that his "performance on this contract will be reported to the Judge to monitor your status in treatment." From all of this, it is clear that Rogers' participation in the drug court program occurred pursuant to a contract; moreover, that contract incorporated the terms of the Drug Court Guilty Plea Form, the Drug Court Participant's Handbook, and the Phase I—Contract. It is this contract that governs Rogers' participation and termination from the drug court program.

A review of the purposes and policies underlying the Ada County Drug Court program confirms that contract law rather than due process law is applicable in cases such as this. Drug courts in Idaho "closely supervise, monitor, test and treat substance abusers" and are based on partnerships among the courts, law enforcement, corrections and social welfare agencies. They offer a therapeutic setting involving "a regimen of graduated sanctions and rewards, substance abuse treatment, close court monitoring and supervision of progress, educational or vocational counseling as appropriate, and other requirements." The therapeutic effectiveness of these programs relies on a drug court's ability to immediately reward or punish participants for their behavior—the ultimate sanction, of course, being termination from the program. By contract, drug court participants, like Rogers, agree to subject themselves to this type of treatment regimen with eyes wide open; the signed Drug Court Guilty Plea Form, the Drug Court Participant Handbook, and the Phase I—Contract provide ample notice of the program's conditions and terms and that failure to comply, i.e., breach of the agreement, could result in sanctions or termination from the program.

Here, Rogers entered an agreement by which the drug court agreed to keep Rogers in the program as long as he did not violate its terms or conditions. The record shows that Rogers had violated drug court terms and conditions numerous times before he actually was terminated. Instead of terminating Rogers' participation for these violations, however, the court simply continued the matter and Rogers' participation in the program, instead choosing to impose intermediate sanctions in order to further the program's therapeutic goals. Eventually, however, the drug court judge learned of certain behavior by Rogers—that is, his alleged attempt to start an illegal prostitution ring involving other drug court participants—that, taking into account all of Rogers' previous breaches, provided the catalyst prompting the judge to expel Rogers from the program. Indeed, the record contains evidence that Rogers handed out business cards and discussed matters with other drug court participants pertaining to his fledgling business venture, Desire, Inc. While a review of the Phase I—Contract, Drug Court Participant Handbook, and Drug Court Guilty Plea Form does not reveal that drug court members are prohibited from engaging in illegal activity, such a condition is easily viewed as an implied promise on the part of Rogers. Rogers' involvement in illegal activity thus breached the agreement and excused the district court from retaining him in the drug court program. Moreover, even if Rogers' activities involved nothing more than the formation of a legal escort service, as he claimed, the inappropriate nature of this sort of action revealed a dangerous "attitude" which, by the terms of the Drug Court Participant Handbook, constituted grounds for termination. Due to Rogers' breach of the agreement, the court was excused from its obligation to continue Rogers in the drug court program, and Rogers was thus properly terminated.

A contract law analysis in the context of a participant's termination from drug court adequately addresses the due process concerns raised by the dissent. That is, the participant has remedies available under the law of contracts to ensure that he is not terminated unfairly.

By this opinion we do not wish to dissuade a judge from following termination procedures in drug court akin to those employed in a probation revocation process. To the contrary, in order to eliminate uncertainty and the appearance of unfairness, we encourage courts to do so. What is recommended is not, however, the equivalent of what is required. We decline to hold that Rogers was entitled to due process protections regarding his termination from the Ada County Drug Court program.

NOTES AND QUESTIONS:

Rumor Has It. What standard of proof should apply to a treatment revocation hearing? In *Torres v. Berbary*,[27] the defendant entered a guilty plea, after which the judge released him to a treatment facility and stated that "If you work out, you will be allowed to come back, re-plead to a misdemeanor, and I will sentence you [to] time served. If you don't work out, you will get at least four and a half to nine years in jail."[28] After less than a month, he was dismissed from the residential program and was provided a "Client Discharge Form" which stated "Although we have been unable to obtain physical evidence, we have received information from residents that clearly implicates this individual in an organized attempt to sell drugs in this facility."[29] Although Torres denied the allegations and requested a hearing, the judge merely stated that the treatment facility "does not want him," so he imposed the original sentence of four-and-a-half to nine years.

The Second Circuit reversed, analogizing the case to probation and parole revocation, as well as loss of "good-time credits" in prison. In all these situations, the United States Supreme Court has held that the defendant is entitled to basic due process. While hearings are generally less formal, defendants are entitled to written notice, a hearing, and the right to present evidence. The court must use a preponderance of the evidence standard. The Second Circuit held that treatment revocation requires "some kind of hearing" that would comport with due process.

C. MENTAL HEALTH COURTS

Mental health courts serve similar objectives to those of drug courts. Prior to the 18th century, the "insane" were usually held in "madhouses"—essentially jails—in appalling conditions. It was not unusual for patients to be chained, whipped, starved, beaten, and isolated. That began to change in the late 18th and early 19th centuries, when reformers began to call for implementation of the "moral treatment." Based on kindness and patience, the moral treatment sought to help the insane regain their sanity in tranquil, spacious, and bucolic settings. State legislatures dedicated significant funds to the construction of mental health institutions. These were often palatial

---

[27] 340 F.3d 63 (2d Cir, 2003).

[28] *Id.* at 64–65.

[29] *Id.* at 65.

estates, designed by famous architects, for the sole purpose of caring for the mentally ill.

By the beginning of the 20th century, the moral treatment waned as asylums grew more crowded. Pressured to admit more patients, and influence by both the eugenics movement and Freudian theories, institutional administrators once again turned to punitive measures designed to control—rather than cure—patients. Techniques such as electroconvulsive therapy, forced over-medication, work without pay, and involuntary lobotomization became commonplace.

Reformers began to call for an end to mental institutions. Deinstitutionalization began in 1955 with the introduction of the first effective antipsychotic medication. The process of deinstitutionalization involved moving the severely mentally ill out of institutions, closing the institutions, and replacing inpatient care programs with community-based clinics. In 1955, there were 558,239 severely mentally ill people in the nation's public psychiatric hospitals. In 1994, there were only 71,619.

Many of those who were moved out of hospitals were severely ill or disabled. Between 50 and 60 percent of them were diagnosed with schizophrenia. Between 20 and 30 percent were diagnosed with manic-depression, severe depression, organic brain diseases, or traumatic brain injuries. Finally, some had mental retardation, psychosis, autism, or brain damage caused by alcohol or drug use.

While deinstitutionalization moved patients away from institutional abuse in highly restrictive settings, often no replacement was offered. Over the intervening 60 years, state legislatures and Congress moved money away from mental health treatment, leaving crowded public inpatient treatment centers and few community resources. Overcrowding meant long waits and heavy competition for too-few beds. Simultaneously, civil commitment became more difficult. In many states, the proponent of commitment has to prove that the mentally ill person poses a threat to themselves or others. This is often a difficult standard to meet.

The impact of these reforms caused a huge ripple in the criminal justice system. By the mid-1970s jail administrators and academics noticed a swell in the percentage of patients who were mentally ill. The numbers climbed steadily. By the late 1990s some jails and prisons reported that more than 10% of their patients exhibited signs of mental illness, ranging from depression to schizophrenia. Patients cycled from jail to homelessness with little or no treatment or follow-up care.

Studies found a causal relationship between mental illness and criminality. On the extreme end, some patients committed crimes as a result of hearing voices or having other delusions. Others were arrested or charged with crimes endemic to homelessness, such as trespassing, petty theft, or public urination. Mentally ill inmates were more likely to be arrested multiple times, often generating long arrest records. They were sometimes held beyond the term of their sentence, or held even without pending charges, awaiting a hospital bed.

While jails and prisons tried to deal with the influx of mentally ill inmates, judges also began to recognize that punitive sentences did little to cure the underlying cause of the criminal behavior. In response, some jurisdictions created courts with a specialized docket for defendants with certain severe mental illnesses. Like drug court, mental health courts combine community-based mental health treatment, access to medication, and support services such as access to housing, with judicial supervision. Many courts partner with jail administrators to make sure mentally ill inmates receive medication and appropriate treatment while in custody. The goal is to stabilize the defendants' conditions, thus closing the revolving-door between court, jail, and homelessness.

Today there are over 300 mental health courts scattered across almost every state in the union. Like drug courts, mental health courts are designed to cure the underlying cause of the criminal behavior rather than to punish the behavior itself.

D. OTHER SPECIALTY COURTS

As the number of drug courts grew, reformers and judges began to argue that rehabilitative philosophies could be implemented in other settings.

> On Saturday, July 15, 1989, some 80 Vietnam veterans gathered in the handball court of San Diego High School. It wasn't a demonstration or a reunion. They had come to surrender to a municipal court judge on outstanding arrest warrants. Their crimes: sleeping on sidewalks, drinking in public, jaywalking and the like.
>
> When they were arrested, they were on the streets without the money to pay San Diego's stiff fines, and they had skipped their court dates. Now they wanted to come clean and resolve their unfinished business with the law.
>
> The public defender's office had worked out the details with the prosecutor and court ahead of time. The judge would hear only misdemeanors that day and come up with creative sentences that made more sense than either a fine, which the defendants were not able to pay, or jail time, which would leave the defendants homeless again when they got out.
>
> Scores of defense attorneys and prosecutors went to the high school that day to cut deals for the city's homeless fugitives. And thus, the country's first homeless court was born.[30]

[30] Wendy Davis, *Special Problems for Specialty Courts: Clients Get Needed Treatment Rather Than Jail Time, But Prosecutors and Defense Lawyers Alike Worry About Compromising Their Roles as Advocates*, 89 A.B.A.J. 32, 32–34 (2003).

Similarly, in 2008 a New York City judge, noticing an increase in the numbers of veterans appearing on his Drug and Mental Health Court dockets, founded the first Veterans' Treatment Court. There are now six federal veterans' courts, as well as a number of state veterans' courts.

Numerous other problem-solving courts have followed. As of 2016, there were more than 3,000 problem-solving courts around the nation dealing with issues as disparate as drugs, alcohol, mental health, domestic violence, truancy, and sexual offenses.

§ 6.4 THE BALANCE BETWEEN INFORMALITY AND CONSTITUTIONAL RIGHTS

Despite their popularity, problem-solving courts have their critics as well. Some defense counsel worry that defendants give up too many constitutional rights in order to receive the benefit of treatment programs, particularly in cases they might win in a traditional forum or in courts that require entry of a guilty plea rather than a plea in abeyance prior to the start of treatment.[31] Prosecutors, however, prefer upfront guilty pleas because they lack the ability to preserve evidence for years while waiting to see if a defendant will successfully complete treatment. Judges may also prefer upfront pleas, finding that coerced treatment is more effective than purely voluntary treatment.

Defense counsel and commentators also express concern that defendants often spend much more time in jail, and pay hundreds or thousands more in fines and court costs, under drug court supervision than they would had they pled guilty to the initial offense. Judges often impose short-term jail stays as a consequence for failing to follow program rules, and defendants must generally pay for treatment and for regular urinalysis tests.

Judicial supervision of treatment programs raises serious concerns about the role of a judge. Most judges lack any formal training in substance abuse, mental health, or social work. At the same time, problem solving court judges have the power to incarcerate defendants at any point during the treatment process, as well as to determine when an offender may "graduate" from the court program. Some critics even question the programs' ultimate goals and methodology.[32]

NOTES AND QUESTIONS

1. **The Opportunity for Abuse.** Does the informal nature of problem-solving courts make vulnerable populations even more vulnerable? In one Eighth Circuit case, five female defendants enrolled in a post-plea treatment and rehabilitation program sued a drug court supervisor, the county, the

---

[31] *Id.* at 36.

[32] Candace McCoy, *The Politics of Problem-Solving: An Overview of the Origins and Development of Therapeutic Courts*, 40 AM. CRIM. L. REV. 1513 (2003).

sheriff, and a lieutenant in the sheriff's department.[33] The plaintiffs alleged that the lieutenant, a "tracker" for the drug court, repeatedly sexually assaulted them. As a tracker, the lieutenant had the power to "conduct home visits, inspect participants' homes for indications of drug and/or alcohol use, curfew compliance, conduct breathalyzer tests, on-site UA [urine analysis] tests and employment verification," as well as the power to take non-compliant participants into custody.[34]

In another federal case, a drug-court judge invited a defendant into chambers to ask if she could procure hydrocodone for him.[35] He ultimately began a sexual relationship with the defendant, purchased drugs from her supplier, and intervened in several criminal cases on her behalf. The judge was convicted on several federal charges of misprision of felony, essentially as if he were part of a conspiracy to violate federal drug laws.

Do the broad extra-constitutional powers given to drug-court judges and officials create additional risks for participants, or are these cases simply emblematic of problems that exist in any justice system?

2. **Gotcha.** Federal courts have had to confront the question of whether a guilty plea in state drug court, which was the basis for entry into a treatment program, counts as a prior conviction for sentencing in a later federal proceeding. The Ninth Circuit concluded that it was a prior conviction because the drug court "deferred sentence" included a "custodial or supervisory" component.[36] Other courts have come to the opposite conclusion.[37]

---

33 S.M. v. Krigbaum, 808 F.3d 335 (8th Cir. 2015).

34 *Id.* at 338.

35 United States v. Baumgartner, 581 Fed. App'x. 522 (6th Cir. 2014).

36 United States v. Franco-Flores, 558 F.3d 978 (9th Cir. 2009).

37 *See, e.g.*, United States v. Martinez-Melgar, 591 F.3d 733 (4th Cir. 2010).

CHAPTER 7

Alternatives to Traditional Litigation

> The courts of this country should not be the places where resolution of disputes begins. They should be the places where the disputes end after alternative methods of resolving disputes have been considered and tried.[1]
>
> – Justice Sandra Day O'Connor

The public's perception of the legal process is often shaped by news, TV shows, and movies where drama is propelled by the trial process. When the public thinks "lawyer," it tends to think of people in suits in court, battling it out, defending the little guy, and having Perry Mason moments. Similarly, when the public thinks "judge," it thinks of a person in black robes sitting on the bench and dispensing justice (or, at least, pontificating about the law).

In reality, however, most lawyers spend their days researching and writing. Similarly, most judges spend their days reading, editing, and meeting with parties to help guide and direct the litigation process. Relatively little of their work occurs on the bench.

In recent years, an increasing amount of a judge's work has moved from bench to desk. Over the past 50 years, the number of jury trials has dropped precipitously. In 2003, the American Bar Association launched an initiative to study the degree to which trials in federal courts were being replaced by other dispositions. One year later, Professor Marc Galanter from the University of Wisconsin Law School wrote an article called *The Vanishing Trial: An Examination of Trials and Related Matters in Federal and State Courts*.[2] The article chronicled a sea change in the way litigation is conducted in the United States. In 1962, 11.5 percent of all civil cases in federal court went to trial. By 2002, that number had fallen to 1.8 percent. The drop was not due to a decline in the number of cases filed: over the same 40-year period dispositions in the federal courts quintupled. Similar statistical shifts occurred in state

---

1 While Justice O'Connor is widely credited with this quote, its original source is unknown. However, it has been cited by numerous sources, including the American Bar Association. Amy Lin Meyerson, *The Chair's Corner: Alternative Dispute Resolution*, A.B.A. http://www.americanbar.org/publications/gp_solo/2015/january-february/the_chairs_corner_alternative_dispute_resolution.html [https://perma.cc/K2V7-V2X6] (last visited Sept. 14, 2016).

2 Marc Galanter, *The Vanishing Trial: An Examination of Trials and Related Matters in Federal and State Courts*, 1 J. EMPIRICAL LEGAL STUD. 459 (2004).

courts, where the majority of litigation is conducted. In 1976, 36.1 percent of state cases went to trial. By 2002, that rate was cut almost in half.

The cause of the decline is a matter of debate. However, it is undoubtedly related, at least in part, to both the rise of alternative dispute resolution (ADR) and the increasing number of pro se parties in the system. Most explanations for partial abandonment of the courtroom include both expense and delay. Reform of the Anglo-American adversarial system has been a subject of debate and even federal legislation over the last century.[3]

§ 7.1 DECLINE OF THE JURY TRIAL

While the decline of the jury trial and rise of ADR are clear and well-documented, the reasons for that shift are not entirely known. It is likely the result of both internal and external factors: changes in the legal system from both within and without.

A. CAUSE

Litigation is an expensive and inefficient model for solving problems. It has never been more expensive to take a civil case from inception through a jury verdict. A 2013 study by the National Center for State Courts found that taking an average automobile tort case through trial averaged $43,000, although costs varied widely depending on the experience and seniority of counsel, the complexity of the case, and the fees charged by experts. Property and contract cases averaged $60,000, while the median cost to take a malpractice case through trial was over $122,000. The trial phase of the case accounted for between one-third and one-half of the fees.

The high cost of litigation undoubtedly dissuades clients and attorneys alike from going to trial. A number of other factors also influence the decision. The American system of allocating attorney's fees, in which parties bear their own costs, means that most litigants cannot shift the expense of litigation to the opposing party. Statutory caps on jury awards make litigation less lucrative for both plaintiffs and their attorneys, who may be working on a contingency basis. Electronic discovery has driven up the cost of pretrial discovery and caused some jurisdictions to limit discovery. The Federal Arbitration Act and mandatory arbitration agreements have put pressure on plaintiffs to arbitrate, as have mandatory mediation rules adopted by many courts. Judges are also increasingly involved in case management. Because many judges are evaluated on their disposition rates, they are under pressure to resolve cases as quickly as possible.

---

[3] Although we don't explore the topic here, ample literature is available on the subject. *See, e.g.*, Carl Tobias, *Did the Civil Justice Reform Act of 1990 Actually Expire?*, 31 U. MICH. J.L. REFORM 887, 892 (1998) (exploring the uncertainty regarding whether the CJRA expired and whether local plans adopted pursuant to it are still effective).

B. EFFECT

Regardless of the cause, the demise of the jury trial has had an irrevocable effect on the judicial system. Because there are fewer trials, fewer attorneys are getting all-important trial experience and training. Because attorneys lack trial experience and skill, they may tend to steer their clients toward settlement.

Settlements, particularly those reached in arbitration, are often shielded from public view. As a result, the pleadings, testimony, and discovery may not be available for later litigants. The settlements may not serve as a negotiation guide for later cases. Ultimately, the lack of adversarial litigation means a lack of precedent and, with it, a slowing of the development of the common law. In addition to the loss of legal doctrine, the ADR system may encourage the emergence of a private society of legal dispute resolution professionals, specialty courts for the rare trial, or perhaps movement toward the European "inquisitorial" model.[4]

Finally, the system is losing the important and intangible social benefits that flow from public trials.[5] Trials can be about catharsis and healing. Trials can educate and enlighten. They can be a catalyst for change. Trials can bring the light of public scrutiny into what would otherwise be the dark corners of our social landscape. The loss of the jury trial also means the loss of the opportunity to serve on a jury. "The jury trial—with all of its faults—is democracy and self-governance in action. Beyond the passive act of voting, jury service may be the only opportunity most citizens have to participate in any aspect of government."[6] Without firsthand participation in the system, the public perception of the court system can be warped by the picture created in the media.

§ 7.2 ALTERNATIVE DISPUTE RESOLUTION (ADR)

Abraham Lincoln, as part of his *Notes for a Law Lecture*, urged lawyers to

> [d]iscourage litigation. Persuade your neighbors to compromise whenever you can. Point out to them how the nominal winner is often a real loser—in fees, expenses, and waste of time. As a peacemaker the lawyer has a superior opportunity of being a good man. There will still be business enough.[7]

---

[4] Stephan Landsman, *So What? Possible Implications of the Vanishing Trial Phenomenon*, 1 J. EMPIRICAL LEGAL STUD. 973, 982 (2004).

[5] Georgetown Law Professor Paul Butler, among others, has made this observation.

[6] Patricia Lee Refo, *The Vanishing Trial Introduction*, 1 J. EMPIRICAL LEGAL STUD. v, vi (2004).

[7] *Abraham Lincoln's Notes for a Law Lecture*, A.B.A. (July 1, 1850), http://www.americanbar.org/content/dam/aba/administrative/professional_responsibility/39th_conference_session_7_did_lincoln_practice_law_the_way_he_practiced_politics.authcheckdam.pdf [https://perma.cc/L9C7-53PP].

Many litigants have taken Lincoln's advice to heart, resolving cases through alternative dispute resolution. When two parties with a dispute, particularly those who have had some ongoing relationship such as a marriage or business arrangement, find themselves in an important disagreement they may turn to any of a number of options before considering litigation. The phrase "alternative dispute resolution" encompasses a range of processes, all designed to resolve cases before they reach trial.

Early Evaluation. The first step in ADR is usually referred to as case evaluation. It asks whether the parties have a legal dispute or just an easily resolvable misunderstanding. Each party evaluates the cost and benefits of bringing a lawsuit versus attempting an amicable resolution. When parties are represented, each may ask a neutral third party, usually an attorney, to conduct a neutral case evaluation. The attorney's job is to provide an unbiased opinion of the merits of the case.

Negotiation and Settlement. If the parties choose formal dispute resolution, they will usually engage the services of attorneys. The attorneys almost always attempt to settle the matter through informal negotiation. Where informal negotiation fails, attorneys are likely to attempt other forms of ADR.

The catalog of ADR techniques is long, but the most common are mediation, arbitration, and mini-trials. Any of the techniques may be used before or after a case has been filed.

Mediation. In mediation, a neutral third party, preferably well-trained and licensed, attempts to bring the parties to an agreement. The mediator usually will sit with both parties together to explain the process, then talk to each party separately to determine what is most important and what each might be willing to accept. The mediator may meet with both parties together or separately but cannot disclose to either side what the other is willing to give up. The mediator does not "decide" the case. Instead, the mediator's role is to help the opposing sides identify possible common ground where they can compromise. This obviously requires skill and tact on the part of the mediator. Once the parties reach an agreement, they may ask the judge to issue an enforceable order consistent with the terms of the negotiated agreement.

Arbitration. The arbitration process looks more like litigation but with some private control. The parties agree that, rather than sending the case to a judge or jury, an arbitrator may decide the case after reviewing the evidence and hearing arguments. Arbitration is sometimes conducted by a single arbitrator and sometimes by a panel of arbitrators. The arbitrator does not have to follow the rules of evidence, and in some cases does not need to apply the governing law or make legal rulings. As a result, arbitration is generally faster and less expensive than traditional litigation. Additionally, arbitrators—unlike judges—often have some knowledge of the industry or technology involved in the case.

The arbitrator may either make an award with no explanation (a "bare bones" award) or an award with an explanation for the award (a "reasoned" award). Arbitration may be either binding or non-binding. A binding decision is final, enforceable, and rarely appealable. A non-binding decision is merely advisory. The parties are free to continue with litigation if they choose to reject the decision.

Mini-trial. Parties may choose a private abbreviated trial conducted by attorneys for both sides. The mini-trial is generally a brief presentation of the evidence and arguments each side intends to present at a full-blown trial. The mini-trial may take place in front of opposing counsel, a neutral attorney acting as judge, a small neutral jury, representatives for each party (often the business executives who have the power to settle the case), or some combination of these. A mini-trial allows the parties to see how their case would look and sound to others. The objective is to encourage settlement after a more realistic assessment of the evidence on either side.

There are many additional kinds of ADR, such as private judging, where the parties agree to hire a neutral, private, and often retired judge; and neutral fact-finding, where a neutral third party investigates the case and reports to the court.

The judge assigned to the case will also often encourage settlement, sometimes after extensive work has been done on pleadings, motions, and discovery. The judge may conduct a settlement conference at one or more stages of the case to facilitate this process. These conferences are a formal part of the litigation process. Many appellate courts now also encourage, or even require, ADR as part of the appeals process.

All of these methods are variations on the same theme: reaching a conclusion in the dispute while avoiding the cost and risk of litigation or appeal.

§ 7.3 MANDATORY MEDIATION

Over the past few decades, either by court rule or by statute, many states have adopted requirements that parties attempt to mediate their dispute before proceeding with litigation.[8] These statutes cover a wide variety of cases, including domestic relations, small claims, landlord-tenant, medical malpractice, and even appellate cases. Courts are cognizant that parties are generally happier and feel better about the judicial process when they participate in the decision-making process.

[8] *See, e.g.*, CAL. FAM. CODE § 3170 (requiring mediation on all contested issues dealing with child custody and visitation); UTAH CODE ANN. § 30–3–39 (establishing mandatory mediation for divorce actions); IOWA CODE § 654A.6 (establishing mandatory mediation for suits to enforce debts against agricultural property); S.D. CODIFIED LAWS § 54–13–10 (same); CONN. GEN. STAT. § 52–190c (establishing mandatory mediation for negligence claims against health care providers); WASH. REV. CODE § 7.70.100 (same); FLA. STAT. § 766.108 (establishing mandatory mediation and settlement conferences for suits involving medical negligence); P.R. LAWS ANN. tit. 32 § 2882 (establishing mandatory mediation for foreclosure proceedings in Puerto Rico).

Mediation also helps cut court costs, reduces the burden on an overloaded docket, and encourages post-divorce harmony and co-parenting. On the downside, it might be thought to serve the interests of certain industries such as landlords and health care providers by imposing barriers to litigation. Whatever the motivations, some mediation efforts will succeed, while others will fail.

Some litigants have attempted to bypass these mandatory mediation rules by claiming that they interfere with state constitutional guarantees of access to the courts. Given that the statutes are usually promoted by the courts, it is not surprising that they usually reject these arguments. Parties who object to mandatory mediation often balk at bearing a portion of the cost of a mediator.

In re Atlantic Pipe Corp.

304 F.3d 135 (1st Cir. 2002)

■ SELYA, CIRCUIT JUDGE.

This mandamus proceeding requires us to resolve an issue of importance to judges and practitioners alike: Does a district court possess the authority to compel an unwilling party to participate in, and share the costs of, non-binding mediation conducted by a private mediator? We hold that a court may order mandatory mediation pursuant to an explicit statutory provision or local rule. We further hold that where, as here, no such authorizing medium exists, a court nonetheless may order mandatory mediation through the use of its inherent powers as long as the case is an appropriate one and the order contains adequate safeguards. Because the mediation order here at issue lacks such safeguards (although it does not fall far short), we vacate it and remand the matter for further proceedings.

I. BACKGROUND

[In a hugely complex litigation stemming from construction and rupture of an aqueduct in Puerto Rico, there was what the court referred to as a "googol of claims." Among the many parties was Atlantic Pipe Corp. (APC), who moved to dismiss the proceedings in federal court while other cases were pending in the local courts of Puerto Rico.]

While this motion was pending before the district court, Thames-Dick asked that the case be referred to mediation and suggested Professor Eric Green as a suitable mediator. The district court granted the motion over APC's objection and ordered non-binding mediation to proceed before Professor Green. The court pronounced mediation likely to conserve judicial resources; directed all parties to undertake mediation in good faith; stayed discovery pending completion of the mediation; and declared that participation in the mediation would not prejudice the parties' positions vis-a-vis the pending motion or the litigation as a whole.

The court also stated that if mediation failed to produce a global settlement, the case would proceed to trial.

After moving unsuccessfully for reconsideration of the mediation order, APC sought relief by way of mandamus. Its petition alleged that the district court did not have the authority to require mediation (especially in light of unresolved questions as to the court's subject-matter jurisdiction) and, in all events, could not force APC to pay a share of the expenses of the mediation. We invited the other parties and the district judge to respond. Several entities opposed the petition. Two others filed a brief in support of APC. We assigned the case to the oral argument calendar and stayed the contemplated mediation pending our review.

Prior to argument in this court, two notable developments occurred. First, the district court considered and rejected the challenges to its exercise of jurisdiction. Second, APC rejected an offer by Thames-Dick to pay its share of the mediator's fees.

II. JURISDICTION

In an effort to shut off further debate, the respondents asseverate that mandamus is improper because APC will not suffer irreparable harm in the absence of such relief. They rest this asseveration on the notion that "mandamus is ordinarily appropriate [only] in those rare cases in which the issuance (or nonissuance) of an order presents a question anent the limits of judicial power, poses some special risk of irreparable harm to the appellant, and is palpably erroneous." The problem, however, is that these limitations typically apply only to *supervisory* mandamus. In the tiny class of cases in which advisory mandamus is appropriate, irreparable harm need not be shown.

We believe that this case is fit for advisory mandamus because the extent of a trial court's power to order mandatory mediation presents a systemically important issue as to which this court has not yet spoken. Moreover, that issue is capable of significant repetition prior to effective review. That fact militates in favor of advisory mandamus. We conclude, therefore, that invoking advisory mandamus is prudent under the circumstances. Consequently, the existence *vel non* of irreparable harm is a non-issue. We turn, then, to the merits.

III. THE MERITS

There are four potential sources of judicial authority for ordering mandatory non-binding mediation of pending cases, namely, (a) the court's local rules, (b) an applicable statute, (c) the Federal Rules of Civil Procedure, and (d) the court's inherent powers. Because the district court did not identify the basis of its assumed authority, we consider each of these sources.

A. *The Local Rules.*

A district court's local rules may provide an appropriate source of authority for ordering parties to participate in mediation. In Puerto Rico, however, the local rules contain only a single reference to any form of alternative dispute resolution (ADR). That reference is embodied in the district court's Amended Civil Justice Expense and Delay Reduction Plan (CJR Plan) [Rule V].

The respondents concede that the mediation order in this case falls outside the boundaries of the mediation program envisioned by Rule V. It does so most noticeably because it involves mediation before a private mediator, not a judicial officer. Seizing upon this discrepancy, APC argues that the local rules limit the district court in this respect, and that the court exceeded its authority thereunder by issuing a non-conforming mediation order (i.e., one that contemplates the intervention of a private mediator). The respondents counter by arguing that the rule does not bind the district court because, notwithstanding the unambiguous promise of the CJR Plan (which declares that the district court "shall adopt a method of Alternative Dispute Resolution"), no such program has been adopted to date.

APC does not contradict the respondents' assurance that the relevant portion of the CJR Plan has remained unimplemented, and we take judicial notice that there is no formal, ongoing ADR program in the Puerto Rico federal district court. Because that is so, we conclude that the District of Puerto Rico has no local rule in force that dictates the permissible characteristics of mediation orders. Consequently, APC's argument founders.

B. *The ADR Act.*

There is only one potential source of statutory authority for ordering mandatory non-binding mediation here: the Alternative Dispute Resolution Act of 1998 (ADR Act), 28 U.S.C. §§ 651–658. Congress passed the ADR Act to promote the utilization of alternative dispute resolution methods in the federal courts and to set appropriate guidelines for their use. The Act lists mediation as an appropriate ADR process. Moreover, it sanctions the participation of "professional neutrals from the private sector" as mediators. Finally, the Act requires district courts to obtain litigants' consent only when they order arbitration, not when they order the use of other ADR mechanisms (such as non-binding mediation).

Despite the broad sweep of these provisions, the Act is quite clear that some form of the ADR procedures it endorses must be adopted in each judicial district by local rule. In the absence of such local rules, the ADR Act itself does not authorize any specific court to use a particular ADR mechanism. Because the District of Puerto Rico has not yet complied with the Act's mandate, the mediation order here at issue cannot be justified under the ADR Act.

We add, however, that although the respondents cannot use the ADR Act as a justification, neither can APC use it as a nullification. Noting that the Act requires the adoption of local rules establishing a formal ADR program, APC equates the absence of such rules with the absence of power to employ an ADR procedure (say, mediation) in a specific case. But that is wishful thinking: if one assumes that district judges possessed the power to require mediation prior to the passage of the ADR Act, there is nothing in the Act that strips them of that power.

C. *The Civil Rules.*

The respondents next argue that the district court possessed the authority to require mediation by virtue of the Federal Rules of Civil Procedure. They concentrate their attention on Fed. R. Civ. P. 16, which states in pertinent part that "the court may take appropriate action with respect to . . . (9) settlement and the use of special procedures to assist in resolving the dispute when authorized by statute or local rule . . . ." Fed. R. Civ. P. 16(c)(9). But the words "when authorized by statute or local rule" are a frank limitation on the district courts' authority to order mediation thereunder, and we must adhere to that circumscription.

D. *Inherent Powers.*

Even apart from positive law, district courts have substantial inherent power to manage and control their calendars. This inherent power takes many forms. By way of illustration, a district court may use its inherent power to compel represented clients to attend pretrial settlement conferences, even though such a practice is not specifically authorized in the Civil Rules.

Of course, a district court's inherent powers are not infinite. There are at least four limiting principles. First, inherent powers must be used in a way reasonably suited to the enhancement of the court's processes, including the orderly and expeditious disposition of pending cases. Second, inherent powers cannot be exercised in a manner that contradicts an applicable statute or rule. Third, the use of inherent powers must comport with procedural fairness. And, finally, inherent powers "must be exercised with restraint and discretion."

At one time, the inherent power of judges to compel unwilling parties to participate in ADR procedures was a hot-button issue for legal scholars. Although many federal district courts have forestalled further debate by adopting local rules that authorize specific ADR procedures and outlaw others, the District of Puerto Rico is not among them. Thus, we have no choice but to address the question head-on.

When mediation is forced upon unwilling litigants, it stands to reason that the likelihood of settlement is diminished. Requiring parties to invest substantial amounts of time and money in mediation under such circumstances may well be inefficient. *Cf.* Richard A. Posner, *The Summary Jury Trial and Other Methods of Alternative Dispute Resolution: Some Cautionary Observations*, 53 U. Chi. L. Rev. 366, 369–

72 (1986) (offering a model to evaluate ADR techniques in terms of their capacity to encourage settlements).

The fact remains, however, that none of these considerations establishes that mandatory mediation is always inappropriate. There may well be specific cases in which such a protocol is likely to conserve judicial resources without significantly burdening the objectors' rights to a full, fair, and speedy trial. Much depends on the idiosyncracies of the particular case and the details of the mediation order.

In some cases, a court may be warranted in believing that compulsory mediation could yield significant benefits even if one or more parties object. After all, a party may resist mediation simply out of unfamiliarity with the process or out of fear that a willingness to submit would be perceived as a lack of confidence in her legal position. In such an instance, the party's initial reservations are likely to evaporate as the mediation progresses, and negotiations could well produce a beneficial outcome, at reduced cost and greater speed, than would a trial. While the possibility that parties will fail to reach agreement remains ever present, the boon of settlement can be worth the risk.

This is particularly true in complex cases involving multiple claims and parties. The fair and expeditious resolution of such cases often is helped along by creative solutions—solutions that simply are not available in the binary framework of traditional adversarial litigation. Mediation with the assistance of a skilled facilitator gives parties an opportunity to explore a much wider range of options, including those that go beyond conventional zero-sum resolutions. Mindful of these potential advantages, we hold that it is within a district court's inherent power to order non-consensual mediation in those cases in which that step seems reasonably likely to serve the interests of justice.

E. *The Mediation Order.*

Our determination that the district courts have inherent power to refer cases to non-binding mediation is made with a recognition that any such order must be crafted in a manner that preserves procedural fairness and shields objecting parties from undue burdens. We thus turn to the specifics of the mediation order entered in this case. As with any exercise of a district court's inherent powers, we review the entry of that order for abuse of discretion.

As an initial matter, we agree with the lower court that the complexity of this case militates in favor of ordering mediation. At last count, the suit involves twelve parties, asserting a welter of claims, counterclaims, cross-claims, and third-party claims predicated on a wide variety of theories. The pendency of nearly parallel litigation in the Puerto Rican courts, which features a slightly different cast of characters and claims that are related to but not completely congruent with those asserted here, further complicates the matter. Untangling the intricate web of relationships among the parties, along with the difficult and fact-intensive arguments made by each, will be time-consuming and will impose significant costs on the parties and the court. Against this backdrop, mediation holds out the dual prospect of advantaging the litigants and conserving scarce judicial resources.

APC posits that the appointment of a private mediator proposed by one of the parties is per se improper (and, thus, invalidates the order). We do not agree. The district court has inherent power to appoint persons unconnected with the court to aid judges in the performance of specific judicial duties. In the context of non-binding mediation, the mediator does not decide the merits of the case and has no authority to coerce settlement. Thus, in the absence of a contrary statute or rule, it is perfectly acceptable for the district court to appoint a qualified and neutral private party as a mediator. The mere fact that the mediator was proposed by one of the parties is insufficient to establish bias in favor of that party.

We hasten to add that the litigants are free to challenge the qualifications or neutrality of any suggested mediator (whether or not nominated by a party to the case). APC, for example, had a full opportunity to present its views about the suggested mediator both in its opposition to the motion for mediation and in its motion for reconsideration of the mediation order. Despite these opportunities, APC offered no convincing reason to spark a belief that Professor Green, a nationally recognized mediator with significant experience in sprawling cases, is an unacceptable choice. When a court enters a mediation order, it necessarily makes an independent determination that the mediator it appoints is both qualified and neutral. Because the court made that implicit determination here in a manner that was procedurally fair (if not ideal), we find no abuse of discretion in its selection of Professor Green.[7]

APC also grouses that it should not be forced to share the costs of an unwanted mediation. We have held, however, that courts have the power under Fed. R. Civ. P. 26(f) to issue pretrial cost-sharing orders in complex litigation. Given the difficulties facing trial courts in cases involving multiple parties and multiple claims, we are hesitant to limit that power to the traditional discovery context. This is especially true in complicated cases, where the potential value of mediation lies not only in promoting settlement but also in clarifying the issues remaining for trial.

The short of the matter is that, without default cost-sharing rules, the use of valuable ADR techniques (like mediation) becomes hostage to the parties' ability to agree on the concomitant financial arrangements. This means that the district court's inherent power to order private mediation in appropriate cases would be rendered nugatory absent the corollary power to order the sharing of reasonable mediation costs. To

---

[7] We say "not ideal" because, in an ideal world, it would be preferable for the district court, before naming a mediator, to solicit the names of potential nominees from all parties and to provide an opportunity for the parties to comment upon each others' proposed nominees.

avoid this pitfall, we hold that the district court, in an appropriate case, is empowered to order the sharing of reasonable costs and expenses associated with mandatory non-binding mediation.

The remainder of APC's arguments are not so easily dispatched. Even when generically appropriate, a mediation order must contain procedural and substantive safeguards to ensure fairness to all parties involved. The mediation order in this case does not quite meet that test. In particular, the order does not set limits on the duration of the mediation or the expense associated therewith.

We need not wax longiloquent. As entered, the order simply requires the parties to mediate; it does not set forth either a timetable for the mediation or a cap on the fees that the mediator may charge. The figures that have been bandied about in the briefs—$ 900 per hour or $ 9,000 per mediation day—are quite large and should not be left to the mediator's whim. Relatedly, because the mediator is to be paid an hourly rate, the court should have set an outside limit on the number of hours to be devoted to mediation. Equally as important, it is trite but often true that justice delayed is justice denied. An unsuccessful mediation will postpone the ultimate resolution of the case—indeed, the district court has stayed all discovery pending the completion of the mediation—and, thus, prolong the litigation. For these reasons, the district court should have set a definite time frame for the mediation.

A court intent on ordering non-consensual mediation should take other precautions as well. For example, the court should make it clear (as did the able district court in this case) that participation in mediation will not be taken as a waiver of any litigation position. The important point is that the protections we have mentioned are not intended to comprise an exhaustive list, but, rather, to illustrate that when a district court orders a party to participate in mediation, it should take care to assuage legitimate concerns about the possible negative consequences of such an order.

To recapitulate, we rule that a mandatory mediation order issued under the district court's inherent power is valid in an appropriate case. We also rule that this is an appropriate case. We hold, however, that the district court's failure to set reasonable limits on the duration of the mediation and on the mediator's fees dooms the decree.

IV. CONCLUSION

We admire the district court's pragmatic and innovative approach to this massive litigation. Our core holding—that ordering mandatory mediation is a proper exercise of a district court's inherent power, subject, however, to a variety of terms and conditions—validates that approach. We are mindful that this holding is in tension with the opinions of the Sixth and Seventh Circuits, but we believe it is justified by the important goal of promoting flexibility and creative problem-solving in the handling of complex litigation.

NOTES AND QUESTIONS

1. **Pay to Play.** The First Circuit in *Atlantic Pipe* held that ordering mediation is within the district court's inherent power. This seems appropriate considering the statutory authority to provide for efficient and fair adjudicatory procedures. But is efficient always fair? Why should an unwilling litigant be required to pay exorbitant fees for a service that it does not want?

2. **That's Counterintuitive.** The court, citing Judge Posner, notes that forced mediation may diminish the likelihood of settlement. This proposition appears counter-intuitive when the stated purpose of mediation is an attempt to reach an amicable settlement.

The article by Judge Posner cited for this proposition actually addresses summary jury trials rather than mediation. Judge Posner used a set of mathematical models to calculate the total cost of ADR when applied to all cases. One may or may not be convinced by his calculations or their underlying assumptions, now 30 years old, but the model is exceedingly difficult to apply to court-ordered mediation.

3. **That's Not Fair.** A party who is ready to go to trial may resent mediation, but no party is ever forced to settle. If one party refuses to engage in the mediation process, what should the court do about allocating the cost of the mediator's time? Should the recalcitrant party pay as much as parties who stay and attempt to come to a solution? Should the recalcitrant party be required to stay at the mediation session for a particular period of time? Could a recalcitrant party be held in contempt for insisting on its right to a trial?

4. **Protecting Procedural Rights.** The First Circuit is very careful to assert that the rights of the litigants are protected. The right of confidentiality is the most obvious concern, but non-coercion, timeliness, discovery, and witness coaching may all come into play as well.

5. **Creditors Need Not Apply.** In a case arising from the perilous economics of the agricultural industry, the Iowa Supreme Court recited the long history of a mandatory mediation statute—and then decided that the statute did not apply.

The American Midwest was hit by an epidemic of farm foreclosures in the 1970s and 1980s. That crisis resulted in a statutory mediation requirement. Before a creditor could seek foreclosure on a farm mortgage, it was required to mediate the case. Here, however, the court held that a creditor need not pursue mediation when the owner of the farm files a lawsuit first, even if the creditor seeks to foreclose by counterclaim. Because the creditor did not initiate the action, the court held that the mediation provision did not apply.[9] The farm crisis was an important and heart-rending chapter in American history. Why, though, would a court delve so extensively into the history of a statute that it would choose not to apply?

---

[9] Schaefer v. Putnam, 841 N.W.2d 68, 83 (Iowa 2013).

§ 7.4 MANDATORY ARBITRATION AGREEMENTS

While ADR is often a win-win proposition for litigants, ideally both parties agree to participate. In recent years, however, companies have discovered that mandatory binding arbitration agreements significantly reduce litigation costs. While this is not necessarily a bad thing, consumers often find themselves unwilling participants in an ADR system that is stacked against them.

Arbitration agreements now crop up in dozens of different types of daily interactions. When you signed up with a cell phone carrier, accepted a job, opened a bank account, hired a mover, bought a car, or went to the doctor, you probably signed an arbitration agreement.

In addition to forcing binding arbitration, these agreements often contain a host of other provisions. Mandatory arbitration agreements may control venue, the amount of discovery available, the scope of judicial review, and the amount and types of damages available. They also generally forbid the filing of class action suits and prohibit creation of a public record of the dispute. They often leave the choice of arbitrator up to the company. Critics charge that companies choose particular arbitrators because they rule in favor of the company. Because the companies provide repeat business, the arbitrators have a financial interest in ruling against consumers. In 2007, a consumer watchdog group alleged that the National Arbitration Forum, one of the largest consumer arbitration companies, ruled against consumers 94% of the time.

Arbitration clauses come under the ambit of the Federal Arbitration Act. The Federal Arbitration Act (FAA), passed in 1925, provides:

> A written provision in any maritime transaction or a contract evidencing a transaction involving commerce to settle by arbitration a controversy thereafter arising out of such contract or transaction . . . shall be valid, irrevocable, and enforceable, save upon such grounds as exist at law or in equity for the revocation of any contract.[10]

The Act also provides that an arbitration award is enforceable in any action over which the federal courts would have subject matter jurisdiction.[11] The standard for judicial review of the award is contained in 9 U.S.C. § 10:

> **(a)** In any of the following cases the United States court in and for the district wherein the award was made may make an order vacating the award upon the application of any party to the arbitration—

---

10 9 U.S.C. § 2.

11 9 U.S.C. § 4.

> **(1)** where the award was procured by corruption, fraud, or undue means;
>
> **(2)** where there was evident partiality or corruption in the arbitrators, or either of them;
>
> **(3)** where the arbitrators were guilty of misconduct in refusing to postpone the hearing, upon sufficient cause shown, or in refusing to hear evidence pertinent and material to the controversy; or of any other misbehavior by which the rights of any party have been prejudiced; or
>
> **(4)** where the arbitrators exceeded their powers, or so imperfectly executed them that a mutual, final, and definite award upon the subject matter submitted was not made.

The Supreme Court noted its history:

> Congress enacted the FAA in response to widespread judicial hostility to arbitration. This text reflects the overarching principle that arbitration is a matter of contract. And consistent with that text, courts must rigorously enforce arbitration agreements according to their terms, including terms that specify with whom the parties choose to arbitrate their disputes, and the rules under which that arbitration will be conducted. That holds true for claims that allege a violation of a federal statute, unless the FAA's mandate has been overridden by a contrary congressional command.[12]

Mandatory arbitration clauses came under attack in the mid 2000s. In *AT&T Mobility v. Concepcion*,[13] consumers brought suit in a California federal court after they were charged $30.22 in sales tax on a phone that AT&T advertised as free. The complaint was consolidated with a putative class action in which the plaintiffs alleged that AT&T had engaged in false advertising and fraud. AT&T moved to compel arbitration under the terms of its contract. The district court denied the motion on the grounds that the provision was unconscionable under California law. The Ninth Circuit agreed, but the Supreme Court reversed five-to-four. Justice Scalia, writing for the Court, concluded that the FAA preempted California's law.

The issue returned one year later in an apparently more compelling situation.[14] CompuCredit marketed Visa cards to people with low credit scores. After signing up for the credit card, customers discovered numerous hidden fees. For example, a card promoted as having a credit line of $300 included fees of $257. Customers filed a class action suit, alleging that CompuCredit violated the Credit Repair Organization Act (CROA). The company moved to compel arbitration, and once again the

[12] American Express Co. v. Italian Colors Rest., 133 S. Ct. 2304, 2308–09 (2013).

[13] 131 S. Ct. 1740 (2011).

[14] *See* CompuCredit Corp. v. Greenwood, 565 U.S. 95 (2012).

district court and the Ninth Circuit ruled for the consumer. The Supreme Court, however, reversed in an eight-to-one decision. Once again, Justice Scalia wrote the majority opinion:

> Like the District Court and the Ninth Circuit, respondents focus on the CROA's disclosure and nonwaiver provisions. The former sets forth a statement that the credit repair organization must provide to the consumer before any contract is executed. One sentence of that required statement reads, "You have a right to sue a credit repair organization that violates the Credit Repair Organization Act." The Act's nonwaiver provision states, "Any waiver by any consumer of any protection provided by or any right of the consumer under this subchapter—(1) shall be treated as void; and (2) may not be enforced by any Federal or State court or any other person."
>
> The Ninth Circuit adopted the following line of reasoning, urged upon us by respondents here: The disclosure provision gives consumers the "right to sue," which "clearly involves the right to bring an action in a court of law." Because the nonwaiver provision prohibits the waiver of "any right of the consumer under this subchapter," the arbitration agreement—which waived the right to bring an action in a court of law—cannot be enforced.
>
> The flaw in this argument is its premise: that the disclosure provision provides consumers with a right to bring an action in a court of law. It does not. Rather, it imposes an obligation on credit repair organizations to supply consumers with a specific statement set forth (in quotation marks) in the statute. The only consumer right it creates is the right to receive the statement, which is meant to describe the consumer protections that the law *elsewhere* provides.[15]

Finally, in 2013, the Supreme Court addressed whether the courts must enforce a contractual waiver of class actions in cases where the plaintiffs' costs to arbitrate far exceed the possible damages.[16] In a short opinion, again written by Justice Scalia, the Court held five-to-three that they must. The plaintiff merchants, led by Italian Colors Restaurant, alleged that American Express used its monopoly power to require them to accept charge cards (bank-issued cards that require the customer to pay off the balance in full every billing cycle) as a condition of accepting regular American Express credit cards. It then charged the plaintiffs 30% higher fees on charge cards. Because many business travelers used regular American Express cards, the merchants could not afford to refuse American Express. They sued for violation of federal antitrust laws, and American Express moved to invoke the "no class actions" clause in the

---

[15] *Id.* at 98–99.

[16] American Express Co. v. Italian Colors Rest., 133 S. Ct. 2304 (2013).

contract. The merchants argued that their individual damages were worth less than $39,000, yet each would be required to hire an expert to conduct an economic analysis at a cost of several hundred thousand dollars or more. Thus, the ability to bring a class action was the only way to seek redress of their claims. The Court disagreed.

> No contrary congressional command requires us to reject the waiver of class arbitration here. Respondents argue that requiring them to litigate their claims individually—as they contracted to do—would contravene the policies of the antitrust laws. But the antitrust laws do not guarantee an affordable procedural path to the vindication of every claim. Congress has taken some measures to facilitate the litigation of antitrust claims—for example, it enacted a multiplied-damages remedy. *See* 15 U.S.C. § 15 (treble damages). In enacting such measures, Congress has told us that it is willing to go, in certain respects, beyond the normal limits of law in advancing its goals of deterring and remedying unlawful trade practice. But to say that Congress must have intended whatever departures from those normal limits advance antitrust goals is simply irrational. "[N]o legislation pursues its purposes at all costs."[17]

Justice Kagan dissented, giving the Court credit for its forthrightness, but not its analysis:

> Here is the nutshell version of this case, unfortunately obscured in the Court's decision. The owner of a small restaurant (Italian Colors) thinks that American Express (Amex) has used its monopoly power to force merchants to accept a form contract violating the antitrust laws. The restaurateur wants to challenge the allegedly unlawful provision (imposing a tying arrangement), but the same contract's arbitration clause prevents him from doing so. That term imposes a variety of procedural bars that would make pursuit of the antitrust claim a fool's errand. So if the arbitration clause is enforceable, Amex has insulated itself from antitrust liability—even if it has in fact violated the law. The monopolist gets to use its monopoly power to insist on a contract effectively depriving its victims of all legal recourse.
>
> And here is the nutshell version of today's opinion, admirably flaunted rather than camouflaged: Too darn bad.[18]

NOTES AND QUESTIONS

1. **You (Sometimes) Get a Second Chance.** In *Szetela v. Discover Bank*,[19] a Discover credit card customer brought a class action suit, alleging

---

[17] *Id.* at 2309.

[18] *Id.* at 2313 (Kagan, J., dissenting).

[19] 118 Cal. Rptr. 2d 862 (2002).

that Discover charged unfair fees. Although a lower court upheld the class action ban contained in an arbitration clause in the customer's contract, the California Court of Appeals reversed. It concluded that the contract was "not only substantively unconscionable, it violates public policy by granting Discover a 'get out of jail free' card while compromising important consumer rights."[20]

Chief Justice Roberts, who in 2002 was still in private practice, represented Discover Bank on appeal. Roberts sought certiorari on the issue of whether the class action ban in the credit card contract preempted the FAA, but the United States Supreme Court declined to take the case. The lawsuit eventually settled. Ten years later, with Roberts sitting as Chief Justice, the Court took up a nearly identical issue in *Italian Colors*. Should Chief Justice Roberts have recused himself in *Italian Colors*? Even without his vote, the outcome would have been the same.

2. **That Proves My Point.** *Szetela* was refiled as a class action lawsuit. It eventually settled for $15 million. Does this case prove the point that arbitration agreements are good for the legal system? Although it is unclear how much the plaintiff's attorneys were paid, they likely made millions of dollars. Were the lawyers the real winners in *Szetela*?

3. **One Statute Deserves Another.** There has been some movement toward reversing the Supreme Court's FAA rulings by statute. The Dodd-Frank Wall Street Reform and Consumer Protection Act required the Consumer Finance Protection Bureau (CFPB) to study the use of arbitration clauses in consumer financial markets. It also gave the Bureau the power to issue regulations if they are in the public's interest. In 2015, the CFPB announced that it was considering rules that would ban consumer finance companies from using mandatory arbitration clauses to block class action suits.

4. **Bourbon—with a Side of Bitter.** The owner of the Italian Colors Restaurant made one change in his menu after he lost in the Supreme Court. He added a special bourbon cocktail to the menu. "I call it the Scalia," he said. "It's bitter and tough to swallow."

§ 7.5 PRO SE LITIGANTS

Abraham Lincoln is also credited with saying, "He who represents himself has a fool for a client." If Lincoln was correct, then a vast number of litigants in American courts are fools.

A rising number of litigants in American courts appear pro se, a Latin phrase for "on one's own behalf." It is easy to see pro se litigants as clogging the court system with frivolous claims. However, many pro se parties have legitimate claims or defenses but little means with which to advance them. Lacking an attorney, they are often at a significant disadvantage. The explosion of pro se cases creates problems for the litigants, as well as the attorneys, court staff, and judges who must find

[20] *Id.* at 868.

ways to handle the influx of tens of thousands of non-lawyers in the legal system.

A. PRO SE PARTIES: WHO, HOW MANY, AND WHY

The right to represent oneself stretches back to the Judiciary Act of 1789. That statute, enacted by the first Congress, provided that "in all the courts of the United States, the parties may plead and manage their own causes personally or by the assistance of counsel." That right has been codified in 28 U.S.C. § 1654(a) (2012): "In all courts of the United States the parties may plead and conduct their own cases personally or by counsel as, by the rules of such courts, respectively, are permitted to manage and conduct causes therein." In *Faretta v. California*,[21] the United States Supreme Court concluded that the right to appear pro se extended to criminal cases as well.

Parties are more likely to represent themselves in certain kinds of cases. These include domestic relations (divorce and child custody), immigration, bankruptcy, small claims, misdemeanor criminal cases, and housing. Numerous jurisdictions have done studies over the past 30 years to measure the number of pro se litigants appearing in their courts.[22] A 1976 Connecticut study found that just 2.5% of litigants were pro se.[23] By 2010, studies in more than a dozen jurisdictions documented pro se rates in domestic relations courts ranging from 49% to almost 90%. Although rates in other kinds of civil cases were lower, they still ranged from 35 percent to more than 90 percent in some jurisdictions.[24]

While more pro se parties appear in state courts, the federal courts have not been immune to the pro se trend. In 2013, more than 77,000 pro se cases were filed in United States district courts.[25] Surprisingly, by 2012, at least 50 percent of appeals in the United States Circuit Courts of Appeal were pro se, although a not-insubstantial number were filed by prisoners or involved a review of agency decisions.[26]

Litigants appear by themselves for a variety of reasons. Many litigants have difficulty finding affordable representation. A 2006 Utah survey found that 60 percent of pro se litigants made less than $36,000 per year. In the same study, between 30 percent and 60 percent of respondents believed—sometimes erroneously—that their cases were not

---

[21] 422 U.S. 806 (1975).

[22] Thanks to Professor Linda F. Smith of the University of Utah for her help in providing information for this section.

[23] Linda F. Smith & Barry Stratford, *DIY in Family Law: A Case Study of a Brief Advice Clinic for Pro Se Litigants*, 14 J.L. & FAM. STUD. 167 (2012).

[24] *Id.*

[25] ADMIN. OFFICE OF THE U.S. COURTS, TABLE C-13: CIVIL PRO SE AND NON-PRO SE FILINGS, BY DISTRICT, DURING THE 12-MONTH PERIOD ENDING SEPTEMBER 30, 2013 1 (2013), http://www.uscourts.gov/statistics/table/c-13/judicial-business/2013/09/30 [https://perma.cc/F4M6-TQ5C].

[26] *U.S. Courts Of Appeals—Judicial Business 2012*, ADMIN. OFFICE OF THE COURTS, http://www.uscourts.gov/statistics-reports/us-courts-appeals-judicial-business-2012 [https://perma.cc/32F8-RLXT] (last visited Sept. 20, 2016).

complicated enough to justify hiring a lawyer. More than 10 percent had consulted a lawyer prior to appearing in court.[27] Others weren't sure how to find a lawyer, assumed that hiring a lawyer would be prohibitively expensive, didn't trust lawyers, or thought that a lawyer would slow down their case. The rise of the Internet has made legal information widely available, including fairly accurate guides to litigation. In a modern incarnation of Roscoe Pound's 1906 observation, many litigants share "the general popular assumption that the administration of justice is an easy task, to which anyone is competent."[28]

Many "self-help" companies have also moved into the gap. These range from the large and fairly reputable (like Legal Zoom) to small companies that help litigants fill out forms but do not provide actual representation. These for-profit businesses legitimately fill a need but often engage in the unauthorized practice of law. Most pernicious are *Notario Publicos*. In many Spanish-speaking countries *notorio publicos* are authorized to perform some legal services. American companies sometimes take advantage of non-English speakers, who assume that notaries public in the United States are authorized to provide these same services.

The cost of legal representation contributes to the rise in pro se litigation. Attorneys often have substantial student loan debt, making it more difficult for them to provide low-cost representation. Federal support for legal services has precipitously declined as well. Statutory caps on some kinds of tort recovery have made attorneys less willing to take on some kinds of civil cases. State Bars have also been slow to approve limited representation, unbundled legal services, and other nontraditional means of representation.

NOTES AND QUESTIONS

1. **The Pen(cil) is Mightier Than the Sword.** Many pro se cases have merit. Some have even been responsible for major shifts in the law. Clarence Gideon's petition for certiorari in the United States Supreme Court was handwritten in pencil on prison stationary. The Court took the case and, in *Gideon v. Wainwright*,[29] held that indigent defendants in state felony cases must be provided counsel.

2. **The Right to Make a Fool of Oneself.** Not all Supreme Court Justices were on board with giving criminal defendants the right to represent themselves. In *Faretta v. California*,[30] Chief Justice Burger commented that

> [t]his case . . . is another example of the judicial tendency to constitutionalize what is thought "good" . . . . [T]here is nothing

[27] Smith & Stratford, *supra* note 23.

[28] Roscoe Pound, The Causes of Popular Dissatisfaction with the Administration of Justice, Presentation at the Annual Convention of the American Bar Association (1906), https://law.unl.edu/RoscoePound.pdf [https://perma.cc/UJK4-M8LQ].

[29] 372 U.S. 335 (1963).

[30] 422 U.S. 806 (1975).

> desirable or useful in permitting every accused person, even the most uneducated and inexperienced, to insist upon conducting his own defense to criminal charges. Moreover, there is no constitutional basis for the Court's holding, and it can only add to the problems of an already malfunctioning criminal justice system.[31]

Justice Blackmun also dissented, expressing his concern that "the right to self-representation constitutionalized today frequently will cause procedural confusion without advancing any significant strategic interest of the defendant."[32] He ended with a zinger: "If there is any truth to the old proverb 'one who is his own lawyer has a fool for a client,' the Court by its opinion today now bestows a *constitutional* right on one to make a fool of himself."[33]

3. **Calling the Shots.** A criminal defendant with counsel only controls whether to plead guilty or not guilty, whether or not to testify, and whether to have a jury trial. Counsel makes all other tactical decisions. Some criminal defendants bridle at these restrictions and represent themselves in order to exert more control over the trial proceedings.

4. **The Problem with Prisoners.** The rise in civil rights cases was also impacted by the exploding number of prisoners. In the 1970s, less than 500,000 people were incarcerated in the United States.[34] By 2013, that number had jumped to more than 2.2 million.[35] Prisoners had ample time, if not ample resources, to challenge their living conditions and treatment.

Some prisoner litigation has been curtailed by the Prison Litigation Reform Act of 1995 (PLRA). The PLRA imposed new restrictions on prisoner litigation. It required prisoners to exhaust administrative grievance procedures before filing suit, imposed fees and costs on inmates, and required district court judges to review complaints filed by prisoners "as soon as practicable" to determine if the complaint may be dismissed under Rule 12(b)(6) or governmental immunity statutes.

5. **Just Not in Our Court.** Although federal statutes and Supreme Court case law affirm the right to represent one's self, in 2013 the Supreme Court codified its long-standing practice of appointing counsel for pro se cases in which it grants certiorari. The Rules of the Supreme Court now provide that "[o]ral arguments may be presented only by members of the Bar of this Court,"[36] officially closing a door on the admittedly extremely rare practice of non-lawyers arguing before the Court.

---

[31] 422 U.S. at 836–37 (Burger, C.J., dissenting).

[32] *Id.* at 846 (Blackmun, J., dissenting).

[33] *Id.* at 852 (Blackmun, J., dissenting).

[34] THE PUNISHING DECADE: PRISON AND JAIL ESTIMATES AT THE MILLENNIUM, JUSTICE POLICY INST. (May 2000), http://www.justicepolicy.org/images/upload/00-05_rep_punishing decade_ac.pdf [https://perma.cc/TT2D-5D28] (citing BUREAU OF JUSTICE STATISTICS, SOURCEBOOK OF CRIMINAL JUSTICE STATISTICS 1997 (1999).

[35] LAUREN E. GLAZE & DANIELLE KAEBLE, BUREAU OF JUSTICE STATISTICS, CORRECTIONAL POPULATIONS IN THE UNITED STATES, 2013 (Dec. 2014), http://www.bjs.gov/content/pub/pdf/cpus13.pdf [https://perma.cc/45J4-MGLU].

[36] SUP. CT. R. 28.8.

B. THE PROBLEM FOR ATTORNEYS

A lawyer might assume that any case with a non-lawyer on the other side is an easy win. That's far from true. Pro se litigants have only a limited (and often mistaken) understanding of the law, are unfamiliar with basic rules of procedure, are not subject to the rules of professional conduct that govern lawyers' behavior, and assume that courts function in real life the way they do on television. Given these shortcomings, pro se parties are often given significant leeway by judges.

Attorneys face a number of ethical issues when dealing with pro se parties. First, unrepresented litigants often ask the lawyer on the other side of the table for legal advice. However, the Model Rules of Professional Conduct provide:

> In dealing on behalf of a client with a person who is not represented by counsel, a lawyer shall not state or imply that the lawyer is disinterested. When the lawyer knows or reasonably should know that the unrepresented person misunderstands the lawyer's role in the matter, the lawyer shall make reasonable efforts to correct the misunderstanding. The lawyer shall not give legal advice to an unrepresented person, other than the advice to secure counsel, if the lawyer knows or reasonably should know that the interests of such a person are or have a reasonable possibility of being in conflict with the interests of the client.[37]

Thus, while a lawyer may give legal *information* to an unrepresented party, she may not give legal *advice*, except for the advice to obtain counsel. The rule also requires a lawyer to correct any misunderstanding an unrepresented person may have about the lawyer's role or the lawyer's impartiality. Because a lawyer cannot settle a case without talking to the pro se party, she must consistently and repeatedly make clear that she is not the pro se party's attorney and cannot give the pro se party any legal advice.

Second, Rule 3.4 requires a lawyer to comply with obligations imposed by the rules of a tribunal. Thus, a lawyer has to play by the usual rules, even when the pro se litigant doesn't. Third, Rule 3.3 provides that a lawyer must "disclose to the tribunal legal authority in the controlling jurisdiction known to the lawyer to be directly adverse to the position of the client and not disclosed by opposing counsel." Because there is no "opposing counsel," the attorney may find herself doing the work of two.

The legal profession has reacted to the influx of pro se litigants in a number of ways. Many attorneys now participate in brief advice clinics provided by law schools or through bar associations. There has been a renewed push for attorneys to take pro bono or "low bono" cases, where clients pay nothing or a sliding scale fee. Some states now allow attorneys

---

[37] MODEL RULES OF PROF'L CONDUCT r. 4.3 (AM. BAR ASS'N 2015).

to offer unbundled legal services, allowing clients to hire an attorney to handle part, but not all, of a case. Finally, some states are considering creating Limited License Legal Technicians. LLLTs are the legal equivalent of nurse practitioners. They attend a one-year training program and must pass an exam. They are then allowed to help clients in family law cases. They consult, advise, and help with document preparation and court scheduling. They may not, however, appear in court on behalf of a client. To date, Washington is the only state to have implemented a LLLT program, in part because of pushback from licensed members of the Bar who are concerned that LLLTs will unfairly compete with attorneys for business.

C. THE PROBLEM FOR COURTS

As the number of pro se litigants grew, many court clerks found themselves pressed into service. They were asked daily for procedural and substantive guidance they were not allowed—or even equipped—to provide. Although clerks are allowed to provide litigants with information, they may not provide legal advice. The distinction was often lost on pro se parties, who left the courthouse little wiser and significantly more frustrated.

Over the past ten years, courts around the country have developed a variety of pro se assistance programs. Many courts have simplified and standardized their forms. They have also made forms and instructions publicly available in the courthouse, by mail, and on the Internet. For example, a court may provide simplified petitions for dissolution of marriage or checklists with all legal defenses to eviction notices. Other courts have created in-house clinics or help lines staffed by attorneys who have access to court records and the ability to give visitors and callers case-specific guidance. Courts and the local bar association may work closely together, sponsoring self-help programs and encouraging counsel to take pro bono or low bono cases. Many courts have leveraged technology by putting standardized forms on the internet, creating electronic case filing platforms for pro se litigants, placing self-help kiosks in courts, and making electronic case filing available to non-attorneys.

A 2011 study of United States District Court judges by the Federal Judicial Center found that a large majority of chief judges identified five major problems present in most pro se cases:

1. pleadings or submissions that are unnecessary, illegible, or cannot be understood;
2. problems with pro se litigants' responses to motions to dismiss or for summary judgment;
3. pro se litigants' lack of knowledge about legal decisions or other information that would help their cases;

4. pro se litigants' failure to know when to object to testimony or evidence; and
5. pro se litigants' failure to understand the legal consequences of their actions or inactions (e.g., failure to plead statute of limitation, failure to respond to requests for admissions).[38]

The chief judges also indicated that

> pro se litigants appear to have a difficult time presenting the substance of their cases to the court.
>
> Prisoner and non-prisoner pro se cases do not necessarily present the same issues for chambers. Prisoner cases present special problems in discerning the substance of the case, whereas non-prisoner cases present special issues involving the litigants themselves, who are more likely than prisoner pro se litigants to demand things a court cannot provide or to be irrational, unreasonable, or mentally unstable. Judges identified procedural problems as being present in both prisoner and non-prisoner pro se cases, but they noted that frivolous cases or logistical problems pose more of a problem for prisoner cases.[39]

As a result of the unique problems posed by pro se parties, many judges have implemented special practices or procedures to help pro se cases through the system. Many broadly construe pro se submissions, ignore technical mistakes in pleadings, provide flexibility on deadlines, relax the rules of evidence, and accept letters in lieu of motions. District court judges may also assign preliminary matters to magistrate judges; take a more active role in shepherding the case; and, where necessary, appoint counsel.

Bending the rules for pro se parties might appear unfair. Rule 2.2 of the ABA's Model Code of Judicial Conduct provides that "[a] judge shall uphold and apply the law, and shall perform all duties of judicial office fairly and impartially." While the implementation of more flexible rules for pro se parties might appear to violate this Rule, Comment 4 to Rule 2.2 clarifies that "[i]t is not a violation of this Rule for a judge to make reasonable accommodations to ensure pro se litigants the opportunity to have their matters fairly heard."

Judges continue to struggle with how closely to hold pro se litigants to the same rules that govern licensed attorneys. Some judges are arguably too strict, others perhaps too helpful, and some are frustrated

---

[38] DONNA STIENSTRA, JARED BATAILLON, & JASON A. CANTONE, ASSISTANCE TO PRO SE LITIGANTS IN U.S. DISTRICT COURTS: A REPORT ON SURVEYS OF CLERKS OF COURT AND CHIEF JUDGES vii (2011), http://www.fjc.gov/public/pdf.nsf/lookup/proseusdc.pdf/$file/proseusdc.pdf [https://perma.cc/PU66-PPSP].

[39] *Id.*

by the truly bizarre. All are subject to reversal if they get the balance wrong.

Dioguardi v. Durning

139 F.2d 774 (2d Cir. 1944)

■ CLARK, CIRCUIT JUDGE.

In his complaint, obviously home drawn, plaintiff attempts to assert a series of grievances against the Collector of Customs at the Port of New York growing out of his endeavors to import merchandise from Italy "of great value," consisting of bottles of "tonics." We may pass certain of his claims as either inadequate or inadequately stated and consider only these two: (1) that on the auction day, October 9, 1940, when defendant sold the merchandise at "public custom," "he sold my merchandise to another bidder with my price of $110, and not of his price of $120," and (2) "that three weeks before the sale, two cases, of 19 bottles each case, disappeared." Plaintiff does not make wholly clear how these goods came into the collector's hands, since he alleges compliance with the revenue laws; but he does say he made a claim for "refund of merchandise which was two-thirds paid in Milano, Italy," and that the collector denied the claim. These and other circumstances alleged indicate (what, indeed, plaintiff's brief asserts) that his original dispute was with his consignor as to whether anything more was due upon the merchandise, and that the collector, having held it for a year (presumably as unclaimed merchandise under 19 U.S.C.A. § 1491), then sold it, or such part of it as was left, at public auction. For his asserted injuries plaintiff claimed $5,000 damages, together with interest and costs, against the defendant individually and as collector. This complaint was dismissed by the District Court, with leave, however, to plaintiff to amend, on motion of the United States Attorney, appearing for the defendant, on the ground that it "fails to state facts sufficient to constitute a cause of action."

Thereupon plaintiff filed an amended complaint, wherein, with an obviously heightened conviction that he was being unjustly treated, he vigorously reiterates his claims, including those quoted above and now stated as that his "medicinal extracts" were given to the Springdale Distilling Company "with my betting [bidding?] price of $ 110: and not their price of $120," and "It isnt so easy to do away with two cases with 37 bottles of one quart. Being protected, they can take this chance." An earlier paragraph suggests that defendant had explained the loss of the two cases by "saying that they had leaked, which could never be true in the manner they were bottled." On defendant's motion for dismissal on the same ground as before, the court made a final judgment dismissing the complaint, and plaintiff now comes to us with increased volubility, if not clarity.

It would seem, however, that he has stated enough to withstand a mere formal motion, directed only to the face of the complaint, and that here is another instance of judicial haste which in the long run makes waste. Under the new rules of civil procedure, there is no pleading requirement of stating "facts sufficient to constitute a cause of action," but only that there be "a short and plain statement of the claim showing that the pleader is entitled to relief," Federal Rules of Civil Procedure, rule 8(a); and the motion for dismissal under Rule 12(b) is for failure to state "a claim upon which relief can be granted." The District Court does not state why it concluded that the complaints showed no claim upon which relief could be granted; and the United States Attorney's brief before us does not help us, for it is limited to the prognostication—unfortunately ill founded so far as we are concerned—that "the most cursory examination" of them will show the correctness of the District Court's action.

We think that, however inartistically they may be stated, the plaintiff has disclosed his claims that the collector has converted or otherwise done away with two of his cases of medicinal tonics and has sold the rest in a manner incompatible with the public auction he had announced—and, indeed, required by [federal statute] and the Treasury Regulations promulgated under it. As to this latter claim, it may be that the collector's only error is a failure to collect an additional ten dollars from the Springdale Distilling Company; but giving the plaintiff the benefit of reasonable intendments in his allegations (as we must on this motion), the claim appears to be in effect that he was actually the first bidder at the price for which they were sold, and hence was entitled to the merchandise. Of course, defendant did not need to move on the complaint alone; he could have disclosed the facts from his point of view, in advance of a trial if he chose, by asking for a pre-trial hearing or by moving for a summary judgment with supporting affidavits. But, as it stands, we do not see how the plaintiff may properly be deprived of his day in court to show what he obviously so firmly believes and what for present purposes defendant must be taken as admitting. It appears to be well settled that the collector may be held personally for a default or for negligence in the performance of his duties.

On remand, the District Court may find substance in other claims asserted by plaintiff, which include a failure properly to catalogue the items (as the cited Regulations provide), or to allow plaintiff to buy at a discount from the catalogue price just before the auction sale (a claim whose basis is not apparent), and a violation of an agreement to deliver the merchandise to the plaintiff as soon as he paid for it, by stopping the payments. In view of plaintiff's limited ability to write and speak English, it will be difficult for the District Court to arrive at justice unless he consents to receive legal assistance in the presentation of his case. The record indicates that he refused further help from a lawyer suggested by the court, and his brief (which was a recital of facts, rather than an argument of law) shows distrust of a lawyer of standing at this bar. It is the plaintiff's privilege to decline all legal help; but we fear that he will be indeed ill advised to attempt to meet a motion for summary judgment or other similar presentation of the merits without competent advice and assistance.

Judgment is reversed and the action is remanded for further proceedings not inconsistent with this opinion.

NOTES AND QUESTIONS

1. **Proper Pleading.** *Dioguardi* is the seminal case for interpretation of "notice pleading." Judge Clark was the reporter (the principal draftsman) of the committee that drafted the Federal Rules of Civil Procedure, which went into effect in 1938. Judge Clark explained that the principles of notice pleading were to show the "type of case brought" for further procedural purposes, and to make the claim sufficiently clear to apply res judicata later.[40]

2. **Not Even That.** Many pro se plaintiffs were unable to meet even the relatively low bar set by Rule 8. Kathleen Tokar was a pro se plaintiff who was injured while working for the city of Chicago and was not allowed to return to her former job. She filed suit against the Union after it failed to help her with her employment grievance. In a footnote, the court commented:

> Plaintiff filed a form complaint. The form provides boxes for a plaintiff to check to indicate her claims and blank lines wherein a plaintiff may describe her claims in greater detail. Plaintiff checked nearly every box on the complaint form including ones where the form instructions read "check one." So, for example, plaintiff checked the box accompanying text stating that "[p]laintiff was hired by and is still employed by defendant" and also checked the box stating that "[p]laintiff was employed but is no longer employed by defendant."[41]

The court went on to note other deficiencies in pleading and prosecuting the case:

> First, plaintiff filed several hundred pages of documents with the court in violation of Local Rule 9 which limits briefs in support or opposition to motions to fifteen pages. Second, most of these documents are illegibly handwritten. Third, plaintiff submitted multiple copies of many documents and presented them in a disorderly fashion. Fourth, after spending many hours and days combing through this tall stack of papers, attempting to read them and discern the time line of events leading up to this lawsuit, I found that Tokar hardly alleged any facts supporting a claim for relief. Finally, Tokar frivolously included no fewer than six claims in her complaint that exceeded the scope of her EEOC charge. Unlike the classic case of *Dioguardi v. Durning*, 139 F.2d 774 (2d Cir. 1944) where the plaintiff was a native Italian speaker, Tokar,

[40] Hon. Charles E. Clark, *Simplified Pleading*, 2 F.R.D. 456, 457 (1943).

[41] Tokar v. Int'l Bhd. of Teamsters, Local 726, 1997 U.S. Dist. LEXIS 98, at *2 n.1 (N.D. Ill. Jan. 3, 1997).

an American, did not merely plead "inartfully." Rather, her pleadings and briefs were lengthy beyond reason and yet failed in large measure to state allegations entitling her to relief. All of these defects in addition to the fact that Tokar served defendant late convinces me to dismiss the one remaining claim of disability discrimination. Plaintiff stated in her brief that all she ever wanted was to be reassigned to rodent patrol. Surely there are numerous better ways she could have sought to satisfy this rather modest desire for relief than by submitting hundreds of pages of garbled and irrelevant statements to the court.[42]

3. **A Change of Plan.** *Conley v. Gibson*[43] concluded that Rule 8 merely requires enough to "give the defendant fair notice of what the plaintiff's claim is and the grounds upon which it rests."[44] After *Conley*, a complaint could be dismissed only if "it appears beyond doubt that the plaintiff can prove no set of facts" on which to recover.[45] Fifty years later, in *Bell Atlantic v. Twombly*,[46] the Court decided that the "no set of facts" language should "be retired."[47] The Court now requires "facts to state a claim to relief that is plausible on its face."[48] *Twombly*, however, does not apply equally to pro se plaintiffs.[49]

Erickson v. Pardus

551 U.S. 89 (2007)

■ PER CURIAM.

Imprisoned by the State of Colorado and alleging violations of his Eighth and Fourteenth Amendment protections against cruel and unusual punishment, William Erickson, the petitioner in this Court, filed suit against prison officials in the United States District Court for the District of Colorado. He alleged that a liver condition resulting from hepatitis C required a treatment program that officials had commenced but then wrongfully terminated, with life-threatening consequences. Deeming these allegations, and others to be noted, to be "conclusory," the Court of Appeals for the Tenth Circuit affirmed the District Court's dismissal of petitioner's complaint. The holding departs in so stark a manner from the pleading standard mandated by the Federal Rules of Civil Procedure that we grant review. We vacate the court's judgment and remand the case for further consideration.

---

42 *Id.* at *16–17.

43 355 U.S. 41 (1957).

44 *Id.* at 47.

45 *Id.* at 45–46.

46 550 U.S. 544 (2007).

47 *Id.* at 578–79.

48 *Id.* at 570.

49 *See, e.g.*, Loaisiga-Cruz v. Hosp. San Juan Bautista, 681 F. Supp. 2d 130 (D.P.R. 2010) (dismissing a pro se complaint because even the *Conley* standard was met when the complaint showed there could be no recovery against the defendant hospital).

Petitioner based his claim on the following allegations, which we assume to be true for purposes of review here: Officials at Colorado's Department of Corrections (Department) diagnosed petitioner as requiring treatment for hepatitis C. After completing the necessary classes and otherwise complying with the protocols set forth by the Department, petitioner began treatment for the disease. The treatment, which would take a year to complete, involved weekly self-injections of medication by use of a syringe Soon after petitioner began this treatment, prison officials were unable to account for one of the syringes made available to petitioner (and other prisoners) for medical purposes. Upon searching, they found it in a communal trash can, modified in a manner suggestive of use for injection of illegal drugs.

Prison officials, disbelieving petitioner's claim not to have taken the syringe, found that his conduct constituted a violation of the Colorado Code of Penal Discipline for possession of drug paraphernalia. This conduct, according to the officials, led to the "reasonable inference" that petitioner had intended to use drugs, so the officials removed petitioner from his hepatitis C treatment. "The successful treatment of Hepatitis C is incumbent upon the individual remaining drug and alcohol free to give the liver a better chance of recovery," they indicated, an explanation they later offered to defend against petitioner's allegations of cruel and unusual punishment [in the motion to dismiss]. Assuming that a person in the course of this treatment takes illicit drugs, the prison's protocol mandates a waiting period of one year followed by a mandatory drug education class lasting six months. Petitioner therefore could face a delay of some 18 months before he would be able to restart treatment.

In his complaint petitioner alleged Dr. Bloor had "removed [him] from [his] hepatitis C treatment" in violation of Department protocol, "thus endangering [his] life." Petitioner attached to the complaint certain grievance forms. In these he claimed, among other things, he was suffering from "continued damage to [his] liver" as a result of the nontreatment. The complaint requested relief including damages and an injunction requiring that the Department treat petitioner for hepatitis C "under the standards of the treatment [protocol] established by [the Department]."

Three months after filing his complaint, and well before the District Court entered a judgment against him, petitioner filed a Motion for Expedited Review. Indicating it was "undisputed" that he had hepatitis C, that he met the Department's standards for treatment of the disease, and that "furtherance of this disease can cause irreversible damage to [his] liver and possible death," petitioner alleged that "numerous inmates" in his prison community had died of the disease and that he was "in imminent danger" himself "due to [the Department's] refusal to treat him." He had identified similar allegations in an earlier filing, explaining that "his liver is suffering irreversible damage" due to the decision to remove him from treatment and that he "will suffer irreparable damage if his disease goes untreated."

Respondents answered these filings with a motion to dismiss. The Magistrate Judge recommended, as relevant, that the District Court dismiss the complaint on the ground it failed to allege Dr. Bloor's actions had caused petitioner "substantial harm." The District Court issued a short order indicating its agreement with the Magistrate Judge and dismissing the complaint.

The Court of Appeals affirmed.

It may in the final analysis be shown that the District Court was correct to grant respondents' motion to dismiss. That is not the issue here, however. It was error for the Court of Appeals to conclude that the allegations in question, concerning harm caused petitioner by the termination of his medication, were too conclusory to establish for pleading purposes that petitioner had suffered "a cognizable independent harm" as a result of his removal from the hepatitis C treatment program.

Federal Rule of Civil Procedure 8(a)(2) requires only "a short and plain statement of the claim showing that the pleader is entitled to relief." Specific facts are not necessary; the statement need only "give the defendant fair notice of what the . . . claim is and the grounds upon which it rests."

The complaint stated that Dr. Bloor's decision to remove petitioner from his prescribed hepatitis C medication was "endangering [his] life." It alleged this medication was withheld "shortly after" petitioner had commenced a treatment program that would take one year, that he was "still in need of treatment for this disease," and that the prison officials were in the meantime refusing to provide treatment. This alone was enough to satisfy Rule 8(a)(2). Petitioner, in addition, bolstered his claim by making more specific allegations in documents attached to the complaint and in later filings.

The Court of Appeals' departure from the liberal pleading standards set forth by Rule 8(a)(2) is even more pronounced in this particular case because petitioner has been proceeding, from the litigation's outset, without counsel. A document filed *pro se* is to be liberally construed, and a *pro se* complaint, however inartfully pleaded, must be held to less stringent standards than formal pleadings drafted by lawyers. *Cf.* Fed. Rule Civ. Proc. 8(f) ("All pleadings shall be so construed as to do substantial justice").

Whether petitioner's complaint is sufficient in all respects is a matter yet to be determined, for respondents raised multiple arguments in their motion to dismiss. In particular, the proper application of the controlling legal principles to the facts is yet to be determined. The case cannot, however, be dismissed on the ground that petitioner's allegations of harm were too conclusory to put these matters in issue. Certiorari and leave to proceed *in forma pauperis* are granted, the judgment of the Court of Appeals is vacated, and the case is remanded for further proceedings consistent with this opinion.

It is so ordered.

Rowe v. Gibson

798 F.3d 622 (7th Cir. 2015)

■ POSNER, CIRCUIT JUDGE.

An Indiana prison inmate named Jeffrey Rowe, the plaintiff in this suit under 42 U.S.C. § 1983, charges administrators and prison staff with deliberate indifference to a serious medical need—that is, with knowing of a serious risk to inmate health or safety but responding ineffectually (as by departing substantially from accepted professional judgment) or not at all. Rowe charges gratuitous infliction of physical pain and potentially very serious medical harm—cogent examples of cruel and unusual punishment. The district judge granted summary judgment in favor of the defendants on both claims, dismissing Rowe's suit and precipitating this appeal.

In 2009, already an inmate at Pendleton, Rowe was diagnosed with reflux esophagitis, also known as gastroesophageal reflux disease (GERD). *See* National Institutes of Health, "Gastroesophageal reflux disease," www.nlm.nih.gov/medlineplus/ency/article/000265.htm (visited August 17, 2015, as were the other websites cited in this opinion). The Mayo Clinic explains that "a valve-like structure called the lower esophageal sphincter usually keeps the acidic contents of the stomach out of the esophagus. If this valve opens when it shouldn't or doesn't close properly, the contents of the stomach may back up into the esophagus (gastroesophageal reflux). . . . [GERD] is a condition in which this backflow of acid is a frequent or ongoing problem. A complication of GERD is chronic inflammation and tissue damage in the esophagus." Mayo Clinic, "Diseases and Conditions, Esophagitis: Reflux Esophagitis," www.mayoclinic.org/diseases-conditions/esophagitis/basics/causes/con–20034313. As we explained in a recent case in which, as in this case, a prison inmate complained of failure to treat his GERD (and we reversed the grant of summary judgment in favor of the prison staff), "GERD can . . . produce persistent, agonizing pain and discomfort. It can also produce 'serious complications. Esophagitis can occur as a result of too much stomach acid in the esophagus. Esophagitis may cause esophageal bleeding or ulcers. In addition, a narrowing or stricture of the esophagus may occur from chronic scarring. Some people develop a condition known as Barrett's esophagus. This condition can increase the risk of esophageal cancer.' WebMD, Heartburn/GERD Health Center, "What Are the Complications of Long-Term GERD?" www.webmd.com/heartburn-gerd/guide/reflux-disease-gerd1?page=4. Miller v. Campanella, 794 F.3d 878, 880, 2015 WL 4523799, at *2 (7th Cir. July 27, 2015). Rowe complains of pain based on neglect of his need for symptomatic relief; continued neglect will endanger him more profoundly.

The prison physician who diagnosed Rowe with GERD told him to take a 150-milligram Zantac pill twice a day. Zantac inhibits the production of stomach acid and is commonly used to treat esophagitis (as we'll abbreviate the name of Rowe's disease). Although technically "Zantac" is merely the trade name for ranitidine manufactured by GlaxoSmithKline (in prescription strengths) and Boehringer Ingelheim (in over-the-counter strengths), it is often used as a synonym for ranitidine, see Wikipedia, "Ranitidine," http://en.wikipedia.org/wiki/Ranitidine, because Glaxo was the first, and remains the best-known, manufacturer. "Zantac" is the only word for the drug that appears in the briefs, and so we too will call the drug that Rowe received "Zantac."

After the diagnosis Rowe was given Zantac pills and was permitted to keep them in his cell and take them when he felt the need to. This regimen continued for more than a year. But in January 2011 his pills were confiscated and he was told that he would be allowed to take a Zantac pill only when a prison nurse gave it to him, and that would be at 9:30 a.m. and then at 9:30 p.m. He complained that he needed to take Zantac with his meals, which were, oddly enough, scheduled by the prison for 4 a.m. and 4 p.m. (why these times, we are not told). The prison had decided that inmates such as Rowe who take psychiatric medications should not be allowed to keep any pills in their cells—yet the head of health care at the prison told Rowe that he could keep in his cell (and thus take whenever he wanted) any Zantac pills that he bought at the prison commissary—which, however, as we're about to see, he couldn't afford. No reason has been articulated for forbidding him to keep Zantac given him by prison staff while permitting him to keep Zantac that he bought at the commissary and take it whenever he needs to in order to prevent or alleviate pain. There is no suggestion that Zantac is a narcotic or otherwise consumed for nonmedical as well as medical reasons.

The defendants question Rowe's inability to pay for the pills. They point out that in one 13-month period he spent approximately $60 at the commissary. But the prison commissary charges $3.28 for just four 75-mg Zantac pills (and recall that Rowe was to take two 150-mg pills daily), meaning that he would have to pay almost $1300 for a 13-month supply. And he was forbidden to buy more than eight days' worth of Zantac a month from the commissary, which was only about a quarter of the amount that he needed.

To continue the narrative of what seems a senseless series of decisions by the prison's medical staff, as well as heartless given what the staff knew about the disease and Rowe's continuous claims of severe pain: at the beginning of July 2011, a month after he filed suit, he ceased receiving Zantac because his "prescription" (that is, his authorization to receive over-the-counter Zantac free of charge on a continuing basis) had lapsed. He made a series of requests for the drug beginning on July 3, but the nurse defendants denied all of them because he had no prescription. When he complained he was told by the administrative director of the medical staff: "Your chronic care condition does not warrant the continued use of Zantac. The continual use of over-the-counter medications can create further health problems in many instances. You will have to purchase this off of commissary if you wish to continue taking it." Notice the contradiction (illustrating the run around to which Rowe was continually subjected) in denying Rowe free Zantac because it could create "further health problems" but permitting him to buy and use it at will, though he couldn't afford to buy it. Nor is there any suggestion that Zantac is one of the over-the-counter medications that can create health problems if taken daily for a protracted period of time. And finally, if over-the-counter medicines are to be barred, why wasn't Rowe given a prescription for 300-mg Zantac pills; these are not only prescription rather than over-the-counter drugs but one such pill a day may be sufficient to control one's GERD, compared to two or more when an over-the-counter strength Zantac is prescribed.

On July 13, 2011, in response to Rowe's continued requests for a renewed prescription for Zantac, a physician who works at the prison (though employed by Corizon) named William H. Wolfe, whose professional specialty is preventive medicine, about which see American College of Preventive Medicine: Physicians Dedicated to Prevention, www.acpm.org/, rather than gastroenterology, see healthgrades, "Dr. William H. Wolfe, MD.," www. healthgrades.com/physician/dr–william–wolfe–2fgkl/background–check, and who is a frequent defendant in prisoner civil rights suits, reviewed Rowe's medical records and opined that his condition didn't require Zantac at all—this despite the fact that Rowe had been continuously prescribed Zantac for almost two years and that Wolfe himself had been the prescribing doctor for a quarter of that period. But though initially refusing to provide a new prescription for Zantac, Wolfe later relented and on August 2 prescribed it though he later stated in an affidavit that he had done so as a "courtesy" to Rowe and not out of medical necessity. (Prescribing drugs for prison inmates as a "courtesy" seems very odd; it is not explained.) The upshot was that Rowe had no access to Zantac for more than a month (between July 1 and August 3)—a significant deprivation. Even after Zantac was restored to him, he continued to be allowed to take it only at 9:30 a.m. and 9:30 p.m., both times being many hours distant from his meals.

In another affidavit Wolfe stated that "it does not matter what time of day Mr. Rowe receives his Zantac prescription. Each Zantac pill is fully effective for twelve hour increments. Zantac does not have to be taken before or with a meal to be effective." However, according to Boehringer Ingelheim, the manufacturer of over-the-counter Zantac, while Zantac can be taken at any time "to relieve symptoms," in order "to prevent symptoms" it should be taken "30 to 60 minutes before eating food or drinking beverages that cause heartburn." Zantac, "Maximum Strength

Zantac 150," www.zantacotc.com/zantac-maximumstrength.html#faqs, and this advice is repeated on the labels of the boxes in which over-the-counter Zantac is sold. Were Zantac equipotent whenever taken, the manufacturer would not tell consumers to take it 30 to 60 minutes before eating, for having to remember when to take a pill adds a complication that the consumer would rather do without. There is thus no reason for the manufacturer to be lying, and it would be absurd to think that Dr. Wolfe, a defendant who is not a gastroenterologist, knows more about treatment of esophagitis with Zantac than the manufacturer does.

Rowe's aim was pain prevention, so having to take Zantac six and a half hours before a meal did not do the trick. It left him in pain for five and a half hours during and after the meal, until he got his next Zantac pill. Wolfe's statement that "each Zantac pill is fully effective for twelve hour increments" is also contradicted by the Zantac website, which states that one 150-mg pill "lasts up to 12 hours" (emphasis added). Thus a pill taken six and half hours before a meal might not be effective in alleviating the pain caused by acid secretions stimulated by the meal.

It might be thought that a corporate website, such as that of the Zantac manufacturer, would be a suspect source of information. Not so; the manufacturer would be taking grave risks if it misrepresented the properties of its product. In any event, the Mayo Clinic's website, as we'll see in a moment, confirms the manufacturer's claims.

Wolfe's affidavit states that Rowe was complaining just of "alleged heartburn [that] was not a serious medical condition warranting a prescription for Zantac"—but if so why did he prescribe Zantac for Rowe during the very period in which, according to the affidavit, Rowe's condition was not serious? (The affidavit fails to mention that it was Wolfe who had prescribed Zantac for Rowe, but that's conceded.)

It's true that the Mayo Clinic's website, at "Drugs and Supplements: Histamine H2 Antagonist (Oral Route, Injection Route, Intravenous Route)," www.mayoclinic.org/drugs–supplements/histamine–h2–antagonist–oralroute–injection–route–intravenous–route/proper–use/drg–20068584, after listing various drugs (including ranitidine) for treatment of the cluster of ailments that includes esophagitis, states that "for this class of drugs . . . patients taking two doses a day are instructed: 'Take one in the morning and one before bedtime.' " But this dosing, Mayo goes on to state, is appropriate "only for patients taking the prescription strengths of these medicines." The 150-mg pills that Rowe was taking are available over the counter; a prescription is required only for the 300-mg version. Both the Boehringer Ingelheim and Mayo websites also say that the patient shouldn't take Zantac for more than two weeks unless directed by a doctor—but Rowe was of course directed by Wolfe, as well as by other doctors earlier, to take Zantac on a continuing basis.

Not only wasn't Rowe allowed to take Zantac with his meals; he was not, as the Mayo website recommends, allowed to take it with water a half hour or an hour before eating a meal or drinking beverages that might cause him esophageal pain. As the Mayo website explains, for "adults and teenagers-150 mg with water taken thirty to sixty minutes before eating a meal or drinking beverages you expect to cause symptoms. Do not take more than 300 mg in twenty-four hours" (emphasis added).

Stomach acid is of course integral to the digestion of food, and indeed thirty percent of total gastric acid secretion is stimulated by the anticipation, smell, and taste of food, before the food ever reaches the stomach. Thomas A. Miller, Modern Surgical Care: Physiologic Foundations and Clinical Applications 344–45 (2006). "The foods you eat affect the amount of acid your stomach produces," and "many people with GERD find that certain foods trigger their symptoms." Healthline, "Diet and Nutrition for GERD," www.healthline.com/health/gerd/diet nutrition#Overview1. So it is no surprise that Rowe experiences painful symptoms when he eats without having been allowed to take a Zantac pill shortly before the meal.

The Physicians' Desk Reference, "PDR Search: Full Prescribing Information: Zantac 150 and 300 Tablets," www.pdr.net/full–prescribing information/zantac–150–and–300–tablets?druglabelid=241, states that a 150-mg dose of Zantac inhibits 79 percent of food-stimulated acid secretion for up to three hours after it's taken. This implies that the drug's efficacy decreases over time and so supports Rowe's claim *627 that a 150-mg dose does not suppress his food-stimulated acid secretions when taken six and a half hours before a meal. The Physicians' Desk Reference also says that "symptomatic relief commonly occurs within 24 hours after starting therapy with ZANTAC 150 mg twice daily," which could be misread to mean that it does not matter what time of day the pills are taken, but which actually means that it takes a day for the body to recognize Zantac as a source of relief from esophageal distress. This interpretation is confirmed by Mayo, which states (at the website cited earlier): "It may take several days before this medicine begins to relieve stomach pain."

The evidence that Rowe was in pain for five and a half hours after eating is his repeated attestation—in his verified federal complaint and his declarations—that he experienced pain for that length of time when he was not allowed to take Zantac with or shortly before his meals. For purposes of summary judgment his attestations of extreme pain must be credited. *See* 28 U.S.C. § 1746; Fed.R.Civ.P. 56(c). There was no plausible contrary evidence. The affidavits of the only expert witness on the proper times at which to take Zantac, defendants' witness Wolfe, were highly vulnerable. Wolfe is not a gastroenterologist. He says that Rowe didn't need Zantac yet prescribed Zantac for him. He opined with confidence about what Rowe needed or didn't need—yet never examined him—and offered no basis for his off-the-cuff medical opinion. A court should not admit opinion evidence that is connected to existing data only by the ipse dixit of the expert.

Remember that Rowe had been diagnosed with esophagitis back in 2009 and that for the ensuing two years physicians had prescribed Zantac to treat his condition. Furthermore, the Indiana Department of Correction permits such continuous treatment only to treat a serious health condition, so presumably the prescribing physicians thought Rowe's condition serious. None of this evidence or inference is undermined by Dr. Wolfe's evidence.

A member of a prison's staff is deliberately indifferent and thus potentially liable to an inmate if he knows of and disregards an excessive risk to inmate health. [The court holds there is "substantial evidence" of deliberate indifference on the part of Dr. Wolfe and some of the other prison medical staff.]

. . . .

In citing even highly reputable medical websites in support of our conclusion that summary judgment was premature we may be thought to be "going outside the record" in an improper sense. It may be said that judges should confine their role to choosing between the evidentiary presentations of the opposing parties, much like referees of athletic events. But judges and their law clerks often conduct research on cases, and it is not always research confined to pure issues of law, without disclosure to the parties. We are not like the English judges of yore, who under the rule of "orality" were not permitted to have law clerks or other staff, or libraries, or even to deliberate—at the end of the oral argument in an appeal the judges would state their views seriatim as to the proper outcome of the appeal.

We don't insulate judges like that, but we must observe proper limitations on judicial research. We must acknowledge the need to distinguish between judicial web searches for mere background information that will help the judges and the readers of their opinions understand the case, web searches for facts or other information that judges can properly take judicial notice of (such as when it became dark on a specific night, a question we answered on the basis of an Internet search in Owens v. Duncan, 781 F.3d 360, 362 (7th Cir.2015), and web searches for facts normally determined by the factfinder after an adversary procedure that produces a district court or administrative record. When medical information can be gleaned from the websites of highly reputable medical centers, it is not imperative that it instead be presented by a testifying witness. Such information tends to fall somewhere between facts that require adversary procedure to determine and facts of which a court can take judicial notice, but it is closer to the second in a case like this in which the evidence presented by the defendants in the district court was sparse and the appellate court need only determine whether there is a factual dispute sufficient to preclude summary judgment.

Rule 201 of the Federal Rules of Evidence makes facts of which judicial notice is properly taken conclusive, and therefore requires that their accuracy be indisputable for judicial notice to be taken of them. We are not deeming the Internet evidence cited in this opinion conclusive or even certifying it as being probably correct, though it may well be correct since it is drawn from reputable medical websites. We use it only to underscore the existence of a genuine dispute of material fact created in the district court proceedings by entirely conventional evidence, namely Rowe's reported pain.

There is a high standard for taking judicial notice of a fact, and a low standard for allowing evidence to be presented in the conventional way, by testimony subject to cross-examination, but is there no room for anything in between? Must judges abjure visits to Internet web sites of premier hospitals and drug companies, not in order to take judicial notice but to assure the existence of a genuine issue of material fact that precludes summary judgment? Are we to forbear lest we be accused of having "entered unknown territory"? This year the bar associations are busy celebrating the eight hundredth anniversary of Magna Carta. The barons who forced King John to sign that notable document were certainly entering unknown territory, and risking their lives to boot. Shall the unreliability of the unalloyed adversary process in a case of such dramatic inequality of resources and capabilities of the parties as this case be an unalterable bar to justice? Must our system of justice allow the muddled affidavit of a defendant who may well be unqualified to be an expert witness in this case to carry the day against a pro se plaintiff helpless to contest the affidavit?

It is heartless to make a fetish of adversary procedure if by doing so feeble evidence is credited because the opponent has no practical access to offsetting evidence. To say for example that however implausible Dr. Wolfe's evidence is, it must be accepted because not contested, is to doom the plaintiff's case regardless of the merits simply because the plaintiff lacks the wherewithal to obtain and present conflicting evidence. Rowe did not move to exclude Wolfe as an expert witness on the ground that Wolfe neither qualified to give expert evidence in this case (because he is not a gastroenterologist) nor, as a defendant, was likely to be even minimally impartial. But Rowe does not have the legal knowledge that would enable him to file such a motion.

We have decided to reverse the judgment. We base this decision on Rowe's declarations, the timeline of his inability to obtain Zantac, the manifold contradictions in Dr. Wolfe's affidavits, and, last, the cautious, limited Internet research that we have conducted in default of the parties' having done so. We add that the judge erred not only by giving undue weight to Wolfe's internally contradictory affidavit but also by relying on a defendant (Wolfe) as the expert witness. There are expert witnesses offered by parties and neutral (court-appointed) expert witnesses, but defendants serving as expert witnesses?—and in cases in which the plaintiff doesn't have an expert witness because he doesn't know how to find such a witness and anyway couldn't afford to pay the witness? And how could an unrepresented prisoner be expected to challenge the affidavit of a hostile medical doctor (in this case really hostile since he's a defendant in the plaintiff's suit) effectively? Is this adversary procedure?

Rowe's allegations alone were sufficient to preclude summary judgment, and were enhanced by the defendants' own evidence, which included both Wolfe's contradictory evidence (among other things, he asserted that Rowe does not need Zantac and yet prescribed it for him) and the absurd opinion by the medical director that over-the-counter medications should not be provided to prisoners. Allowing Wolfe to be an expert witness in the case despite his being a defendant and not practicing the medical specialty at issue was another boost to the plaintiff's case, though again not one that an unrepresented, indigent prisoner could exploit.

We are coming to the end of this long opinion but we need to change gears for a moment: Besides arguing deliberate indifference to a serious medical need, Rowe accuses several of the defendants, in particular Dr. Wolfe and Nurse Bagienski, of retaliating against him for filing a lawsuit. He says they told him that going without Zantac for a month would make him "think twice about bringing lawsuits about inadequate medical care." If indeed they said this—an issue that cannot be determined without a trial—Rowe has a solid claim of retaliation.

Although reversing, we are not ordering that judgment be entered in Rowe's favor. As we've explained, we are not invoking Fed.R.Evid. 201 and thus not taking judicial notice of any facts outside the district court record. The remaining defendants are entitled to try to rebut any evidence whether or not presented in the district court, including any evidence found on the Internet. Like the conventional forms of evidentiary inquiry, Internet research must be conducted with circumspection. In particular it must not be allowed to extinguish reasonable opportunities for rebuttal.

Because of the profound handicaps under which the plaintiff is litigating and the fact that his claim is far from frivolous, we urge the district judge to give serious consideration to recruiting a lawyer to represent Rowe; appointing a neutral expert witness, authorized by Fed.R.Evid. 706, to address the medical issues in the case; or doing both. We are mindful that district courts don't have budgets for paying expert witnesses. But the medical issues in the case are not complex; there should be no difficulty in the judge's persuading a reputable gastroenterologist to speak to Rowe and some of the prison medical personnel (Rowe's prison is only 30 miles from Indianapolis, and there are 128 gastroenterologists in or near Indianapolis, healthgrades, www.healthgrades.com/gastroenterology-directory/in-indiana/indianapolis), to sit for a deposition, and, if necessary, to testify. Rule 706(c)(2) states that a court-appointed expert "is entitled to a reasonable compensation, as set by the court," and that "the compensation is payable . . . in any . . .

civil case [not involving just compensation under the Fifth Amendment] by the parties in the proportion and at the time that the court directs—and the compensation is then charged like other costs." In light of Rowe's indigency, the court if it appoints its own expert witness will have to order the defendants to pay the expert a reasonable fee if the expert is unwilling to work for nothing. Most prisons are strapped for cash, and this is something for the district court to bear in mind in deciding on whether and how large a fee to order the defendants to pay a court-appointed expert witness in a case (such as this case) that has sufficient merit to warrant such an appointment.

A substantial academic literature identifies serious deficiencies in the provision of health care in American prisons and jails. See, e.g., Andrew P. Wilper et al., "The Health and Health Care of U.S. Prisoners: Results of a Nationwide Survey," 99 Am. J. Public Health 666 (2009), and the studies posted by the Academic Consortium on Criminal Justice Health, www.accjh.org/. On the quality of treatment problems of Corizon, the employer of Dr. Wolfe and the other medical staff members sued by Rowe, see David Royse, "Medical Battle Behind Bars: Big Prison Healthcare Firm Corizon Struggles to Win Contracts," April 11, 2015, www.modernhealthcare.com/article/20150411/MAGAZINE/304119981; also Human Rights Defense Center, Prison Legal News, "Corizon Needs a Checkup: Problems with Privatized Correctional Healthcare," March 2014, www.prisonlegalnews.org/news/2014/mar/15/corizon-needs-a-checkup-problems-with-privatized-correctionalhealthcare/. The present case illustrates the problems that this literature has identified.

AFFIRMED IN PART, REVERSED IN PART, AND REMANDED

■ HAMILTON, CIRCUIT JUDGE, concurring in part and dissenting in part.

I agree with the majority's disposition of most claims and issues: affirming summary judgment for defendants on several claims and reversing on Rowe's retaliation claim and his claim for complete denial of his Zantac medicine for 33 days in July and August 2011.

I must dissent, however, from the reversal of summary judgment on Rowe's claim regarding the timing for administering his medicine between January and July 2011 and after August 2011. On that claim, the reversal is unprecedented, clearly based on "evidence" this appellate court has found by its own internet research. The majority has pieced together information found on several medical websites that seems to contradict the only expert evidence actually in the summary judgment record. With that information, the majority finds a genuine issue of material fact on whether the timing of Rowe's Zantac doses amounted to deliberate indifference to a serious health need, and reverses summary judgment. (The majority denies at a couple of points that its internet research actually makes a difference to the outcome of the case, but when the opinion is read as a whole, the decisive role of the majority's internet research is plain.)

The majority writes that adherence to rules of evidence and precedent makes a "heartless . . . fetish of adversary procedure." Yet the majority's decision is an unprecedented departure from the proper role of an appellate court. It runs contrary to long-established law and raises a host of practical problems the majority fails to address.

NOTES AND QUESTIONS

1. **Twice as Nice.** Linda Reed, a pro se plaintiff, had at least two separate lawsuits that went to the Seventh Circuit. Reed had tardive dyskinesia, a neurological condition characterized by involuntary movements. She also suffered from post-traumatic stress disorder, bipolar disorder, and severe anxiety. In the first case, Reed filed a personal injury suit.[50] Reed requested six accommodations at trial: a note-taker, podium, additional recesses, interpreter, microphone, and a jury instruction on her disability. The court granted the first three requests and denied the last three. After Reed lost at trial, she appealed to the Illinois Court of Appeals. Before that court could rule, she filed a separate federal suit arguing that the lack of accommodations "rendered her communications less effective than her defense attorney counterpart, who [did] not have the same impairments."[51] The second lawsuit was dismissed by the federal district court, which held that her claims were barred by collateral estoppel. The Seventh Circuit, however, reversed.[52] It concluded that, while the threshold elements of collateral estoppel were satisfied, equity—based on her disability and pro se status—required the court to hear her claims.

Reed, again pro se, later sued Columbia St. Mary's Hospital alleging that the hospital discriminated against her on the basis of her disability during her stay there.[53] The federal district court dismissed her claims without prejudice, concluding that even an amended complaint failed to state a claim for relief under Federal Rule of Civil Procedure 8(a)(2). Less than a month later, Reed filed the same case in the same court but before a new judge. In it, she expanded on the allegations deemed insufficient in the first case. The second case was also dismissed at screening. Reed appealed the dismissal, and the Seventh Circuit again reversed. On remand the district court agreed to attempt to recruit appointed counsel, noting that although "there is no right to court-appointed counsel in federal civil litigation, a district court has discretion to recruit counsel to represent an indigent plaintiff under 28 U.S.C. § 1915(e)(1)."[54]

To what extent do Linda Reed's cases represent the average pro se party? Does her repeated success in the Seventh Circuit indicate that she doesn't need the help of counsel to litigate, or are her appeals representative of the problems experienced by pro se parties?

---

[50] Reed v. Moore, 2012 IL App 113442–U.

[51] Reed v. Illinois, 2014 U.S. Dist. LEXIS 30381, at *3–4 (N.D. Ill. Mar. 10, 2014).

[52] Reed v. Illinois, 808 F.3d 1103 (7th Cir. 2015).

[53] Reed v. Columbia St. Mary's Hospital, 782 F.3d 331 (7th Cir. 2015).

[54] Reed v. Columbia St. Mary's Hospital, 2015 U.S. Dist. LEXIS 53998, at *4–5 (E.D. Wis. Apr. 24, 2015).

1. SOVEREIGN CITIZENS

Perhaps no pro se cases are as frustrating as sovereign citizen cases. The sovereign citizen movement is nurtured on the internet, and its members hold bizarre and complex antigovernment beliefs. Its adherents believe that they are not subject to the laws of any governmental body or the jurisdiction of the courts. They believe they are not required to pay taxes or adhere to regulatory requirements such as getting driver's licenses or social security cards. Some sovereign citizens file innumerable false tax returns, spurious lawsuits, and false liens against officials' homes for perceived wrongs. Eliminating these liens to clear the officials' title to their property can be not only time-consuming but expensive as well.[55]

When called to account in federal court, they often file strange and incoherent pleadings, full of archaic and irrelevant references. The information comes from sovereign citizen law lessons sold on-line, and pleadings often cite the Uniform Commercial Code, maritime law, and the Bible. Their copious filings can double the size of a normal docket.[56]

United States v. Hakeem El Bey

No. 1:14-cr-00447 (N.D. Ill. Feb. 20, 2015) ECF No. 46

ORDER OF FEBRUARY 20, 2015

Defendant Hakeem El Bey has been indicted by the federal government for defrauding and attempting to defraud the Internal Revenue Service in violation of Title 18 of the federal code. I have been assigned to conduct his trial, which is scheduled to begin on March 2. The defendant has chosen to represent himself, as he is entitled to do provided he is at least minimally competent. I appointed standby counsel as a resource to the defendant in preparing his case.

I have been concerned by a series of affidavits that the defendant has filed over the course of the pretrial proceedings, and statements that he has made at our preconference hearings. As I have reminded him repeatedly, most recently in an order of February 12, he must not at trial attempt to introduce evidence, testimony, or argument regarding the Uniform Commercial Code, the Federal Rules of Civil Procedure, admiralty and maritime law, or the Foreign Sovereign Immunities Act.

---

[55] *See* Erica Goode, *In Paper War, Flood of Liens Is the Weapon*, N.Y. TIMES (Aug. 23, 2013), http://www.nytimes.com/2013/08/24/us/citizens-without-a-country-wage-battle-with-liens.html?_r=0 [https://perma.cc/6KGZ-465B]; *see also* Bill Morlin, *Sovereign Citizen Gets 10 Years for Filing Bogus Liens*, S. POVERTY LAW CTR (Dec. 7, 2015), https://www.splcenter.org/hatewatch/2015/12/07/sovereign-citizen-gets-10-years-filing-bogus-liens [https://perma.cc/5ET3-C3UY ("Tyrone Eugene Jordan, described as an antigovernment sovereign citizen, will spend 10 years in prison for filing $6.5 million in bogus liens against a federal judge and prosecutor.").

[56] Lorelei Laird, *'Sovereign citizens' plaster courts with bogus legal filings—and some turn to violence*, A.B.A.J. (May 1, 2014, 10:20 AM), http://www.abajournal.com/magazine/article/sovereign_citizens_plaster_courts_with_bogus_legal_filings/ [https://perma.cc/5NZP-TLW7]

These bodies of law are totally irrelevant to this criminal prosecution. Nor may he argue at trial that this court lacks jurisdiction over him because he is a "sovereign citizen" or citizen of the Cherokee nation (he is in fact a U.S. citizen), that the U.S. Government is a corporation or is insolvent, or that the Internal Revenue Service has been dismantled. These are all utterly irrelevant and frivolous contentions.

But I seem unable to convince him, and I am losing confidence that he will obey my order. Since I issued it he has submitted two additional affidavits. The first, dated the day before the issuance of the order I just mentioned, asks that the government pay him $367,500 in "redemption" of damages he has suffered as a result of property theft and kidnapping (by whom not specified, though he seems to be accusing the government). He also asserts "Lack of Jurisdiction over the Person (contracted Artificial Subject vs Natural Borne)"—whatever that means. He also asserts that "Queen of England, entered into a Treaty with the Federal Government For the Taxing of Alcoholic beverages and cigarettes sold in America. The Treaty is called—The Stamp Act and in this Act, the Queen ordained that her Subject, the American people, are Exonerated of all other Federal Taxes. So the Federal Income Tax and the State Income Taxes Levied against all Americans is Contrary to an International Treaty and against the Sovereign Orders of the Queen."

The Stamp Act was enacted by the Parliament of Great Britain in 1765. It did not relieve Americans of any taxes; on the contrary, it imposed a comprehensive tax on the use of paper by Americans. The Act was not a treaty between Britain and the federal government of the United States, for there was no United States; there were just the 13 British colonies that 11 years later declared independence from Great Britain. There were no federal taxes that the Act could have relieved Americans from having to pay. The sovereign of Britain at the time was a King, not a Queen; the King's wife (Princess Charlotte of Mecklenburg-Strelitz) was Great Britain's Queen but had no governmental authority.

In the defendant's second recent filing, signed several days after this Court's February 12 Order, the defendant once again asks the Court to dismiss the case for want of jurisdiction, invokes the Uniform Commercial Code and the Foreign Sovereign Immunities Act, and claims that the proper court to hear this case is the Court of International Trade. This filing borders on incoherence, as where it states "This Case Reference to 28 USC–2461, since all Tax Revenue case are done 'within the Admiralty.' Court of International Trade is the proper Jurisdiction. The Foreign Sovereign Immunity Act—This provision as Application since the Foreign Sovereign—Judge—Clerk Attorney and Agents ect [*sic*], are Liable for Damages while doing business in the United States." In this filing he also asks for $367,500 in damages.

If as is increasingly becoming apparent, the defendant refuses to refrain from injecting utterly irrelevant, patently inaccurate, and sometimes unintelligible contentions into this case, I will not be able to allow him to represent himself at the trial. I do not believe that he is mentally deficient; indeed he strikes me as an intelligent person, and he has been unfailingly polite at our pretrial conferences.

I want him to have a fair trial. He cannot have a fair trial if as I fear his defense will be based solely on the "affidavits of truth" that culminate with the latest two such affidavits summarized above. A defendant who has the cognitive ability to represent himself in a legal proceeding but refuses to confine his defense to testimony and other evidence, and to argument, that are permissible in a legal proceeding—refuses in effect to cooperate with the court and obey the law governing the proceeding—forfeits his right to defend himself. I reaffirm my order of February 12 and thus remind the defendant that he will not be permitted to present at trial the arguments to which I have referred, however deeply and sincerely he believes them to be valid.

CHAPTER 8

JUDICIAL POWER & INDEPENDENCE

> All the rights secured to the citizens under the Constitution are worth nothing, and a mere buble [sic], except guaranteed to them by an independent and virtuous Judiciary.[1]
>
> – President Andrew Jackson

§ 8.1 THE HISTORY OF JUDICIAL INDEPENDENCE

The phrase "judicial independence" means different things to different people. To some, it means a judiciary that is separate from, and not beholden to, the executive or legislative branches. To others, it means a judiciary that is free to make unpopular decisions, ensuring that the minority is protected from the tyranny of the majority[2] and "that the strong might not harm the weak."[3]

The American system, in which federal judges are independent of the other branches as well as the people, has its roots in British history. Its boundaries have been repeatedly tested over the past 225 years.

A. THE BRITISH EXPERIENCE

In the mid-18th century, Britain and most European parliamentary systems blended the legislative and executive functions. For much of British history, the judiciary likewise answered to the Crown. From 1178, when Henry II formalized a small court system, until 1701, British judges were considered "Lions under the King's Throne."[4] They served at the pleasure of the sovereign and were often removed for failing to rule as the sovereign wished.

That changed in 1701 with the passage of the Act of Settlement (also known as "An Act for the Further Limitation of the Crown and Better Securing the Rights and Liberties of the Subject"). Primarily designed to address issues of royal succession and conflicts with the Roman Catholic Church, the Act also provided that no member of the monarch's staff

---

[1] Letter from Andrew Jackson to Andrew Jackson Donelson (July 5, 1822) (on file with the Donelson Papers, Library of Congress).

[2] Both the phrase and the idea of the "tyranny of the majority" have been used by many writers, including John Adams, Alexis de Tocqueville, John Stuart Mill, and James Madison.

[3] *Epilogue* to THE CODE OF HAMMURRABI (ca. 1780 BCE).

[4] FRANCIS BACON, OF JUDICATURE, THE ESSAYS OR COUNSELS, CIVIL AND MORAL OR FRANCIS BACON 365, 377 (Harvey Reynolds ed., Oxford Press 1890).

could be a Member of Parliament. Further, it provided that "after the said limitations [concerning royal succession] shall take effect, as aforesaid, judges' commissions be made *quamdiu se bene gesserint* [as long as they behave well], and their salaries ascertained and established but upon the address of both Houses of Parliament it may be lawful to remove them."[5] Thus, judges were to hold their positions during "good behaviour," and could only be fired by the Houses of Parliament. Judicial independence was born.

Judicial independence in the century prior to the American Revolution was not perfect. Judges could still be removed through a variety of methods. Monarchs sometimes ignored the Act of Settlement. Judges could be removed through impeachment. Other methods were also available for removal, including the *writ of scire facias* and the use of a criminal information.

French lawyer and philosopher Charles de Secondat, Baron de Montesquieu, famously described and critiqued the British system in his 1748 work *The Spirit of the Laws*.[6] Seventeen years later, Blackstone's *Commentaries on the Laws of England* furthered Montesquieu's ideas:

> In this distinct and separate existence of the judicial power in a peculiar body of men, nominated indeed, but not removable at pleasure by the Crown, consists one main preservative of the public's liberty which cannot subsist long in any state, unless the administration of justice be in some degree separated both from the legislative and also from the executive power.[7]

Despite the work of Montesquieu and Blackstone, a clear separation of power never existed in Britain. Some judges remained members in the House of Lords. One, Lord High Chancellor of Great Britain, embodied multiple branches of government. He was appointed by the king or queen on the advice of the prime minister, was a member of the cabinet, the presiding officer of the House of Lords, and the Head of the Judiciary in England and Wales. Similarly, the Master of the Rolls continued to sit in the House of Lords until the Judicature Acts in the early 1870s.

Further, the power of judicial review, at least as Americans conceive it, did not exist in Britain. Instead, the House of Lords applied the doctrine of "parliamentary supremacy," often called "parliamentary sovereignty."

> Parliament could make or unmake any law whatever. The courts can only interpret and may not question the validity of Acts of Parliament. No Parliament can bind its successor;

[5] 12 & 13 Will. 3, c. 2 (Eng.). *See also* James E. Pfander, *Removing Federal Judges*, 74 U. CHI. L. REV. 1227, 1235 (2007) ("The Act of Settlement, adopted in 1701 as a cornerstone of constitutional monarchy, provided that the judges . . . were to hold their offices during good behavior [and] were subject to removal upon parliamentary address.").

[6] CHARLES DE SECONDAT, BARON DE MONTESQUIEU, THE SPIRIT OF THE LAWS (1748).

[7] 1 WILLIAM BLACKSTONE, *Of the King's Prerogative*, *in* COMMENTARIES ON THE LAWS OF ENGLAND 259, 259 (1765–69).

> otherwise the supremacy of succeeding Parliaments would be limited. The Bill of Rights [passed in 1688] could be cast overboard by the same process as a Prevention of Damage by Pests Act, namely by a repealing measure passed in ordinary form.[8]

In 1608, Chief Justice Coke articulated a different vision:

> And it appears in our books, that in many cases, the common law will controul Acts of Parliament, and sometimes adjudge them to be utterly void: For when an Act of Parliament is against common right and reason, or repugnant, or impossible to be performed, the common law will controul it, and adjudge such Act to be void.[9]

Lord Coke lost not only this argument but also his position as Chief Justice. Later struggles between Parliament and the Crown ultimately produced the Glorious Revolution of 1688, in which William and Mary of Orange took the throne promising that total lawmaking authority would lie with Parliament. That development also coincided with the 1689 publication of the leading treatise on liberal democracy: John Locke's *Second Treatise on Civil Government*.

While the British courts do not exert the power of judicial review, the common law retains a presumption that Parliament does not change rights of British personhood without explicitly saying so. The presumption applies to individual liberties such as criminal procedure rights, property law, and access to the courts. As a practical matter, the common law stands as a check on Parliament. Statutes are interpreted to preserve common-law rights until Parliament takes on the political risk of abrogating that right.

For example, in 1920, Ireland was separated into two distinct entities. The south, a predominantly Catholic area of the island, became the independent Republic of Ireland. The north, a predominantly Protestant area, remained part of the United Kingdom. "The Troubles" was a violent 30-year conflict over the constitutional status of Northern Ireland. The overwhelmingly Protestant loyalists in Northern Ireland wanted to remain part of the United Kingdom, while the overwhelmingly Catholic nationalists wanted Northern Ireland to become part of one united Ireland. Beginning in the late 1960s, paramilitary groups and British state security forces engaged in violent clashes and guerilla attacks through the United Kingdom. Parliament dealt with The Troubles by permitting executive detention of suspected terrorists, searches without warrants, and trial of terrorist offenses without a jury.[10] Although many of these emergency powers were a direct

---

[8] EMLYN C.S. WADE & GEORGE G. PHILLIPS, CONSTITUTIONAL LAW 46 (8th ed. 1970).

[9] *Dr. Bonham's Case* (1610), 77 Eng. Rep. 638.

[10] Northern Ireland (Emergency Provisions) (Amendment) Act 1975, c. 62 (UK), http://www.legislation.gov.uk/ukpga/1975/62/pdfs/ukpga_19750062_en.pdf [https://perma.cc/5BLN-BTUX].

contradiction to the rights of British subjects, they were not seriously questioned by the courts.[11] The Emergency Powers Acts were repealed and replaced by more comprehensive provisions in the Civil Contingencies Act of 2004.

For many decades, the highest judicial body in Britain was the Committee of Law Lords, appointed members of the House of Lords.[12] The British judiciary looks very different today, but many of the reforms were recent. The Constitutional Reform Act of 2005 split the post of Lord High Chancellor, making the Lord Chief Justice head of the judiciary. It also abolished the system of Law Lords sitting in the House of Lords, created a separate Supreme Court, and established a new Judicial Appointments Commission.[13] Because of the principle of parliamentary sovereignty, however, the Supreme Court has no judicial review function over Acts of Parliament except in a very limited sense.[14] In a slight variation from the presumption of the common law, neither the European Union Charter (EU) nor the European Convention of Human Rights (ECHR) is fully incorporated into domestic law, but they do serve as guides to interpretation of domestic law. A Ministry of Justice was created in May 2007 and given power over courts, prisons, probation, and constitutional affairs.

The British courts have historically been less "activist" than American courts. An exhibit at the British National Library in 2009 called *Taking Liberties* was a marvelous collection of historical documents beginning with the Domesday Book (a survey of British citizens, lands, and assets commissioned by William the Conqueror after the Norman invasion) through the Magna Carta, the Civil Rights Bill of 1835, and modern grants of universal suffrage and rights of sexual liberties. Perhaps the most fascinating aspect of this parade of British civil liberties was the absence of a single court case.[15] The British judiciary's reticence to engage in political debate has lessened somewhat in recent years. Predictably, these changes have caused some Ministers

---

[11] *See Ex Parte Lynch*, [1980] NI 126.

[12] *Law Lords*, U.K. PARLIAMENT, http://www.parliament.uk/about/mps-and-lords/about-lords/lords-types/law-lords/ [https://perma.cc/JN9A-9TWJ] (last visited Sept. 25, 2016); *The Supreme Court*, U.K. COURTS AND TRIBUNALS JUDICIARY, https://www.judiciary.gov.uk/about-the-judiciary/the-justice-system/the-supreme-court/ [https://perma.cc/H79S-UQP7] (last visited Sept. 25, 2016). In 2009, the judicial functions of the House of Lords was moved to the Supreme Court of the United Kingdom.

[13] *Judicial Independence*, POLITICS, http://www.politics.co.uk/reference/judicial-independence [https://perma.cc/2YG2-MP9R] (last visited Sept. 20, 2016).

[14] In one instance, Parliament did provide some limited judicial review. The Human Rights Act of 1998 authorizes a competent court to issue a "declaration of incompatibility" between an Act and the European Convention on Human Rights (ECHR). *A v. Secretary of State for the Home Department*, [2004] UKHL 56. In this landmark case, the House of Lords declared that emergency powers of executive detention granted in the Anti-Terrorism, Crime, and Security Act of 2001 were incompatible with British obligations under the ECHR. As a declaration, however, the effect of the decision was merely advice to Parliament and the Ministers that important participants saw a legal problem that needed to be addressed.

[15] Imagine a similar exhibit detailing the growth of civil rights in the U.S. without the leading opinions of the Supreme Court.

to accuse judges of attempting to usurp the democratic process—a debate that looks very much like our own.[16]

B. THE AMERICAN EXPERIENCE

The British experience undoubtedly shaped the views of the Founding Fathers. Hamilton attributed the idea of separation of powers, articulated in *The Federalist Papers* # 78, to "[t]he celebrated Montesquieu." *The Spirit of the Laws* was hugely influential on both Alexis de Tocqueville and American writers.

References to the British system of government appear before the start of the Revolutionary War. The Declaration of Independence accused King George III of acting in ways forbidden in England: "He has obstructed the Administration of Justice, by refusing his Assent to Laws for establishing Judiciary powers. He has made Judges dependent on his Will alone, for the tenure of their offices, and the amount and payment of their salaries."[17] Prior to the War, Thomas Paine likewise argued for a separation of crown from bench: "[I]n absolute governments the king is law," but "[i]n America the law is king."[18] In 1780, echoing the sentiments of Thomas Paine and Aristotle, John Adams enshrined the concept of "a government of laws, not of men" in the 1780 Massachusetts state constitution.

The Articles of Confederation, in effect from 1781 to 1789, did not provide for a national judiciary. Congress had sole jurisdiction over boundary disputes between the states and was also given the power to create courts with jurisdiction over prize cases (related to the capture and seizure of enemy ships). All other judicial matters were left to the states.

The post-Revolution Constitution attempted to address issues of judicial independence much as the Act of Settlement addressed it almost 100 years earlier. It vested the judicial power of the new government in federal judges "who shall hold their offices during good behaviour, and shall, at stated times, receive for their services a compensation, which shall not be diminished during their continuance in office." The authors of *The Federalist Papers*, John Jay, Alexander Hamilton, and James Madison, argued in favor of ratification of the proposed Constitution, including provisions that would ensure an independent judiciary. In *The Federalist Papers*, Hamilton described life tenure and salary as the foremost guarantee of decisional independence.

---

[16] "The Attorney General is fully entitled to insist on the proper limits of judicial authority, but he is wrong to stigmatise judicial decision-making as in some way undemocratic . . . . The effect is not, of course, to override the sovereign legislative authority of the Queen in Parliament, since if primary legislation is declared to be incompatible, the validity of the legislation is unaffected and the remedy lies with the appropriate minister who is answerable to Parliament. The 1998 Act gives the courts a very specific, wholly democratic, mandate." *A v. Home Secretary*, [2004] UKHL 56.

[17] THE DECLARATION OF INDEPENDENCE paras. 10–11 (U.S. 1776).

[18] Thomas Paine, Common Sense (1776).

> [I]ndependence of the judges is equally requisite to guard the Constitution and the rights of individuals from the effects of those ill humors, which the arts of designing men or the influence of particular conjunctures sometimes disseminate among the people themselves; and which, though they speedily give place to better information and more deliberate reflection, have a tendency, in the meantime, to occasion dangerous innovations in the government, and serious oppressions of the minor party in the community.[19]

Hamilton also expanded on the views of Montesquieu and Blackstone, writing that the power of judicial review must exist in a written constitution, for otherwise there would be no point in writing down rights of personhood.

While modern discourse often assumes that the "Founding Fathers" acted with one mind, in reality, they differed on many things, including the powers that should be bestowed on the judiciary. The proper balance between judicial independence and democratic accountability was a source of discussion and discord. James Madison argued that the judiciary must derive all its power directly or indirectly from the great body of the people.[20] Thomas Jefferson, writing toward the end of his life, agreed:

> [O]ur judges are effectually independent of the nation. But this ought not to be. I would not, indeed, make them dependent on the Executive authority, as they formerly were in England; but I deem it indispensable to the continuance of this government, that they should be submitted to some practical & impartial control; and that this, to be imparted, must be compounded of a mixture of State and Federal authorities. It is not enough that honest men are appointed judges. All know the influence of interest on the mind of man, and how unconsciously his judgment is warped by that influence.[21]

Hamilton had addressed these concerns 30 years prior, writing that the judiciary would be the least dangerous branch, as it "has no influence over either the sword or the purse; no direction either of the strength or of the wealth of the society."[22] Further, Congress retained the check of impeachment. "There never can be danger that the judges, by a series of deliberate usurpations on the authority of the legislature, would hazard the united resentment of the body intrusted with it, while this body was possessed of the means of punishing their presumption, by degrading them from their stations."[23]

---

[19] THE FEDERALIST NO. 78 (Alexander Hamilton).

[20] THE FEDERALIST NOS. 37, 39 (James Madison).

[21] THOMAS JEFFERSON, THE AUTOBIOGRAPHY OF THOMAS JEFFERSON (1821).

[22] THE FEDERALIST NO. 78 (Alexander Hamilton).

[23] THE FEDERALIST NO. 81 (Alexander Hamilton).

The same positions staked out by the Founders are echoed in our political discourse today. More "conservative" academics and politicians often argue that the courts are too independent and quick to discard the will of Congress or the people. The "liberals" champion a more independent judiciary, in which the courts act as a robust barrier, rebalancing the rights of the minority against the rights of the majority. Indeed, many of the constitutional battles addressed in the coming chapters come down to this question: should the people, in the form of their representatives, decide the meaning of Constitutional rights, or is that job better left to the courts?

§ 8.2 POWER AND INDEPENDENCE OF THE COURTS

That a federal court had authority to declare acts of congress unconstitutional was not always a given. In *The Federalist Papers* Hamilton noted that "there is not a syllable in the plan under consideration which *directly* empowers the national courts to construe the laws according to the spirit of the Constitution, or which gives them any greater latitude in this respect than may be claimed by the courts of every State."[24]

Hamilton stated clearly, however, that the power of judicial review was implicit in the structure of the Constitution:

> The complete independence of the courts of justice is peculiarly essential in a limited Constitution. By a limited Constitution, I understand one which contains certain specified exceptions to the legislative authority; such, for instance, as that it shall pass no bills of attainder, no *ex post facto* laws, and the like. Limitations of this kind can be preserved in practice no other way than through the medium of courts of justice, whose duty it must be to declare all acts contrary to the manifest tenor of the Constitution void. Without this, all the reservations of particular rights or privileges would amount to nothing.[25]

Interestingly, when the issue of judicial review came before the Supreme Court in *Marbury v. Madison*, Chief Justice Marshall made this very argument without mentioning the Federalist Papers.

In the decade after the ratification, the judiciary remained secondary to the other branches. In 1801, President John Adams nominated John Jay to be Chief Justice of the Supreme Court. Jay declined the post, at least in part because

> the Efforts repeatedly made to place the judicial Departmt. on a proper Footing [with the other branches], have proved fruitless—

[24] THE FEDERALIST NO. 81 (Alexander Hamilton).

[25] THE FEDERALIST NO. 78 (Alexander Hamilton).

> I left the Bench perfectly convinced that under a System so defective, it would not obtain the Energy weight and Dignity which are essential to its affording due support to the national Governmt.; nor acquire the public Confidence and Respect, which, as the last Resort of the Justice of the Nation, it should possess. Hence I am induced to doubt both the Propriety and Expediency of my returning to the Bench under the present System[.][26]

The trajectory of the new federal courts changed radically with the celebrated case of *Marbury v. Madison*. A case that purported to be a model of judicial restraint was also an audacious power-grab by the Supreme Court.

A. THE POWER OF JUDICIAL REVIEW

In 1801, John Adams was replaced as President by his erstwhile friend Thomas Jefferson. Adams was a Federalist who believed in a more powerful federal government. Jefferson was a Republican who believed in a smaller and more restrained federal government. Jefferson was deeply wary of a powerful federal judicial system.

Prior to Adams' departure, Congress passed the Judiciary Act of 1801. Among other things, the Act created 16 new circuit court judgeships—the so-called "midnight judges." Adams began to hurriedly pack the judiciary in the weeks before he left office. As part of this process, Adams convinced Supreme Court Chief Justice Ellsworth to resign and replaced him with Adams' Secretary of State, John Marshall. Jefferson wrote Mrs. Adams that these political appointments were the "one act of Mr. Adams's life, and one only, [that] ever gave me a moment's personal displeasure."[27] Jefferson recognized that the appointments "were [selected] from among my most ardent political enemies,"[28] purposely chosen in the knowledge that they would work against Jefferson.

One of these last-minute political appointments was William Marbury, who was appointed Justice of the Peace in the District of Colombia by Adams. Marbury was nominated, confirmed by the Senate, and his commission was signed by Adams. However, the commission was not delivered before the expiration of Adams' term. Marbury sued James Madison, Jefferson's new Secretary of State, to force delivery of the commission. The suit came by way of a writ of mandamus in the Supreme Court. A writ of mandamus, Latin for "we command," is "issued by a

[26] Letter from John Jay to John Adams, (Jan. 2, 1801), http://founders.archives.gov/documents/Adams/99-02-02-4745 [https://perma.cc/USA7-929B].

[27] Letter from Thomas Jefferson to Abigail Adams (June 13, 1804). https://www.loc.gov/item/mtjbib013519/.

[28] *Id.*

superior court to compel a lower court or a government officer to perform mandatory or purely ministerial duties correctly."[29]

Because Marbury filed his petition for the writ of mandamus directly in the Supreme Court, the Court needed to be able to exercise original jurisdiction over the case in order to have the power to hear it. The Constitution provided original jurisdiction "[i]n all Cases affecting Ambassadors, other public Ministers and Consuls, and those in which a State shall be a Party."[30] Section 13 of the Judiciary Act of 1789, however, provided that

> [t]he Supreme Court shall also have appellate jurisdiction from the circuit courts and courts of the several states, in the cases herein after provided for; *and shall have power to issue writs of prohibition to the district courts [. . .] and writs of mandamus [. . .]* to any courts appointed, or persons holding office, under the authority of the United States.[31]

Marbury argued that the Judiciary Act of 1789 granted the Supreme Court jurisdiction over petitions for writs of mandamus.

Thus, the Court was tasked with deciding whether Congress could expand the original jurisdiction of the Supreme Court. However, the Court also faced a fundamental practical problem: the Constitution hadn't set out the power of judicial review, and the idea didn't have widespread acceptance. If the Court issued the writ of mandamus, there was a very real possibility that Jefferson would simply ignore it. The Court would lose both power and face. If the Court appeared afraid to issue the writ of mandamus despite the clear direction in the Judiciary Act, the Court would lose both power and face. Marshall ingeniously solved the problem: he concluded that Congress lacked the power to bestow supplemental jurisdiction. He handed Jefferson a win, but in the process greatly expanded the Court's ability to review acts of Congress.

Marbury v. Madison

5 U.S. 137 (1 Cranch 137) (1803)

■ MARSHALL, C.J.:

The very essence of civil liberty certainly consists in the right of every individual to claim the protection of the laws, whenever he receives an injury. One of the first duties of government is to afford that protection. In Great Britain the king himself is sued in the respectful form of a petition, and he never fails to comply with the judgment of his court.

---

[29] *Writ of Mandamus*, BLACK'S LAW DICTIONARY (7th ed. 1999).

[30] U.S. CONST., Art. III, § 2, Cl. 2.

[31] The Judiciary Act of 1789 § 13, 1 Stat. 77 (1789) (emphasis added).

In the 3d vol. of his commentaries, p. 23, Blackstone states two cases in which a remedy is afforded by mere operation of law.

"In all other cases," he says, "it is a general and indisputable rule, that where there is a legal right, there is also a legal remedy by suit or action at law, whenever that right is invaded."

The government of the United States has been emphatically termed a government of laws, and not of men. It will certainly cease to deserve this high appellation, if the laws furnish no remedy for the violation of a vested legal right.

If this obloquy is to be cast on the jurisprudence of our country, it must arise from the peculiar character of the case.

Is the act of delivering or withholding a commission to be considered as a mere political act, belonging to the executive department alone, for the performance of which, entire confidence is placed by our constitution in the supreme executive; and for any misconduct respecting which, the injured individual has no remedy.

That there may be such cases is not to be questioned; but that every act of duty, to be performed in any of the great departments of government, constitutes such a case, is not to be admitted.

By the constitution of the United States, the President is invested with certain important political powers, in the exercise of which he is to use his own discretion, and is accountable only to his country in his political character, and to his own conscience. To aid him in the performance of these duties, he is authorized to appoint certain officers, who act by his authority and in conformity with his orders.

In such cases, their acts are his acts; and whatever opinion may be entertained of the manner in which executive discretion may be used, still there exists, and can exist, no power to control that discretion. The subjects are political. They respect the nation, not individual rights, and being entrusted to the executive, the decision of the executive is conclusive. The application of this remark will be perceived by adverting to the act of congress for establishing the department of foreign affairs. This officer, as his duties were prescribed by that act, is to conform precisely to the will of the President. He is the mere organ by whom that will is communicated. The acts of such an officer, as an officer, can never be examinable by the courts.

But when the legislature proceeds to impose on that officer other duties; when he is directed peremptorily to perform certain acts; when the rights of individuals are dependent on the performance of those acts; he is so far the officer of the law; is amenable to the laws for his conduct; and cannot at his discretion sport away the vested rights of others.

The conclusion from this reasoning is, that where the heads of departments are the political or confidential agents of the executive, merely to execute the will of the President, or rather to act in cases in which the executive possesses a constitutional or legal discretion, nothing can be more perfectly clear than that their acts are only politically examinable. But where a specific duty is assigned by law, and individual rights depend upon the performance of that duty, it seems equally clear that the individual who considers himself injured, has a right to resort to the laws of his country for a remedy.

The constitution vests the whole judicial power of the United States in one supreme court, and such inferior courts as congress shall, from time to time, ordain and establish. This power is expressly extended to all cases arising under the laws of the United States; and consequently, in some form, may be exercised over the present case; because the right claimed is given by a law of the United States.

In the distribution of this power it is declared that "the supreme court shall have original jurisdiction in all cases affecting ambassadors, other public ministers and consuls, and those in which a state shall be a party. In all other cases, the supreme court shall have appellate jurisdiction."

The authority, therefore, given to the supreme court, by the act establishing the judicial courts of the United States, to issue writs of mandamus to public officers, appears not to be warranted by the constitution; and it becomes necessary to enquire whether a jurisdiction, so conferred, can be exercised.

The question, whether an act, repugnant to the constitution, can become the law of the land, is a question deeply interesting to the United States; but, happily, not of an intricacy proportioned to its interest. It seems only necessary to recognize certain principles, supposed to have been long and well established, to decide it.

That the people have an original right to establish, for their future government, such principles as, in their opinion, shall most conduce to their own happiness, is the basis, on which the whole American fabric has been erected. The exercise of this original right is a very great exertion; nor can it, nor ought it to be frequently repeated. The principles, therefore, so established, are deemed fundamental. And as the authority, from which they proceed, is supreme, and can seldom act, they are designed to be permanent.

This original and supreme will organizes the government, and assigns, to different departments, their respective powers. It may either stop here; or establish certain limits not to be transcended by those departments.

The government of the United States is of the latter description. The powers of the legislature are defined, and limited; and that those limits may not be mistaken, or forgotten, the constitution is written. To what purpose are powers limited, and to what purpose is that limitation committed to writing, if these limits may, at any time, be passed by those intended to be restrained? The distinction, between a government with limited and unlimited powers, is abolished, if those limits do not confine the persons on whom they are imposed, and if acts prohibited and acts allowed, are of equal obligation. It is a proposition too plain to be contested, that the constitution controls any legislative act repugnant to it; or, that the legislature may alter the constitution by an ordinary act.

Between these alternatives there is no middle ground. The constitution is either a superior, paramount law, unchangeable by ordinary means, or it is on a level with ordinary legislative acts, and like other acts, is alterable when the legislature shall please to alter it.

If the former part of the alternative be true, then a legislative act contrary to the constitution is not law: if the latter part be true, then written constitutions are absurd attempts, on the part of the people, to limit a power, in its own nature illimitable.

Certainly all those who have framed written constitutions contemplate them as forming the fundamental and paramount law of the nation, and consequently the theory of every such government must be, that an act of the legislature, repugnant to the constitution, is void.

This theory is essentially attached to a written constitution, and is consequently to be considered, by this court, as one of the fundamental principles of our society. It is not therefore to be lost sight of in the further consideration of this subject.

If an act of the legislature, repugnant to the constitution, is void, does it, notwithstanding its invalidity, bind the courts, and oblige them to give it effect? Or, in other words, though it be not law, does it constitute a rule as operative as if it was a law? This would be to overthrow in fact what was established in theory; and would seem, at first view, an absurdity too gross to be insisted on. It shall, however, receive a more attentive consideration.

It is emphatically the province and duty of the judicial department to say what the law is. Those who apply the rule to particular cases, must of necessity expound and interpret that rule. If two laws conflict with each other, the courts must decide on the operation of each.

So if a law be in opposition to the constitution; if both the law and the constitution apply to a particular case, so that the court must either decide that case conformably to the law, disregarding the constitution; or conformably to the constitution, disregarding the law; the court must determine which of these conflicting rules governs the case. This is of the very essence of judicial duty.

If then the courts are to regard the constitution; and the constitution is superior to any ordinary act of the legislature; the constitution, and not such ordinary act, must govern the case to which they both apply.

Those then who controvert the principle that the constitution is to be considered, in court, as a paramount law, are reduced to the necessity of maintaining that courts must close their eyes on the constitution, and see only the law.

This doctrine would subvert the very foundation of all written constitutions. It would declare that an act, which, according to the principles and theory of our government, is entirely void; is yet, in practice, completely obligatory. It would declare, that if the legislature shall do what is expressly forbidden, such act, notwithstanding the express prohibition, is in reality effectual. It would be giving to the legislature a practical and real omnipotence, with the same breath which professes to restrict their powers within narrow limits. It is prescribing limits, and declaring that those limits may be passed as pleasure.

That it thus reduces to nothing what we have deemed the greatest improvement on political institutions—a written constitution—would of itself be sufficient, in America, where written constitutions have been viewed with so much reverence, for rejecting the construction.

NOTES AND QUESTIONS

1. **A Logical Conclusion.** Chief Justice Marshall declared that when a statute and the Constitution collide, the Constitution wins. He also declared that the Supreme Court has the power to interpret the Constitution. His argument is built on a series of premises: first, the Court decides cases according to law; second, the constitution is law, just as statutes are law. Because the Court has the power to decide cases, it has the power of judicial review.

2. **The Fox Guarding the Henhouse.** Could the case have come out differently? Could Congress simply police itself? The British system seemed to have accomplished just that.

3. **What One Hand Giveth, the Other Taketh Away.** Marshall's opinion in *Marbury* was a brilliant way to carve out power for the Court. With it, he handed Jefferson a win: Jefferson was not required to deliver Marbury's commission. However, while Marshall gave with one hand, he took away with another: Jefferson could not wrest back the power of judicial review.

4. **Beating Him at His Own Game.** Could Jefferson have beaten Marshall at his own game? What would have happened if Jefferson had ordered Madison to deliver Marbury's commission before the case reached the Supreme Court?

B. POWER OVER STATE COURTS

Marbury v. Madison stood for two propositions: Constitutional supremacy and the power of judicial review. Left open, however, was whether the United States Supreme Court had appellate power over state court rulings on federal issues. The state courts argued that they had co-equal power to address issues of federal law and that the Supreme

Court lacked appellate power in those cases. That issue was addressed in *Martin v. Hunter's Lessee*.

Martin v. Hunter's Lessee

14 U.S. (1 Wheat.) 304, 4 L. Ed. 97 (1816)

[Lord Fairfax, a citizen of Virginia, willed his Virginia estates to his nephew, Denny Martin, a British subject. Following the American Revolution, treaties of 1783 and 1794 between the United States and Great Britain protected British lands in the United States. In 1789, Virginia attempted to confiscate lands owned by British subjects and granted title over the Fairfax lands to David Hunter. Hunter brought an action of ejectment against Martin. The Virginia Court of Appeals held for Hunter on the basis that Virginia's title to the land was perfected prior to the enactment of the treaties. In *Fairfax's Devisee v. Hunter's Lessee*, 11 U.S. (7 Cranch) 603 (1813), the U.S. Supreme Court reversed the Virginia Court of Appeals. The mandate of the Supreme Court directed the Virginia Court of Appeals to enter judgment for Martin. That court refused to obey the Supreme Court's decree on the ground that § 25 of the Judiciary Act of 1789, which conferred appellate jurisdiction on the Supreme Court over the decisions of a state's highest tribunal, was unconstitutional.

[Judge Cabell of the Virginia court had presented this argument in refusing to obey the Supreme Court:

> [It has been contended that the constitution . . . intended to give to the Supreme Court of the United States appellate jurisdiction in all cases of federal cognizance. But this argument proves too much, and what is utterly inadmissible. It would give appellate jurisdiction, as well over the courts of England or France, as over the State courts; for, although I do not think the state courts are foreign courts in relation to the federal courts, yet I consider them not less independent than foreign courts.]

■ STORY, J., delivered the opinion of the court:

This is a writ of error from the Court of Appeals of Virginia, founded upon the refusal of that court to obey the mandate of this court, requiring the judgment rendered in this very cause, at February term, 1813, to be carried into due execution.

The third article of the constitution is that which must principally attract our attention. The judicial power of the United States shall be vested (not may be vested) in one supreme court, and in such inferior courts as Congress may, from time to time, ordain and establish.

The next consideration is as to the courts in which the judicial power shall be vested. It is manifest that a supreme court must be established; but [if] a discretion be vested in Congress to establish, or not to establish, inferior courts at their own pleasure, and Congress should not establish such courts, the appellate jurisdiction of the Supreme Court would have nothing to act upon, unless it could act upon cases pending in the state courts. Under such circumstances it must be held that the appellate power would extend to state courts; for the constitution is peremptory that it shall extend to certain enumerated cases, which cases could exist in no other courts. Any other construction, upon this supposition, would involve this strange contradiction—that a discretionary power vested in Congress, and which they might rightfully omit to exercise, would defeat the absolute injunctions of the constitution in relation to the whole appellate power.

But it is plain that the framers of the constitution did contemplate that cases within the judicial cognizance of the United States not only might but would arise in the state courts, in the exercise of their ordinary jurisdiction. With this view the sixth article declares, that "this constitution, and the laws of the United States which shall be made in pursuance thereof, and all treaties made, or which shall be made, under the authority of the United States, shall be the supreme law of the land, and the judges in every state shall be bound thereby, anything in the constitution or laws of any state to the contrary notwithstanding." From the very nature of their judicial duties they would be called upon to pronounce the law applicable to the case in judgment. They were not to decide merely according to the laws or constitution of the state, but according to the constitution, laws and treaties of the United States—"the supreme law of the land."

It must, therefore, be conceded that the constitution not only contemplated, but meant to provide for cases within the scope of the judicial power of the United States, which might yet depend before state tribunals. It was foreseen that in the exercise of their ordinary jurisdiction, state courts would incidentally take cognizance of cases arising under the constitution, the laws and treaties of the United States. Yet to all these cases the judicial power, by the very terms of the constitution, is to extend. It cannot extend by original jurisdiction if that was already rightfully and exclusively attached in the state courts, which (as has been already shown) may occur; it must, therefore, extend by appellate jurisdiction, or not at all. It would seem to follow that the appellate power of the United States must, in such cases, extend to state tribunals; and if in such cases, there is no reason why it should not equally attach upon all others within the purview of the constitution.

It is a mistake that the constitution was not designed to operate upon states, in their corporate capacities. It is crowded with provisions which restrain or annul the sovereignty of the states in some of the highest branches of their prerogatives. The tenth section of the first article contains a long list of disabilities and prohibitions imposed upon the states. Surely, when such essential portions of state sovereignty are taken away, or prohibited to be exercised, it cannot be correctly asserted that the constitution does not act upon the states.

Nor can such a right be deemed to impair the independence of state judges. It is assuming the very ground in controversy to assert that they possess an absolute independence of the United States. In respect to the powers granted to the United States, they are not independent; they are expressly bound to obedience by the letter of the constitution; and if they should unintentionally transcend their authority, or misconstrue the constitution, there is no more reason for giving their judgments an absolute and irresistible force than for giving it to the acts of the other coordinate departments of state sovereignty.

This is not all. A motive of another kind, perfectly compatible with the most sincere respect for state tribunals, might induce the grant of appellate power over their decisions. That motive is the importance, and even necessity of uniformity of decisions throughout the whole United States, upon all subjects within the purview of the constitution. Judges of equal learning and integrity, in different states, might differently interpret a statute, or a treaty of the United States, or even the constitution itself. If there were no revising authority to control these jarring and discordant judgments, and harmonize them into uniformity, the laws, the treaties, and the constitution of the United States would be different in different states, and might, perhaps, never have precisely the same construction, obligation, or efficacy, in any two states.

On the whole, the court are of opinion that the appellate power of the United States does extend to cases pending in the state courts; and that the 25th section of the judiciary act, which authorizes the exercise of this jurisdiction in the specified cases, by a writ of error, is supported by the letter and spirit of the constitution. We find no clause in that instrument which limits this power; and we dare not interpose a limitation where the people have not been disposed to create one.

We have not thought it incumbent on us to give any opinion upon the question, whether this court have authority to issue a writ or mandamus to the Court of Appeals to enforce the former judgments, as we do not think it necessarily involved in the decision of this cause. It is the opinion of the whole court that the judgment of the Court of Appeals of Virginia, rendered on the mandate in this cause, be reversed, and the judgment of the District Court, held at Winchester, be, and the same is hereby affirmed.

NOTES AND QUESTIONS

1. **Forum Shopping.** What would have happened if Virginia's view of judicial review had prevailed? If the federal law had a different meaning in different states, what would prevent litigants from forum shopping?

2. **Independent and Adequate State Grounds.** *Martin* did not hold that the United States Supreme Court could review all cases coming from the state courts. The Court's appellate power extends only to federal

questions and diversity cases (which, under the *Erie*[32] doctrine, must be decided using appropriate state law). The Court is not empowered to review cases where an "independent and adequate state ground" exists for the ruling.

3. **Criminal Cases, Too.** In 1821, *Cohens v. Virginia*[33] extended *Martin* to criminal cases. *Cohens* held that the Supreme Court may exercise jurisdiction in state criminal cases and cases where the state is a party if there is a constitutional question. The Court reasoned that Article III applies to all cases that involve federal questions, not just civil cases.

§ 8.3 CHALLENGES TO JUDICIAL POWER

Unsurprisingly, there have been many attempts over the years to curtail the power of Article III courts. Although it would be possible to limit the courts' power through a constitutional amendment, the process is arduous. Other avenues of political control have been more manageable, if not always successful. These include limiting the courts' jurisdiction by statute, employing the power of impeachment, packing the courts with friendly judges, and statutorily directing the outcome of cases.

A. JURISDICTION STRIPPING

One way to control the Supreme Court is to limit its jurisdiction. Article III, § 2 of the Constitution provides:

> In all cases affecting ambassadors, other public ministers and consuls, and those in which a state shall be party, the Supreme Court shall have original jurisdiction. In all the other cases before mentioned, the Supreme Court shall have appellate jurisdiction, both as to law and fact, with such exceptions, and under such regulations as the Congress shall make.[34]

Thus, while the Supreme Court has both original and appellate jurisdiction, its appellate jurisdiction is subject to "such exceptions . . . as the Congress shall make." Congress has the power either to move a particular case to a different venue or to insulate particular cases from judicial review. Moving a case from one venue to another is known as jurisdiction-conferring or jurisdiction-stripping. It does not take away substantive rights from the parties and is quite commonplace. Consider, for example, the "amount in controversy" requirement in the federal jurisdiction statutes. This requirement effectively allows the federal courts to hear some state law claims but not others. Insulating certain kinds of cases from judicial review is more problematic, but has been done.

---

32 Erie R.R. Co. v. Tompkins, 304 U.S. 64 (1938).

33 19 U.S. 264 (1821).

34 U.S. CONST. Art. 3 § 2.

During and immediately after the Civil War, both the president and Congress attempted to limit the federal courts' jurisdiction over some kinds of cases with varying success. During the War, President Abraham Lincoln dealt with insurrection in a number of ways, including by suspending the writ of habeas corpus and establishing military tribunals. Habeas corpus, Latin for "you have the body," empowers the courts to demand that an official bring a prisoner before a civil court and to justify the arrest and detainment. The writ had a long history in England. It was enshrined in the Habeas Corpus Act of 1679, which Blackstone called "another Magna Carta." In *Ex parte Merryman*,[35] Chief Justice Roger Taney, sitting not as a Supreme Court justice but as a United States Circuit Court judge, held that only Congress had the power to suspend the writ under Article I, Section 9 of the Constitution. Taney's opinion, delivered to President Lincoln and widely published in the papers, represented an eloquent defense of judicial power.[36] Congress reacted by passing the Habeas Corpus Suspension Act, which gave Lincoln the power to suspend habeas corpus at his discretion during the pendency of the War.

The constitutionality of military tribunals came before the Court a few years later. In 1864, Lambden Milligan was arrested in Indiana, charged with conspiracy before a military commission rather than a civilian court, convicted, and sentenced to death by hanging. His habeas corpus petition was granted by the Supreme Court unanimously.[37] Although the nine Justices disagreed over whether the defects in the proceedings were constitutional or statutory, Justice Davis, for the five-vote majority, held that Congress could not authorize the use of military commissions, even for violations of the "laws and usages of war," in areas outside the "theater of operations" and in which the civilian courts were open and operating.

> It can serve no useful purpose to inquire what those laws and usages [of war] are, whence they originated, where found, and on whom they operate; they can never be applied to citizens in states which have upheld the authority of the government, and where the courts are open and their process unobstructed. This court has judicial knowledge that in Indiana the Federal authority was always unopposed, and its courts always open to hear criminal accusations and redress grievances; and no usage of war could sanction a military trial there for any offence whatever of a citizen in civil life, in nowise connected with the military service. Congress could grant no such power; and to the honor of our national legislature be it said, it has never been provoked by the state of the country even to attempt its exercise.

---

[35] 17 F. Cas. 144 (1861).

[36] Bruce A. Ragsdale, Ex parte Merryman and Debates on Civil Liberties During the Civil War (2007), http://www.fjc.gov/history/docs/merryman.pdf [https://perma.cc/9XFA-A5YF].

[37] *Ex parte Milligan*, 71 U.S. (4 Wall.) 2 (1866).

> One of the plainest constitutional provisions was, therefore, infringed when Milligan was tried by a court not ordained and established by Congress, and not composed of judges appointed during good behavior.[38]

Chief Justice Chase, writing for the four-vote minority, believed that Congress could have authorized the use of military commissions under these circumstances but had not done so.

After the War, Radical Republicans feared that *Milligan* would adversely affect their plans for military rule in the South. Its desire to protect the Reconstruction effort resulted in a series of statutes that gave rise to *Ex parte McCardle*.

Ex parte McCardle

74 U.S. (7 Wall.) 506 (1869)

[McCardle, a sympathizer with the Southern cause, had published some editorials criticizing the federal military occupation of Mississippi in the Vicksburg, Mississippi Times between October 2 and November 6, 1867. The substance of these editorials resulted in McCardle's arrest and detention by the commanding general of the federal military government in Mississippi. A military commission was convened to try McCardle on charges, including disturbing the peace, inciting insurrection, and impeding reconstruction. McCardle sought a writ of habeas corpus from the federal court and invoked the Act of February 5, 1867, which gave the federal courts jurisdiction to grant writs of habeas corpus in cases where persons were detained in violation of law. The statute also provided for appeal to the United States Supreme Court. The federal court denied the writ, and McCardle appealed to the Supreme Court. McCardle filed his appeal on December 23, 1867. After oral argument was heard in *McCardle*, Congress, by a bill enacted over veto on March 27, 1868, repealed that part of the Habeas Corpus Act of February 5, 1867 which gave appellate jurisdiction to the Supreme Court.]

■ [CHIEF JUSTICE SALMON P. CHASE] delivered the opinion of the Court.

The first question necessarily is that of jurisdiction; for, if the act of March 1868, takes away the jurisdiction defined by the act of February, 1867, it is useless, if not improper, to enter into any discussion of other questions. It is quite true, as was argued by the counsel for the petitioner, that the appellate jurisdiction of this Court is not derived from acts of Congress. It is, strictly speaking, conferred by the Constitution. But it is conferred "with such exceptions and under such regulations as Congress shall make."

It is unnecessary to consider whether, if Congress had made no exceptions and no regulations, this Court might not have exercised general appellate jurisdiction under rules prescribed by itself. For among

---

38 *Id.* at 121–22.

the earliest acts of the first Congress, at its first session, was the act of September 24th, 1789, to establish the judicial courts of the United States. That act provided for the organization of this Court, and prescribed regulations for the exercise of its jurisdiction.

The provision of the act of 1867, affirming the appellate jurisdiction of this Court in cases of habeas corpus is expressly repealed. It is hardly possible to imagine a plainer instance of positive exception.

We are not at liberty to inquire into the motives of the legislature. We can only examine into its power under the Constitution: and the power to make exceptions to the appellate jurisdiction of this Court is given by express words. What, then, is the effect of the repealing act upon the case before us? We cannot doubt as to this. Without jurisdiction the Court cannot proceed at all in any cause. Jurisdiction is power to declare the law, and when it ceases to exist, the only function remaining to the Court is that of announcing the fact and dismissing the cause. And this is not less clear upon authority than upon principle.

It is quite clear, therefore, that this Court cannot proceed to pronounce judgment in this case, for it has no longer jurisdiction of the appeal; and judicial duty is not less fitly performed by declining ungranted jurisdiction than in exercising firmly that which the Constitution and the laws confer.

Counsel seem to have supposed, if effect be given to the repealing act in question, that the whole appellate power of the Court, in cases of habeas corpus, is denied. But this is an error. The act of 1868 does not except from that jurisdiction any cases but appeals from Circuit Court under the act of 1867. It does not affect the jurisdiction which was previously exercised.

NOTES AND QUESTIONS

1. **Not So Fast.** In *Ex parte Yerger*,[39] the Court immediately suggested limits on *McCardle*, both as to the specifics of habeas corpus jurisdiction and the general authority of Congress. Yerger was being held for trial by a military court just as McCardle had been. His petition for a writ of habeas corpus was denied by the lower courts. The Supreme Court asked for briefing and argument solely on the question of the Court's appellate jurisdiction. The Court held that, indeed, it had jurisdiction to hear the case.

The Court pointed out that Congress had granted habeas corpus jurisdiction in several statutory provisions, including acts of 1789 (prisoners pending trial by United States authorities, committed for trial by United States courts, or to be brought into court to testify), 1833 (prisoners confined under any authority, state or federal, for acts done under color of federal authority), 1842 (foreign citizens acting under color of foreign authority), and 1867 (any person confined in violation of federal constitution, treaty, or statute). Although the 1867 habeas corpus provision had been repealed, the

[39] 75 U.S. (8 Wall.) 75 (1869).

courts and the Supreme Court still possessed other means, in view of the earlier legislation, to free a prisoner from unlawful confinement.

The Court limited its decision in *Yerger* to the issue of jurisdiction. The case ultimately became moot on the merits when Yerger was transferred to civilian custody.

2. **More Jurisdiction Stripping.** Legislation has surfaced from time to time that would prevent the Supreme Court from hearing cases related to school prayer, segregation in public schools, legislative apportionment, abortion, and any number of other issues. These proposals often follow controversial rulings from the Court. Ironically, of course, if the Supreme Court were stripped of jurisdiction after ruling in a prior case, then the prior case would stand as the precedent to be followed by lower courts. If the lower courts were stripped of jurisdiction, then the state courts would be forced to choose between following Supreme Court precedent or developing independent and potentially conflicting interpretations.

B. IMPEACHMENT

Adams' appointment of the midnight judges in 1801 rankled Jefferson and the Republicans. In a private letter written in 1801, Jefferson complained that the Federalists

> have retired into the Judiciary as a stronghold. There the remains of Federalism are to be preserved and fed from the treasury, and from that battery all the works of Republicanism are to be beaten down and erased. By fraudulent use of the constitution, which has made the judges irremovable, they have multiplied those officers merely to strengthen their phalanx.[40]

While Jefferson's complaint may have been legitimate, his conclusion was not entirely correct. First, the Court held in *Stuart v. Laird* that Congress could deprive duly appointed Article III judges of their positions by statutorily reorganizing the federal courts. Second, federal judges are subject to impeachment.

The first impeachment came just weeks after *Marbury* and *Laird* were decided. John Pickering, a district court judge from New Hampshire, was impeached on charges of being mentally deranged and intoxicated on the bench. He was convicted and removed in 1804. The same day that Pickering was convicted, the House of Representatives impeached Supreme Court Justice Samuel Chase on charges of arbitrary and oppressive conduct of trials. "Justice Samuel Chase was the most controversial judge in the Sedition Act trials and became the target of Republican accusations about the politicization of the federal bench. Chase's domineering and even arrogant manner provoked conflicts

---

[40] Letter from Thomas Jefferson to John Dickinson (Dec. 19, 1801).

throughout his career and often overshadowed his formidable and original legal mind."[41]

Many of the complaints against Chase were valid by today's terms. As a circuit judge presiding over a trial, Chase argued to the jury in favor of conviction. In the Delaware circuit court, he coerced the district attorney and grand jury into considering an indictment of a Republican printer he suspected of seditious libel. In 1800, he openly campaigned for the reelection of John Adams. He then used a grand jury charge to denounce Republicans for the repeal of the Judiciary Act of 1801.

Acquitted by the Senate in 1805, Chase's impeachment curtailed both overtly political behavior by federal judges and immediate attempts to impeach them as a method of political control. It was 25 years before Congress attempted another impeachment. There have been a few modern attempts to impeach Supreme Court justices, most notably the "Impeach Earl Warren" movement of the 1960s. It became moot when Warren left the Court in 1969.

C. COURT-PACKING

Congress has the power to create inferior courts under both the congressional powers clause in Article I, § 8 and the judicial vesting clause in Article III. Adams' plan to pack the judiciary involved creating new judgeships and reducing the number of Supreme Court justices from six to five. The plan allowed him to both place his own appointees in key positions and prevent Jefferson from doing the same. Although Adams' plan to pack the courts with the midnight judges was the first court-packing plan, it was by no means the last.

Congress's most significant attempt to pack the court occurred in the years after the Civil War. In 1863, Congress increased the number of sitting Supreme Court justices to ten. Just three years later, it reduced the number to six via a scheme whereby retiring justices were not replaced. Arguably, the change came amid fears that President Andrew Johnson would appoint conservative justices who would invalidate Reconstruction legislation favored by the Radical Republicans. Johnson was impeached, he narrowly escaped conviction, and he lost the nomination for reelection. Congress restored the Supreme Court to nine justices in 1869 after Ulysses S. Grant was safely in office.

The most famous Presidential court-packing plan was proposed by President Franklin Roosevelt. In the 1930s a series of Supreme Court cases struck down portions of Roosevelt's New Deal legislation. Many were close votes, with the majority including swing voters Chief Justice Charles Evans Hughes and Justice Owen J. Roberts. In response, Roosevelt proposed the Judicial Procedures Reform Bill of 1937. The bill

---

[41] *The Sedition Act Trials—Historical Background and Documents, Biographies: Samuel Chase* (1741–1811), FED. JUDICIAL CTR., http://www.fjc.gov/history/home.nsf/page/tu_sedbio_chase.html [https://perma.cc/69VC-7V5A] (last visited Sept. 21, 2016).

would have allowed Roosevelt to appoint one new justice for every member of the Court over age 70½. The plan would have allowed for the appointment of six additional justices, bringing the total on the bench to fifteen. Three weeks after Roosevelt announced his plan, the Court upheld a minimum wage law in *West Coast Hotel Co. v. Parrish*. The ruling was 5-to-4, and came about when Justice Roberts joined justices who were supportive of the New Deal. His vote was called "the switch in time that saved nine." Later records revealed that Justice Roberts' vote had been cast before Roosevelt's announced proposal. With the retirement of conservative Justice Willis Van Devanter in 1937, the New Deal was safe. Van Devanter was ultimately replaced by Roosevelt appointee Hugo Black. The Judicial Procedures Reform Bill ultimately died in committee.

NOTES AND QUESTION

1. **Political Patsy or Protector of Independence?** Although Justice Roberts has been criticized for bowing to political pressure, it is now fairly apparent that his vote in *Parrish* was cast before President Roosevelt proposed the court-packing legislation. Even assuming, however, that Justice Roberts changed his vote in response to Roosevelt's plan, did the ends justify the means?

2. **You Dance with the One That Brung You.** Presidents are often accused of court-packing when they nominate jurists who appear friendly to their political agenda. Unfortunately, what you see is not always what you get. Presidents are not infrequently surprised by the way their nominees vote once on the Court. President Nixon, a conservative, appointed the now notoriously liberal Justice Blackmun—best known for penning *Roe v. Wade*. Similarly, conservative President Eisenhower appointed Justices William Brennan and Earl Warren. Blackmun and Brennan became two of the most liberal justices on the Court, while Warren guided the Court through *Brown v. Board of Education*, *Gideon v. Wainwright*, and *Miranda v. Arizona*.

D. DIRECTING THE OUTCOME OF CASES

Even when the federal courts have jurisdiction to hear a case, Congress has sometimes attempted to direct the outcome of the case through legislation. Once again, Congressional efforts have met with varying degrees of success.

United States v. Klein

80 U.S. (13 Wall.) 128 (1872)

[Following the Civil War, as part of Reconstruction, Congress provided that former members of the rebellion would forfeit their property to the United States. The Court of Claims was created to adjudicate title to property confiscated by the government. President Johnson offered pardons to rebels who would take an oath of loyalty. In return, they could have their property back. When the Supreme Court held that the Court of Claims must enforce the President's promise, Congress passed a statute stating that a pardon had the effect of establishing guilt, directing the Court of Claims to deny claims from pardoned rebels, and withdrawing appellate jurisdiction by the Supreme Court over the Court of Claims.]

■ CHIEF JUSTICE SALMON P. CHASE delivered the opinion of the Court:

Undoubtedly the legislature has complete control over the organization and existence of that court and may confer or withhold the right of appeal from its decisions. And if this act did nothing more, it would be our duty to give it effect. If it simply denied the right of appeal in a particular class of cases, there could be no doubt that it must be regarded as an exercise of the power of Congress to make "such exceptions from the appellate jurisdiction" as should seem to it expedient.

But the language of this proviso shows plainly that it does not intend to withhold appellate jurisdiction except as a means to an end. Its great and controlling purpose is to deny to pardons granted by the President the effect which this court had adjudged them to have. The proviso declares that pardons shall not be considered by this court on appeal. We had already decided that it was our duty to consider them and give them effect, in cases like the present as equivalent to proof of loyalty.

The court is required to ascertain the existence of certain facts and thereupon to declare that its jurisdiction on appeal has ceased, by dismissing the bill. What is this but to prescribe a rule for the decision of the cause in a particular way? In the case before us, the Court of Claims has rendered judgment for the claimant and an appeal has been taken to this court. We are directed to dismiss the appeal, if we find that the judgment must be affirmed, because of a pardon granted to the intestate of the claimants. Can we do so without allowing one party to the controversy to decide it in its own favor? Can we do so without allowing that the legislature may prescribe rules of decision to the Judicial Department of the government in cases pending before it? We must think that Congress has inadvertently passed the limit which separates the legislative from the judicial power.

The rule prescribed is also liable to just exception as impairing the effect of a pardon, and thus infringing the constitutional power of the Executive. To the executive alone is intrusted the power of pardon; and it is granted without limit. Pardon includes amnesty. It blots out the offence pardoned and removes all its penal consequences. It may be granted on conditions. In these particular pardons, that no doubt might exist as to their character, restoration of property was expressly pledged, and the pardon was granted on condition that the person who availed himself of it should take and keep a prescribed oath. Now it is clear that the legislature cannot change the effect of such a pardon any more than the executive can change a law. Yet this is attempted by the provision under consideration. This certainly impairs the executive authority and directs the court to be instrumental to that end.

NOTES AND QUESTIONS

1. **Righting the Ship.** From 1798 to 1800, American law allowed the capture and seizure of French ships. In 1800, the French schooner *Peggy* was captured and libeled in the District Court of Connecticut. While the case was on appeal, America and France signed the Treaty of Môrtefontaine. That treaty provided that "[p]roperty captured and not yet definitively condemned . . . shall be mutually restored." The Supreme Court held that the treaty applied retroactively to the case, essentially directing the outcome of pending litigation. Justice Marshall noted:

> It is true that in mere private cases between individuals, a court will and ought to struggle hard against a construction which will, by a retrospective operation, affect the rights of parties, but in great national concerns where individual rights, acquired by war, are sacrificed for national purposes, the contract making the sacrifice ought always to receive a construction conforming to its manifest import; and if the nation has given up the vested rights of its citizens, it is not for the court but for the government to consider whether it be a case proper for compensation.[42]

2. **The Last Word of the Judicial Department.** In 1991, the Supreme Court decided that a one-year statute of limitations applied to suits brought under section 10(b) of the Securities and Exchange Act for fraud in securities trading.[43] Congress, in response to widespread criticism of this holding, passed a statute not only setting a longer limitations period, but also mandating "reinstatement" of civil actions that had been dismissed prior to the 1991 holding. Justice Scalia, writing for the majority of the Court, held that the new statute was an unconstitutional attempt to determine the outcome of judicial proceedings:

> Section 27A(b) effects a clear violation of the separation-of-powers principle . . . . It is, of course, retroactive legislation, that is, legislation that prescribes what the law was at an earlier time, when the act whose effect is controlled by the legislation occurred—in this case, the filing of the initial Rule 10b-5 action in the District Court. When retroactive legislation requires its own application in a case already finally adjudicated, it does no more and no less than reverse a determination once made, in a particular case.
>
> It is true, as petitioners contend, that Congress can always revise the judgments of Article III courts in one sense: When a new law makes clear that it is retroactive, an appellate court must apply that law in reviewing judgments still on appeal that were rendered before the law was enacted, and must alter the outcome accordingly. But a distinction between judgments from which all

---

[42] United States v. Schooner Peggy, 5 U.S. 103 (1801).

[43] Plaut v. Spendthrift Farms, 514 U.S. 211 (1995).

appeals have been forgone or completed, and judgments that remain on appeal (or subject to being appealed), is implicit in what Article III creates: not a batch of unconnected courts, but a judicial department composed of "inferior Courts" and "one supreme Court." Within that hierarchy, the decision of an inferior court is not (unless the time for appeal has expired) the final word of the department as a whole. It is the obligation of the last court in the hierarchy that rules on the case to give effect to Congress's latest enactment, even when that has the effect of overturning the judgment of an inferior court, since each court, at every level, must decide according to existing laws. Having achieved finality, however, a judicial decision becomes the last word of the judicial department with regard to a particular case or controversy, and Congress may not declare by retroactive legislation that the law applicable to that very case was something other than what the courts said it was.[44]

Robertson v. Seattle Audubon Society

503 U.S. 429 (1992)

■ JUSTICE THOMAS delivered the opinion of the [unanimous] Court.

In this case we must determine the operation of § 318 of the Department of the Interior and Related Agencies Appropriations Act, 1990.

I

This case arises out of two challenges to the Federal Government's continuing efforts to allow the harvesting and sale of timber from old-growth forests in the Pacific Northwest. These forests are home to the northern spotted owl, a bird listed as threatened under the Endangered Species Act of 1973 since June 1990. Harvesting the forests, say environmentalists, would kill the owls. Restrictions on harvesting, respond local timber industries, would devastate the region's economy.

Petitioner Robertson is Chief of the United States Forest Service, which manages 13 national forests in Oregon and Washington known to contain the northern spotted owl. In 1988, the Service amended its regional guide to prohibit timber harvesting on certain designated areas within those forests. Respondent Seattle Audubon Society (joined by various other environmental groups) and the Washington Contract Loggers Association (joined by various other industry groups) filed separate lawsuits in the District Court for the Western District of Washington, complaining respectively that the amendment afforded the owl either too little protection, or too much.

---

[44] *Id.* at 225–28.

[Multiple lawsuits resulted.] Twice before reversing (on grounds not relevant here), the Court of Appeals for the Ninth Circuit enjoined some of the challenged harvesting pending appeal.

In response to this ongoing litigation, Congress enacted § 318 of the Department of the Interior and Related Agencies Appropriations Act, 1990, popularly known as the Northwest Timber Compromise. The Compromise established a comprehensive set of rules to govern harvesting within a geographically and temporally limited domain. By its terms, it applied only to "the thirteen national forests in Oregon and Washington and [BLM] districts in western Oregon known to contain northern spotted owls." It expired automatically on September 30, 1990, the last day of fiscal year 1990, except that timber sales offered under § 318 were to remain subject to its terms for the duration of the applicable sales contracts.

The Compromise both required harvesting and expanded harvesting restrictions. Subsections (a)(1) and (a)(2) required the Forest Service and the BLM respectively to offer for sale specified quantities of timber from the affected lands before the end of fiscal year 1990. On the other hand, subsections (b)(3) and (b)(5) prohibited harvesting altogether from various designated areas within those lands, expanding the applicable administrative prohibitions and then codifying them for the remainder of the fiscal year. In addition, subsections (b)(1), (b)(2), and (b)(4) specified general environmental criteria to govern the selection of harvesting sites by the Forest Service. Subsection (g)(1) provided for limited, expedited judicial review of individual timber sales offered under § 318.

This controversy centers around the first sentence of subsection (b)(6)(A), which stated in part:

> The Congress hereby determines and directs that management of areas according to subsections (b)(3) and (b)(5) of this section on the thirteen national forests in Oregon and Washington and Bureau of Land Management lands in western Oregon known to contain northern spotted owls is adequate consideration for the purpose of meeting the statutory requirements that are the basis for the consolidated cases captioned *Seattle Audubon Society et al., v. F. Dale Robertson*, Civil No. 89–160 and *Washington Contract Loggers Assoc. et al., v. F. Dale Robertson*, Civil No. 89–99 (order granting preliminary injunction) and the case *Portland Audubon Society et al., v. Manuel Lujan, Jr.*, Civil No. 87–1160–FR.

Subsection (b)(6)(A) also declined to pass upon "the legal and factual adequacy" of the administrative documents produced by the 1988 Forest Service amendment and the 1987 BLM agreement.

After § 318 was enacted, both the *Seattle Audubon* and *Portland Audubon* defendants sought dismissal, arguing that the provision had temporarily superseded all statutes on which the plaintiffs' challenges had been based. The plaintiffs resisted on the ground that the first sentence of subsection (b)(6)(A), because it purported to direct the results in two pending cases, violated Article III of the Constitution.

II

The first sentence of subsection (b)(6)(A) provided that "management of areas according to subsections (b)(3) and (b)(5) . . . is adequate consideration for the purpose of meeting the statutory requirements that are the basis for [*Seattle Audubon*] and [*Portland Audubon*]." The Ninth Circuit held that this language did not "amend" any previously existing "laws," but rather "directed" certain "factual findings" and "specific result[s]" under those laws. Petitioners interpret the provision differently. They argue that subsection (b)(6)(A) replaced the legal standards underlying the two original challenges with those set forth in subsections (b)(3) and (b)(5), without directing particular applications under either the old or the new standards. We agree.

We conclude that subsection (b)(6)(A) compelled changes in law, not findings or results under old law. Before subsection (b)(6)(A) was enacted, the original claims would fail only if the challenged harvesting violated none of five old provisions. Under subsection (b)(6)(A), by contrast, those same claims would fail if the harvesting violated neither of two new provisions. Its operation, we think, modified the old provisions. Moreover, we find nothing in subsection (b)(6)(A) that purported to direct any particular findings of fact or applications of law, old or new, to fact.

Finally, respondents emphasize that subsection (b)(6)(A) explicitly made reference to pending cases identified by name and caption number. The reference to *Seattle Audubon* and *Portland Audubon*, however, served only to identify the five "statutory requirements that are the basis for" those cases—namely, pertinent provisions of MBTA, NEPA, NFMA, FLPMA, and OCLA. Subsection (b)(6)(A) named two pending cases in order to identify five statutory provisions. To the extent that subsection (b)(6)(A) affected the adjudication of the cases, it did so by effectively modifying the provisions at issue in those cases.

We have no occasion to address any broad question of Article III jurisprudence. The Court of Appeals held that subsection (b)(6)(A) was unconstitutional under *Klein* because it directed decisions in pending cases without amending any law. Because we conclude that subsection (b)(6)(A) *did* amend applicable law, we need not consider whether this reading of *Klein* is correct. The Court of Appeals stated additionally that a statute would be constitutional under *Wheeling Bridge* if it did amend law. Respondents' *amicus* Public Citizen challenges this proposition. It contends that even a change in law, prospectively applied, would be unconstitutional if the change swept no more broadly, or little more broadly, than the range of applications at issue in the pending cases. This alternative theory was neither raised below nor squarely considered by the Court of Appeals; nor was it advanced by respondents in this Court.

Accordingly, we decline to address it here. The judgment of the Court of Appeals is reversed, and the case is remanded for further proceedings consistent with this opinion.

It is so ordered.

NOTES AND QUESTIONS

1. You Can Bank On It. *Klein* held that Congress may not "prescribe rules of decision to the Judicial Department of the government in cases pending before it." *Robertson* held that, while Congress could not direct the outcome of pending cases, it could amend the applicable law without running afoul of separation of powers.

A new challenge to *Klein* was heard by the Court in January of 2016 (prior to Justice Scalia's death). *Bank Markazi v. Peterson*[45] involved a series of lawsuits brought by the family members of Americans killed in Iranian-sponsored terrorist attacks. While Iran would normally have sovereign immunity from suit, Congress withdrew the immunity from foreign governments that sponsor terrorism. When Iran refused to pay (or even defend against the suit), the plaintiffs claimed almost $2 billion in assets from the Iranian Central Bank.

While the suit was pending, Congress passed 22 U.S.C § 8872. Titled "Iran Threat Reduction and Syria Human Rights Act of 2012," the statute allowed the plaintiffs to seize "the financial assets that are identified in and the subject of proceedings in the United States District Court for the Southern District of New York in Peterson et al. v. Islamic Republic of Iran et al., Case No. 10 Civ. 4518 (BSJ) (GWG) . . . ."[46] Thus, Congress ensured that the plaintiffs in *Bank Markazi* won. The Bank ultimately appealed the case to the Supreme Court, which granted certiorari on the issue of "[w]hether § 8772—a statute that effectively directs a particular result in a single pending case—violates the separation of powers."[47]

In oral arguments, the Justices initially appeared inclined to give Congress wide latitude, "even as to particular controversies." Their views seemed to shift, however, as the arguments went on. The Deputy Solicitor General asserted that, although Congress might not act blatantly, it could instead achieve a particular outcome by "tweaking the law." Chief Justice Roberts responded, "You're saying that Congress has to be cute about it. They can't say Smith wins. But they can say in the case of *Jones v. Smith* where the critical issue is this, we can change that in a way so Smith wins."[48] Justice Breyer retorted, "Congress has 4,000 ways of being cute. And I can't quite see this Court trying to police those ways."[49]

---

[45] 136 S. Ct. 1310 (2016).

[46] 22 U.S.C § 8872(b).

[47] 14–770 Bank Markazi v. Peterson: Questions Presented, U.S. Supreme Court (Oct. 1, 2015), https://www.supremecourt.gov/qp/14-00770qp.pdf [https://perma.cc/X3G6-KBWJ].

[48] Transcript of Oral Argument at 49, Bank Markazi v. Peterson, 136 S. Ct. 1310 (2016) (No. 14–770), https://www.supremecourt.gov/oral_arguments/argument_transcripts/14-770_m64o.pdf [https://perma.cc/QK9M-VLYN].

[49] *Id.*

In April of 2016, the Court held that § 8772 does not violate separation of powers.[50] The Court reiterated that, while Congress may not prescribe rules of decision to courts in pending cases, it may amend applicable law. The Court concluded that § 8772 simply requires a court to apply a new legal standard in a pending post-judgment enforcement proceeding. The fact that the new legal standard made the outcome a foregone conclusion was irrelevant.

2. **Just a Tweak.** Is there a difference between directing that the court enter judgment for a particular party and "tweaking" the substantive law to effectively guarantee a win? Is that a distinction with a difference? *Bank Markazi* seems to indicate that it is not.

3. **Ten to One.** Does it matter whether Congress passes a law that affects ten cases instead of just one? What if Congress passes a law just prior to the inception of a lawsuit knowing the suit is about to be filed?

4. **Foreign Affairs.** What if the law arguably touches on foreign affairs? The Court indicated in *Bank Markazi* that the political branches have historically had unfettered power both to control the disposition of foreign state-owned property and to determine when a grant of sovereign immunity is appropriate.

5. **Similarly Situated Parties.** If Congress acted constitutionally in *Bank Markazi*, could it go one step further and enact legislation dictating disparate outcomes in legally identical cases? Does equal protection play a role in the analysis?

6. **This Legislation is for You.** What is the difference between the legislation at issue in *Bank Markazi* and a private bill? Legislators introduce hundreds of private bills each year, each designed to affect the rights, remedies, or responsibilities of an individual person or corporation. In 2015, private bills were introduced to address the immigration status of private parties, authorize the president to bestow the Medal of Honor on various veterans, transfer assets from the General Omar Bradley Foundation to his heirs, and award attorney's fees in a dispute with the BLM over water rights in the Snake River Basin.

7. **Off With Her Head.** Where a private law is enacted punitively it is called a bill of attainder. A bill of attainder declares a particular person guilty of a crime without trial. Once popular in England, bills of attainder resulted in the execution of Thomas Cromwell; King Henry VIII's fifth wife, Catherine Howard; and Anne Boleyn's sister-in-law and one-time accuser, Lady Jane Rochford. They are forbidden by Article I, section 9, of the United States Constitution.

§ 8.4 STATE ELECTORAL CHALLENGES

As discussed in Chapter 5, many states in the U.S. have judicial elections, either contested elections or retention votes in which the judge merely runs on his or her own record. Many observers believe that the

[50] *Bank Markazi*, 136 S. Ct. at 1317.

voters should have no say in either selection or retention of judges. The reasons are basically those laid out by Alexander Hamilton in 1788:

> The standard of good behavior for the continuance in office of the judicial magistracy, is certainly one of the most valuable of the modern improvements in the practice of government. In a monarchy it is an excellent barrier to the despotism of the prince; in a republic it is a no less excellent barrier to the encroachments and oppressions of the representative body. And it is the best expedient which can be devised in any government, to secure a steady, upright, and impartial administration of the laws.[51]

The counter-argument that has prevailed in many states is that the judicial function is inherently political and thus should be politically accountable. This has led to some notorious examples of voter interference in the judicial process. In 1986, three Justices of the California Supreme Court were defeated in retention votes. The principal issue revolved around the death penalty. Chief Justice Bird had voted to reverse all 61 death penalty cases that had come before her. Justices Reynoso and Grodin had the misfortune to be on the ballot at the same time and also lost the retention election, leaving the then-conservative Governor with three new appointments to the bench. Similarly, in Idaho, a ruling on water rights cost one sitting judge her seat in 2000 and came close to unseating another judge two years later.

Texas has a particularly ripe legacy of justice for sale. In the early 1980s, the plaintiffs' bar decided that the courts were leaning too heavily to the side of insurance companies against injured persons. They joined together and funded campaigns to get their sympathizers on the court. Soon after, insurance companies and hospitals mounted a concerted effort to elect judges sympathetic to their interests. Donors heavily funded various campaigns. Between 1992 and 1997, "the seven winning candidates for the Texas Supreme Court raised nearly $9.2 million dollars. Of this $9.2 million, more than 40% was contributed by parties or lawyers with cases before the court or by contributors linked to those parties."[52]

In 2014, the Kansas legislature adopted a provision stripping the Kansas Supreme Court of its power to appoint lower court chief judges (chosen from among sitting judges, not new appointments). The corresponding budget bill provided that the entire judiciary would lose much of its funding if the Supreme Court struck down the law on appointments. On December 23, 2015, the state's Supreme Court declared the appointment statute unconstitutional, stating that

---

[51] THE FEDERALIST NO. 78 (Alexander Hamilton).

[52] *Judicial Campaigns and Elections: Texas: Campaign Financing*, NAT'L CTR. FOR STATE COURTS, http://www.judicialselection.us/judicial_selection/campaigns_and_elections/campaign_financing.cfm?state=TX [http://perma.cc/7PMN-SGRR] (last visited Sept. 21, 2016).

> the means of assigning positions responsible to the Supreme Court and charged with effectuating Supreme Court policy must be in the hands of the Supreme Court, not the legislature. By enacting sec. 11 of H.B. 2338, the legislature asserted significant control over a constitutionally established essential power of the Supreme Court.[53]

The Court closed with this rather dry comment: "We note only that our holding appears to have practical adverse consequences to the judiciary budget, which the legislature may wish to address, even though those concerns played no part in our analysis."[54] The next step was that several Republican legislators tried to adopt a measure making it an impeachable offense for a judge to "attempt[ ] to usurp the power" of another branch.[55]

We have already seen one of the most notorious "justice for sale" cases—that of the West Virginia judge who was elected to the state Supreme Court after a coal company spent $3 million on his campaign. When he then voted for the company in a pending lawsuit, the U.S. Supreme Court took the case and ruled that the judge's participation amounted to a denial of due process because of the extreme probability of actual bias.[56]

§ 8.5 ADMINISTRATIVE LAW JUDGES

Different issues affect the independence of administrative law judges. As pointed out in Chapter 2, administrative law judges are not Article III judges. Instead, they are located in the executive branch under statutory authority from Congress. ALJs have none of the protections of Article III. Instead, they are hired by the federal Office of Personnel Management as career civil servants. The agency "may remove, suspend, reduce in level, reduce in pay, or furlough for 30 days or less an administrative law judge only for good cause established and determined by the Merit Systems Protection Board on the record and after opportunity for a hearing before the Board."[57]

Congress did not define what constitutes "good cause." "The general rule appears to be that '[a]ctions by an ALJ that undermine confidence in the administrative adjudicatory process constitute good cause for disciplinary action.' "[58] However, the agency may not "improperly interfere[ ] with an ALJ's performance, such as 'interference with the

---

53 Solomon v. State of Kansas, 364 P.3d 536, 549 (2015).

54 *Id.* at 550.

55 *Frustrated Kansas GOP Lawmakers Weigh Move to Impeach Top Judges*, KANSAS CITY (Mar. 7, 2016 1:44 PM), http://www.kansascity.com/news/state/kansas/article64574032.html [https://perma.cc/LVK3-K95Y].

56 Caperton v. A. T. Massey Coal Co., 556 U.S. 868 (2009).

57 5 U.S.C. § 7521 (2012).

58 VANESSA K. BURROWS, ADMINISTRATIVE LAW JUDGES: AN OVERVIEW 8 (Apr. 13, 2010), http://ssaconnect.com/tfiles/ALJ-Overview.pdf (citing A GUIDE TO FEDERAL AGENCY ADJUDICATION 172 (Michael Asimow, ed., 2003) [hereinafter Asimow]).

writing of opinions or interference with the way in which an ALJ conducts hearings.' "[59] ALJs have 45 days after briefing to issue an opinion, and judges have been disciplined for "a high rate of significant adjudicatory errors."[60] In 2014, the Association of Administrative Law Judges challenged a directive by the Social Security Administration's chief law judge requiring ALJs to issue "500–700 legally sufficient decisions each year."

Association of Administrative Law Judges v. Colvin

777 F.3d 402 (7th Cir. 2014)

■ POSNER, CIRCUIT JUDGE.

The Association of Administrative Law Judges (its cumbersome official name is given in the caption) is a union that, so far as relates to this case, represents the Social Security Administration's administrative law judges in collective bargaining with the Administration, pursuant to the Federal Labor-Management Relations Act. The Association, together with three administrative law judges employed by the Social Security Administration, are the plaintiffs in this suit, which, though the named defendant is the head of the Administration, is really a suit against the Administration itself because she is being sued in her official capacity.

The plaintiffs contend that, by requiring its administrative law judges to decide at least 500 social security disability cases a year the Administration has interfered with the administrative law judges' decisional independence, in violation of the Administrative Procedure Act, which provides that when conducting a hearing an administrative law judge is not subject to direction or supervision by other employees of the agency that he is employed by and may not be assigned duties inconsistent with his duties and responsibilities as an administrative law judge.

In October 2007 the Social Security Administration's chief administrative law judge issued a directive setting as a "goal" for the administrative law judges that each one "manage their docket in such a way that they will be able to issue 500–700 legally sufficient decisions each year." (When the directive was issued, 56 percent of the administrative law judges were deciding fewer than 500 cases a year.) Although it is described as a goal, the plaintiffs claim in their 37-page, 126-paragraph complaint that the Administration has taken formal and informal disciplinary measures to enforce it, so that it is in effect an enforceable and enforced quota. The purpose of the goal or quota is to reduce the backlog of disability cases.

---

[59] *Id.* (citing Asimow at 176–77).

[60] Asimow, at 172–76.

The district court dismissed the complaint for want of subject-matter jurisdiction, holding that the Civil Service Reform Act of 1978 precludes the plaintiffs' resort to the Administrative Procedure Act. The Civil Service Reform Act creates remedies for "prohibited personnel practices" taken against federal employees, and defines "personnel practices" to include "significant change in duties, responsibilities, or working conditions." 5 U.S.C. §§ 2302(a)(1), (2)(A)(xii), (b). Subsection (b) has a long list of the prohibited personnel practices, most of which are various types of discrimination. The district judge ruled that the plaintiffs were alleging a "significant change in duties, responsibilities, or working conditions," and if this is correct, their exclusive remedy is under the Civil Service Reform Act. It is correct. Increasing an employee's production quota changes his or her duties and responsibilities, and therefore working conditions. But the plaintiffs have no remedy under that Act either, even if they're right that the challenged order is a quota rather than a goal, because the Act does not prohibit an increase in a production quota unless the increase violates a prohibition listed in 5 U.S.C. § 2302(b), and the increase challenged in this case does not.

The plaintiffs argue that because it takes less time for an administrative law judge to award social security disability benefits than to deny benefits, because an award is not judicially appealable and therefore the administrative law judge doesn't have to be as careful in his analysis of the disability claim (doesn't, in short, have to try to make his decision appeal proof), the effect of the quota (as we'll call the "goal," thus giving the plaintiffs the benefit of the doubt) is to induce administrative law judges to award more benefits: were it not for the quota, they would deny benefits whenever they thought the applicant wasn't entitled to them under the law, even if making that determination took a lot of time. The argument is thus that the quota alters the administrative law judges' preferred ratio of grants to denials of benefits and by doing so infringes their decision-making independence.

The argument would have merit if the Social Security Administration had imposed the quota because it wanted a higher rate of benefits awards, but that is not contended. If the result of the quota is that the percentage of such awards has risen—and in fact there is evidence that the administrative law judges who decide the most cases per year also award benefits in a higher percentage of their cases than do the administrative law judges who decide fewer cases per year—this is not contended to be an aim of the quota, but an unintended and presumably unwanted byproduct. Because the social security disability insurance trust fund is on the verge of being exhausted [according to published reports], the Social Security Administration is under pressure to reduce, not increase, the aggregate disability benefits that its administrative law judges award—which in 2012 was $137 billion. U.S. Social Security Administration, Office of Retirement and Disability Policy, Annual Statistical Supplement, 2013, "Highlight and Trends."

The aim of the quota is to speed up decision-making rather than to prod administrative law judges to grant more applications for disability benefits.

Of course any change in work duties, responsibilities, or working conditions might affect an administrative law judge's decision-making. Beyond some point, increasing a worker's quota is going to induce him to spend less time on each task. If he is a worker on a poultry processing assembly line and the conveyor belt that carries the chickens to his work station for deboning is speeded up, he will spend less time deboning each chicken than he might think desirable to make sure no bits of bone are left in the chicken when it leaves his work station on the conveyor belt. In other words, the quality of his output would decline. Yet he would not be heard to claim that his decisional independence was being compromised. His situation would parallel that of the administrative law judges. The time pressure on him would result in a reduction in the quality of his work. Similarly, the plaintiffs allege that because of the quota, the quality of the administrative law judges' work decreases because they grant benefits in cases in which, had they more time, they would have denied benefits; the quota thus affected their decision-making.

Suppose the Social Security Administration hired more administrative law judges, thus reducing the workload of each one. With less pressure to grant benefits in order to make the quota, the administrative law judges might, because they were spending more time on each case, increase the fraction of benefit denials. But who would argue that increasing a work force is an actionable interference with the workers' decisional independence?

In the 1960s and 1970s there were very steep increases in federal court caseloads, and increases in the number of judgeships lagged. So each judge had to work harder. Maybe some judges responded by dismissing more cases earlier than they would have preferred to do. Would this have meant that by failing to increase the number of judges in proportion to the increase in caseload, the government was interfering with federal judges' decisional independence? The answer is no, and it is no here as well, and were it otherwise the courts would be flooded with cases brought by civil servants complaining that, as an incidental and unintended effect of a change in their working conditions, they had decided to reduce the amount of effort they devoted to each task they were assigned. An incidental and unintentional effect of a change in working conditions is not actionable under the Administrative Procedure Act.

We are mindful that the District of Columbia Circuit went even further, ruling that *any* action alleged to interfere with an administrative law judge's decisional independence is a personnel action governed exclusively by the Civil Service Reform Act even though that Act provides no remedy for personnel actions that interfere—even that intentionally interfere—with decisional independence. That ruling, if sound, would nullify the express protection of such independence in the Administrative Procedure Act. We doubt that it's sound but need not pursue the issue in this case. The other cases cited in Judge Ripple's concurring opinion do not involve claims relating to the infringement of decisional independence. But we are mindful of his suggestion that administrative law judges whose decisional independence is interfered with by their superiors might have a constitutional remedy. Although the suggestion opens up a rather frightening vista of constitutional claims by administrative law judges employed by the federal government, of whom some 1400 are employed by the Social Security Administration alone, we can imagine a case in which a change in working conditions could have an unintentional effect on decisional independence so great as to create a serious issue of due process. Suppose that solely for the sake of administrative efficiency the Social Security Administration ordered that disability hearings were to last no more than 15 minutes. The quality of justice meted out by the administrative law judges would be dangerously diminished. But all that matters for the decision of the present case is that the administrative law judges' remedy under the Administrative Procedure Act for interference with their decisional independence does not extend to the incidental consequences of a bona fide production quota.

AFFIRMED.

§ 8.6 INTERNATIONAL JUDICIAL INDEPENDENCE

A. INTERNATIONAL STANDARDS

There are numerous organizations around the world with codes that promote the independence of judges. Many of these are collected on the website of the International Commission of Jurists, although the ICJ does not itself promulgate a code.[61] Perhaps the most influential code is that of the International Bar Association, which emphasizes independence from the executive branch:[62]

IBA MINIMUM STANDARDS OF JUDICIAL INDEPENDENCE

(Adopted 1982)

A. JUDGES AND THE EXECUTIVE

1. Individual judges should enjoy personal independence and substantive independence.

---

[61] *International standards on the independence and accountability of judges, lawyers and prosecutors*, INT'L COMM'N OF JURISTS, http://www.icj.org/themes/centre-for-the-independence-of-judges-and-lawyers/international-standards/ [https://perma.cc/YZ5N-NK6F] (last visited Sept. 22, 2016).

[62] IBA MINIMUM STANDARDS OF JUDICIAL INDEPENDENCE, INT'L BAR ASS'N (1982), http://icj.wpengine.netdna-cdn.com/wp-content/uploads/2014/10/IBA_Resolutions_Minimum_Standards_of_Judicial_Independence_1982.pdf [http://perma.cc/R2NQ-673W].

a. Personal independence means that the terms and conditions of judicial service are adequately secured so as to ensure that individual judges are not subject to executive control.

b. Substantive independence means that in the discharge of his/her judicial function a judge is subject to nothing but the law and the commands of his/her conscience.

The International Association of Judicial Independence and World Peace, a group of volunteer lawyers and professors, states that "Judicial Independence is essential for democracy, liberty, world peace, and International Trade."[63] Unfortunately, judicial corruption is still common in the developing world.[64]

B. THE CONTINENTAL EXPERIENCE

With the obvious exception of Great Britain, most of the European judicial systems are built around the basics of the civil law model. In this model, law school graduates typically choose one of several routes in the profession, one of which may be the judicial route.

> Judges typically enter judicial service at the lower levels of the judiciary—they enter directly from law school after passing state qualifying examinations. Judicial service is analogous to a career in civil service in the United States, with judges moving up the court hierarchy based on seniority and merit. The standard image of the civil-law judge is one of "a civil servant who performs important but essentially uncreative functions."[65]

Despite this initial unflattering assessment, the Federal Judicial Center goes on to recognize that the many gaps and ambiguities in civil codes require interpretation, and civil-law judges take on an increasingly important role in building a coherent body of law.

In many countries the professional judiciary is subject to influence by executive ministerial decisions. The Minister of Justice often has the power to move a judge from one court to another and, in some instances,

---

[63] *Home*, INT'L ASS'N OF JUDICIAL INDEP. AND WORLD PEACE, http://www.jiwp.org/ [https://perma.cc/E5VP-WMYT] (last visited Sept. 22, 2016). One might question why "Trade" is capitalized while the other concepts are not, but that's a minor quibble.

[64] *See, e.g.*, Aislinn Laing, *Ghana Suspends Seven High Court Judges Over Bribe-Taking Film*, TELEGRAPH (Oct. 6, 2016, 9:00 PM), http://www.telegraph.co.uk/news/worldnews/africaandindianocean/ghana/11915763/Ghana-suspends-seven-high-court-judges-over-bribe-taking-film.html [https://perma.cc/E5MB-N898] (addressing judicial bribe-taking in Ghana); Ruth Sherlock, *Turkey Continues With Huge Purge of Judges and Police*, TELEGRAPH (Jan 22, 2014, 6:08 PM), http://www.telegraph.co.uk/news/worldnews/europe/turkey/10590399/Turkey-continues-with-huge-purge-of-judges-and-police.html [https://perma.cc/UR6F-MZW5] (addressing judicial corruption in Turkey); Muyiwa Adeyemi & Ado Ekiti, *Judiciary is corrupt, says Fayose*, GUARDIAN (Oct. 21, 2015, 4:40 AM), http://www.ngrguardiannews.com/2015/10/judiciary-is-corrupt-says-fayose/ [https://perma.cc/HAN5-9HPM] (addressing judicial corruption in Nigeria).

[65] JAMES G. APPLE & ROBERT P. DEYLING, FED. JUDICIAL CTR., A PRIMER ON THE CIVIL-LAW SYSTEM 30, http://www.fjc.gov/public/pdf.nsf/lookup/CivilLaw.pdf/$file/CivilLaw.pdf [https://perma.cc/E7WL-QA3C] (last visited Oct. 2, 2016).

to remove the judge altogether. Without the prospect of life tenure, therefore, judges are part of a three-way political discussion, or negotiation, with the executive and legislature. Indeed, in the classic parliamentary system, all three branches are in constant consultation despite the concept of separation of powers elaborated by Montesquieu.

C. JUDICIARIES IN TIMES OF CONFLICT

It is tempting to conclude that the Rule of Law effort is fruitless in a society plagued by violence and corruption, as it is unrealistic to expect people to turn to law when their very lives are at risk on a daily basis. The Rule of Law is designed to create stable social conditions conducive to economic and personal development—in other words, a peaceful and healthy society. Conversely, the Rule of Law is not generally possible in conditions where more powerful actors operate with impunity. The conundrum is that a justice system cannot operate in the midst of chaos, but chaos is difficult to forestall without a functioning justice system. Following the Cold War and the end of colonialism, many regions and countries around the world, including the Middle East, Russia, Eastern Europe, and the Southern Hemisphere, have undergone significant disruptions in pursuit of systems of governance.

1. THE MIDDLE EAST

The Arab Spring of 2011 appeared to be a democratic revolution sweeping across Northern Africa and into the Middle East. As existing totalitarian regimes toppled under the weight of combined grassroots and organized resistance, much of the world rejoiced that democracy was coming to a power-starved populace. The Arab Spring was, however, immediately followed by a difficult and chaotic transition sometimes referred to as the "Arab Winter."[66] Iraq and Libya are excellent examples of the pattern of uncertainty that dominates a nation undergoing rapid and chaotic transition.

Following the U.S. invasion and ouster of the Baathist regime of Saddam Hussein in Iraq, the Coalition Provisional Authority dismissed the former leadership of the military and the executive branch but left much of the judiciary in place. Iraq had centuries of judicial traditions dating back to the Code of Hammurabi, but these were interrupted by the Ottoman Empire, the British rule after WWII, and the dictatorship established in 1958. Following the 2003 U.S. invasion, there was hope for a stable judiciary that could overcome the Shi'a-Sunni tension in the country. Although the judiciary is functioning reasonably well in some parts of the country, the central government (and thus the judiciary) has lost control to ISIS in much of the country.

---

[66] Richard Spencer, *Middle East Review of 2012: The Arab Winter*, TELEGRAPH (Dec. 31, 2012, 9:00 AM GMT), http://www.telegraph.co.uk/news/worldnews/middleeast/9753123/Middle-East-review-of-2012-the-Arab-Winter.html [https://perma.cc/73Y6-AJ7U].

The judiciary in Turkey was rocked in early 2014 by the dismissal and reassignment of numerous judges. The chaos resulted from a corruption scandal that then-Prime Minister Erdogan said was engineered by a former ally turned bitter opponent. Erdogan said the judicial shakeup was intended to halt a "foreign plot" that was targeting corruption within the Erdogan government and family.[67] In February 2014, the legislature strengthened the role of the minister of justice, a move that was widely criticized by the international community. Turkey was making progress toward membership in the EU and is the pivot point of the flow of refugees from Syria, but the EU heavily criticized these moves as interference with human rights and judicial independence.[68] The aborted military coup in the summer of 2016 has led to further executive control over the judiciary.

2. RUSSIA

Russia has now had a quarter century of nominally democratic institutions, yet according to some observers, the old phenomenon of "telephone justice" is still alive and well.[69] Russia suffers from both public perceptions of corruption (tied with Nigeria in the Transparency International index of corruption)[70] and public reports by international leaders about the difficulties of the country's judiciary.

Dismissal of high-level judges and intervention into political trials implicate corruption and free expression with at least a hint of some political pressure on the judiciary. In 2012, the International Commission of Jurists reported on a number of issues within Russia, noting that "[t]he right to a fair trial and to an effective remedy for violations of human rights continues to be hampered by a weak judiciary that is vulnerable to undue influence from both private and public interests."[71]

The most specific development regarding judicial independence in the post-USSR is the 2014 report by UN Special Rapporteur on the Independence of Judges and Lawyers. Her report included observations about appointment and removal of judges by the executive, as well as threats against, and even murder of, some lawyers. She concluded with

---

[67] Sherlock, *supra* note 66.

[68] Laurence Norman & Emre Peker, *EU Criticizes Turkey for Backsliding on Judicial Independence, Media Freedoms*, WALL ST. J. (Nov 10, 2015 12:49 PM ET), http://www.wsj.com/articles/eu-criticizes-turkey-for-backsliding-on-judicial-independence-media-freedoms-1447142972 [https://perma.cc/7MPZ-KTAC].

[69] Alena Ledeneva, *Behind the Facade: "Telephone Justice", in* DICTATORSHIP OR REFORM? THE RULE OF LAW IN RUSSIA 24 (2006), https://www.files.ethz.ch/isn/26626/FULL_Dictatorship_Reform_Russia.pdf [https://perma.cc/8JA4-LDDQ].

[70] *Corruption by Country/Territory: Russia*, TRANSPARENCY INT'L, https://www.transparency.org/country/#RUS [https://perma.cc/UM8W-ELCR] (last visited Sept. 22, 2016).

[71] UNITED NATIONS HUMAN RIGHTS COUNCIL, INTERNATIONAL COMMISSION OF JURISTS (ICJ) SUBMISSION TO THE UNIVERSAL PERIODIC REVIEW OF THE RUSSIAN FEDERATION 2 (Oct. 2012), http://lib.ohchr.org/HRBodies/UPR/_layouts/15/WopiFrame.aspx?sourcedoc=/HRBodies/UPR/Documents/Session16/RU/ICJ_UPR_RUS_S16_2013_InternationalCommissionofJurists_E.pdf&action=default&DefaultItemOpen=1 [https://perma.cc/XL4S-MPNG].

49 specific recommendations, including taking appointment of judges away from the executive and creating independent procedures for judicial conduct review.[72]

The Human Rights Committee of the UN concluded in 2015 that there was an urgent need for reforms that would ensure judicial independence and stop the harassment of, and attacks on, lawyers.

3. EASTERN EUROPE

Romania was one member of the former Soviet bloc, along with Hungary and the Czech Republic, which seemed to be making strides toward joining the EU as a stable democracy. Then, in 2012, there were reports of executive "slashing" through the judiciary to install judges friendly to the leftist government.[73] The European Union also severely criticized Romania for failing to enact judicial reform.[74] Despite the government's alleged widespread corruption, at least one observer credits the judiciary with making significant progress:

> At the end of ten years of reform, the results are extraordinary: people above the law in the past, are now in prison, convicted for serious corruption offenses; prosecutors conduct investigations in a neutral way, destroying crime networks comprising businessmen, politicians and even judges.[75]

Poland was the subject of a 2010 UN Human Rights Committee report, which commented on a number of matters regarding human rights, including such matters as hate crimes (especially against the Roma), gender and sexual orientation, domestic violence, and length of pretrial detention. Significantly, the Committee had no comments about the independence of the judiciary beyond urging the appointment of more women judges.[76]

Then, in a rather sudden surge of conservatism, the right-wing Law and Justice Party (PiS) won a majority in Parliament in October 2015. Some of its immediate actions prompted the head of the European

---

[72] HUMAN RIGHTS COUNCIL, UNITED NATIONS GENERAL ASSEMBLY, REPORT OF THE SPECIAL RAPPORTEUR ON THE INDEPENDENCE OF JUDGES AND LAWYERS—MISSION TO THE RUSSIAN FEDERATION (A/HRC/26/32/ADD.1) 18–22 (APR. 30, 2014), http://www.ohchr.org/EN/Countries/ENACARegion/Pages/RUIndex.aspx [https://perma.cc/FAN8-E4H5].

[73] Kim Lane Scheppele, *Guest Post: Romania Unravels the Rule of Law*, N.Y. TIMES (July 4, 2012), http://krugman.blogs.nytimes.com/2012/07/05/guest-post-romania-unravels-the-rule-of-law [http://perma.cc/H86Z-7D9J].

[74] L.C, *What Will Happen to Romania's Judiciary?* ECONOMIST (Jan. 7, 2013), http://www.economist.com/blogs/easternapproaches/2013/01/romania-2013 [https://perma.cc/MZ6T-2RPD].

[75] *Thoughts on the Romanian Judicial System*, CEELI (October 21, 2014), http://ceeliinstitute.org/thoughts-on-the-romanian-judicial-system/ [https://perma.cc/XY77-SJRP].

[76] HUMAN RIGHTS COMM., INT'L COVENANT ON CIVIL AND POLITICAL RIGHTS, CONSIDERATION OF REPORTS SUBMITTED BY STATES PARTIES UNDER ARTICLE 40 OF THE COVENANT 3 (Nov. 15, 2010), http://tbinternet.ohchr.org/_layouts/treatybodyexternal/Download.aspx?symbolno=CCPR/C/POL/CO/6&Lang=En [https://perma.cc/MQ4W-VQFT].

Parliament to describe the new government as a "coup."[77] The new Parliament "voided" the appointment of several members of the Constitutional Court and substituted five of its own choices in their place. The Court declared this move unconstitutional and Parliament responded with legislation requiring decisions by the Court to be made by a two-thirds majority. In August 2016, the confrontation was boiling to a new head. "The PiS government is attempting an unconstitutional takeover of the tribunal—ignoring its rulings, trying to pack it with new judges, and, most recently, threatening the head judge with prosecution."[78]

4. THE SOUTHERN HEMISPHERE

Some former colonies in Asia and the southern hemisphere inherited the British system of government and have remained relatively stable. These include Australia, New Zealand, Malaysia, Singapore, and India. South Africa, after its experience with apartheid, settled into a reasonably stable situation based on its former Dutch colonial governance.

Elsewhere, much of the southern hemisphere has been chaotic. Africa has seen myriad civil wars. Even those countries that have stabilized their basic government structures are often besieged by corruption. South America has pockets of stability, but other areas are dominated by drug lords, oil-rich despotic regimes, and poverty that fuels instability.

Prior to colonization, many areas of the world had their own robust dispute resolution systems, both formal and informal in character. Developed over centuries, the informal systems could create stable structures usually based on adjudication by tribal or village elders. European colonizers imposed Western systems of government, often dismantling traditional culture in the process. After independence, some newly formed countries were able to reintegrate their historical systems of governance, while others were left without cultural roots or stable systems. These latter countries often experienced political and social upheavals resulting in violence and even collapse.[79]

5. CONCLUSION

As this brief summary of some of the more chaotic regions of the world indicates, it is extremely difficult to identify the state of the judiciary in areas undergoing upheaval, especially those in states of

[77] *Poland's New Right-Wing Leaders Have Crossed a Line*, WASH. POST (Dec. 22, 2015), https://www.washingtonpost.com/opinions/polands-new-right-wing-leaders-cross-a-line/2015/12/22/54d42ea4-a8d3-11e5-8058-480b572b4aae_story.html [https://perma.cc/G5QU-HTYD].

[78] R. Daniel Kelemen, *Poland's Constitutional Crisis: How the Law and Justice Party is Threatening Democracy*, FOREIGN AFF. (Aug. 25, 2016), https://www.foreignaffairs.com/articles/poland/2016-08-25/polands-constitutional-crisis [https://perma.cc/3SJX-UMYK].

[79] For a collection of essays elaborating aspects of this phenomenon, see PROMOTING THE RULE OF LAW ABROAD (Thomas Carothers ed., 2006).

violent civil war. An independent judiciary is vital to the Rule of Law, which itself is vital to the health of a community and economy.

CHAPTER 9

COMMON LAW REASONING & STATUTORY INTERPRETATION

> We are not final because we are infallible, but we are infallible only because we are final.
>
> – United States Supreme Court Justice Robert H. Jackson[1]

How do judges make decisions? What do they do when the law isn't clear? Do judges make law? Find law? Make emotional decisions without law? Do they have the power to do any of these things, or must they always be subservient to the legislature? Partial answers may lie in the history and traditions of the common law, as well as the framework for statutory interpretation.

§ 9.1 DECISION-MAKING AT COMMON LAW

The heart of the common law process is the role of stare decisis, an abbreviation of the Latin phrase *stare decisis et non quieta movere*: to stand by decisions and not disturb settled matters. It is one of the first concepts taught in law school, and its roots go back almost 1,000 years.

A. HISTORY OF THE COMMON LAW

In September 1066, William, Duke of Normandy, invaded the south coast of England. Arriving on the shore and falling into the sand, he announced, "I have taken possession of England with both my hands."[2]

Also known as William the Bastard (because his parents were not married) and William the Conqueror, he set about destroying everything in his path. Although he had himself crowned King of England on Christmas Day in 1066, he actually controlled only a small part of the country. William spent the next 18 years pacifying the countryside, particularly the rebellious north. While he initiated a campaign of cruelty and brutality, he simultaneously created a Norman aristocracy and gave the new nobles land, wealth, and power.

---

1 Brown v. Allen, 344 U.S. 443, 540 (1953) (Jackson, J., concurring).

2 WILLIAM FRANCIS COLLIER, HISTORY OF ENGLAND: WITH A SKETCH OF OUR INDIAN AND COLONIAL EMPIRE 80 (1864), https://books.google.com/books?id=n1kBAAAAQAAJ&pg=PA80&lpg=PA80&dq=I+have+taken+England+with+both+my+hands.&source=bl&ots=vP6k6m0zBS&sig=jHApUsD3t6CTqNWsWGS97AdlaVc&hl=en&sa=X&ved=0ahUKEwjM2LSLnPnOAhVW1WMKHXkLDAsQ6AEIODAG#v=onepage&q=I%20have%20takenËngland%20with%20both%20my%20hands.&f=false [https://perma.cc/6DZY-52H7].

Prior to the ascent of the Normans, English law was local. It was rooted in local customs, as well as canonical laws, and was known and enforced by local courts. However, as Norman nobility centralized power, it took over the local courts. These new national courts didn't know local customs, local law, or even the local language—even William never learned to speak English. French became the language of the law, although it eventually merged with Middle English to create modern English. As the courts became more centralized, even the English began to look to the King's courts rather than their local authorities. There was no Parliament and, thus, no statutory law.

Under Henry II, the King began to send judges from central courts to the countryside. They would return to London to discuss and record their rulings. They made an effort to harmonize their rulings, and treated prior rulings as (at least somewhat) binding on later cases. Thus, the "common" law was born. The judges applied basic rules that every medieval society required. As new situations arose, the judges reasoned by analogy. They often acted as if this law had been there all along. They came to realize that following precedent was also efficient: they didn't have to struggle with an issue if someone else had already decided it. In addition, the common law provided much-needed predictability at a time when the middle class was beginning to drive the economic life of the country. Those tenets of efficiency and predictability stand today as the cornerstones of the common law system.

Thus, since the 1100s the courts have had either sole or co-equal authority to make law. "Legislating from the bench" is a historical and legitimate role of the court.

B. COMMON LAW REASONING

Perhaps the most famous of all observations on both the art of statutory construction and common law reasoning was from the late professor and legal scholar Karl Llewellyn. He began with a discussion of how courts viewed prior cases.[3] His article continues with a discussion of statutory construction, excerpted in § 9.02(A)(1) below.

Karl N. Llewellyn
Remarks on the Theory of Appellate Decision and the Rules of Canons About How Statutes are to be Construed

ONE DOES NOT PROGRESS far into legal life without learning that there is no single right and accurate way of reading one case, or of reading a bunch of cases. For

[3] Karl N. Llewellyn, *Remarks on the Theory of Appellate Decision and the Rules of Canons About How Statutes are to be Construed*, 3 VAND. L. REV. 395 (1950), republished with permission.

(1) Impeccable and correct doctrine makes clear that a case "holds" with authority only so much of what the opinion says as is absolutely necessary to sustain the judgment. Anything else is unnecessary and "distinguishable" and noncontrolling for the future. Indeed, if the judgment rests on two, three or four rulings, any of them can be rightly and righteously knocked out, for the future, as being thus "unnecessary." Moreover, any distinction on the facts is rightly and righteously a reason for distinguishing and therefore disregarding the prior alleged holding. But

(2) Doctrine equally impeccable and correct makes clear that a case "holds" with authority the rule on which the court there chose to rest the judgment; more, that that rule covers, with full authority, cases which are plainly distinguishable on their facts and their issue, whenever the reason for the rule extends to cover them. Indeed, it is unnecessary for a rule or principle to have led to the decision in the prior case, or even to have been phrased therein, in order to be seen as controlling in the new case: (a) "We there said . . . " (b) "That case necessarily decided . . . "

These divergent and indeed conflicting correct ways of handling or reading a single prior case as one "determines" what it authoritatively holds, have their counterparts in regard to the authority of a series or body of cases. Thus

(1) It is correct to see that "That rule is too well settled in this jurisdiction to be disturbed"; and so to apply it to a wholly novel circumstance. But

(2) It is no less correct to see that "The rule has never been extended to a case like the present"; and so to refuse to apply it: "We here limit the rule." Again,

(3) It is no less correct to look over the prior "applications" of "the rule" and rework them into a wholly new formulation of "the true rule" or "true principle" which knocks out some of the prior cases as simply "misapplications" and then builds up the others.

In the work of a single opinion-day I have observed 26 different, describable ways in which one of our best state courts handled its own prior cases, repeatedly using three to six different ways within a single opinion.

What is important is that *all* 26 ways (plus a dozen others which happened not to be in use that day) are correct. They represent not "evasion," but sound use, application and development of precedent. They represent not "departure from," but sound continuation of, our system of precedent as it has come down to us. The major defect in that system is a mistaken idea which many lawyers have about it—to wit, the idea that the cases themselves and in themselves, plus the correct rules on how to handle cases, provide one single correct answer to a disputed issue of law. In fact the available correct answers are two, three, or ten. The question is: *Which* of the available correct answers will the court *select*—and *why*?

For since there is always more than one available correct answer, the court always has to select.

C. COMMON LAW REASONING AT WORK

The common law frequently develops as communities progress socially, economically, and politically. For example, the British courts initially had a choice between two opposing views of injuries: one in which a person who caused harm to another paid regardless of the circumstances (a rule that prevails today in many primitive cultures), or one in which the injured person could recover compensation only if the other were at fault. Courts opted for the latter position under the pressure of increasing urbanization and the complexities of emerging technological changes (such as buggies on crowded streets).

Once that principle was established many other questions arose. What is the duty of care that one person owes to another? What if the injured person assumed the risk of danger? These and other questions were answered through the courts' use of both analogies and public policy. The result was that the landed gentry were protected by the courts, and liability varied based on the class of plaintiff, be they a trespasser, a licensee, or an invitee.

Modern courts must struggle to apply these distinctions to a changed society. They have the tools of common law reasoning at their disposal: reasoning by analogy, applying "common sense" applications, and determining the best public policy for parties in today's courts.

Chicago, B. & Q. R. Co. v. Krayenbuhl

65 Neb. 889, 91 N.W. 880 (1902)

■ Opinion by ALBERT, C.

This action was brought on behalf of Leo Krayenbuhl, against the Chicago, Burlington & Quincy Railroad Company, to recover for personal injuries received by the plaintiff while playing on a turntable belonging to the defendant.

[The railroad operated a "turntable," a device which you can see in operation today at the end of the cable car lines in San Francisco, by which a train can be turned around at the end of one line and pointed either back along the same line or in a different direction. The four-year-old plaintiff lived with his father, an employee of the railroad, near this turntable.]

On [the day of the injury], in company with some other members of the family, the oldest of whom was eleven years old, and some other children, the oldest of whom was fourteen, were playing with a push car, moving it up and down on the railroad track. The agent in charge of the station joined them, and rode a short distance on the car. He then left them, and went to his rooms in the station. The children continued to push the car, and finally reached the turntable. There is evidence sufficient to sustain a finding that they found the turntable unlocked and unguarded, but the evidence is conflicting on that point. The plaintiff and some of the other children got on the turntable, while two of the others set it in motion. While it was in motion the plaintiff's foot was caught between the rails, and severed at the ankle joint. The injury thus sustained is that for which damages is sought in this action. A trial was had to a jury, which resulted in a verdict and judgment for the plaintiff. The defendant brings error.

The [turntable] doctrine, as we gather it from the cases cited, is that where a turntable is so situated that its owner may reasonably expect that children too young to appreciate the danger will resort to it, and amuse themselves by using it, it is guilty of negligence for a failure to take reasonable precautions to prevent such use. It has not been permitted to pass as law unchallenged. On the contrary, it has been expressly repudiated in many cases.

The defendant insists that the doctrine is unsound, and asks that it be repudiated by the court. The argument in this behalf rests on the proposition that the owner of dangerous premises owes no active duty to trespassing children. The proposition is not universally true. There may be, and often are, circumstances under which one owes some active duty to a trespasser upon his premises. If a man wilfully lies down upon a railroad track the engineer must not wantonly run his engine over him. One may not set a snare or spring-gun for trespassers, and, knowing that some stranger had placed the snare or spring-gun, if he wantonly allows it to remain he will be responsible for the consequences. A well may be so contrived as to act as a dangerous trap, and one who allows it so to remain upon his premises will, under some circumstances, be liable. If adults, or children of such age as to ordinarily be capable of discerning and avoiding danger are injured while trespassing upon the premises of another, they may be without remedy, while under similar circumstances children of three or four years of age would be protected. If I know that there is an open well upon my premises and know that children of such tender years as to have no notion of their danger are continually playing around it and I can obviate the danger with very little trouble to myself and without injuring the premises or interfering with my own free use thereof, I owe an active duty to those children, and if I neglect that duty and they fall into the well and are killed it is through my negligence. I cannot urge their negligence as a defense, even though I have never invited or encouraged them expressly or impliedly to go upon the premises.

It is true [that] "the business of life must go forward"; the means by which it is carried forward cannot be rendered absolutely safe. Ordinarily, it can be best carried forward by the unrestricted use of private property by the owner; therefore, the law favors such use to the fullest extent consistent with the main purpose for which, from a social standpoint, such business is carried forward, namely, the public good.

Hence, in order to determine the extent to which such use may be enjoyed, its bearing on such main purpose must be taken into account, and a balance struck between its advantages and disadvantages. If, on the whole, such use defeats rather than promotes the main purpose, it should not be permitted; on the other hand, if the restrictions proposed would so operate, they should not be imposed. The business of life is better carried forward by the use of dangerous machinery; hence the public good demands its use, although occasionally such use results in the loss of life or limb. It does so because the danger is insignificant, when weighed against the benefits resulting from the use of such machinery, and for the same reason demands its reasonable, most effective and unrestricted use, up to the point where the benefits resulting from such use no longer outweigh the danger to be anticipated from it. At that point the public good demands restrictions. For example, a turntable is a dangerous contrivance, which facilitates railroading; the general benefits resulting from its use outweigh the occasional injuries inflicted by it; hence the public good demands its use. We may conceive of means by which it might be rendered absolutely safe, but such means would so interfere with its beneficial use that the danger to be anticipated would not justify their adoption; therefore the public good demands its use without them. But the danger incident to its use may be lessened by the use of a lock which would prevent children, attracted to it, from moving it; the interference with the proper use of the turntable occasioned by the use of such lock is so slight that it is outweighed by the danger to be anticipated from an omission to use it; therefore the public good, we think, demands the use of the lock. The public good would not require the owner of a vacant lot on which there is a pond to fill up the pond or enclose the lot with an impassible wall to insure the safety of children resorting to it, because the burden of doing so is out of all proportion to the danger to be anticipated from leaving it undone. But where there is an open well on a vacant lot, which is frequented by children, of which the owner of the lot has knowledge, he is liable for injuries sustained by children falling into the well, because the danger to be anticipated from the open well, under the circumstances, outweighs the slight expense or inconvenience that would be entailed in making it safe.

Hence, in all cases of this kind, in the determination of the question of negligence, regard must be had to the character and location of the premises, the purpose for which they are used, the probability of injury therefrom, the precautions necessary to prevent such injury, and the relations such precautions bear to the beneficial use of the premises. The nature of the precautions would depend on the particular facts in each case. In some cases, a warning to the children or the parents might be sufficient; in others, more active measures might be required. But in every case they should be such as a man of ordinary care and prudence would observe under like circumstances. If, under all the circumstances, the owner omits such precautions as a man of ordinary care and prudence, under like circumstances, would observe, he is guilty of negligence. We are fully satisfied that the principle under consideration is sound, and that its application would not operate oppressively on the owner. We see no good reason for receding from the position already taken by this court in cases of this character.

NOTES AND QUESTIONS

1. **Benefits and Burdens, Weighed and Measured.** The court in *Krayenbuhl* openly weighs the benefits of protecting the public against the cost of remediation. It sanctions the "public good" of railroad turntables, despite the occasional "loss of life or limb." Is this balancing callous? Does it give a putative defendant sufficient notice of required safety measures?

The task of weighing benefits and burdens eventually gave rise to Judge Learned Hand's famous algebraic formula for assessing negligence. After reviewing a number of cases involving accidents that might have been avoided by the expenditure of additional funds or care, he stated the weighing of burdens: "if the probability be called P; the injury, L; and the burden, B; liability depends upon whether B is less than L multiplied by P: i.e., whether B less than PL."[4]

The result is this formula: If B<PL, then liability. Thus, if the burden on the defendant of additional safeguards is less than the probable serious harm, then those additional safeguards should be taken.

Does Judge Hand's formula make public policy determinations more scientific, or does it just add a patina of neutrality to what is inherently a discretionary task?

2. **Whose Job Is It, Anyway?** Who is in the best position to assess the relative burdens and benefits to society from particular mechanical or societal changes? Should judges determine the "public good," and is there any principled way for a judge to make that determination? How did judges obtain the power to create such a rubric? Did "We the People" delegate this power? Was it inherited from the roles assigned to judges by British kings? Does it exist because legislatures have abdicated the role?

3. **Analogies and Inductive Reasoning.** The court compares the railroad turntable to ponds and open wells, reasoning by analogy to its conclusion. This graphic illustration shows how the first case might determine the outcome of two others:

a. If A and B while X, then liability.

b. If A and B while Y, then?

c. If A and C while X, then?

How would you answer either question (b) or (c)? We need to know how similar fact Y is to fact X in the second case, or how similar fact C is to fact B in the third case. But that means that we need to know on what basis to make the comparisons. Here is a simple syllogism that attempts to fill in one of the blanks:

---

[4] United States v. Carroll Towing Co., 159 F.2d 169, 173 (2d Cir. 1947).

If A and B while X, then liability.

Y is similar to X.

Therefore, if A and B while Y, then liability.

The problem with this syllogism is that we do not yet know on what basis someone decided that Y was similar to X. That is the purpose behind opinion writing by common law judges. They reason by analogy and they are obligated to explain the reasons for their conclusions.

The syllogism also shows a genuine risk in the common law method. What the judge is trying to do in reasoning by analogy is to glean a principle from past experience to apply to a future case. The gleaning of a principle from specific cases is called induction, while the application of a principle to a particular case is deduction. There is no certainty in the inductive phase of the reasoning process. It is often said that just because the sun has come up in the east for thousands of years there is no guarantee that it will do so in the future.

Further, we may need additional precedents to fill in gaps in our understanding of principles to be applied.

Given [1, 2, 3 . . .], what is the next number?

At this point, the available data would justify an inference that any of three different sets is involved:

a. 1, 2, 3, 4, 5, 6, 7 . . . [All integers in sequence]

b. 1, 2, 3, 5, 7, 11, 13 . . . [All prime numbers—that is, numbers divisible only by 1 and themselves]

c. 1, 2, 3, 5, 8, 13, 21 . . . [A Fibonacci series, in which each succeeding term is the sum of the two immediately preceding numbers]

This simple example illustrates Llewellyn's point that we cannot know the future use of a case just by knowing what was held in that case. Future experience will fill in gaps in our understanding of what principles are explaining the outcomes of cases. Of course, to the extent that judges explain their reasoning lucidly and candidly, future judges are more able to grasp the reason for the prior holding and decide for themselves whether to agree or disagree.[5]

4. **No Phone Zone.** Imagine one case in which a driver was found negligent for reading a newspaper while driving, and then analogize that to a driver reaching under the seat for a lost item. Is reaching under the seat the same as reading a newspaper? Is either the same as talking on a phone or texting while driving? How should a judge decide?

Some judges would consider only deductive reasoning, while others would consider the purpose of the law or the consequences of a particular outcome.

---

[5] *See* Lee Teitelbaum & Wayne McCormack, *A Simplified Introduction to Legal Argument*, 2006 UTAH L. REV. 35 (2006).

What if the legislature passes a statute making texting while driving a crime? What impact does that statute have on existing common law? What advantages or disadvantages does a statute have over common law?

5. **Judicial Empathy.** What role should empathy have in judicial decision-making? Some commentators have held up United States District Court Judge Jack Weinstein as a model of the empathetic judge:

> His judicial philosophy places great weight on the responsibility of the judge to seek out a broad understanding not only of the litigants' situations, but also of the societal context in which their cases arise. He says quite movingly: "Were it possible, judges would want to crawl into the skin of society, acquiring all knowledge and understanding all feelings. . . . Judges cannot make accurate findings of fact or evaluate the effect of their decisions unless they have some understanding of society."[6]

Judge Weinstein emphasized treating "every person appearing before the judge [as a] human being [ ] entitled to be treated with dignity, and that often requires that we speak face-to-face and try to . . . appreciate that we have a human being before us."[7]

Is empathy different from sympathy? For example, a judge in a landlord-tenant case might be troubled by the prospect of evicting a family from an apartment after a three-day notice. The sympathetic judge might feel compassion for the tenant, but have no difficulty applying the law. The empathetic judge, however, might put herself in the shoes of the tenant, making it tremendously difficult to apply the law. Is empathy a necessary, or even desirable, trait in a judge?

6. **Fact and Law.** The common law may not dictate whether a particular issue should be decided by the judge or the jury. Issues of law are for the judge, issues of fact are for the jury, and mixed questions such as negligence may be for either or both. One way to resolve the difficulty is for the judge to consider negligence as a question of law under the heading of "scope of duty," while giving essentially the same question to the jury under the heading of "proximate cause." Is there wisdom in the common law lack of clarity, because it allows for community standards of behavior to evolve?

§ 9.2 THE INTERSECTION BETWEEN COMMON LAW AND STATUTES

For all the history and care that has gone into the creation of the common law, it can be incomplete, inconsistent, or anachronistic. It necessarily creeps along, developing slowly and only as necessary.

If one purpose of law is to provide clear and workable standards for a society, the common law can fall woefully short. For example, how does an event manager know whether his or her duty to spectators has been

---

6 Susan Bandes, *Empathy and Article III: Judge Weinstein, Cases and Controversies*, 64 DEPAUL L. REV. 317, 318 (2015).

7 *Id.* at 317 (citations omitted).

fulfilled? How does a doctor know when to conduct another test? How does a car manufacturer know whether it is necessary to include air bags or collision avoidance devices?

In addition to potentially leaving gaps in the law, common law created by judges—sometimes hundreds of years ago—may run counter to the more rapidly-evolving preferences of the people and the legislature. For example, common law norms regarding liability may interfere with the protection a legislature would like to provide for industries such as hospitals or ski resorts.

To resolve uncertainties, legislatures are importuned to create statutory "rules." No matter how thoughtful the legislative process or how careful the drafting, however, no statute can close every loophole and anticipate every factual variation. As a result, courts must once again step in and interpret the statute.

Whether the legislature is attempting to clarify the common law, overturn the common law, or fill in a gap in the law, a court charged with determining the meaning of a statute has a range of options. A court is not supposed to substitute its own best judgment about what a statute should or should not do. Instead, it must start with the plain meaning of the statute. However, English is a complicated language, and the meaning of words can change over time. New facts creep up, sometimes precipitated by technological or societal change. Sometimes statutes are deliberately vague, often because of compromises made by the drafters. When "plain meaning" fails—and it often does—courts must apply an established tool of statutory construction.

A. CODIFIED LAWS ON STATUTORY CONSTRUCTION

Every jurisdiction has codified laws on statutory construction. These laws are designed to guide a court tasked with interpreting the legislation. Some apply to an entire code. For example, Title 1 of the United States Code provides universal definitions for a variety of words scattered throughout sections of the federal laws, including "county," "vessel," "vehicle," "company," and "products of American fisheries." It also directs courts that the singular includes the plural, the masculine the feminine, and the present the future.

Many statutes also have definitions or rules of construction designed to direct interpretation of a limited portion of the code. For example, 21 U.S.C. § 853(o) tells courts that the code on investment of illicit drug profits "shall be liberally construed to effectuate its remedial purposes." Similarly, 18 U.S.C. § 700(c) informs courts that "[n]othing in this section shall be construed as indicating an intent on the part of Congress to deprive any State, territory, possession, or the Commonwealth of Puerto Rico of jurisdiction over any offense over which it would have jurisdiction in the absence of this section."

Finally, some codes may be prefaced by a purpose or intent section. 15 U.S.C. § 1127 provides that

> [i]n the construction of this chapter, unless the contrary is plainly apparent from the context. . . . The intent of this chapter is to regulate commerce within the control of Congress by making actionable the deceptive and misleading use of marks in such commerce; to protect registered marks used in such commerce from interference by State, or territorial legislation; to protect persons engaged in such commerce against unfair competition; to prevent fraud and deception in such commerce by the use of reproductions, copies, counterfeits, or colorable imitations of registered marks; and to provide rights and remedies stipulated by treaties and conventions respecting trademarks, trade names, and unfair competition entered into between the United States and foreign nations.

Courts use these statutory sections to help effectuate the intent of the legislature where possible.

B. CANONS OF STATUTORY CONSTRUCTION

In the absence of instructions from a law-making authority, courts rely on common law rules, also known as canons of statutory construction. These rules are well-known and are generally understood by legislators engaged in the drafting process.

Courts have adopted and relied on canons for more than four centuries. In 1584, Lord Coke laid out the rules "for the sure and true interpretation of all statutes in general (be they penal or beneficial, restrictive or enlarging of the common law):

> 1st. What was the common law before the making of the Act.
>
> 2nd. What was the mischief and defect for which the common law did not provide.
>
> 3rd. What remedy the Parliament hath resolved and appointed to cure the disease of the commonwealth. And,
>
> 4th. The true reason of the remedy; and then the office of all the Judges is always to make such construction as shall suppress the mischief, and advance the remedy, and to suppress subtle inventions and evasions for continuance of the mischief, *pro privato commodo*, and to add force and life to the cure and remedy, according to the true intent of the makers of the Act, *pro bono publico*.[8]

Coke's rule, also known as the mischief rule, construes statutes to effectuate the intended remedy. Other judges and academics have

---

[8] *Heydon's Case* (1584), 76 Eng. Rep. 637, 628 (L.R. Exch.) (internal citations omitted) (paragraph structure added).

emphasized the plain meaning of the language in the statute, the intent of the legislators, and the practical results of particular interpretations.

William Blackstone
Commentaries on the Laws of England Section the Second: Of the Nature of Laws in General[9]

The fairest and most rational method to interpret the will of the legislator, is by exploring his intentions at the time when the law was made, by signs the most natural and probable. And these signs are either the words, the context, the subject-matter, the effects and consequence, or the spirit and reason of the law. Let us take a short view of them all.

1. Words are generally to be understood in their usual and most known signification; not so much regarding the propriety of grammar, as their general and popular use. Thus the law mentioned by Puffendorf, which forbad a layman to lay hands on a priest, was adjudged to extend to him, who had hurt a priest with a weapon. Again; terms of art, or technical terms, must be taken according to the acceptation of the learned in each art, trade, and science. So in the act of settlement, where the crown of England is limited "to the princess Sophia, and the heirs of her body, being protestants," it becomes necessary to call in the assistance of lawyers, to ascertain the precise idea of the words "heirs of her body;" which in a legal sense comprize only certain of her lineal descendants.

2. If words happen to be still dubious, we may establish their meaning from the context; with which it may be of singular use to compare a word, or a sentence, whenever they are ambiguous, equivocal, or intricate. Thus the proeme, or preamble, is often called in to help the construction of an act of parliament. Of the same nature and use is the comparison of a law with other laws, that are made by the same legislator, that have some affinity with the subject, or that expressly relate to the same point.

Thus, when the law of England declares murder to be felony without benefit of clergy, we must resort to the same law of England to learn what the benefit of clergy is: and when the common law censures simoniacal contracts, it affords great light to the subject to consider what the canon law has adjudged to be simony [buying or selling of ecclesiastical privilege].

3. As to the subject-matter, words are always to be understood as having a regard thereto; for that is always supposed to be in the eye of the legislator, and all his expressions directed to that end. Thus, when a law of our Edward III. forbids all ecclesiastical persons to purchase provisions at Rome, it might seem to prohibit the buying of grain and

---

[9] WILLIAM BLACKSTONE, *Section the Second: Of the Nature of Laws in General*, *in* COMMENTARIES ON THE LAWS OF ENGLAND (1753), http://avalon.law.yale.edu/18th_century/blackstone_intro.asp#2 [https://perma.cc/6FLP-DPSC].

other victuals; but when we consider that the statute was made to repress the usurpations of the papal see, and that the nominations to benefices by the pope were called provisions, we shall see that the restraint is intended to be laid upon such provisions only.

4. As to the effects and consequence, the rule is, that where words bear either none, or a very absurd signification, if literally understood, we must a little deviate from the received sense of them. Therefore the Bolognian law, mentioned by Puffendorf, which enacted "that whoever drew blood in the streets should be punished with the utmost severity," was held after a long debate not to extend to the surgeon, who opened the vein of a person that fell down in the street with a fit.

5. But, lastly, the most universal and effectual way of discovering the true meaning of a law, when the words are dubious, is by considering the reason and spirit of it; or the cause which moved the legislator to enact it. For when this reason ceases, the law itself ought likewise to cease with it. An instance of this is given in a case put by Cicero, or whoever was the author of the treatise inscribed to Herennius. There was a law, that those who in a storm forsook the ship, should forfeit all property therein; and that the ship and lading should belong entirely to those who staid in it. In a dangerous tempest all the mariners forsook the ship, except only one sick passenger, who by reason of his disease was unable to get out and escape. By chance the ship came safe to port. The sick man kept possession, and claimed the benefit of the law. Now here all the learned agree, that the sick man is not within the reason of the law; for the reason of making it was, to give encouragement to such as should venture their lives to save the vessel: but this is a merit, which he could never pretend to, who neither staid in the ship upon that account, nor contributed anything to its preservation.

From this method of interpreting laws, by the reason of them, arises what we call equity; which is thus defined by Grotius, "the correction of that, wherein the law (by reason of its universality) is deficient." For since in laws all cases cannot be foreseen or expressed, it is necessary, that when the general decrees of the law come to be applied to particular cases, there should be somewhere a power vested of defining those circumstances, which (had they been foreseen) the legislator himself would have expressed. And these are the cases which, according to Grotius, "*lex non exacte definit, sed arbitrio boni viri permittit.*"

Equity thus depending, essentially, upon the particular circumstances of each individual case, there can be no established rules and fixed precepts of equity laid down, without destroying its very essence, and reducing it to a positive law. And, on the other hand, the liberty of considering all cases in an equitable light, must not be indulged too far; lest thereby we destroy all law, and leave the decision of every question entirely in the breast of the judge. And law, without equity, though hard and disagreeable, is much more desirable for the public good, than equity without law: which would make every judge a legislator, and introduce most infinite confusion; as there would then be almost as many different rules of action laid down in our courts, as there are differences of capacity and sentiment in the human mind.

Karl N. Llewellyn
Remarks on the Theory of Appellate Decision and the Rules of Canons About How Statutes are to be Construed[10]

If a statute is to make sense, it must be read in the light of some assumed purpose. A statute merely declaring a rule, with no purpose or objective, is nonsense.

If a statute is to be merged into a going system of law, moreover, the court must do the merging, and must in so doing take account of the policy of the statute or else substitute its own version of such policy. Creative re-shaping of the net result is thus inevitable.

But the policy of a statute is of two wholly different kinds—each kind somewhat limited in effect by the statute's choice of measures, and by the statute's choice of fixed language. On the one hand there are the ideas consciously before the draftsmen, the committee, the legislature: a known evil to be cured, a known goal to be attained, a deliberate choice of one line of approach rather than another. Here talk of "intent" is reasonably realistic; committee reports, legislative debate, historical knowledge of contemporary thinking or campaigning which points up the evil or the goal can have significance.

But on the other hand—and increasingly as a statute gains in age—its language is called upon to deal with circumstances utterly uncontemplated at the time of its passage. Here the quest is not properly for the sense originally intended by the statute, for the sense sought originally to be put into it, but rather for the sense which can be quarried out of it in the light of the new situation. Broad purposes can indeed reach far beyond details known or knowable at the time of drafting. A "dangerous weapon" statute of 1840 can include tommy guns, tear gas or atomic bombs. "Vehicle," in a statute of 1840, can properly be read, when sense so suggests, to include an automobile, or a hydroplane that lacks wheels. But for all that, the sound quest does not run primarily in terms of historical intent. It runs in terms of what the words can be made to bear, in making sense in the light of the unforeseen.

III

When it comes to presenting a proposed construction in court, there is an accepted conventional vocabulary. As in argument over points of case-law, the accepted convention still, unhappily requires discussion as if only one single correct meaning could exist. Hence there are two opposing canons on almost every point. An arranged selection is

---

10 Llewellyn, *supra* note 3.

appended. Every lawyer must be familiar with them all: they are still needed tools of argument. At least as early as Fortescue the general picture was clear, on this, to any eye which would see.[11]

Plainly, to make any canon take hold in a particular instance, the construction contended for must be sold, essentially, by means other than the use of the canon: The good sense of the situation and a simple construction of the available language to achieve that sense, by tenable means, out of the statutory language.

NOTES AND QUESTIONS

1. An Equal and Opposite Mode of Interpretation. Llewellyn lists 28 examples of competing canons of construction.

Compare Llewellyn's two columns in the sample canons below. For every method of interpretation there is an equal and opposite method. Does this fact call the entire enterprise into question?

Canons of Construction

1. A statute cannot go beyond its text.	1. To effect its purpose, a statute may be implemented beyond its text.
2. Statutes in derogation of the common law will not be extended by construction.	2. Such acts will be liberally construed if their nature is remedial.
3. Statutes are to be read in the light of the common law, and a statute affirming a common law rule is to be construed in accordance with the common law.	3. The common law gives way to a statute which is consistent with it, and when a statute is designed as a revision of the whole body of law applicable to a given subject, it supercedes the common law.
7. A statute imposing a new penalty or forfeiture, or a new liability or disability, or creating a new right of action will not be construed as having a retroactive effect.	7. Remedial statutes are to be liberally construed and if a retroactive interpretation will promote the ends of justice, they should receive such.
8. Where design has been distinctly stated, no place is left for construction.	8. Courts have the power to inquire into real—as distinct from ostensible—purpose.

[11] [Sir John Fortesque (1394–1476): English jurist. A supporter of the Lancastrian king Henry VI, he was chief justice of the Court of King's Bench from 1442 until 1461, when Henry was deposed by the Yorkist Edward IV. Fortescue was attainted and fled to France with the royal family.]

9. Definitions and rules of construction contained in an interpretation clause are part of the law and binding.	9. Definitions and rules of construction in a statute will not be extended beyond their necessary import nor allowed to defeat intention otherwise manifested.
16. Every word and clause must be given effect.	16. If inadvertently inserted or if repugnant to the rest of the statute, they may be rejected as surplusage.
17. The same language used repeatedly in the same connection is presumed to bear the same meaning throughout the statute.	17. This presumption will be disregarded where it is necessary to assign different meanings to make the statute consistent.
20. Expression of one thing excludes another [*expressio unius est exclusion alterius*].	20. The language may fairly comprehend many different cases where some only are expressly mentioned by way of example.
22. [*ejusdem generis*] It is a general rule of construction that where general words follow an enumeration they are to be held as applying only to persons and things of the same general kind or class specifically mentioned.	22. They may be limited by specific terms with which they are associated or by the scope and purpose of the statute.

2. "The True Reason of the Remedy." In reading a statute that is not entirely clear, judges often ask what the "purpose" of the statute was. Unfortunately, that starts to sound as if the judge is trying to "crawl into the mind" of the statutes' authors when what she really wants is an observable objective. Once a judge knows why a decision was made or what the objective of a rule is, she is well on the way to a principle that can be applied in the new situation. This theme will recur in the realm of constitutional interpretation.

3. Tug of War. The common law canon of construction requires that "statutes in derogation of the common law are to be strictly construed" unless "the statute is remedial" in nature. Many statutes derogate a common law rule, partially repealing or abolishing it, while others entirely repeal or annul it. Sometimes judges are called upon to interpret these statutes.

Legislation in most states reacted by statutorily abrogating the common law rule of strict construction. Many look like Kansas' statute:

> Common law. The common law as modified by constitutional and statutory law, judicial decisions, and the conditions and wants of the people, shall remain in force in aid of the General Statutes of this state; but the rule of the common law, that statutes in derogation thereof shall be strictly construed, shall not be

> applicable to any general statute of this state, but all such statutes shall be liberally construed to promote their object.[12]

Courts have developed a number of devices that allow them to circumvent derogation statutes, even in the face of clear edicts by legislatures. By circumventing the derogation statute, the court is free to construe the substantive statute strictly, thereby leaving the common law in place. Devices for getting around derogation statutes include requiring a specific statute to derogate the common law clearly or simply ignoring a general derogation statute. For example, in some circumstances, the Supreme Court of Kansas has simply ignored the derogation statute, noting that "when the legislature has intended to abolish a common-law rule, it has done so in an explicit manner. In the absence of such an expression of legislative intent, the common law remains part of our law."[13]

§ 9.3 STATUTORY INTERPRETATION AT WORK

The cases in this section are emblematic of the intersection between the common law, state statutes, and the judicial interpretation of those statutes.

A. INHERENT RISK STATUTES

The common law developed rules over hundreds of years that dictated compensation for plaintiffs injured through the negligence of others. In some circumstances, state legislatures enacted statutes designed to shield particular defendants from liability, apparently for the purpose of promoting a particular industry or protecting a particular profession. Courts have interpreted these statutes in light of their purpose and plain meaning, employing codified laws and canons of construction.

Clover v. Snowbird Ski Resort

808 P.2d 1037 (Utah 1991)

■ CHIEF JUSTICE HALL:

Plaintiff Margaret Clover sought to recover damages for injuries sustained as the result of a ski accident in which Chris Zulliger, an employee of defendant Snowbird Corporation ("Snowbird"), collided with her. From the entry of summary judgment in favor of defendants, Clover appeals. Many of the facts underlying Clover's claims are in dispute. Review of an order granting summary judgment requires that the facts be viewed in a light most favorable to the party opposing summary judgment.

---

[12] KAN. STAT. ANN. § 77–109 (2015).

[13] Am. Gen. Fin. Servs., Inc. v. Carter, 184 P.3d 273, 277 (2008) (citing *In re* Estate of Mettee, 694 P.2d 1325, 1328 (Kan. 1985), *aff'd*, 702 P.2d 1381 (Kan. 1985)).

At the time of the accident, Chris Zulliger was employed by Snowbird as a chef at the Plaza Restaurant. Zulliger was supervised by his father, Hans Zulliger, who was the head chef at both the Plaza, which was located at the base of the resort, and the Mid-Gad Restaurant, which was located halfway to the top of the mountain. Zulliger was instructed by his father to make periodic trips to the Mid-Gad to monitor its operations. Prior to the accident, the Zulligers had made several inspection trips to the restaurant. On at least one occasion, Zulliger was paid for such a trip. He also had several conversations with Peter Mandler, the manager of the Plaza and Mid-Gad Restaurants, during which Mandler directed him to make periodic stops at the Mid-Gad to monitor operations.

On December 5, 1985, the date of the accident, Zulliger was scheduled to begin work at the Plaza Restaurant at 3 p.m. Prior to beginning work, he had planned to go skiing with Barney Norman, who was also employed as a chef at the Plaza. Snowbird preferred that their employees know how to ski because it made it easier for them to get to and from work. As part of the compensation for their employment, both Zulliger and Norman received season ski passes. On the morning of the accident, Mandler asked Zulliger to inspect the operation of the Mid-Gad prior to beginning work at the Plaza.

Zulliger and Norman stopped at the Mid-Gad in the middle of their first run. At the restaurant, they had a snack, inspected the kitchen, and talked to the personnel for approximately fifteen to twenty minutes. Zulliger and Norman then skied four runs before heading down the mountain to begin work. On their final run, Zulliger and Norman took a route that was often taken by Snowbird employees to travel from the top of the mountain to the Plaza. About mid-way down the mountain, at a point above the Mid-Gad, Zulliger decided to take a jump off a crest on the side of an intermediate run. He had taken this jump many times before. A skier moving relatively quickly is able to become airborne at that point because of the steep drop off on the downhill side of the crest. Due to this drop off, it is impossible for skiers above the crest to see skiers below the crest. The jump was well known to Snowbird. In fact, the Snowbird ski patrol often instructed people not to jump off the crest. There was also a sign instructing skiers to ski slowly at this point in the run. Zulliger, however, ignored the sign and skied over the crest at a significant speed. Clover, who had just entered the same ski run from a point below the crest, either had stopped or was traveling slowly below the crest. When Zulliger went over the jump, he collided with Clover, who was hit in the head and severely injured.

Clover brought claims against Zulliger and Snowbird, alleging that (1) Zulliger's reckless skiing was a proximate cause of her injuries, (2) Snowbird is liable for Zulliger's negligence because at the time of the collision, he was acting within the scope of his employment, (3) Snowbird negligently designed and maintained its ski runs, and (4) Snowbird breached its duty to adequately supervise its employees. Zulliger settled separately with Clover. Under two separate motions for summary judgment, the trial judge dismissed Clover's claims against Snowbird for the following reasons: (1) as a matter of law, Zulliger was not acting within the scope of his employment at the time of the collision, (2) Utah's Inherent Risk of Skiing Statute, Utah Code Ann. §§ 78–27–51 to –54 (Supp. 1986), bars plaintiff's claim of negligent design and maintenance, and (3) an employer does not have a duty to supervise an employee who is acting outside the scope of employment.

I. STANDARD OF REVIEW

Summary judgment is proper in cases where there is no genuine issue of material fact and the moving party is entitled to a judgment as a matter of law. In cases where the facts are in dispute, summary judgment is only granted when, viewing the facts in a light most favorable to the party opposing summary judgment, the moving party is entitled to judgment. Therefore, when reviewing an order granting summary judgment, the facts are to be liberally construed "in favor of the parties opposing the motion, and those parties are to be given the benefit of all inferences which might reasonably be drawn from the evidence." The determination of whether the facts, viewed in this light, justify the entry of judgment is a question of law. We accord the trial court's conclusions of law no deference, but review them for correctness.

II. SCOPE OF EMPLOYMENT

Under the doctrine of *respondeat superior*, employers are held vicariously liable for the torts their employees commit when the employees are acting within the scope of their employment. Clover's *respondeat superior* claim was dismissed on the ground that as a matter of law, Zulliger's actions at the time of the accident were not within the scope of his employment.

Under the circumstances of the instant case, it is entirely possible for a jury to reasonably believe that at the time of the accident, Zulliger had resumed his employment and that Zulliger's deviation was not substantial enough to constitute a total abandonment of employment.

III. NEGLIGENT DESIGN AND MAINTENANCE

The trial court dismissed Clover's negligent design and maintenance claim on the ground that such a claim is barred by Utah's Inherent Risk of Skiing Statute, Utah Code Ann. §§ 78–27–51 to –54 (Supp. 1986). This ruling was based on the trial court's findings that "Clover was injured as a result of a collision with another skier, and/or the variation of steepness in terrain." Apparently, the trial court reasoned that regardless of a ski resort's culpability, the resort is not liable for an injury occasioned by one or more of the dangers listed in section 78–27–52(1). This reasoning, however, is based on an incorrect interpretation of sections 78–27–51 to –54.

Utah Code Ann. §§ 78–27–51 and –52(1) read in part:

Inherent risks of skiing—Public policy

> The Legislature finds that the sport of skiing is practiced by a large number of residents of Utah and attracts a large number of nonresidents, significantly contributing to the economy of this state.
>
> It further finds that few insurance carriers are willing to provide liability insurance protection to ski area operators and that the premiums charged by those carriers have risen sharply in recent years due to confusion as to whether a skier assumes the risks inherent in the sport of skiing. It is the purpose of this act, therefore, to clarify the law in relation to skiing injuries and the risks inherent in that sport, and to establish as a matter of law that certain risks are inherent in that sport, and to provide that, as a matter of public policy, no person engaged in that sport shall recover from a ski operator for injuries resulting from those inherent risks.

Inherent risk of skiing—Definitions

> As used in this act:
>
> (1) "Inherent risk of skiing" means those dangers or conditions which are an integral part of the sport of skiing, including, but not limited to: changing weather conditions, variations or steepness in terrain; snow or ice conditions; surface or subsurface conditions such as bare spots, forest growth, rocks, stumps, impact with lift towers and other structures and their components; collisions with other skiers; and a skier's failure to ski within his own ability.

Section 78–27–53 states that notwithstanding anything to the contrary in Utah's comparative fault statute, a skier cannot recover from a ski area operator for an injury caused by an inherent risk of skiing. Section 78–27–54 requires ski area operators to "post trail boards at one or more prominent locations within each ski area which shall include a list of the inherent risks of skiing and the limitations on liability of ski area operators as defined in this act."

It is clear that sections 78–27–51 to –54 protect ski area operators from suits initiated by their patrons who seek recovery for injuries caused by an inherent risk of skiing. The statute, however, does not purport to grant ski area operators complete immunity from all negligence claims initiated by skiers. While the general parameters of the act are clear, application of the statute to specific circumstances is less certain. In the instant case, both parties urge different interpretations of the act. Snowbird claims that any injury occasioned by one or more of the dangers listed in section 78–27–52(1) is barred by the statute because, as a matter of law, such an accident is caused by an inherent risk of skiing. Clover, on the other hand, argues that a ski area operator's negligence is not an inherent risk of skiing and that if the resort's negligence causes a collision between skiers, a suit arising from that collision is not barred by sections 78–27–51 to –54.

Although the trial court apparently agreed with Snowbird, we decline to adopt such an interpretation. The basis of Snowbird's argument is that the language of section 78–27–52(1) stating that " 'inherent risk of skiing' means those dangers or conditions which are an integral part of the sport of skiing, including but not limited to: . . . collision with other skiers" must be read as defining all collisions between skiers as inherent risks. The wording of the statute does not compel such a reading. To the contrary, the dangers listed in section 78–27–52(1) are modified by the term "integral part of the sport of skiing." Therefore, ski area operators are protected from suits to recover for injuries caused by one or more of the dangers listed in section 78–27–52(1) only to the extent that those dangers, under the facts of each case, are integral aspects of the sport of skiing. Indeed, the list of dangers in section 78–27–52(1) is expressly nonexclusive. The statute, therefore, contemplates that the determination of whether a risk is inherent be made on a case-by-case basis, using the entire statute, not solely the list provided in section 78–27–52(1).

Furthermore, when the act is read in its entirety, no portion thereof is rendered meaningless. When reading section 78–27–52(1) in connection with section 78–27–54, it becomes clear that the relevance of section 78–27–52(1) is in insuring that ski area operators provide skiers with sufficient notice of the risks they face when participating in the sport of skiing, as well as ski area operators' liability in connection with these risks. It should also be noted that the interpretation urged by Snowbird would result in a wide range of absurd consequences. For example, if a skier loses control and falls by reason of the negligence of an operator, recovery for injury would depend on whether, in the fall, the skier collides with a danger listed in section 78–27–52(1). Such a result is entirely arbitrary.

To the extent that the wording of section 78–27–52(1) creates uncertainty regarding the specific application of the act, that confusion should be resolved through the use of the rules of statutory construction. A rule of construction which this court has commonly applied is that the terms of a statute should be interpreted in accord with their usual and accepted meanings. Another rule is that a statute should not be construed in a piecemeal fashion but as a comprehensive whole. Furthermore, "if there is doubt or uncertainty as to the meaning or application of the provisions of an act, it is appropriate to analyze the act in its entirety, in light of its objective, and to harmonize its provisions in accordance with its intent and purpose." In cases such as this, where a statement of the statute's purpose is codified in the statute, this method of construction is particularly appropriate. It is also proper in construing a statute which deals with tort claims to interpret the statute in accord with relevant tort law. Finally, in dealing with an unclear statute, this court renders interpretations that will "best promote the protection of the public."

Finally, it is to be noted that without a duty, there can be no negligence. Such an interpretation, therefore, harmonizes the express purpose of the statute, protecting ski area operators from suits arising out of injuries caused by the inherent risks of skiing, with the fact that the statute does not purport to abrogate a skier's traditional right to recover for injuries caused by ski area operators' negligence.

A similar analysis leads to the conclusion that the duties sections 78–27–51 to –54 impose on ski resorts are the duty to use reasonable care for the protection of its patrons and, under section 78–27–54, the duty to warn its patrons of the inherent risks of skiing. Beyond the general warning prescribed by section 78–27–54, however, a ski area operator is under no duty to protect its patrons from the inherent risks of skiing. The inherent risks of skiing are those dangers that skiers wish to confront as essential characteristics of the sport of skiing or hazards that cannot be eliminated by the exercise of ordinary care on the part of the ski area operator.

As noted above, the purpose of the statute is to prohibit suits seeking recovery for injuries caused by an inherent risk of skiing. The term "inherent risk of skiing," using the ordinary and accepted meaning of the term "inherent," refers to those risks that are essential characteristics of skiing—risks that are so integrally related to skiing that the sport cannot be undertaken without confronting these risks. Generally, these risks can be divided into two categories. The first category of risks consists of those risks, such as steep grades, powder, and mogul runs, which skiers wish to confront as an essential characteristic of skiing. Under sections 78–27–51 to –54, a ski area operator is under no duty to make all of its runs as safe as possible by eliminating the type of dangers that skiers wish to confront as an integral part of skiing.

The second category of risks consists of those hazards which no one wishes to confront but cannot be alleviated by the use of reasonable care on the part of a ski resort. It is without question that skiing is a dangerous activity. Hazards may exist in locations where they are not readily discoverable. Weather and snow conditions can suddenly change and, without warning, create new hazards where no hazard previously existed. Hence, it is clearly foreseeable that a skier, without skiing recklessly, may momentarily lose control or fall in an unexpected manner. Ski area operators cannot alleviate these risks, and under sections 78–27–51 to –54, they are not liable for injuries caused by such risks. The only duty ski area operators have in regard to these risks is the requirement set out in section 78–27–54 that they warn their patrons, in the manner prescribed in the statute, of the general dangers patrons must confront when participating in the sport of skiing. This does not mean, however, that a ski area operator is under no duty to use ordinary care to protect its patrons. In fact, if an injury was caused by an unnecessary hazard that could have been eliminated by the use of ordinary care, such a hazard is not, in the ordinary sense of the term, an inherent risk of skiing and would fall outside of sections 78–27–51 to –54.

In light of the genuine issues of material fact in regard to each of Clover's claims, summary judgment was inappropriate.

Reversed and remanded for further proceedings.

NOTES AND QUESTIONS

1. **Who Needs a Statute Anyway?** Courts have dealt with a variety of recreational activities in which injured persons sought to show that the proprietor was negligent and, thus, the injury was not an "inherent risk" of the sport. Would the presence or absence of an inherent risk statute matter in these cases? For example, courts have addressed whether injuries from horseback riding,[14] off-road vehicles,[15] and high-diving[16] are inherent dangers in a sport. The California Supreme Court has recognized that one has no duty to mitigate the dangers inherent in a sport:

> Although persons generally owe a duty of due care not to cause an unreasonable risk of harm to others, some activities—and, specifically, many sports—are inherently dangerous. Imposing a duty to mitigate those inherent dangers could alter the nature of the activity or inhibit vigorous participation. In a game of touch football, for example, there is an inherent risk that players will collide; to impose a general duty on coparticipants to avoid the risk of harm arising from a collision would work a basic alteration—or cause abandonment—of the sport.[17]

If courts eventually reach the same outcome as that mandated by a statute, is there any advantage to the legislative process?

2. **They Said It and We Mean It.** Faced with other "inherent risk" statutes, courts have reached a variety of outcomes. In *Skene v. Fileccia*,[18] the court was quite emphatic about following the letter of the inherent risk statute as it applied to a roller skater:

> Here, the statute is clear and unambiguous. By participating in the sport of roller-skating, plaintiff accepted the dangers that

---

[14] Sapone v. Grand Targhee, 308 F.3d 1096, 1104 (10th Cir. 2002) ("[W]e disagree with the district court's conclusion that falling from this particular bolting horse is an inherent risk of horseback riding. Daya presented evidence to show that the injury may have been caused not by an inherent risk, but rather by a risk that was atypical, uncharacteristic, [and] not intrinsic to the recreational activity of horseback riding.").

[15] Lorette v. Peter-Sam Inv. Props., 697 A.2d 1386, 1389–90 (N.H. 1997) (concluding that a landowner was not responsible for leaving an excavation pit on property known to be used by OHRV riders.).

[16] Kahn v. E. Side Union High Sch. Dist., 75 P.3d 30, 37 (Cal. 2003).

[17] *Id.*

[18] 539 N.W.2d 531 (Mich. 1995).

> inhere in the sport insofar as they are obvious and necessary. Specifically included within such dangers are "injuries that result from collisions with other roller skaters." Because the act is clear and unambiguous, this Court must apply the act as written. Here, plaintiff was injured from an obvious and necessary danger of roller-skating and may not recover damages.[19]

Other courts have varied in their interpretation of "inherent risks." While courts have found that being struck from behind,[20] hitting the "lone tree growing on a ski slope,"[21] and falling out of the ski lift[22] are all inherent risks; other courts have held that hitting a boulder on a groomed run[23] and falling down an unmarked ravine were not inherent risks.[24] What accounts for these seemingly contradictory outcomes from nearly identical statutes?

The Utah court drew a dissent when it concluded that flying over a "cat track" (a road smoothed by a snow machine) on a ski resort was not "an integral part or essential characteristic of the sport of skiing."[25] The lone dissent had this to say:

> The majority opinion contradicts the plain language of the inherent risks of skiing statute, which clearly and unambiguously states that any danger or condition integral to the sport of skiing is "as a matter of law" an inherent risk of skiing and that no skier may recover from any ski area operator for injury resulting from any of the inherent risks of skiing. . . .
>
> According to the unambiguous language of the statute as a whole, (1) any danger or condition integral to the sport of skiing is as a matter of law an inherent risk of skiing and (2) a skier cannot recover from ski area operators for injuries resulting from the inherent risks of skiing.
>
> While the majority has correctly applied the law as set forth in *Clover*, I believe that *Clover* is clearly wrong and constitutes nothing more than judicial legislation. It should be abandoned as precedent.[26]

B. COMPARATIVE FAULT STATUTES

At common law, an injured person would not be able to recover if he or she were found to be contributorily negligent. As a result, even a defendant who engaged in reprehensible behavior would be absolved of

---

19 *Id.* at 533.

20 Grieb v. Alpine Valley Ski Area, Inc., 400 N.W.2d 653 (Mich. Ct. App. 1986).

21 Schmitz v. Cannonsburg Skiing Corp., 428 N.W.2d 742 (Mich. Ct. App. 1988).

22 Chepkevich v. Hidden Valley Resort, L.P., 2 A.3d 1174 (Pa. 2010).

23 Kopeikin v. Moonlight Basin Mgmt., LLC, 981 F. Supp. 2d 936 (D. Mont. 2013).

24 Graven v. Vail Assocs., Inc., 909 P.2d 514, 515 (Colo. 1995), as modified on denial of reh'g (Jan. 16, 1996).

25 White v. Deseelhorst, 879 P.2d 1371, 1374 (Utah 1994).

26 *Id.* at 1377–78.

responsibility if the plaintiff were even just slightly negligent herself. To remedy this anomaly, some courts adopted a rule of comparative fault, while other states adopted the same approach by statute. In general, comparative fault simply means that the jury apportions the degree of fault to each of the parties and applies that apportionment to the amount of damages.

Difficulties with this approach, however, abound. How should the law treat an intentional tortfeasor, such as an assailant, who injures a somewhat careless victim? Moreover, what if the intentional assailant has fled the scene leaving behind a somewhat careless third party, such as a landowner? In addition, there are some activities that occasion strict liability under either a statute (such as dram shop liability) or a common law rule (such as those for dangerous animals or defective products). Should these long-standing strict liability rules be modified by the doctrine of comparative fault?

Some courts have found answers in definitions of the term "fault" while others have searched diligently for legislative intent, public policy, or common sense results.

Clark v. Connor

843 N.W.2d 785 (Minn. Ct. App. 2014)

■ HOOTEN, JUDGE.

FACTS

A pit bull barked at and chased respondent Faron Clark into the street, where he collided with appellant Vydell Jones's passing van. Respondent sustained serious injuries to his hip, left arm, and head. He sued (a) appellant for common-law negligence and (b) the dog owners, defendants Sheri and Timothy Connor, for both common-law negligence and statutory liability under Minn. Stat. § 347.22, commonly known as the dog-attack statute. Respondent eventually settled his claims against the dog owners and executed a release. His remaining claim against appellant was resolved in a jury trial.

The jury found that the negligent conduct of respondent, appellant, and the dog owners combined to directly cause respondent's injuries, attributing 10% fault to respondent, 10% to appellant, and 80% to the dog owners. The jury also found that the dog attacked or injured respondent while he was acting peaceably in a place he was entitled to be. Based on this jury finding, appellant requested that the district court relieve her of all liability. The district court denied appellant's request, concluding that "[w]hile Minn. Stat. § 347.22 precludes considering the comparative fault of the plaintiff, it does not preclude comparative fault as between defendants nor preclude a consideration of causation." Accordingly, the district court determined that appellant is liable for 10% of damages.

ANALYSIS

Interpretation of a statute presents a question of law, which we review de novo. Application of a statute to the undisputed facts of a case involves a question of law, and the district court's decision is not binding on this court.

Under the comparative-fault statute, "[w]hen two or more persons are severally liable, contributions to awards shall be in proportion to the percentage of fault attributable to each." Minn. Stat. § 604.02, subd. 1. " 'Fault' includes acts or omissions that are in any measure negligent . . . or that subject a person to strict tort liability." Minn. Stat. § 604.01, subd. 1a (2012). Under the dog-attack statute, "If a dog, without provocation, attacks or injures any person who is acting peaceably in any place where the person may lawfully be, the owner of the dog is liable in damages to the person so attacked or injured to the full amount of the injury sustained."

Appellant argues that, in light of the jury's finding that the dog attacked or injured respondent while he was acting peaceably in a place he was entitled to be, in violation of Minn. Stat. § 347.22, the district court erred in applying the comparative-fault statute to allocate fault between her and the dog owners. We disagree.

As an initial matter, appellant's argument ignores the jury's finding that the dog owners are liable under both theories of statutory liability and common-law negligence. Respondent properly sought recovery under both theories. Because the comparative-fault statute allows the allocation of fault for negligent conduct, the district court properly allocated fault between appellant and the dog owners.

Even if the jury had found the dog owners liable solely on the basis of statutory liability, we find no persuasive support for appellant's argument. The comparative-fault statute allows the allocation of fault based on "acts or omissions that are in any measure negligent" and fault based on "acts or omissions . . . that subject a person to strict tort liability." The dog-attack statute "leaves the dog owner . . . with the strict liability of an insurer." Accordingly, the comparative-fault statute allows comparing a dog owner's liability stemming from the dog-attack statute with a co-tortfeasor's negligence.

Appellant relies on *Seim v. Garavalia*, in which the Supreme Court "conclude[d] that section 347.22 was meant to provide absolute statutory strict liability." 306 N.W.2d 806, 812 (Minn. 1981). "The doctrine of absolute liability is applicable when the legislature, by enacting a particular statute, intends to preclude certain defenses and place the entire responsibility for the injury upon the individual who violated the statute." Applying this doctrine, the *Seim* court determined that despite "the specific inclusion of 'strict tort liability' in the comparative fault statute's definition of fault," the dog-attack statute precludes the comparison of a dog owner's strict liability with a dog-attack victim's negligence.

But *Seim* did not examine whether the dog-attack statute precludes the comparison of a dog owner's strict liability with a co-tortfeasor's negligence. Appellant asserts that "[i]t should not matter, as a matter of policy, whether the comparative fault is that of the plaintiff or, as in this case, that of a co-defendant." But because this court is limited in its function to correcting errors it cannot create public policy. Moreover, we see no policy served by appellant's proposal to extend *Seim*. In "recogniz[ing] the principle that the legislative body that enacted the comparative fault statute has the authority to carve out or preserve exceptions to the statute in the interest of public policy," the *Seim* court concluded that violators of the dog-attack statute cannot have their liability reduced due to the victim's own negligence so that "recovery is insured in all cases" and that the law "provide[s] for recovery of full damage irrespective of contributory fault." This interest in guaranteeing full recovery for a victim is satisfied by allocating fault between a dog owner and a co-tortfeasor in a way that it cannot be satisfied by allocating fault between a dog owner and the victim. Accordingly, *Seim* does not support appellant's argument.

Appellant also relies on *Hill v. Sacka*, in which the Michigan Court of Appeals interpreted Michigan's dog-attack statute. 256 Mich. App. 443, 666 N.W.2d 282 (Mich. Ct. App. 2003). There, a two-year-old child "was bitten, gnawed, and mauled by defendants' German shepherd." Because a jury found the child's father 75% at fault, the dog owners requested that the judgment against them be reduced accordingly. But the Michigan court held that "the fault or negligence of a third person, *i.e.*, not the dog owner or the direct victim of the dog bite, is . . . not relevant."

Appellant's reliance on *Hill* is misplaced for three reasons. First, the Michigan court's interpretation of Michigan's statute is not binding on us when interpreting our own statute. Second, Michigan's dog-attack statute would not apply here anyway because it imposes liability only for dog bites and not for no-contact dog attacks like the one suffered by respondent. And finally, *Hill* is procedurally distinguishable. In that case, "[t]he negligence claim was summarily dismissed pursuant to agreement of the parties. The jury heard and decided the remaining statutory claim." This case reaches us in the opposite procedural posture-the claims against the dog owners were settled, leaving only the negligence claim against appellant to be tried. The Michigan court in *Hill*, therefore, never considered the issue before us.

Finally, appellant argues that because section 347.22 renders a dog owner liable "to the full amount of the injury sustained," "[t]he legislative intent would suggest that a co-defendant whose liability is premised on negligence would, under principles of equity, be entitled to indemnity from a dog owner whose liability is established as absolute under the statute." Appellant contends that respondent "should not benefit from the hammer of absolute liability to reach a settlement with the dog owner[s] 'to the full amount of the injury sustained,' and then be allowed to pursue the same damages against other parties under a negligence theory."

We are not persuaded. Appellant interprets the phrase "the full amount of the injury sustained" to mean that a dog owner is liable for any and all injuries sustained during an accident involving a dog attack, regardless of whether such accident involves a third party's negligence and whether the dog attack is the sole direct cause of the injuries. But section 347.22 states that "the owner of the dog is liable in damages to the person *so attacked or injured* to the full amount of the injury sustained." (Emphasis added.) Accordingly, the statute imposes liability on a dog owner only for injuries caused by the dog. Appellant's interpretation would mean that if a dog attack is ever a direct cause in any series of unfortunate and tortious events, then the dog owner is solely liable for all injuries sustained and all other tortfeasors are absolved of liability. This interpretation is contrary to the plain language of the statute and would produce absurd results. *See* Minn. Stat. § 645.17 (2012) (instructing that we should presume that "the legislature does not intend a result that is absurd").

DECISION

Because the comparative-fault statute allows the allocation of fault for both negligent conduct and conduct that subjects one to strict liability, and because we conclude that the legislature did not intend the dog-attack statute to preclude the allocation of fault between a dog owner and a co-tortfeasor, the district court did not err in determining that appellant is liable for 10% of damages.

Slager v. HWA Corp.

435 N.W.2d 349 (Iowa 1989)

■ LAVORATO, J.:

The sole issue here is whether comparative fault under Iowa Code chapter 668 (1987) has any application as a defense to a dram shop action under Iowa Code section 123.92. The district court ruled it did not. We agree and affirm.

Defendant HWA Corporation owned and operated the College St. Club, a liquor establishment in Iowa City. Ramon Jose DeSantiago, a minor, was sold and served intoxicating beverages at the College St. Club while he was intoxicated or until he became intoxicated. DeSantiago left the club in an intoxicated condition and began tampering with a motorcycle belonging to John E. Slager. Slager confronted DeSantiago as DeSantiago was tampering with the motorcycle. At that point DeSantiago shot and seriously injured Slager.

When sued, HWA denied the general allegations of the petition and alleged as an affirmative defense that the comparative fault of persons other than HWA had contributed to John's injuries. The plaintiffs moved to strike the affirmative defense. They contended that, as a matter of law, the comparative fault defense is not available to a defendant in a dram shop action. The trial court sustained the motion to strike, holding that "comparative fault does not apply in dram shop cases."

In determining the legislature's intent, we consider the language of the statute, the objects sought to be accomplished, and the evils sought to be remedied. We also consider the consequences of a particular construction. In determining the legislature's intent on this question, we must keep in mind that our function is not to question the wisdom of legislation. Nor is it our function to write into law what the legislature might or should have said.

Applying these principles of statutory construction, we are convinced the legislature did not intend comparative fault to be a defense to a dram shop action. We can see several important indicia of legislative intent against such a result.

What would be the consequences if we said comparative fault is a defense to dram shop liability? As we mentioned, this is a legitimate concern in the interpretation of statutes.

Were we to reach a different result we think the dram shop statute's use as a meaningful remedy would be seriously impaired.

The following scenario is a good example of how the remedy could be impaired. In our hypothetical dram shop case, the plaintiff is seriously injured in an automobile collision with an intoxicated person who, shortly before the accident, became intoxicated in the defendant tavern. The plaintiff had nothing to do with the intoxicated tortfeasor's drinking activities and was unaware of the person's condition. The intoxicated tortfeasor is insolvent, a fact the plaintiff is well aware of when suit is filed. Consequently, only the tavern is sued.

The tavern's strategy, of course, is to avoid as much fault as possible. So in its answer, it alleges comparative fault as a defense to plaintiff's dram shop allegations and joins the intoxicated tortfeasor as a third-party defendant.

At trial the plaintiff, of course, is limited as to what fault the plaintiff may establish against the tavern. The tavern, on the other hand, is not handicapped in this way. The facts show that the collision was due, in large part, to the intoxicated tortfeasor's negligence resulting from that person's impaired condition. The plaintiff's own negligence was also a cause. Consequently, the tavern easily convinces the jury to assign seventy percent of the fault to the intoxicated tortfeasor and ten percent to the plaintiff. The plaintiff is only able to convince the jury to assign the remaining twenty percent to the tavern.

The practical result is that the plaintiff is forced to financially assume eighty percent of the damages: ten percent due to the plaintiff's own fault and seventy percent due to the intoxicated tortfeasor's fault. In contrast, the tavern, which violated the provisions of section 123.92, pays only twenty percent of the damages and is insulated against the other eighty percent. Of course, absent the availability of comparative fault as a defense, the tavern would be responsible for all the damages, because under our hypothetical facts the plaintiff is an innocent party.

The scenario we have just described is not an unlikely one. In a dram shop case, an intoxicated tortfeasor is usually involved in an underlying tort of some kind that is easily provable. Often, such a tortfeasor is insolvent. The jury might find it difficult to overcome the temptation to apportion most of the fault to the intoxicated tortfeasor, as the dram shop defendant would be urging.

NOTES AND QUESTIONS

1. **Negligently Encountering Harm.** In *McLain v. Training & Development Corp.*,[27] a young man sought to enter the Marines but failed the written exam. He then enrolled in a Job Corps program run by a private company, which assigned him to a training instructor. The instructor "told McLain that he could get into the Marines through physical 'tests' . . . [but] not to tell anyone of this secret way into the Marines or both of them would be 'in trouble.' "[28] Over a period of a few months, the instructor put the young man through painful and humiliating exercises before his mother learned what was happening and informed law enforcement. In the ensuing lawsuit, the Maine court held that the intentional torts of the employee were imputed to the employer and that the comparative fault statute did not allow the young man's negligence to be considered.

> From a review of the law prevailing prior to the enactment of [the statute], it appears without exception that contributory negligence never has been considered a good defense to an intentional tort such as a battery, and it would likewise appear contrary to sound policy to reduce a plaintiff's damages under comparative fault for his "negligence" in encountering the defendant's deliberately inflicted harm.[29]

2. **What Happens Next?** *Shin v. Sunriver Preparatory School, Inc.*[30] involved a plaintiff who was born and raised in Korea. As a high school sophomore she enrolled at Sunriver Preparatory, a private boarding school. During her junior year, a teacher with whom she was living discovered that she had been sexually molested by her father since age four. When Shin's father visited Oregon from Korea, the teacher attempted to intervene. The teacher was eventually fired by the school principal, and Shin's father

---

[27] 572 A.2d 494 (Me. 1990).

[28] *Id.* at 495.

[29] *Id.* at 497 (citing PROSSER & KEATON ON TORTS § 67, at 477–78 (5th ed. 1984)).

[30] 111 P.3d 762 (Or. Ct. App. 2003).

further abused her during the visit. In this lawsuit, the trial judge refused to apportion liability between the school, which was allegedly negligent, and the father, who committed a series of intentional torts.

In what might seem an unusual maneuver, the plaintiff sought to exclude the intentional tortfeasor father in the allocation of fault while the school sought to include him. There are several possible explanations for the plaintiff's approach, including her frequently stated fear of him and the possibility that the Oregon court could not obtain jurisdiction over him.

Whatever the strategic reasons, the court held that intentional tortfeasors are not to be included in the apportionment of fault:

> In conclusion, we hold that, when the legislature changed "negligence" to "fault" in the comparative fault statutes, it intended to extend comparative fault to tortious conduct to which contributory negligence was a valid defense at common law. References to "fault" in [the] statutes do not encompass intentional conduct to which contributory negligence was not a defense; apportionment of liability between negligent and intentional tortfeasors therefore is not permitted under those statutes.[31]

What is the practical effect of this holding? Does the intentional tortfeasor go scot-free? Did the court intend to hold both intentional and negligent tortfeasors liable for the full amount of damage? Does the concept of "joint and several liability" become infused into a comparative fault regime?

3. Cases in Harmony. In a series of cases under the Utah comparative fault statute, the courts have been unable to reach an intelligible conclusion. First, in *Cortez v. University Mall*,[32] federal Magistrate Judge Boyce refused to apportion fault between a shopping mall and an unknown assailant when the shopping mall allegedly had inadequate security lighting. Judge Boyce held instead that "[i]ntentional tort forms of conduct were apparently not intended to be within the concept of 'fault' contemplated by the Utah Legislature."[33]

Then, in a virtually identical case, a fractured Utah Supreme Court held that "Utah's comparative fault scheme requires comparison of negligent and intentional conduct," but the statute does not "require[ ] attribution of fault to [the] nonparty, unknown assailant."[34]

Later, the Utah Supreme Court made a heroic attempt to harmonize the various views in a case that involved only intentional tortfeasors: a group of teenagers who beat and seriously injured a student from a rival school. After assessing the earlier conflicting opinions, the court concluded that the "solution to the riddle . . . is that whether the [statute] applies to intentional torts remains an open question."[35]

---

31 *Id.* at 778.

32 941 F. Supp. 1096 (D. Utah 1996).

33 *Id.* at 1100.

34 Field v. Boyer Co., 952 P.2d 1078, 1082 (Utah 1998).

35 Jedrziewski v. Smith, 128 P.3d 1146, 1151 (2005).

In this sequence of cases the courts struggled with statutory interpretation in light of settled common law on the same subject. These cases may reflect a debate over statutory interpretation, or may reflect a larger policy dispute over which party the court should protect.

§ 9.4 STATUTORY CONSTRUCTION IN THE UNITED STATES SUPREME COURT

The United States Supreme Court follows the same conventions of statutory interpretation employed by state courts. The justices often split over which of Llewellyn's canons of construction should be applied to a particular statute, as well as the relative role of the courts vis-à-vis Congress.

National Federation of Independent Business v. Sebelius

132 S. Ct. 2566 (2012)

■ CHIEF JUSTICE ROBERTS delivered the opinion of the Court [with respect to the use of taxing power]:

In 2010, Congress enacted the Patient Protection and Affordable Care Act. The Act aims to increase the number of Americans covered by health insurance and decrease the cost of health care.

The individual mandate requires most Americans to maintain "minimum essential" health insurance coverage. 26 U.S.C. § 5000A. Many individuals will receive the required coverage through their employer, or from a government program such as Medicaid or Medicare. But for individuals who are not exempt and do not receive health insurance through a third party, the means of satisfying the requirement is to purchase insurance from a private company.

Beginning in 2014, those who do not comply with the mandate must make a "[s]hared responsibility payment" to the Federal Government. § 5000A(b)(1). That payment, which the Act describes as a "penalty," is calculated as a percentage of household income, subject to a floor based on a specified dollar amount and a ceiling based on the average annual premium the individual would have to pay for qualifying private health insurance. In 2016, for example, the penalty will be 2.5 percent of an individual's household income, but no less than $695 and no more than the average yearly premium for insurance that covers 60 percent of the cost of 10 specified services (e.g., prescription drugs and hospitalization).

The Act provides that the penalty will be paid to the Internal Revenue Service with an individual's taxes, and "shall be assessed and collected in the same manner" as tax penalties, such as the penalty for claiming too large an income tax refund. The Act, however, bars the IRS from using several of its normal enforcement tools, such as criminal prosecutions and levies. And some individuals who are subject to the mandate are nonetheless exempt from the penalty—for example, those with income below a certain threshold and members of Indian tribes.

In the Affordable Care Act, Congress addressed the problem of those who cannot obtain insurance coverage because of preexisting conditions or other health issues. It did so through the Act's "guaranteed-issue" and "community-rating" provisions. These provisions together prohibit insurance companies from denying coverage to those with such conditions or charging unhealthy individuals higher premiums than healthy individuals.

The guaranteed-issue and community-rating reforms do not, however, address the issue of healthy individuals who choose not to purchase insurance to cover potential health care needs. In fact, the reforms sharply exacerbate that problem, by providing an incentive for individuals to delay purchasing health insurance until they become sick, relying on the promise of guaranteed and affordable coverage. The reforms also threaten to impose massive new costs on insurers, who are required to accept unhealthy individuals but prohibited from charging them rates necessary to pay for their coverage. This will lead insurers to significantly increase premiums on everyone.

The individual mandate was Congress's solution to these problems. By requiring that individuals purchase health insurance, the mandate prevents cost-shifting by those who would otherwise go without it. In addition, the mandate forces into the insurance risk pool more healthy individuals, whose premiums on average will be higher than their health care expenses. This allows insurers to subsidize the costs of covering the unhealthy individuals the reforms require them to accept. The Government claims that Congress has power under the Commerce and Necessary and Proper Clauses to enact this solution.

The individual mandate does not regulate existing commercial activity. It instead compels individuals to become active in commerce by purchasing a product, on the ground that their failure to do so affects interstate commerce. Construing the Commerce Clause to permit Congress to regulate individuals precisely because they are doing nothing would open a new and potentially vast domain to congressional authority. Every day individuals do not do an infinite number of things. In some cases they decide not to do something; in others they simply fail to do it. Allowing Congress to justify federal regulation by pointing to the effect of inaction on commerce would bring countless decisions an individual could potentially make within the scope of federal regulation, and—under the Government's theory—empower Congress to make those decisions for him.

That is not the end of the matter. Because the Commerce Clause does not support the individual mandate, it is necessary to turn to the Government's second argument: that the mandate may be upheld as within Congress's enumerated power to "lay and collect Taxes." Art. I, § 8, cl. 1.

The Government's tax power argument asks us to view the statute differently than we did in considering its commerce power theory. In making its Commerce Clause argument, the Government defended the mandate as a regulation requiring individuals to purchase health insurance. The Government does not claim that the taxing power allows Congress to issue such a command. Instead, the Government asks us to read the mandate not as ordering individuals to buy insurance, but rather as imposing a tax on those who do not buy that product.

The text of a statute can sometimes have more than one possible meaning. To take a familiar example, a law that reads "no vehicles in the park" might, or might not, ban bicycles in the park. And it is well established that if a statute has two possible meanings, one of which violates the Constitution, courts should adopt the meaning that does not do so. Justice Story said that 180 years ago: "No court ought, unless the terms of an act rendered it unavoidable, to give a construction to it which should involve a violation, however unintentional, of the constitution." *Parsons v. Bedford*, 28 U.S. 433, 3 Pet. 433, 448–449 (1830). Justice Holmes made the same point a century later: "[T]he rule is settled that as between two possible interpretations of a statute, by one of which it would be unconstitutional and by the other valid, our plain duty is to adopt that which will save the Act." *Blodgett v. Holden*, 275 U.S. 142, 148 (1927) (concurring opinion).

The most straightforward reading of the mandate is that it commands individuals to purchase insurance. After all, it states that individuals "shall" maintain health insurance. Congress thought it could enact such a command under the Commerce Clause, and the Government primarily defended the law on that basis. But, for the reasons explained above, the Commerce Clause does not give Congress that power. Under our precedent, it is therefore necessary to ask whether the Government's alternative reading of the statute—that it only imposes a tax on those without insurance—is a reasonable one.

Under the mandate, if an individual does not maintain health insurance, the only consequence is that he must make an additional payment to the IRS when he pays his taxes. Under that theory, the mandate is not a legal command to buy insurance. Rather, it makes going without insurance just another thing the Government taxes, like buying gasoline or earning income. And if the mandate is in effect just a tax hike on certain taxpayers who do not have health insurance, it may be within Congress's constitutional power to tax.

The question is not whether that is the most natural interpretation of the mandate, but only whether it is a fairly possible one. As we have explained, every reasonable construction must be resorted to, in order to save a statute from unconstitutionality.

It is of course true that the Act describes the payment as a "penalty," not a "tax."

We have [in the past] held that exactions not labeled taxes nonetheless were authorized by Congress's power to tax. In the *License Tax Cases*, for example, we held that federal licenses to sell liquor and lottery tickets—for which the licensee had to pay a fee—could be sustained as exercises of the taxing power. 5 Wall., at 471. And in *New York v. United States* we upheld as a tax a "surcharge" on out-of-state nuclear waste shipments, a portion of which was paid to the Federal Treasury. 505 U.S., at 171. We thus ask whether the shared responsibility payment falls within Congress's taxing power, "[d]isregarding the designation of the exaction, and viewing its substance and application."

[T]he shared responsibility payment may for constitutional purposes be considered a tax, not a penalty: First, for most Americans the amount due will be far less than the price of insurance, and, by statute, it can never be more. It may often be a reasonable financial decision to make the payment rather than purchase insurance. Second, the individual mandate contains no scienter requirement. Third, the payment is collected solely by the IRS through the normal means of taxation—except that the Service is not allowed to use those means most suggestive of a punitive sanction, such as criminal prosecution. The reasons the Court in [*Bailey v.*] *Drexel Furniture* held that what was called a "tax" there was a penalty support the conclusion that what is called a "penalty" here may be viewed as a tax.

Our precedent demonstrates that Congress had the power to impose the exaction in § 5000A under the taxing power, and that § 5000A need not be read to do more than impose a tax. That is sufficient to sustain it.

■ JUSTICES SCALIA, KENNEDY, THOMAS, and ALITO, dissenting.

Congress has set out to remedy the problem that the best health care is beyond the reach of many Americans who cannot afford it. It can assuredly do that, by exercising the powers accorded to it under the Constitution. The question in this case, however, is whether the complex structures and provisions of the Patient Protection and Affordable Care Act (Affordable Care Act or ACA) go beyond those powers. We conclude that they do.

The Government's second theory in support of the Individual Mandate is that § 5000A is valid because it is actually a regulation of activities having a substantial relation to interstate commerce, i.e., activities that substantially affect interstate commerce. This argument takes a few different forms, but the basic idea is that § 5000A regulates the way in which individuals finance their participation in the health-care market. That is, the provision directs the manner in which individuals purchase health care services and related goods (directing that they be purchased through insurance) and is therefore a straightforward exercise of the commerce power.

The primary problem with this argument is that § 5000A does not apply only to persons who purchase all, or most, or even any, of the health care services or goods that the mandated insurance covers. Indeed, the main objection many have to the Mandate is that they have no intention of purchasing most or even any of such goods or services and thus no need to buy insurance for those purchases. The Government responds that the health-care market involves "essentially universal participation." The principal difficulty with this response is that it is, in the only relevant sense, not true. It is true enough that everyone consumes "health care," if the term is taken to include the purchase of a bottle of aspirin. But the health care "market" that is the object of the Individual Mandate not only includes but principally consists of goods and services that the young people primarily affected by the Mandate do not purchase. They are quite simply not participants in that market, and cannot be made so (and thereby subjected to regulation) by the simple device of defining participants to include all those who will, later in their lifetime, probably purchase the goods or services covered by the mandated insurance. Such a definition of market participants is unprecedented, and were it to be a premise for the exercise of national power, it would have no principled limits.

In a variation on this attempted exercise of federal power, the Government points out that Congress in this Act has purported to regulate economic and financial decisions to forgo health insurance coverage and to attempt to self-insure, since those decisions have a substantial and deleterious effect on interstate commerce. But as the discussion above makes clear, the decision to forgo participation in an interstate market is not itself commercial activity (or indeed any activity at all) within Congress'[s] power to regulate. It is true that, at the end of the day, it is inevitable that each American will affect commerce and become a part of it, even if not by choice. But if every person comes within the Commerce Clause power of Congress to regulate by the simple reason that he will one day engage in commerce, the idea of a limited Government power is at an end.

NOTES AND QUESTIONS

1. **Ingenious or Disingenuous?** Plaintiffs argued that they were being taxed because they might one day need health care, and thus being required to buy a good that they didn't need or want. The real issue, however, was that younger and healthier individuals were needed in the pool to help subsidize the entire system. In essence, it was as if they were being required to join a pool like the Social Security system and were being taxed for the general welfare. Politically, a single-payer system was impossible to implement because the health insurance industry had been dominated for decades by private insurers as a result of the McCarran-Ferguson Act of 1945. Thus, the healthy individual was given a choice to participate in the private system or pay a tax. The statute could have been created as a tax that exempted those who bought health insurance.

When you make an argument as a lawyer, is it proper to mold the opposition's argument to your advantage? Is it proper for a judge to accept this seemingly disingenuous argument and respond to it rather than the more salient argument? Was all this confusion caused by Congress' attempt to avoid the political difficulty of a federal health insurance system? If so, did Chief Justice Roberts simply do Congress a favor by changing Congress's words while leaving the congressional system intact?

2. Jiggery-Pokery. The Affordable Care Act came back to the Supreme Court three years later in *King v. Burwell*.[36] This time, the issue involved the creation of "Exchanges" (brokerage pools) in each state, and again, Chief Justice Roberts delivered the opinion of the Court. Under the statute, low-income filers receive a federal tax credit for purchasing insurance through "an Exchange established by the State." The Act provided elsewhere that if the State did not create an Exchange, the federal government could step in to create one for that state.

> The issue in this case is whether the Act's tax credits are available in States that have a Federal Exchange rather than a State Exchange. The Act initially provides that tax credits "shall be allowed" for any "applicable taxpayer." The Act then provides that the amount of the tax credit depends in part on whether the taxpayer has enrolled in an insurance plan through "an Exchange established by the State." [The IRS interpreted the Act to include credits for Federal Exchanges established in a State.]
>
> [Several] provisions suggest that the Act may not always use the phrase "established by the State" in its most natural sense. Thus, the meaning of that phrase may not be as clear as it appears when read out of context.
>
> The upshot of all this is that the phrase "an Exchange established by the State under [42 U. S. C. § 18031]" is properly viewed as ambiguous. The phrase may be limited in its reach to State Exchanges. But it is also possible that the phrase refers to all Exchanges—both State and Federal—at least for purposes of the tax credits.
>
> Petitioners' arguments about the plain meaning of Section 36B are strong. But while the meaning of the phrase "an Exchange established by the State under [42 U. S. C. § 18031]" may seem plain "when viewed in isolation," such a reading turns out to be "untenable in light of [the statute] as a whole." In this instance, the context and structure of the Act compel us to depart from what would otherwise be the most natural reading of the pertinent statutory phrase.
>
> In a democracy, the power to make the law rests with those chosen by the people. Our role is more confined—"to say what the law is." *Marbury v. Madison*, 5 U.S. 137, 1 Cranch 137, 177 (1803). That is easier in some cases than in others. But in every case we

[36] 135 S. Ct. 2480 (2015).

> must respect the role of the Legislature, and take care not to undo what it has done. A fair reading of legislation demands a fair understanding of the legislative plan.
>
> Congress passed the Affordable Care Act to improve health insurance markets, not to destroy them. If at all possible, we must interpret the Act in a way that is consistent with the former, and avoids the latter. Section 36B can fairly be read consistent with what we see as Congress's plan, and that is the reading we adopt.[37]

Justice Scalia, predictably, dissented, joined by Justices Thomas and Alito:

> The Court holds that when the Patient Protection and Affordable Care Act says "Exchange established by the State" it means "Exchange established by the State or the Federal Government." That is of course quite absurd, and the Court's 21 pages of explanation make it no less so.
>
> Lawmakers sometimes repeat themselves—whether out of a desire to add emphasis, a sense of belt-and-suspenders caution, or a lawyerly penchant for doublets (aid and abet, cease and desist, null and void). Lawmakers do not, however, tend to use terms that "have no operation at all." So while the rule against treating a term as a redundancy is far from categorical, the rule against treating it as a nullity is as close to absolute as interpretive principles get. The Court's reading does not merely give "by the State" a duplicative effect; it causes the phrase to have no effect whatever.
>
> Perhaps the Patient Protection and Affordable Care Act will attain the enduring status of the Social Security Act or the Taft-Hartley Act; perhaps not. But this Court's two decisions on the Act will surely be remembered through the years. The somersaults of statutory interpretation they have performed ("penalty" means tax, "established by the State" means not established by the State) will be cited by litigants endlessly, to the confusion of honest jurisprudence. And the cases will publish forever the discouraging truth that the Supreme Court of the United States favors some laws over others, and is prepared to do whatever it takes to uphold and assist its favorites.[38]

Scalia's dissent contained some of the more memorable lines from the case, including "pure applesauce," and "interpretive jiggery-pokery." He ends with a now well-known line suggesting that the Court repeatedly engaged in intellectual dishonesty in order to save the Affordable Care Act: "We should start calling this law SCOTUScare."[39]

3. When Is The Right To Sue Not a Right to Sue? In *CompuCredit Corp. v. Greenwood*,[40] discussed in chapter 7, an eight-to-one majority held

---

[37] *Id.* at 2487–96.

[38] *Id.* at 2496–2507.

[39] *Id.* at 2507.

[40] 132 S. Ct. 665 (2012).

that mandatory arbitration agreements could be enforced despite the language of the Credit Repair Organizations Act (CROA). CROA dealt with the practice of issuing credit cards for the purpose of restoring a debtor's credit worthiness. The Act spells out the consumer's right to sue for violations of the Act, including the right to class actions and punitive damages.[41] In addition, the Act requires

> a statement that a credit repair organization must provide to the consumer before any contract is executed. One sentence of that required statement reads, "You have a right to sue a credit repair organization that violates the Credit Repair Organization Act." The Act's nonwaiver provision states, "Any waiver by any consumer of any protection provided by or any right of the consumer under this subchapter—(1) shall be treated as void; and (2) may not be enforced by any Federal or State court or any other person."[42]

Despite the apparently plain meaning of the statute, the majority opinion interpreted the "right to sue" as subservient to the Federal Arbitration Act. It held that the "right" conferred on the creditor by the Act is a right to receive a specific statement describing the consumer protections in the law, not the substantive right to a class action.

What happens to the "right to sue" contained elsewhere in the statute? One explanation is that the right to sue contained in the statute is waived by the debtor's agreement to arbitration contained in the credit card application. The right is there, but only if the debtor hasn't signed it away. Given the non-waiver provision, another explanation could be that the right still exists but it is essentially worthless because the individual arbitrations will have produced awards against the consumer that are then enforceable themselves. Debtors are usually the losers in arbitration because of the disparity in resources between the credit card companies and the consumers.[43]

Why didn't the Court read the Act in light of its remedial purposes rather than apply a strict construction of the language? Perhaps the answer lies in the concurrence by Justice Sotomayor throwing the burden back on Congress to fix the problem.

4. **Legislative History is Not Your Friend.** In *Milavetz, Gallop & Milavetz, P.A. v. United States*,[44] the Court decided that the Bankruptcy Abuse Prevention and Consumer Protection Act of 2005 included attorneys within the definition of "debt relief agenc[ies]"—*i.e.*, professionals who provide bankruptcy assistance to consumer debtors.

In an opinion by Justice Sotomayor, the Court held that the regulation of attorneys' conduct and disclosure requirements did not violate their First

---

[41] 15 U.S.C. § 1679g.

[42] *Id.* at 98–99.

[43] *See* Collin Koenig, *If It Only Had a Heart: Supreme Court Eschews Compassion for CashStrapped Consumers in Upholding the Validity of Arbitration Clauses in Credit Repair Contracts*, 2012 J. DISP. RESOL. 627 (2012); Casenote, *Arbitration and Class Actions—National Labor Relations Act—District Court Enforces Class Action Waiver in Employment Arbitration Agreement*, 126 HARV. L. REV. 1122 (2013).

[44] 559 U.S. 229 (2010).

Amendment rights. The court inserted text and a footnote on the use of legislative history in the case:

> As already noted, a debt relief agency is "any person who provides any bankruptcy assistance to an assisted person" in return for payment. By definition, "bankruptcy assistance" includes several services commonly performed by attorneys. Indeed, some forms of bankruptcy assistance, including the "provi[sion of] legal representation with respect to a case or proceeding," may be provided only by attorneys. *See* § 110(e)(2) (prohibiting bankruptcy petition preparers from providing legal advice). Moreover, in enumerating specific exceptions to the definition of debt relief agency, Congress gave no indication that it intended to exclude attorneys. Thus, as the Government contends, the statutory text clearly indicates that attorneys are debt relief agencies when they provide qualifying services to assisted persons.[3]
>
> > [Footnote 3: Although reliance on legislative history is unnecessary in light of the statute's unambiguous language, we note the support that record provides for the Government's reading. Statements in a Report of the House Committee on the Judiciary regarding the Act's purpose indicate concern with abusive practices undertaken by attorneys as well as other bankruptcy professionals. *See*, e.g., H.R.Rep. No. 109–31, pt. 1, p. 5 (2005) (hereinafter H.R. Rep.). And the legislative record elsewhere documents misconduct by attorneys. *See, e.g.*, Hearing on H.R. 3150 before the Subcommittee on Commercial and Administrative Law of the House Committee on the Judiciary, 105th Cong., 2d Sess., pt. III, p. 95 (1998) (hereinafter 1998 Hearings). (While the 1998 Hearings preceded the BAPCPA's enactment by several years, they form part of the record cited by the 2005 House Report. *See* H.R. Rep., at 7.)][45]

Justice Scalia concurred in the judgment, but objected to footnote three:

> I join the opinion of the Court, except for footnote 3, which notes that the legislative history supports what the statute unambiguously says. The Court first notes that statements in the Report of the House Committee on the Judiciary "indicate concern with abusive practices undertaken by attorneys." Perhaps, but only the concern of the author of the Report. Such statements tell us nothing about what the statute means, since (1) we do not know that the members of the Committee read the Report, (2) it is almost certain that they did not vote on the Report (that is not the practice), and (3) even if they did read and vote on it, they were not, after all, those who made this law. The statute before us is a law because its text was approved by a majority vote of the House and the Senate, and was signed by the President. Even indulging the extravagant assumption that Members of the House other than

---

[45] *Id.* at 236, 236 n.3.

members of its Committee on the Judiciary read the Report (and the further extravagant assumption that they agreed with it), the Members of the Senate could not possibly have read it, since it did not exist when the Senate passed the Bankruptcy Abuse Prevention and Consumer Protection Act of 2005. And the President surely had more important things to do.

> The Court acknowledges that nothing can be gained by this superfluous citation (it admits the footnote is "unnecessary in light of the statute's unambiguous language"). But much can be lost. Our cases have said that legislative history is irrelevant when the statutory text is clear. The footnote advises conscientious attorneys that this is not true, and that they must spend time and their clients' treasure combing the annals of legislative history in all cases: To buttress their case where the statutory text is unambiguously in their favor; and to attack an unambiguous text that is against them. If legislative history is relevant to confirm that a clear text means what it says, it is presumably relevant to show that an apparently clear text does not mean what it seems to say. Even for those who believe in the legal fiction that committee reports reflect congressional intent, footnote 3 is a bridge too far.[46]

5. There is No Such Thing as Legislative Intent. In *Edwards v. Aguilard*,[47] the Court dealt with a Louisiana requirement that schools teach "creation science" whenever they teach the "theory of evolution." The Court held that the requirement was unconstitutional, in large part because some legislative statements indicated that the Louisiana Legislature intended to promote religion. Justice Scalia dissented, noting that it is extremely difficult to discern the intent of a single legislator, much less the entire legislature:

> [W]hile it is possible to discern the objective "purpose" of a statute (i. e., the public good at which its provisions appear to be directed), or even the formal motivation for a statute where that is explicitly set forth (as it was, to no avail, here), discerning the subjective motivation of those enacting the statute is, to be honest, almost always an impossible task. The number of possible motivations, to begin with, is not binary, or indeed even finite. In the present case, for example, a particular legislator need not have voted for the Act either because he wanted to foster religion or because he wanted to improve education. He may have thought the bill would provide jobs for his district, or may have wanted to make amends with a faction of his party he had alienated on another vote, or he may have been a close friend of the bill's sponsor, or he may have been repaying a favor he owed the Majority Leader, or he may have hoped the Governor would appreciate his vote and make a fundraising appearance for him, or he may have been pressured to vote for a bill he disliked by a wealthy contributor or by a flood of

[46] *Id.* at 253–54 (Scalia, J., concurring).

[47] 482 U.S. 578 (1987).

constituent mail, or he may have been seeking favorable publicity, or he may have been reluctant to hurt the feelings of a loyal staff member who worked on the bill, or he may have been settling an old score with a legislator who opposed the bill, or he may have been mad at his wife who opposed the bill, or he may have been intoxicated and utterly unmotivated when the vote was called, or he may have accidentally voted "yes" instead of "no," or, of course, he may have had (and very likely did have) a combination of some of the above and many other motivations. To look for *the sole purpose* of even a single legislator is probably to look for something that does not exist.[48]

§ 9.5 GRAMMAR AND PUNCTUATION

In addition to considering the plain meaning, history, and purpose of the statute, courts will also consider the grammar and structure used by drafters. These canons create presumptions about various parts of speech, including the use of "and" versus "or" and the use of the permissive "may" versus the mandatory "shall." Courts presume that the drafter intentionally placed commas, colons, and other punctuation.[49] Finally, courts apply some little-known rules of grammar, including the rule of the last antecedent. That rule "limits the operation of qualifying phrases to the last phrase in a sentence (rather than applying that limitation to the entire sentence). It is a partner to the punctuation rule: if a proviso is set off from other phrases by a comma, the qualifying phrase should apply to all preceding phrases—not just the last one."[50]

Many legislatures have codified an "out," however, for grammatical mistakes. These "bad grammar" statutes preserve laws even when the drafter makes a mistake. They often allow the transposition, deletion, or addition of words and subordinate poor grammar to the intent of the legislature.

Barnhart v. Thomas

540 U.S. 20 (2003)

■ JUSTICE SCALIA delivered the opinion of the Court.

Under the Social Security Act, the Social Security Administration (SSA) is authorized to pay disability insurance benefits and Supplemental Security Income to persons who have a "disability." A person qualifies as disabled, and thereby eligible for such benefits, "only if his physical or mental impairment or impairments are of such severity that he is not only unable to do his previous work but cannot, considering his age, education, and work experience, engage in any other kind of

---

[48] *Id.* at 636–37.

[49] Jacob Scott, *Codified Canons and the Common Law of Interpretation*, 98 GEO. L.J. 341, 357 (2010).

[50] *Id.* at 358.

substantial gainful work which exists in the national economy." 42 U.S.C. §§ 423(d)(2)(A), 1382c(a)(3)(B). The issue we must decide is whether the SSA may determine that a claimant is not disabled because she remains physically and mentally able to do her previous work, without investigating whether that previous work exists in significant numbers in the national economy.

I

Pauline Thomas worked as an elevator operator for six years until her job was eliminated in August 1995. In June 1996, at age 53, Thomas applied for disability insurance benefits under Title II and Supplemental Security Income under Title XVI of the Social Security Act.

After the SSA denied Thomas's application initially and on reconsideration, she requested a hearing before an Administrative Law Judge (ALJ). The ALJ found that Thomas had "hypertension, cardiac arrythmia, [and] cervical and lumbar strain/sprain." He concluded, however, that Thomas was not under a "disability" because her "impairments do not prevent [her] from performing her past relevant work as an elevator operator." He rejected Thomas's argument that she is unable to do her previous work because that work no longer exists in significant numbers in the national economy. The SSA's Appeals Council denied Thomas's request for review.

Thomas then challenged the ALJ's ruling in the United States District Court for the District of New Jersey, renewing her argument that she is unable to do her previous work due to its scarcity. The District Court affirmed the ALJ, concluding that whether Thomas's old job exists is irrelevant under the SSA's regulations. The Court of Appeals for the Third Circuit, sitting en banc, reversed and remanded. Over the dissent of three of its members, it held that the statute unambiguously provides that the ability to perform prior work disqualifies from benefits only if it is "substantial gainful work which exists in the national economy." That holding conflicts with the decisions of four other Courts of Appeals. We granted the SSA's petition for certiorari.

II

As relevant to the present case, Title II of the Act defines "disability" as the "inability to engage in any substantial gainful activity by reason of any medically determinable physical or mental impairment which can be expected to result in death or which has lasted or can be expected to last for a continuous period of not less than 12 months." That definition is qualified, however, as follows:

> "An individual shall be determined to be under a disability only if his physical or mental impairment or impairments are of such severity that he is *not only unable to do his previous work* but cannot, considering his age, education, and work experience, *engage in any other kind of substantial gainful work which exists in the national economy. . . .*" § 423(d)(2)(A) (emphases added).

"[W]ork which exists in the national economy" is defined to mean "work which exists in significant numbers either in the region where such individual lives or in several regions of the country." Title XVI of the Act, which governs Supplemental Security Income for disabled indigent persons, employs the same definition of "disability" used in Title II, including a qualification that is verbatim the same as § 423(d)(2)(A). For simplicity's sake, we will refer only to the Title II provisions, but our analysis applies equally to Title XVI.

Section 423(d)(2)(A) establishes two requirements for disability. First, an individual's physical or mental impairment must render him "unable to do his previous work." Second, the impairment must also preclude him from "engag[ing] in any other kind of substantial gainful work." The parties agree that the latter requirement is qualified by the clause that immediately follows it—"which exists in the national economy." The issue in this case is whether that clause also qualifies "previous work."

The SSA has answered this question in the negative. Acting pursuant to its statutory rulemaking authority, the agency has promulgated regulations establishing a five-step sequential evaluation process to determine disability. If at any step a finding of disability or nondisability can be made, the SSA will not review the claim further. At the first step, the agency will find nondisability unless the claimant shows that he is not working at a "substantial gainful activity." At step two, the SSA will find nondisability unless the claimant shows that he has a "severe impairment," defined as "any impairment or combination of impairments which significantly limits [the claimant's] physical or mental ability to do basic work activities." At step three, the agency determines whether the impairment which enabled the claimant to survive step two is on the list of impairments presumed severe enough to render one disabled; if so, the claimant qualifies. If the claimant's impairment is not on the list, the inquiry proceeds to step four, at which the SSA assesses whether the claimant can do his previous work; unless he shows that he cannot, he is determined not to be disabled. If the claimant survives the fourth stage, the fifth, and final, step requires the SSA to consider so-called "vocational factors" (the claimant's age, education, and past work experience), and to determine whether the claimant is capable of performing other jobs existing in significant numbers in the national economy.

As the above description shows, step four can result in a determination of no disability without inquiry into whether the claimant's previous work exists in the national economy; the regulations explicitly reserve inquiry into the national economy for step five. Thus, the SSA has made it perfectly clear that it does not interpret the clause "which exists in the national economy" in § 423(d)(2)(A) as applying to "previous work." The issue presented is whether this agency interpretation must be accorded deference.

As we held in *Chevron U.S.A., Inc. v. Natural Resources Defense Council, Inc.*, 467 U.S. 837, 843 (1984), when a statute speaks clearly to the issue at hand we "must give effect to the unambiguously expressed intent of Congress," but when the statute "is silent or ambiguous" we must defer to a reasonable construction by the agency charged with its implementation. The Third Circuit held that, by referring first to "previous work" and then to "any other kind of substantial gainful work which exists in the national economy," the statute unambiguously indicates that the former is a species of the latter. "When," it said, "a sentence sets out one or more specific items followed by 'any other' and a description, the specific items must fall within the description." We disagree. For the reasons discussed below, the interpretation adopted by SSA is at least a reasonable construction of the text and must therefore be given effect.

The Third Circuit's reading disregards—indeed, is precisely contrary to—the grammatical "rule of the last antecedent," according to which a limiting clause or phrase (here, the relative clause "which exists in the national economy") should ordinarily be read as modifying only the noun or phrase that it immediately follows (here, "any other kind of substantial gainful work"). While this rule is not an absolute and can assuredly be overcome by other indicia of meaning, we have said that construing a statute in accord with the rule is "quite sensible as a matter of grammar."

An example will illustrate the error of the Third Circuit's perception that the specifically enumerated "previous work" "must" be treated the same as the more general reference to "any other kind of substantial gainful work." Consider, for example, the case of parents who, before leaving their teenage son alone in the house for the weekend, warn him, "You will be punished if you throw a party or engage in any other activity that damages the house." If the son nevertheless throws a party and is caught, he should hardly be able to avoid punishment by arguing that the house was not damaged. The parents proscribed (1) a party, and (2) any other activity that damages the house. As far as appears from what they said, their reasons for prohibiting the home-alone party may have had nothing to do with damage to the house—for instance, the risk that underage drinking or sexual activity would occur. And even if their only concern was to prevent damage, it does not follow from the fact that the same interest underlay both the specific and the general prohibition that proof of impairment of that interest is required for both. The parents, foreseeing that assessment of whether an activity had in fact "damaged" the house could be disputed by their son, might have wished to preclude all argument by specifying and categorically prohibiting the one activity—hosting a party—that was most likely to cause damage and most likely to occur.

The Third Circuit suggested that interpreting the statute as does the SSA would lead to "absurd results." The court could conceive of "no plausible reason why Congress might have wanted to deny benefits to an otherwise qualified person simply because that person, although unable to perform any job that actually exists in the national economy, could perform a previous job that no longer exists." But on the very next page the Third Circuit conceived of just such a plausible reason, namely, that "in the vast majority of cases, a claimant who is found to have the capacity to perform her past work also will have the capacity to perform other types of work." The conclusion which follows is that Congress could have determined that an analysis of a claimant's physical and mental capacity to do his previous work would "in the vast majority of cases" serve as an effective and efficient administrative proxy for the claimant's ability to do some work that does exist in the national economy. Such a proxy is useful because the step-five inquiry into whether the claimant's cumulative impairments preclude him from finding "other" work is very difficult, requiring consideration of "each of th[e] [vocational] factors and . . . an individual assessment of each claimant's abilities and limitations." There is good reason to use a workable proxy that avoids the more expansive and individualized step-five analysis. As we have observed, "[t]he Social Security hearing system is 'probably the largest adjudicative agency in the western world.' . . . The need for efficiency is self-evident."

The Third Circuit rejected this proxy rationale because it would produce results that "may not always be true, and . . . may not be true in this case." 294 F.3d, at 576. That logic would invalidate a vast number of the procedures employed by the administrative state. To generalize is to be imprecise. Virtually every legal (or other) rule has imperfect applications in particular circumstances. *Cf. Bowen v. Yuckert*, 482 U.S. 137 (1987) (O'Connor, J., concurring) ("To be sure the Secretary faces an administrative task of staggering proportions in applying the disability benefits provisions of the Social Security Act. Perfection in processing millions of such claims annually is impossible"). It is true that, under the SSA's interpretation, a worker with severely limited capacity who has managed to find easy work in a declining industry could be penalized for his troubles if the job later disappears. It is also true, however, that under the Third Circuit's interpretation, impaired workers in declining or marginal industries who cannot do "other" work could simply refuse to return to their jobs—even though the jobs remain open and available—and nonetheless draw disability benefits. The proper *Chevron* inquiry is not whether the agency construction can give rise to undesirable results in some instances (as here both constructions can), but rather whether, in light of the alternatives, the agency construction is reasonable. In the present case, the SSA's authoritative interpretation certainly satisfies that test.

We have considered respondent's other arguments and find them to be without merit.

NOTES AND QUESTIONS

Bad Grammar. Is the bad grammar rule just another way of allowing a court to interpret a statute any way it wishes, or is a presumption that legislatures normally use proper grammar implied in the bad grammar rule?

§ 9.6 PARTIALLY UNCONSTITUTIONAL STATUTES

Courts sometimes conclude that a portion of a statute is unconstitutional. When that happens, there may be a portion of the statute that remains good law. Many legislatures write "escape" clauses into their statute. These provisions tell the court what to do when a portion of a statute is struck down and a portion remains.

Severability clauses provide that if a portion of an act is held unconstitutional, that portion should be stricken but the remainder should remain in force. For example, 20 U.S.C. § 3506 provides that "neither the remainder of this Act nor the application of such provision to other persons or circumstances shall be affected thereby."

Non-severability clauses do the opposite. These provisions tell the courts that an entire section of the code must fall if any one section is held unconstitutional. For example, 4 U.S.C. § 125 provides that "[i]f a court of competent jurisdiction enters a final judgment on the merits that . . . substantially limits or impairs the essential elements of sections 116 through 126 of this title, then sections 116 through 126 of this title are invalid and have no legal effect as of the date of entry of such judgment."

CHAPTER 10

CONSTITUTIONAL INTERPRETATION

> [A]n independent judiciary with the authority to finally interpret a written constitution . . . is one of the crown jewels of our system of government today.
>
> – United States Supreme Court Chief Justice William Rehnquist[1]

Hermeneutics is the theory and methodology of interpretation. There are basically three tools available for any interpretational task: text, history, and structure. The tools are the same regardless of whether an author is interpreting law, religious texts, or literature.

In law, the text is always the starting point. In some instances, it is also the ending point. Some provisions of the United States Constitution, such as the requirement that Presidents be at least 35 years old,[2] are so straightforward that they require no further interpretation. History is also often an important guide, not only for those who seek the "original" meaning of a text but also for those who look for meaning in societal evolution. Finally, "structure" may refer to the structure of the text but may also consider the structure of the institutions created or molded by the Constitution.

To the extent that Americans are familiar with the role of the courts, they are most aware when the courts engage in Constitutional interpretation. The United States Supreme Court's constitutional decisions often generate heated debates in academia, social media, and the political arena. These decisions highlight the political importance of the Supreme Court, and turn seemingly esoteric arguments about constitutional theory into practical realities.

§ 10.1 THEORIES OF CONSTITUTIONAL INTERPRETATION

The Constitution, said Supreme Court Justice David Souter, "embodies the desire of the American people, like most people, to have

---

[1] Chief United States Supreme Court Justice William Rehnquist, Address at American University's Washington College of Law (Apr. 9, 1996).

[2] U.S. CONST. art. II, § 1.

things both ways. We want order and security, and we want liberty. And we want not only liberty but equality as well."[3]

For a federal judge, constitutional interpretation is both obligatory and fraught. As Chief Justice Marshall declared, it is "emphatically the province and duty of the judicial department to say what the law is."[4] Although there are a variety competing interpretive theories, each is based on text, history, or structure. Underlying each is a debate about the power and legitimacy of the court and the court's position vis-à-vis the other branches of government and the people. While single theories of interpretation are often attributed to a particular Justice, various modes of interpretation may overlap, or a single judge may employ multiple theories in pursuit of the most sensible approach to a given case.

A. ORIGINALISM

The goal of originalism is to discern the original meaning of the Constitution at the time of its creation. The word originalism encompasses a family of theories. First, the original intent theory requires courts to interpret the Constitution consistently with what was meant by those who drafted and ratified it. Second, the original meaning theory, closely related to textualism, requires courts to interpret the Constitution consistently with what reasonable persons living at the time of its adoption would have declared the ordinary meaning of the text to be. Most originalists, including Justice Scalia, are associated with the original meaning theory.

Proponents argue that originalism is the more democratic of the theories. It looks to a higher authority—the original drafters—to give the Constitution meaning and shape. That meaning remains relatively static over time. Any changes come not through the work of the Court, but through the democratic process. Thus originalism requires, at least in theory, fewer policy decisions on the part of the court.

Like other modes of interpretation, originalism has its drawbacks. While it looks to "the framers" for meaning, the historical record is not always as clear or available as an originalist might wish. The framers did not thoroughly debate every provision and, where they did, there may be an incomplete record of that debate. Just as with legislatures, not every framer agreed on the meaning of each provision. Additionally, the existing historical records may be slanted by the author. As a result, different originalists, relying on the same historical record, may reach different conclusions. More existentially, originalism assumes that the framers themselves believed that the Constitution would be a static document.

---

[3] Associate United States Supreme Court Justice David H. Souter, Harvard University Commencement Address (May 27, 2010), http://news.harvard.edu/gazette/story/2010/05/text-of-justice-david-souters-speech/ [https://perma.cc/393R-738B].

[4] Marbury v. Madison, 5 U.S. 137, 177 (1803).

Further, it is not always clear who is or is not a framer. The Constitutional Convention lasted for more than two months at a time when travel was time-consuming and difficult. Not all states sent delegates, not all delegates appointed by the states were able to attend, not all delegates attended the entire Convention, and not all those who did attend signed the final document. Importantly, many of those whom we might consider framers did not attend the Convention. Thomas Jefferson, John Adams, Patrick Henry, John Hancock, and Samuel Adams were all absent for a variety of reasons.

The difficulties of divining the intent of a large group of people from an incomplete historical record has led opponents to argue that originalism is what Justice Brennan called "arrogance cloaked as humility."[5] While originalism purports to emphasize the democratic process and limit the role of judges, it is sometimes the least democratic mode of interpretation. A purely originalist view of the Constitution would result in the disenfranchisement of the portions of the population disenfranchised in 1787. Further, because originalism attempts to ignore current societal trends, it may subvert the will of today's people to the will of a small group of dead white men.

B. TEXTUALISM

Textualism is often used in statutory interpretation as well as constitutional interpretation. Textualism asks "not what this man meant, but what those words would mean in the mouth of a normal speaker of English, using them in the circumstances in which they were used .... We do not inquire what the legislature meant; we ask only what the statutes mean."[6]

Textualism comes in several forms. The first is the plain meaning approach, in which one looks only at the document itself. A second form of textualism gives primary weight to the text of the Constitution, but may look further for its plain meaning. This approach eschews questions of legislative intent, the problem that a particular provision was intended to remedy, and substantive questions of the justice and rectitude of a particular law. However, it still looks to the language and structure of the text as it would have been understood at the time of adoption.

Plain meaning is sufficient for some fairly simple and concrete constitutional provisions. Other more nuanced or nebulous provisions, however, are ill-suited to a plain meaning approach. Many Constitutional

---

5 Associate United States Supreme Court Justice William J. Brennan, Jr., Speech at the Georgetown University Text and Teaching Symposium (Oct. 12, 1985), http://www.pbs.org/wnet/supremecourt/democracy/sources_document7.html [https://perma.cc/LKS2-WCDZ].

6 Oliver Wendell Holmes, *The Theory of Legal Interpretation*, 12 HARV. L. REV. 417, 417–19 (1899).

provisions, including equal protection, due process, and the "majestic generalities" in the Bill of Rights are "both luminous and obscure."[7]

C. THE LIVING CONSTITUTION

The living constitutionalist believes that the Constitution isn't a static document, nor should it be. The framers did not, and could not, consider every possible factual permutation. The framers did not, and could not, act with one unified mind. Instead, they created a blueprint, largely written in general terms, that provides both the structure and the flexibility to create a functioning society.

Proponents of living constitutionalism argue that, while many constitutional provisions are specific enough to be applied with little debate, others are hopelessly anachronistic. It makes little sense to apply the Seventh Amendment literally, as the value of every controversy now exceeds $20. Other provisions were written so generally as to be ambiguous—perhaps purposely so. The requirement of due process of law is perhaps the most obvious example. Finally, some provisions are unworkable without refinement. The First Amendment's proscription of laws which abridge the freedom of speech cannot be employed in its naked form. A law that allows any citizen to make any statement, at any time, and in any place plainly collides with other political and societal needs.

Therefore, the living constitutionalist reads the Constitution as a floor for government responsibilities and individual rights, but concludes that the document must also reflect the judgment and needs of the times. Furthermore, viewing the Constitution through a historical majoritarian lens ignores one point of the Constitution: to protect the rights of the minority from the tyranny of the majority.

Critics of the living constitution theory argue that it gives judges too much freedom to impose their own morals, ethics, or political values on the country at large. Living constitutionalists may appear to lack objective, neutral criteria upon which to base decisions, giving judges immense power and freedom. Those opposed to living constitutionalism also argue that it usurps states' rights and the power of the people to reach consensus through the political process.

D. TRADITIONALISM

Traditionalists are concerned with maintaining long-standing legal, political, and social principles. The court looks not only at its own legal practices but also those of other branches of government or social institutions. It may also consider cultural norms.

---

[7] Brennan, *supra* note 5. The phrase "majestic generalities" is most often attributed to Justice Robert Jackson.

Traditionalist constitutional interpretation draws parallels with originalism. Like originalism, traditionalism focuses on history. However, it is less single-minded in scope. Rather than looking only at the intent or beliefs of one group of people at one moment in time, it looks for continuity in particular beliefs over a period of time. Unlike living constitutionalism, traditionalism doesn't deviate from continuous and long-standing practices without an overwhelming reason to do so.

E. FORMALISM AND FUNCTIONALISM

Formalism seeks to apply settled principles of law—often bright-line rules—to facts in a mechanical way. It emphasizes deductive reasoning based on authoritative premises, separation of powers, and a limited role for the courts. Formalism gives "priority to rule of law values such as transparency, predictability, and continuity in law."[8] It is often placed in opposition to "functionalism," a school of thought that emphasizes "pragmatic values like adaptability, efficacy, and justice in law."[9]

§ 10.2 THE ROLE OF FEDERALISM IN CONSTITUTIONAL INTERPRETATION

Constitutional interpretation frequently implicates questions of federalism and separation of powers. The Court is called on to address the balance of power between the states and the federal government, the power of each branch of the federal government in relation to the others, and the role of the Court in dictating the boundaries of those relationships.

District of Columbia v. Heller

554 U.S. 570 (2008)

■ JUSTICE SCALIA for the Court:

The Second Amendment provides: "A well regulated Militia, being necessary to the security of a free State, the right of the people to keep and bear Arms, shall not be infringed." In interpreting this text, we are guided by the principle that the Constitution was written to be understood by the voters; its words and phrases were used in their normal and ordinary as distinguished from technical meaning. Normal meaning may of course include an idiomatic meaning, but it excludes secret or technical meanings that would not have been known to ordinary citizens in the founding generation.

---

8 William N. Eskridge, Jr., *Relationships Between Formalism and Functionalism in Separation of Powers Cases*, 22 HARV. J.L. & PUB. POL'Y, 21, 22 (1998).

9 *Id.*; *see also* ANTONIN SCALIA, A MATTER OF INTERPRETATION: FEDERAL COURTS AND THE LAW 25 (1997); Antonin Scalia, *The Rule of Law as a Law of Rules*, 56 U. CHI. L. REV. 1175 (1989).

The two sides in this case have set out very different interpretations of the Amendment. Petitioners and today's dissenting Justices believe that it protects only the right to possess and carry a firearm in connection with militia service. Respondent argues that it protects an individual right to possess a firearm unconnected with service in a militia, and to use that arm for traditionally lawful purposes, such as self-defense within the home.

The Second Amendment is naturally divided into two parts: its prefatory clause and its operative clause. The former does not limit the latter grammatically, but rather announces a purpose.

The first salient feature of the operative clause is that it codifies a "right of the people." In other provisions of the Constitution [such as the First and Ninth Amendments] that mention "the people," the term unanimously refers to all members of the political community, not an unspecified subset. This contrasts markedly with the phrase "the militia" in the prefatory clause. The "militia" in colonial America consisted of a subset of "the people"—those who were male, able bodied, and within a certain age range.

Some have made the argument, bordering on the frivolous, that only those arms in existence in the 18th century are protected by the Second Amendment. We do not interpret constitutional rights that way. Just as the First Amendment protects modern forms of communications, and the Fourth Amendment applies to modern forms of search, the Second Amendment extends, prima facie, to all instruments that constitute bearable arms, even those that were not in existence at the time of the founding.

From our review of founding-era sources, we conclude that this natural meaning was also the meaning that "bear arms" had in the 18th century. In numerous instances, "bear arms" was unambiguously used to refer to the carrying of weapons outside of an organized militia.

Putting all of these textual elements together, we find that they guarantee the individual right to possess and carry weapons in case of confrontation. This meaning is strongly confirmed by the historical background of the Second Amendment. We look to this because it has always been widely understood that the Second Amendment, like the First and Fourth Amendments, codified a pre-existing right. The very text of the Second Amendment implicitly recognizes the pre-existence of the right and declares only that it "shall not be infringed."

[JUSTICE SCALIA then reviewed Britain's history of limiting weapons for the purpose of suppressing dissent.]

We reach the question, then: Does the preface fit with an operative clause that creates an individual right to keep and bear arms? It fits perfectly, once one knows the history that the founding generation knew and that we have described above. That history showed that the way tyrants had eliminated a militia consisting of all the able-bodied men was not by banning the militia but simply by taking away the people's arms, enabling a select militia or standing army to suppress political opponents. This is what had occurred in England that prompted codification of the right to have arms in the English Bill of Rights.

It is therefore entirely sensible that the Second Amendment's prefatory clause announces the purpose for which the right was codified: to prevent elimination of the militia. The prefatory clause does not suggest that preserving the militia was the only reason Americans valued the ancient right; most undoubtedly thought it even more important for self-defense and hunting. But the threat that the new Federal Government would destroy the citizens' militia by taking away their arms was the reason that right—unlike some other English rights—was codified in a written Constitution.

We also recognize another important limitation on the right to keep and carry arms. [*United States v.*] *Miller* [307 U.S. 174 (1939)] said that the sorts of weapons protected were those "in common use at the time." It may be objected that if weapons that are most useful in military service—M-16 rifles and the like—may be banned, then the Second Amendment right is completely detached from the prefatory clause. But as we have said, the conception of the militia at the time of the Second Amendment's ratification was the body of all citizens capable of military service, who would bring the sorts of lawful weapons that they possessed at home to militia duty. It may well be true today that a militia, to be as effective as militias in the 18th century, would require sophisticated arms that are highly unusual in society at large. Indeed, it may be true that no amount of small arms could be useful against modern-day bombers and tanks. But the fact that modern developments have limited the degree of fit between the prefatory clause and the protected right cannot change our interpretation of the right.

NOTES AND QUESTIONS

1. **How Many Modes of Interpretation Can Fit on the Head of a Pin?** In *Heller*, Justice Scalia employed numerous modes of interpretation. Does this blend of interpretive techniques speak to the richness of the options, or to the frailties of individual techniques?

2. **The Eye of the Beholder.** Two judges may look at the same historical record and come to two different conclusions. For example, the dissenting justices in *Heller* use text, history, institutional structure, modern technology, and societal norms to conclude that the Second Amendment does not limit the authority of Congress to regulate the use or possession of firearms for civilian purposes. Given that justices may use the same evidence to reach entirely different results, is there any salient reason to construct "theories of interpretation"? Are these theories just a cover for the wisdom, judgment, and persuasive power of a judge?

United States v. Comstock

560 U.S. 126 (2010)

[The Adam Walsh Child Protection and Safety Act, named after a six-year-old child who was kidnapped and murdered in 1981, allowed a federal district court to order the indefinite civil commitment of any mentally ill, sexually dangerous federal prisoner, even one who had completed his criminal sentence. Five convicted sex offenders moved to dismiss civil-commitment proceedings instituted under the statute, arguing that the statute violated double jeopardy, substantive due process, and equal protection guarantees. They also argued that Congress lacked the constitutional power to enact the statute.

The Supreme Court granted certiorari only on the issue of whether the Necessary and Proper Clause, found in Art. I, § 8, cl. 18, grants Congress the necessary authority. The Court held that it did because the statute was rationally related to Congress's power to regulate commerce through criminal enforcement.]

■ JUSTICE THOMAS, with whom JUSTICE SCALIA joins in all but Part III-A-1-b, dissenting.

* * *

The Constitution plainly sets forth the "few and defined" powers that Congress may exercise. Article I "vest[s]" in Congress "[a]ll legislative Powers herein granted," § 1, and carefully enumerates those powers in § 8. The final clause of § 8, the Necessary and Proper Clause, authorizes Congress "[t]o make all Laws which shall be necessary and proper for carrying into Execution the foregoing Powers, and all other Powers vested by this Constitution in the Government of the United States, or in any Department or Officer thereof." As the Clause's placement at the end of § 8 indicates, the "foregoing Powers" are those granted to Congress in the preceding clauses of that section. The "other Powers" to which the Clause refers are those "vested" in Congress and the other branches by other specific provisions of the Constitution.

Chief Justice Marshall famously summarized Congress' authority under the Necessary and Proper Clause in *McCulloch*, which has stood for nearly 200 years as this Court's definitive interpretation of that text:

"Let the end be legitimate, let it be within the scope of the constitution, and all means which are appropriate, which are plainly adapted to that end, which are not prohibited, but consist with the letter and spirit of the constitution, are constitutional." 4 Wheat., at 421.

McCulloch's summation is descriptive of the Clause itself, providing that federal legislation is a valid exercise of Congress' authority under the Clause if it satisfies a two-part test: First, the law must be directed toward a "legitimate" end, which *McCulloch* defines as one "within the scope of the [C]onstitution"—that is, the powers expressly delegated to the Federal Government by some provision in the Constitution. Second, there must be a necessary and proper fit between the "means" (the federal law) and the "end" (the enumerated power or powers) it is designed to serve. *McCulloch* accords Congress a certain amount of discretion in assessing means-end fit under this second inquiry. The means Congress selects will be deemed "necessary" if they are "appropriate" and "plainly adapted" to the exercise of an enumerated power, and "proper" if they are not otherwise "prohibited" by the Constitution and not "[in]consistent" with its "letter and spirit."

Critically, however, *McCulloch* underscores the linear relationship the Clause establishes between the two inquiries: Unless the end itself is "legitimate," the fit between means and end is irrelevant. In other words, no matter how "necessary" or "proper" an Act of Congress may be to its objective, Congress lacks authority to legislate if the objective is anything other than "carrying into Execution" one or more of the Federal Government's enumerated powers. Art. I, § 8, cl. 18.

This limitation was of utmost importance to the Framers. During the state ratification debates, Anti-Federalists expressed concern that the Necessary and Proper Clause would give Congress virtually unlimited power. *See, e.g., Essays of Brutus*, in 2 THE COMPLETE ANTI-FEDERALIST 421 (H. Storing ed. 1981). Federalist supporters of the Constitution swiftly refuted that charge, explaining that the Clause did not grant Congress any freestanding authority, but instead made explicit what was already implicit in the grant of each enumerated power. Referring to the "powers declared in the Constitution," Alexander Hamilton noted that "it is expressly to execute these powers that the sweeping clause . . . authorizes the national legislature to pass all necessary and proper laws." THE FEDERALIST No. 33, at 245. James Madison echoed this view, stating that "the sweeping clause . . . only extend[s] to the enumerated powers." 3 J. ELLIOT, THE DEBATES IN THE SEVERAL STATE CONVENTIONS ON THE ADOPTION OF THE FEDERAL CONSTITUTION 455 (1836) (hereinafter Elliot). Statements by delegates to the state ratification conventions indicate that this understanding was widely held by the founding generation. *E.g., id.*, at 245–246 (statement of George Nicholas) ("Suppose [the Necessary and Proper Clause] had been inserted, at the end of every power, that they should have power to make laws to carry that power into execution; would that have increased their powers? If, therefore, it could not have increased their powers, if placed at the end of each power, it cannot increase them at the end of all").

Roughly 30 years after the Constitution's ratification, *McCulloch* firmly established this understanding in our constitutional jurisprudence. Since then, our precedents uniformly have maintained that the Necessary and Proper Clause is not an independent fount of congressional authority, but rather a *caveat* that Congress possesses all the means necessary to carry out the specifically granted "foregoing" powers of § 8 "and all other Powers vested by this Constitution."

NOTES AND QUESTIONS

1. **Vale of Tiers.** When President Truman seized steel mills that were threatened with a strike during the Korean War, the Supreme Court held that he had overstepped his powers. The majority opinion in *Youngstown Sheet & Tube v. Sawyer*[10] referred to it as an exercise of executive lawmaking, but it is Justice Jackson's concurrence that has survived as a landmark opinion. Jackson took a functionalist view in describing the President's actions in three tiers: those specifically authorized by Congress, those taken in the face of legislative silence, and those taken against the express will of Congress. In the latter instance, the President's "power is at its lowest ebb, for then he can rely only upon his own constitutional powers minus any constitutional powers of Congress."[11]

Although there is little in the text of the Constitution from which to derive Jackson's formulation, his exegesis of power allocations is so persuasive that it has become virtually "black letter" law. Is this an example of formalism or functionalism? Does it matter what we call it if it works?

2. **Form over Function.** Most cases involving conflicts between Congress and the Executive are decided with some attention to both the form and substance of government processes. Because the lines between the branches are not cleanly drawn, "separation" has given way to a "system of checks and balances."

3. **A Triumph of Formalism.** Section 244(c)(2) of the Immigration and Nationality Act allowed either the House or Senate to overrule a decision of the Immigration and Naturalization Service and order an alien deported. In *INS v. Chadha*,[12] the Supreme Court held that § 244(c)(2) was unconstitutional. Although the House Resolution in *Chadha* applied to a single person, the Court held that action taken by the House was legislative in nature, and therefore must meet the requirements of bicameralism (passage by both houses) and presentment to the President for signature or veto.

To the dissenters, the one-house legislative veto was a useful device that allowed Congress to check abuse of the powers delegated to administrative agencies. Legislative vetoes existed in about 200 statutes. All were called into question because of one immigration decision.

Chadha has been called a triumph of "formalism" over "functionalism" for its refusal to allow Congress to implement an efficient method of delegation and control. Chief Justice Burger's majority opinion answered this assertion by stating that "the fact that a given law or procedure is efficient, convenient, and useful . . . will not save it if it is contrary to the Constitution. Convenience and efficiency are not the primary objectives—or the hallmarks—of democratic government . . . ."[13]

---

10 343 U.S. 579 (1952).

11 *Id.* at 637 (Jackson, J., concurring).

12 462 U.S. 929 (1983).

13 *Id.* at 944.

4. Market Forces. Constitutional scholar John Hart Ely proposed a middle ground between the apparent extremes of originalism and interpretivism. He argued that the job of a judge was to protect and enhance the democratic process, ensuring that it remains open and fair.[14] He called his approach "representation reinforcing." "Rather than dictate the substantive result," judges should intervene "only when the 'market,' in our case the political market, is systematically malfunctioning."[15] Is *Baker v. Carr* an instance when the Court's intervention was warranted?

Baker v. Carr

369 U.S. 186 (1962)

■ MR. JUSTICE BRENNAN delivered the opinion of the Court.

[The Tennessee state constitution required that the legislature redraw legislative districts every 10 years. In 1901, the legislature drew districts that reflected the number of qualified voters counted in the 1900 federal census. Between 1901 and 1960, the Tennessee population both increased substantially and moved from rural areas to cities. Because the districts were not redrawn to reflect these changes, a single vote in a rural area represented significantly more political power than did a single vote in a metropolitan area.]

* * * *

We come, finally, to the ultimate inquiry whether our precedents as to what constitutes a nonjusticiable 'political question' bring the case before us under the umbrella of that doctrine. A natural beginning is to note whether any of the common characteristics which we have been able to identify and label descriptively are present. We find none: The question here is the consistency of state action with the Federal Constitution. We have no question decided, or to be decided, by a political branch of government coequal with this Court. Nor do we risk embarrassment of our government abroad, or grave disturbance at home if we take issue with Tennessee as to the constitutionality of her action here challenged. Nor need the appellants, in order to succeed in this action, ask the Court to enter upon policy determinations for which judicially manageable standards are lacking. Judicial standards under the Equal Protection Clause are well developed and familiar, and it has been open to courts since the enactment of the Fourteenth Amendment to determine, if on the particular facts they must, that a discrimination reflects no policy, but simply arbitrary and capricious action.

---

[14] Adam Liptak, *John Hart Ely, a Constitutional Scholar, Is Dead at 64*, N.Y. TIMES (Oct. 27, 2003), http://www.nytimes.com/2003/10/27/us/john-hart-ely-a-constitutional-scholar-is-dead-at-64.html [https://perma.cc/8YRN-9GG7].

[15] JOHN HART ELY, DEMOCRACY AND DISTRUST: A THEORY OF JUDICIAL REVIEW 103 (1980).

■ MR. JUSTICE FRANKFURTER, whom MR. JUSTICE HARLAN joins, dissenting.

The Court today reverses a uniform course of decision established by a dozen cases, including one by which the very claim now sustained was unanimously rejected only five years ago. The impressive body of rulings thus cast aside reflected the equally uniform course of our political history regarding the relationship between population and legislative representation—a wholly different matter from denial of the franchise to individuals because of race, color, religion or sex. Such a massive repudiation of the experience of our whole past in asserting destructively novel judicial power demands a detailed analysis of the role of this Court in our constitutional scheme. Disregard of inherent limits in the effective exercise of the Court's 'judicial Power' not only presages the futility of judicial intervention in the essentially political conflict of forces by which the relation between population and representation has time out of mind been and now is determined. It may well impair the Court's position as the ultimate organ of 'the supreme Law of the Land' in that vast range of legal problems, often strongly entangled in popular feeling, on which this Court must pronounce. The Court's authority—possessed of neither the purse nor the sword—ultimately rests on sustained public confidence in its moral sanction. Such feeling must be nourished by the Court's complete detachment, in fact and in appearance, from political entanglements and by abstention from injecting itself into the clash of political forces in political settlements.

A hypothetical claim resting on abstract assumptions is now for the first time made the basis for affording illusory relief for a particular evil even though it foreshadows deeper and more pervasive difficulties in consequence. The claim is hypothetical and the assumptions are abstract because the Court does not vouchsafe the lower courts—state and federal—guidelines for formulating specific, definite, wholly unprecedented remedies for the inevitable litigations that today's umbrageous disposition is bound to stimulate in connection with politically motivated reapportionments in so many States. In such a setting, to promulgate jurisdiction in the abstract is meaningless. It is as devoid of reality as 'a brooding omnipresence in the sky,' for it conveys no intimation what relief, if any, a District Court is capable of affording that would not invite legislatures to play ducks and drakes with the judiciary. For this Court to direct the District Court to enforce a claim to which the Court has over the years consistently found itself required to deny legal enforcement and at the same time to find it necessary to withhold any guidance to the lower court how to enforce this turnabout, new legal claim, manifests an odd—indeed an esoteric—conception of judicial propriety. One of the Court's supporting opinions, as elucidated by commentary, unwittingly affords a disheartening preview of the mathematical quagmire (apart from divers judicially inappropriate and elusive determinants) into which this Court today catapults the lower courts of the country without so much as adumbrating the basis for a legal calculus as a means of extrication. Even assuming the indispensable intellectual disinterestedness on the part of judges in such matters, they do not have accepted legal standards or criteria or even reliable analogies to draw upon for making judicial judgments. To charge courts with the task of accommodating the incommensurable factors of policy that underlie these mathematical puzzles is to attribute, however flatteringly, omnicompetence to judges. The Framers of the Constitution persistently rejected a proposal that embodied this assumption and Thomas Jefferson never entertained it.

Recent legislation, creating a district appropriately described as 'an atrocity of ingenuity,' is not unique. Considering the gross inequality among legislative electoral units within almost every State, the Court naturally shrinks from asserting that in districting at least substantial equality is a constitutional requirement enforceable by courts. Room continues to be allowed for weighting. This of course implies that geography, economics, urban-rural conflict, and all the other non-legal factors which have throughout our history entered into political districting are to some extent not to be ruled out in the undefined vista now opened up by review in the federal courts of state reapportionments. To some extent—aye, there's the rub. In effect, today's decision empowers the courts of the country to devise what should constitute the proper composition of the legislatures of the fifty States. If state courts should for one reason or another find themselves unable to discharge this task, the duty of doing so is put on the federal courts or on this Court, if State views do not satisfy this Court's notion of what is proper districting.

We were soothingly told at the bar of this Court that we need not worry about the kind of remedy a court could effectively fashion once the abstract constitutional right to have courts pass on a state-wide system of electoral districting is recognized as a matter of judicial rhetoric, because legislatures would heed the Court's admonition. This is not only a euphoric hope. It implies a sorry confession of judicial impotence in place of a frank acknowledgment that there is not under our Constitution a judicial remedy for every political mischief, for every undesirable exercise of legislative power. The Framers carefully and with deliberate forethought refused so to enthrone the judiciary. In this situation, as in others of like nature, appeal for relief does not belong here. Appeal must be to an informed, civically militant electorate. In a democratic society like ours, relief must come through an aroused popular conscience that sears the conscience of the people's representatives. In any event there is nothing judicially more unseemly nor more self-defeating than for this Court to make *in terrorem* pronouncements, to indulge in merely empty rhetoric, sounding a word of promise to the ear, sure to be disappointing to the hope.

NOTES AND QUESTIONS

1. **A Political Thicket.** Fifteen years prior to *Baker*, in *Colegrove v. Green*,[16] a plurality of the Supreme Court held that Congressional redistricting was a political question:

> We are of opinion that the petitioners ask of this Court what is beyond its competence to grant. This is one of those demands on judicial power which cannot be met by verbal fencing about 'jurisdiction.' It must be resolved by considerations on the basis of which this Court, from time to time, has refused to intervene in controversies. It has refused to do so because due regard for the effective working of our Government revealed this issue to be of a peculiarly political nature and therefore not meet for judicial determination.[17]

Justice Frankfurter, writing for the plurality, went on,

> To sustain this action would cut very deep into the very being of Congress. Courts ought not to enter this political thicket. The remedy for unfairness in districting is to secure State legislatures that will apportion properly, or to invoke the ample powers of Congress. The Constitution has many commands that are not enforceable by courts because they clearly fall outside the conditions and purposes that circumscribe judicial action. Thus, 'on Demand of the executive Authority,' Art. IV, s 2, of a State it is the duty of a sister State to deliver up a fugitive from justice. But the fulfillment of this duty cannot be judicially enforced. The duty to see to it that the laws are faithfully executed cannot be brought under legal compulsion. Violation of the great guaranty of a republican form of government in States cannot be challenged in the courts. The Constitution has left the performance of many duties in our governmental scheme to depend on the fidelity of the executive and legislative action and, ultimately, on the vigilance of the people in exercising their political rights.[18]

2. **A Little Judicial Pregnancy.** Although *Baker v. Carr* was a six-to-two decision, it caused significant consternation on the Court. Initially argued in April of 1961, the case was held over for reargument in the October 1962 term after no clear majority emerged. The Court was deeply divided, and the stress of the decision purportedly led to Justice Charles Evans Whittaker's nervous breakdown and eventual resignation from the Court.

Baker was also a stinging defeat for Justice Frankfurter. He harshly criticized his colleagues in the majority, writing to a former clerk and Yale law professor, "Am I right in assuming that your head note for *Baker v. Carr* would be '*Held*, a little judicial pregnancy is permissible?"[19] Frankfurter suffered a stroke less than two weeks after *Baker* was decided, and resigned

---

[16] 328 U.S. 549 (1946).

[17] *Id.* at 552.

[18] *Id.* at 556.

[19] J. DOUGLAS SMITH, ON DEMOCRACY'S DOORSTEP: THE INSIDE STORY OF HOW THE SUPREME COURT BROUGHT "ONE PERSON ONE VOTE" TO THE UNITED STATES 92 (2014).

from the court that term. He reportedly blamed his stroke on the stress of *Baker v. Carr*.[20]

3. **The Most Vital Decision.** Chief Justice Warren called *Baker v. Carr* the most vital decision of his fifteen-year tenure on the Court. It ushered in redistricting throughout the country, marked a shift in the relationship between the Court and state governments, and was the font of the "one person, one vote" revolution formally adopted by the Court in 1964.[21]

4. **From Tennessee to Florida to the White House.** Some scholars have argued that *Baker v. Carr* laid the groundwork for *Bush v. Gore*,[22] the 2000 Supreme Court case which held that Florida's standardless manual recounts of votes in the 2000 presidential election violated the equal protection clause in the Fourteenth Amendment. The decision effectively gave the presidential election to George W. Bush.[23] Is *Bush v. Gore* a sign that Justice Frankfurter's dissent in *Baker v. Carr* was correct?

§ 10.3 THE ROLE OF HISTORY AND TRADITION IN CONSTITUTIONAL INTERPRETATION

Michael H. & Victoria D. v. Gerald D.

491 U.S. 110 (1989)

■ JUSTICE SCALIA announced the judgment of the Court and delivered an opinion, in which THE CHIEF JUSTICE joins, and in all but note 6 of which JUSTICES O'CONNOR and KENNEDY join.

[Michael H. had "an adulterous affair" with Carole D. while she was married to Gerald D. Victoria D. was born to Carole, and blood tests showed that there was a 98.07% probability that Michael was the father of Victoria. During Victoria's first three years, she resided exclusively with her mother, who at times lived with Michael. On these occasions, Michael established a relationship with the child and held her out as his daughter. Carole eventually reconciled with Gerald, and she and Victoria had been living with him since 1984.

[Michael filed suit to establish his paternity and a right to visitation. Victoria, through her guardian ad litem, filed a cross-complaint asserting that she was entitled to maintain her filial relationship with both Michael and Gerald. Gerald intervened in the action and ultimately moved for summary judgment under § 621 of the California Evidence Code, which provides that a child born to a married woman living with her husband, who is neither impotent nor sterile, is presumed to be a

---

[20] Interview by Thomas Hilbink with Archibald Cox, (June 19–20, 2010) (transcript available at Columbia University Oral History Research Office), http://www.columbia.edu/cu/lweb/digital/collections/oral_hist/cox/interview.html [https://perma.cc/6UJ3-SR66].

[21] *See* Reynolds v. Sims, 377 U.S. 533 (1964).

[22] 531 U.S. 98 (2000).

[23] *See, e.g.*, Nelson Lund, *From Baker v. Carr to Bush v. Gore, and Back*, 62 CASE W. RES. L. REV. 947 (2012); Robert J. Pushaw, Jr., *Bush v. Gore: Looking at Baker v. Carr in a Conservative Mirror*, 18 CONST. COMM. 359 (2001).

child of the marriage. That presumption may only be rebutted by the husband or wife, and then only in limited circumstances. There were no triable issues of fact as to Victoria's paternity. The California Superior Court granted Gerald's motion for summary judgment, concluding that the evidence presented sufficed to demonstrate that Gerald and Carole were cohabitating at conception and birth and that Gerald was neither sterile nor impotent. The Court also denied visitation rights to Michael because it would impugn the integrity of the family unit.

[On appeal, Michael claimed that the Superior Court's application of § 621 violated his procedural and substantive due process rights. Victoria claimed that her due process and equal protection rights were violated because only the father or mother, and not the child, could rebut the presumption. The California Court of Appeals affirmed the grant of summary judgment, upheld the statute, and denied visitation rights. The California Supreme Court denied discretionary review. The United States Supreme Court affirmed the judgment.]

We address first the claims of Michael. At the outset, it is necessary to clarify what he sought and what he was denied. California law, like nature itself, makes no provision for dual fatherhood. Michael was seeking to be declared the father of Victoria. The immediate benefit he evidently sought to obtain from that status was visitation rights. But if Michael were successful in being declared the father, other rights would follow—most importantly, the right to be considered as the parent who should have custody. All parental rights, including visitation, were automatically denied by denying Michael status as the father.

Michael contends as a matter of substantive due process that because he has established a parental relationship with Victoria, protection of Gerald's and Carole's marital union is an insufficient state interest to support termination of that relationship. This argument is, of course, predicated on the assertion that Michael has a constitutionally protected liberty interest in his relationship with Victoria.

It is an established part of our constitutional jurisprudence that the term "liberty" in the Due Process Clause extends beyond freedom from physical restraint. In an attempt to limit and guide interpretation of the Clause, we have insisted not merely that the interest denominated as a "liberty" be "fundamental" (a concept that, in isolation, is hard to objectify), but also that it be an interest traditionally protected by our society.

This insistence that the asserted liberty interest be rooted in history and tradition is evident, as elsewhere, in our cases according constitutional protection to certain parental rights. As we view them, they rest not upon such isolated factors but upon the historic respect—indeed, sanctity would not be too strong a term—traditionally accorded to the relationships that develop within the unitary family.[3] In *Stanley*, for example, we forbade the destruction of such a family when, upon the death of the mother, the state had sought to remove children from the custody of a father who had lived with and supported them and their mother for 18 years.

Thus, the legal issue in the present case reduces to whether the relationship between persons in the situation of Michael and Victoria has been treated as a protected family unit under the historic practices of our society, or whether on any other basis it has been accorded special protection. We think it impossible to find that it has. In fact, quite to the contrary, our traditions have protected the marital family (Gerald, Carole, and the child they acknowledge to be theirs) against the sort of claim Michael asserts.

We have found nothing in the older sources, nor in the older cases, addressing specifically the power of the natural father to assert parental rights over a child born into a woman's existing marriage with another man. What Michael asserts here is a right to have himself declared the natural father and thereby to obtain parental prerogatives. What he must establish, therefore, is not that our society has traditionally allowed a natural father in his circumstances to establish paternity, but that it has traditionally accorded such a father parental rights, or at least has not traditionally denied them. What counts is whether the States in fact award substantive parental rights to the natural father of a child conceived within and born into an extant marital union that wishes to embrace the child. We are not aware of a single case, old or new, that has done so. This is not the stuff of which fundamental rights qualifying as liberty interests are made.[6]

---

[3] Justice Brennan asserts that only "a pinched conception of 'the family' " would exclude Michael, Carole and Victoria from protection. We disagree. The family unit accorded traditional respect in our society, which we have referred to as the "unitary family," is typified, of course, by the marital family, but also includes the household of unmarried parents and their children. Perhaps the concept can be expanded even beyond this, but it will bear no resemblance to traditionally respected relationships—and will thus cease to have any constitutional significance—if it is stretched so far as to include the relationship established between a married woman, her lover and their child, during a three-month sojourn in St. Thomas, or during a subsequent 8-month period when, if he happened to be in Los Angeles, he stayed with her and the child.

[6] Justice Brennan criticizes our methodology in using historical traditions specifically relating to the rights of an adulterous natural father, rather than inquiring more generally "whether parenthood is an interest that historically has received our attention and protection."

We do not understand why, having rejected our focus upon the societal tradition regarding the natural father's rights *vis-a-vis* a child whose mother is married to another man, Justice Brennan would choose to focus instead upon "parenthood." Why should the relevant category not be even more general—perhaps "family relationships"; or "personal relationships"; or even "emotional attachments in general"? Though the dissent has no basis for the level of generality it would select, we do: We refer to the most specific level at which a relevant tradition protecting, or denying protection to, the asserted right can be identified. If, for example, there were no societal tradition, either way, regarding the rights of the natural father of a child adulterously conceived, we would have to consult, and (if possible) reason from, the traditions regarding natural fathers in general. But there is such a more specific tradition, and it unqualifiedly denies protection to such a parent.

■ JUSTICE O'CONNOR, with whom JUSTICE KENNEDY joins, concurring in part.

I concur in all but footnote 6 of Justice Scalia's opinion. This footnote sketches a mode of historical analysis to be used when identifying liberty interests protected by the Due Process Clause of the Fourteenth Amendment that may be somewhat inconsistent with our past decisions in this area. On occasion the Court has characterized relevant traditions protecting asserted rights at levels of generality that might not be "the most specific level" available. I would not foreclose the unanticipated by the prior imposition of a single mode of historical analysis.

■ JUSTICE BRENNAN, with whom JUSTICES MARSHALL and BLACKMUN join, dissenting.

In a case that has yielded so many opinions as has this one, it is fruitful to begin by emphasizing the common ground shared by a majority of this Court. Five Members of the Court refuse to foreclose "the possibility that a natural father might ever have a constitutionally protected interest in his relationship with a child whose mother was married to and cohabiting with another man at the time of the child's conception and birth." (Stevens, J., concurring in judgment). Five Justices agree that the flaw inhering in a conclusive presumption that terminates a constitutionally protected interest without any hearing whatsoever is a procedural one. (White, J., dissenting); (Stevens, J., concurring in judgment). Four Members of the Court agree that Michael H. has a liberty interest in his relationship with Victoria (White, J., dissenting), and one assumes for purposes of this case that he does (Stevens, J., concurring in judgment).

In contrast, only two Members of the Court fully endorse Justice Scalia's view of the proper method of analyzing questions arising under the Due Process Clause. (O'Connor, J., concurring in part). Nevertheless,

---

One would think that Justice Brennan would appreciate the value of consulting the most specific tradition available, since he acknowledges that "[e]ven if we can agree . . . that 'family' and 'parenthood' are part of the good life, it is absurd to assume that we can agree on the contents of those terms and destructive to pretend that we do." Because such general traditions provide such imprecise guidance, they permit judges to dictate rather than discern the society's views. The need, if arbitrary decision-making is to be avoided, to adopt the most specific tradition as the point of reference—or at least to announce, as Justice Brennan declines to do, some other criterion for selecting among the innumerable relevant traditions that could be consulted—is well enough exemplified by the fact that in the present case Justice Brennan's opinion and Justice O'Connor's opinion, which disapproves this footnote, both appeal to tradition, but on the basis of the tradition they select reach opposite results. Although assuredly having the virtue (if it be that) of leaving judges free to decide as they think best when the unanticipated occurs, a rule of law that binds neither by text nor by any particular, identifiable tradition, is no rule of law at all.

Finally, we may note that this analysis is not inconsistent with the result in cases such as *Griswold v. Connecticut*, or *Eisenstadt v. Baird*. None of those cases acknowledged a longstanding and still extant societal tradition withholding the very right pronounced to be the subject of a liberty interest and then rejected it. Justice Brennan must do so here. In this case, the existence of such a tradition, continuing to the present day, refutes any possible contention that the alleged right is "so rooted in the traditions and conscience of our people as to be ranked as fundamental," *Snyder v. Massachusetts*, or "implicit in the concept of ordered liberty," *Palko v. Connecticut*.

because the plurality opinion's exclusively historical analysis portends a significant and unfortunate departure from our prior cases and from sound constitutional decision-making, I devote a substantial portion of my discussion to it.

Once we recognized that the "liberty" protected by the Due Process Clause of the Fourteenth Amendment encompasses more than freedom from bodily restraint, today's plurality opinion emphasizes, the concept was cut loose from one natural limitation on its meaning. This innovation paved the way, so the plurality hints, for judges to substitute their own preferences for those of elected officials. Dissatisfied with this supposedly unbridled and uncertain state of affairs, the plurality casts about for another limitation on the concept of liberty.

It finds this limitation in "tradition." Apparently oblivious to the fact that this concept can be as malleable and as elusive as "liberty" itself, the plurality pretends that tradition places a discernible border around the Constitution. The pretense is seductive; it would be comforting to believe that a search for "tradition" involves nothing more idiosyncratic or complicated than poring through dusty volumes on American history. Because reasonable people can disagree about the content of particular traditions, and because they can disagree even about which traditions are relevant to the definition of "liberty," the plurality has not found the objective boundary that it seeks.

Even if we could agree, moreover, on the content and significance of particular traditions, we still would be forced to identify the point at which a tradition becomes firm enough to be relevant to our definition of liberty and the moment at which it becomes too obsolete to be relevant any longer. The plurality supplies no objective means by which we might make these determinations.

It is not that tradition has been irrelevant to our prior decisions. Throughout our decisionmaking in this important area runs the theme that certain interests and practices—freedom from physical restraint, marriage, childbearing, childrearing, and others—form the core of our definition of "liberty." Our solicitude for these interests is partly the result of the fact that the Due Process Clause would seem an empty promise if it did not protect them, and partly the result of the historical and traditional importance of these interests in our society. In deciding cases arising under the Due Process Clause, therefore, we have considered whether the concrete limitation under consideration impermissibly impinges upon one of these more generalized interests.

Today's plurality, however, does not ask whether parenthood is an interest that historically has received our attention and protection; the answer to that question is too clear for dispute. Instead, the plurality asks whether the specific variety of parenthood under consideration—a natural father's relationship with a child whose mother is married to another man—has enjoyed such protection.

If we had looked to tradition with such specificity in past cases, many a decision would have reached a different result. Surely the use of contraceptives by unmarried couples, or even by married couples; the freedom from corporal punishment in schools; the freedom from an arbitrary transfer from a prison to a psychiatric institution; and even the right to raise one's natural but illegitimate children, were not "interest[s] traditionally protected by our society," at the time of their consideration by this Court. If we had asked, therefore, in *Eisenstadt, Griswold, Ingraham, Vitek,* or *Stanley* itself whether the specific interest under consideration had been traditionally protected, the answer would have been a resounding "no." That we did not ask this question in those cases highlights the novelty of the interpretive method that the plurality opinion employs today.

The plurality's interpretive method is more than novel; it is misguided. It ignores the good reasons for limiting the role of "tradition" in interpreting the Constitution's deliberately capacious language. In the plurality's constitutional universe, we may not take notice of the fact that the original reasons for the conclusive presumption of paternity are out of place in a world in which blood tests can prove virtually beyond a shadow of a doubt who sired a particular child and in which the fact of illegitimacy no longer plays the burdensome and stigmatizing role it once did.

Moreover, by describing the decisive question as whether Michael and Victoria's interest is one that has been "traditionally protected by our society," rather than one that society traditionally has thought important (with or without protecting it), and by suggesting that our sole function is to "discern the society's views," the plurality acts as if the only purpose of the Due Process Clause is to confirm the importance of interests already protected by a majority of the States. Transforming the protection afforded by the Due Process Clause into a redundancy mocks those who, with care and purpose, wrote the Fourteenth Amendment.

In construing the Fourteenth Amendment to offer shelter only to those interests specifically protected by historical practice, moreover, the plurality ignores the kind of society in which our Constitution exists. We are not an assimilative, homogeneous society, but a facilitative, pluralistic one, in which we must be willing to abide someone else's unfamiliar or even repellant practice because the same tolerant impulse protects our own idiosyncracies. Even if we can agree, therefore, that "family" and "parenthood" are part of the good life, it is absurd to assume that we can agree on the content of those terms and destructive to pretend that we do. In a community such as ours, "liberty" must include the freedom not to conform. The plurality today squashes this freedom by requiring specific approval from history before protecting anything in the name of liberty.

The document that the plurality construes today is unfamiliar to me. It is not the living charter that I have taken to be our Constitution; it is instead a stagnant, archaic, hidebound document steeped in the prejudices and superstitions of a time long past. This Constitution does not recognize that times change, does not see that sometimes a practice or rule outlives its foundations. I cannot accept an interpretive method that does such violence to the charter that I am bound by oath to uphold.

NOTES AND QUESTIONS

1. **A Footnote in History.** Why did Justice O'Connor think that footnote 6 was sufficiently important to warrant a separate opinion? Was it really to avoid foreclosing "the unanticipated by the prior imposition of a single mode of historical analysis"? Is it possible that she actually disagreed with the "most narrow" mode of Justice Scalia's history?

2. **Nature v. Nurture.** Is the disagreement between Justice Scalia and Justice Brennan about the nature of the Constitution, or about the role of the courts and Justices in interpreting ambiguous or vague language? Could the dispute simply be a dispute over the content of unenumerated rights?

Graham v. Florida

560 U.S. 48 (2010)

■ JUSTICE KENNEDY delivered the opinion of the Court.

[Terrance Graham was a 16-year-old who was sentenced to life in prison for burglary. He challenged the sentence under the Eighth Amendment's Cruel and Unusual Punishments Clause.]

The Eighth Amendment states: "Excessive bail shall not be required, nor excessive fines imposed, nor cruel and unusual punishments inflicted." To determine whether a punishment is cruel and unusual, courts must look beyond historical conceptions to the evolving standards of decency that mark the progress of a maturing society. This is because the standard of extreme cruelty is not merely descriptive, but necessarily embodies a moral judgment. The standard itself remains the same, but its applicability must change as the basic mores of society change.

[In Eighth Amendment cases involving] categorical rules the Court has taken the following approach. The Court first considers objective indicia of society's standards, as expressed in legislative enactments and state practice to determine whether there is a national consensus against the sentencing practice at issue. Next, guided by the standards elaborated by controlling precedents and by the Court's own understanding and interpretation of the Eighth Amendment's text, history, meaning, and purpose, the Court must determine in the exercise of its own independent judgment whether the punishment in question violates the Constitution.

[The Court looked to "objective indicia of national consensus," including the number of jurisdictions that permitted life without parole for juveniles, and the number of jurisdictions that actually imposed these sentences. It also considered whether the sentences serve legitimate penological goals, international juvenile sentencing standards, cognitive science, and its own "reasoned judgment."]

A State is not required to guarantee eventual freedom to a juvenile offender convicted of a nonhomicide crime. What the State must do, however, is give defendants like Graham some meaningful opportunity to obtain release based on demonstrated maturity and rehabilitation. . . . Terrance Graham's sentence guarantees he will die in prison without any meaningful opportunity to obtain release, no matter what he might do to demonstrate that the bad acts he committed as a teenager are not representative of his true character, even if he spends the next half century attempting to atone for his crimes and learn from his mistakes. The State has denied him any chance to later demonstrate that he is fit to rejoin society based solely on a nonhomicide crime that he committed while he was a child in the eyes of the law. This the Eighth Amendment does not permit.

* * *

The Constitution prohibits the imposition of a life without parole sentence on a juvenile offender who did not commit homicide. A State need not guarantee the offender eventual release, but if it imposes a sentence of life it must provide him or her with some realistic opportunity to obtain release before the end of that term. The judgment of the First District Court of Appeal of Florida is reversed, and the case is remanded for further proceedings not inconsistent with this opinion.

It is so ordered.

■ JUSTICE STEVENS, with whom JUSTICE GINSBURG and JUSTICE SOTOMAYOR join, concurring.

In his dissenting opinion, Justice Thomas argues that today's holding is not entirely consistent with the controlling opinions in *Lockyer v. Andrade*, 538 U.S. 63 (2003), *Ewing v. California*, 538 U.S. 11 (2003), *Harmelin v. Michigan*, 501 U.S. 957 (1991), and *Rummel v. Estelle*, 445 U.S. 263. Given that "evolving standards of decency" have played a central role in our Eighth Amendment jurisprudence for at least a century, this argument suggests the dissenting opinions in those cases more accurately describe the law today than does Justice Thomas's rigid interpretation of the Amendment. Society changes. Knowledge accumulates. We learn, sometimes, from our mistakes. Punishments that did not seem cruel and unusual at one time may, in the light of reason and experience, be found cruel and unusual at a later time; unless we are to abandon the moral commitment embodied in the Eighth Amendment, proportionality review must never become effectively obsolete.

While Justice Thomas would apparently not rule out a death sentence for a $50 theft by a 7-year-old, the Court wisely rejects his static approach to the law. Standards of decency have evolved since 1980. They will never stop doing so.

■ JUSTICE THOMAS, with whom JUSTICE SCALIA joins, and with whom JUSTICE ALITO joins as to Parts I and III, dissenting.

The Court holds today that it is "grossly disproportionate" and hence unconstitutional for any judge or jury to impose a sentence of life without parole on an offender less than 18 years old, unless he has committed a homicide. Although the text of the Constitution is silent regarding the permissibility of this sentencing practice, and although it would not have offended the standards that prevailed at the founding, the Court insists that the standards of American society have evolved such that the Constitution now requires its prohibition.

The news of this evolution will, I think, come as a surprise to the American people. Congress, the District of Columbia, and 37 States allow judges and juries to consider this sentencing practice in juvenile nonhomicide cases, and those judges and juries have decided to use it in the very worst cases they have encountered.

The Court does not conclude that life without parole itself is a cruel and unusual punishment. It instead rejects the judgments of those legislatures, judges, and juries regarding what the Court describes as the "moral" question whether this sentence can ever be proportionate when applied to the category of offenders at issue here.

I am unwilling to assume that we, as members of this Court, are any more capable of making such moral judgments than our fellow citizens. Nothing in our training as judges qualifies us for that task, and nothing in Article III gives us that authority.

I respectfully dissent.

NOTES AND QUESTIONS

A $50 Theft by a 7-Year-Old. Justice Stevens writes a separate concurrence in large part to address Justice Thomas's dissent.

Justice Thomas begins his dissent with a reference to the "original understanding" of the Cruel and Unusual Punishments Clause. He notes that proportionality in sentencing was not considered a constitutional command, and that early statutes prescribed capital punishment for offenses ranging from " 'run[ning] away with . . . goods or merchandise to the value of fifty dollars,' " to "murder on the high seas." Thomas continued in a footnote,

> The Court ignores entirely the threshold inquiry of whether subjecting juvenile offenders to adult penalties was one of the "modes or acts of punishment that had been considered cruel and unusual at the time that the Bill of Rights was adopted." As the Court has noted in the past, however, the evidence is clear that, at the time of the Founding, "the common law set a rebuttable presumption of incapacity to commit any felony at the age of 14, and theoretically permitted [even] capital punishment to be imposed on a person as young as age 7." It thus seems exceedingly

unlikely that the imposition of a life-without-parole sentence on a person of Graham's age would run afoul of those standards.[24]

Would Justice Thomas really conclude that a modern statute that imposed the death penalty on a child of seven, or even fourteen, was constitutional? The Court considered the application of the death penalty to children under the age of 16 prior to Justice Thomas's appointment.[25] However, in 2005, the Court held that the execution of individuals who were under 18 years old at the time they committed a capital crime was prohibited by the Eighth and Fourteenth Amendments.[26] Thomas joined Justice Scalia's dissent in that case.[27] Justice Scalia's dissent, however, largely criticized the majority's use of "national consensus" and its "own judgment" to reach the result.[28]

§ 10.4 CONSTITUTIONAL INTERPRETATION AND UNENUMERATED RIGHTS

Interpretive theories are often discussed in stark and simplistic precepts. In reality, however, decisions rarely fall into clean categories. Justices struggle with how to manage a Constitution that is stable enough to survive the centuries, yet flexible enough to survive in the face of changing circumstances and norms. In at least one area of the law, however, intense disagreement over Constitutional interpretation may directly affect the outcome: the issue of whether it is appropriate for the Supreme Court to recognize a "right" that has not been enforced before.

Griswold v. Connecticut

381 U.S. 479 (1965)

■ JUSTICE DOUGLAS delivered the opinion of the Court.

Appellant Griswold is Executive Director of the Planned Parenthood League of Connecticut. Appellant Buxton is a licensed physician and a professor at the Yale Medical School who served as Medical Director for the League at its Center in New Haven—a center open and operating from November 1 to November 10, 1961, when appellants were arrested. They gave information, instruction, and medical advice to married persons as to the means of preventing conception. They examined the wife and prescribed the best contraceptive device or material for her use. Fees were usually charged, although some couples were serviced free.

---

[24] Graham v. Florida, 560 U.S. 48, 106 n.3 (2010).

[25] Thompson v. Oklahoma, 487 U.S. 815 (1988) (holding that the Eighth and Fourteenth Amendments prohibited execution of a defendant convicted of first-degree murder for offense committed when defendant was 15 years old).

[26] Roper v. Simmons, 543 U.S. 551 (2005).

[27] *Id.* at 607–08 (Scalia, J., dissenting).

[28] *Id.* at 607–29 (Scalia, J., dissenting).

The statutes whose constitutionality is involved in this appeal are §§ 53–32 and 54–196 of the General Statutes of Connecticut (1958 rev.). The former provides:

Any person who uses any drug, medicinal article or instrument for the purpose of preventing conception shall be fined not less than fifty dollars or imprisoned not less than sixty days nor more than one year or be both fined and imprisoned.

Section 54–196 provides:

> Any person who assists, abets, counsels, causes, hires or commands another to commit any offense may be prosecuted and punished as if he were the principal offender.

The appellants were found guilty as accessories and fined $100 each, against the claim that the accessory statute as so applied violated the Fourteenth Amendment. The Supreme Court of Errors affirmed that judgment.

[The Court initially held that the appellants had "standing to raise the constitutional rights of the married people with whom they had a professional relationship."]

Coming to the merits, we are met with a wide range of questions that implicate the Due Process Clause of the Fourteenth Amendment. Overtones of some arguments suggest that *Lochner v. New York* should be our guide. But we decline that invitation. We do not sit as a super-legislature to determine the wisdom, need, and propriety of laws that touch economic problems, business affairs, or social conditions. This law, however, operates directly on an intimate relation of husband and wife and their physician's role in one aspect of that relation.

The association of people is not mentioned in the Constitution nor in the Bill of Rights. The right to educate a child in a school of the parents' choice—whether public or private or parochial—is also not mentioned. Nor is the right to study any particular subject or any foreign language. Yet the First Amendment has been construed to include certain of those rights. By *Pierce v. Society of Sisters* [268 U.S. 510 (1925)], the right to educate one's children as one chooses is made applicable to the States by the force of the First and Fourteenth Amendments. By *Meyer v. Nebraska* [262 U.S. 390 (1923)], the same dignity is given the right to study the German language in a private school. In other words, the State may not, consistently with the spirit of the First Amendment, contract the spectrum of available knowledge. The right of freedom of speech and press includes not only the right to utter or to print, but the right to distribute, the right to receive, the right to read and freedom of inquiry, freedom of thought, and freedom to teach—indeed the freedom of the entire university community. Without those peripheral rights the specific rights would be less secure. And so we reaffirm the principle of the *Pierce* and the *Meyer* cases.

In other words, the First Amendment has a penumbra where privacy is protected from governmental intrusion. In like context, we have protected forms of "association" that are not political in the customary sense but pertain to the social, legal, and economic benefit of the members. The right of "association," like the right of belief, is more than the right to attend a meeting; it includes the right to express one's attitudes or philosophies by membership in a group or by affiliation with it or by other lawful means. Association in that context is a form of expression of opinion; and while it is not expressly included in the First Amendment its existence is necessary in making the express guarantees fully meaningful.

The foregoing cases suggest that specific guarantees in the Bill of Rights have penumbras, formed by emanations from those guarantees that help give them life and substance. Various guarantees create zones of privacy. The right of association contained in the penumbra of the First Amendment is one. The Third Amendment in its prohibition against the quartering of soldiers "in any house" in time of peace without the consent of the owner is another facet of that privacy. The Fourth Amendment explicitly affirms the "right of the people to be secure in their persons, houses, papers, and effects, against unreasonable searches and seizures." The Fifth Amendment in its Self-Incrimination Clause enables the citizen to create a zone of privacy which government may not force him to surrender to his detriment. The Ninth Amendment provides: "The enumeration in the Constitution, of certain rights, shall not be construed to deny or disparage others retained by the people." We have had many controversies over these penumbral rights of "privacy and repose." These cases bear witness that the right of privacy which presses for recognition here is a legitimate one.

The present case, then, concerns a relationship lying within the zone of privacy created by several fundamental constitutional guarantees. And it concerns a law which, in forbidding the use of contraceptives rather than regulating their manufacture or sale, seeks to achieve its goals by means having a maximum destructive impact upon that relationship. Such a law cannot stand in light of the familiar principle, so often applied by this Court, that a governmental purpose to control or prevent activities constitutionally subject to state regulation may not be achieved by means which sweep unnecessarily broadly and thereby invade the area of protected freedoms. Would we allow the police to search the sacred precincts of marital bedrooms for telltale signs of the use of contraceptives? The very idea is repulsive to the notions of privacy surrounding the marriage relationship.

We deal with a right of privacy older than the Bill of Rights—older than our political parties, older than our school system. Marriage is a coming together for better or for worse, hopefully enduring, and intimate to the degree of being sacred. It is an association that promotes a way of life, not causes; a harmony in living, not political faiths; a bilateral loyalty, not commercial or social projects. Yet it is an association for as noble a purpose as any involved in our prior decisions.

■ JUSTICE GOLDBERG, whom CHIEF JUSTICE WARREN and JUSTICE BRENNAN join, concurring.

I agree with the Court that Connecticut's birth-control law unconstitutionally intrudes upon the right of marital privacy, and I join in its opinion and judgment. Although I have not accepted the view that "due process" as used in the Fourteenth Amendment incorporates all of the first eight Amendments, I do agree that the concept of liberty protects those personal rights that are fundamental, and is not confined to the specific terms of the Bill of Rights. My conclusion that the concept of liberty is not so restricted and that it embraces the right of marital privacy though that right is not mentioned explicitly in the Constitution is supported both by numerous decisions of this Court, referred to in the Court's opinion, and by the language and history of the Ninth Amendment. In reaching the conclusion that the right of marital privacy is protected, as being within the protected penumbra of specific guarantees of the Bill of Rights, the Court refers to the Ninth Amendment. I add these words to emphasize the relevance of that Amendment to the Court's holding.

This Court, in a series of decisions, has held that the Fourteenth Amendment absorbs and applies to the States those specifics of the first eight amendments which express fundamental personal rights. The language and history of the Ninth Amendment reveal that the Framers of the Constitution believed that there are additional fundamental rights, protected from governmental infringement, which exist alongside those fundamental rights specifically mentioned in the first eight constitutional amendments.

The Ninth Amendment is almost entirely the work of James Madison. It was introduced in Congress by him and passed the House and Senate with little or no debate and virtually no change in language. It was proffered to quiet expressed fears that a bill of specifically enumerated rights could not be sufficiently broad to cover all essential rights and that the specific mention of certain rights would be interpreted as a denial that others were protected.

While this Court has had little occasion to interpret the Ninth Amendment, it cannot be presumed that any clause in the constitution is intended to be without effect." The Ninth Amendment to the Constitution may be regarded by some as a recent discovery and may be forgotten by others, but since 1791 it has been a basic part of the Constitution which we are sworn to uphold. To hold that a right so basic and fundamental and so deep-rooted in our society as the right of privacy in marriage may be infringed because that right is not guaranteed in so many words by the first eight amendments to the Constitution is to ignore the Ninth Amendment and to give it no effect whatsoever. Moreover, a judicial construction that this fundamental right is not protected by the

Constitution because it is not mentioned in explicit terms by one of the first eight amendments or elsewhere in the Constitution would violate the Ninth Amendment, which specifically states that "[t]he enumeration in the Constitution, of certain rights, shall not be construed to deny or disparage others retained by the people." (Emphasis added.)

A dissenting opinion suggests that my interpretation of the Ninth Amendment somehow "broaden[s] the powers of this Court." With all due respect, I believe that it misses the import of what I am saying. I do not take the position of my Brother Black in his dissent in *Adamson v. California* that the entire Bill of Rights is incorporated in the Fourteenth Amendment, and I do not mean to imply that the Ninth Amendment is applied against the States by the Fourteenth. Nor do I mean to state that the Ninth Amendment constitutes an independent source of rights protected from infringement by either the States or the Federal Government. Rather, the Ninth Amendment shows a belief of the Constitution's authors that fundamental rights exist that are not expressly enumerated in the first eight amendments and an intent that the list of rights included there not be deemed exhaustive. As any student of this Court's opinions knows, this Court has held, often unanimously, that the Fifth and Fourteenth Amendments protect certain fundamental personal liberties from abridgment by the Federal Government or the States. The Ninth Amendment simply shows the intent of the Constitution's authors that other fundamental personal rights should not be denied such protection or disparaged in any other way simply because they are not specifically listed in the first eight constitutional amendments. I do not see how this broadens the authority of the Court; rather it serves to support what this Court has been doing in protecting fundamental rights.

Nor am I turning somersaults with history in arguing that the Ninth Amendment is relevant in a case dealing with a State's infringement of a fundamental right. While the Ninth Amendment—and indeed the entire Bill of Rights—originally concerned restrictions upon federal power, the subsequently enacted Fourteenth Amendment prohibits the States as well from abridging fundamental personal liberties. And, the Ninth Amendment, in indicating that not all such liberties are specifically mentioned in the first eight amendments, is surely relevant in showing the existence of other fundamental personal rights, now protected from state, as well as federal, infringement. In sum, the Ninth Amendment simply lends strong support to the view that the "liberty" protected by the Fifth and Fourteenth Amendments from infringement by the Federal Government or the States is not restricted to rights specifically mentioned in the first eight amendments.

In determining which rights are fundamental, judges are not left at large to decide cases in light of their personal and private notions. Rather, they must look to the "traditions and [collective] conscience of our people" to determine whether a principle is "so rooted [there] as to be ranked as fundamental." "Liberty" also "gains content from the emanations of specific [constitutional] guarantees" and "from experience with the requirements of a free society."

I agree fully with the Court that, applying these tests, the right of privacy is a fundamental personal right, emanating "from the totality of the constitutional scheme under which we live." Mr. Justice Brandeis, dissenting in *Olmstead v. United States*, comprehensively summarized the principles underlying the Constitution's guarantees of privacy:

> The protection guaranteed by the [Fourth and Fifth] Amendments is much broader in scope. The makers of our Constitution undertook to secure conditions favorable to the pursuit of happiness. They recognized the significance of man's spiritual nature, of his feelings and of his intellect. They knew that only a part of the pain, pleasure and satisfactions of life are to be found in material things. They sought to protect Americans in their beliefs, their thoughts, their emotions and their sensations. They conferred, as against the Government, the right to be let alone—the most comprehensive of rights and the right most valued by civilized men.

The entire fabric of the Constitution and the purposes that clearly underlie its specific guarantees demonstrate that the rights to marital privacy and to marry and raise a family are of similar order and magnitude as the fundamental rights specifically protected.

The logic of the dissents would sanction federal or state legislation that seems to me even more plainly unconstitutional than the statute before us. Surely the Government, absent a showing of a compelling subordinating state interest, could not decree that all husbands and wives must be sterilized after two children have been born to them. Yet by their reasoning such an invasion of marital privacy would not be subject to constitutional challenge because, while it might be "silly," no provision of the Constitution specifically prevents the Government from curtailing the marital right to bear children and raise a family.

Finally, it should be said of the Court's holding today that it in no way interferes with a State's proper regulation of sexual promiscuity or misconduct.

■ JUSTICE HARLAN, concurring in the judgment.

I fully agree with the judgment of reversal, but find myself unable to join the Court's opinion. The reason is that it seems to me to evince an approach to this case very much like that taken by my Brothers Black and Stewart in dissent, namely: the Due Process Clause of the Fourteenth Amendment does not touch this Connecticut statute unless the enactment is found to violate some right assured by the letter or penumbra of the Bill of Rights.

In my view, the proper constitutional inquiry in this case is whether this Connecticut statute infringes the Due Process Clause of the

Fourteenth Amendment because the enactment violates basic values "implicit in the concept of ordered liberty," *Palko v. Connecticut*. For reasons stated at length in my dissenting opinion in Poe v. Ullman, I believe that it does. While the relevant inquiry may be aided by resort to one or more of the provisions of the Bill of Rights, it is not dependent on them or any of their radiations. The Due Process Clause of the Fourteenth Amendment stands, in my opinion, on its own bottom.

While I could not more heartily agree that judicial "self restraint" is an indispensable ingredient of sound constitutional adjudication, I do submit that the formula [Justice Black] suggested for achieving it is more hollow than real. "Specific" provisions of the Constitution, no less than "due process," lend themselves as readily to "personal" interpretations by judges whose constitutional outlook is simply to keep the Constitution in supposed "tune with the times." Judicial self-restraint will be achieved in this area, as in other constitutional areas, only by continual insistence upon respect for the teachings of history, solid recognition of the basic values that underlie our society, and wise appreciation of the great roles that the doctrines of federalism and separation of powers have played in establishing and preserving American freedoms.

■ JUSTICE WHITE, concurring in the judgment.

In my view this Connecticut law as applied to married couples deprives them of "liberty" without due process of law, as that concept is used in the Fourteenth Amendment. I therefore concur in the judgment of the Court reversing these convictions under Connecticut's aiding and abetting statute. Prior decisions affirm that there is a realm of family life which the state cannot enter without substantial justification.

The Connecticut anti-contraceptive statute deals rather substantially with this relationship. For it forbids all married persons the right to use birth-control devices, regardless of whether their use is dictated by considerations of family planning, health, or indeed even of life itself. The clear effect of these statutes, as enforced, is to deny disadvantaged citizens of Connecticut, those without either adequate knowledge or resources to obtain private counseling, access to medical assistance and up-to-date information in respect to proper methods of birth control. In my view, a statute with these effects bears a substantial burden of justification when attacked under the Fourteenth Amendment.

There is no serious contention that Connecticut thinks the use of artificial or external methods of contraception immoral or unwise in itself, or that the anti-use statute is founded upon any policy of promoting population expansion. Rather, the statute is said to serve the State's policy against all forms of promiscuous or illicit sexual relationships, be they premarital or extramarital, concededly a permissible and legitimate legislative goal.

Without taking issue with the premise that the fear of conception operates as a deterrent to such relationships in addition to the criminal proscriptions Connecticut has against such conduct, I wholly fail to see how the ban on the use of contraceptives by married couples in any way reinforces the State's ban on illicit sexual relationships. I find nothing in this record justifying the sweeping scope of this statute, with its telling effect on the freedoms of married persons, and therefore conclude that it deprives such persons of liberty without due process of law.

■ JUSTICE BLACK, with whom JUSTICE STEWART joins, dissenting.

The Court talks about a constitutional "right of privacy" as though there is some constitutional provision or provisions forbidding any law ever to be passed which might abridge the "privacy" of individuals. But there is not. There are, of course, guarantees in certain specific constitutional provisions which are designed in part to protect privacy at certain times and places with respect to certain activities. Such, for example, is the Fourth Amendment's guarantee against "unreasonable searches and seizures." But I think it belittles that Amendment to talk about it as though it protects nothing but "privacy." The average man would very likely not have his feelings soothed any more by having his property seized openly than by having it seized privately and by stealth. He simply wants his property left alone. And a person can be just as much, if not more, irritated, annoyed and injured by an unceremonious public arrest by a policeman as he is by a seizure in the privacy of his office or home.

One of the most effective ways of diluting or expanding a constitutionally guaranteed right is to substitute for the crucial word or words of a constitutional guarantee another word or words more or less flexible and more or less restricted in meaning. "Privacy" is a broad, abstract and ambiguous concept which can easily be shrunken in meaning but which can also, on the other hand, easily be interpreted as a constitutional ban against many things other than searches and seizures. I like my privacy as well as the next one, but I am nevertheless compelled to admit that government has a right to invade it unless prohibited by some specific constitutional provision. For these reasons I cannot agree with the Court's judgment and the reasons it gives for holding this Connecticut law unconstitutional.

Our Court certainly has no machinery with which to take a Gallup Poll. And the scientific miracles of this age have not yet produced a gadget which the Court can use to determine what traditions are rooted in the "[collective] conscience of our people." Moreover, one would certainly have to look far beyond the language of the Ninth Amendment to find that the Framers vested in this Court any such awesome veto powers over lawmaking, either by the States or by the Congress. Nor does anything in the history of the Amendment offer any support for such a shocking doctrine. That Amendment was passed, not to broaden the powers of this Court or any other department of "the General Government," but, as every student of history knows, to assure the people that the Constitution in all its provisions was intended to limit the

Federal Government to the powers granted expressly or by necessary implication. This fact is perhaps responsible for the peculiar phenomenon that for a period of a century and a half no serious suggestion was ever made that the Ninth Amendment, enacted to protect state powers against federal invasion, could be used as a weapon of federal power to prevent state legislatures from passing laws they consider appropriate to govern local affairs. Use of any such broad, unbounded judicial authority would make of this Court's members a day-to-day constitutional convention.

■ JUSTICE STEWART, whom JUSTICE BLACK joins, dissenting.

I think this is an uncommonly silly law. As a practical matter, the law is obviously unenforceable, except in the oblique context of the present case. As a philosophical matter, I believe the use of contraceptives in the relationship of marriage should be left to personal and private choice, based upon each individual's moral, ethical, and religious beliefs. As a matter of social policy, I think professional counsel about methods of birth control should be available to all, so that each individual's choice can be meaningfully made. But we are not asked in this case to say whether we think this law is unwise, or even asinine. We are asked to hold that it violates the United States Constitution. And that I cannot do.

What provision of the Constitution, then, does make this state law invalid? The Court says it is the right of privacy "created by several fundamental constitutional guarantees." With all deference, I can find no such general right of privacy in the Bill of Rights, in any other part of the Constitution, or in any case ever before decided by this Court.

NOTES AND QUESTIONS

1. **I Know My Rights.** How should one read the Ninth Amendment's assurance that there are unenumerated rights "retained by the people?" Where would we look for the source of these rights? If they are in the rights of British personhood prior to 1776 or 1791, then is Blackstone the basic source? If so, then at what level of generality would we view his assurance of "life, liberty, and property?" Because the British courts operated on the common law, with its sense of evolving rights, is Justice Goldberg on sound footing to rely on "liberty" generally rather than the specific aspects of liberty protected in 1791?

2. **Tradition, Tradition.** Justice Harlan's *Griswold* concurrence emphasizes the role of tradition as a check on excessive judicial "activism." That concurrence is built on his dissent in *Poe v. Ullman*, where he formulated his classic statement on fundamental rights:[29]

> Due process has not been reduced to any formula; its content cannot be determined by reference to any code. The best that can be said is that through the course of this Court's decisions it has

[29] 367 U.S. 497, 542–44 (1961) (Harlan, J., dissenting).

represented the balance which our Nation, built upon postulates of respect for the liberty of the individual, has struck between that liberty and the demands of organized society. The balance of which I speak is the balance struck by this country, having regard to what history teaches are the traditions from which it developed as well as the traditions from which it broke. That tradition is a living thing. A decision of this Court which radically departs from it could not long survive, while a decision which builds on what has survived is likely to be sound. No formula could serve as a substitute, in this area, for judgment and restraint. . . .

[I]nasmuch as this context is one not of words, but of history and purposes, the full scope of the liberty guaranteed by the Due Process Clause cannot be found in or limited by the precise terms of the specific guarantees elsewhere provided in the Constitution. This "liberty" is not a series of isolated points pricked out in terms of the taking of property; the freedom of speech, press, and religion; the right to keep and bear arms; the freedom from unreasonable searches and seizures; and so on. It is a rational continuum which, broadly speaking, includes a freedom from all substantial arbitrary impositions and purposeless restraints, and which also recognizes, what a reasonable and sensitive judgment must, that certain interests require particularly careful scrutiny of the state needs asserted to justify their abridgment.[30]

3. **Home Is Where the Right to Privacy Is.** Prior to *Griswold*, the Court had found privacy interests in both search and seizure and self-incrimination cases. Four years after *Griswold*, the Court struck down a Georgia law that made possession of obscene materials illegal, even in one's own home. The Court cited both the First Amendment and the right to privacy.[31] It emphasized that the home was a critical locus of privacy, and that thoughts and beliefs were essential parts of the "right to be let alone."

What relationship does the "privacy" protected in these cases bear to the right of privacy fashioned in *Griswold*? Is the right recognized in *Griswold* limited to marriage and familial privacy? Does it logically extend to all matters relating to sex? To the use of one's own body? To all matters relating to one's personality?

Justice White, concurring in *Griswold*, argued that "the State's policy against all forms of promiscuous or illicit sexual relationships" was "a permissible and legitimate legislative goal."[32] Is this statement reconcilable with the logic of *Griswold*? Justice White authored the opinion of the Court in the subsequent case of *Bowers v. Hardwick*,[33] which refused to recognize a right to engage in homosexual conduct.

---

[30] *Id.* at 542–43.

[31] Stanley v. Georgia, 394 U.S. 557 (1969).

[32] Griswold v. Connecticut, 381 U.S. 479, 505 (1965) (White, J., concurring).

[33] Bowers v. Hardwick, 478 U.S. 186 (1986), *overruled by* Lawrence v. Texas, 539 U.S. 558 (2003).

Justice Harlan similarly assumed the validity of laws proscribing adultery and other sexual conduct but emphasized that the contraceptive law raised the specter of the state's intrusion into the marital unit, even into the bedroom, thus triggering the right of privacy.

4. **What About Everyone Else?** If *Griswold* protected only the right of married couples to use contraceptives, then statutes limiting access to contraceptives by unmarried persons would appear to be constitutional. In *Eisenstadt v. Baird*,[34] however, the Court struck down a Massachusetts statute which, while allowing distribution of contraceptives to married persons by medical personnel, prohibited their distribution to unmarried persons. While the case was decided on equal protection grounds, the opinion indicated that the right of privacy recognized in *Griswold* had broader application:

> We need not and do not, however, decide [whether a statute that bans contraception on the grounds of immorality] because, whatever the rights of the individual to access to contraceptives may be, the rights must be the same for the unmarried and the married alike. If under *Griswold* the distribution of contraceptives to married persons cannot be prohibited, a ban on distribution to unmarried persons would be equally impermissible. It is true that in *Griswold* the right of privacy in question inhered in the marital relationship. Yet the marital couple is not an independent entity with a mind and heart of its own, but an association of two individuals each with a separate intellectual and emotional makeup. If the right of privacy means anything, it is the right of the individual, married or single, to be free from unwarranted governmental intrusion into matters so fundamentally affecting a person as the decision whether to bear or beget a child.[35]

Is this language from *Eisenstadt* a logical extension of *Griswold*? Does the right of privacy go beyond even marriage, family and sexual relationships to "intimate associations"?

5. **Anchoring the Justices.** After *Griswold* and its progeny, are Justices free to apply their own values to the American public? Justice Harlan addressed the problem and its possible solution:

> Judicial self-restraint will not, I suggest, be brought about in the 'due process' area by the historically unfounded incorporation formula long advanced by my Brother BLACK, and now in part espoused by my Brother STEWART. It will be achieved in this area, as in other constitutional areas, only by continual insistence upon respect for the teachings of history, solid recognition of the basic values that underlie our society, and wise appreciation of the great roles that the doctrines of federalism and separation of powers have played in establishing and preserving American freedoms. Adherence to these principles will not, of course, obviate all constitutional differences of opinion among judges, nor should it.

[34] 405 U.S. 438 (1972).

[35] *Id.* at 453.

> Their continued recognition will, however, go farther toward keeping most judges from roaming at large in the constitutional field than will the interpolation into the Constitution of an artificial and largely illusory restriction on the content of the Due Process Clause.[36]

Are those principles enough to prevent judges from imposing their own values on the Constitution? Do they lead inexorably to Justice Scalia's adherence to "tradition" in *Michael H. v. Gerald D.*?

6. It's All in the Framing. In *Bowers v. Hardwick*, Michael Hardwick was charged with violating Georgia's criminal anti-sodomy statute in the bedroom of his home. After the District Attorney tentatively decided not to bring the case to the grand jury, Hardwick sued in federal district court, challenging the constitutionality of the statute to the extent it criminalized consensual sodomy. The Court of Appeals, relying on cases such as *Griswold v. Connecticut*, held the statute unconstitutional. The Supreme Court, in an opinion by Justice White, reversed:

> [W]e think it evident that none of the rights announced in [*inter alia Griswold v. Connecticut, Carey v. Population Services International, Loving v. Virginia,* and *Roe v. Wade*] bears any resemblance to the claimed constitutional right of homosexuals to engage in acts of sodomy that is asserted in this case. No connection between family, marriage, or procreation on the one hand and homosexual activity on the other has been demonstrated, either by the Court of Appeals or by respondent. Moreover, any claim that these cases nevertheless stand for the proposition that any kind of private sexual conduct between consenting adults is constitutionally insulated from state proscription is unsupportable.[37]

Justice White sounded very much like critics of *Griswold* and its progeny when he noted that

> [t]he Court is most vulnerable and comes nearest to illegitimacy when it deals with judge-made constitutional law having little or no cognizable roots in the language or design of the Constitution. . . . There should be, therefore, great resistance to expand the substantive reach of [the Fifth and Fourteenth Amendments], particularly if it requires redefining the category of rights deemed to be fundamental. Otherwise, the Judiciary necessarily takes to itself further authority to govern the country without express constitutional authority. The claimed right pressed on us today falls far short of overcoming this resistance.[38]

Justice Blackmun, speaking for four Justices, dissented, arguing that the case was not about "a fundamental right to engage in homosexual sodomy," as the majority asserted. Rather, it was about a fundamental "right to be let alone." He added that "the Court's almost obsessive focus on

---

36 Griswold v. Connecticut, 381 U.S. 479, 501–02 (1965) (Harland, J., concurring).

37 Bowers, 478 U.S. at 190–91.

38 *Id.* at 194–95.

homosexual activity is particularly hard to justify in light of the broad language Georgia has used. . . . The sex or status of the persons who engage in the act is irrelevant as a matter of state law."[39]

Seventeen years later, *Bowers* was overruled by *Lawrence v. Texas.*

Lawrence v. Texas

539 U.S. 558 (2003)

■ JUSTICE KENNEDY delivered the opinion of the Court.

Liberty protects the person from unwarranted government intrusions into a dwelling or other private places. In our tradition the State is not omnipresent in the home. And there are other spheres of our lives and existence, outside the home, where the State should not be a dominant presence. Freedom extends beyond spatial bounds. Liberty presumes an autonomy of self that includes freedom of thought, belief, expression, and certain intimate conduct. The instant case involves liberty of the person both in its spatial and in its more transcendent dimensions.

I

The question before the Court is the validity of a Texas statute making it a crime for two persons of the same sex to engage in certain intimate sexual conduct.

[John Geddes Lawrence and Tyron Garner were observed by police officers engaging in homosexual sex in Lawrence's home. They were charged with engaging in "deviate sexual intercourse with another individual of the same sex."]

II

We conclude the case should be resolved by determining whether the petitioners were free as adults to engage in the private conduct in the exercise of their liberty under the Due Process Clause of the Fourteenth Amendment to the Constitution. For this inquiry we deem it necessary to reconsider the Court's holding in *Bowers*.

The Court began its substantive discussion in *Bowers* as follows: "The issue presented is whether the Federal Constitution confers a fundamental right upon homosexuals to engage in sodomy and hence invalidates the laws of the many States that still make such conduct illegal and have done so for a very long time." That statement, we now conclude, discloses the Court's own failure to appreciate the extent of the liberty at stake. To say that the issue in *Bowers* was simply the right to engage in certain sexual conduct demeans the claim the individual put forward, just as it would demean a married couple were it to be said marriage is simply about the right to have sexual intercourse. The laws involved in *Bowers* and here are, to be sure, statutes that purport to do

---

[39] *Id.* at 200 (Blackmun, J., dissenting).

no more than prohibit a particular sexual act. Their penalties and purposes, though, have more far-reaching consequences, touching upon the most private human conduct, sexual behavior, and in the most private of places, the home. The statutes do seek to control a personal relationship that, whether or not entitled to formal recognition in the law, is within the liberty of persons to choose without being punished as criminals.

This, as a general rule, should counsel against attempts by the State, or a court, to define the meaning of the relationship or to set its boundaries absent injury to a person or abuse of an institution the law protects. It suffices for us to acknowledge that adults may choose to enter upon this relationship in the confines of their homes and their own private lives and still retain their dignity as free persons. When sexuality finds overt expression in intimate conduct with another person, the conduct can be but one element in a personal bond that is more enduring. The liberty protected by the Constitution allows homosexual persons the right to make this choice.

Having misapprehended the claim of liberty there presented to it, and thus stating the claim to be whether there is a fundamental right to engage in consensual sodomy, the *Bowers* Court said proscriptions against that conduct have ancient roots. In academic writings, and in many of the scholarly amicus briefs filed to assist the Court in this case, there are fundamental criticisms of the historical premises relied upon by the majority and concurring opinions in *Bowers*. We need not enter this debate in the attempt to reach a definitive historical judgment, but the following considerations counsel against adopting the definitive conclusions upon which *Bowers* placed such reliance.

At the outset it should be noted that there is no longstanding history in this country of laws directed at homosexual conduct as a distinct matter. Beginning in colonial times there were prohibitions of sodomy derived from the English criminal laws passed in the first instance by the Reformation Parliament of 1533. The English prohibition was understood to include relations between men and women as well as relations between men and men. Nineteenth-century commentators similarly read American sodomy, buggery, and crime-against-nature statutes as criminalizing certain relations between men and women and between men and men. The absence of legal prohibitions focusing on homosexual conduct may be explained in part by noting that according to some scholars the concept of the homosexual as a distinct category of person did not emerge until the late 19th century. Thus early American sodomy laws were not directed at homosexuals as such but instead sought to prohibit nonprocreative sexual activity more generally. This does not suggest approval of homosexual conduct. It does tend to show that this particular form of conduct was not thought of as a separate category from like conduct between heterosexual persons.

It was not until the 1970's that any State singled out same-sex relations for criminal prosecution, and only nine States have done so. Post-*Bowers* even some of these States did not adhere to the policy of suppressing homosexual conduct. Over the course of the last decades, States with same-sex prohibitions have moved toward abolishing them.

In summary, the historical grounds relied upon in *Bowers* are more complex than the majority opinion and the concurring opinion by Chief Justice Burger indicate. Their historical premises are not without doubt and, at the very least, are overstated.

It must be acknowledged, of course, that the Court in *Bowers* was making the broader point that for centuries there have been powerful voices to condemn homosexual conduct as immoral. The condemnation has been shaped by religious beliefs, conceptions of right and acceptable behavior, and respect for the traditional family. For many persons these are not trivial concerns but profound and deep convictions accepted as ethical and moral principles to which they aspire and which thus determine the course of their lives. These considerations do not answer the question before us, however. The issue is whether the majority may use the power of the State to enforce these views on the whole society through operation of the criminal law. Our obligation is to define the liberty of all, not to mandate our own moral code.

In all events we think that our laws and traditions in the past half century are of most relevance here. These references show an emerging awareness that liberty gives substantial protection to adult persons in deciding how to conduct their private lives in matters pertaining to sex. History and tradition are the starting point but not in all cases the ending point of the substantive due process inquiry. This emerging recognition should have been apparent when *Bowers* was decided.

Bowers was not correct when it was decided, and it is not correct today. It ought not to remain binding precedent. *Bowers v. Hardwick* should be and now is overruled.

The present case does not involve minors. It does not involve persons who might be injured or coerced or who are situated in relationships where consent might not easily be refused. It does not involve public conduct or prostitution. It does not involve whether the government must give formal recognition to any relationship that homosexual persons seek to enter. The case does involve two adults who, with full and mutual consent from each other, engaged in sexual practices common to a homosexual lifestyle. The petitioners are entitled to respect for their private lives. The State cannot demean their existence or control their destiny by making their private sexual conduct a crime. Their right to liberty under the Due Process Clause gives them the full right to engage in their conduct without intervention of the government. It is a promise of the Constitution that there is a realm of personal liberty which the government may not enter. The Texas statute furthers no legitimate state interest which can justify its intrusion into the personal and private life of the individual.

Had those who drew and ratified the Due Process Clauses of the Fifth Amendment or the Fourteenth Amendment known the components of liberty in its manifold possibilities, they might have been more specific. They did not presume to have this insight. They knew times can blind us to certain truths and later generations can see that laws once thought necessary and proper in fact serve only to oppress. As the Constitution endures, persons in every generation can invoke its principles in their own search for greater freedom.

The judgment of the Court of Appeals for the Texas Fourteenth District is reversed, and the case is remanded for further proceedings not inconsistent with this opinion.

It is so ordered.

■ JUSTICE SCALIA, with whom THE CHIEF JUSTICE and JUSTICE THOMAS join, dissenting.

Liberty finds no refuge in a jurisprudence of doubt. That was the Court's sententious response, barely more than a decade ago, to those seeking to overrule *Roe v. Wade*. The Court's response today, to those who have engaged in a 17-year crusade to overrule *Bowers v. Hardwick* is very different. The need for stability and certainty presents no barrier.

Most of the rest of today's opinion has no relevance to its actual holding—that the Texas statute "furthers no legitimate state interest which can justify" its application to petitioners under rational-basis review. Though there is discussion of "fundamental propositions," and "fundamental decisions," nowhere does the Court's opinion declare that homosexual sodomy is a "fundamental right" under the Due Process Clause; nor does it subject the Texas law to the standard of review that would be appropriate (strict scrutiny) if homosexual sodomy were a "fundamental right." Thus, while overruling the outcome of *Bowers*, the Court leaves strangely untouched its central legal conclusion: "[R]espondent would have us announce . . . a fundamental right to engage in homosexual sodomy. This we are quite unwilling to do." Instead the Court simply describes petitioners' conduct as "an exercise of their liberty"—which it undoubtedly is—and proceeds to apply an unheard-of form of rational-basis review that will have far-reaching implications beyond this case.

Countless judicial decisions and legislative enactments have relied on the ancient proposition that a governing majority's belief that certain sexual behavior is "immoral and unacceptable" constitutes a rational basis for regulation. State laws against bigamy, same-sex marriage, adult incest, prostitution, masturbation, adultery, fornication, bestiality, and obscenity are likewise sustainable only in light of *Bowers'* validation of laws based on moral choices. Every single one of these laws is called into question by today's decision; the Court makes no effort to cabin the scope of its decision to exclude them from its holding. The impossibility of distinguishing homosexuality from other traditional "morals" offenses is precisely why *Bowers* rejected the rational-basis challenge. "The law," it said, "is constantly based on notions of morality, and if all laws representing essentially moral choices are to be invalidated under the Due Process Clause, the courts will be very busy indeed." What a massive disruption of the current social order, therefore, the overruling of *Bowers* entails.

To tell the truth, it does not surprise me, and should surprise no one, that the Court has chosen today to revise the standards of stare decisis set forth in *Casey*. It has thereby exposed *Casey's* extraordinary deference to precedent for the result-oriented expedient that it is.

The Court is quite right that history and tradition are the starting point but not in all cases the ending point of the substantive due process inquiry. An asserted fundamental liberty interest must not only be deeply rooted in this Nation's history and tradition, but it must also be implicit in the concept of ordered liberty, so that neither liberty nor justice would exist if it were sacrificed. Moreover, liberty interests unsupported by history and tradition, though not deserving of "heightened scrutiny," are still protected from state laws that are not rationally related to any legitimate state interest. As I proceed to discuss, it is this latter principle that the Court applies in the present case.

Proscriptions against that conduct have ancient roots. Sodomy was a criminal offense at common law and was forbidden by the laws of the original 13 States when they ratified the Bill of Rights. In 1868, when the Fourteenth Amendment was ratified, all but 5 of the 37 States in the Union had criminal sodomy laws. In fact, until 1961, all 50 States outlawed sodomy, and today, 24 States and the District of Columbia continue to provide criminal penalties for sodomy performed in private and between consenting adults. Against this background, to claim that a right to engage in such conduct is 'deeply rooted in this Nation's history and tradition' or 'implicit in the concept of ordered liberty' is, at best, facetious. It is (as *Bowers* recognized) entirely irrelevant whether the laws in our long national tradition criminalizing homosexual sodomy were "directed at homosexual conduct as a distinct matter." Whether homosexual sodomy was prohibited by a law targeted at same-sex sexual relations or by a more general law prohibiting both homosexual and heterosexual sodomy, the only relevant point is that it was criminalized—which suffices to establish that homosexual sodomy is not a right "deeply rooted in our Nation's history and tradition." The Court today agrees that homosexual sodomy was criminalized and thus does not dispute the facts on which *Bowers* actually relied.

The Texas statute undeniably seeks to further the belief of its citizens that certain forms of sexual behavior are "immoral and unacceptable,"—the same interest furthered by criminal laws against fornication, bigamy, adultery, adult incest, bestiality, and obscenity.

Bowers held that this was a legitimate state interest. The Court today reaches the opposite conclusion. The Texas statute, it says, "furthers no legitimate state interest which can justify its intrusion into the personal and private life of the individual." The Court embraces instead Justice STEVENS' declaration in his *Bowers* dissent, that " 'the fact that the governing majority in a State has traditionally viewed a particular practice as immoral is not a sufficient reason for upholding a law prohibiting the practice.' " This effectively decrees the end of all morals legislation. If, as the Court asserts, the promotion of majoritarian sexual morality is not even a legitimate state interest, none of the above-mentioned laws can survive rational-basis review.

Today's opinion is the product of a Court, which is the product of a law-profession culture, that has largely signed on to the so-called homosexual agenda, by which I mean the agenda promoted by some homosexual activists directed at eliminating the moral opprobrium that has traditionally attached to homosexual conduct. I noted in an earlier opinion the fact that the American Association of Law Schools (to which any reputable law school must seek to belong) excludes from membership any school that refuses to ban from its job-interview facilities a law firm (no matter how small) that does not wish to hire as a prospective partner a person who openly engages in homosexual conduct.

One of the most revealing statements in today's opinion is the Court's grim warning that the criminalization of homosexual conduct is "an invitation to subject homosexual persons to discrimination both in the public and in the private spheres." It is clear from this that the Court has taken sides in the culture war, departing from its role of assuring, as neutral observer, that the democratic rules of engagement are observed. Many Americans do not want persons who openly engage in homosexual conduct as partners in their business, as scoutmasters for their children, as teachers in their children's schools, or as boarders in their home. They view this as protecting themselves and their families from a lifestyle that they believe to be immoral and destructive. The Court views it as "discrimination" which it is the function of our judgments to deter. So imbued is the Court with the law profession's anti-anti-homosexual culture, that it is seemingly unaware that the attitudes of that culture are not obviously "mainstream"; that in most States what the Court calls "discrimination" against those who engage in homosexual acts is perfectly legal; that proposals to ban such "discrimination" under Title VII have repeatedly been rejected by Congress, see Employment Non-Discrimination Act of 1994; Civil Rights Amendments of 1975; that in some cases such "discrimination" is mandated by federal statute, see 10 U.S.C. § 654(b)(1) (mandating discharge from the Armed Forces of any service member who engages in or intends to engage in homosexual acts); and that in some cases such "discrimination" is a constitutional right, see Boy Scouts of America v. Dale, 530 U.S. 640 (2000).

Let me be clear that I have nothing against homosexuals, or any other group, promoting their agenda through normal democratic means. Social perceptions of sexual and other morality change over time, and every group has the right to persuade its fellow citizens that its view of such matters is the best. That homosexuals have achieved some success in that enterprise is attested to by the fact that Texas is one of the few remaining States that criminalize private, consensual homosexual acts. But persuading one's fellow citizens is one thing, and imposing one's views in absence of democratic majority will is something else. I would no more require a State to criminalize homosexual acts—or, for that matter, display any moral disapprobation of them—than I would forbid it to do so. What Texas has chosen to do is well within the range of traditional democratic action, and its hand should not be stayed through the invention of a brand-new "constitutional right" by a Court that is impatient of democratic change. It is indeed true that later generations can see that laws once thought necessary and proper in fact serve only to oppress; and when that happens, later generations can repeal those laws. But it is the premise of our system that those judgments are to be made by the people, and not imposed by a governing caste that knows best.

One of the benefits of leaving regulation of this matter to the people rather than to the courts is that the people, unlike judges, need not carry things to their logical conclusion. The people may feel that their disapprobation of homosexual conduct is strong enough to disallow homosexual marriage, but not strong enough to criminalize private homosexual acts—and may legislate accordingly. The Court today pretends that it possesses a similar freedom of action, so that we need not fear judicial imposition of homosexual marriage, as has recently occurred in Canada (in a decision that the Canadian Government has chosen not to appeal).

At the end of its opinion—after having laid waste the foundations of our rational-basis jurisprudence—the Court says that the present case "does not involve whether the government must give formal recognition to any relationship that homosexual persons seek to enter." Do not believe it. More illuminating than this bald, unreasoned disclaimer is the progression of thought displayed by an earlier passage in the Court's opinion, which notes the constitutional protections afforded to "personal decisions relating to marriage, procreation, contraception, family relationships, child rearing, and education," and then declares that "[p]ersons in a homosexual relationship may seek autonomy for these purposes, just as heterosexual persons do." Today's opinion dismantles the structure of constitutional law that has permitted a distinction to be made between heterosexual and homosexual unions, insofar as formal recognition in marriage is concerned. If moral disapprobation of homosexual conduct is "no legitimate state interest" for purposes of proscribing that conduct; and if, as the Court coos (casting aside all pretense of neutrality), "[w]hen sexuality finds overt expression in intimate conduct with another person, the conduct can be but one element in a personal bond that is more enduring"; what justification could there possibly be for denying the benefits of marriage to homosexual couples exercising "[t]he liberty protected by the Constitution,"? Surely not the encouragement of procreation, since the sterile and the elderly are allowed to marry. This case "does not involve" the issue of homosexual marriage only if one entertains the belief that principle and logic have nothing to do with the decisions of this Court. Many will hope that, as the Court comfortingly assures us, this is so.

■ JUSTICE THOMAS, dissenting.

I write separately to note that the law before the Court today "is . . . uncommonly silly." Griswold v. Connecticut, 381 U.S. 479, 527 (1965) (Stewart, J., dissenting). If I were a member of the Texas Legislature, I would vote to repeal it. Punishing someone for expressing his sexual preference through noncommercial consensual conduct with another adult does not appear to be a worthy way to expend valuable law enforcement resources.

Notwithstanding this, I recognize that as a Member of this Court I am not empowered to help petitioners and others similarly situated. My duty, rather, is to decide cases agreeably to the Constitution and laws of the United States. And, just like Justice Stewart, I can find neither in the Bill of Rights nor any other part of the Constitution a general right of privacy, or as the Court terms it today, the "liberty of the person both in its spatial and more transcendent dimensions."

Obergefell v. Hodges

135 S. Ct. 2584 (2015)

■ KENNEDY, J., delivered the opinion of the Court, in which GINSBURG, BREYER, SOTOMAYOR, and KAGAN, JJ., joined. ROBERTS, C. J., filed a dissenting opinion, in which SCALIA and THOMAS, JJ., joined. SCALIA, J., filed a dissenting opinion, in which THOMAS, J., joined. THOMAS, J., filed a dissenting opinion, in which SCALIA, J., joined. ALITO, J., filed a dissenting opinion, in which SCALIA and THOMAS, JJ., joined.

■ JUSTICE KENNEDY delivered the opinion of the Court.

The Constitution promises liberty to all within its reach, a liberty that includes certain specific rights that allow persons, within a lawful realm, to define and express their identity. The petitioners in these cases seek to find that liberty by marrying someone of the same sex and having their marriages deemed lawful on the same terms and conditions as marriages between persons of the opposite sex.

II

Before addressing the principles and precedents that govern these cases, it is appropriate to note the history of the subject now before the Court.

A

From their beginning to their most recent page, the annals of human history reveal the transcendent importance of marriage. The lifelong union of a man and a woman always has promised nobility and dignity to all persons, without regard to their station in life. Marriage is sacred to those who live by their religions and offers unique fulfillment to those who find meaning in the secular realm. Its dynamic allows two people to find a life that could not be found alone, for a marriage becomes greater than just the two persons. Rising from the most basic human needs, marriage is essential to our most profound hopes and aspirations.

The centrality of marriage to the human condition makes it unsurprising that the institution has existed for millennia and across civilizations. Since the dawn of history, marriage has transformed strangers into relatives, binding families and societies together. Confucius taught that marriage lies at the foundation of government. This wisdom was echoed centuries later and half a world away by Cicero, who wrote, "The first bond of society is marriage; next, children; and then the family." There are untold references to the beauty of marriage in religious and philosophical texts spanning time, cultures, and faiths, as well as in art and literature in all their forms. It is fair and necessary to say these references were based on the understanding that marriage is a union between two persons of the opposite sex.

That history is the beginning of these cases. The respondents say it should be the end as well. To them, it would demean a timeless institution if the concept and lawful status of marriage were extended to two persons of the same sex. Marriage, in their view, is by its nature a gender-differentiated union of man and woman. This view long has been held—and continues to be held—in good faith by reasonable and sincere people here and throughout the world.

The petitioners acknowledge this history but contend that these cases cannot end there. Were their intent to demean the revered idea and reality of marriage, the petitioners' claims would be of a different order. But that is neither their purpose nor their submission. To the contrary, it is the enduring importance of marriage that underlies the petitioners' contentions. This, they say, is their whole point. Far from seeking to devalue marriage, the petitioners seek it for themselves because of their respect—and need—for its privileges and responsibilities. And their immutable nature dictates that same-sex marriage is their only real path to this profound commitment.

Recounting the circumstances of three of these cases illustrates the urgency of the petitioners' cause from their perspective. Petitioner James Obergefell, a plaintiff in the Ohio case, met John Arthur over two decades ago. They fell in love and started a life together, establishing a lasting, committed relation. In 2011, however, Arthur was diagnosed with amyotrophic lateral sclerosis, or ALS. [They] traveled from Ohio to Maryland, where same-sex marriage was legal. Three months later,

Arthur died. Ohio law does not permit Obergefell to be listed as the surviving spouse on Arthur's death certificate. By statute, they must remain strangers even in death, a state-imposed separation Obergefell deems "hurtful for the rest of time." He brought suit to be shown as the surviving spouse on Arthur's death certificate.

April DeBoer and Jayne Rowse are co-plaintiffs in the case from Michigan. They celebrated a commitment ceremony to honor their permanent relation in 2007. They both work as nurses, DeBoer in a neonatal unit and Rowse in an emergency unit. In 2009, DeBoer and Rowse fostered and then adopted a baby boy. Later that same year, they welcomed another son into their family. The new baby, born prematurely and abandoned by his biological mother, required around-the-clock care. The next year, a baby girl with special needs joined their family. Michigan, however, permits only opposite-sex married couples or single individuals to adopt, so each child can have only one woman as his or her legal parent. If an emergency were to arise, schools and hospitals may treat the three children as if they had only one parent. And, were tragedy to befall either DeBoer or Rowse, the other would have no legal rights over the children she had not been permitted to adopt. This couple seeks relief from the continuing uncertainty their unmarried status creates in their lives.

Army Reserve Sergeant First Class Ijpe DeKoe and his partner Thomas Kostura, co-plaintiffs in the Tennessee case, fell in love. In 2011, DeKoe received orders to deploy to Afghanistan. Before leaving, he and Kostura married in New York. A week later, DeKoe began his deployment, which lasted for almost a year. When he returned, the two settled in Tennessee, where DeKoe works full-time for the Army Reserve. Their lawful marriage is stripped from them whenever they reside in Tennessee, returning and disappearing as they travel across state lines. DeKoe, who served this Nation to preserve the freedom the Constitution protects, must endure a substantial burden.

Under the Due Process Clause of the Fourteenth Amendment, no State shall "deprive any person of life, liberty, or property, without due process of law." The fundamental liberties protected by this Clause include most of the rights enumerated in the Bill of Rights. In addition these liberties extend to certain personal choices central to individual dignity and autonomy, including intimate choices that define personal identity and beliefs.

The nature of injustice is that we may not always see it in our own times. The generations that wrote and ratified the Bill of Rights and the Fourteenth Amendment did not presume to know the extent of freedom in all of its dimensions, and so they entrusted to future generations a charter protecting the right of all persons to enjoy liberty as we learn its meaning. When new insight reveals discord between the Constitution's central protections and a received legal stricture, a claim to liberty must be addressed.

The four principles and traditions to be discussed demonstrate that the reasons marriage is fundamental under the Constitution apply with equal force to same-sex couples.

A first premise of the Court's relevant precedents is that the right to personal choice regarding marriage is inherent in the concept of individual autonomy. This abiding connection between marriage and liberty is why *Loving* [*v. Virginia*] invalidated interracial marriage bans under the Due Process Clause.

The nature of marriage is that, through its enduring bond, two persons together can find other freedoms, such as expression, intimacy, and spirituality. This is true for all persons, whatever their sexual orientation. There is dignity in the bond between two men or two women who seek to marry and in their autonomy to make such profound choices.

A second principle in this Court's jurisprudence is that the right to marry is fundamental because it supports a two-person union unlike any other in its importance to the committed individuals. As this Court held in *Lawrence* [*v. Texas*], same-sex couples have the same right as opposite-sex couples to enjoy intimate association. *Lawrence* invalidated laws that made same-sex intimacy a criminal act. And it acknowledged that "[w]hen sexuality finds overt expression in intimate conduct with another person, the conduct can be but one element in a personal bond that is more enduring." But while *Lawrence* confirmed a dimension of freedom that allows individuals to engage in intimate association without criminal liability, it does not follow that freedom stops there. Outlaw to outcast may be a step forward, but it does not achieve the full promise of liberty.

A third basis for protecting the right to marry is that it safeguards children and families and thus draws meaning from related rights of childrearing, procreation, and education. Under the laws of the several States, some of marriage's protections for children and families are material. But marriage also confers more profound benefits. By giving recognition and legal structure to their parents' relationship, marriage allows children "to understand the integrity and closeness of their own family and its concord with other families in their community and in their daily lives." Marriage also affords the permanency and stability important to children's best interests.

Fourth and finally, this Court's cases and the Nation's traditions make clear that marriage is a keystone of our social order. Alexis de Tocqueville recognized this truth on his travels through the United States almost two centuries ago:

> There is certainly no country in the world where the tie of marriage is so much respected as in America. . . . [W]hen the American retires from the turmoil of public life to the bosom of his family, he finds in it the image of order and of peace . . . . [H]e afterwards carries [that image] with him into public

affairs. 1 DEMOCRACY IN AMERICA 309 (H. Reeve transl., rev. ed. 1990).

For that reason, just as a couple vows to support each other, so does society pledge to support the couple, offering symbolic recognition and material benefits to protect and nourish the union. Indeed, while the States are in general free to vary the benefits they confer on all married couples, they have throughout our history made marriage the basis for an expanding list of governmental rights, benefits, and responsibilities. These aspects of marital status include: taxation; inheritance and property rights; rules of intestate succession; spousal privilege in the law of evidence; hospital access; medical decisionmaking authority; adoption rights; the rights and benefits of survivors; birth and death certificates; professional ethics rules; campaign finance restrictions; workers' compensation benefits; health insurance; and child custody, support, and visitation rules. Valid marriage under state law is also a significant status for over a thousand provisions of federal law. The States have contributed to the fundamental character of the marriage right by placing that institution at the center of so many facets of the legal and social order.

There is no difference between same- and opposite-sex couples with respect to this principle. Yet by virtue of their exclusion from that institution, same-sex couples are denied the constellation of benefits that the States have linked to marriage. This harm results in more than just material burdens. Same-sex couples are consigned to an instability many opposite-sex couples would deem intolerable in their own lives.

There may be an initial inclination in these cases to proceed with caution—to await further legislation, litigation, and debate. The respondents warn there has been insufficient democratic discourse before deciding an issue so basic as the definition of marriage. In its ruling on the cases now before this Court, the majority opinion for the Court of Appeals made a cogent argument that it would be appropriate for the respondents' States to await further public discussion and political measures before licensing same-sex marriages.

Of course, the Constitution contemplates that democracy is the appropriate process for change, so long as that process does not abridge fundamental rights. The dynamic of our constitutional system is that individuals need not await legislative action before asserting a fundamental right. The Nation's courts are open to injured individuals who come to them to vindicate their own direct, personal stake in our basic charter. An individual can invoke a right to constitutional protection when he or she is harmed, even if the broader public disagrees and even if the legislature refuses to act. The idea of the Constitution "was to withdraw certain subjects from the vicissitudes of political controversy, to place them beyond the reach of majorities and officials and to establish them as legal principles to be applied by the courts." This is why "fundamental rights may not be submitted to a vote; they depend on the outcome of no elections." It is of no moment whether advocates of same-sex marriage now enjoy or lack momentum in the democratic process. The issue before the Court here is the legal question whether the Constitution protects the right of same-sex couples to marry.

No union is more profound than marriage, for it embodies the highest ideals of love, fidelity, devotion, sacrifice, and family. In forming a marital union, two people become something greater than once they were. As some of the petitioners in these cases demonstrate, marriage embodies a love that may endure even past death. It would misunderstand these men and women to say they disrespect the idea of marriage. Their plea is that they do respect it, respect it so deeply that they seek to find its fulfillment for themselves. Their hope is not to be condemned to live in loneliness, excluded from one of civilization's oldest institutions. They ask for equal dignity in the eyes of the law. The Constitution grants them that right.

■ CHIEF JUSTICE ROBERTS, with whom JUSTICE SCALIA and JUSTICE THOMAS join, dissenting.

Petitioners make strong arguments rooted in social policy and considerations of fairness. They contend that same-sex couples should be allowed to affirm their love and commitment through marriage, just like opposite-sex couples. That position has undeniable appeal; over the past six years, voters and legislators in eleven States and the District of Columbia have revised their laws to allow marriage between two people of the same sex.

But this Court is not a legislature. Whether same-sex marriage is a good idea should be of no concern to us. Under the Constitution, judges have power to say what the law is, not what it should be. The people who ratified the Constitution authorized courts to exercise "neither force nor will but merely judgment." THE FEDERALIST No. 78, p. 465 (C. Rossiter ed. 1961) (A. Hamilton) (capitalization altered).

Although the policy arguments for extending marriage to same-sex couples may be compelling, the legal arguments for requiring such an extension are not. The fundamental right to marry does not include a right to make a State change its definition of marriage. And a State's decision to maintain the meaning of marriage that has persisted in every culture throughout human history can hardly be called irrational. In short, our Constitution does not enact any one theory of marriage. The people of a State are free to expand marriage to include same-sex couples, or to retain the historic definition.

The legitimacy of this Court ultimately rests upon the respect accorded to its judgments. That respect flows from the perception—and reality—that we exercise humility and restraint in deciding cases according to the Constitution and law. The role of the Court envisioned by the majority today, however, is anything but humble or restrained. Over and over, the majority exalts the role of the judiciary in delivering social change. In the majority's telling, it is the courts, not the people, who are responsible for making "new dimensions of freedom . . . apparent to new generations," for providing "formal discourse" on social issues, and for ensuring "neutral discussions, without scornful or disparaging commentary."

If you are among the many Americans—of whatever sexual orientation—who favor expanding same-sex marriage, by all means celebrate today's decision. Celebrate the achievement of a desired goal. Celebrate the opportunity for a new expression of commitment to a partner. Celebrate the availability of new benefits. But do not celebrate the Constitution. It had nothing to do with it.

I respectfully dissent.

■ JUSTICE SCALIA, with whom JUSTICE THOMAS joins, dissenting.

I join THE CHIEF JUSTICE's opinion in full. I write separately to call attention to this Court's threat to American democracy.

The substance of today's decree is not of immense personal importance to me. The law can recognize as marriage whatever sexual attachments and living arrangements it wishes, and can accord them favorable civil consequences, from tax treatment to rights of inheritance. Those civil consequences—and the public approval that conferring the name of marriage evidences—can perhaps have adverse social effects, but no more adverse than the effects of many other controversial laws. So it is not of special importance to me what the law says about marriage. It is of overwhelming importance, however, who it is that rules me. Today's decree says that my Ruler, and the Ruler of 320 million Americans coast-to-coast, is a majority of the nine lawyers on the Supreme Court. The opinion in these cases is the furthest extension in fact—and the furthest extension one can even imagine—of the Court's claimed power to create "liberties" that the Constitution and its Amendments neglect to mention. This practice of constitutional revision by an unelected committee of nine, always accompanied (as it is today) by extravagant praise of liberty, robs the People of the most important liberty they asserted in the Declaration of Independence and won in the Revolution of 1776: the freedom to govern themselves.

Buried beneath the mummeries and straining-to-be-memorable passages of the opinion is a candid and startling assertion: No matter *what* it was the People ratified, the Fourteenth Amendment protects those rights that the Judiciary, in its "reasoned judgment," thinks the Fourteenth Amendment ought to protect. That is so because "[t]he generations that wrote and ratified the Bill of Rights and the Fourteenth Amendment did not presume to know the extent of freedom in all of its dimensions . . . ." One would think that sentence would continue: " . . . and therefore they provided for a means by which the People could amend the Constitution," or perhaps " . . . and therefore they left the creation of additional liberties, such as the freedom to marry someone of the same sex, to the People, through the never-ending process of legislation." But no. What logically follows, in the majority's judge-empowering estimation, is: "and so they entrusted to future generations a charter protecting the right of all persons to enjoy liberty as we learn its meaning." The "we," needless to say, is the nine of us. "History and tradition guide and discipline [our] inquiry but do not set its outer boundaries." Thus, rather than focusing on *the People's* understanding of "liberty"-at the time of ratification or even today-the majority focuses on four "principles and traditions" that, *in the majority's view*, prohibit States from defining marriage as an institution consisting of one man and one woman.

This is a naked judicial claim to legislative—indeed, *super*-legislative—power; a claim fundamentally at odds with our system of government. Except as limited by a constitutional prohibition agreed to by the People, the States are free to adopt whatever laws they like, even those that offend the esteemed Justices' "reasoned judgment." A system of government that makes the People subordinate to a committee of nine unelected lawyers does not deserve to be called a democracy.

Judges are selected precisely for their skill as lawyers; whether they reflect the policy views of a particular constituency is not (or should not be) relevant. Not surprisingly then, the Federal Judiciary is hardly a cross-section of America. Take, for example, this Court, which consists of only nine men and women, all of them successful lawyers who studied at Harvard or Yale Law School. Four of the nine are natives of New York City. Eight of them grew up in east- and west-coast States. Only one hails from the vast expanse in-between. Not a single Southwesterner or even, to tell the truth, a genuine Westerner (California does not count). Not a single evangelical Christian (a group that comprises about one quarter of Americans), or even a Protestant of any denomination. The strikingly unrepresentative character of the body voting on today's social upheaval would be irrelevant if they were functioning as *judges*, answering the legal question whether the American people had ever ratified a constitutional provision that was understood to proscribe the traditional definition of marriage. But of course the Justices in today's majority are not voting on that basis; *they say they are not*. And to allow the policy question of same-sex marriage to be considered and resolved by a select, patrician, highly unrepresentative panel of nine is to violate a principle even more fundamental than no taxation without representation: no social transformation without representation.

But what really astounds is the hubris reflected in today's judicial Putsch. The five Justices who compose today's majority are entirely comfortable concluding that every State violated the Constitution for all of the 135 years between the Fourteenth Amendment's ratification and Massachusetts' permitting of same-sex marriages in 2003. They have discovered in the *Fourteenth Amendment* a "fundamental right" overlooked by every person alive at the time of ratification, and almost everyone else in the time since. They see what lesser legal minds—minds like Thomas Cooley, John Marshall Harlan, Oliver Wendell Holmes, Jr., Learned Hand, Louis Brandeis, William Howard Taft, Benjamin Cardozo, Hugo Black, Felix Frankfurter, Robert Jackson, and Henry Friendly—could not. They are certain that the People ratified the Fourteenth Amendment to bestow on them the power to remove questions from the democratic process when that is called for by their "reasoned judgment." These Justices *know* that limiting marriage to one man and one woman is contrary to reason; they *know* that an institution as old as government itself, and accepted by every nation in history until 15 years ago, cannot possibly be supported by anything other than ignorance or bigotry. And they are willing to say that any citizen who does not agree with that, who adheres to what was, until 15 years ago, the unanimous judgment of all generations and all societies, stands against the Constitution.

The opinion is couched in a style that is as pretentious as its content is egotistic. It is one thing for separate concurring or dissenting opinions to contain extravagances, even silly extravagances, of thought and expression; it is something else for the official opinion of the Court to do so. Of course the opinion's showy profundities are often profoundly incoherent. "The nature of marriage is that, through its enduring bond, two persons together can find other freedoms, such as expression, intimacy, and spirituality." (Really? Who ever thought that intimacy and spirituality [whatever that means] were freedoms? And if intimacy is, one would think Freedom of Intimacy is abridged rather than expanded by marriage. Ask the nearest hippie. Expression, sure enough, *is* a freedom, but anyone in a long-lasting marriage will attest that that happy state constricts, rather than expands, what one can prudently say.) Rights, we are told, can "rise . . . from a better informed understanding of how constitutional imperatives define a liberty that remains urgent in our own era." (Huh? How can a better informed understanding of how constitutional imperatives [whatever that means] define [whatever that means] an urgent liberty [never mind], give birth to a right?) And we are told that, "[i]n any particular case," either the Equal Protection or Due Process Clause "may be thought to capture the essence of [a] right in a more accurate and comprehensive way," than the other, "even as the two Clauses may converge in the identification and definition of the right." (What say? What possible "essence" does substantive due process "capture" in an "accurate and comprehensive way"? It stands for nothing whatever, except those freedoms and entitlements that this Court *really* likes.) I could go on. The world does not expect logic and precision in poetry or inspirational pop-philosophy; it demands them in the law. The stuff contained in today's opinion has to diminish this Court's reputation for clear thinking and sober analysis.

Hubris is sometimes defined as o'erweening pride; and pride, we know, goeth before a fall. The Judiciary is the "least dangerous" of the federal branches because it has "neither Force nor Will, but merely judgment; and must ultimately depend upon the aid of the executive arm" and the States, "even for the efficacy of its judgments." With each decision of ours that takes from the People a question properly left to them—with each decision that is unabashedly based not on law, but on the "reasoned judgment" of a bare majority of this Court—we move one step closer to being reminded of our impotence.

NOTES AND QUESTIONS

The Least Dangerous Branch. Is Justice Scalia's scathing dissent in *Obergefell* justified? What is the point of having judicial review if the Court is required to follow the desires of majority will? Isn't the goal of constitutional safeguards, as described originally by Hamilton, to enforce those safeguards against what first John Adams and then Alexis deToqueville called the tyranny of the majority?

Justice Scalia laments a decision that "takes from the People a question properly left to them"—but how are we to know which decisions are "properly left to the People" and which are for the judiciary? Are the Justices arguing about the role of the Court, or about what unenumerated rights should be recognized over time?

§ 10.5 THE ROLE OF FOREIGN AND INTERNATIONAL LAW IN CONSTITUTIONAL INTERPRETATION

Prior to Justice Scalia's death, he was locked in a debate with other members of the Court over the validity of citing foreign or treaty law in Supreme Court opinions.

The dispute appeared sporadically in a variety of cases. For example, in *Lawrence v. Texas,*[40] Justice Kennedy asserted that *Bowers* was wrong both in its description of national historical practice but also its depiction of foreign law and standards. The debate appeared more prominently and repeatedly in a series of death penalty cases[41] culminating in a holding that application of the death penalty to offenders under the age of 18 would be cruel and unusual punishment.[42] In all of these cases, the Court had noted the practices of other countries. In the concluding case, Justice Kennedy made reliance on international law more explicit:

> Our determination that the death penalty is disproportionate punishment for offenders under 18 finds confirmation in the

[40] 539 U.S. 558 (2003).

[41] *See* Atkins v. Virginia, 536 U.S. 304 (2002) (invalidating the death penalty for mentally retarded defendants); Thompson v. Oklahoma, 487 U.S. 815 (1988) (eliminating the death penalty for juvenile offenders under the age of 16 at the time of the offense); Enmund v. Florida, 458 U.S. 782 (1982) (holding that application of the death penalty to a defendant who was convicted of first-degree murder only as an "aider and abettor" was unconstitutional); Coker v. Georgia, 433 U.S. 584 (1977) (holding that the death penalty was cruel and unusual in cases of rape when the victim survived).

[42] Roper v. Simmons, 543 U.S. 551 (2005).

stark reality that the United States is the only country in the world that continues to give official sanction to the juvenile death penalty. This reality does not become controlling, for the task of interpreting the Eighth Amendment remains our responsibility. Yet at least from the time of the Court's decision in [Trop v. Dulles, 356 U.S. 86 (1958)], the Court has referred to the laws of other countries and to international authorities as instructive for its interpretation of the Eighth Amendment's prohibition of "cruel and unusual punishments."

As respondent and a number of *amici* emphasize, Article 37 of the United Nations Convention on the Rights of the Child, which every country in the world has ratified save for the United States and Somalia, contains an express prohibition on capital punishment for crimes committed by juveniles under 18. No ratifying country has entered a reservation to the provision prohibiting the execution of juvenile offenders. Parallel prohibitions are contained in other significant international covenants.

Respondent and his *amici* have submitted, and petitioner does not contest, that only seven countries other than the United States have executed juvenile offenders since 1990: Iran, Pakistan, Saudi Arabia, Yemen, Nigeria, the Democratic Republic of Congo, and China. Since then each of these countries has either abolished capital punishment for juveniles or made public disavowal of the practice. In sum, it is fair to say that the United States now stands alone in a world that has turned its face against the juvenile death penalty.

Though the international covenants prohibiting the juvenile death penalty are of more recent date, it is instructive to note that the United Kingdom abolished the juvenile death penalty before these covenants came into being. The United Kingdom's experience bears particular relevance here in light of the historic ties between our countries and in light of the Eighth Amendment's own origins. The Amendment was modeled on a parallel provision in the English Declaration of Rights of 1689, which provided: "[E]xcessive Bail ought not to be required nor excessive Fines imposed; nor cruel and unusual Punishments inflicted."

It is proper that we acknowledge the overwhelming weight of international opinion against the juvenile death penalty, resting in large part on the understanding that the instability and emotional imbalance of young people may often be a factor in the crime. The opinion of the world community, while not

> controlling our outcome, does provide respected and significant confirmation for our own conclusions.[43]

Justice O'Connor, although she disagreed with the Court's ultimate holding, saw nothing wrong in referring to international law:

> [T]he evidence of an international consensus does not alter my determination that the Eighth Amendment does not, at this time, forbid capital punishment of 17-year-old murderers in all cases.
>
> Nevertheless, I disagree with Justice SCALIA's contention that foreign and international law have no place in our Eighth Amendment jurisprudence. Over the course of nearly half a century, the Court has consistently referred to foreign and international law as relevant to its assessment of evolving standards of decency. This inquiry reflects the special character of the Eighth Amendment, which, as the Court has long held, draws its meaning directly from the maturing values of civilized society. Obviously, American law is distinctive in many respects, not least where the specific provisions of our Constitution and the history of its exposition so dictate. But this Nation's evolving understanding of human dignity certainly is neither wholly isolated from, nor inherently at odds with, the values prevailing in other countries. On the contrary, we should not be surprised to find congruence between domestic and international values, especially where the international community has reached clear agreement—expressed in international law or in the domestic laws of individual countries—that a particular form of punishment is inconsistent with fundamental human rights. At least, the existence of an international consensus of this nature can serve to confirm the reasonableness of a consonant and genuine American consensus. The instant case presents no such domestic consensus, however, and the recent emergence of an otherwise global consensus does not alter that basic fact.[44]

Justice Scalia vehemently dissented:

> Though the views of our own citizens are essentially irrelevant to the Court's decision today, the views of other countries and the so-called international community take center stage.
>
> Unless the Court has added to its arsenal the power to join and ratify treaties on behalf of the United States, I cannot see how this evidence favors, rather than refutes, its position. That the Senate and the President—those actors our Constitution empowers to enter into treaties—have declined to join and ratify treaties prohibiting execution of under-18 offenders can only

---

[43] *Id.* at 575–78.

[44] *Id.* at 604–05 (O'Connor, J., dissenting).

> suggest that our country has either not reached a national consensus on the question, or has reached a consensus contrary to what the Court announces.[45]

In the years after *Roper*, Justices Scalia and Breyer appeared together on several occasions to discuss constitutional interpretation. As those debates unfolded, it became apparent that what was really at stake was not the use of foreign or international law but the role of the Justices and the validity of an unelected judiciary making important decisions.[46]

> SCALIA: But if you're looking for the evolving standards of decency of American society, why would you look to France? The only way in which it makes sense is if you have a third approach to the interpretation of the Constitution, and that is I am not looking for the evolving standards of decency of American society; I'm looking for what is the best answer in my mind as an intelligent judge. And for that purpose I look to other intelligent people, and I talk sometimes about conversations with judges and lawyers and law students. Do you think you're representative of American society? Do you not realize you are a small cream at the top, and that your views on innumerable things are not the views of America at large? And doesn't it seem somewhat arrogant for you to say, I can make up what the moral values of America should be on all sorts of issues, such as penology, the death penalty, abortion, whatever? . . . I suggest that change is based not upon the theory that you're looking for what the moral perceptions of America is, but that you're looking for moral perceptions of the justices. And I frankly don't want to undertake that responsibility. I don't want to do it with foreign law, and I don't want to do it without foreign law. I sleep very well at night, because I read old English cases. (Laughter.) And there's my answer.
>
> JUSTICE BREYER: I think that's pretty good. I think that's really what's worrying people. And of course I think that underneath that my own views, it's really because I think, and I think many judges think, that your own moral views are not the answer; that people look other places for trying to find out in those few cases where [moral views are] determinative how to find answers that aren't [my own but other respected opinions].

For those who believe that constitutional principles were established in 1787 and 1791, there is no room for importing standards from any

---

[45] *Id.* at 622–23 (Scalia, J., dissenting).

[46] Associate United States Supreme Court Justice Antonin Scalia & Associate United States Supreme Court Justice Stephen Breyer, American University Washington College of Law, U.S. Association of Constitutional Law Discussion on Constitutional Relevance of Foreign Court Decisions (Jan. 13, 2005), http://domino.american.edu/AU/media/mediarel.nsf/1D265343BDC2189785256B810071F238/1F2F7DC4757FD01E85256F890068E6E0?OpenDocument [https://perma.cc/P2VZ-N63Q].

source whatever. Others believe that changing norms are necessarily implicated in interpretation of words and phrases such as "due process," "cruel and unusual," "unreasonable," "liberty," "association," and "equal protection." This group, sometimes described as adhering to a "living constitution," any source may be helpful in discerning what the current norms for individual rights should be. An international consensus on an issue could be persuasive.

The United States has been, in some respects, intellectually and geographically isolated over the centuries. That isolation has made it possible to argue that America has a unique set of values that should not be influenced by the importation of values from other nations. That isolation is, however, rapidly dissipating with globalization in the 21st century. Judges are likely to accelerate their reference to, and reliance on, international law. The only questions remaining are the degree to which some of those other values will be explicitly incorporated and the speed at which these developments will occur.

§ 10.6 TIERED INTERPRETATION AND JUDICIAL PHILOSOPHY

Under equal protection and due process analysis, most legislative acts are considered constitutional if they pass the rational basis test. Under that test, "statutory classifications are valid if they bear a rational relation to a legitimate governmental purpose. Statutes are subjected to a higher level of scrutiny if they interfere with the exercise of a fundamental right, such as freedom of speech, or employ a suspect classification, such as race."[47] Racial classifications receive strict scrutiny. They are "constitutional only if they are narrowly tailored measures that further compelling governmental interests."[48] Classifications based on gender receive heightened scrutiny. They are constitutional "only if they serve important governmental objectives and the discriminatory means employed are substantially related to the achievement of those objectives."[49]

The Justices have differed on the legitimacy of these categories. Justice Marshall argued that the Court should abandon this "rigid three-tiered approach" to constitutional analysis. He argued that there should be a single "spectrum," or quasi-sliding scale, of judicial review based "on the constitutional and societal importance of the interest adversely affected and the recognized invidiousness of the basis upon which the particular classification is drawn."[50]

---

47 Regan v. Taxation With Representation of Washington, 461 U.S. 540, 547 (1983).

48 Kimel v. Florida Bd. of Regents, 528 U.S. 62, 84 (2000) (quotations and citations omitted).

49 *Id.* (quotations and citations omitted).

50 San Antonio Ind. Sch. Dist. v. Rodriguez, 411 U.S. 1, 99 (1973) (Marshall, J., dissenting).

At the other end of judicial philosophy, the mantle of strict constructivism has passed to Justice Thomas, who took Marshall's seat on the Court and turned it 180 degrees. Justice Thomas has challenged an entire structure of constitutional review that requires greater justification for state encroachment on some rights than on others. Most recently, he described the famous footnote four of *Carolene Products*[51] as the source of unprincipled distinctions among different types of rights: those enumerated in the Constitution or affecting "discrete and insular minorities," and all other rights. In Justice Thomas' view,

> Eighty years on, the Court has come full circle. The Court has simultaneously transformed judicially created rights like the right to abortion into preferred constitutional rights, while disfavoring many of the rights actually enumerated in the Constitution. But our Constitution renounces the notion that some constitutional rights are more equal than others. A plaintiff either possesses the constitutional right he is asserting, or not—and if not, the judiciary has no business creating ad hoc exceptions so that others can assert rights that seem especially important to vindicate. A law either infringes a constitutional right, or not; there is no room for the judiciary to invent tolerable degrees of encroachment. Unless the Court abides by one set of rules to adjudicate constitutional rights, it will continue reducing constitutional law to policy-driven value judgments until the last shreds of its legitimacy disappear.
>
> * * *
>
> Today's decision [in *Whole Woman's Health v. Hellerstedt*] will prompt some to claim victory, just as it will stiffen opponents' will to object. But the entire Nation has lost something essential. The majority's embrace of a jurisprudence of rights-specific exceptions and balancing tests is "a regrettable concession of defeat—an acknowledgement that we have passed the point where 'law,' properly speaking, has any further application.[52]

This statement perhaps exemplifies the fundamental dispute over the role of the judiciary. Should courts view law as a set of rules to which they must adhere, or should courts view law as consisting of principles to be applied in pursuit of justice? This debate is endemic to the judicial function.

---

[51] United States v. Carolene Products Co., 304 U.S. 144, 152–153 n.4 (1938).

[52] Whole Woman's Health v. Hellerstedt, 136 S. Ct. 2292, 2329–30 (2016) (Thomas, J., dissenting) (quoting Scalia, *The Rule of Law as a Law of Rules*, 56 U. CHI. L. REV. 1175, 1182 (1989)); *see also* Evan Bernick, *Justice Thomas' Abortion Dissent And The Decline Of The Rule of Law*, HUFFINGTON POST (July 10, 2016 10:53 AM), http://www.huffingtonpost.com/evan-bernick/justice-thomas-abortion-d_b_10915136.html [https://perma.cc/EE43-U479].

CHAPTER 11

CIVIL LAW AND OTHER SYSTEMS

> It is more proper that law should govern than any one of the citizens: upon the same principle, if it is advantageous to place the supreme power in some particular persons, they should be appointed to be only guardians, and the servants of the laws.
>
> – Aristotle[1]

Common wisdom has it that there are two types of legal systems in the world: common law (uncodified and adversarial) and civil law (code based and inquisitorial).[2] Some understanding of the civil law systems will be critical as both business and criminal sanctions become increasingly international in scope.

As the Anglo-American system moves away from adversarial trials to more judge-ordered models, the civil law and Continental systems are moving toward more adversarial models. As we become more like them and they become more like us, the judicial processes of Anglo-Europe may meet somewhere in the middle.

There is a third set of courts with great influence on both of these systems: permanent international courts. For example, the International Court of Justice (ICJ) is the primary and permanent judicial branch of the United Nations. The ICJ hears disputes between nations but only when the nations have consented to the tribunal's authority. Compliance with the Court's judgments is also voluntary, even when the losing party consented to the jurisdiction. Only the Security Council or military action can force a losing country to obey the ICJ's rulings.

Similarly, the European Convention on Human Rights (ECHR) created the European Court of Human Rights (ECtHR). Until 1998, only the European Commission on Human Rights could submit a case to the court. Today, however, individuals may file a petition directly with the Court alleging that a member state has violated the Convention. The ECHR allows individuals to challenge a range of state-sponsored

---

1 ARISTOTLE, POLITICS Bk III, Chapter 16 (c. 335 B.C.E.).

2 For an overview and comparison of the two systems, see SCOTT N. CARLSON, INT'L NETWORK TO PROMOTE THE RULE OF LAW, INTRODUCTION TO CIVIL LAW LEGAL SYSTEMS (2009), http://www2.fjc.gov/sites/default/files/2015/Introduction%20to%20Civil%20Law%20Legal%20 Systems.pdf [https://perma.cc/6TTE-38FD]. *See also*, *The Common Law and civil Law Traditions*, THE ROBINS COLLECTION, UNIV. OF CAL. AT BERKELEY COLLEGE OF LAW https://www.law.berkeley.edu/library/robbins/CommonLawCivilLawTraditions.html [https://perma.cc/5EUX-RMUE].

activities, including torture, unlawful detention, and collective expulsion of aliens. Its rulings are binding on member states.[3]

Since the creation of the ECHR, there have been a number of tribunals created by the United Nations and the European Union. The International Criminal Court is the only permanent body of its type, but a number of ad hoc courts have been created to deal with war crimes and related offenses from Yugoslavia, Rwanda, and Sierra Leone. At the EU level, the European Court of Justice deals with disputes among member nations. In addition, "hybrid" courts operate within the domestic systems of Cambodia and Lebanon with international lawyers and judges participating.

All of these courts, and many domestic courts in various nations, have an official known as the Registrar. For example, in the ECHR, the "task of the Registry is to provide legal and administrative support to the Court in the exercise of its judicial functions."[4] In addition to administrative functions, the staff lawyers in these offices function in similar fashion to the law clerks of American courts.

Chapter 7 noted the role of informal dispute resolution systems such as village and tribal courts. These are still prevalent in many parts of the world. Some informal systems claim roots in religious tenets but are sadly lacking in fundamentals of human rights, while others are well-regarded cultural institutions.

Finally, non-governmental organizations (NGOs) play a role in dispute resolution. In some instances, an NGO may be an arbitral entity created by inter-governmental treaty. These possess a quasi-governmental capacity, and include organizations such as the World Trade Organization and the General Agreement on Tariffs and Trade tribunal. Others, such as sports federations like the IOC and FIFA, have only limited government involvement; while a nation may name members, the organization operates essentially as a mere commercial enterprise.

§ 11.1 COMPARING THE CIVIL AND COMMON LAW SYSTEMS

The common law system arose from the multiplicity of baronial "courts" in medieval England, in which the lord of the feoff would dispense "justice" according to his own needs. Over time, and with the advent of the ecclesiastical courts in the domain of the Roman and Anglican churches, the norms harmonized. By the 12th Century, the

---

[3] EUROPEAN COURT OF HUMAN RIGHTS, COUNCIL OF EUR., QUESTIONS & ANSWERS 4, http://www.echr.coe.int/Documents/Questions_Answers_ENG.pdf [https://perma.cc/N2R5-ZWAB] (last visited Oct. 4, 2016).

[4] EUROPEAN COURT OF HUMAN RIGHTS, COUNCIL OF EUR., ECHR REGISTRY 1, http://www.echr.coe.int/Documents/Registry_ENG.pdf [https://perma.cc/5VLP-HS9J] (last visited Oct. 4, 2016).

King's courts were applying "rules" that were thought to have arisen naturally from the community.

By contrast, the European continent developed legal systems from the Code of Justinian, a collection of laws developed during the sixth century under the Byzantine emperor Justinian I. These were similarly amplified by Church doctrines and learned commentators. The tradition of a code of laws was formalized in 1648. The Treaty of Westphalia, which ended the brutal Thirty Years' War that had engulfed much of Europe, ensured each of the principalities its own sovereignty. By that time, the judicial systems in each area had already become well entrenched, each with its own unique set of procedures, but all stemming from the code tradition.

"Common law is generally uncodified. . . . Civil law, in contrast, is codified."[5] Just as the cornerstone of common law is *stare decisis*, the cornerstone of civil law is the code. A judge must follow the legislation and cannot be bound by the rulings of other judges—after all, that would mean that the prior judge had made law. At the same time, civil law judges often refer to "commentators" or learned "jurists" to guide them on the meaning of the code.

But who are the commentators and from what sources would they draw their commentary? European law professors read the opinions of judges and listen to their oral conclusions. They then write about the meaning of the code, using the opinions of other learned judges and observers. Their work is then read by the next judge with a similar case. In reality, the two systems are similar in their use of precedent.[6] The complexities of 20th century life, and commerce in particular, "led to what is sometimes referred to as the 'decodification' of Civil Law" or the trend in civil law systems toward using precedent as common law systems do.[7] This only makes sense given all the reasons for the rule of *stare decisis*—efficiency and predictability being among the most important. The role of *stare decisis*, however, is not the only difference between the civil and common law systems. There are several structural differences as well.

The common law system is also known as an adversarial system. The adversarial model pits two opponents in a contest before a neutral arbiter, the judge. In that model, the judge is thought to be rather passive, merely ruling on the issues and facts presented by the parties. Most civil law countries, however, use an inquisitorial model. The inquisitorial model puts the judge in the active role of controlling the

---

5 INTRODUCTION TO CIVIL LAW LEGAL SYSTEMS, *supra* note 2.

6 *See* Mitchel de S.-O.-l'E. Lasser, *Comparative Law and Comparative Literature: A Project in Progress*, 1997 UTAH L. REV. 471 (1997). Professor Lasser also notes that decisions of the European Court of Human Rights criticizing the French system have further pushed the civil-law system closer to the techniques of the common law system. Mitchel de S.-O.-l'E. Lasser, *The European Pasteurization of French Law*, 90 CORNELL L. REV. 995 (2005).

7 CARLSON, *supra* note 1, at 4.

entire proceedings. Indeed, in some versions, the judge is the only person in the room allowed to ask questions of a witness.

The roles of counsel in inquisitorial systems vary widely. To understand the structural differences, it is easiest to begin with the roles of prosecutors and defense counsel in criminal cases.

The early medieval British law did not distinguish between civil and criminal proceedings. Every case was brought to the king's courts as an allegation that the defendant had done something that threatened "the king's peace," and there was no official known as a prosecutor. Although the prosecutor in today's adversarial system is said to be a servant of justice and given wide discretion to dismiss cases when appropriate, the general nature of the adversarial system remains dependent on "zealous" representation of the client. In the case of the prosecutor, the "client" is the state or the people with the mandate of putting criminals in jail.

In the inquisitorial system, conversely, the prosecutor is a member of the judicial system and works with the investigative judge to put together a case. When the evidence has been assembled, the case is presented to a trial judge, but there may never be a single event similar to a common law trial. The trying of a case is sometimes described as a series of meetings among the judge and counsel. The judge may or may not take fresh testimony; he or she may instead rule on the basis of the file presented by the prosecutor and assembled under the direction of the investigating magistrate.

Civil law counsel or litigants may play a role in formulating questions for the judges to pose, but a direct active role for litigants, such as cross-examination of witnesses, is unusual. "The limited role of Civil Law litigants is not only a function of judicial authority, but also it reflects the Civil Law system's bias against witness-based evidence. Civil Law systems commonly consider witness testimony one of the lowest standards of proof."[8]

Many observers have noted ways in which the two systems are drawing closer together. The "vanishing trial" in the American system parallels an increasing role for advocates in the civil law systems. Section 11.02 highlights international courts that have consciously taken aspects from both systems.

Parliamentary systems often rely on ministries that carry out executive functions within the confines of the parliamentary structure. Those ministries may also include elements of the judiciary and even exercise oversight of judicial performance.

For example, the Netherlands Ministry of Security and Justice consists of many segments, including the Judiciary, Public Prosecution Service, Police, National Coordinator for Counterterrorism and Security, Child Care and Protection Agency, Prison System, and Fire Brigade. It

---

[8] *Id.* at 11.

might seem that this single ministry combines many functions that would be separated in most parts of the Anglo-American world, but in most parliamentary systems, there is no bright-line division among the three branches of government. The Council for the Judiciary is part of the judicial system and carries out operational tasks such as allocation of budgets, financial management, and personnel policy.

Typically, the prosecutor in a civil-law system is a member of the judiciary. In some countries, the prosecutor is answerable directly to a magistrate while, in others, the Prosecutor's Office is an independent part of the judicial branch. In the magisterial model, the role of the police is to "detect crime," at which point they hand the matter over to the prosecution. There may be an investigating magistrate who directs the prosecution in its gathering of evidence. The magistrate may order a suspect or witness to be brought in for questioning, may issue search warrants or direct wiretaps. In many cases, if the police or prosecution questions a person without permission of the magistrate any evidence obtained is inadmissible in later proceedings.

In models based on a more independent prosecutor, the police work with the prosecutor's office in much the same way that police and prosecutors work in the Anglo-American system.

§ 11.2 MOVING TOWARD MORE UNIFIED MODELS

Chapter 7 discussed the various ways in which the Anglo-American system is moving away from trials and taking on aspects of judicially-controlled proceedings. This trend is evident in the Anglo-American methods of dispute resolution, judge-directed case management, and problem-solving courts.

Meanwhile the civil law systems are becoming more open and adversarial, with less secret judicial decision-making and more reliance on counsel. The pressure of the European international courts in this direction has been inexorable, including direct pressure from the European Court of Human Rights and more subtle pressure from the European Court of Justice.

The following are examples of ECtHR holdings with regard to some features of the French system, one criminal case and one civil. These cases illustrate both the operation of the French inquisitorial system, which is typical of systems in Europe, and also some emerging international limitations on national approaches.

A. ECTHR AND FAIR TRIAL

Case of Reinhardt and Slimane-Kaïd v. France

(1998–11 Eur. Ct. H.R. 640)

AS TO THE FACTS

I. CIRCUMSTANCES OF THE CASE

[Slimane-Kaïd and Reinhardt formed three companies (Provex, Servec, and Urka) which took "cab chassis" from Iveco for resale to coachbuilders. Iveco allegedly delivered many vehicles for which it was never paid.]

4. The description of the facts set out in this and the next paragraph is based on the documents from the domestic proceedings produced to the Court.

At Iveco's request, a bailiff inspected Servec's premises and drew up an official report on 11 May 1984. A court-appointed expert carried out an inspection on 25 July 1984 and an interim attachment was made on 28 August 1984. It was found on the first of those three dates that 155 vehicles were missing, on the second that 198 were missing and on the third that 211 were missing. Iveco obtained restitution of only 43 vehicles; the others had been registered and sold [521 missing vehicles].

5. On 27 July 1984 an Iveco representative reported certain of these matters to the Versailles Regional Criminal Investigation Department ("RCID"). Inquiries were made by Detective Inspector Renaud. In a report of 24 September 1984 he said that the test certificates and certificates of sale of 116 Iveco vehicles that had been filed by Provex for registration purposes with the prefecture were forgeries; he went on to say that offences may have been committed under the companies acts and insolvency legislation in connection with Servec /Provex and to conclude that a judicial investigation was necessary.

The judicial investigation

1. The first judicial investigation

Preferment of charges against Mr Slimane-Kaïd of misappropriation and procuring the issue of administrative documents by means of false information, certificates or statements

6. On 25 September 1984 the Chartres public prosecutor made a written application for an investigation to be opened into offences by an unnamed person of misappropriation and procuring the issue of administrative documents by means of false information, certificates or statements. Mr Candau, the investigating judge, who was assigned to the case that day, sent instructions on 27 September 1984 to the head of the Versailles RCID to "... continue the investigation with a view to identifying the persons who committed the offences, their co-principals and accomplices ...".

7. On 2 October 1984 Mr Slimane-Kaïd was taken into police custody and questioned. On 4 October 1984 the Versailles RCID's report was received, Mr Slimane-Kaïd was charged with misappropriation and procuring the issue of administrative documents by means of false information, certificates or statements, and remanded in custody (until 8 January 1985, when the investigating judge ordered his release under judicial supervision). On the same day the investigating judge sent instructions to the Versailles RCID to pursue the investigation.

[Other charges of forgery and bank fraud came about later.]

13. Between 9 October 1984 and 27 March 1985 the Versailles RCID carried out a number of searches and seizures at Mr Slimane-Kaïd's home address and on the premises of Provex; but they also carried out searches and seizures on 16 October 1984 at Mrs Reinhardt's home (the registered office of Urka)—while she was in custody—and on 18 October 1984 in a house rented by Urka. On 14 November 1984 Mrs Reinhardt was questioned by a police investigator.

14. On 2 November 1984 the investigating judge had made an order transmitting the file to the public prosecutor for submissions (*ordonnance de soit-communiqué*).

19. Mrs Reinhardt was arrested on 6 February 1985; the next day, following an application by the Chartres public prosecutor for a further investigation to be opened, she was charged with aiding and abetting the misappropriation of company assets and of handling misappropriated company assets.

The remainder of the investigation

20. On 7 February 1985 the investigating judge sent instructions to the Versailles RCID to pursue the investigation into the offences with which Mr Slimane-Kaïd, Mr G. and Mrs Reinhardt had been charged.

21. On 25 March 1985 Mr Slimane-Kaïd's lawyer sent a letter to the investigating judge enclosing documents for the file.

22. On 31 May 1985 the Versailles RCID sent in its report pursuant to the investigating judge's instructions of 7 February 1985.

23. Mr Slimane-Kaïd and Mr G. were questioned on 4 and 5 December 1985 respectively and Mrs Reinhardt—who had been summoned to appear before the investigating judge on 4 December 1985, but had not done so—on 11 February 1986.

24. On 25 March 1986 the investigating judge made an order transmitting the file to the public prosecutor for submissions.

25. On 16 July 1986 Mr Slimane-Kaïd wrote to the investigating judge enclosing documents for the file.

[Numerous orders from the investigating judge were carried out by the prosecution and police. Meanwhile, the defendants were also submitting documents to the judge.]

Judgment and appeals

1. Proceedings in the Chartres Criminal Court

54. The Chartres Criminal Court held a hearing on 11 June 1990.

On 25 June 1990 Mr Slimane-Kaïd's lawyer wrote to the president of that court enclosing documents for the file, as did Iveco's lawyer on 8 August 1990. Mr Slimane-Kaïd's lawyer forwarded further documents on 25 August.

On 22 and 25 October 1990 respectively Iveco and Mr Slimane-Kaïd's lawyers wrote to the president of that court enclosing documents for the file.

55. Judgment was delivered on 14 November 1990. Mr Slimane-Kaïd was found guilty of misappropriation, forging private, commercial or banking documents, fraud, false accounting and misappropriation of company assets and sentenced to five years' imprisonment, three of which were suspended; he was barred from carrying on any business activity for ten years. Mr G. was given a sentence of eighteen months' imprisonment for forging private, commercial or banking documents and aiding and abetting the forgery of commercial documents and Mrs Reinhardt a one-year suspended sentence for aiding and abetting the misappropriation of company assets. The court declared the civil party claims of Iveco and VPL inadmissible.

2. Proceedings in the Versailles Court of Appeal

56. Mr Slimane-Kaïd appealed to the Versailles Court of Appeal on 14 November 1990, as did the public prosecutor's office, Mrs Reinhardt, Mr G. and Iveco on 15, 16, 20 and 26 November 1990 respectively.

60. On 2 April 1992 the Versailles Court of Appeal acquitted Mr Slimane-Kaïd on the count of misappropriation of company assets, upheld the guilty verdict on the other counts and confirmed the sentence. It increased Mrs Reinhardt's sentence to a term of eighteen months' imprisonment, suspended, and reduced Mr G.'s sentence to one year. It upheld the judgment of the trial court in all other respects.

3. Proceedings in the Court of Cassation

61. Mrs Reinhardt and Mr G. lodged appeals on points of law with the Court of Cassation that same day. Mr Slimane-Kaïd and Iveco did likewise on 3 and 6 April. Mr G. also appealed.

The case file was sent to the Court of Cassation on 29 April 1992 and assigned to a reporting judge on 2 June 1992.

Iveco lodged written pleadings on 31 August 1992, followed by Mr G. and Mrs Reinhardt on 1 September 1992. On 12 October 1992 Iveco lodged one, and Mr Slimane-Kaïd two, written pleadings.

The reporting judge filed his report on 20 November 1992 and the advocate-general was appointed on 30 November.

Mr Slimane-Kaïd filed written pleadings on 18 February and 9 March 1993. VPL and Mr Mariani filed pleadings on 11 March 1993.

62. According to the Government, it is unlikely that the advocate-general prepared his submissions in writing as he intended to present them orally at the hearing.

The Government further maintained that at the hearing of the Court of Cassation on 15 March 1993, which took place without the applicant's representatives being present, the reporting judge addressed the court and oral submissions were made by the advocate-general.

63. In a decision delivered on 15 March 1993, the Court of Cassation, relying on the reporting judge's report, the parties' pleadings and the submissions of the advocate-general, dismissed the appeals of those who had been convicted.

II. RELEVANT DOMESTIC LAW AND PRACTICE

Organisation of the Court of Cassation

64. The Court of Cassation is composed of the president, the divisional presidents, the judges, the auxiliary judges, Principal State Counsel, the Principal Advocate-General, the advocates-general, the senior registrar and the divisional registrars (Article L. 121–1 of the Judicature Code).

It is divided into five civil divisions and one criminal division, each comprising a divisional president, judges, auxiliary judges, one or more advocates-general and a divisional registrar (Articles L. 121–3, R. 121–3 and R. 121–4). The divisions are subdivided into sections, in which formation most appeals are heard.

Appeals to the Court of Cassation

65. Judgments of an Indictment Division and judgments delivered by an assize court, a criminal court or a police court sitting as a court of last instance may, if they are not in accordance with the law, be set aside on an appeal on points of law by either the public prosecutor's office attached to the court which delivered the judgment or the party adversely affected (Article 567 of the Code of Criminal Procedure).

In criminal cases, Principal State Counsel at the Court of Cassation may appeal to that court only for the purposes of clarifying the law (*pourvoi dans l'intérêt de la loi*). In such cases, he appeals either on formal instructions from the Minister of Justice (Article 620) or of his own motion against a judgment delivered by an assize court, a criminal court or a police court sitting as a court of last instance where none of the parties has entered an appeal within the set time-limit (Article 621); in the event of an appeal by Principal State Counsel of his own motion, if the appeal is allowed the judgment is reversed but the parties may not rely on the Court of Cassation's ruling to contest execution of the judgment that has been set aside (ibid.).

The reporting judge's report

66. As soon as the case file is received by the registry of the Criminal Division of the Court of Cassation, the president of that division appoints a reporting judge (Article 587 of the Code of Criminal Procedure) from among the judges and the auxiliary judges; the latter have a vote at deliberations on appeals in which they are appointed as reporting judge (Article L. 131–7 of the Judicature Code).

67. The reporting judge draws up a written report in which he carries out a thorough review of the case, sets out the legal arguments deduced from the grounds of appeal, indicates what research he has carried out into legal opinion and case-law on the basis of the grounds of appeal and states his recommendations. He also prepares a draft judgment, which is distributed to each of his colleagues as a basis for discussion at deliberations.

The case file lodged by the reporting judge is sent by the registry, with the report and draft judgment, to the advocate-general assigned to the case by Principal State Counsel. Counsel for the parties are informed of the recommendation in the report (appeal to be declared inadmissible, or to be dismissed, allowed in part or in full) by an entry in the list of cases that is distributed a week before the hearing to lawyers practising in the *Conseil d'Etat* and Court of Cassation.

In principle, any additional pleading filed at this stage will be declared inadmissible. However, the Court of Cassation has a discretion and it appears that examples of its declaring inadmissible pleadings filed late are rare (see Y. Monnet, Principal Advocate-General at the Court of Cassation, "*Pourvoi en cassation*", *Juris-classeur procédure pénale*, 1993, *fascicule* 40).

The role of Principal State Counsel's Office at the Court of Cassation

68. Principal State Counsel's Office at the Court of Cassation does not act as a prosecuting authority before that court. Except in appeals made for the purposes of clarifying the law, it acts only as a party joined to the criminal proceedings. Its role is not to argue the prosecution's case but to ensure that the law is correctly applied.

69. [Principal State Counsel assigns the advocate-general to a case.]

"The value of the work [of the advocate-general], which is performed after the reporting judge has completed his task, is as a 'second opinion'. Either the advocate-general agrees with the report, in which eventuality the decision to be taken will be clearer, or he disagrees, and will have triggered the necessary debate. In all cases his role is somewhat 'maieutic'."

70. The advocate-general's submissions do not have to be in writing.

The hearing

72. A few days before the hearing a preparatory "meeting" is held between the president and the senior judge of the division and the

advocate-general on duty for that week; they systematically review the cases on the list and exchange views. In parallel, the reporting judge's report is studied in detail by the offices of the president and the senior judge, which give a reasoned opinion in writing. Their opinion, together with the submissions of the advocate-general, are communicated to the reporting judge a few days before the hearing.

73. The procedure before the Court of Cassation is in written form; the parties' lawyers are not required to appear at hearings. In the Criminal Division there is an oral hearing only in the (rare) cases where the parties' lawyers have expressly requested one.

At the hearing the reporting judge is the first to address the court. He reads out his report but does not disclose his recommendations. If there are to be oral submissions, counsel for the appellant addresses the court first followed by counsel for the respondent; they may not submit any new legal argument. The advocate-general is the last to address the court; he makes submissions that are confined to legal issues and may concern the consideration of a ground of appeal raised by the court of its own motion. It would appear that where oral submissions are made it is customary to allow the parties to reply to the advocate-general's submissions, either orally or by a note addressed to the court in deliberations.

Deliberations and adoption of the judgment

74. After the public hearing, the members of the court deliberate in private. The reporting judge gives his opinion; the other judges and the president then express their views. Following a vote on whether the recommendations of the report should be adopted, the draft judgment, which each judge will have received eight days beforehand, is then considered. The advocate-general generally attends the deliberations.

75. The judgment in its adopted form is then finalised and delivered at a public hearing, in most cases immediately after the deliberations.

AS TO THE LAW

I. SCOPE OF THE CASE

II. ALLEGED VIOLATIONs OF ARTICLE 6 OF THE CONVENTION

83. The applicants stated that they had not been tried "within a reasonable time" and considered that the proceedings in the Court of Cassation had been unfair. They relied on Article 6 §§ 1 and 3 (b) of the Convention, which reads:

> 1. In the determination of . . . any criminal charge against him, everyone is entitled to a fair . . . hearing within a reasonable time by [a] . . . tribunal. . . .
>
> 3. Everyone charged with a criminal offence has the following minimum rights:

(b) to have adequate time and facilities for the preparation of his defence;

[The Court decided that delays in the proceedings were unreasonable as a result of unexplained gaps in the investigating judge's decisions.]

Whether the proceedings in the Court of Cassation were fair

95. The applicants maintained that they had not had a fair hearing in the Court of Cassation. Neither they nor their counsel had received the reporting judge's report before the hearing, whereas the advocate-general had.

Nor had they had an opportunity to reply to the advocate-general's submissions. Yet, as society's representative before the Court of Cassation he had been the applicants' opponent so that, under the adversarial principle, the applicants should have been able to reply.

99. It was common ground that well before the hearing the advocate-general had received the report and draft judgment that had been prepared by the reporting judge. As the Government said, the report was in two parts: the first contained a description of the facts, procedure and grounds of appeal and the second a legal analysis of the case and an opinion on the merits of the appeal.

Those documents were not communicated to either the applicants or their lawyers. Currently, parties' lawyers are informed of the recommendation in the report (whether an appeal is to be declared inadmissible, to be dismissed, or to be allowed in whole or in part—see paragraph 73 above) by a note in the list of cases that is distributed a week before the hearing to lawyers practising in the *Conseil d'Etat* and Court of Cassation.

Mrs Reinhardt's and Mr Slimane-Kaïd's lawyers could have made oral submissions if they had so requested; at the hearing they would have had the right to address the court after the reporting judge, which would have meant that they would have been able to hear the first part of his report and to comment on it. The second part of the report and the draft judgment—which were legitimately privileged from disclosure as forming part of the deliberations—could not in any event be communicated to them; at best, they would thus have learnt of the recommendation in the reporting judge's report a few days before the hearing.

Given the importance of the reporting judge's report (and in particular the second part thereof), the advocate-general's role and the consequences of the outcome of the proceedings for Mrs Reinhardt and Mr Slimane-Kaïd, the imbalance thus created by the failure to give like disclosure of the report to the applicants' advisers is not reconcilable with the requirements of a fair trial.

100. The fact that the advocate-general's submissions were not communicated to the applicants is likewise questionable. In the light of

the fact that only questions of pure law are argued before the Court of Cassation and that the parties are represented in that court by highly specialised lawyers, that practice affords parties an opportunity of apprising themselves of the advocate-general's submissions and commenting on them in a satisfactory manner. It has not, however, been shown that such a practice existed at the material time.

101. Consequently, regard being had to the circumstances referred to above, there has been a violation of Article 6 § 1.

FOR THESE REASONS, THE COURT

Holds unanimously that there has been a violation of Article 6 § 1 of the Convention in that the applicants' case was not heard within a reasonable time;

Holds by nineteen votes to two that there has been a violation of Article 6 § 1 of the Convention in that the applicants did not have a fair hearing in the Court of Cassation;

Done in English and in French, and delivered at a public hearing in the Human Rights Building, Strasbourg, on 31 March 1998.

B. ECTHR AND "ADMINISTRATIVE" COURTS

In addition to the "regular" court system that culminates with the *Cour de Cassation*, France also has a separate system of "Administrative Courts" which are a product of the Napoleonic Code and are emulated in a number of Western European countries. Their role is to deal with challenges to government institutions, which in France include universities and hospitals. These courts report up to the *Conseil d'Etat* rather than the Court of Cassation.

The procedures in the *Conseil d'Etat* are very similar to those in the *Cour de Cassation*. A reporting judge does a preliminary report which is reviewed by an official known as the Government Commissioner. The Commissioner may then make suggestions for changes.

Following the decision in *Slimane-Kaïd v. France,* the next logical challenge was to the presence and role of the Government Commissioner in the proceedings of the *Conseil d'Etat*.

The difference between the Government Commissioner and the Advocate-General, however, is that the former was appointed from among the judges themselves. This difference was almost determinative for the ECHR but not quite—the "appearance" of bias was too much to swallow.

Kress v. France[9] was a medical malpractice claim brought by a woman who suffered severe neurological damage following surgery. Her claim was heard in the Administrative Courts because the hospital was

---

[9] ECHR *39594/98* (2001).

a state institution. When the court-appointed experts found no lack of care by the physicians, she appealed to the *Conseil d'Etat*, which affirmed the judgment with the participation of the Government Commissioner.

At the ECtHR, she made the same arguments that had prevailed with the Advocate-General, but the ECtHR determined that the Commissioner's appointment as a judge made his role different. Nevertheless, the ECtHR held that the "appearance" of inequality was a violation of the right of fair trial:

> 74. Lastly, the doctrine of appearances must also come into play. In publicly expressing his opinion on the rejection or acceptance of the grounds submitted by one of the parties, the Government Commissioner could legitimately be regarded by the parties as taking sides with one or other of them.
>
> In the Court's view, a litigant not familiar with the mysteries of administrative proceedings may quite naturally be inclined to view as an adversary a Government Commissioner who submits that his appeal on points of law should be dismissed. Conversely, a litigant whose case is supported by the Commissioner would see him as his ally.
>
> The Court can also imagine that a party may have a feeling of inequality if, after hearing the Commissioner make submissions unfavourable to his case at the end of the public hearing, he sees him withdraw with the judges of the trial bench to attend the deliberations held in the privacy of chambers.
>
> 75. [T]he Court has noted on numerous occasions that while the independence and impartiality of the Advocate-General or similar officer at certain supreme courts were not open to criticism, the public's increased sensitivity to the fair administration of justice justified the growing importance attached to appearances.
>
> It is for this reason that the Court has held that regardless of the acknowledged objectivity of the Advocate-General or his equivalent, that officer, in recommending that an appeal on points of law should be allowed or dismissed, became objectively speaking the ally or opponent of one of the parties and that his presence at the deliberations afforded him, if only to outward appearances, an additional opportunity to bolster his submissions in private, without fear of contradiction.
>
> 76. The Court sees no reason to depart from the settled case-law referred to above, even though it is the Government Commissioner who is in issue, whose opinion does not derive its authority from that of a State counsel's office.
>
> 78. In the Court's opinion, the benefit for the trial bench of this purely technical assistance is to be weighed against the higher interest of the litigant, who must have a guarantee that the

Government Commissioner will not be able, through his presence at the deliberations, to influence their outcome. That guarantee is not afforded by the current French system.

79. The Court is confirmed in this approach by the fact that at the Court of Justice of the European Communities the Advocate General, whose role is closely modelled on that of the Government Commissioner, does not attend the deliberations (Article 27 of the Rules of Procedure of the Court of Justice).

FOR THESE REASONS, THE COURT

1. *Holds* unanimously that there has been no violation of Article 6 § 1 of the Convention with regard to the applicant's complaint that she did not receive the Government Commissioner's submissions in advance of the hearing and was unable to reply to him at the end of it;

2. *Holds* by ten votes to seven that there has been a violation of Article 6 § 1 of the Convention on account of the Government Commissioner's participation in the *Conseil d'Etat*'s deliberations.

NOTES AND QUESTIONS

1. **(Some) Change Is Going to Come.** [T]he French reaction has consisted not of one response, but of two. For its part, the Conseil d'Etat has simply refused to abandon its proud Napoleonic ethos and corresponding habits, offering the stiffest possible resistance by all but ignoring the ECHR's decisions. The Cour de Cassation, on the other hand, led by formidable Chief Justice Guy Canivet, has adopted a startling array of reforms that not only satisfy the ECHR's mandates, but could also mark a turning point in the history of French law.[10]

2. **Appearances Matter.** Notice that the holding in *Kress* regarding a fair trial was only that, as a matter of appearances, the Government Commissioner should not sit as a member of the court. The ECtHR did accept the argument that the Commissioner was fully a judge and not an advocate for the Government. Given that this holding on the "appearance of fairness" was, itself, a ten-to-seven vote, is it not reasonable for the Conseil d'Etat to maintain its historic practices?

§ 11.3 INTERNATIONAL TRIBUNALS—UNIQUE AND HYBRID SYSTEMS

The growth of international tribunals is important to both current and future lawyers. An increasing number of clients will require guidance on both procedures and policies in an increasingly globalized world.

---

[10] Lasser, *supra* note 5, 90 CORNELL L. REV. at 1000.

International tribunals are different from both the civil law and the Anglo-American systems. To an extent, they borrow aspects of both, which raises some potentially confusing questions. First, what procedures and interpretive techniques will the tribunals employ—the common law adversarial/precedent model or the civil law inquisitorial/code model? Second, somewhat related to the precedent/code question, what law applies?

There are two sources of international law: treaties (documents signed by nations) and customary law (practices of "civilized nations" as pronounced by recognized commentators). The customary Law of War, now known as the Law of Armed Conflict (LOAC) has ancient roots. It is at least 3500 years old, but began to be codified in the 19th century by a few nations in their domestic law and in treaties such as the Hague Conventions of 1899 and 1907.

At the end of World War II, the Nuremberg Trials and related tribunals were based on the London Charter. Signed by the four victorious nations, the London Charter borrowed the definition of three crimes—war crimes, crimes against humanity, and crimes of aggression—from all the prior sources. The Nuremberg Trials treated genocide as a subset of crimes against humanity, but subsequent treaties have separated the crime of genocide from crimes against humanity.

Thus the law governing criminal liability for mass atrocities is both codified and customary. To satisfy due process concerns, a crime based on customary law must be sufficiently established such that the accused would have known that it was universally regarded as criminal behavior among knowledgeable sources.

The Types of International Tribunals

There are a growing number of courts that have borrowed features from both the common law and civil law traditions. Some are unique multinational creations. Others are special courts embedded within domestic systems using international law and foreign personnel. These are sometimes referred to as "hybrid" courts.

The first example of a permanent international court was the European Court of Human Rights (ECtHR) located in Strasbourg, which took its mandate from the European Convention on Human Rights (ECHR). It is "blended" in the sense that it uses some of the argumentative style and reliance on precedent of the common law system, but the structure of the system and the rhetorical style of opinions are more in the civil law tradition.

Hybrid courts, by contrast, are divisions within a domestic court system, in which "foreign judges sit alongside their domestic counterparts to try cases prosecuted and defended by teams of local lawyers working with those from other countries. . . . [A]t the same time, the judges apply domestic law that has been reformed to include international standards."[11]

In recent decades, a number of tribunals have been instituted to deal with the atrocities of violent regimes and internal conflicts. These have given rise to a permanent court known as the International Criminal Court (ICC). The International Criminal Court has jurisdiction over international law of armed conflict in signatory countries, but it has no police power of its own.

A prime example of a distinct ad hoc tribunal is the International Criminal Tribunal for the former Yugoslavia (ICTY) established by the United Nations and located in The Hague. The Bosnian conflict was the worst of the several conflicts occurring from the breakup of Yugoslavia into the component republics of Croatia, Slovenia, Serbia, and Bosnia-Herzegovina. The ICTY was established to pursue war crimes committed during that conflict.

From 1992 to 1995, ending with the negotiated Dayton Peace Accords, some 100,000 people died and about 2.2 million people were displaced from their homes. Although war crimes were committed on all sides of the conflict, the genocidal effort of Serbian forces and sympathizers against Bosniak (Muslim) residents included torture, murder, and the rape of somewhere between 20,000 to 50,000 women, most of them Bosniak.

> Legal scholar and anthropologist Robert Hayden has estimated that the ICTY will have spent about $14 million per individual trial. The ICTY's budget for 2012–13 was approximately $251 million. By way of comparison, this year's total annual budget of the UN High Commission for Refugees, the primary international agency tasked with assisting some three hundred thousand refugees and internally displaced persons in southeastern Europe, is $50.9 million.[12]

Between its inception in 1993 and its projected closure in 2016, the ICTY will have spent over $2 billion—approximately $250 million per year. As of late 2015, the tribunal had convicted 80 persons, dismissed or acquitted 54 others and still had seven cases involving 14 persons pending. More to the point in terms of procedure, in the 20 years of its operation, it had consumed 10,800 trial days, heard 4650 witnesses, and generated 2.5 million pages of transcripts.[13]

---

[11] Laura A. Dickinson, *The Relationship Between Hybrid Courts and International Courts: The Case of Kosovo*, 37 NEW ENG. L. REV. 1059, 1059 (2003).

[12] Gordon N. Bardos, *Trials and Tribulations: Politics as Justice at the ICTY*, WORLD AFF. J. (Sept/Oct 2013), http://www.worldaffairsjournal.org/article/trials-and-tribulations-politics-justice-icty [https://perma.cc/B64X-B5FR].

[13] *ICTY Facts & Figures*, UNITED NATIONS: INT'L CRIM. TRIBUNAL FOR THE FORMER YUGOSLAVIA, http://www.icty.org/en/content/infographic-icty-facts-figures [https://perma.cc/439R-MED8] (last visited Oct. 6, 2016).

In fairness, some cases in the U.S. may take years to complete because of pretrial preparation or delays on court calendars, but the trial portion itself is usually continuous and comparatively brief.

NOTES AND QUESTIONS

1. **The Long and the Short of It.** Some opinions of the ICTY and ICTR have run 500 pages or more, giving rise to some criticism that the courts' rulings are exceedingly difficult to understand even for knowledgeable observers, let alone affected persons. There are three reasons for the length and style of these opinions.

First, the initial opinions were important to justify the role of the tribunals themselves. The judges were speaking not just to the international community providing their funding, but also to the affected communities: Muslim, Serbian, and Croatian in one instance; Hutu and Tutsi in the other.

Second, the opinions found "established facts" that could be used in later prosecutions. But does using facts found in one case against another accused comport with basic due process? To the extent that the established facts relate to general background and not to the actions of the accused themselves, they are useful as context open to public scrutiny and critique rather than evidence against the accused.

Third, the style of the opinions reflect the continental style of academics. The repetitive style (law, then history, then facts, then findings, then conclusions) is highly formalistic, much more so than opinions in common law countries. This is likely because continental academics were accustomed to having to persuade academic commentators that they had covered every part of every base.

2. **Living in the Past.** It is an open question whether the trials in the ICTY will help dispel the religious/cultural tensions of the Balkan region. It could be argued that the cases merely held open the countries' festering wounds. Rather than advancing the cause of peace-building, 20 years of legal action have kept the fires of hostility burning. In contrast, other post-conflict societies have turned more quickly to "restorative justice" models with mixed results, as illustrated in the next note.

3. **Truth and Reconciliation Commissions.** Between 20 and 30 truth and reconciliation commissions have been established in the wake of civil unrest or open conflict in the last 30 years.[14] The most well-known reconciliation commissions include:

a. **South Africa.** The TRC was established by statute at the end of apartheid in 1995. It operated from 1996 to 1998 under a mandate that allowed witnesses of human rights violations to tell their stories. It also permitted perpetrators to come forward to give testimony and seek amnesty. In the latter sense, it was something like confession and forgiveness. The TRC has been widely hailed as a success because there has been no organized racial violence in South Africa since the end of

---

[14] *See* TRUTH V. JUSTICE: THE MORALITY OF TRUTH COMMISSIONS (Robert Rotberg & Dennis Thompson eds., 2000) (a collection of thirteen essays on the commission phenomenon).

Apartheid. However, some criticize the TRC on the ground that it allowed perpetrators of atrocities a "free pass" by just telling their stories.[15]

b. **Guatemala.** The Historical Clarification Commission was a rare entity created as part of peace negotiations during an ongoing civil war. It was created in 1994, and concluded its work with a 1999 report titled *Memory of Silence*. The Commission estimated that over 200,000 people disappeared or were killed during the civil war, and that 93 percent of abuses were attributable to the government.

c. **Ecuador.** This "democracy" went through periods of turmoil and ouster of elected governments from the 1970s until recently. *La Comisión de la Verdad* was appointed to investigate and report on abuses occurring from 1984 to 1988.

d. **El Salvador.** The *Comisión de la Verdad para El Salvador* was established by the UN as part of peace accords ending a civil war between a military junta and leftist militias. The war lasted from late 1979 to 1992, and is thought to have seen the disappearance of more than 75,000 persons. The U.S. supported the government despite multiple human rights violations on both sides.

e. **Liberia and Sierra Leone.** The civil war in Sierra Leone lasted from 1991 to 2003. As portrayed in the movie "Blood Diamonds," the war was fueled, in part, by Charles Taylor's National Patriotic Front of Liberia. Accused of multiple war crimes, slavery, rape, and use of child soldiers, Taylor was tried in The Hague by the Special Court for Sierra Leone and sentenced to 50 years in prison. Both countries conducted Truth and Reconciliation Commissions, but there is little evidence that they had much impact. Peace and the rule of law in both countries remains somewhat tenuous.

f. **Rwanda.** The Gacaca of Rwanda came into the international spotlight as part of an effort to reunify the country after the atrocities of 1994.

To address the fact that thousands of accused still awaited trial in the national court system, and to bring about justice and reconciliation at the grassroots level, the Rwandan government in 2005 re-established the traditional community court system called "Gacaca" (pronounced GA-CHA-CHA).

In the Gacaca system, communities at the local level elected judges to hear the trials of genocide suspects accused of all crimes except planning of genocide. The courts gave lower sentences if the person was repentant and sought reconciliation with the community. Often, confessing prisoners returned home without further penalty or merely received community service orders. More than 12,000 community-based courts tried more than 1.2 million cases throughout the country.

---

[15] *See* MARTHA MINOW, BETWEEN VENGEANCE AND FORGIVENESS: FACING HISTORY AFTER GENOCIDE AND MASS VIOLENCE 89 (2000) ("The repertoire of societal responses to collective violence must include prosecutions, but it must not be limited to them.")

The Gacaca trials served to promote reconciliation by providing a means for victims to learn the truth about the death of their family members and relatives. They also gave perpetrators the opportunity to confess their crimes, show remorse, and ask for forgiveness in front of their community. The Gacaca courts officially closed on May 4, 2012.[16]

§ 11.4 INFORMAL AND RELIGIOUS COURTS

A. INFORMAL TRIBUNALS

In addition to common law systems, civil law systems, and hybrid systems, there are many variations on the theme of informal dispute resolution. The most common are practiced through tribal or village elders. The Jirga of Islamic countries and the Gacaca of Rwanda are only two prominent examples of what is undoubtedly the oldest system of justice in the world.

The Jirga and Shura are similar terms in Arab culture. The former refers to a gathering of village elders or leaders, often for the purpose of dispute resolution, while Shura refers to a council or gathering, usually for the purpose of making governance decisions.

Jirga is primarily a Pashtun concept used in Afghanistan to identify the village or tribal elders who sit down to settle a dispute: "The consensus among historians, political scientists, and anthropologists is of the Jirga as a communal institution that deals with dispute settlement or conflict resolution and is limited to tribal or semi-tribal communities, especially among the Pashtuns."[17]

A variation of the Jirga is the Loya Jirga, or "grand assembly." The Loya Jirga brings together thousands of elders and community leaders to discuss matters of national importance. A Loya Jirga was called by Afghan President Hamid Karzai to discuss a 2014 security agreement with the United States.[18] Another was brought together to write a Constitution for the Republic of Afghanistan.

The concept of Shura has a much broader meaning. It refers to the entire process of consultation. In some Islamic teachings, even the religious leaders are required to consult with the people, although this is

---

[16] OUTREACH PROGRAMME ON THE RWANDA GENOCIDE AND THE UNITED NATIONS, THE JUSTICE AND RECONCILIATION PROCESS IN RWANDA (2014), http://www.un.org/en/preventgenocide/rwanda/pdf/Backgrounder%20Justice%202014.pdf [https://perma.cc/A4JB-GHVN].

[17] U.S. AGENCY INT'L DEV., AFGHANISTAN RULE OF LAW PROJECT: FIELD STUDY OF INFORMAL AND CUSTOMARY JUSTICE IN AFGHANISTAN AND RECOMMENDATIONS ON IMPROVING ACCESS TO JUSTICE AND RELATIONS BETWEEN FORMAL COURTS AND INFORMAL BODIES 7 (2005), http://www.usip.org/sites/default/files/file/usaid_afghanistan.pdf [https://perma.cc/U59T-RAV9].

[18] Greg Myre, *Everything You Wanted To Know About An Afghan Loya Jirga*, NPR (Nov. 21, 2013), http://www.npr.org/sections/parallels/2013/11/21/246536898/everything-you-wanted-to-know-about-an-afghan-loya-jirga [https://perma.cc/8XQC-7RWA].

a matter of some dispute. In Iraq, the Shura has taken on a much more formal role and is only slightly subordinate to the Parliament or High Court.

> The Shura Council is a venerable Iraqi Institution with a basis in law dating back to 1933 .... [T]he Shura Council is comparable with the Conseil D'Etat in France and has a number of functions including:
>
> 1. Acting as an administrative court;
> 2. Vetting of draft primary legislation to ensure constitutionality and avoid contradictions with the Iraqi legal system prior to the draft being passed to the Council of Representatives;
> 3. Vetting of secondary legislation issued by the various Ministries.[19]

The Iraqi Shura is not generally regarded as a mechanism for dispute resolution except with respect to disputes between citizen and government (the "administrative court" parallel to the *Conseil d'Etat*).

B. RELIGIOUS LAW AND COURTS

Religious law and secular law have been closely related for centuries. The British common law of contracts originated in the Ecclesiastical courts of medieval England because a promise (or its breach) was considered a religious matter. Similarly, Roman law—the basis of modern civil law—was heavily influenced by the Vatican in the Renaissance period.

Today, religious courts flourish in many countries in the world. For example, Israeli secular courts will yield jurisdiction to religious courts in some matters of marriage and divorce, subject to supervision of the civil courts. Moreover, in countries with purely secular court systems the courts may apply portions of religious law to disputes. For example, the Italian courts are divided on whether Islamic family law can be employed in the domestic court system.

1. ISRAEL

The application of religious law to family law in Israel was first introduced under Ottoman rule and continued under the British Mandate (1917–1948) until establishment of the State of Israel.

Today, Israel has two coexisting legal systems: religious courts (Jewish, Muslim, Christian, and Druze) and civil courts. Hebrew or Rabbinic law is based on the Talmud, which in turn is an amalgam of scholarly commentaries elaborating on the written words found in the

---

[19] *Shura Council*, U. OF UTAH S.J. QUINNEY C.L: GLOBAL JUST. PROJECT: IRAQ http://gjpi.org/library/primary/state-shura-council/ [https://perma.cc/EHS2-GDQ9] (last visited Oct. 6, 2016).

scriptural Law of Moses. Similarly, Islamic law (usually transliterated as Shari'a) is the commentary of learned jurists derived from the Quran as well as the Sunnah (sayings of the Prophet) and Hadith (practices of the Prophet and Caliphs). Shari'a is divided into four Sunni schools of thought and one of Shi'a principles, the most widespread of which is the Sunni Hanafi School.

In general, only matters of marriage and divorce may be taken to religious courts, although "marriage and divorce matters" may include some financial affairs such as estate distribution. When a Jewish couple is about to divorce, the husband tends to race to a rabbinical court, while the wife rushes to a civil court. Although the divorce itself has to go through the rabbinical court, the court in which the case is filed first has jurisdiction over alimony, child custody, and division of property (provided that these matters were included in the first suit), and civil courts are known to be more generous to women than rabbinical courts. The Family Courts Law, enacted in 1995, established a new category of civil courts to adjudicate these matters.[20]

> The Supreme Court of Israel held recently that religious courts must apply statutory principles of equality between spouses, unless the parties have expressly consented to the application of religious law.[21] This decision brings to the forefront the tensions inherent in a highly volatile constitutional structure in which secular and religious courts, both part of one legal system, sometimes come into conflict, and exposes the dangers of such a clash of authorities.[22]

For example, commentators have argued that the Women's Equal Rights Law of 1951 requires the "religious courts to follow the principle of community of property, which does not exist in Jewish law."[23] The Rabbinical courts, however, have refused to apply secular law on the ground that the parties have chosen the religious law by coming to the religious courts.

Religious law applies to marriage and divorce in the Israeli Muslim community as well. According to the Israeli Ministry of Justice,

> The Sharia Courts have existed since the time of the Ottoman Empire when they functioned as the official court of the State. During the British Mandate, the legal situation which preceded it was left in place; however changes were introduced which

---

[20] *Israel Judicial Branch: Rabbinical Courts vs Civil Courts*, JEWISH VIRTUAL LIBR., https://www.jewishvirtuallibrary.org/jsource/Politics/courts.html [https://perma.cc/EK8C-BDN4] (last visited Oct. 6, 2016).

[21] [Yemini v. Great Rabbinical Court, HJC 9734/03 (2006).]

[22] Anat Scolnicov, *Religious Law, Religious Courts and Human Rights Within Israeli Constitutional Structure*, 4 INT'L J. CONST. L. 732, 732 (2006).

[23] *Id.*

limited the jurisdiction of the Sharia Courts to personal status issues within the Muslim community.[24]

With the ability to decide matters of family finances and inheritance, the Islamic courts in Israel potentially have a significant role to play in the judicial system. Moreover, the parties may have to decide which "school of Shari'a" will be applied.

Religious courts in Israel have limited jurisdiction. Perhaps most importantly, religious courts do not have jurisdiction over commercial cases. Because Shari'a generally prohibits payment of interest or the purchase of insurance, application of Shari'a law could have a destabilizing effect on business matters.

2. SHARI'A

Islamic law, generally transliterated as Shari'a or Shari'ah, prevails in many countries, notably those formed or revolutionized in the last century. Islamic scholars dispute whether Shari'a is intended to be a social construct or is intended for civil governance, a dispute that exists in the Judeo-Christian world as well. "Many majority Muslim countries have a dual system in which the government is secular but Muslims can choose to bring familial and financial disputes to sharia courts."[25]

The Constitution of the Islamic Republic of Afghanistan states that "No law shall contravene the tenets and provisions of the holy religion of Islam in Afghanistan."[26] The country has both a formal system of courts, controlled by the state and applying codified law, and an informal system of dispute resolution.[27] The Afghan courts tend to look mostly to the Sunni Hanafi school, but there is no uniform consensus. Moreover, the formal judicial system is less important in most parts of the country than the informal system. As the United States Institute of Peace puts it, "informal dispute resolution bodies, which handle the bulk of disputes across the country, involve a blend of customary and tribal norms along with interpretations of Islamic law that are often enforced through local tribal bodies and regional power-brokers."[28]

---

[24] *The Sharia Courts*, ISR. MINISTRY OF JUST., http://www.justice.gov.il/En/Units/ShariaCourts/Pages/default.aspx (last visited Oct. 6, 2016).

[25] *See* Toni Johnson & Mohammed Aly Sergie, *Islam: Governing Under Sharia (Aka Shariah, Shari'a)*, COUNCIL OF FOREIGN REL. (July 25, 2014), http://www.cfr.org/religion/islam-governing-under-sharia/p8034 [https://perma.cc/S6D6-XC8U].

[26] THE CONSTITUTION OF THE ISLAMIC REPUBLIC OF AFGHANISTAN Jan. 26, 2004, Ch. 1, Art 3, http://www.afghanembassy.com.pl/afg/images/pliki/TheConstitution.pdf [https://perma.cc/69GL-RTV2].

[27] Hamid Khan, *Clarifying the Role of Islamic Law in Afghanistan's Justice System*, U.S. INST. OF PEACE (June 12, 2012), http://www.usip.org/publications/clarifying-the-role-islamic-law-in-afghanistans-justice-system-0 [https://perma.cc/H6GV-B6U3].

[28] *Id.*

In Saudi Arabia, Islamic law (Shari'ah in the Saudi transliteration) is the basis of law. The position of the Saudi monarchy is that Shari'ah is the governing law for both religious and secular affairs.[29]

Similar to the French system, the Saudi system long had separate courts for criminal matters, ordinary disputes, and "administrative" matters. There is currently a reform movement underway consolidating the court systems into one with a Supreme Court at the top of the pyramid.

A 2007 effort at judicial reform has yet to bear visible results—the king is still both lawgiver and overseer of the courts. Some progress in women's rights, such as the right to vote, occurred under King Abdullah, who was succeeded by King Salman in 2015. In 2016, Prince Mohammed became known as a young reformer with significant power and more modern views than most of his elders.

C. CLAIMS AND MYTHS ABOUT SHARI'A

Shari'a is a governing principle in the Islamic Republics of Iraq, Iran, and Afghanistan, although the courts of Iraq and Afghanistan are secularly created. Saudi Arabia had an overtly religious system that was the subject of some superficially secular reforms in 2007.

The many debates about the nature of Islam and Shari'a have arisen from two central factors: the claims of violent jihadists and the mistreatment of women in some Islamic countries. While critics tend to treat these judicial systems as identical, each of the Islamic Republics has a separate formal judicial system in addition to the codes of conduct imposed by either culture or religion. Further, many of the most abusive practices are not rooted in Shari'a but are, instead, cultural artifacts.

Religious law is different from religious culture. For example, nothing in Islamic law (Shari'a) dictates women's clothing other than a general exhortation to modesty. The practice of covering the face or hair is known as hijab. The choice of item (burqa, Shayla, chador, etc.) is governed by custom, and sometimes law, in different Muslim countries or communities. It is not, however, part of religious law. Just as most Roman Catholic women wore hats or scarves to church prior to Vatican II but then immediately removed them when leaving church, some women do the same at mosques today in many predominantly Muslim countries.

Nor is the practice of "honor killing" explicitly condoned by Shari'a. In particular, the practice of killing a rape victim because of her dishonor is not only considered contrary to Shari'a, it is also formally acknowledged as murder in the law of most Muslim nations. The pervasive notion that mistreatment of women is part of a code derived

[29] *See* Johnson & Sergie, *supra* note 23.

from scripture has been debated and often debunked by any number of scholars and popular authors.[30]

Many Americans believe that Shari'a is "Islamic law." Shari'a is not generally regarded by Muslims as an enforceable legal code. It is instead "fiqh" or "rules of right action," more in the nature of a moral code. Shari'a is also not a legal code standing alone. In those countries that proclaim their law to be "based on Shari'a," there are other influences at work in the civil law.

Commentators have also challenged the belief that Islam is inherently hostile to women: although there is a verse in the Koran referring to men as "protectors" of women, it reflects both the time and gender roles of nomadic peoples. Other "anti-woman" legislation has been cherry-picked, and often doesn't accurately reflect fiqh.[31]

Westerners also often believe that Islam is brutal, both in its punishments and in its quest for geographical conquest. "It's true that sharia permits harsh corporal punishment, including amputation of limbs, but fiqh restricts its application."[32] While the Koran may permit harsh sentences, they often come with numerous caveats or extremely high burdens of proof. Contrary to the actions of the Islamic State and other extremist groups, "the Koran's prohibition of wanton violence . . . forbids attacks on civilians, property, houses of worship and even animals." Further, nothing in the Koran commands conquest or spreading of the faith by force.[33]

In many ways the history and modern interpretations of Islam reflect the history of Judaism and Christianity, as well as modern debates of how ancient religious texts should be implemented in the modern world.

§ 11.5 IGO AND NGO PROCEEDINGS

There are literally dozens of entities operating under the banner of the United Nations, which is the global intergovernmental organization. Similarly, the EU could be considered an intergovernmental organization. While both entities have created formal court systems, discussed in section 11.2, both also employ dispute resolution systems of nongovernmental or quasi-governmental entities.

---

[30] *E.g.*, Asifa Quraishi-Landes, *Five Myths About Sharia*, WASH. POST (June 24, 2016), https://www.washingtonpost.com/opinions/five-myths-about-sharia/2016/06/24/7e3efb7a-31ef-11e6-8758-d58e76e11b12_story.html [https://perma.cc/YRB2-STYN].

[31] *Id.*

[32] *Id.*

[33] *Id.* For a more complete rendering of these issues, see MOHAMMAD HAHIM KAMALI, SHAR'IA LAW: AN INTRODUCTION (2008).

A. INTER-GOVERNMENTAL ORGANIZATIONS (IGO)

The most prominent organizations with formal dispute resolution mechanisms are the World Trade Organization (WTO) and its General Agreement on Tariffs and Trade (GATT). In general, the WTO works to produce free or near-free trade across national boundaries, a highly controversial aspect of the globalized economy. A shirt made in Bangladesh by low-paid workers may produce two controversies. First, companies will employ workers in the lowest economic settings. Second, there are no regulations for labor conditions. The WTO has instituted a series of agreements designed to "cover goods, services and intellectual property. They spell out the principles of liberalization and the permitted exceptions. They include individual countries' commitments to lower customs tariffs and other trade barriers, and to open and keep open services markets. They set procedures for settling disputes."[34] The WTO dispute resolution process is modeled on arbitration principles covered in Chapter 7.

In the post-Soviet era, the Organization for Security and Cooperation in Europe (OSCE) stepped in to attempt to alleviate some of the tensions inherent in the breakup of the Soviet Union and the resulting impacts of organized crime on newly capitalist systems. The OSCE attempts to broker peaceful solutions to difficult transborder issues—efforts that conclude with the OSCE Court of Conciliation and Arbitration.

> The main mechanism offered by the Convention is conciliation, which aims at proposing terms of settlement to the States Parties to a dispute. This mechanism can be activated unilaterally by any State party to the Convention for a dispute between it and one or more other States parties. At the conclusion of the proceedings, the conciliation commission presents a report and recommendations to the Parties. The Parties then have thirty days to decide whether they accept those or not. If there is no agreement within that period, and if the parties have agreed to submit to arbitration, an ad hoc arbitral tribunal may be set up whose ruling will be legally binding on the Parties. Arbitral proceedings may also be initiated by agreement between States parties concerned.[35]

B. IGO—TREATIES AND ARBITRATION PROVISIONS

One potentially powerful tool of the globalized market is the existence of arbitration provisions in free-trade or fair-trade agreements. One critic has dubbed this system "investor-state dispute settlement"

---

[34] *Understanding the WTO: What We Do*, WORLD TRADE ORG., https://www.wto.org/english/thewto_e/whatis_e/what_we_do_e.htm [https://perma.cc/6BVK-A57Q] (last visited Oct. 8, 2016).

[35] *OSCE Court of Conciliation and Arbitration*, Org. for Security and Co-operation in Eur., http://www.osce.org/cca [https://perma.cc/8CGQ-QPT3] (last visited Oct. 8, 2016).

(ISDS) and proclaimed arbitrators to be a "Super Court" with power to overturn not just normal domestic national laws, but even force relinquishment of criminal convictions for corruption, toxic waste pollution, and other illegal practices.[36] Whether these assertions are accurate or overblown, international arbitration will continue to be a force, for better or worse, in the globalized economy. Thus far, the U.S. courts have treated these decisions as binding only to the extent that the political branches choose to make them so.

One of the best-known examples of adjudication of disputes under trade agreements is the U.S.-Mexico dispute over dolphin-safe tuna fishing under the General Agreement on Tariffs and Trade (GATT). This dispute over safe fishing methods has been pending before the GATT bodies since 2008.[37]

One interesting example of the role (or non-role) of IGO dispute resolution is the decision of the WTO that the United States may not prevent transnational internet gambling. In a prosecution under U.S. law, however, a federal district court held that the WTO's ruling was not binding on the courts unless Congress chose to make it so:

> Defendants have no standing to assert a defense based on the obligations of the United States under GATS. A failure on the part of the United States to comply with a decision of the Appellate Body may give rise to WTO sanctions against the United States under GATS. However, whether to accept those sanctions, modify federal law, or renegotiate its GATS commitments is a matter committed to the discretion of Congress. It is the Court's role to apply federal law to the case at hand as found in the Wire Act. Any provision of GATS to the contrary "shall have [no] effect."[38]

C. NGO ADJUDICATORS—THE EXAMPLE OF INTERNATIONAL SPORTS FEDERATIONS

International sports federations essentially exist as commercial entities. They govern transnational competitions, attempt to obtain greater exposure for the sport, and settle disputes over rules violations. Recall Professor Rosenberg's use of sports in Chapter 3 as examples of the types of discretion afforded to decision makers.

The largest of these is the International Olympic Committee, which disclaims authority over any single sport, leaving eligibility in each sport to the federations such as International Association of Athletic Federations (IAAF) (track and field), Fédération Internationale de

[36] Chris Hamby, *The Court that Rules the World,* BUZZFEED (Aug. 28, 2016, 7:00 AM), https://www.buzzfeed.com/chrishamby/super-court [https://perma.cc/S8ZH-W22A].

[37] *United States—Measures Concerning the Importation, Marketing and Sale of Tuna and Tuna Products*, WORLD TRADE ORG., https://www.wto.org/english/tratop_e/dispu_e/cases_e/ds381_e.htm [https://perma.cc/T4E3-HZRW] (last visited Oct. 8, 2016).

[38] United States v. Lombardo, 639 F. Supp. 2d 1271, 1290 (D. Utah 2007).

Football Association (FIFA) (what the US calls soccer and the rest of the world calls football), and Union Cycliste International (UCI) (cycling).

The World Anti-Doping Agency (WADA) is entrusted by most sports federations with the development and administration of tests for performance-enhancing drugs and prohibited biological substances (*e.g.*, blood doping). Pursuant to calls for greater regularity, WADA turned to the former President of the European Court of Human Rights to incorporate procedural protections into investigations and imposition of sanctions.

A number of recent sports scandals have featured the involvement of international NGOs, many of which acted in an adjudicatory capacity. For example, the lifetime ban of cyclist Lance Armstrong and the stripping of a Tour de France victory from Floyd Landis involved investigations, reports, and decisions by the United States Anti-Doping Agency, the anti-doping agencies of several European countries, the Italian Cycling Federation, the Union Cycliste Internationale, the World Triathlon Corporation, the IOC, and the WADA. Similarly, the decision to ban some members of the 2016 Russian Olympic team involved the IAAF, the IOC, the International Weightlifting Federation, the World Rowing Federation, and others. The "Cold War Basketball Game" described in Chapter 3 is illustrative of the power of NGOs in major economic arenas.

CHAPTER 12

BIAS IN THE JUDICIAL PROCESS

> Bias is easy to attribute to others and difficult to discern in oneself.
>
> – United States Supreme Court Justice Anthony Kennedy[1]

Bias, whether blatant or latent, forms early in life as a result of cultural, religious, societal, and familial messages.[2] Blatant bias may have become less acceptable over the past 60 years, yet both blatant and latent biases remain and can be difficult to combat.

Beginning in the 1970s, a cadre of scholars, collectively known as the Critical Legal Studies movement, looked specifically at law through the lens of class, race, and gender. They argued that the legal system was geared toward preserving the status quo, and was biased on behalf of the wealthy—particularly wealthy white males.

While the Critical Legal Studies movement has waned in recent years, the American public has begun to discuss how race and ethnicity impact public policy and the law. Allegations of bias in judicial selection, jury selection, criminal sentencing, application of the death penalty, police practices, and immigration policy have all made national news. Explicit bias, implicit bias, and stereotypes impact equality in the judicial system—on both sides of the bench.

§ 12.1 RACIAL EQUALITY ON THE BENCH

Macon B. Allen, born a free man in Indiana, passed the Maine Bar examination and was licensed to practice law in 1844. Twenty-five years later, in 1869, the first black man graduated with a degree in law. That same year, Howard University opened a law school for newly-freed African-Americans.

The numbers of black lawyers in the United States rose steadily after the Civil War, but dropped during the Jim Crow era.[3] It was not until 1937 that the first black man was appointed to the federal district

---

1 Williams v. Pennsylvania, 136 S. Ct. 1899, 1905 (2016).

2 Annie Murphy Paul, *Where Bias Begins: The Truth About Stereotypes*, PSYCHOL. TODAY (May 1, 1998), https://www.psychologytoday.com/articles/199805/where-bias-begins-the-truth-about-stereotypes [https://perma.cc/HH8W-DFES].

3 M. Marshall, *Jim Crow Constitution Stifled Virginia's Black Lawyers*, U. VA. SCH. L. (Oct. 13, 2003), http://www.law.virginia.edu/html/news/2003_fall/hylton.htm [https://perma.cc/U2CD-7E9A].

court bench, and not until 1950 that the same judge, William Henry Hastie, was confirmed as the first black federal appellate judge. Seventeen years later, Thurgood Marshall was the first African-American appointed to the Supreme Court.

Despite attempts by law schools and state bar associations to increase diversity in the legal profession, 89 percent of judges in the United States are white. Only six percent are African-American, and three percent are Hispanic. Conversely, only 60 percent of Americans are white, 13 percent are African-American, and 17 percent are Hispanic.[4]

The current Justices have publicly expressed different opinions on the value of racial diversity on the bench. On one end of the spectrum, Justice Thomas consistently votes against affirmative action, even though he is a product of it. Thomas, who was born into a poor rural family in Georgia, acknowledges that he was accepted to Yale Law School because of affirmative action. He argues, however, that affirmative action did him no favors, and in fact made it harder for him to find a job after graduation. He famously took a 15-cent sticker off a cigar box, stuck it on his Yale diploma, and put the diploma in the basement.

In his memoir, *My Grandfather's Son*, Thomas says he felt "tricked" by paternalistic whites at Yale who recruited black students.

> "I was bitter toward the white bigots whom I held responsible for the unjust treatment of blacks," he wrote, "but even more bitter toward those ostensibly unprejudiced whites who pretended to side with black people while using them to further their own political and social ends."[5]

Conversely, Justice Sotomayor, born into a similarly poor family in the South Bronx, has embraced the role affirmative action played in her admission to Princeton. In 2001, she gave a speech declaring that the ethnicity and sex of a judge "may and will make a difference in our judging."[6] Contrary to Justices Ginsburg and O'Connor, she openly questioned the notion that a wise old man and a wise old woman would reach the same conclusion when deciding cases. "I would hope that a wise Latina woman with the richness of her experiences would more often than not reach a better conclusion than a white male who hasn't lived that life," said Judge Sotomayor.[7] "Whether born from experience or inherent physiological or cultural differences," she said, for jurists who

---

[4] *Quick Facts: United States*, U.S. CENSUS BUREAU, https://www.census.gov/quickfacts/table/PST045215/00 [https://perma.cc/9WUX-7VUV] (last visited Oct. 9, 2016).

[5] Elizabeth Flock, *Clarence Thomas Suggests Affirmative Action is Like Jim Crow*, U.S. NEWS (June 24, 2013 12:15 PM), http://www.usnews.com/news/articles/2013/06/24/clarence-thomas-suggests-affirmative-action-is-like-jim-crow [https://perma.cc/S948-V9QW]. *See also* Kevin Merida & Michael Fletcher, SUPREME DISCOMFORT: THE DIVIDED SOUL OF CLARENCE THOMAS (2008).

[6] Charlie Savage, *A Judge's View of Judging Is on the Record*, N.Y. TIMES (May 14, 2009), http://www.nytimes.com/2009/05/15/us/15judge.html [https://perma.cc/QH8F-FPDP].

[7] *Id.*

are women and nonwhite, "our gender and national origins may and will make a difference in our judging."[8]

§ 12.2 RACIAL EQUALITY IN THE CIVIL SYSTEM

A. HISTORICALLY

Dred Scott was a slave taken from Alabama to Missouri where he was sold to an Army officer. The officer moved with him on several occasions, sometimes residing in Illinois and Wisconsin where slavery was prohibited. After a complex series of transactions, Scott, his wife, and his two children ended up back in Missouri, which had long followed the rule of "once free, always free." Under that rule, Scott's one-time presence in a free state meant that he would be free in Missouri. Faced with the issue in Dred Scott's case, the Missouri courts reversed prior doctrine and ruled that he was a slave. In the meantime, Scott's owner died and left titular ownership of the family to a New York citizen, Sanford (whose name was misspelled by clerical error at the Supreme Court). Scott then sued for his freedom in federal court on the basis of diversity of citizenship.

The case represented high stakes for the nation for several reasons. The Missouri Compromise was an effort in 1820 to keep a balance of free and slave states by admitting Missouri as a slave state and carving Maine out from Massachusetts as a free state. In addition, the legislation purported to decree that, in the future, all areas west of the Mississippi River and north of a line starting at the bottom of Missouri would be free. The areas south of that line would be slaveholding. The Compromise was repealed in 1854, two years before the *Dred Scott* case was decided by the Supreme Court. The Court, however, blithely decided that the Compromise had been unconstitutional anyway.

To modern readers, *Dred Scott* is an aggressively racist and offensive case. However, it accurately reflects the attitudes of the time. It also articulates legal principles that would dominate U.S. law for another century. The case turned on the issue of whether Scott was a citizen for purposes of diversity jurisdiction.

Dred Scott v. Sandford

60 U.S. 393 (1856)

The words "people of the United States" and "citizens" are synonymous terms, and mean the same thing. They both describe the political body who, according to our republican institutions, form the sovereignty, and who hold the power and conduct the Government through their representatives. They are what we familiarly call the "sovereign people," and every citizen is one of this people, and a

[8] *Id.*

constituent member of this sovereignty. The question before us is, whether the class of persons described in the plea in abatement compose a portion of this people, and are constituent members of this sovereignty? We think they are not, and that they are not included, and were not intended to be included, under the word "citizens" in the Constitution, and can therefore claim none of the rights and privileges which that instrument provides for and secures to citizens of the United States. On the contrary, they were at that time considered as a subordinate and inferior class of beings, who had been subjugated by the dominant race, and, whether emancipated or not, yet remained subject to their authority, and had no rights or privileges but such as those who held the power and the Government might choose to grant them.

The question arises, whether the provisions of the Constitution, in relation to the personal rights and privileges to which the citizen of a State should be entitled, embraced the negro African race, at that time in this country, or who might afterwards be imported, who had then or should afterwards be made free in any State; and to put it in the power of a single State to make him a citizen of the United States, and endue him with the full rights of citizenship in every other State without their consent? Does the Constitution of the United States act upon him whenever he shall be made free under the laws of a State, and raised there to the rank of a citizen, and immediately cloth [sic] him with all the privileges of a citizen in every other State, and in its own courts?

In the opinion of the court, the legislation and histories of the times, and the language used in the Declaration of Independence, show, that neither the class of persons who had been imported as slaves, nor their descendants, whether they had become free or not, were then acknowledged as a part of the people, nor intended to be included in the general words used in that memorable instrument.

They had for more than a century before been regarded as beings of an inferior order, and altogether unfit to associate with the white race, either in social or political relations; and so far inferior, that they had no rights which the white man was bound to respect; and that the negro might justly and lawfully be reduced to slavery for his benefit. He was bought and sold, and treated as an ordinary article of merchandise and traffic, whenever a profit could be made by it. This opinion was at that time fixed and universal in the civilized portion of the white race. It was regarded as an axiom in morals as well as in politics, which no one thought of disputing, or supposed to be open to dispute; and men in every grade and position in society daily and habitually acted upon it in their private pursuits, as well as in matters of public concern, without doubting for a moment the correctness of this opinion.

The language of the Declaration of Independence is equally Conclusive:

It begins by declaring that, "when in the course of human events it becomes necessary for one people to dissolve the political bands which have connected them with another, and to assume among the powers of the earth the separate and equal station to which the laws of nature and nature's God entitle them, a decent respect for the opinions of mankind requires that they should declare the causes which impel them to the separation."

It then proceeds to say: "We hold these truths to be self-evident: that all men are created equal; that they are endowed by their Creator with certain unalienable rights; that among them is life, liberty, and the pursuit of happiness; that to secure these rights, Governments are instituted, deriving their just powers from the consent of the governed."

The general words above quoted would seem to embrace the whole human family, and if they were used in a similar instrument at this day would be so understood. But it is too clear for dispute, that the enslaved African race were not intended to be included, and formed no part of the people who framed and adopted this declaration; for if the language, as understood in that day, would embrace them, the conduct of the distinguished men who framed the Declaration of Independence would have been utterly and flagrantly inconsistent with the principles they asserted; and instead of the sympathy of mankind, to which they so confidently appeared, they would have deserved and received universal rebuke and reprobation.

Yet the men who framed this declaration were great men—high in literary acquirements—high in their sense of honor, and incapable of asserting principles inconsistent with those on which they were acting. They perfectly understood the meaning of the language they used, and how it would be understood by others; and they knew that it would not in any part of the civilized world be supposed to embrace the negro race, which, by common consent, had been excluded from civilized Governments and the family of nations, and doomed to slavery. They spoke and acted according to the then established doctrines and principles, and in the ordinary language of the day, no one misunderstood them. The unhappy black race were separated from the white by indelible marks, and laws long before established, and were never thought of or spoken of except as property, and when the claims of the owner or the profit of the trader were supposed to need protection.

No one of that race had ever migrated to the United States voluntarily; all of them had been brought here as articles of merchandise. The number that had been emancipated at that time were but few in comparison with those held in slavery; and they were identified in the public mind with the race to which they belonged, and regarded as a part of the slave population rather than the free. It is obvious that they were not even in the minds of the framers of the Constitution when they were conferring special rights and privileges upon the citizens of a State in every other part of the Union.

The legislation of the States . . . shows, in a manner not to be mistaken, the inferior and subject condition of that race at the time the

Constitution was adopted, and long afterwards, throughout the thirteen States by which that instrument was framed; and it is hardly consistent with the respect due to these States, to suppose that they regarded at that time, as fellow-citizens and members of the sovereignty, a class of beings whom they had thus stigmatized; whom, as we are bound, out of respect to the State sovereignties, to assume they had deemed it just and necessary thus to stigmatize, and upon whom they had impressed such deep and enduring marks of inferiority and degradation; or, that when they met in convention to form the Constitution, they looked upon them as a portion of their constituents, or designed to include them in the provisions so carefully inserted for the security and protection of the liberties and rights of their citizens. It cannot be supposed that they intended to secure to them rights, and privileges, and rank, in the new political body throughout the Union, which every one of them denied within the limits of its own dominion. More especially, it cannot be believed that the large slaveholding States regarded them as included in the word citizens, or would have consented to a Constitution which might compel them to receive them in that character from another State. For if they were so received, and entitled to the privileges and immunities of citizens, it would exempt them from the operation of the special laws and from the police regulations which they considered to be necessary for their own safety. It would give to persons of the negro race, who were recognized as citizens in any one State of the Union, the right to enter every other State whenever they pleased, singly or in companies, without pass or passport, and without obstruction, to sojourn there as long as they pleased, to go where they pleased at every hour of the day or night without molestation, unless they committed some violation of law for which a white man would be punished; and it would give them the full liberty of speech in public and in private upon all subjects upon which its own citizens might speak; to hold public meetings upon political affairs, and to keep and carry arms wherever they went. And all of this would be done in the face of the subject race of the same color, both free and slaves, and inevitably producing discontent and insubordination among them, and endangering the peace and safety of the State.

What the construction was at that time, we think can hardly admit of doubt. We have the language of the Declaration of Independence and of the Articles of Confederation, in addition to the plain words of the Constitution itself; we have the legislation of the different States, before, about the time, and since, the Constitution was adopted; we have the legislation of Congress, from the time of its adoption to a recent period; and we have the constant and uniform action of the Executive Department, all concurring together, and leading to the same result. And if anything in relation to the construction of the Constitution can be regarded as settled, it is that which we now give to the word "citizen" and the word "people."

And upon a full and careful consideration of the subject, the court is of opinion, that, upon the facts stated in the plea in abatement, Dred Scott was not a citizen of Missouri within the meaning of the Constitution of the United States, and not entitled as such to sue in its courts; and, consequently, that the Circuit Court had no jurisdiction of the case, and that the judgment on the plea in abatement is erroneous.

NOTES AND QUESTIONS

1. **On the Heels of *Marbury*.** *Dred Scott* was only the second time that the Supreme Court held an act of Congress unconstitutional. The first was *Marbury v. Madison* in 1801. The Court did not hold another act unconstitutional until after the Civil War.

2. **North and South.** In addition to holding that no person descended from an American slave was a citizen for Article III purposes, the Court held the Missouri Compromise unconstitutional. Having already decided that the Court lacked jurisdiction, and given that the Missouri Compromise had already been repealed prior to the Court's decision, this portion of the opinion was dicta several times over.

While some hoped this holding would end "the slavery question," it only exacerbated tensions between the North and South. Hailed by Southerners as a proper constitutional analysis and limitation on federal power, it empowered a furious anti-slavery Republican party and fueled violence between slave owners and abolitionists.

3. **Self-Inflicted Wounds.** *Dred Scott* is universally condemned by modern scholars. It usually makes the list of "worst Supreme Court opinions,"[9] and Chief Justice Hughes called it one of the Court's greatest "self-inflicted wounds."[10] In 2016, the Kansas Attorney General withdrew a brief that had cited *Dred Scott* and apologized for its inclusion.[11]

4. **Behind the Curtain.** The decision was, at least partially, the result of both the Justices' personal prejudices and politics. Five of the Justices were from slave-holding families. The newly-elected President James Buchanan was eager to have the case decided before his inauguration. Buchanan pressured Justice Grier, a northerner, to join the southern majority in order to give the appearance of impartiality. Buchanan also likely had advance notice of the decision. He mentioned it in his inaugural address—two days before the decision was issued.

5. **Free at Last.** The children of Dred Scott's first master paid for at least a portion of his legal fees. After *Dred Scott v. Sandford* was decided they

---

[9] Sarah Mui, *What Are the Worst Supreme Court Decisions Ever?*, A.B.A.J. (May 7, 2014 7:10 PM), http://www.abajournal.com/news/article/what_are_the_worst_scotus_decisions_ever [https://perma.cc/6CXF-V6SS].

[10] CHARLES HUGHES, THE SUPREME COURT OF THE UNITED STATES: ITS FOUNDATION, METHODS AND ACHIEVEMENTS: AN INTERPRETATION 50 (1928).

[11] *Kansas attorney general apologizes for Dred Scott citation in abortion brief*, ABA JOURNAL,http://www.abajournal.com/news/article/kansas_attorney_general_apologizes_for_dred_scott_citation_in_abortion_brie (Oct. 20, 2016) [https://perma.cc/KX3E-FW9R].

purchased Scott and his wife for $750 and then set them free. Dred Scott died nine months later.

6. **The End of *Dred Scott*.** Following the Civil War, the Thirteenth, Fourteenth, and Fifteenth Amendments directly overturned *Dred Scott*. Today, all people born or naturalized in the United States are American citizens, as specified by the Fourteenth Amendment in 1868:

> Section 1. All persons born or naturalized in the United States, and subject to the jurisdiction thereof, are citizens of the United States and of the State wherein they reside. No State shall make or enforce any law which shall abridge the privileges or immunities of citizens of the United States; nor shall any State deprive any person of life, liberty, or property, without due process of law; nor deny to any person within its jurisdiction the equal protection of the laws.
>
> . . .
>
> Section 5. The Congress shall have power to enforce, by appropriate legislation, the provisions of this article.

Plessy v. Ferguson

163 U.S. 537 (1896)

[Louisiana passed a statute in 1890 that required railroad companies "provide equal but separate accommodations for the white and colored races." The statute required that passengers sit in their assigned seats or coaches. Homer Plessy, who was "seven-eighths Caucasian and one-eighth African blood" was charged with violating the statute after he insisted on sitting in the "white" coach.]

■ MR. JUSTICE BROWN.

The constitutionality of this act is attacked upon the ground that it conflicts both with the thirteenth amendment of the constitution, abolishing slavery, and the fourteenth amendment, which prohibits certain restrictive legislation on the part of the states.

By the fourteenth amendment, all persons born or naturalized in the United States, and subject to the jurisdiction thereof, are made citizens of the United States and of the state wherein they reside; and the states are forbidden from making or enforcing any law which shall abridge the privileges or immunities of citizens of the United States, or shall deprive any person of life, liberty, or property without due process of law, or deny to any person within their jurisdiction the equal protection of the laws.

The proper construction of this amendment was first called to the attention of this court in the *Slaughter-House Cases*, which involved, however, not a question of race, but one of exclusive privileges. The case did not call for any expression of opinion as to the exact rights it was intended to secure to the colored race, but it was said generally that its main purpose was to establish the citizenship of the negro, to give definitions of citizenship of the United States and of the states, and to protect from the hostile legislation of the states the privileges and immunities of citizens of the United States, as distinguished from those of citizens of the states.

The object of the amendment was undoubtedly to enforce the absolute equality of the two races before the law, but, in the nature of things, it could not have been intended to abolish distinctions based upon color, or to enforce social, as distinguished from political, equality, or a commingling of the two races upon terms unsatisfactory to either. Laws permitting, and even requiring, their separation, in places where they are liable to be brought into contact, do not necessarily imply the inferiority of either race to the other, and have been generally, if not universally, recognized as within the competency of the state legislatures in the exercise of their police power. The most common instance of this is connected with the establishment of separate schools for white and colored children, which have been held to be a valid exercise of the legislative power even by courts of states where the political rights of the colored race have been longest and most earnestly enforced.

We consider the underlying fallacy of the plaintiff's argument to consist in the assumption that the enforced separation of the two races stamps the colored race with a badge of inferiority. If this be so, it is not by reason of anything found in the act, but solely because the colored race chooses to put that construction upon it. The argument necessarily assumes that if, as has been more than once the case, and is not unlikely to be so again, the colored race should become the dominant power in the state legislature, and should enact a law in precisely similar terms, it would thereby relegate the white race to an inferior position. We imagine that the white race, at least, would not acquiesce in this assumption. The argument also assumes that social prejudices may be overcome by legislation, and that equal rights cannot be secured to the negro except by an enforced commingling of the two races. We cannot accept this proposition. If the two races are to meet upon terms of social equality, it must be the result of natural affinities, a mutual appreciation of each other's merits, and a voluntary consent of individuals. If the civil and political rights of both races be equal, one cannot be inferior to the other civilly or politically. If one race be inferior to the other socially, the constitution of the United States cannot put them upon the same plane.

Brown v. Board of Education of Topeka

347 U.S. 483 (1954)

[*Brown v. Board of Education* consolidated four lawsuits brought in separate states. The parents of African-American children challenged various statutes that required public schools to be segregated based on race. They argued that the statutes violated the Equal Protection clause because the schools were not substantially equal. The plaintiffs, with one exception, lost in the lower courts under the "separate but equal" doctrine announced in *Plessy v. Ferguson*.]

■ MR. CHIEF JUSTICE WARREN delivered the opinion of the Court.

We come then to the question presented: Does segregation of children in public schools solely on the basis of race, even though the physical facilities and other 'tangible' factors may be equal, deprive the children of the minority group of equal educational opportunities? We believe that it does.

In *Sweatt v. Painter* in finding that a segregated law school for Negroes could not provide them equal educational opportunities, this Court relied in large part on 'those qualities which are incapable of objective measurement but which make for greatness in a law school.' In *McLaurin v. Oklahoma State Regents*, the Court, in requiring that a Negro admitted to a white graduate school be treated like all other students, again resorted to intangible considerations: 'his ability to study, to engage in discussions and exchange views with other students, and, in general, to learn his profession.' Such considerations apply with added force to children in grade and high schools. To separate them from others of similar age and qualifications solely because of their race generates a feeling of inferiority as to their status in the community that may affect their hearts and minds in a way unlikely ever to be undone. The effect of this separation on their educational opportunities was well stated by a finding in the Kansas case by a court which nevertheless felt compelled to rule against the Negro plaintiffs:

> "Segregation of white and colored children in public schools has a detrimental effect upon the colored children. The impact is greater when it has the sanction of the law; for the policy of separating the races is usually interpreted as denoting the inferiority of the negro group. A sense of inferiority affects the motivation of a child to learn. Segregation with the sanction of law, therefore, has a tendency to [retard] the educational and mental development of negro children and to deprive them of some of the benefits they would receive in a racial[ly] integrated school system."

Whatever may have been the extent of psychological knowledge at the time of *Plessy v. Ferguson*, this finding is amply supported by modern authority. Any language in *Plessy v. Ferguson* contrary to this finding is rejected.

We conclude that in the field of public education the doctrine of 'separate but equal' has no place. Separate educational facilities are inherently unequal. Therefore, we hold that the plaintiffs and others similarly situated for whom the actions have been brought are, by reason of the segregation complained of, deprived of the equal protection of the laws guaranteed by the Fourteenth Amendment. This disposition makes unnecessary any discussion whether such segregation also violates the Due Process Clause of the Fourteenth Amendment.

JUSTICE SOUTER'S 2010 HARVARD COMMENCEMENT ADDRESS[12]

Now let me tell a second story, not one illustrating the tensions within constitutional law, but one showing the subtlety of constitutional facts. Again the story is about a famous case, and a good many of us here remember this one, too: *Brown v. Board of Education* from 1954, in which the Supreme Court unanimously held that racial segregation in public schools imposed by law was unconstitutional, as violating the guarantee of equal protection of the law.

Brown ended the era of separate-but-equal, whose paradigm was the decision in 1896 of the case called *Plessy v. Ferguson*, where the Supreme Court had held it was no violation of the equal protection guarantee to require black people to ride in a separate railroad car that was physically equal to the car for whites. One argument offered in *Plessy* was that the separate black car was a badge of inferiority, to which the court majority responded that if black people viewed it that way, the implication was merely a product of their own minds. Sixty years later, *Brown* held that a segregated school required for black children was inherently unequal.

For those whose exclusive norm for constitutional judging is merely fair reading of language applied to facts objectively viewed, *Brown* must either be flat-out wrong or a very mystifying decision. Those who look to that model are not likely to think that a federal court back in 1896 should have declared legally mandated racial segregation unconstitutional. But if *Plessy* was not wrong, how is it that *Brown* came out so differently? The language of the Constitution's guarantee of equal protection of the laws did not change between 1896 and 1954, and it would be hard to say that the obvious facts on which *Plessy* was based had changed, either. While *Plessy* was about railroad cars and *Brown* was about schools, that distinction was no great difference. Actually, the best clue to the difference between the cases is the dates they were decided, which I think lead to the explanation for their divergent results.

As I've said elsewhere, the members of the Court in *Plessy* remembered the day when human slavery was the law in much of the land. To that generation, the formal equality of an identical railroad car meant progress. But the generation in power in 1954 looked at enforced separation without the revolting background of slavery to make it look unexceptional by contrast. As a consequence, the judges of 1954 found a meaning in segregating the races by law that the majority of their predecessors in 1896 did not see. That meaning is not captured by descriptions of physically identical schools or physically identical

---

[12] Justice David H. Souter, Address at Harvard University Commencement (May 27, 2010), http://news.harvard.edu/gazette/story/2010/05/text-of-justice-david-souters-speech/ [https://perma.cc/Z9NF-S34Q].

railroad cars. The meaning of facts arises elsewhere, and its judicial perception turns on the experience of the judges, and on their ability to think from a point of view different from their own. Meaning comes from the capacity to see what is not in some simple, objective sense there on the printed page. And when the judges in 1954 read the record of enforced segregation it carried only one possible meaning: It expressed a judgment of inherent inferiority on the part of the minority race. The judges who understood the meaning that was apparent in 1954 would have violated their oaths to uphold the Constitution if they had not held the segregation mandate unconstitutional.

Again, a rhetorical question. Did the judges of 1954 cross some limit of legitimacy into law making by stating a conclusion that you will not find written in the Constitution? Was it activism to act based on the current meaning of facts that at a purely objective level were about the same as *Plessy's* facts 60 years before? Again, you know my answer. So much for the assumption that facts just lie there waiting for an objective judge to view them.

B. CURRENT ISSUES

Some studies indicate that both civil litigants and criminal defendants have different outcomes depending on the race of the presiding judge. Although these studies are difficult to design given the numerous variables that go into every judicial decision, African-American and Hispanic defendants are generally incarcerated at a higher rate and receive longer sentences than do their white counterparts. African-American judges tend to sentence criminal defendants more uniformly than do their white peers.[13] Similarly, plaintiffs who appeared before African-American judges in racial harassment cases, such as employment discrimination, had a higher success rate than plaintiffs whose cases were presided over by white judges.[14]

At the same time, recent research in neuropsychology has addressed the degree to which decisions makers are influenced by emotional and physical factors, including conscious bias, unconscious bias, and stereotyping.[15] In 2016, the Department of Justice brought the vast majority of federal immigration judges to a training seminar on combatting bias. Judges discussed the difficulty of ignoring race, class, age, and gender in a system with 500,000 pending cases:

---

[13] David S. Abrams, Marianne Bertrand & Sendhil Mullainathan, *Do Judges Vary In Their Treatment of Race?* 41 J. LEGAL STUD. 347, 350 (2012).

[14] Pat K. Chew & Robert E. Kelley, Myth of the Color-Blind Judge: An Empirical Analysis of Racial Harassment Cases, 86 WASH. U. L. REV. 1117, 1121 (2009).

[15] Caitlin Dickerson, *How U.S. Immigration Judges Battle Their Own Prejudice*, N.Y. TIMES (Oct. 4, 2016), http://www.nytimes.com/2016/10/05/us/us-immigration-judges-bias.html [https://perma.cc/LX34-BL7G].

> When the brain has to process large volumes of information quickly, there is a tendency to rely on experiences rather than on unique details in the present. In judging people, for instance, this can mean falling back on generalizations about race, age, country of origin, religion, or gender.[16]

Fisher v. University of Texas at Austin

133 S. Ct. 2411 (2013)

■ JUSTICE KENNEDY delivered the opinion of the Court.

The University of Texas at Austin considers race as one of various factors in its undergraduate admissions process. Race is not itself assigned a numerical value for each applicant, but the University has committed itself to increasing racial minority enrollment on campus. It refers to this goal as a "critical mass." Petitioner, who is Caucasian, sued the University after her application was rejected. She contends that the University's use of race in the admissions process violated the Equal Protection Clause of the Fourteenth Amendment.

The parties asked the Court to review whether the judgment below was consistent with "this Court's decisions interpreting the Equal Protection Clause of the Fourteenth Amendment, including *Grutter v. Bollinger*." The Court concludes that the Court of Appeals did not hold the University to the demanding burden of strict scrutiny articulated in *Grutter* and *Regents of Univ. of Cal. v. Bakke*. . . . [Remanded for reconsideration.]

■ JUSTICE THOMAS, concurring.

I join the Court's opinion because I agree that the Court of Appeals did not apply strict scrutiny to the University of Texas at Austin's (University) use of racial discrimination in admissions decisions. I write separately to explain that I would overrule *Grutter v. Bollinger*, and hold that a State's use of race in higher education admissions decisions is categorically prohibited by the Equal Protection Clause.

III

While I find the theory advanced by the University to justify racial discrimination facially inadequate, I also believe that its use of race has little to do with the alleged educational benefits of diversity. I suspect that the University's program is instead based on the benighted notion that it is possible to tell when discrimination helps, rather than hurts, racial minorities. The worst forms of racial discrimination in this Nation have always been accompanied by straight-faced representations that discrimination helped minorities.

---

[16] *Id.*

A

Slaveholders argued that slavery was a "positive good" that civilized blacks and elevated them in every dimension of life. A century later, segregationists similarly asserted that segregation was not only benign, but good for black students. They argued, for example, that separate schools protected black children from racist white students and teachers. And they even appealed to the fact that many blacks agreed that separate schools were in the "best interests" of both races.

Following in these inauspicious footsteps, the University would have us believe that its discrimination is likewise benign. I think the lesson of history is clear enough: Racial discrimination is never benign. Benign carries with it no independent meaning, but reflects only acceptance of the current generation's conclusion that a politically acceptable burden, imposed on particular citizens on the basis of race, is reasonable. It is for this reason that the Court has repeatedly held that strict scrutiny applies to *all* racial classifications, regardless of whether the government has benevolent motives. The University's professed good intentions cannot excuse its outright racial discrimination any more than such intentions justified the now denounced arguments of slaveholders and segregationists.

B

While it does not, for constitutional purposes, matter whether the University's racial discrimination is benign, I note that racial engineering does in fact have insidious consequences. There can be no doubt that the University's discrimination injures white and Asian applicants who are denied admission because of their race. But I believe the injury to those admitted under the University's discriminatory admissions program is even more harmful.

Blacks and Hispanics admitted to the University as a result of racial discrimination are, on average, far less prepared than their white and Asian classmates. In the University's entering class of 2009, for example, among the students admitted outside the Top Ten Percent plan, blacks scored at the 52d percentile of 2009 SAT takers nationwide, while Asians scored at the 93d percentile. Blacks had a mean GPA of 2.57 and a mean SAT score of 1524; Hispanics had a mean GPA of 2.83 and a mean SAT score of 1794; whites had a mean GPA of 3.04 and a mean SAT score of 1914; and Asians had a mean GPA of 3.07 and a mean SAT score of 1991.

Tellingly, neither the University nor any of the 73 *amici* briefs in support of racial discrimination has presented a shred of evidence that black and Hispanic students are able to close this substantial gap during their time at the University. "It is a fact that in virtually all selective schools . . . where racial preferences in admission is practiced, the majority of [black] students end up in the lower quarter of their class." S. Cole & E. Barber, Increasing Faculty Diversity: The Occupational

Choices of High-Achieving Minority Students 124 (2003). There is no reason to believe this is not the case at the University.

Furthermore, the University's discrimination does nothing to increase the number of blacks and Hispanics who have access to a college education generally. Instead, the University's discrimination has a pervasive shifting effect. The University admits minorities who otherwise would have attended less selective colleges where they would have been more evenly matched. But, as a result of the mismatching, many blacks and Hispanics who likely would have excelled at less elite schools are placed in a position where underperformance is all but inevitable because they are less academically prepared than the white and Asian students with whom they must compete. Setting aside the damage wreaked upon the self-confidence of these overmatched students, there is no evidence that they learn more at the University than they would have learned at other schools for which they were better prepared. Indeed, they may learn less.

Moreover, the University's discrimination stamps blacks and Hispanics with a badge of inferiority. It taints the accomplishments of all those who are admitted as a result of racial discrimination. And, it taints the accomplishments of all those who are the same race as those admitted as a result of racial discrimination. In this case, for example, most blacks and Hispanics attending the University were admitted without discrimination under the Top Ten Percent plan, but no one can distinguish those students from the ones whose race played a role in their admission. The question itself is the stigma—because either racial discrimination did play a role, in which case the person may be deemed 'otherwise unqualified,' or it did not, in which case asking the question itself unfairly marks those who would succeed without discrimination. Although cloaked in good intentions, the University's racial tinkering harms the very people it claims to be helping.

Schuette v. Coalition to Defend Affirmative Action, Integration and Immigrant Rights and Fight for Equality by any Means Necessary (BAMN)

134 S. Ct. 1623 (2014)

[A 2006 amendment to the Michigan Constitution prohibited the state from granting race-based preferences in a variety of actions and decisions including college admissions. The Coalition sued, arguing that the Michigan amendment violated the Equal Protection clause of the Fourteenth Amendment. The Supreme Court held, six to two, that the provision was valid.]

■ JUSTICE KENNEDY announced the judgment of the Court and delivered an opinion, in which THE CHIEF JUSTICE and JUSTICE ALITO join.

The question here concerns not the permissibility of race-conscious admissions policies under the Constitution but whether, and in what manner, voters in the States may choose to prohibit the consideration of racial preferences in governmental decisions, in particular with respect to school admissions.

The respondents in this case insist that a difficult question of public policy must be taken from the reach of the voters, and thus removed from the realm of public discussion, dialogue, and debate in an election campaign. Quite in addition to the serious First Amendment implications of that position with respect to any particular election, it is inconsistent with the underlying premises of a responsible, functioning democracy. One of those premises is that a democracy has the capacity—and the duty—to learn from its past mistakes; to discover and confront persisting biases; and by respectful, rationale deliberation to rise above those flaws and injustices. That process is impeded, not advanced, by court decrees based on the proposition that the public cannot have the requisite repose to discuss certain issues. It is demeaning to the democratic process to presume that the voters are not capable of deciding an issue of this sensitivity on decent and rational grounds. The process of public discourse and political debate should not be foreclosed even if there is a risk that during a public campaign there will be those, on both sides, who seek to use racial division and discord to their own political advantage. An informed public can, and must, rise above this. The idea of democracy is that it can, and must, mature. Freedom embraces the right, indeed the duty, to engage in a rational, civic discourse in order to determine how best to form a consensus to shape the destiny of the Nation and its people. These First Amendment dynamics would be disserved if this Court were to say that the question here at issue is beyond the capacity of the voters to debate and then to determine.

■ [JUSTICES SCALIA, THOMAS, and BREYER concurred.]

■ JUSTICE SOTOMAYOR, with whom JUSTICE GINSBURG joins, dissenting.

We are fortunate to live in a democratic society. But without checks, democratically approved legislation can oppress minority groups. For that reason, our Constitution places limits on what a majority of the people may do. This case implicates one such limit: the guarantee of equal protection of the laws.

[T]o know the history of our Nation is to understand its long and lamentable record of stymieing the right of racial minorities to participate in the political process. At first, the majority acted with an open, invidious purpose. Notwithstanding the command of the Fifteenth Amendment, certain States shut racial minorities out of the political process altogether by withholding the right to vote. This Court intervened to preserve that right. The majority tried again, replacing outright bans on voting with literacy tests, good character requirements, poll taxes, and gerrymandering. The Court was not fooled; it invalidated those measures, too. The majority persisted. This time, although it allowed the minority access to the political process, the majority changed the ground rules of the process so as to make it more difficult for the minority, and the minority alone, to obtain policies designed to foster racial integration. Although these political restructurings may not have been discriminatory in purpose, the Court reaffirmed the right of minority members of our society to participate meaningfully and equally in the political process.

This case involves this last chapter of discrimination: A majority of the Michigan electorate changed the basic rules of the political process in that State in a manner that uniquely disadvantaged racial minorities. Prior to the enactment of the constitutional initiative at issue here, all of the admissions policies of Michigan's public colleges and universities—including race-sensitive admissions policies—were in the hands of each institution's governing board. The members of those boards are nominated by political parties and elected by the citizenry in statewide elections. After over a century of being shut out of Michigan's institutions of higher education, racial minorities in Michigan had succeeded in persuading the elected board representatives to adopt admissions policies that took into account the benefits of racial diversity. And this Court twice blessed such efforts—first in *Regents of Univ. of Cal. v. Bakke*, and again in *Grutter v. Bollinger*, a case that itself concerned a Michigan admissions policy.

As a result of § 26, there are now two very different processes through which a Michigan citizen is permitted to influence the admissions policies of the State's universities: one for persons interested in race-sensitive admissions policies and one for everyone else. A citizen who is a University of Michigan alumnus, for instance, can advocate for an admissions policy that considers an applicant's legacy status by meeting individually with members of the Board of Regents to convince them of her views, by joining with other legacy parents to lobby the Board, or by voting for and supporting Board candidates who share her position. The same options are available to a citizen who wants the Board to adopt admissions policies that consider athleticism, geography, area of study, and so on. The one and only policy a Michigan citizen may not seek through this long-established process is a race-sensitive admissions policy that considers race in an individualized manner when it is clear that race-neutral alternatives are not adequate to achieve diversity.

The plurality's decision fundamentally misunderstands the nature of the injustice worked by § 26. This case is not, as the plurality imagines, about "who may resolve" the debate over the use of race in higher education admissions. I agree wholeheartedly that nothing vests the resolution of that debate exclusively in the courts or requires that we remove it from the reach of the electorate. Rather, this case is about *how* the debate over the use of race-sensitive admissions policies may be resolved, that is, it must be resolved in constitutionally permissible ways. While our Constitution does not guarantee minority groups victory in the political process, it does guarantee them meaningful and equal access to that process.

Like the plurality, I have faith that our citizenry will continue to learn from this Nation's regrettable history; that it will strive to move beyond those injustices towards a future of equality. And I, too, believe in the importance of public discourse on matters of public policy. But I part ways with the plurality when it suggests that judicial intervention in this case "impede[s]" rather than "advance[s]" the democratic process and the ultimate hope of equality. I firmly believe that our role as judges includes policing the process of self-government and stepping in when necessary to secure the constitutional guarantee of equal protection.

My colleagues are of the view that we should leave race out of the picture entirely and let the voters sort it out. We have seen this reasoning before. It is a sentiment out of touch with reality, one not required by our Constitution, and one that has properly been rejected as not sufficient to resolve cases of this nature. While the enduring hope is that race should not matter, the reality is that too often it does. Racial discrimination is not ancient history.

Race matters. Race matters in part because of the long history of racial minorities' being denied access to the political process. Race also matters because of persistent racial inequality in society—inequality that cannot be ignored and that has produced stark socioeconomic disparities. And race matters for reasons that really are only skin deep, that cannot be discussed any other way, and that cannot be wished away. Race matters to a young man's view of society when he spends his teenage years watching others tense up as he passes, no matter the neighborhood where he grew up. Race matters to a young woman's sense of self when she states her hometown, and then is pressed, "No, where are you *really* from?", regardless of how many generations her family has been in the country. Race matters to a young person addressed by a stranger in a foreign language, which he does not understand because only English was spoken at home. Race matters because of the slights, the snickers, the silent judgments that reinforce that most crippling of thoughts: "I do not belong here."

In my colleagues' view, examining the racial impact of legislation only perpetuates racial discrimination. This refusal to accept the stark reality that race matters is regrettable. The way to stop discrimination on the basis of race is to speak openly and candidly on the subject of race, and to apply the Constitution with eyes open to the unfortunate effects of centuries of racial discrimination. As members of the judiciary tasked with intervening to carry out the guarantee of equal protection, we ought not sit back and wish away, rather than confront, the racial inequality that exists in our society. It is this view that works harm, by perpetuating the facile notion that what makes race matter is acknowledging the simple truth that race *does* matter.

NOTES AND QUESTIONS

1. **Not in My Experience.** Several justices, while coming to different conclusions about the constitutionality of affirmative action, use their personal experience in making those decisions. Does that speak to the role race and gender play in the judicial process? To what extent should a judge use his or her personal experience in deciding cases?

2. **When Helping Hurts.** Some observers have argued that well-meaning attempts to address inequality can isolate and marginalize the intended beneficiaries:

> A 2004 empirical study led by Harvard University psychologist James Sidanius (who is African American) concluded that "there was no indication that the experiences in [ ] ethnically oriented . . . organizations increased the students' sense of common identity with members of other groups or their sense of belonging to the wider university community. Furthermore . . . the evidence suggested that membership in ethnically oriented student organizations actually *increased* the perception that ethnic groups are locked into zero-sum competition with one another and the feeling of victimization by virtue of one's ethnicity."[17]

3. **Manufacturing Cases.** Many of the most famous civil rights cases, including *Plessy v. Ferguson*, *Lawrence v. Texas*, and *Brown v. Board of Education*, were "manufactured," or "cultivated" cases. Activists and attorneys sought out "perfect plaintiffs" who had standing to challenge particular laws. While civil rights attorneys perfected this method of challenging discriminatory legislation, it has been used with great effect by conservative activists to successfully challenge affirmative action in a variety of contexts.[18]

4. **Free Speech for Some.** Attempts to silence "hate speech," or even less vituperative opinions such as the "All Lives Matter" movement, abound. Some student activists have sought dismissal of university faculty and administrators who make statements they regard as "microaggressions."[19]

---

[17] Fareed Zakaria, *On College Campuses, Separate Is Still Unequal*, WASH. POST (Nov. 26, 2015), https://www.washingtonpost.com/opinions/on-college-campuses-separate-is-still-unequal/2015/11/26/59e89c04-93b6-11e5-b5e4-279b4501e8a6_story.html?utm_term=.5b293b08b1c2 [https://perma.cc/84D4-V2LX].

[18] Krissah Thompson, *Edward Blum Defies Odds in Getting Cases to Supreme Court*, WASH. POST (Feb. 25, 2013), https://www.washingtonpost.com/lifestyle/style/edward-blum-defies-odds-in-getting-cases-to-supreme-court/2013/02/25/2d6e06ac-7b8e-11e2-a044-676856536b40_story.html [https://perma.cc/2NVE-U7YZ]. *See also* Bush v. Vera, 517 U.S. 952 (1996) (congressional districting), Fisher v. University of Texas at Austin, 133 S. Ct. 2411 (2013) (use of race in college admissions), Shelby County v. Holder, 133 S. Ct. 1236 (2013) (section 5 of the Voting Rights Act).

[19] For example, the Dean of Students at Claremont McKenna College resigned her position after sending an e-mail to one student with the comment that "the college needed to do a better job of serving students who *'don't fit our C.M.C. mold.'* " Ian Lovett, *Dean at Claremont McKenna College Resigns Amid Protests*, N.Y. TIMES (Nov. 12, 2015), http://www.nytimes.com/2015/11/13/

A number of western governments have attempted, over the years, to criminalize certain kinds of speech. Germany criminalized Nazi speech and Holocaust denial. Conversely, the U.K. criminalized boycotts by governmental entities against Israeli settlements. This essential question may be unanswerable: does freedom require tolerance of some degree of intolerance?

§ 12.3 RACIAL EQUALITY IN THE CRIMINAL JUSTICE SYSTEM

McCleskey v. Kemp

481 U.S. 279 (1987)

[Warren McCleskey, a black man, was convicted of killing a white police officer in the course of a robbery. McCleskey argued, based on a statistical study known as "the Baldus study," that the death penalty in Georgia was applied in a racially discriminatory fashion because the imposition of the death penalty in Georgia depended to some extent on the race of the victim and the accused.]

■ JUSTICE POWELL delivered the opinion of the Court.

[Baldus] found that the death penalty was assessed in 22% of the cases involving black defendants and white victims; 8% of the cases involving white defendants and white victims; 1% of the cases involving black defendants and black victims; and 3% of the cases involving white defendants and black victims. Similarly, Baldus found that prosecutors sought the death penalty in 70% of the cases involving black defendants and white victims; 32% of the cases involving white defendants and white victims; 15% of the cases involving black defendants and black victims; and 19% of the cases involving white defendants and black victims.

Baldus subjected his data to an extensive analysis, taking account of 230 variables that could have explained the disparities on nonracial grounds. One of his models concludes that, even after taking account of 39 nonracial variables, defendants charged with killing white victims were 4.3 times as likely to receive a death sentence as defendants charged with killing blacks. According to this model, black defendants were 1.1 times as likely to receive a death sentence as other defendants. Thus, the Baldus study indicates that black defendants, such as McCleskey, who kill white victims have the greatest likelihood of receiving the death penalty.

II

A

Our analysis begins with the basic principle that a defendant who alleges an equal protection violation has the burden of proving the

us/dean-at-claremont-mckenna-college-resigns-amid-protests.html [https://perma.cc/9KGW-AMRK].

existence of purposeful discrimination. A corollary to this principle is that a criminal defendant must prove that the purposeful discrimination had a discriminatory effect on him. Thus, to prevail under the Equal Protection Clause, McCleskey must prove that the decisionmakers in *his* case acted with discriminatory purpose. He offers no evidence specific to his own case that would support an inference that racial considerations played a part in his sentence. The Baldus study is clearly insufficient to support an inference that any of the decisionmakers in McCleskey's case acted with discriminatory purpose.

IV

B

Because of the risk that the factor of race may enter the criminal justice process, we have engaged in unceasing efforts to eradicate racial prejudice from our criminal justice system. [However] McCleskey's argument that the Constitution condemns the discretion allowed decisionmakers in the Georgia capital sentencing system is antithetical to the fundamental role of discretion in our criminal justice system. Discretion in the criminal justice system offers substantial benefits to the criminal defendant. Not only can a jury decline to impose the death sentence, it can decline to convict or choose to convict of a lesser offense. Whereas decisions against a defendant's interest may be reversed by the trial judge or on appeal, these discretionary exercises of leniency are final and unreviewable. Similarly, the capacity of prosecutorial discretion to provide individualized justice is firmly entrenched in American law. As we have noted, a prosecutor can decline to charge, offer a plea bargain, or decline to seek a death sentence in any particular case. Of course, the power to be lenient [also] is the power to discriminate, but a capital punishment system that did not allow for discretionary acts of leniency would be totally alien to our notions of criminal justice.

C

At most, the Baldus study indicates a discrepancy that appears to correlate with race. Apparent disparities in sentencing are an inevitable part of our criminal justice system. The discrepancy indicated by the Baldus study is a far cry from the major systemic defects identified in *Furman* [*v. Georgia*]. As this Court has recognized, any mode for determining guilt or punishment has its weaknesses and the potential for misuse. Specifically, there can be no perfect procedure for deciding in which cases governmental authority should be used to impose death. Despite these imperfections, our consistent rule has been that constitutional guarantees are met when the mode for determining guilt or punishment itself has been surrounded with safeguards to make it as fair as possible. Where the discretion that is fundamental to our criminal process is involved, we decline to assume that what is unexplained is invidious. In light of the safeguards designed to minimize racial bias in the process, the fundamental value of jury trial in our criminal justice system, and the benefits that discretion provides to criminal defendants, we hold that the Baldus study does not demonstrate a constitutionally significant risk of racial bias affecting the Georgia capital sentencing process.

V

Two additional concerns inform our decision in this case. First, McCleskey's claim, taken to its logical conclusion, throws into serious question the principles that underlie our entire criminal justice system. The Eighth Amendment is not limited in application to capital punishment, but applies to all penalties. Thus, if we accepted McCleskey's claim that racial bias has impermissibly tainted the capital sentencing decision, we could soon be faced with similar claims as to other types of penalty.

Second, McCleskey's arguments are best presented to the legislative bodies. It is not the responsibility—or indeed even the right—of this Court to determine the appropriate punishment for particular crimes. It is the legislatures, the elected representatives of the people, that are constituted to respond to the will and consequently the moral values of the people. Legislatures also are better qualified to weigh and evaluate the results of statistical studies in terms of their own local conditions and with a flexibility of approach that is not available to the courts. Capital punishment is now the law in more than two-thirds of our States. It is the ultimate duty of courts to determine on a case-by-case basis whether these laws are applied consistently with the Constitution. Despite McCleskey's wide-ranging arguments that basically challenge the validity of capital punishment in our multiracial society, the only question before us is whether in his case the law of Georgia was properly applied. We agree with the District Court and the Court of Appeals for the Eleventh Circuit that this was carefully and correctly done in this case.

NOTES AND QUESTIONS

1. **Wrong Again.** *McCleskey* has been named one of the worst Supreme Court decisions of the modern era, and has been compared to both *Dred Scott* and *Plessy v. Ferguson*.[20] Are there parallels among the cases?

2. **What's the Alternative?** Did the Supreme Court decide *McCleskey* correctly? Justice Powell wrote the majority opinion in *McCleskey*. After Powell retired, his biographer asked whether, given the chance, Powell would change his vote in any case. "Yes," Justice Powell said. "*McCleskey v. Kemp*."[21] He added that he now found capital punishment itself unworkable

---

[20] *See e.g.*, Scott E. Sundby, *The Loss of Constitutional Faith:* McCleskey v. Kemp *and the Dark Side of Procedure*, 10 OHIO ST. J. CRIM. L. 5, 5 (2012), http://moritzlaw.osu.edu/students/groups/osjcl/files/2012/12/2.-Sundby.pdf [https://perma.cc/KT9C-6QMN]; David G. Savage, *How Did They Get It So Wrong?*, A.B.A.J. (Jan. 1, 2009 6:30 AM), http://www.abajournal.com/magazine/article/how_did_they_get_it_so_wrong [https://perma.cc/DMJ5-D2SD].

[21] *Justice Powell's New Wisdom*, N.Y. TIMES, (June 11, 1994), http://www.nytimes.com/1994/06/11/opinion/justice-powell-s-new-wisdom.html [https://perma.cc/U3Y8-W7J6].

and would vote against it in any case. If *McCleskey* was incorrectly decided, what should the Court have done? Was there was a workable alternative?

3. **Similarly-Situated Parties.** If the Rule of Law means that similarly situated parties are treated similarly, did the Court follow the Rule of Law?

4. **Hide the Evidence.** Georgia prosecutors had obtained the most damaging evidence against McCleskey, his alleged admission that he was the triggerman, from a jailhouse informant who was planted by Atlanta police. The state hid the informant's status for a decade. In 1991, the Supreme Court ruled that McCleskey had waited too long to raise the claim, despite the fact that prosecutors hid the needed evidence.[22] Just prior to McCleskey's execution, two former jurors told the Georgia Board of Pardons and Paroles that their votes to sentence McCleskey to death would have been different had they known the informant was a police plant.[23] Do these facts shed any additional light on the correctness of the Court's decision?

5. **One in Three.** At the beginning of 2016, experts estimated that one in three African-American males will enter state or federal prison at some point in his lifetime.[24] While African-Americans make up only 12 percent of the U.S. population, as of October 2016, they comprise 38 percent of inmates—the second-largest single ethnic group behind bars.[25]

6. **One of Four.** Warren McCleskey was executed by electrocution in Georgia on September 25, 1991. He was the only one of the four co-defendants executed.

Batson v. Kentucky

476 U.S. 79 (1986)

[James Batson, a black man, was convicted by an all-white jury of burglary and receipt of stolen goods. The prosecutor used his peremptory challenges to strike all four black persons on the venire.]

■ JUSTICE POWELL delivered the opinion of the Court.

More than a century ago, the Court decided that the State denies a black defendant equal protection of the laws when it puts him on trial before a jury from which members of his race have been purposefully excluded. That decision laid the foundation for the Court's unceasing efforts to eradicate racial discrimination in the procedures used to select the venire from which individual jurors are drawn. Exclusion of black

---

22 McCleskey v. Zant, 499 U.S. 467, 497–99 (1991).

23 *Warren McCleskey Is Dead*, N.Y. TIMES, (Sept. 29, 1991), http://www.nytimes.com/1991/09/29/opinion/warren-mccleskey-is-dead.html [https://perma.cc/5TDY-9EFY].

24 THE SENTENCING PROJECT, REPORT OF THE SENTENCING PROJECT TO THE UNITED NATIONS HUMAN RIGHTS COMMITTEE: REGARDING RACIAL DISPARITIES IN THE UNITED STATES CRIMINAL JUSTICE SYSTEM 1 (AUG. 2013), http://sentencingproject.org/wp-content/uploads/2015/12/Race-and-Justice-Shadow-Report-ICCPR.pdf [https://perma.cc/5CBS-SLTP].

25 *Statistics: Inmate Race*, FED. BUREAU OF PRISONS, https://www.bop.gov/about/statistics/statistics_inmate_race.jsp (last updated Oct. 29, 2016); George Gao, *Chart of the Week: The Black-White Gap in Incarceration Rates*, PEW RES. CTR. (July 18, 2014), http://www.pewresearch.org/fact-tank/2014/07/18/chart-of-the-week-the-black-white-gap-in-incarceration-rates/ [https://perma.cc/2FEX-3B3M].

citizens from service as jurors constitutes a primary example of the evil the Fourteenth Amendment was designed to cure.

In holding that racial discrimination in jury selection offends the Equal Protection Clause, however, a defendant has no right to a petit jury composed in whole or in part of persons of his own race. But the defendant does have the right to be tried by a jury whose members are selected pursuant to nondiscriminatory criteria.

Purposeful racial discrimination in selection of the venire violates a defendant's right to equal protection because it denies him the protection that a trial by jury is intended to secure. The very idea of a jury is a body . . . composed of the peers or equals of the person whose rights it is selected or summoned to determine; that is, of his neighbors, fellows, associates, persons having the same legal status in society as that which he holds.

Accordingly, the component of the jury selection process at issue here, the State's privilege to strike individual jurors through peremptory challenges, is subject to the commands of the Equal Protection Clause. Although a prosecutor ordinarily is entitled to exercise permitted peremptory challenges for any reason at all, as long as that reason is related to his view concerning the outcome of the case to be tried, the Equal Protection Clause forbids the prosecutor to challenge potential jurors solely on account of their race or on the assumption that black jurors as a group will be unable impartially to consider the State's case against a black defendant.

III

C

A defendant may establish a prima facie case of purposeful discrimination in selection of the petit jury solely on evidence concerning the prosecutor's exercise of peremptory challenges at the defendant's trial. To establish such a case, the defendant first must show that he is a member of a cognizable racial group, and that the prosecutor has exercised peremptory challenges to remove from the venire members of the defendant's race. Second, the defendant is entitled to rely on the fact, as to which there can be no dispute, that peremptory challenges constitute a jury selection practice that permits those to discriminate who are of a mind to discriminate. Finally, the defendant must show that these facts and any other relevant circumstances raise an inference that the prosecutor used that practice to exclude the veniremen from the petit jury on account of their race. This combination of factors in the empaneling of the petit jury, as in the selection of the venire, raises the necessary inference of purposeful discrimination.

Once the defendant makes a prima facie showing, the burden shifts to the State to come forward with a neutral explanation for challenging black jurors. Though this requirement imposes a limitation in some cases on the full peremptory character of the historic challenge, we emphasize that the prosecutor's explanation need not rise to the level justifying exercise of a challenge for cause. But the prosecutor may not rebut the defendant's prima facie case of discrimination by stating merely that he challenged jurors of the defendant's race on the assumption-or his intuitive judgment-that they would be partial to the defendant because of their shared race. Just as the Equal Protection Clause forbids the States to exclude black persons from the venire on the assumption that blacks as a group are unqualified to serve as jurors so it forbids the States to strike black veniremen on the assumption that they will be biased in a particular case simply because the defendant is black. Nor may the prosecutor rebut the defendant's case merely by denying that he had a discriminatory motive or affirming his good faith in making individual selections.

NOTES AND QUESTIONS

1. **Discrimination by Extension.** *Batson* was later extended to peremptory challenges by criminal defendants,[26] peremptory challenges based on gender,[27] and peremptory challenges in civil cases.[28] Is there anything wrong with extending *Batson* to these types of cases?

2. **What if the Prosecution Were Right?** Prosecutors often struck black veniremen—those called for jury service and questioned as potential members of the jury—because they thought a black juror would be less likely to convict a black defendant. In recent years a number of studies have addressed whether certain groups of jurors, including people of color and women, are more or less likely to convict certain defendants. Academics have also studied whether certain groups of jurors are more or less likely to favor certain witnesses. Not surprisingly, studies have found a positive correlation between the race, ethnicity, or gender of a juror and his or her beliefs about the guilt of defendants or the veracity of witnesses. How do these studies affect *Batson*? Should they?

3. **The Real Justice Powell.** Both *McCleskey* and *Batson* were written by Justice Powell. Can the two cases be reconciled?

4. **The Thirty Years' War.** In 2015, the Supreme Court heard the case of *Foster v. Chatman*.[29] Timothy Foster is a black man convicted by an all-white jury of killing an elderly white woman. The prosecution used a combination of challenges for cause and peremptory challenges to dismiss five black veniremen.

After his conviction and death sentence Foster used the open records law to obtain copies of the prosecution's trial notes. The notes show that the prosecution invented race neutral reasons to dismiss the black jurors. The prosecutor's statements in closing also poignantly showed the team's racism. For example, the prosecutor cautioned the jury that "[w]e have got to believe

---

[26] Georgia v. McCollum, 505 U.S. 42 (1992).

[27] J.E.B. v. Alabama ex rel. T.B, 511 U.S. 127 (1994).

[28] Edmonson v. Leesville Concrete Co., 500 U.S. 614 (1991).

[29] 136 S. Ct. 1737 (2016).

that if you send somebody to death, that you deter other people out there in the projects from doing the same again."[30]

In a seven-to-one decision authored by Justice Roberts, the Court held that Foster established that the prosecutor purposefully discriminated when it dismissed two of the jurors. The only dissent came from Justice Thomas.

The murder in *Foster* occurred the same year that *Batson* was decided, so it is not remarkable that prosecutors were using peremptory challenges impermissibly. What is remarkable is that they were still defending it 30 years later.

5. **What About My Rights?** Does the prosecutor have a right to a fair trial? Litigants have historically been able to use peremptory challenges for any reason, or no reason at all. Is there a way to balance the constitutional rights of the defendant with the prosecution's "right" to use peremptory challenges?

6. **Canary in a Coal Mine.** In 2016, the Court addressed the issue of race in the Fourth Amendment context. Edward Strieff, a white man, was stopped and detained after exiting a suspected drug house. Although the officer lacked probable cause, he stopped and detained Strieff, ran a warrants check, found an outstanding small traffic warrant, and then discovered methamphetamine and a drug pipe during a search incident to arrest. The Court held that the evidence was admissible, despite the Fourth Amendment violation, because the warrant sufficiently attenuated the illegal conduct from the arrest.

Justice Thomas, writing for the majority, thought it was "unlikely" that officers would take advantage of the large number of outstanding warrants in poor and minority communities and conduct dragnet searches without probable cause, essentially banking that they would find an outstanding warrant.[31]

Justice Sotomayor, in a strongly worded dissent, disagreed. Writing "only for myself, and drawing on my professional experiences," she noted:

> For generations, black and brown parents have given their children "the talk"—instructing them never to run down the street; always keep your hands where they can be seen; do not even think of talking back to a stranger—all out of fear of how an officer with a gun will react to them.
>
> By legitimizing the conduct that produces this double consciousness, this case tells everyone, white and black, guilty and innocent, that an officer can verify your legal status at any time. It says that your body is subject to invasion while courts excuse the violation of your rights. It implies that you are not a citizen of a democracy but the subject of a carceral state, just waiting to be cataloged.

---

[30] Petition for Writ of Certiorari at 22, Foster v. Chatman, 136 S. Ct. 290 (2015) (No. 14–8349), 2015 WL 2457657 at * 22.

[31] Utah v. Strieff, 136 S. Ct. 2056 (2016).

> We must not pretend that the countless people who are routinely targeted by police are "isolated." They are the canaries in the coal mine whose deaths, civil and literal, warn us that no one can breathe in this atmosphere. They are the ones who recognize that unlawful police stops corrode all our civil liberties and threaten all our lives. Until their voices matter too, our justice system will continue to be anything but.[32]

§ 12.4 GENDER EQUALITY ON THE BENCH

The first woman to act as an attorney in the newly-formed North American colonies was Margaret Brent.[33] After arriving in "the New World" in 1638, she received a land grant, became executrix for Governor Leonard Calvert of Maryland, and was appointed attorney-in-fact for Lord Baltimore. She appeared before the provincial court in suits against her own debtors and as an attorney for Lord Baltimore.[34]

In 1869, Iowa became the first state to admit women to the Bar after Arabella Mansfield challenged a state statute that excluded her.[35] The first African-American woman licensed to practice law, Charlotte E. Ray, was admitted to the District of Columbia Bar in 1872 after she applied under the name C. E. Ray. The admissions committee thought the Howard University graduate was male.[36]

By the 1870s, lawyers around the country were forming professional state-based bar associations. These associations mimicked the ancient "guild" system, and were designed to organize, professionalize, and influence the legal profession. While a few women graduated from law school and were admitted to state bar associations in the late 19th century, many others found themselves barred from both.

Bradwell v. Illinois

83 U.S. 130 (1872)

[An Illinois statute required that attorneys be licensed to practice law. Myra Bradwell qualified for a license, but her application was denied. The State of Illinois justified the decision on the grounds that Bradwell would be unable to practice law because, as a married woman, she was not allowed to enter into any contracts—including the implied contract between attorney and client. She appealed, arguing that the denial

---

[32] *Id.* at 2070–71.

[33] Lois Green Carr, *Margaret Brent (ca. 1601–1671)*, MD. ST. ARCHIVES, http://msa.maryland.gov/megafile/msa/speccol/sc3500/sc3520/002100/002177/html/bio.html [https://perma.cc/44WK-KJ9G] (last visited Oct. 9, 2016).

[34] *Id.*

[35] *Women Lawyer "Firsts"*, NAT'L CONF. OF WOMEN'S BAR ASS'NS, http://ncwba.org/history/women-lawyer-firsts/ [https://perma.cc/KD44-NEYD] (last visited Oct. 9, 2016).

[36] *Women Lawyers and State Bar Admission*, LIBR. OF CONGRESS, https://memory.loc.gov/ammem/awhhtml/awlaw3/women_lawyers.html [https://perma.cc/SKW9-RGZF] (last visited Oct. 9, 2016).

violated both the privileges and immunities clause and the Fourteenth Amendment. The Supreme Court held that the privileges and immunities clause only guarantees privileges and immunities to citizens of other states, the right to practice law in the state courts is not a privilege or immunity of a citizen of the United States, and the "power of a State to prescribe the qualifications for admission to the bar of its own courts is unaffected by the fourteenth amendment, and this court cannot inquire into the reasonableness or propriety of the rules it may prescribe."]

■ MR. JUSTICE BRADLEY:

I concur in the judgment of the court in this case, by which the judgment of the Supreme Court of Illinois is affirmed, but not for the reasons specified in the opinion just read.

It certainly cannot be affirmed, as an historical fact, that [the practice of law] has ever been established as one of the fundamental privileges and immunities of the sex. On the contrary, the civil law, as well as nature herself, has always recognized a wide difference in the respective spheres and destinies of man and woman. Man is, or should be, woman's protector and defender. The natural and proper timidity and delicacy which belongs to the female sex evidently unfits it for many of the occupations of civil life. The constitution of the family organization, which is founded in the divine ordinance, as well as in the nature of things, indicates the domestic sphere as that which properly belongs to the domain and functions of womanhood. The harmony, not to say identity, of interest and views which belong, or should belong, to the family institution is repugnant to the idea of a woman adopting a distinct and independent career from that of her husband. So firmly fixed was this sentiment in the founders of the common law that it became a maxim of that system of jurisprudence that a woman had no legal existence separate from her husband, who was regarded as her head and representative in the social state; and, notwithstanding some recent modifications of this civil status, many of the special rules of law flowing from and dependent upon this cardinal principle still exist in full force in most States. One of these is, that a married woman is incapable, without her husband's consent, of making contracts which shall be binding on her or him. This very incapacity was one circumstance which the Supreme Court of Illinois deemed important in rendering a married woman incompetent fully to perform the duties and trusts that belong to the office of an attorney and counsellor.

It is true that many women are unmarried and not affected by any of the duties, complications, and incapacities arising out of the married state, but these are exceptions to the general rule. The paramount destiny and mission of woman are to fulfil the noble and benign offices of wife and mother. This is the law of the Creator. And the rules of civil society must be adapted to the general constitution of things, and cannot be based upon exceptional cases.

NOTES AND QUESTIONS

Finally. In 1890, the Illinois Supreme Court, acting on its own motion, approved Bradwell's original application for a license to practice law.[37]

A smattering of women were appointed to state benches in the late 19th and early 20th centuries. The first female judge on the federal bench was appointed in 1928.[38] Today, approximately one-third of the active Article III judges are women. Likewise, one-third of all state court judges in the United States are women.[39] However, women are not equally represented in all courts. There are still six district courts around the country where there has never been a female judge.

A number of scholars have studied whether the gender of a judge makes a difference in the outcome of a case. The results have varied, perhaps in part, because of the difficulty in designing such studies. Many studies looked at gender, race, ideology, and political affiliation together. However, several studies have found that female judges are more likely to favor plaintiffs in sexual harassment and discrimination cases.[40]

In the 1980s and 1990s, the majority of state courts undertook systematic studies of gender bias in the courts.[41] By 1996, at least 35 reports detailed problems that had largely gone undetected.[42] Many of these studies recommended a variety of improvements, including helping mothers in divorce proceedings receive higher child support awards,[43] dealing more aggressively with domestic violence, and increasing the roles of women in the court system itself.

Some also included guidelines designed to encourage equal access to the courts and appropriate decorum. Some states included requirements in their judicial codes of conduct providing that judges shall not, by "word or conduct

---

[37] Julie A. Neubauer, *Why Celebrate Women in the Profession?*, CATALYST, Feb. 2014, https://www.isba.org/committees/women/newsletter/2014/02/whycelebratewomenintheprofession [https://perma.cc/764F-FX48].

[38] *Women as 'Way Pavers' in the Federal Judiciary*, ADMIN. OFF. OF THE U.S. COURTS (Feb. 26, 2015), http://www.uscourts.gov/news/2015/02/26/women-way-pavers-federal-judiciary [https://perma.cc/FRX7-D5AN].

[39] COMM'N ON WOMEN IN THE PROFESSION, A.B.A., A CURRENT GLANCE AT WOMEN IN THE LAW 5 (May 2016), http://www.americanbar.org/content/dam/aba/marketing/women/current_glance_statistics_may2016.authcheckdam.pdf [https://perma.cc/RWZ4-LA5P].

[40] Jennifer L. Peresie, Note, *Female Judges Matter: Gender and Collegial Decisionmaking in the Federal Appellate Courts*, 114 YALE L.J. 1759, 1761 (2005).

[41] For a summary, see *Gender and Racial Fairness Resource Guide*, NAT'L CTR. ST. CTS., http://www.ncsc.org/Topics/Access-and-Fairness/Gender-and-Racial-Fairness/Resource-Guide.aspx [https://perma.cc/UP9R-AELN] (last visited Oct. 9, 2016).

[42] *See* Judith Resnik, *Asking About Gender in Courts*, 21 SIGNS: J. OF WOMEN IN CULTURE AND SOC'Y 952 (1996); Jeannette F. Swent, *Gender Bias at the Heart of Justice: an Empirical Study Of State Task Forces*, 6 S. CAL. REV. L. & WOMEN'S STUD. 1, 6 (1996).

[43] One rather unexpected result of these studies was an increased movement for "Fairness to Dads," challenging perceptions that mothers received unduly generous treatment in custody disputes and in alimony settlements.

manifest bias or prejudice" based on sex.[44] In 1996, California issued guidelines to judges reminding them to "treat all court staff, litigants, witnesses and attorneys with courtesy and dignity regardless of their sex, race or any other characteristic."[45] The guidelines were fairly simple: address both attorneys and witnesses by their title and last name; refrain from referring to female attorneys, law clerks, secretaries, and courtroom deputies as "young lady," "girls," "little girl," or "office help"; and avoid sexually suggestive jokes or commentary.

Despite significant improvement, gender bias is still readily apparent in courts and law firms. Clarence Darrow famously told a group of women lawyers,

> You can't be shining lights at the Bar because you are too kind. You can never be corporation lawyers because you are not cold-blooded. You have not a high grade of intellect. You can never expect to get the fees men get. I doubt you could ever make a living.[46]

Today it is still not unusual for female attorneys to be criticized for being "too hard" or "too soft."[47] Their clothing is often criticized for being too masculine or too "sexy," as in federal district court judge Richard Kopf's 2014 blog post titled, *On being a dirty old man and how young women lawyers dress*.[48] Salaries for female attorneys are approximately 20 percent lower than the salaries of male attorneys, even at the equity partner level.[49] Women also leave the legal profession at a higher rate.

§ 12.5 GENDER EQUALITY IN THE CIVIL SYSTEM

In March of 1776, Abigail Adams wrote to her husband John about the new laws that would be created by the Continental Congress:

> I long to hear that you have declared an independency. And, by the way, in the new code of laws which I suppose it will be necessary for you to make, I desire you would remember the ladies and be more generous and favorable to them than your ancestors. Do not put such unlimited power into the hands of

---

[44] CAL. CODE OF JUDICIAL ETHICS Canon 3B(5) (1996). See also *The Effects of Gender In the Federal Courts: The Final Report of the Ninth Circuit Gender Bias Task Force*, 67 S. CAL. L. REV. 745, 959 (1994) ("Judges set the tone and establish the norms of proper behavior . . . Judges can lead by example and by using their authority and influence to ensure that the . . . courts offer truly equal access to men and women judges, lawyers, employees, and litigants.")

[45] JUDICIAL COUNCIL ADVISORY COMM. ON ACCESS AND FAIRNESS & ORANGE CTY. BAR ASS'N GENDER EQUITY COMM., GENDER BIAS: GUIDELINES FOR JUDICIAL OFFICERS AVOIDING THE APPEARANCE OF BIAS 10 (Aug. 1996), http://www.courts.ca.gov/documents/genderb.pdf [https://perma.cc/7V25-S3BN].

[46] Beatrice Dinerman, *Sex Discrimination in the Legal Profession*, 55 A.B.A.J. 951, (1969) (citations omitted).

[47] Estate of Vermont v. Forte, 624 A.2d 352, 562–65 (1993) (Morse, J., dissenting) (criticizing the trial court's description of female prosecutor as too "emotionally involved" and "a fury seldom seen this side of hell.").

[48] Judge Richard Kopf, *On Being a Dirty Old Man and How Young Women Lawyers Dress*, HERCULES AND THE UMPIRE (March 25, 2014), https://wednesdaywiththedecentlyprofane.me/2014/03/25/on-being-a-dirty-old-man-and-how-young-women-lawyers-dress/ [https://perma.cc/S8PD-FEVR].

[49] Comm'n on Women in the Profession, A.B.A, *supra* note 29, at 6.

> the husbands. Remember, all men would be tyrants if they could. If particular care and attention is not paid to the ladies, we are determined to foment a rebellion, and will not hold ourselves bound by any laws in which we have no voice or representation.[50]

The future president replied, "As to your extraordinary Code of Laws, I cannot but laugh. We have been told that our Struggle has loosened the bands of Government every where. . . . Depend upon it, We know better than to repeal our Masculine systems."[51]

Reed v. Reed

404 U.S. 71 (1971)

[Idaho's Probate Code required that courts prefer males over females when appointing estate administrators. Sally and Cecil Reed, who were married but separated, both applied to be administrators of their son's estate. Cecil Reed was appointed because he was male, and Sally Reed appealed, arguing that the statute violated the equal protection clause of the Fourteenth Amendment.]

■ MR. CHIEF JUSTICE BURGER delivered the opinion for a unanimous Court.

In applying [the Equal Protection] clause, this Court has consistently recognized that the Fourteenth Amendment does not deny to States the power to treat different classes of persons in different ways. The Equal Protection Clause of that amendment does, however, deny to States the power to legislate that different treatment be accorded to persons placed by a statute into different classes on the basis of criteria wholly unrelated to the objective of that statute. A classification must be reasonable, not arbitrary, and must rest upon some ground of difference having a fair and substantial relation to the object of the legislation, so that all persons similarly circumstanced shall be treated alike. The question presented by this case, then, is whether a difference in the sex of competing applicants for letters of administration bears a rational relationship to a state objective that is sought to be advanced by the operation of §§ 15–312 and 15–314.

In upholding the latter section, the Idaho Supreme Court concluded that its objective was to eliminate one area of controversy when two or more persons, equally entitled under § 15–312, seek letters of administration and thereby present the probate court 'with the issue of which one should be named.' The court also concluded that where such persons are not of the same sex, the elimination of females from consideration 'is neither an illogical nor arbitrary method devised by the

---

[50] Letter from Abigail Adams to John Adams, (Mar. 31, 1776), https://www.masshist.org/digitaladams/archive/doc?id=L17760331aa [https://perma.cc/A9BP-VW8U].

[51] Letter from John Adams to Abigail Adams, (Apr. 14, 1776), https://www.masshist.org/digitaladams/archive/doc?id=L17760414ja [https://perma.cc/SK3V-R3KT].

legislature to resolve an issue that would otherwise require a hearing as to the relative merits * * * of the two or more petitioning relatives * * *.'

Clearly the objective of reducing the workload on probate courts by eliminating one class of contests is not without some legitimacy. The crucial question, however, is whether § 15–314 advances that objective in a manner consistent with the command of the Equal Protection Clause. We hold that it does not. To give a mandatory preference to members of either sex over members of the other, merely to accomplish the elimination of hearings on the merits, is to make the very kind of arbitrary legislative choice forbidden by the Equal Protection Clause of the Fourteenth Amendment; and whatever may be said as to the positive values of avoiding intrafamily controversy, the choice in this context may not lawfully be mandated solely on the basis of sex.

We note finally that if § 15–314 is viewed merely as a modifying appendage to § 15–312 and as aimed at the same objective, its constitutionality is not thereby saved. The objective of § 15–312 clearly is to establish degrees of entitlement of various classes of persons in accordance with their varying degrees and kinds of relationship to the intestate. Regardless of their sex, persons within any one of the enumerated classes of that section are similarly situated with respect to that objective. By providing dissimilar treatment for men and women who are thus similarly situated, the challenged section violates the Equal Protection Clause.

NOTES AND QUESTIONS

1. America's "Long and Unfortunate History of Sex Discrimination." *Reed v. Reed* applied rational basis scrutiny to the Idaho Probate Code. In the years after *Reed*, the Court struggled to decide the appropriate level of scrutiny to give gender classifications.

A plurality of the Court first applied intermediate scrutiny in *Frontiero v. Richardson*.[52] The plurality, addressing a statute that provided benefits to wives of service members but not husbands, argued for a strict standard of judicial scrutiny for gender classifications due to America's "long and unfortunate history of sex discrimination."

Various members of the court objected to further subdivision of standards of review, concluded that the cases could be resolved under rational basis review, or thought it would be more appropriate to wait to decide the issue until the Equal Rights Amendment was considered by the states.

The issue was resolved in *Craig v. Boren*,[53] although not without dissent. A five-member majority of the Court applied an intermediate standard of review to a statute that allowed women to purchase 3.2 percent alcoholic beverages at age 18, but required men to wait until age 21.

---

[52] 411 U.S. 677 (1973).

[53] 429 U.S. 190 (1976).

2. **Equality of Rights Under the Law.** In 1972, Congress passed the Equal Rights Amendment (ERA). The ERA provided quite simply that "[e]quality of rights under the law shall not be denied or abridged by the United States or by any state on account of sex."[54] Although quickly passed by Congress, it faced opposition from business groups, conservative religious groups, and organizations such as the Eagle Forum. Despite receiving an extension from Congress, the ERA was only ratified by 35 of the necessary 38 states prior to the 1982 deadline.

3. **Men Can Be Nurses, Too.** That same year, in *Mississippi University for Women v. Hogan*,[55] the Court addressed a university policy that denied men admission to nursing school. Applying intermediate scrutiny, it held that denying otherwise qualified males the right to enroll in a baccalaureate nursing program violated the Equal Protection Clause. It made no difference to the standard of review or the outcome that the statute discriminated against men instead of women.

The University argued that its policy constituted educational affirmative action for women. The Court, however, was unpersuaded given that women have not traditionally lacked opportunities in the nursing field. Further, the Court, in an opinion authored by the Court's first female justice, concluded that the statute "tends to perpetuate the stereotyped view of nursing as an exclusively women's job."[56]

Should the Court apply the same heightened scrutiny to gender classifications that discriminate against men, rather than women?

4. **But Can Women Sell Lawnmowers?** Despite the holding in *Mississippi University for Women v. Hogan*, parties continued to argue that women should be excluded from certain jobs because their gender made them less-interested in, or fit for, the position. One long-running Title VII case challenged Sears Roebuck's decision to exclude most women from commission jobs. Sears presented testimony that women applicants tended to be less interested in commission roles, and goods sold on commission were "big-ticket" items such as appliances, roofing, and furnaces, with which women tended to be less experienced. Sears argued that many women preferred "non-commission selling because it was more enjoyable and friendly."[57]

EEOC v. Sears, Roebuck & Co. raised the same issue that appears next in *United States v. Virginia*: should women demand modifications to job descriptions, or should they accept the requirements of competition?

The issue sharply divided feminists, two of whom testified on opposite sides as experts. That debate spilled over into issues of maternity care and family leave. It continues today in both politics and popular culture.

---

[54] Equal Rights Amendment § 1 (1972) (proposed as an amendment but never ratified).

[55] 458 U.S. 718 (1982).

[56] *Id.* at 729.

[57] EEOC v. Sears, Roebuck & Co., 628 F. Supp. 1264, 1307 (N.D. Ill. 1986).

United States v. Virginia

518 U.S. 515 (1996)

[Founded in 1839, the Virginia Military Institute (VMI) was Virginia's only exclusively male public undergraduate institution. The United States sued the state of Virginia, alleging that the male-only admissions policy violated the Equal Protection Clause. In response, the state created the Virginia Women's Institute for Leadership (VWIL). It argued that this parallel women's program offered "substantively comparable" educational benefits.]

■ JUSTICE GINSBURG delivered the opinion of the Court.

Virginia's public institutions of higher learning include an incomparable military college, Virginia Military Institute (VMI). The United States maintains that the Constitution's equal protection guarantee precludes Virginia from reserving exclusively to men the unique educational opportunities VMI affords. We agree.

Founded in 1839, VMI is today the sole single-sex school among Virginia's 15 public institutions of higher learning. VMI's distinctive mission is to produce "citizen-soldiers," men prepared for leadership in civilian life and in military service. VMI pursues this mission through pervasive training of a kind not available anywhere else in Virginia. Assigning prime place to character development, VMI uses an "adversative method" modeled on English public schools and once characteristic of military instruction. VMI constantly endeavors to instill physical and mental discipline in its cadets and impart to them a strong moral code. The school's graduates leave VMI with heightened comprehension of their capacity to deal with duress and stress, and a large sense of accomplishment for completing the hazardous course.

VMI has notably succeeded in its mission to produce leaders; among its alumni are military generals, Members of Congress, and business executives. The school's alumni overwhelmingly perceive that their VMI training helped them to realize their personal goals. VMI's endowment reflects the loyalty of its graduates; VMI has the largest per-student endowment of all public undergraduate institutions in the Nation.

Neither the goal of producing citizen-soldiers nor VMI's implementing methodology is inherently unsuitable to women. And the school's impressive record in producing leaders has made admission desirable to some women. Nevertheless, Virginia has elected to preserve exclusively for men the advantages and opportunities a VMI education affords.

IV

We note, once again, the core instruction of this Court's pathmarking decisions in *J.E.B. v. Alabama ex rel. T. B.* and *Mississippi Univ. for Women*: Parties who seek to defend gender-based government action must demonstrate an "exceedingly persuasive justification" for that action.

Today's skeptical scrutiny of official action denying rights or opportunities based on sex responds to volumes of history. As a plurality of this Court acknowledged a generation ago, "our Nation has had a long and unfortunate history of sex discrimination." *Frontiero v. Richardson.* Through a century plus three decades and more of that history, women did not count among voters composing "We the People";[5] not until 1920 did women gain a constitutional right to the franchise. And for a half century thereafter, it remained the prevailing doctrine that government, both federal and state, could withhold from women opportunities accorded men so long as any "basis in reason" could be conceived for the discrimination.

In 1971, for the first time in our Nation's history, this Court ruled in favor of a woman who complained that her State had denied her the equal protection of its laws. Since *Reed* [*v. Reed*], the Court has repeatedly recognized that neither federal nor state government acts compatibly with the equal protection principle when a law or official policy denies to women, simply because they are women, full citizenship stature—equal opportunity to aspire, achieve, participate in and contribute to society based on their individual talents and capacities.

A

Single-sex education affords pedagogical benefits to at least some students, Virginia emphasizes, and that reality is uncontested in this litigation. Similarly, it is not disputed that diversity among public educational institutions can serve the public good. But Virginia has not shown that VMI was established, or has been maintained, with a view to diversifying, by its categorical exclusion of women, educational opportunities within the Commonwealth. In cases of this genre, our precedent instructs that "benign" justifications proffered in defense of categorical exclusions will not be accepted automatically; a tenable justification must describe actual state purposes, not rationalizations for actions in fact differently grounded.

B

Virginia argues that VMI's adversative method of training provides educational benefits that cannot be made available, unmodified, to women. Alterations to accommodate women would necessarily be "radical," so "drastic," Virginia asserts, as to transform, indeed "destroy,"

[5] As Thomas Jefferson stated the view prevailing when the Constitution was new: "Were our State a pure democracy . . . there would yet be excluded from their deliberations . . . [w]omen, who, to prevent depravation of morals and ambiguity of issue, could not mix promiscuously in the public meetings of men." "Were our State a pure democracy . . . there would yet be excluded from their deliberations . . . [w]omen, who, to prevent depravation of morals and ambiguity of issue, could not mix promiscuously in the public meetings of men." Letter from Thomas Jefferson to Samuel Kercheval (Sept. 5, 1816), in 10 Writings of Thomas Jefferson 45–46, n. 1 (P. Ford ed. 1899).

VMI's program. Neither sex would be favored by the transformation, Virginia maintains: Men would be deprived of the unique opportunity currently available to them; women would not gain that opportunity because their participation would "eliminat[e] the very aspects of [the] program that distinguish [VMI] from . . . other institutions of higher education in Virginia."

The District Court forecast from expert witness testimony, and the Court of Appeals accepted, that coeducation would materially affect "at least these three aspects of VMI's program—physical training, the absence of privacy, and the adversative approach." And it is uncontested that women's admission would require accommodations, primarily in arranging housing assignments and physical training programs for female cadets. It is also undisputed, however, that "the VMI methodology could be used to educate women." The District Court even allowed that some women may prefer it to the methodology a women's college might pursue. "[S]ome women, at least, would want to attend [VMI] if they had the opportunity," the District Court recognized, and "some women," the expert testimony established, "are capable of all of the individual activities required of VMI cadets." The parties, furthermore, agree that "some women can meet the physical standards [VMI] now impose[s] on men." In sum, as the Court of Appeals stated, "neither the goal of producing citizen soldiers," VMI's raison d'être, "nor VMI's implementing methodology is inherently unsuitable to women."

It may be assumed, for purposes of this decision, that most women would not choose VMI's adversative method. As Fourth Circuit Judge Motz observed, however, in her dissent from the Court of Appeals' denial of rehearing en banc, it is also probable that "many men would not want to be educated in such an environment." (On that point, even our dissenting colleague might agree.) Education, to be sure, is not a "one size fits all" business. The issue, however, is not whether "women—or men—should be forced to attend VMI"; rather, the question is whether the Commonwealth can constitutionally deny to women who have the will and capacity, the training and attendant opportunities that VMI uniquely affords.

The notion that admission of women would downgrade VMI's stature, destroy the adversative system and, with it, even the school, is a judgment hardly proved, a prediction hardly different from other self-fulfilling prophecies, once routinely used to deny rights or opportunities.

VI

In the second phase of the litigation, Virginia presented its remedial plan—maintain VMI as a male-only college and create VWIL as a separate program for women.

A

A remedial decree, this Court has said, must closely fit the constitutional violation; it must be shaped to place persons unconstitutionally denied an opportunity or advantage in the position they would have occupied in the absence of discrimination. The constitutional violation in this suit is the categorical exclusion of women from an extraordinary educational opportunity afforded men. A proper remedy for an unconstitutional exclusion, we have explained, aims to eliminate so far as possible the discriminatory effects of the past and to bar like discrimination in the future.

Virginia chose not to eliminate, but to leave untouched, VMI's exclusionary policy. For women only, however, Virginia proposed a separate program, different in kind from VMI and unequal in tangible and intangible facilities. Having violated the Constitution's equal protection requirement, Virginia was obliged to show that its remedial proposal directly addressed and related to the violation,

VWIL affords women no opportunity to experience the rigorous military training for which VMI is famed. Instead, the VWIL program deemphasizes military education, and uses a "cooperative method" of education "which reinforces self-esteem." Virginia deliberately did not make VWIL a military institute.

Virginia maintains that these methodological differences are "justified pedagogically," based on "important differences between men and women in learning and developmental needs," "psychological and sociological differences" Virginia describes as "real" and "not stereotypes." The Task Force charged with developing the leadership program for women, drawn from the staff and faculty at Mary Baldwin College, determined that a military model and, especially VMI's adversative method, would be wholly inappropriate for educating and training most women.

As earlier stated, generalizations about "the way women are," estimates of what is appropriate for most women, no longer justify denying opportunity to women whose talent and capacity place them outside the average description.

VII

A prime part of the history of our Constitution, historian Richard Morris recounted, is the story of the extension of constitutional rights and protections to people once ignored or excluded. VMI's story continued as our comprehension of "We the People" expanded. There is no reason to believe that the admission of women capable of all the activities required of VMI cadets would destroy the Institute rather than enhance its capacity to serve the "more perfect Union."

■ JUSTICE SCALIA, dissenting.

Today the Court shuts down an institution that has served the people of the Commonwealth of Virginia with pride and distinction for over a century and a half. To achieve that desired result, it rejects (contrary to our established practice) the factual findings of two courts below, sweeps aside the precedents of this Court, and ignores the history of our people. As to facts: It explicitly rejects the finding that there exist "gender-based developmental differences" supporting Virginia's restriction of the "adversative" method to only a men's institution, and the finding that the all-male composition of the Virginia Military Institute (VMI) is essential to that institution's character. As to precedent: It drastically revises our established standards for reviewing sex-based classifications. And as to history: It counts for nothing the long tradition, enduring down to the present, of men's military colleges supported by both States and the Federal Government.

Much of the Court's opinion is devoted to deprecating the closed-mindedness of our forebears with regard to women's education, and even with regard to the treatment of women in areas that have nothing to do with education. Closed-minded they were—as every age is, including our own, with regard to matters it cannot guess, because it simply does not consider them debatable. The virtue of a democratic system with a First Amendment is that it readily enables the people, over time, to be persuaded that what they took for granted is not so, and to change their laws accordingly. That system is destroyed if the smug assurances of each age are removed from the democratic process and written into the Constitution. So to counterbalance the Court's criticism of our ancestors, let me say a word in their praise: They left us free to change. The same cannot be said of this most illiberal Court, which has embarked on a course of inscribing one after another of the current preferences of the society (and in some cases only the counter-majoritarian preferences of the society's law-trained elite) into our Basic Law. Today it enshrines the notion that no substantial educational value is to be served by an all-men's military academy—so that the decision by the people of Virginia to maintain such an institution denies equal protection to women who cannot attend that institution but can attend others. Since it is entirely clear that the Constitution of the United States—the old one—takes no sides in this educational debate, I dissent.

The all-male constitution of VMI comes squarely within a governing tradition. Founded by the Commonwealth of Virginia in 1839 and continuously maintained by it since, VMI has always admitted only men. And in that regard it has not been unusual. For almost all of VMI's more than a century and a half of existence, its single-sex status reflected the uniform practice for government-supported military colleges. Another famous Southern institution, The Citadel, has existed as a state-funded school of South Carolina since 1842. And all the federal military colleges—West Point, the Naval Academy at Annapolis, and even the Air Force Academy, which was not established until 1954—admitted only males for most of their history. Their admission of women in 1976 (upon which the Court today relies) came not by court decree, but because the people, through their elected representatives, decreed a change. In other words, the tradition of having government-funded military schools for men is as well rooted in the traditions of this country as the tradition of sending only men into military combat. The people may decide to change the one tradition, like the other, through democratic processes; but the assertion that either tradition has been unconstitutional through the centuries is not law, but politics-smuggled-into-law.

Today, however, change is forced upon Virginia, and reversion to single-sex education is prohibited nationwide, not by democratic processes but by order of this Court. Even while bemoaning the sorry, bygone days of "fixed notions" concerning women's education, the Court favors current notions so fixedly that it is willing to write them into the Constitution of the United States by application of custom-built "tests." This is not the interpretation of a Constitution, but the creation of one.

NOTES AND QUESTIONS

1. **Modify or Adapt?** The first women graduated from VMI in 2001. Although VMI originally held women cadets to the same physical requirements and training as male cadets, in 2008, VMI adopted "gender-normed" training standards.

2. **Protecting the Peremptory Challenge.** *J.E.B. v. Alabama ex rel. T.B.*, referenced in *United States v. Virginia*, was a paternity and child support suit brought by the state of Alabama against a putative father. Alabama used its challenges to strike nine of ten men from the jury. The father used all but one of his strikes to remove female jurors. All the selected jurors were female. Somewhat ironically, the father then appealed the case on the grounds that the state's use of peremptory challenges to strike male jurors was a violation of the Equal Protection clause.

The Court agreed and extended *Batson v. Kentucky*[58] to gender-based peremptory challenges. It held that "[i]ntentional discrimination on the basis of gender by state actors violates the Equal Protection Clause, particularly where, as here, the discrimination serves to ratify and perpetuate invidious, archaic, and overbroad stereotypes about the relative abilities of men and women."[59] Much of the Court's analysis was based on historical discrimination against women in the jury selection process.

3. **Keep the Legislation Coming.** The Civil Rights Act also changed the face of gender equality. The 1964 civil rights legislation outlawed discrimination based on race, color, religion, sex, or national origin. It eliminated unequal application of voter registration requirements, racial segregation in public accommodations and public facilities, and employment discrimination. It was further supplemented by the Pregnancy Discrimination Act of 1978[60] and Title IX of the Education Amendments Act of 1972.[61] The latter prohibits sex discrimination in federally funded education programs and activities.

---

[58] 476 U.S. 79 (1986).

[59] *J.E.B.* v. Alabama ex rel. T.B., 511 U.S. 127, 131 (1994).

[60] 42 U.S.C. §§ 2000e et seq.

[61] 20 U.S.C. § 1681.

4. No Means No. Gender discrimination is patently obvious in proceedings such as the "Stanford rapist" sentencing.[62] Despite improvements in statutes and codes such as Federal Rule of Evidence 412, it is not uncommon for judges to excuse rape on the grounds that the victim failed to aggressively resist, dressed suggestively, or the defendant or victim were under the influence of alcohol or drugs.[63]

---

[62] Liam Stack, *Light Sentence for Brock Turner in Stanford Rape Case Draws Outrage*, N.Y. TIMES (June 6, 2016), http://www.nytimes.com/2016/06/07/us/outrage-in-stanford-rape-case-over-dueling-statements-of-victim-and-attackers-father.html [https://perma.cc/7UM8-BUX4].

[63] *See, e.g.*, Catchpole v. Brannon, 36 Cal.App.4th 237, 258–59 (1995); *Mike McIntyre Rape Victim 'Inviting,' So No Jail: Judge Rules Woman's Clothes, Conduct Ease Blame on Attacker*, BRANDON SUN (Feb. 26, 2011 6:05 PM), http://www.brandonsun.com/breaking-news/rape-victim-inviting-so-no-jail—rape-victim-inviting-so-no-jail-116801578.html?viewAll Comments=y [https://perma.cc/47ZE-XP3K]; Lauren R.D. Fox, *Judge Gives Rapist Light Sentence Because 14-Year-Old Girl "Wasn't the Victim She Claimed to Be,"* MADAME NOIRE (May 5, 2014), http://madamenoire.com/425765/judge-gives-rapist-light-sentence/ [https://perma.cc/W5FG-FNCB]; Stack, *supra* note 63.

CHAPTER 13

WRITING FOR CLERKS

> Writing is easy. You simply sit down at the typewriter, open your veins, and bleed.
>
> – Pulitzer Prize-winning *New York Times* sportswriter Walter Wellesley "Red" Smith[1]

Writing is a lawyer's stock-in-trade. Unfortunately, most law students don't have the opportunity to read, study, and practice good writing. Many legal texts are full of moribund opinions, often written with little structure and even less clarity. Academic writing suffers from the same faults. Most problematic, law students frequently have little opportunity to practice their writing and editing skills.

The best way to learn about writing is to read good writing.[2] Lawyers must also write often and receive detailed feedback on that writing from an experienced editor. Fortunately, most judicial clerks and interns have that opportunity when working for a judge.

§ 13.1 TYPES OF WRITING PROJECTS

The type of writing projects delegated to clerks varies by the court and judge. Trial courts spend much of their time ruling on, and writing orders for, Rule 12(b)(6) motions, Rule 56 motions, motions to suppress, and discovery squabbles. The volume of cases is generally high, the rulings are rarely precedential, and the work must be generated quickly. Appellate courts, conversely, have a lower case load, often must create law that will apply in a variety of future cases, and have the luxury of time and resources.

Judges also vary in their use of clerks. Some involve their clerks at the beginning and end of the opinion-writing process. The clerk performs the legal research at the beginning, as well as the cite-checking, formatting, and proof-reading at the end. The judge writes the opinion herself with little input from the clerks. Others involve their clerks at every stage of the writing process.[3]

---

1 *Walter Winchell In New York*, NAUGATUCK DAILY NEWS, Apr. 6, 1949, at 4.

2 Nina Totenberg, *Skip The Legalese And Keep It Short, Justices Say*, NPR (June 13, 2011 2:01 AM) (quoting Chief Justice Roberts), http://www.npr.org/2011/06/13/137036622/skip-the-legalese-and-keep-it-short-justices-say [https://perma.cc/VMC2-P2W3].

3 *Id.* ("Some justices, like Ginsburg or the retired Justice John Paul Stevens, find it easier to write a first draft and then let their law clerks have a go at it. Others, like Scalia, let the law clerks write the first draft, and then the justice rewrites, edits and refines. [Justice] Thomas

A. WRITING ASSIGNMENTS IN APPELLATE COURTS

1. CERTIORARI MEMORANDUM ("CERT. MEMO")

A certiorari memorandum is used in courts that have discretionary appeals. The judges must choose which petitions for certiorari they should grant. While some judges read every petition for certiorari individually, most rely on cert. memos written by clerks.

Each petition for certiorari that comes into chambers is assigned to a single clerk. The clerk will read through petition, response brief, reply brief, and briefs of *amicus curiae* before crafting the memo. The certiorari memo is written for the judge and is intended to flag cases that the court should consider hearing. One certiorari memo may be shared with other judges who will be voting on whether to hear the case. When multiple judges rely on one clerk to review a single petition it is called a "cert. pool." Almost all Supreme Court Justices participate in the cert. pool. Participants divide the tens of thousands of petitions for certiorari among their judicial clerks. Each cert. memo is then distributed to all the chambers participating in the pool.

Generally, a cert. memo will contain:

1. A summary of the issue presented in the case;
2. Facts;
3. Decisions below;
4. A summary of the parties' arguments for or against certiorari;
5. A summary of the amicus arguments for or against certiorari;
6. A review of the current law on the issue, as well as a notation of open questions of law;
7. An evaluation of the merits of the appeal; and
8. A recommendation on whether to grant certiorari or deny certiorari. In the Supreme Court the clerk may also recommend that the Court call for the view of the Solicitor General.

2. BENCH MEMORANDUM

A bench memorandum is drafted prior to oral arguments and used to prepare the judge for that hearing. It will be read by the judge and may be read by other clerks or judges sitting on an appellate panel.

---

says he never even sees a draft until it has been through three aggressive rewrites by his law clerks.")

Before writing the bench memo, the clerk will review the entire file and research the applicable law. The length of a bench memo will vary, but most include:

1. The docket number, a short caption of the case, and names of members of the panel;
2. The district court and the name of the judge from whom the appeal is taken;
3. The procedural history of the case;
4. A statement of facts, noting both disputed and undisputed facts;
5. A summary of both sides' arguments;
6. The applicable law;
7. A summary of unclear issues, including matters that should be clarified, expanded, or explained during oral argument; and
8. When requested, an evaluation of, and suggested outcome for, the case.

A bench memo will often be used as a template for the final opinion or dissenting opinion.

3. Single-Issue Memorandum

Judges sometimes ask clerks to research and draft a memorandum discussing a single question that has not been clearly answered by the parties, has arisen as a result of new precedent, or that arose after briefing. Single-issue memoranda often address complex legal issues. Their format is fairly simple. They generally require only one section structured as an IRAC analysis.

4. Full Case Memorandum

A full case memorandum is similar to a first-year law student's objective memorandum assignment. It addresses all the issues in a case, the applicable law, the parties' arguments, and each argument's strengths and weaknesses. It will also often recommend a particular outcome in the case. A full case memorandum will often be used as a template for the final opinion or dissenting opinion.

5. Precedential Judicial Opinion

A precedential opinion is an opinion that may be cited by parties in later cases. It is the most formal, heavily-edited, and carefully cite-checked opinion. These are the opinions that appear in textbooks. A precedential opinion is usually issued by an appellate court when the court addresses a novel area of law.

The same basic IRAC, CREAC, or TRAC format taught by legal writing professors around the nation also works well for judicial opinions. If your legal writing class did not teach one of these structures, default to the format you were taught. Judges strive to make sure all work product coming from their chambers is relatively identical, so clerks and interns should use prior opinions as a model.

Every judicial opinion requires the following sections:

1. An opening paragraph or introduction. This paragraph explains the type of case and claims or defenses, the names and positions of the parties, the procedural posture of the case, any prior rulings or judgments, and sometimes the ultimate ruling or outcome in the case.
2. A summary of the issue or issues to be decided.
3. The basis of the court's jurisdiction.
4. A statement of facts.
5. An analysis of each argument, structured accordingly:
    a. The first issue presented;
    b. The governing legal principles for that issue;
    c. An application of the law to that issue;
    d. Any counter-arguments, addressed and refuted;
    e. A conclusion or holding for each individual issue.
6. An overall disposition or conclusion, including specific instructions to the parties or the lower courts.

6. MEMORANDUM OPINION

A memorandum opinion is non-precedential. It is shorter and generally less comprehensive. It is used when the rule of law is clear, the parties are merely arguing about the facts or about the application of the law to the facts, and the decision requires some degree of rationale. The structure of a memorandum opinion is identical to the structure of a precedential opinion.

7. PER CURIAM OPINION

The least common opinion is the per curiam opinion. "Per curiam" is a Latin term meaning "by the court." A per curiam is issued by the court as a single unit. No individual or identifiable judge or justice is the named author. These are generally one-page orders.

B. WRITING ASSIGNMENTS IN TRIAL COURTS

Some of the work of trial courts mimics the work of appellate courts. Judges may hold oral argument on motions, which necessitates a bench memo. A novel issue may arise, which requires the creation of a single-issue memorandum. Just like appellate courts, federal trial courts issue both published and unpublished decisions. However, additional writing projects arise in trial courts.

1. STATEMENT OF FACTS

A statement of facts addresses only the facts in the case, not the law. A law clerk will review the briefs, any appendices or attachments to the briefs, trial exhibits, and hearing notes or transcripts before drafting the statement of facts.

The statement of facts is an accurate and objective recitation of the facts. It should contain notes regarding any disputes, along with citations to evidence supporting each possible interpretation of the facts. It is usually best to write statements of fact chronologically.

2. FINDINGS OF FACT AND CONCLUSIONS OF LAW

When a trial court judge is the finder of fact in an evidentiary hearing such as a motion to suppress, a motion for a preliminary injunction, or a bench trial, the judge may issue findings of fact and conclusions of law.

The document is formatted similarly to a standard opinion. The judge will list the material facts that have been proven to the necessary standard. She will also list her conclusions of law. This section will either list the applicable law or will contain a ruling and reasoning for novel issues of law. Finally, the judge will apply the law to the facts, issuing a ruling in the case. Some judges write findings of fact and conclusions of law in a standard opinion-like narrative form, while others write them with numbered paragraphs.

3. JURY INSTRUCTIONS

Most jurisdictions have "pattern" or model jury instructions that are used in virtually every case. In most courts, the parties will file proposed jury instructions, with citations to legal authority, in advance of the trial. Most of these instructions are based on the pattern instructions. When the parties differ on the inclusion of an instruction or the language of that instruction the judge may rule prior to trial. Additionally, parties may submit additional jury instructions during the trial as the evidence develops. The judge will hear arguments on the instructions, frequently after the jury has been released for the day. Clerks are responsible for researching the applicable law for contested instructions, as well as formatting, proof-reading, and providing the final set of instructions to the parties and the judge.

4. MOTIONS

Much of a trial court's work is made up of rulings on motions. Many rulings on motions are made orally from the bench and require no work by the clerk. Other rulings require only a single sentence order indicating that the motion has been granted or denied.

Some motions, particularly motions to dismiss, motions for summary judgment, and motions to suppress, require a more detailed analysis. In these instances, the judge may issue a precedential opinion, memorandum opinion, or findings of fact and conclusions of law.

5. MISCELLANEOUS COURT ORDERS

Trial courts issue numerous orders in every case. Many of these are routine and are completed by the judge's court clerk or administrative assistant. Often, proposed orders are filed by the parties. The court must also issue a judgment at the completion of the case. Most chambers have stock orders and judgment forms.

§ 13.2 PLANNING THE WORKLOAD

A. GETTING STARTED

When faced with any research or writing project, begin by getting clear instructions. Although newcomers to chambers often want to appear that they already know what they are doing, failing to get clear instructions on the front end can waste significant time as the project develops.

Clerks should:

- Ask for whom they are writing;
- Ask to see a sample of a similar work product to get a sense of organization and style;
- Understand the type of assignment;
- Understand the legal and factual scope of the assignment;
- Ask for both draft and final deadlines;
- Ask how the judge or clerk would like the work product organized and presented;
- Ask whether the judge or clerk would like paper or electronic copies of cases and other sources;
- Determine whether there is a page or word limit; and
- Ask to whom the clerk should bring questions. Often an intern will be supervised by an experienced clerk, and a term clerk may be supervised by a permanent clerk. It is a good idea to ask questions "up the chain of command" before approaching the judge.

The first time you work on any case you should read the entire case file. Chart out the parties, claims, defenses, motions, and rulings. Once you understand the trajectory of the case you may begin to read the applicable motions and briefs. Take separate notes on the parties' arguments and support for those arguments.

After reading through the attorneys' filings, make a research plan before turning on the computer. The parties' legal research is an excellent place to begin, but should never be the end of the inquiry. The clerk has a duty to research independently all the law on any issue presented to the court. As you research, keep a three-ring notebook or electronic folder with copies of cases, statutes, and other research you've completed for the case.

If you get stuck, don't be afraid to ask for help. You should make every effort to answer your own question first. However, a supervising clerk would much rather spend five minutes getting you back on track than spend five hours redoing your work.

B. DRAFTING

A blank word processing page can seem overwhelming. Begin by outlining the assignment. Use the structure outlined in section 13.1 above, or ask for a template or sample document.

Next, write the introduction. This will not only ease you into writing, but will ensure that you understand the type of case, claims and defenses, positions of the parties, and issue presented. Next, write the fact section. This is also a fairly "easy" section to write, gives you forward momentum, and helps you understand the case. When you've finished these two sections you may then begin writing the analysis.

When writing, keep all your citations in long form, or at least in short form. Do not use "*id.*" until you reach the final stages of editing and proof-reading. Sentences are frequently moved, added, or deleted during the editing process. Using "*id.*" early in the writing process will make it difficult or impossible to find a source later. Save this version of the document separately, and make edits in a separate copy of the paper so that you will always know where to find a concept or quote.

C. EDITING

Plan on spending at least 50 percent of your total writing time editing and proof-reading your work. Like revenge, editing is a dish best served cold. If possible, take a break of several days, or at least several hours before editing your work. You are more likely to catch mistakes. Plan to come back and edit multiple times. Take a break again before completing a final proof-read.

Picture editing as a reverse pyramid. Begin by looking at your work from the broadest angle. Start with gross organization, and work your way down to a final word-by-word proof-read.

1. GROSS ORGANIZATION

Have you included all the necessary parts in the opinion?

Are the parts of the opinion in the judge's preferred order?

Have you placed the proper material in the proper section?

2. IRAC, CREAC, OR TRAC

Is your IRAC, CREAC, or TRAC form solid?

Did you choose appropriate cases, explain them fully, and use them in your analysis?

Do you have strong, case-based arguments?

Have you applied the salient facts from the case?

3. TOPIC SENTENCES

Do you have a topic sentence at the beginning of each paragraph?

Is everything in a particular paragraph related to the topic sentence?

4. SENTENCE STRUCTURE AND GRAMMAR

Are you using simple, straight-forward sentences?

Have you checked for the most common errors, including passive voice?

5. WORD CHOICE

Have you been clear? Would someone unfamiliar with the case be able to follow your writing?

Have you been concise? Have you looked for ways to economize both sentences and words?

Have you used appropriate vocabulary? Have you written in English rather than Latin where possible?

Have you chosen the words that best convey your meaning?

Is your language appropriately formal?

6. SPELLING

Have you used spell-check and grammar-check on the entire document?

Have you checked for homonyms?

7. CITATIONS

Have you saved your long-form citations in a separate document?

Have you checked all your citations against the Bluebook rules?

8. FINAL PROOF

Use the speaking function on your computer and have the computer read the text to you while you follow along.

§ 13.3 THE IMPORTANCE OF GOOD BASIC SKILLS

There are copious books on the market designed to teach students, clerks, and judges how to write clear and concise opinions. However, the same rules that apply to any good legal writing apply to judicial opinions.

A. BASIC SENTENCE STRUCTURE

Sentences should be kept short and simple. The subject, verb, and object should be close together in the sentence and generally appear in that order. Legal readers are accustomed to simple declarative sentences. It is better to write many short and clear sentences than one long and convoluted sentence.

B. GRAMMAR AND PUNCTUATION

Student writers tend to make similar grammar, spelling, and punctuation errors, no matter what their background. Most of these errors are due simply to a lack of practice and feedback. Some, such as errors in comma placement, occur because many primary and secondary schools no longer emphasize grammar in the curriculum. A list of the most common grammatical and punctuation errors is below, along with guidance on how to spot and fix those errors.

1. MISPLACED MODIFIERS

A modifier is a word, phrase, or clause that adds detail or specificity to a sentence. A misplaced modifier is a word, phrase, or clause that is improperly separated from the word it modifies or describes. The result is a sentence that is awkward, confusing, or (often) just plain funny. As Groucho Marx said, "The other morning I shot an elephant in my pajamas. How he got into my pajamas I'll never know."[4] If you find that the "lawyer discussed the proposal to fill the drainage ditch with his partners,"[5] you should either call the police or rewrite the sentence.

2. COMMAS

Oscar Wilde is credited with quipping that he spent most of a morning removing a single comma, but upon mature reflection put it

---

[4] ANIMAL CRACKERS (Paramount Pictures 1930).

[5] David S. Levine, THE STATE OF THE LANGUAGE 406 (Leonard Michaels and Christopher Ricks eds., 1980).

back.[6] Commas are a source of frustration for both writers and editors. Many students are told by teachers that they should place a comma where they would naturally pause when speaking the sentence out loud. This is simply bad advice, although it does represent the norm for writing circa 1800. Consider the first line in *Pride and Prejudice*: "It is a truth universally acknowledged, that a single man in possession of a good fortune, must be in want of a wife."[7] While the comma may make sense to a reader speaking aloud, it is indisputably wrong under modern rules of grammar. Writers must ditch the easy "place a comma when pausing" rule and memorize the modern rules.

a. **Punctuation Placement.** Place the punctuation, including commas, on the inside of the quotation mark. There is one exception to this rule: if a question mark or exclamation point is not part of the quotation the question mark or exclamation mark goes outside the final quotation mark.

b. **The Serial Comma.** Use the serial comma (sometimes called "the Oxford comma") to separate every element in a series, including the last two items.

   Journalists rarely follow this rule, but lawyers must. Without the serial comma, it is unclear whether the writer was creating two categories or three. For example, if "Rebecca is proud of her new muffin recipes: blueberry, peanut butter and chocolate chip,"[8] we don't know whether Rebecca makes two kinds of muffins (one that is flavored with blueberries, and the other that is flavored with both peanut butter and chocolate chips) or three kinds of muffins (blueberry, peanut butter, and chocolate chip). This actually is a distinction with a difference, as cases have been won or lost over a single comma.

   Omitting the serial comma can also give your work a funny but false meaning. The most famous example is the apocryphal book dedication: "To my parents, Ayn Rand and God."

c. **FANBOYS.** Use a comma plus a coordinating conjunction to connect two independent clauses. A coordinating

---

[6] Colman McCarthy, *Writing: A Matter of Commas, Blank Pages and Limps*, WASH. POST, Sept. 29, 1969, at A22.

[7] JANE AUSTEN, PRIDE AND PREJUDICE 1 (1813); *see also* Eugene Volokh, *Jane Austen and the Second Amendment*, WASH. POST (Apr. 13, 2015), https://www.washingtonpost.com/news/volokh-conspiracy/wp/2015/04/13/jane-austen-and-the-second-amendment/?utm_term=.0531993200fa [https://perma.cc/8JPW-7NEM]; Ben Yagoda, *Fanfare for the Comma Man*, N.Y. TIMES: OPINIONATOR (Apr. 9, 2012 9:00 PM), http://opinionator.blogs.nytimes.com/2012/04/09/fanfare-for-the-comma-man/?_r=0 [https://perma.cc/96UD-UB4H].

[8] Mignon Fogarty, *Serial Comma*, QUICK AND DIRTY TIPS, http://www.quickanddirtytips.com/education/grammar/serial-comma [https://perma.cc/9YH9-DMQ8] (last visited Oct. 10, 2016).

conjunction is a word that hooks up words, phrases, or clauses. Students of a certain age remember the Schoolhouse Rock video, "Conjunction Junction." Other students remember coordinating conjunctions by memorizing the acronym FANBOYS: for, and, nor, but, or, yet, and so. For example, "I give myself good advice, but I seldom follow it."

d. **Have We Been Introduced?** Use a comma to set off introductory elements: "Running toward third base, he suddenly realized how stupid he looked."

e. **A Side Note.** Use a comma to set off parenthetical elements. A parenthetical element is a part of a sentence that can be removed without changing the essential meaning of that sentence. To test whether you have a parenthetical element, remove the language in question and see if you still have a complete sentence:

London Bridge, which was built in 1824, is falling down.

You know this use of commas is correct because if you strike the material inside the commas you still have a complete sentence:

London Bridge, ~~which was built in 1824~~, is falling down.

Thus, London Bridge is falling down. Your sentence is complete.

f. **Can I Quote You On That?** Generally, use a comma to separate quoted material from the rest of the sentence that explains or introduces the quotation. Illustrating this point, the author writes, "The purpose of the comma is to separate the quoted material from the remainder of the sentence."

Conversely, you should not use commas to set off quoted elements introduced by the word "that" or quoted elements that are embedded in a larger structure. Illustrating this point, the author writes that "[t]he purpose of the comma is to separate the quoted material from the remainder of the sentence."

Sometimes, your attribution will occur in the middle of the sentence, rather than the beginning or the end. When this happens, use two commas to set off an attribution of a quoted element in the middle of the quotation. Use one comma and a quote to place an attribution between two sentences:

"But I don't want to go among mad people," Alice remarked.

"Oh, you can't help that," said the Cat. "We're all mad here. I'm mad. You're mad."

"How do you know I'm mad?" said Alice.

"You must be," said the Cat, "or you wouldn't have come here."[9]

3. COMMA SPLICES

Comma splices incorrectly connect independent clauses with a comma. An independent clause is simply a set of words in a sentence that could stand by itself and make a complete sentence. If the clause on either side of your comma could itself be a complete sentence, you have a comma splice.

For example, the sentence "I didn't like *Alice in Wonderland*, it was too complicated" is itself two sentences: "I didn't like *Alice in Wonderland*" and "It was too complicated." Likewise, the sentence "It's no use going back to yesterday, I was a different person then" is actually two separate sentences: "It's no use going back to yesterday," and "I was a different person then."

Comma splices are easily fixed in one of three ways: First, you could make each independent clause into its own sentence. Second, you can separate the clauses with a semi-colon. Finally, you can separate the clauses with a comma and a coordinating conjunction (for, and, nor, but, or, yet, so).

4. SPLIT INFINITIVES

A full infinitive is "to" in front of a verb: to go, to sprinkle, to run. A split infinitive puts an adverb (a descriptor) between the two parts of the full infinitive: to generously sprinkle, to quickly go, to awkwardly run. The most memorable example of a split infinitive is the famous Star Trek opener: "To boldly go where no man has gone before." "To go" is a full infinitive. By putting the adverb "boldly" between the two words, the author has split the infinitive.

There is a convincing argument to be made that the "rule" against split infinitives is wrong and is based on improperly importing the rule against split infinitives from Latin to English. However, most senior lawyers and judges were taught in grade school never to split an infinitive. Therefore, you should avoid it where possible.

5. ENDING A SENTENCE WITH A PREPOSITION

A preposition is a word that creates a relationship between other words. You can think of prepositions as placing items in time or space. Although there are more than 100 prepositions in the English language, common prepositions[10] include:

---

[9] LEWIS CARROLL, ALICE'S ADVENTURES IN WONDERLAND (1865).

[10] *See, e.g.*, *25 Most Common Prepositions*, ENG. CLUB, https://www.englishclub.com/vocabulary/common-prepositions-25.htm [https://perma.cc/L65U-T24T] (last visited Oct. 10, 2016); *Prepositions*, CAMBRIDGE DICTIONARY, http://dictionary.cambridge.org/us/grammar/british-grammar/prepositions [https://perma.cc/4VPZ-5MQF] (last visited Oct. 10, 2016).

- of
- in
- to
- for
- with
- on
- at
- from
- by
- about
- as
- into
- like
- through
- after
- over
- between
- out
- against
- during
- without
- before
- under
- around
- among

The basic rule is not to end a sentence with a preposition. "Where are you at?" is a painful example of this rule and causes most of us to cringe. However, many sentences ending in prepositions are used in everyday speech. For example, "What did you step on?" generally sounds fine to the modern American ear. It is, however, forbidden by the rule against ending a sentence with a preposition.

There are two ways to solve the problem. The first is to embed the proposition in the sentence: "Upon what did you step?" Embedding the preposition in the sentence may force you to create a formal and somewhat artificial sentence. The second, and usually better, option is to rewrite the sentence: "Did you step on something?"

Many grammarians argue that this "rule" either isn't a rule or should be abandoned altogether. Winston Churchill is (probably falsely) credited with writing, "That is the sort of English up with which I will not put!" However, like split infinitives, a sentence that ends in a preposition sets many readers' teeth on edge, and should therefore be avoided.

6. PASSIVE VOICE

In order to understand passive voice, you must be able to identify the subject, verb, and object in a sentence. In the sentence "I love you," the word "I" is the subject because it is the actor in the sentence. "Love" is the verb because it is the action in the sentence. "You" is the object because "you" is the person or thing upon which the subject is acting. Similarly, in the sentence "Steve killed Sandra in the kitchen with the candlestick," "Steve" is the subject, "killed" is the verb, and "Sandra" is the object.

There are two kinds of passive voice. In the first, the sentence completely lacks a subject. The classic example of passive voice is the politician's phrase, "Mistakes were made." The author (or speaker) doesn't tell us who made the mistake. In a more legal context, a defense attorney might write, "The victim was pushed out the window, but it was an accident." Again, the author hasn't told us who did the pushing. Therefore, the sentence is in passive voice.

The second kind of passive voice occurs when the subject and object are flipped in the sentence. Going back to the first example, "I love you" is active voice. However, if the author wrote, "You are loved by me," it would be passive voice. The subject of the sentence is now "you," but "you" isn't doing anything. Another memorable example comes from the great Marvin Gaye song, "I heard it through the grapevine." As sung, "I heard it through the grapevine" is active voice. However, if the song was, "It was heard by me through the grapevine" the sentence would become passive. "It" is promoted from object to subject, but "it" isn't doing anything.[11]

Active voice sentences are generally shorter and clearer. However, authors will sometimes purposely use passive voice for one of several reasons. First, it allows the author or speaker to avoid responsibility. In the first example, the author avoided saying "*I* made a mistake." To do so would be to take responsibility. Similarly, in the second example the defense attorney avoided placing her client at the scene. Second, passive voice can soften the blow. Telling a customer "your electricity will be cut off" sounds kinder than "we will turn off your electricity." Finally, passive voice may be appropriate if you don't know who the actor is or was. For example, crime reports are often written in passive voice.

Most instances of passive voice are inadvertent. Your word processing program is generally good at pointing out passive voice during a spelling- and grammar-check. Pay attention when it does.

7. THE PROBLEM OF THE SINGULAR GENDER-NEUTRAL PRONOUN

The problem is that we don't have a singular gender-neutral pronoun in the English language.

Pronouns fill in for the noun. English has a masculine singular pronoun (he/him), a feminine singular pronoun (she/her), a singular pronoun for an entity (it), and a plural gender-neutral pronoun (they/them). What we do not have is a singular gender-neutral pronoun: a pronoun to fill in when we mean to refer to a single subject but don't know the gender of that subject. Many writers fill this gap by using the plural gender-neutral pronoun (they). Examples include, "I don't know who my new teacher will be, but I hope they will be nice." "Who owns that car? Their alarm is going off."

While using the plural gender-neutral pronoun is common and even acceptable in day-to-day speech, most writing instructors—and judges—will mark it wrong when it appears in print. There are two ways to fix the problem. The best is to work around the problem by rephrasing the sentence: "I hope my new teacher will be nice." The second is to replace "they" with "he or she." For example, "I don't know who my new teacher

---

[11] Mignon Fogarty, *Active Voice Versus Passive Voice*, QUICK AND DIRTY TIPS, http://www.quickanddirtytips.com/education/grammar/active-voice-versus-passive-voice [https://perma.cc/EYU3-WGHK] (last visited Oct. 10, 2016).

will be, but I hope he or she will be nice." Note that using a simple "he" is considered sexist, and "s/he" is considered clunky.

When you are discussing an entity, replace "they" with "it": "The University has changed its parking system. It no longer issues paper permits"; "The immigration court was very crowded. Its docket was three hours long." Courts are always entities: "The Tenth Circuit addressed the issue in *Smith v. Jones*. It held that a contract requires consideration." A specific judge, however, is referred to as either "he" or "she."

There has been some movement toward using "they" as a singular gender-neutral pronoun.[12] *The Washington Post* officially approved its use in its 2015 manual of style, and the American Dialect Society named it Word of the Year in 2016.[13] Others have pushed for the creation of a new singular gender-neutral pronoun, such as "ze." These activist grammarians analogize "ze" to the title "Ms.," created in the 1970s. A judge or other academic writer, however, is likely to be unmoved by these arguments.

8. WHO VERSUS WHOM

In order to understand who and whom, it is again helpful to understand subjects and objects, explained in the "passive voice" section above. Remember that the subject in a sentence is the actor—it is the person or entity that is doing something. The object is having that thing done to him, her, or it.

Who and whom are pronouns. You use "who" when you refer to the subject of the clause and "whom" when you refer to the object. A quick way to determine whether a sentence requires "who" or "whom" is to ask yourself whether the answer is "he" or "him" (excuse the sexism—the rule is easier to remember this way). If the answer is "he," then "who" is the correct word in the sentence. If the answer is "him," then "whom" is the correct word. You can remember the rule because the 'm' in "him" and the 'm' in "whom" match. For example, "To *whom* does this pencil belong?" "It belongs to *him*." "*Whom* do I love? I love *him*." "*Who* broke the teapot? *He* did." "*Who* killed Sandra with a candlestick? *He* did."

9. THAT VERSUS WHICH

Many copies of Strunk and White's *The Elements of Style* are heavily thumbed on the page explaining "that" and "which."

"That" is restrictive or defining. A restrictive clause is one you can't get rid of because it will change the meaning of the sentence. For

---

[12] Geoff Nunberg, *Everyone Uses Singular 'They,' Whether They Realize It Or Not*, NPR (Jan. 13, 2016 1:00 PM), http://www.npr.org/2016/01/13/462906419/everyone-uses-singular-they-whether-they-realize-it-or-not [https://perma.cc/BW4H-66E8].

[13] Jeff Guo, *Sorry, Grammar Nerds. The Singular 'They' Has Been Declared Word of the Year*, WASH. POST: WONKBLOG (Jan. 8, 2016), https://www.washingtonpost.com/news/wonk/wp/2016/01/08/donald-trump-may-win-this-years-word-of-the-year/ [https://perma.cc/9RC3-8CXF].

example, the sentence, "The lawnmower that is broken is in the garage" tells you that, from among several lawnmowers, the one that is broken is in the garage. Similarly, the sentence "Dogs that bark scare me" tells the reader that not all dogs scare the speaker—only the ones that bark.

"Which" is for nonrestrictive clauses—basically everything else. A nonrestrictive clause can be left off without changing the meaning of the sentence. You can throw out the "which-s" and no harm will be done to the meaning of the sentence. For example, the sentence "The lawnmower, which is broken, is in the garage" tells you something about the one and only lawnmower. It can be found in the garage, and it happens to be broken. Similarly, "London Bridge, which is falling down, was first built in 1824." There is only one London Bridge, and now we know something additional about it: the bridge is falling down.

Non-restrictive clauses are often set off by commas: "Your homework, which is late, is incomplete." Sometimes a non-restrictive clause is only set off my one comma: "The election will be delayed, which is bad news."

Like other rules, some academics argue that the "that" versus "which" construction is invented and not supported by history. Even President Franklin Roosevelt ignored it when announcing, "Yesterday, December 7, 1941—a date which will live in infamy—the United States of America was suddenly and deliberately attacked by naval and air forces of the Empire of Japan."[14] Once again, however, a clerk is not in a position to fight the rules of grammar.

10. COMMONLY CONFUSED WORDS

Commonly confused words include similar-sounding words such as

- as and like;
- ensure and insure;
- affect and effect;
- elicit and illicit;
- emigrate and immigrate;
- than and then;
- further and farther; and
- lay and lie

Writers also commonly confuse possessives and contractions. The difference is sometimes difficult to remember because in some circumstances an apostrophe is used to indicate possession, but in others, the apostrophe is used to indicate a contraction. The words that are mostly commonly confused include:

---

[14] Geoffrey Pullum, *A Rule Which Will Live in Infamy*, CHRON. OF HIGHER LEARNING (Dec. 7, 2012), http://chronicle.com/blogs/linguafranca/2012/12/07/a-rule-which-will-live-in-infamy/?cid=pm&utm_source=pm&utm_medium=en [https://perma.cc/N2JB-PPYZ].

- "Your" (possessive) versus "you're" (a contraction for "you are");
- "Whose" (possessive) versus "who's" (a contraction for "who is");
- "Its" (possessive) versus "it's" (contraction). You can remember the difference by picturing the apostrophe in "it's" as the dot on an "i." This will help you remember that "it's" is the contraction for "it is."

Be on the lookout for homophones such as there, their, and they're; and to, too, and two. Look words up when you're not sure which to use. There are a number of good grammar guides available in print and on the internet.

C. THE BLUEBOOK: A UNIFORM SYSTEM OF CITATION

For many legal writers, the *Bluebook* is A Uniform System of Frustration. No other citation manual receives more bad press—published and otherwise—than the *Bluebook*.[15] It is the bane of most 1Ls, and frustrates all but the most dogged and painstaking writers and cite-checkers. Weighing in at 511 pages, it is more than twice as long as the Official Rules of Baseball. Its rules are often convoluted and unnecessarily complicated. It takes a simple task—making it easy for a reader to recognize and find a source—and turns it into a time-consuming treasure hunt.

Despite its difficulties, the *Bluebook* continues to be the go-to citation manual for the law. Other competitors, including the *ALWD Guide to Legal Citation* and the *Maroonbook*, have had some success but have failed to universally catch on with legal writers, judges, and academics. A new citation manual called *The Indigo Book: A Manual of Legal Citation* was published in 2016 after a protracted and public fight with the Harvard Law Review Association over alleged copyright violations. This on-line, open-source manual is a stripped down and simplified version of the *Bluebook*. Whether it will fare better than its predecessors remains to be seen.

The *Bluebook*'s stamina is more likely due to what good *Bluebook* form says about the writer than what it says about citation form. Judges and senior partners were often members of law review, and law review students spend two years perfecting their *Bluebook* form. Knowing the *Bluebook* tells the reader that you are part of the club: well-educated, possibly on law review, and a meticulous writer and researcher.

---

[15] *See, e.g.*, Richard A. Posner, *Goodbye to the Bluebook*, 53 U. CHI. L. REV. 1343 (1986), http://chicagounbound.uchicago.edu/cgi/viewcontent.cgi?context=journal_articles&article=2797 [https://perma.cc/DT5D-PZB5]; Debra Cassens Weiss, *Posner Says Bluebook Is '560 Pages of Rubbish,' Suggests Changes to Improve Jury Trials*, A.B.A.J. (Mar. 29, 2016 06:15 AM), http://www.abajournal.com/news/article/want_to_even_out_lawyer_quality_and_end_contingent_fees_adopt_a_uniform_pay/ [https://perma.cc/QSQ8-4KBV].

Many authors who are unsure about, or not interested in, *Bluebook* form revert to using the citations generated by Westlaw or Lexis. Both are often almost, but not completely, correct. The *Bluebook*-literate reader will recognize them for what they are: a close-but-not-quite facsimile.

Despite the intricacies of the *Bluebook*, most writers use only a handful of rules. Interns and clerks who learn these basic citation forms by heart have a much easier time writing quickly and accurately. The most important rules to know are:

- Long form case citations
- Short form case citations
- *Id.*
- Parallel citations
- Pinpoint citations
- Block quotes
- Explanatory parentheticals and explanatory phrases
- Prior or subsequent history
- Signals
- String cites
- Long form statutory citations
- Short form statutory citations
- Citations to the Constitution and rules of procedure
- Use of ellipses

The internet is replete with guides intended to help you generate perfect *Bluebook* citations. You should also check to see if your jurisdiction has its own rules for legal citation. Many now do.

§ 13.4 THE SEVEN DEADLY SINS OF LEGAL WRITING

A. FOOTNOTES

Judges have different theories on the use of footnotes. Some heavily footnote their opinions, putting both citations and substantive material in footnotes. Others put all, or many, citations in footnotes but eschew substantive commentary. Finally, some allow no footnotes of any kind.

There is an ongoing debate about whether citations should go in text or footnotes. Bryan Garner, one of the best-known authorities on legal writing, argues that all citations should go in footnotes, but no discussion should be placed there.[16] He, and a number of judges and attorneys

[16] Bryan A. Garner, *Textual Citations Make Legal Writing Onerous, for Lawyers and Nonlawyers Alike*, A.B.A. J. (Feb. 1, 2014 9:00 AM), http://www.abajournal.com/magazine/

around the nation, believe that moving citations to footnotes makes for a document that is cleaner, easier to read, and more accessible to legal and non-legal readers alike.

Others, including Associate Justice Antonin Scalia, disagree and argue that placing bibliographic material in footnotes "force[s] the eyes to bounce repeatedly from text to footnote."[17] Citations are meaningful to the legal reader, and well-crafted citations give the trained reader an immense amount of information, including the persuasiveness of the precedent. Because most readers skip the footnotes, they often miss key information about the strength of the writer's arguments.

Your judge will have a personal preference on the location of citations. However, avoid placing substantive discussion in a footnote unless it is your judge's preferred style. Although the Supreme Court sometimes places valuable material, including discussion, justice-to-justice disagreements, and "zinger" comments in footnotes,[18] student authors often use them because they are worried that they are missing key information. Because the opinion will serve as a guide for later litigation, extraneous information or commentary that is not necessary for the decision in the case may be the font of later argument. Deleting—whether the extraneous material appears in text or footnotes—is often the better choice. Minimize footnotes unless your judge requests that you do otherwise.

B. EXCLAMATION MARKS

Exclamation marks are an attempt to give meaning where your text has failed to do the job. If you are tempted to add an exclamation mark, go back and rethink your text. The same goes for the phrase "in other words." If you have to write "in other words," consider the possibility that you didn't write the sentence properly the first time.

C. OVER-EMPHASIS

Briefs are sometimes peppered with underlining, bold text, or italics. This is the author's way of signaling to the reader that the words are

---

article/textual_citations_make_legal_writing_onerous_for_lawyers_and_nonlawyers/ [https://perma.cc/Z7MU-J7NL].

[17] Rich Cassidy, *Bryan Garner Says: Put Your Citations in Footnotes*, ON LAWYERING (Mar. 3, 2014), http://onlawyering.com/2014/03/bryan-garner-says-put-your-citations-in-footnotes/ [https://perma.cc/QAL7-DYTW].

[18] *See, e.g.*, Obergefell v. Hodges, 135 S. Ct. 2584, 2630 n.22 (2015) (Scalia, J., dissenting) ("If . . . I ever joined an opinion for the Court that began: 'The Constitution promises liberty to all within its reach, a liberty that includes certain specific rights that allow persons, within a lawful realm, to define and express their identity,' I would hide my head in a bag. The Supreme Court of the United States has descended from the disciplined legal reasoning of John Marshall and Joseph Story to the mystical aphorisms of the fortune cookie."); Milavetz v. United States, 559 U.S. 229, 253 (2010) (Scalia, J., concurring in part and dissenting in part) ("I join the opinion of the Court, except for footnote 3, which notes that the legislative history supports what the statute unambiguously says."); United States v. Carolene Products, 304 U.S. 144, 153 n.4 (1938) (laying out the basis of what would become heightened scrutiny).

really important. It indicates both a lack of faith in the author's persuasive abilities and a lack of faith in the reader's ability to read and grasp the meaning of the brief. Trust that your reader is *smart enough to get it*.

Occasionally, some emphasis is helpful. For example, you may wish to draw the reader's attention to a single word or phrase in a long statute or quote. Where some emphasis is necessary, limit yourself to italics.

D. SNARK

Every law clerk comes upon irrelevant, incompetent, or incomplete briefing. At some point, the urge to comment on an attorney's errors can become overwhelming. However, the privilege of the snarky or unkind comment is the judge's alone. The clerk must remain unfailingly polite and professional.

E. VERBOSITY

Your writing should be clear and concise on both micro and macro levels. Opinions should be understandable for the average reader, including parties, journalists, and the public. The average adult reads at the 8th grade level. Most popular novels, including the later Harry Potter novels and F. Scott Fitzgerald's work, are written at this level. Conversely, statutes and academic work are generally written at the 12th grade or college level.

Include no more than 18 words per sentence. Keep your thesaurus use to a minimum. Use the best words to convey your meaning, not the biggest words you can muster. When in doubt, write in English and not in Latin unless the Latin phrase reflects a term of art in the legal field.

Your memoranda and draft opinions should also err on the side of brevity. Chief Justice Roberts once quipped that he never got to the end of the brief and wished it were longer.[19] The same is true for memoranda and opinions.

F. SLOTH

Clerks are human, as are judges. However, a clerk's work is often all that comes between a person and jail, bankruptcy, or injustice. Don't assume that attorneys have done their work, and don't assume that someone else will catch your mistakes. You have an ethical duty to be competent. Research and write as if your liberty or property were on the line.

---

[19] Tony Mauro, *Briefer Briefs Ahead for Supreme Court*, NAT'L L.J. (Feb. 4, 2010, http://www.nationallawjournal.com/id=1202441952705/Briefer-Briefs-Ahead-for-Supreme-Court?slreturn=20160616142458 [https://perma.cc/WUX6-M5T5].

G. MISSTATEMENT

As noted in Chapter 7, most parties want to feel heard. They will forgive a judge for a mistake of law but will not forgive a mistake of fact. When writing facts, err on the side of the losing party. Not only will this ensure that litigants feel that their position was credited, but it will also make your opinion stronger if the case is appealed.

Make sure your judge never has cause to doubt your fair and impartial reading of the law and evidence.

INDEX

References are to Pages

ABA, 77, 78, 124, 130, 143, 165, 206
abuse of discretion, 30, 52, 61, 68, 91, 159, 192, 193
activist, 100, 125, 153, 230, 357, 421, 457
Adams, Abigail, 234, 432, 433
Adams, John, 227, 231, 233, 234, 248, 319, 368, 433
administrative courts, 1, 8, 10, 73, 387
administrative law judges (ALJ), 10, 69, 258–62
Administrative Procedure Act, 68, 259–62
affirmative action, 22, 98, 404, 417, 435
Affordable Care Act, 98, 100, 300, 301, 303, 305, 306
Alito, Samuel, 110, 303, 306, 339, 359, 418
Allen, Macon, 403
alternative dispute resolution (ADR), 13, 16, 184–86, 190–91
American Judicature Society, 124, 143
appearance of impropriety, 28, 30, 33–36, 120, 130, 141
arbitration, 184–87, 190, 196–200, 307, 400–01
Aristotle, 375, 231
Article I, 9, 129, 244, 248, 256, 324
Article IV, 10
assignment of cases, 87–97, 112, 135, 147
assistance of counsel, 71, 159, 201

basketball, 51, 52, 54, 121, 402
bench memorandum, 31, 444
bias, racial equality, 403, 405, 422
bias, gender equality, 429, 432
bias, implicit, 403
bill of attainder, 256
Blackmun, Harry, 203, 249
Blackstone, William, 153, 228, 280
Bluebook, 451, 459
Bork, Robert, 128
Bradwell, Myra, 429
Brennan, William, 26, 249
Breyer, Stephen, 371

canons of construction, 279, 283, 285, 300
certiorari, 200, 202, 203, 212, 255, 311, 324, 444
certiorari memorandum, 444
Chandler, Stephen, 134
Chase, Salmon, 245
Chase, Samuel, 134, 247, 248
citation, 44, 56, 309, 409, 447, 449, 451, 459
civil case, 11, 13, 114, 139, 153, 183, 184, 201, 202, 221, 243, 427
civil law, 263, 375, 430
civil law system, 375, 377–79, 394
civil rights, 9, 10, 12, 88, 92, 95, 118, 144, 203, 215, 230, 357, 421
Civil Rights Act, 53, 441

class action, 12, 31, 105, 113, 196–200, 307
code, 130, 375, 377, 387, 390, 398–99, 431–33, 442
Code of Judicial Conduct, 20, 27, 97, 98, 102, 109, 130, 139, 143, 145, 206
Coke, Sir Edward, 229
collateral consequences, 162
college admissions, 417, 421
comma splices, 454
commas, 310, 451
Commentaries on the Laws of England, 153, 228, 280
common law, 9, 49, 62, 75, 104, 105, 110, 112, 145, 146, 153, 185, 229, 230, 269, 339, 348, 356, 375, 376, 390, 392, 394, 395, 430
common law reasoning, 269, 270, 272
commonly confused words, 458
comparative fault, 288, 292
confidentiality, 19, 21, 158, 195
conflict, societies in, 227, 229, 264, 391, 392, 396
conflict, with judge, 19, 24, 107, 130
constitutional interpretation, 112, 384, 317, 321, 331, 340, 368
constitutional rights, problem-solving courts, 162
Consumer Finance Protection Bureau, 200
court packing, 248
CREAC, 446, 450
Credit Repair Organizations Act, 307
criminal case, 9, 11, 14, 139, 154, 162, 171, 182, 201, 243, 378, 383
criminal law, 12, 75, 151, 156, 353, 354, 356
Crown, British, 153, 227–31

de novo review, 52
death penalty, 128,161, 257, 340, 368, 369, 371, 403, 422
Declaration of Independence, 231, 365, 406, 407, 408
derogation statutes, 285
discipline, attorney, 11, 75, 76, 122
discipline, nurse, 83, 205
drafting, 6, 18, 24, 278–79, 282, 447, 449
drug courts, 163
due process, 24, 71, 73, 82–84, 101, 102, 104–12, 139, 154–64, 165, 258, 262, 320, 324, 332, 334–36, 341, 343, 345–56, 361–62, 367, 372, 390, 392, 410, 413

editing, 18, 183, 443, 449
Eighth Amendment, 161, 337, 338, 369, 370, 424
electoral challenge, 256

Ely, John Hart, 327
equal protection, 22, 114, 256, 320, 324, 327, 331, 332, 350, 367, 372, 410, 411–15, 417–420, 422–27, 433–41
Equal Rights Amendment, 434, 435
equality, gender. See bias, gender equality
equality, racial. See bias, racial equality
ethics, judge, 26, 33, 79, 84, 85, 95, 97, 130, 320
ethics, clerk, 19–26
ethics, general considerations, 20, 26, 84, 85, 363
ethics, judicial, 33
exclamation marks, 461

Federal Arbitration Act, 184, 196, 307
federal court history, 2, 153, 163, 227, 269, 331
federal court structure, 4
Federal Judicial Center, 20, 205, 263
federal jurisdiction, 10, 243
federalism, 247, 321, 346, 350
Federalist Papers, 231, 233
Fifth Amendment, 15, 71, 221, 342, 345, 355
Fifth Circuit Four, 88, 95
final judgment, 59, 207, 315
findings of fact and conclusions of law, 54, 56, 447, 448
First Amendment, 24, 27, 320, 322, 341, 342, 349, 418, 440
footnotes, 44, 460
foreign law, 368, 371
formalism, 321, 326
Fortas, Abe, 45, 101, 127
forum shopping, 242
Fourteenth Amendment, 101, 106, 113, 114, 145, 155, 159, 210, 327, 331, 334, 335, 336, 340, 341, 343–46, 351, 352, 355, 356, 361, 365–67, 410, 412, 415, 417, 426, 430, 433–34
Fourth Amendment, 27, 113, 114, 322, 342, 347, 428
Frankfurter, Felix, 367
full case memorandum, 445
functionalism, 321, 326

gender-neutral pronoun, 456
Gideon, Clarence, 202
Ginsburg, Ruth Bader, 50, 129, 338, 359, 404, 418, 436, 443
grammar, 280, 310, 450, 451

habeas corpus, 11, 16, 155, 244–46
Hand, Learned, 275, 367
Haynsworth, Clement, 101, 127
homeless courts, 151
House of Representatives, 131, 133, 247

immigration, 2, 69, 70, 71, 256, 326, 403, 414, 457
Immigration and Nationality Act, 326
impartiality, 21, 27, 30, 32, 35, 36, 38, 87, 95, 97, 99, 109, 110, 113, 115, 117–21, 126, 130, 143, 204, 388, 409
impeachment, 130–36, 148, 228, 232, 243, 247
informal tribunals, 394
inherent risk statutes, 285, 291
inter-governmental organizations, 400
interlocutory appeal, 132
International Bar Association, 262
international courts, 263, 368, 375, 377–79, 389
IRAC, 445, 446, 450

Jackson, Andrew, 227
Jackson, Robert, 320, 367
Jefferson, Thomas, 232, 234, 319, 329, 437
jirga, 394
Jones, Robert, 135, 136
Judicial Conduct Commission, 25, 73, 130, 136
Judicial Conference, 16, 19, 27, 131, 134
judicial discipline, 130
judicial immunity, 144
judicial independence, 123, 147, 227, 262
judicial independence, British, 227
judicial independence, federal, 231–56
judicial independence, state, 256–58
judicial oversight, 130
judicial sanction, 143
judicial selection, 123, 403
judicial systems, federal, 2, 133, 205, 324, 263, 377
judicial systems, state, 11, 124
judicial systems, civil law, 263, 375, 430
judicial systems, religious, 394
judicial systems, informal, 394
Judiciary Act, 3, 4, 5, 7, 201, 234, 235, 240, 242, 248
jurisdiction stripping, 243
jurisdiction, federal courts, 2, 3, 10, 244, 245
jurisdiction, state courts, 12
jury instructions, 14, 60, 447
jury selection, 123, 403, 426, 441
jury trial, decline of, 53, 183, 184
jury trials, 14, 53, 92, 160, 183, 195, 203, 293, 423
juvenile courts, 151, 153

Kagan, Elena, 6, 98, 129
Kaye, Judith S., 1, 151
Kennedy, Anthony, 128, 403
King George III, 231

law school admissions, 415, 416, 418, 419, 436
legal writing, 443, 460
legislative intent, 278, 279, 280, 282, 285, 289, 293, 295, 297, 309, 310, 319
legislative veto, 326
life without parole, 80, 161, 178, 337, 338, 425
Lincoln, Abraham, 185, 200, 244
living constitution, 320, 372
Llewellyn, Karl, 270

Madison, James, 227, 231, 234, 325, 343
manufactured cases, 421
Marbury, William, 234
Marshall, John, 234, 367, 461
Marshall, Thurgood, 98, 404

McCully, Sharon, 143
mediation, 13, 15, 184, 187
medieval England, 376, 395
memorandum (memoranda), 28, 31, 34, 54, 71, 98, 100, 103, 444–46, 448
mental health courts, 151, 164, 175, 178
misplaced modifiers, 451
Missouri Compromise, 405, 409
misstatement, 50–51, 99, 463
mixed issues, 60
Model Rules of Professional Conduct, 204
Montesquieu, Charles, 228, 231, 232, 26
motions, 24, 25, 29, 30, 31, 32, 36, 63, 71, 98, 102, 108–14, 121, 187, 205, 206, 209, 287, 345, 443, 446–49

Ninth Amendment, 322, 342–44, 347–48
Nixon, Walter, 135
non-governmental organizations (NGOs), 376, 399, 401
nonjusticiable, 111, 327
Notario Publicos, 202
notice pleading, 209
Nottingham, Edward, 134

O'Connor, Sandra Day, 126, 183
originalism, 318, 321, 327
over-emphasis, 461

Paine, Thomas, 231
paper record, 58, 59
Parliament, 224, 228–31, 264, 266, 267, 270, 279, 280, 353, 295
Parliamentary supremacy, 228
partially unconstitutional statutes, 315
passive voice, 450, 455, 457
patent, 7, 10, 40, 224, 442
per curiam, 91, 94, 112, 210, 446
peremptory challenge, 121, 425–28, 441
Pickering, John, 134, 247
plain meaning, 44, 278, 280, 285, 305, 307, 310, 319
political activities, by clerks, 21
Posner, Richard, 40, 42, 43, 191, 195, 213, 259
Powell, Lewis, 422, 424, 425, 427
precedential opinion, 445, 446, 448
preemption, 197, 200
prepositions, 454
Prison Litigation Reform Act, 203
privacy, 27, 128, 342–50, 359, 388, 438
private bill, 256
pro bono, 204, 205, 279
pro se, 24, 184, 200
problem-solving courts. See specialty courts, 162, 181, 379
pronoun, gender neutral, 456
proof reading, 443, 447, 449
public defender, 74, 78, 79, 160, 180
punctuation, 310, 451
punishment. See theories of punishment

rabbinical law, 395
record, 36
recusal, judge, 97
recusal, clerk, 27
recusal, lower courts, 101
recusal, United States Supreme Court, 98
Rehnquist, William, 317
religious courts, 394
resign, 31, 127, 129, 134, 135, 234, 330, 421
restorative justice, 151, 392
retention, 123, 256–57
retire, 23, 131, 134, 136, 138, 142, 187, 210, 247, 249, 260, 362, 424
revocation, 69, 79, 83, 84, 170–73, 178, 196
right to counsel, 154, 155, 160
right to privacy, 349
Ritter, Willis, 121, 135
Roberts, John, 100, 112, 200, 255, 300, 305, 462
role of the clerk, 36
Roosevelt, Franklin, 248, 458
Rosenberg, Maurice, 45
rule of law, 48, 60, 88, 96, 109, 264, 268, 321, 334, 393, 425, 446
rule of the last antecedent, 310, 313
Russia, 264, 265, 402
Rutledge, John, 1

same-sex marriage, 97, 125, 129, 355, 360, 363–66
Scalia, Antonin, 321, 371, 461
Second Amendment, 321–23
segregation, 89, 247, 412, 413–16, 441
Senate, 36, 101, 127–29, 132–35, 234, 248, 308, 309, 326, 343, 370
senior status, 96, 134
sentence structure, 450, 451
separation of powers, 231, 251, 255, 256, 264, 321, 346, 350
settlement, 115, 116, 185–87, 189, 191–95, 227, 228, 231, 280, 296, 328, 394, 400, 422
sexual harassment, 25, 143, 431
Shari'a, 397
shura, 394–96
single issue memorandum, 445
Sixth Amendment. See right to counsel
sloth, 462
Smith, Walter Wellesley, 443
snark, 462
social security, 2, 8, 10, 70, 259, 260, 261, 262, 304, 306, 310, 311, 314
Sotomayor, Sonia, 87
Souter, David, 317
sovereign citizen, 223
Soviet Union, 51, 400
specialty courts, mental health, 151, 164–69, 175, 178
specialty courts, drug court, 163
specialty courts, juvenile, 143, 153
specialty courts, veterans, 151, 181
spelling, 450, 451, 456
split infinitives, 454, 455
sports, 47, 51, 54, 291, 376, 401–02
sports, international, 401
standards of review, de novo, 52, 58–61, 64, 67, 69, 70, 294

standards of review, abuse of discretion, 30, 52, 61, 65, 68, 69, 91, 159, 192, 193
standards of review, clear error, 53, 61, 64, 65, 67
standards of review, substantial evidence, 60, 68–73, 82, 85, 218
standards of review, 14, 45, 52
standards of review, clear and convincing, 74, 138, 139, 140
standards of review, mixed, 60
standards of review, multiple in single case, 62
standards of review, theory behind, 45
standards of review, administrative action, 67–84
stare decisis, 107, 269, 356, 377
state court jurisdiction, 12
state court structure, 1, 11
statement of facts, 445–47
statistics, 97
statutes, 16, 20, 44, 68, 69, 83, 84, 87, 104, 112, 158, 160, 187, 188, 203, 229, 239, 243, 245, 254, 269, 270, 277, 282, 285, 292, 315, 319, 326, 339, 341, 346, 350, 352, 353, 372, 411, 442, 449, 462
statutes, partially unconstitutional, 315
statutory construction, 270, 278, 279, 289, 297, 300
statutory construction, canons of, 279
statutory construction, codified laws, 278
Stevens, John Paul, 443
Stewart, Carl E., 17
substantial deference, 52, 59, 60

Taft, William Howard, 123, 367
textualism, 318, 319
that and which, 457
The Brethren, 23, 24
theories of punishment, 151
Thirteenth Amendment, 410
Thomas, Clarence, 100, 128, 404
tiered interpretation, 372
topic sentences, 450
TRAC, 450
tradition, 4, 49, 107, 152, 183, 264, 320, 331, 377, 390, 440
traditionalism, 320
trial court, 1, 11, 45, 52, 61, 446
Truman, Harry S, 326

unenumerated rights, 337, 340
unified models, 379
United Nations, 85, 265, 369, 375, 376, 391, 394, 399, 425
United States Courts of Appeal, structure of, 7
United States District Courts, structure of, 8
United States Supreme Court, structure of, 4
unprofessional conduct, 82–85

venire, 425–27
verbosity, 462
veterans' courts, 163, 180
village elders, 151, 267, 394

Warren, Earl, 127, 248, 249
Weinstein, Jack, 277
Whittaker, Charles Evans, 330
whom and whom, 457
word choice, 450